W9-DCC-845

Discovering
Smalltalk

The Benjamin/Cummings Series
in Object-Oriented Software Engineering

Grady Booch, Series Editor

Booch, *Object-Oriented Analysis and Design with Applications, Second Edition* (1994)
Booch, *Object Solutions: A Sourcebook for Developers* (1994)
Booch/Bryan, *Software Engineering with Ada, Third Edition* (1994)
Collins, *Designing Object-Oriented User Interfaces* (1995)
LaLonde, *Discovering Smalltalk* (1994)
Pohl, *Object-Oriented Programming Using C++* (1993)

Other Titles of Interest

Fischer/LeBlanc, *Crafting a Compiler in C* (1991)
Kelley/Pohl, *A Book on C, Second Edition* (1990)
Kelley/Pohl, *C by Dissection: The Essentials of C Programming, Second Edition* (1992)
Pohl, *C++ for C Programmers* (1994)
Sebesta, *Concepts of Programming Languages, Second Edition* (1993)
Sobell, *A Practical Guide to the Unix System, Third Edition* (1994)
Weiss, *Data Structures and Algorithm Analysis in C++* (1992)

Discovering Smalltalk

Wilf LaLonde

Carleton University

The Object People, Inc.

QA
76.64
.L337
1994

The Benjamin/Cummings Publishing Company, Inc

Redwood City, California ■ Menlo Park, California
Reading, Massachusetts ■ New York ■ Don Mills, Ontario ■ Wokingham, U.K.
Amsterdam ■ Bonn ■ Sydney ■ Singapore ■ Tokyo ■ Madrid ■ San Juan

Sponsoring editor: *Carter Shanklin*
Editorial assistant: *Melissa Standen*
Production supervisor: *Gwen Larson*
Production management: *Matrix Productions*
Cover design: *Yvo Riezebos*
Proofreader: *Cathy Baehler*

INDIANA-
PURDUE
LIBRARY

WITHDRAWN

MAY 1 6 1997

FORT WAYNE

Apple and Macintosh are trademarks of Apple Computer, Incorporated.
Objectworks, VisualWorks, and Smalltalk-80 are trademarks of ParcPlace Systems.
OS/2 and Presentation Manager are trademarks of International Business Machines.
Paintbrush and Windows are trademarks of Microsoft Corporation.
PARTS, Smalltalk/V for Windows, Smalltalk/V for OS/2, and Smalltalk/V are trademarks of Digitalk, Incorporated.
Widgets/V 286, WindowBuilder/V, and WindowBuilder Pro are trademarks of Objectshare Systems.

Copyright © 1994 by The Benjamin/Cummings Publishing Company, Inc.

All rights reserved. No part of this publication may be reproduced, stored in a retrieval system, or transmitted, in any form or by any means, electronic, mechanical, photocopying, recording, or otherwise, without prior written permission of the publisher. Printed in the United States of America. Published simultaneously in Canada.

Library of Congress Cataloging-in-Publication Data

LaLonde, Wilf, 1947-
      Discovering Smalltalk / Wilf LaLonde.
         p.   cm.
      Includes index.
      ISBN 0-8053-2720-7
        1. Object-oriented programming (Computer science) 2. Smalltalk/V
(Computer program language)   I. Title
QA76.64.L337   1994
005.26'2--dc20   93-6348
                                          CIP

3 4 5 6 7 8 9 10-ARF-98 97 96 95

The Benjamin/Cummings Publishing Company, Inc
390 Bridge Parkway
Redwood City, California, 94065

FTW
AJB7047

Table of Contents

6   Hierarchies of Classes   235

7   Object Containers   317

8   Evolutionary Software Development and Design   371

9   The Smalltalk Library   415

Foreword

Smalltalk is perhaps the quintessential object-oriented programming language. Its features have shaped a whole generation of contemporary languages, and its underlying philosophy has been an important influence to many modern software engineering methods. Indeed, Smalltalk has been one of the primary vehicles in bringing object-oriented technology into the mainstream of industrial-strength software development.

Smalltalk is distinctly not a research language: there exist many examples of its use for critical applications, encompassing such diverse domains as the processing of credit card transactions, the manufacturing of semiconductors, and the monitoring of international securities markets. Not only is Smalltalk a language well-suited to exploratory development, but it also serves as a good first programming language.

Wilf LaLonde's book, Discovering Smalltalk, provides a path for the beginner approaching computers for the first time, as well as for the professional programmer transitioning from more traditional languages into the object paradigm. LaLonde is one of the earliest advocates for bringing object-oriented technology to the undergraduate curriculum, and his work has been an inspiration to others pursuing similar initiatives. Wilf has helped to pioneer the production use of Smalltalk, and his practical experience shows through in this book.

Grady Booch

Preface

Introduction

In the seventies, structured programming revolutionized the way programmers constructed software systems. Today, many are predicting that the object-oriented programming paradigm will be the second major revolution in software engineering and that object-oriented systems will become the predominant programming tools of the nineties. In this book, we introduce many of the important object-oriented concepts in the context of the **Smalltalk** programming language and programming environment.

Smalltalk is a language that consistently adheres to the object-oriented paradigm. It has served both as a model for object-oriented extensions to more traditional procedural languages and as the basis for a new generation of languages supporting inheritance. It can be argued that Smalltalk has had more impact on software development in the last decade than any other programming language.

Smalltalk fosters *programming in the large* and *programming by extension* rather than by *re-invention*. It provides a foundation for window-based applications, for the development of truly reusable class libraries, and for the introduction of on-line tools such as code browsers.

This book provides an introduction to programming that encompasses the Smalltalk environment, the language, the library, and the major object-oriented concepts such as classes, inheritance, and polymorphism. Our aim is to produce practitioners who not only understand the basic ideas but also have the confidence and ability to perform complex programming tasks even when the tasks appear, on the surface, to be beyond their capabilities.

We subscribe to the notion that learning is a series of experiments in which negative results are just as important as positive results. The task of the teacher is to lead the experiments and summarize what has been learned rather than simply present the conclusions to be accepted without question. Indeed, the idea is to foster an environment where questioning is the modus operandi. We learn because we doubt or mistrust the seemingly obvious.

Organization of the Book

This book must introduce the syntax of the Smalltalk language, the Smalltalk library (objects, strings, numbers, characters, ordered collections, dictionaries, graphical objects, and panes to name a few), the Smalltalk environment (workspaces, inspectors, browsers, debuggers), and fundamental object-oriented concepts (classes versus instances, inheritance, methods, method lookup, instance variables, sequencing, binding, meta-level operations, design, etc.) in an interleaved fashion. For example, the internal structure of an object is best explained after a number of specially chosen objects have been inspected. Thus, the topic of inspectors precedes discussion about the details of representation. Similarly, the method lookup algorithm and the message-sending execution semantics are best explained using debuggers to visually illustrate the ramifications. Thus, the subject of debuggers precedes the discussion of detailed message passing semantics.

The success attributed to Smalltalk by its users is as much due to the facilities provided by the programming environment as to the powerful inheritance facilities that it supports. Consequently, mastering the programming environment is a prerequisite to becoming an expert in object-oriented programming with Smalltalk. As a result, these fundamental programming environment facilities cannot be relegated to an appendix nor can they be presented neatly in a series of self-contained chapters. What sense can you make of an inspector if you don't know what an object is? How can you fully understand what a browser is and what you can do with it if you don't understand classes and methods? How can you understand the debugger if you don't know how to program with classes and methods or if you don't have some understanding of variables and message passing? Clearly, these facilities cannot be introduced first and then used to elucidate the important notions nor can they be introduced last once all the prerequisites are understood. Their introduction must be integrated with the important conceptual knowledge in a gradual fashion.

This book adopts a discovery approach to learning; i.e., together, we hypothesize, experiment, and discover as many of the important concepts as we can. This discovery process can at times be relatively lengthy, but it has the side-effect of providing deeper and more detailed understanding. We end each chapter with a summary of all the important facts. This ensures that reviewing can be done without substantial rereading.

Who Should Read This Book?

This book is aimed at those who have never programmed before but who wish to learn the important concepts that are revolutionizing the industry. In particular, it is intended for those who wish to learn how to program in a language that fosters experimentation and that encourages exploration. It is written for those people who are intrigued and challenged by the potential of computers and the languages that are used to program them.

But readers who have some knowledge of traditional programming languages can also benefit from this book. If you program in languages like Pascal, C, Ada, or Fortran, or even if programming is something you used to do, you will find the book revealing and interesting. It can also be used profitably by those planning to learn C++; in fact, it has often been said that some of the best C++ programmers were first Smalltalk programmers.

This book can be used effectively in undergraduate and introductory graduate courses in object-oriented programming where Smalltalk is the language of instruction. It will be particularly valuable for students carrying out extensive projects and theses.

Smalltalk Dialects

There are two major variations of Smalltalk: Smalltalk-80 marketed by ParcPlace Systems[1] under the names Objectworks for Smalltalk-80 and VisualWorks, and Smalltalk/V marketed by Digitalk[2]. Excluding the user-interface classes, there is a great deal of commonality between the Smalltalk/V and Smalltalk-80 class libraries. The range of programming tools is similar, although there are distinct differences in the structure and functionality of specific tools such as the browser, in the method of interaction with the environment, and in the degree of integration with the specific platforms the variations are intended to run on.

In this book, we focus exclusively on the dialect of Smalltalk/V developed for Microsoft Windows.

Where the Book Fits in the Curriculum

This book is designed to support a first course in programming. It is currently used at Carleton University, Ottawa, Canada, in the first semester of an undergraduate computer science program. The course is taught with a machine in the classroom to illustrate all the concepts as they are presented. Students and teachers interract as they attempt to discover together all the important notions they need to know to become expert programmers.

---

[1]ParcPlace Systems, 1550 Plymouth Street, Mountain View, CA, 94043.
[2]Digitalk, Inc., 9841 Airport Road Boulevard, Los Angeles, CA, 90045.

In the second semester, students are introduced to the rudiments of C as part of a course that also introduces assembly language programming. This is in preparation for a more advanced course in the second year that uses C and C++ in greater detail. Learning C after Smalltalk is a revelation rather than a discovery for students, because many of its features are specializations of more advanced Smalltalk facilities. Such a course can also deal with topics that make sense only in procedural programming languages; e.g., call-by-reference versus call-by-value, pointers, and linked list management.

In the second semester, students also take a second course in Smalltalk dealing with applications. This course is concerned with developing a handful of small applications, each consisting of a small number of interacting objects along with an associated user interface. An example might be a check manager that permits a user to add, annotate, view, and modify the checks issued. Another might be an interactive facility that permits a user to view a map of a street district and query the system for information about restaurants in the area. By clicking on a new location, a user can interactively add new restaurants to the map.

In the second year of the computer science program, students take a data types course that focuses on the design and implementation of families of computer science data types; e.g., the family of trees such as binary trees, AVL trees, and B-trees. Because the first course has taught basic programming and conceptual skills and the second course has dealt with applications programming and applications data types, this third course solidly complements the first two. Moreover, it does so from the perspective of families of data types rather than from the viewpoint of isolated independent data types. Students benefit from the organizational aspects and abstraction facilities inspired by Smalltalk. This is in contrast to more conventional approaches that attempt to teach computer science algorithms and computer science data type in addition to basic programming skills, all in the first course.

A brief introduction to object-oriented analysis and design is also provided in second year, although more details are presented in a third-year course that complements it.

To summarize, this book concentrates on the knowledge needed to support a first course in object-oriented programming when Smalltalk is the didactic language of choice. As such, it provides all the basic programming knowledge needed to support later courses—knowledge about the language syntax, programming concepts, the programming environment, and the library.

The book is divided into ten chapters. The first seven are dedicated to providing the expertise that would be expected of a good programmer, without going into too many details about the Smalltalk library. It is the basic material that all first courses should cover. Chapter 8 is an optional chapter that introduces object-oriented analysis and design terminology and can serve as a precursor for more advanced courses on the topic—courses that might also consider more traditional design methodologies. Chapter 9 provides a detailed overview of the basic classes in the Smalltalk library and introduces many advanced concepts that can only be understood with the foundation developed by the earlier chapters. In the first course, we attempt to cover as many of these concepts as possible but we generally have to pick and choose, since there isn't time to cover everything. However, we do try to cover all the important new concepts supported by class Object along with advanced facilities associated with blocks and collections. Because of their importance, many of the notions in this chapter are traditionally reviewed in the second course on applications, since it is a good way of ensuring that students taught by different instructors have a common background. Finally, Chapter 10 is an introduction to building user interfaces—a topic that is the exclusive domain of the second course.

Acknowledgments

First and foremost, I would like to acknowledge the contribution made to the software community by the group of researchers at the Xerox Palo Alto Research Center (PARC) who were responsible for the development of the Smalltalk system. In particular, Alan Kay, Adele Goldberg, and Dan Ingalls, who in 1987 received formal recognition of their work with the 1987 ACM Software Systems Award, were leaders in the development of this new technology. In recognition of the development of a software system that has had a lasting influence, that has reflected contributions to new and still evolving concepts, and that has resulted in commercial acceptance, the Xerox PARC group received the award for seminal contributions to object-oriented programming languages and related programming techniques. Smalltalk was cited as having provided the foundation for explorations in new software methodologies, graphical user-interface designs, and forms of on-line assistance to the software development process.

I also wish to thank the members of the Center for Object-Oriented Programming (COOP), particularly Dave Thomas, John Pugh, and Paul White, whose collective wisdom and energy served to better motivate me. To the many students at Carleton University in Ottawa who had the audacity and nerve to challenge me and correct me, my sincere thanks for helping to improve some of the ideas in this book. Finally, on a more personal note, I thank my wife, Marla Doughty, for her support and understanding, and my children, Brannon and Robin, who forced me to take breaks now and then.

The World of Mice and Windows

What You Will Learn

You will learn the fundamentals of computers and the basics of the Smalltalk programming environment. These introductory notions are as important to programming as an understanding of the parts of a bicycle is to someone learning how to ride. But we can carry the analogy further. Clearly, there is an advantage to understanding the mechanics of bicycle riding, but too detailed a study is apt to frustrate and bore an eager student. The same applies in this endeavor. Although the details of this chapter are important, you need not understand them in depth before progressing onward to subsequent chapters. Indeed, this chapter contains more material than can be grasped during a first reading. A cursory reading now, followed by a more detailed reading after you are more familiar with the first three or four chapters will be more fruitful. This pattern of study follows the analogy suggested above. A cursory knowledge of the mechanics of a bicycle, followed by practice (and play), followed by more detailed study is apt to result in better understanding and more refined skills.

1.1 Introduction

A **command** is an order for someone or something to perform some action. Giving commands is natural to all of us. We command ourselves to get up, to do our homework, to jump as far as we can. We command pets—albeit lovingly—to come with us, to beg, to sit, to stay. We command people to take out the garbage, clean the garage, sweep the floor. We also command devices such as lights to turn on and off; a car to start up, move ahead, and turn left or right; or a radio to decrease its volume. As you can see, commands need not be verbal. They can be signalled by a twitch of the eye when we're in a hurry to leave, by a clap of the hands to cause an electronic flower to dance, or by a push of the foot to cause a riding lawn mower to stop.

Programming is the art of providing someone or something with commands that can be executed at some later time. We program a clock to ring the next morning, a videotape recorder to tape a show on a special evening, or a cruise control to maintain the car's speed. Commands can be specified in many different ways—by hitting special buttons, as in the previous examples; by writing down steps to be followed later by someone else; or by drawing a treasure map to indicate where to go to uncover some hidden gift.

Designing is the act of organizing the commands. A novelist about to write a new book designs by organizing his ideas for the plot and programs by writing down the words for the manuscript. But clearly, his design ideas will also have to be written down lest he forget them. This is programming at a different level and it illustrates that designing and programming are two extreme points in a continuum. In other words, designing is high-level programming. Conversely, programming is low-level designing—after all, there are many ways of writing down the gist of a particular sentence. Designing and programming are inextricably intertwined. It is impossible to simply program without at the same time thinking of improvements to a design.

A **computer** is a machine that can both store and execute commands—assuming, of course, that the commands are in a language or notation it understands. A **programmer** is a person that supplies commands either to be stored and followed at some later time or to be performed immediately. A **designer** is a high-level programmer. When a computer follows commands provided by a programmer, it is said to **execute** or **evaluate** the commands.

Colloquially, we often refer to the computer as **hardware**, since it is relatively resilient to change. Commands, on the other hand, are easy to change and are thus referred to as **software**. More colloquially, programmers often refer to software as **code**[1]. For the most part, this book is concerned primarily about software aspects. Of course, there can be no software without hardware.

In this chapter, we will introduce computers, describe their most important components, and illustrate the typical nontextual commands that might be used to control one; e.g., using a mouse.

---

[1]Historically, early software was often encoded. cryptic, and hard to decipher — hence programmers were thought of as coding.

1.2 Computers

A **computer** (see Figure 1.1) consists of several components: a **processor** that can execute commands, a **memory** that can be used to temporarily store information (including commands) while executing, a **hard disk** that can permanently store information, a **hard disk drive** that can actually retrieve and change old information on the hard disk and store new information, a **floppy disk** that is equivalent to a hard disk but easily carried in a pocket, a **floppy disk drive** that can retrieve and change information on the floppy disk, a **monitor** that can display information on a **screen**, a **keyboard** that can be used to type in information, and a **mouse** that can be used to point at and select items on the screen.

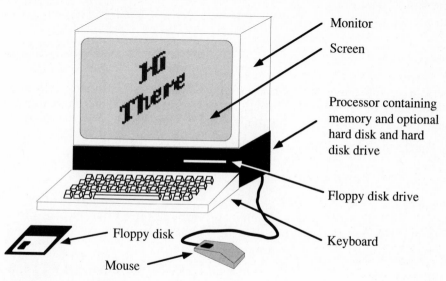

Monitor

Screen

Processor containing memory and optional hard disk and hard disk drive

Floppy disk drive

Keyboard

Floppy disk

Mouse

Figure 1.1 A computer.

The processor, memory, hard disk, hard disk drive, and floppy disk drive are usually hidden inside a special enclosure or **cabinet** (only the cabinet is shown in Figure 1.1). Sometimes, the monitor is integrated with the cabinet, but more often, it is separate. As a rule, hard disks can hold much more information than floppy disks but they cannot be easily carried. Floppy disks are generally used for carrying information between home and work or school.

In general, different manufacturers produce different variations of computers, called **models**. In most cases, the cabinets or monitors of distinct models look different. In other cases, the differences are strictly internal; only the processor or the amount of memory is changed. As a rule, models from distinct major manufacturers not only look different but behave differently. Computers that may (or may not) look different but behave the same way are said to belong to the same **family** of computers. For example, two distinct families of computers includes the Macintosh[1] or the IBM[2] PC family of computers.

In general, all Macintosh systems come equipped with a mouse. A mouse, however, is optional for IBM PCs. Although it is possible to learn and use Smalltalk on a system without a mouse, it is an inconvenience that is easy to eliminate, since the cost of mice is relatively low. Our remarks for the remainder of the book therefore assume that you are working on a system with a mouse. As a rule, Macintosh systems have a one-button mouse (see Figure 1.2), while IBM PCs have a two-button mouse (see Figure 1.3).

Figure 1.2 A one-button Macintosh mouse.

Figure 1.3 A two-button MS-DOS mouse.

On the surface, this seems like quite a difference. However, the missing button on the Macintosh (the right button) is simulated by depressing the **Option key** on the keyboard. The following are the mouse button equivalents:

left button = button on Macintosh = left button on IBM PC
right button = Option key + button on Macintosh = right button IBM PC
button (neither left nor right explicitly specified) = left button

We refer to the process of pressing down on a mouse button followed by an immediate release as **clicking** the mouse button. Doing this twice in rapid succession is referred to as **double-clicking**. Pressing on the mouse button for a long time without releasing is **pressing and holding**.

To use a computer we must first turn it on. The hardware responds by loading software called the **operating system** into the memory and then executing it—this is called **booting** the system. The operating system is responsible for providing the computer with a specific "look and feel." For example, the operating system for a Macintosh—the most current is System 7—might appear as shown in Figure 1.4. There are many candidate operating systems for IBM PCs—MS-DOS[3], Microsoft Windows[4], OS/2[5], each with their own unique look and feel. The particular operating system that we will focus on in this book is Microsoft Windows. An example is shown in Figure 1.5.

A programmer can communicate with the Microsoft Windows operating system by interacting with the **Program Manager**. Each icon in the Program Manager

---

[1]Macintosh is a trademark of Apple Computer, Inc.
[2]IBM stands for International Business Machines Corporation.
[3]MS-DOS is a trademark of Microsoft Corporation.
[4]Microsoft Windows is a trademark of Microsoft Corporation.
[5]OS/2 is a trademark of International Business Machines Corporation.

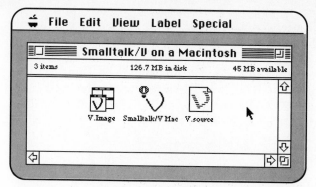

Figure 1.4 A Macintosh as it might appear after booting the system.

window is termed a **program group**. Double-clicking on a program group causes the icon to open up and display its internal icons called **program items** as shown in Figure 1.6.

Associated with each program icon is a specific piece of software termed a **program** that can be executed by double-clicking on the program item. Double-clicking on the program item is said to **activate** the program.

A **file** is simply information saved on a disk in a format that can be retrieved later. A **directory** is a special file that can contain other files. Generally, files are placed on a floppy disk for transportation between computers or on a hard disk for permanent storage on a specific computer. Disks, in general, are simply file recording mediums. Each disk drive is normally referenced by one of a number of special letter prefixes such as **a:**, **b:**, or **c:**. The **file manager** is a special program that can be activated by double-clicking on the file manager program item shown in Figure 1.6. It permits the files in the system to be copied, deleted,

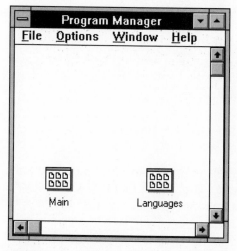

Figure 1.5 An IBM PC as it might appear after booting a Microsoft Windows system.

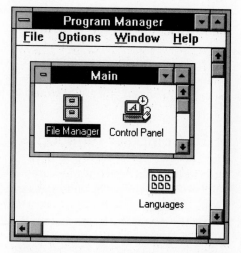

Figure 1.6 The result of double-clicking on the program group called **Main**.

moved, and investigated. Figure 1.7 illustrates the result of activating the file manager on a computer with three drives where the **c**: drive is a hard disk drive and the **a**: and **b**: drives are floppy disk drives. As shown, the currently selected drive is the **c**: drive containing two directories: V20 and Windows. Directory V20, in turn, contains directory Book. The Book directory contains four files: change.log, v.bak, v.exe, and vw.exe. The window to the right containing these files appeared as a result of double-clicking on Book.

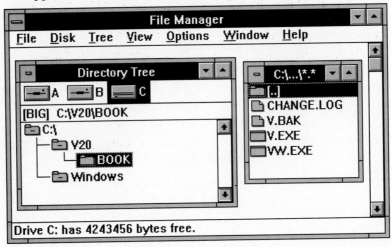

Figure 1.7 Using the file manager to look at files.

In general, different files with the same name could exist in different directories. For example, there might exist another file called vw.exe in the V20 directory. A file can be uniquely identified by specifying the **path name** as in c:\v20\book\vw.exe which includes the drive and the complete **directory hierarchy** in the appropriate order; i.e., drive c: contains a disk with directory V20 which in turn contains directory Book which finally contains file VW.EXE. Uppercase and lowercase characters are equivalent in file names. Hence, we could have specified the file name as vw.exe. By contrast, another file with the same name in directory V20 would be specified as c:\v20\vw.exe.

1.3 Computer Languages

Just as humans can communicate in different languages, so can computers. Some examples of computer languages are BASIC, Fortran, COBOL, Pascal, C, PL/1, Ada, Snobol, Forth, Prolog, Lisp, and Smalltalk. In our case, we will be concerned with the **Smalltalk** language. There are two major dialects of Smalltalk: Smalltalk-80[1] and Smalltalk/V[2] each with its own subdialects. In this book, we

---

[1] ParcPlace Systems, 1550 Plymouth Street, Mountain View, CA 94043.
[2] Digitalk, Inc., 9841 Airport Road Blvd., Los Angeles, CA 90045.

will be concerned with Smalltalk/V Windows, a subdialect of Smalltalk/V that executes under the Microsoft Windows operating system.

As a rule, computers do not understand arbitrary languages (such as the above) without some translation. However, they do understand a much simpler language, called **machine language**. Many variations exist, each unique to the specific kind of processor in the computer. In this book, we will not be concerned with the details of machine languages. What we need is an interface that plays an intermediary role between the Smalltalk language and the computer-specific machine language. Such an interface is a program called a programming environment.

A **programming environment** enables the programmer to communicate in a programmer-oriented language like Smalltalk without having to worry about a specific machine-oriented language, it provides tools that support the programming process in the programmer-oriented language, and provides a library of preprogrammed instructions that can be used to construct more elaborate commands.

1.4   The Smalltalk/V Programming Environment

1.4.1   Starting Up Smalltalk

Before anything can be done in Smalltalk, the Smalltalk programming environment must be **activated** by double-clicking the mouse on the **Smalltalk/V** program item.

Figure 1.8 The Program Manager with two program group icons.

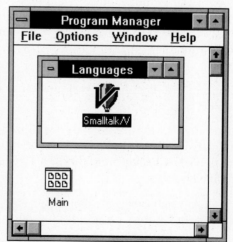

Figure 1.9 After double-clicking on the **Smalltalk/V** program group.

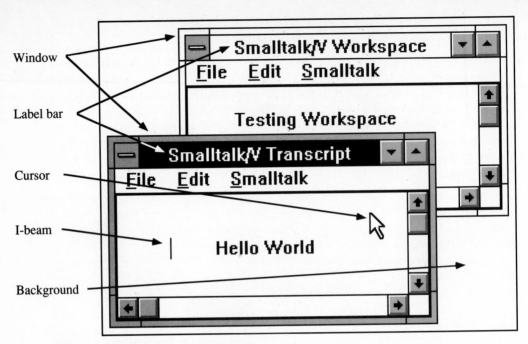

Window

Label bar

Cursor

I-beam

Background

Figure 1.10 A typical start-up screen.

To do this, you must first locate the program group that contains the **Smalltalk/V** program item. Double-click on each of the program groups in the Program Manager until the right one is found. Since program groups can be renamed by knowledgeable programmers, the names in your computer might not correspond to ours. For example, on a system that contains only two program groups such as "Main" and "Languages" (see Figure 1.8), you might find the program item by double-clicking on "Languages" to obtain the program group expansion of Figure 1.9.

Once the "Smalltalk/V" program item is located, double-click on it to start up the Smalltalk/V Windows programming environment. Figure 1.10 illustrates a typical start-up screen.

As shown in Figure 1.10, the Smalltalk/V Windows environment is typically activated with several objects in view; in this case, a cursor, two windows with label bars, a background, and an I-beam. Each of these components is further defined below:

- A **window** is an area on the screen surrounded by a special boundary. In Figure 1.10, two rectangular windows are shown: a transcript window and a workspace window. As we will see, windows can generally be moved around and resized (made bigger or smaller), and they can overlap; e.g., in Figure 1.10, the transcript window overlaps the workspace window.
- A **label bar** is an area (at the top of a window) that contains a title.

- The **background** is the area behind the windows.
- An **I-beam** is a vertical line inside a text window (a window that can accept and display text). The I-beam marks the spot where text is to be inserted or deleted. Note that the I-beam is sometimes confused with the text cursor. In practice, they are easy to distinguish. Moving the mouse, for example, will move the text cursor but not the I-beam.
- A **cursor** is a special icon (or picture) that indicates the location of the mouse on the screen. More than one icon is available, each signaling that a special activity is being performed or can be performed. For example, a **text** cursor indicates that the mouse is over some portion of a window where text can be written, whereas an **arrow** cursor, which could appear over a component such as the label bar, indicates that text cannot be written at that location. An **execute** cursor indicates that some long computation is being performed. A **cross hair** cursor indicates that a selection is expected from the user. and a **window resizing** cursor indicates that the edges or corners of a window can be moved. The complete set of cursor icons is illustrated in Figure 1.11.

Arrow   Cross hair   Execute   Text   Window resizing

Figure 1.11 The complete set of cursor icons.

Clearly, when the mouse is moved on a desk, for example, it is the associated cursor on the screen that we see moving over the components of a window. The association between the mouse and its cursor is so obvious that it is conveninent to omit mentioning the cursor. Rather than, for example, say "move the cursor to the top-left corner of the window and press on the left mouse button," we will simply say "press the left mouse button **over** the top-left corner of the window." Pressing, clicking, or double-clicking the mouse button over an area of the screen is a short form for first moving the cursor to the specified area and then performing the specified mouse button activity.

1.4.2 Saving the Image

As you work with Smalltalk, everything that you do is recorded in two special files:

- The **image**, a file called **v.exe**, that contains the current state of your programming environment (this file cannot be printed).
- The **changes file**, a file called **change.log**, containing all the instructions that you executed while in the Smalltalk environment (this file can be printed).

The current state of the Smalltalk/V environment can be saved at any time. If you make changes to the system (by typing in one of the windows, for example) and you save the image, the next time you start up Smalltalk, it will start up with the latest changes. On the other hand, you can make changes to the system and deliberately choose not to save the image. The next time you start up, you will be back in the same state in which you originally started.

To save the image, follow these steps:

- Move the cursor to the **File** menu, as shown in Figure 1.12, and press and hold left mouse button. A **pull-down menu** will appear, as shown in Figure 1.13.
- Move the cursor to menu command **Save Image...** and release the mouse button. The dialog box shown in Figure 1.14 will then appear, asking if you wish to save the image.
- Click on the **Make Backup** check box if you have room to make a backup—a **backup** is a copy that can be used to replace the original if it should be destroyed. The backup of **v.exe** is called **v.bak**. Generally, if you are running from a diskette, you will not have room. If you are running from a hard disk, you should make a backup.
- Finally, click on **Yes**. Alternatively, click on **No** if you've changed your mind and no longer want to exit.

Note: If there is insufficient space to save the image, the save will result in an error message. In that case, delete unnecessary files and try to save the image again.

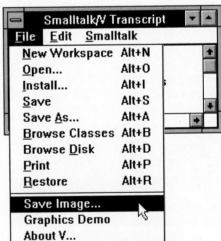

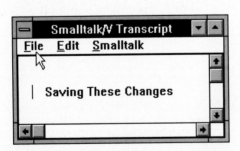

Figure 1.12 The transcript window with the mouse over the **File** menu.

Figure 1.13 Selecting **Save Image...** in the pull-down menu.

Figure 1.14 Responding **Yes** to the dialog box.

1.4.3 Exiting Smalltalk

When you are finished with Smalltalk, you should exit the Smalltalk/V environment. Follow these steps:

- Move the cursor to the top left corner of the transcript window (to the **close box**), as shown in Figure 1.15, and press and hold the left mouse button. A pull-down menu will appear, as shown in Figure 1.16.
- Move the cursor to menu command **Exit Smalltalk/V...** and release the mouse button. The dialog box shown in Figure 1.17 will then appear asking if you wish to save the image.
- If you wish to save the image, we recommend that you choose **Cancel** and explicitly save the image as described in the previous section. If you save while exiting and an error results (because there is insufficient disk space), there is no opportunity to delete files and try again. If you have already saved the image, you should choose **No** (there is no need to save it again).

Figure 1.15 The transcript window with the cursor over the close box.

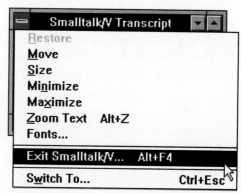

Figure 1.16 Selecting **Exit Smalltalk/V...** in the pull-down menu.

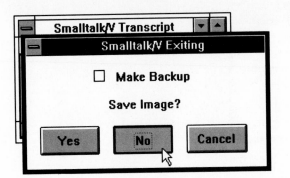

Figure 1.17 Responding **No** to the dialog box.

1.4.4 Recovering Lost Work and Compressing the Image

This section deals with an advanced topic that will not be of interest to you until Chapter 3 or 4. Nevertheless, it belongs in this section because it has to do with how to proceed if you mistakenly forgot to save your image as you hurriedly exited the environment. Alternatively, you might also wish to do this if you inadvertently crashed the system or if the power to the computer was accidentally cut off. This section uses terminology that is defined in future chapters.

Recall that as you work with Smalltalk, everything you do is recorded in the changes file called **change.log**. In general, all the expressions that you executed are in the changes file in the order that you executed them. However, they are all terminated by an exclamation mark. For example, you might find the following in the changes file:

```
1 + 2!
1 - 2!
```

It is possible to open the changes file, select a portion of the file, copy it, and then paste the copied text into a workspace, for example. But you will have to deliberately delete the exclamation marks. They are of no use to you in a workspace. We'll see why the exclamation marks are there in a moment.

In addition to expressions, the changes file also contains your class definitions and the methods associated with those classes (classes and methods are not discussed in this chapter). But be careful! The exclamation marks, in this case, are particularly important. Methods are preceded by a **method prefix**, such as one of the following:

```
!Banana methods !
!Banana class methods !
```

The first prefix precedes instance methods, and the second precedes class methods. All methods following this prefix are terminated by an exclamation mark. The last method associated with a particular prefix is terminated by two exclamations marks separated by a space.

To be able to recover the methods and install them into your current image (as opposed to just copying them into a workspace or browser), you need to select a portion that begins with a method prefix and ends with an exclamation mark. Any number of intervening exclamation marks are permitted. As you might now be able to guess, the programming environment uses these exclamation marks to separate the individual methods when you install them into your environment.

As an example, if we were to scroll to the bottom of the changes file after we created some of the classes and methods of Chapter 4, we might find text like the following:

```
...
(Banana new color: 'yellow') printOn: Transcript!

!Banana methods !
color: aString
        color := aString!

printOn: aWindow
        aWindow nextPutAll: 'a '.
        aWindow nextPutAll: color.
        aWindow nextPutAll: ' Banana'! !

!Banana methods !
printOn: aWindow
        aWindow nextPutAll: 'a '; nextPutAll: color; nextPutAll: ' Banana'! !
```

To recover specific methods, select the desired methods, including the related prefixes and terminating exclamation marks, and click on **File It In** in the **Smalltalk** menu. All lost work can be recovered in this way.

Since everything is recorded in the changes file, this file can get to be quite large after a few weeks of playing with Smalltalk. At some point, it will be necessary to compress this file by executing

Smalltalk **compressChanges**

Compressing the file gets rid of all test expressions and retains only the most recent version of your methods. If you never compress the changes file, you will ultimately run out of space.

1.4.5 Smalltalk Windows: Components, Menus, and Scrolling

An experienced Smalltalk programmer will know all the names for the window components, will be able to manipulate menus that are associated with the windows, and will be able to scroll the windows. This section provides you with all of this information in a somewhat condensed form. There is no need to try to remember it on first reading. We will have plenty of opportunity to learn and relearn this information through practice and exposure in contexts where they are needed. The goal for this section is introduce you to the terminology, so that there is a ring of familiarity when we use the terms later.

Window Components

Windows are not just pictures (see Figure 1.18). They have parts, such as buttons that can be clicked on, for example, to change the size of the window and scroll bars to cause text to move horizontally or vertically. Windows generally consist of a **label bar**, a **border**, one or more **panes** or subwindows (see Figure 1.18), and special window **buttons** (clickable rectangular areas) for manipulating the window. A window button is activated by clicking the mouse button when the cursor is over the window button.

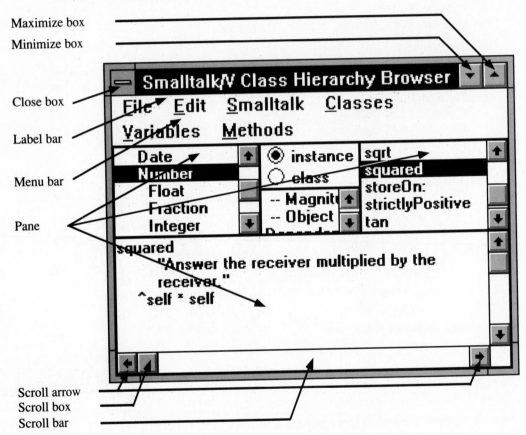

Figure 1.18 A window with three panes.

A short definition of each part of a window is provided below. Refer to the diagrams to properly identify the parts.

- The **maximize box** is a button that causes the window to grow to maximum size when you click over it with the left mouse button. To restore the window to its prior size, click on the maximize box a second time.

- The **minimize box** is a button that causes the window to shrink to its minimum size when you click over it with the left mouse button. In this **collapsed** state, only an icon (a picture) and its label are visible (see Figure 1.19). As a rule, different kinds of windows will have different icons. To restore the window to its prior size, double-click over the icon or its label.

Smalltalk/V Class Hierarchy Browser

Figure 1.19 The window shown in Figure 1.18, minimized.

- The **close box** is a button that causes the window to disappear from the environment when you double-click over it with the left mouse button; as its name implies, it is used to close the window.
- The **label bar** is a rectangular area at the top of the window containing non-editable text called a label (or title).
- The **menu bar** is the rectangular area below the label bar containing a list of menu items; a pull-down menu appears under the item when you press and hold the left mouse button over it (as shown in Figure 1.20). When the window is sufficiently wide to contain all menu items, these appear on a single line; otherwise, they wrap around onto additional lines as shown in Figures 1.18 and 1.20.

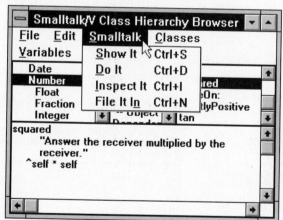

Figure 1.20 Pressing the left mouse button over the **Smalltalk** menu item.

- A **pane** is a subwindow without a label bar or associated window buttons. It may be an area for editing text, drawing pictures, or scrolling lists of items.
- A **scroll bar** is a rectangle that indicates that the pane data can be moved horizontally or vertically; i.e., **scrolled**. Scrolling is achieved in one of three ways: by clicking on a **scroll arrow**, one of the special buttons at the ends of a scroll bar; by dragging the **scroll box**, a square rectangle that can be moved anywhere inside the scroll bar; or by clicking elsewhere inside a scroll bar.

Selecting Window Menus

Generally, each pane in a window has a special task for which it was designed. Consequently, each pane has a number of menu commands that can be selected by the programmer. These menu commands are associated with specific menu items in the menu bar. The commands in each item can be made to appear by pressing the left mouse button over the item. When this is done, the menu commands appear immediately below the item—hence, they are called **pull-down menus**. When there are several panes in a window, the commands apply to the **active** pane—the pane in which you clicked last. Figure 1.21 illustrates how you might choose a menu command to cause "1+2" to be executed. Writing text and highlighting it is covered in detail in chapter 2—here, we are concerned only with the mechanics of obtaining and selecting menu commands. The steps involved are summarized in the following example:

- Press and hold the left mouse button over the word **Smalltalk** in the menu bar (see Figure 1.21). This causes a pull-down menu of commands to appear.
- Still holding down the mouse button, move the cursor down to the command desired (for example, the **Show It** command) and then release the mouse button. Should you wish to change your mind, simply click outside the pull-down menu.

Alternatively, it is possible to "freeze" the pull-down menu so that you don't have to hold down the mouse button as you move the mouse towards the desired command. This is achieved as follows:

- Click over the word **Smalltalk** to cause the pull-down menu to freeze.
- Move the cursor down to the desired command without pressing the mouse button.
- Select a command by clicking over the desired selection.

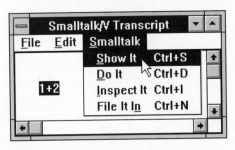

Figure 1.21 Selecting a pane's pull-down menu.

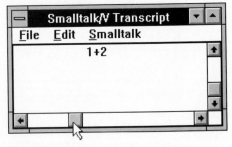

Figure 1.22 Scrolling right while at the bottom.

Window Scrolling

Most Smalltalk windows can be scrolled. An example is a transcript window that contains a **text pane** (a pane that can hold text). In general, the position of the scroll box indicates which part of the data is visible in the pane. For example, if the vertical scroll box is in the middle, then the pane is showing the middle part of the data (the top and bottom parts are consequently not visible). Figure 1.22 provides an illustration.

For text panes, horizontal and vertical scroll bars are permanently visible and scrolling is achieved by clicking on the scroll arrow, the scroll box, or the remaining areas of the scroll bar. However, scrolling can also be initiated by pressing and holding the mouse button over any location in the pane and moving the mouse in the desired direction—the pane will scroll to allow you to select more text, which you can subsequently deselect by clicking anywhere in the pane. In general, scrolling by directly manipulating the scroll bar (or its components) will occur only if there is actually more text to be seen by scrolling. You cannot scroll if everything to be seen is already visible.

1.5   Getting Some Experience with Smalltalk

1.5.1   Playing with Smalltalk Windows: Learning Mouse Mechanics

One of the first things you might do with a new car is sit in it and touch the different parts to develop a feel for it. The same applies to a new environment. Before we can be comfortable with the Smalltalk/V environment, we need to feel that we are in control. The best way to develop our confidence is to play with the system—to play with the windows.

Our task in this section will be to develop windowing expertise—to learn how to create windows (workspace windows, in particular), to move them around, to change their sizes, and to discard them. But wait! Don't we have to worry about making mistakes and breaking the system? The answer is "NO." Indeed, that is what makes it so much fun. You can—in fact, should—try things without really knowing what will happen. In the Smalltalk/V environment, this eagerness to learn by experimentation should be encouraged.

Starting Up

Begin by starting up Smalltalk as discussed at the beginning of Section 1.4. Your start-up screen should be similar to that shown in Figure 1.10. If not, there is no cause for alarm. We will very quickly change things to organize the screen the way we want it.

Creating New Workspace Windows

We can ignore the existing windows and create new ones. In particular, we can create a very special kind of windows, called a **workspace** window, as follows:

- Press and hold the left mouse button over the **File** entry in the menu bar. This will cause a pull-down menu to appear, as shown in Figure 1.23.
- Select menu item **New Workspace** by moving the cursor until it is above the item to be selected (this will cause the item to darken) and releasing the mouse button. The pull-down menu will then disappear and a new workspace window will appear, as shown in Figure 1.24 .

Repeat this procedure until you have created two or three workspace windows. This process of creating window is called **opening** a window.

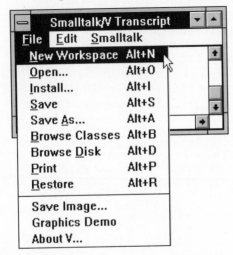

Figure 1.23 Prior to creating a new workspace window.

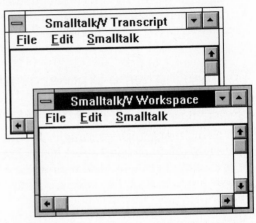

Figure 1.24 After creating a new workspace window.

Activating Windows

No matter how many windows are in the Smalltalk environment, only one window is ever **active** at a time. An active window can be recognized by the fact that the label bar is specially highlighted (see the workspace window in Figure 1.24). An **inactive** window is **activated** by clicking the mouse anywhere inside the window. If the window is partially concealed by some other window, it will rise to the top (or **pop-up**) when it is activated.

Experiment with the system by clicking on successive windows.

Moving Windows

Windows are easily **moved** by pressing and holding the left mouse button over the window's label bar. If the mouse is moved, the window will follow along. When the window has moved to the location desired, release the mouse button.

Experiment with the system by lining up the windows on your screen.

Resizing Windows

To **resize** a window—change its size—do the following:

- Move the cursor to an edge or a corner of the window. The current mouse cursor will change to a window resizing cursor, as shown in Figure 1.25. Which cursor you get will depend on the edge or corner the cursor is over.
- Press the left mouse button and move the mouse. The window's edge or corner should follow. When the edge or corner has moved to the location desired, release the mouse button.

Some experience is needed to master the process. So, experiment by making all your windows smaller. Another task would be to line up your windows in two rows in such a way that they touch each other but do not overlap.

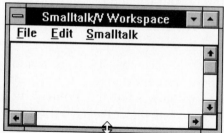

Figure 1.25 Resizing a window (notice the resizing cursor at the bottom).

Closing Windows

A window is discarded by **closing** it. A window can be closed as follows:

- Double-click on the close box at the top left corner of the window.

Alternatively,

- Press on the close box to obtain a pull-down menu.
- Click on menu entry **Close**.

In the Smalltalk/V environment, all windows can be closed. However, closing the transcript window is equivalent to exiting Smalltalk. Don't worry if this is done accidentally, because the resulting dialog box (shown in Figure 1.17) allows you to cancel the operation.

Experiment by closing a few of your windows. If necessary, open new workspace windows and immediately close them.

Collapsing Windows

When a Smalltalk/V window is collapsed, only an icon and the label bar are visible (see Figure 1.20). A window is **collapsed** by clicking the minimize box (the leftmost box at the top right corner of the window).

To restore the collapsed window to its original state, double-click anywhere on the icon or label bar.

Experiment by collapsing a few of your windows. Open new ones, if necessary. Note that collapsed windows can be moved just like their uncollapsed counterparts.

Zooming Windows

When a window contains text to be read or changed, it is convenient to make the window large enough to fill the whole screen; i.e., to **maximize** it. We can do this by resizing the window as explained above. However, it is cumbersome to make the window fit exactly. To make this process simpler, a window can be zoomed by clicking the maximize box (the rightmost box at the top right corner of the window). To unzoom, click on the maximize box a second time.

Experiment by zooming and unzooming a few of your windows.

1.5.2 A Tour of Smalltalk Windows

There are many different kinds of windows in the system. Each kind of window has a specific purpose and a special look. In subsequent chapters, we will consider the details of these different kinds of windows. For the moment, it is sufficient just to see what they look like. (The sampling that follows, illustrated in Figures 1.26-1.31, includes windows whose purpose we do not explain at this stage. This brief listing is provided for later reference.)

- A **workspace** window (or **worskpace** for short) is a text window used by the programmer to display textual information. Workspaces are covered in detail in Chapter 2.
- A **transcript** window (or **transcript** for short) is a workspace window that can be used by the system for displaying messages to the programmer. Transcripts are also investigated in Chapter 2.
- A **class hierarchy browser** (or **browser** for short) is a window used by the programmer to view the class library and to make additions or modifications to this class library. Browsers are considered in detail in Chapter 4. The concept of a class is introduced as early as Chapter 2 but considered in great detail in Chapter 5.
- A **disk browser** is a window used by the programmer to view and modify files on disk. Files have already been covered; filing in and filing out is covered in Chapter 4; also, see Exercise 6 at the end of this chapter.

- An **inspector** window (**inspector** for short) is a window used to look at and modify objects in the system. Inspectors and objects are considered in detail in Chapter 2.
- A **walkback** window appears when a programming command contains an execution error. Such windows are discussed repeatedly in several chapters beginning with Chapter 2.
- A **debugger** window (**debugger** for short) is used by a programmer to investigate and correct an execution error. Debuggers are investigated in Chapter 5.

Figure 1.26 A transcript window.

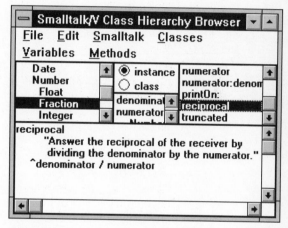

Figure 1.27 A class hierarchy browser.

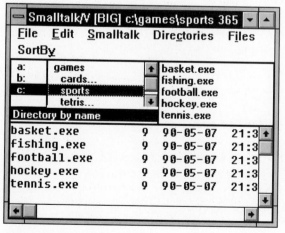

Figure 1.27 A disk browser.

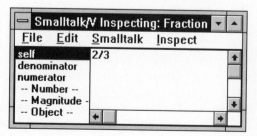

Figure 1.29 An inspector window.

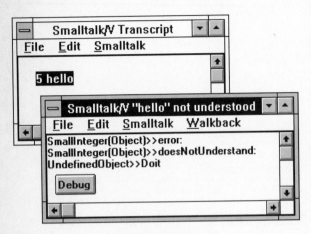

Figure 1.30 A walkback window.

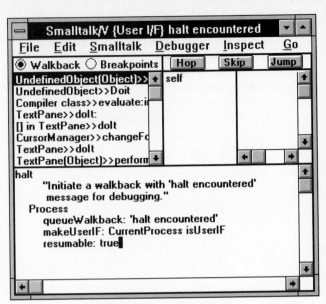

Figure 1.31 A debugger window.

1.6   Summary

This chapter has provided a basic introduction to the Smalltalk user interface. In particular, we have discussed the following notions:

- The typical computer and its components
- Starting up and exiting Smalltalk
- Typical Smalltalk windows and their components
- Opening, closing, moving, collapsing, and resizing windows
- Obtaining pull-down menus
- Scrolling

1.7   What You Did and Did Not Learn

This chapter has given you the basic terminology needed to understand computers and manipulate windows in the Smalltalk programming environment. In particular, you should be reasonably confident about creating, manipulating, and closing windows and controllling the computer via nontextual commands—specifically, by using the mouse.

However, you probably will not remember how to do all the things possible with windows. To develop this expertise requires practice that will be provided by subsequent chapters. Moreover, you have not yet been shown how to use the computer with textual commands—a subject of the next chapter.

1.8 Keywords

computer components: cabinet, computer, disk, disk drive, family of computers, floppy disk, hard disk, keyboard, memory, model, monitor, mouse, processor

computer terminology: activating, booting the system, code, commanding, designer, designing, evaluating, executing, hardware, machine language, operating system, program, programmer, programming, programming environment, software

files: backup, directory, directory hierarchy, disk drive, file, path name

operating systems (Microsoft Windows): Program Manager, program group, program item, file manager

programming environment facilities: changes file, compressing changes, exiting Smalltalk, image, recovering changes, saving an image, starting up Smalltalk

window components: close box, label bar, maximize box, menu bar, minimize box, pane, scroll arrow, scroll bar, scroll box, text pane

window cursors: cursor, arrow cursor, cross hair cursor, execute cursor, text cursor, window resizing cursor

window manipulation: activating windows, closing windows, collapsing windows, maximizing windows, moving windows, opening windows, resizing windows

window menus: menu bar, pull-down menu

window terminology: active window, clicking, collapsed window, double-clicking, background, I-beam, inactive window, scrolling, window

window varieties: class hierarchy browser, debugger window, disk browser, inspector window, transcript window, walkback window, workspace

1.9 Exercises

These exercises are intended to be done in an actual Smalltalk environment—not on paper.

1. Start up Smalltalk and then immediately exit it, taking care not to save the image.
2. Start up Smalltalk, change the layout of the transcript window by moving it around and resizing it, and then immediately exit it, once again taking care not to save the image. When you start up the next time, notice that nothing changed.
3. Repeat step 2 but this time save the image. When you start up, notice that you are continuing from the context of this saved image.
4. Open workspace windows until you have four windows. Adjust them to form two rows of two windows each. Line them up so they just touch and cover the entire screen.
5. Create several small workspaces inside of (or on top of) a larger one. Activate the larger workspace. Can you make the smaller workspaces visible again? Hint: Collapse the larger workspace.
6. Open a disk browser (hint: select **Browse Disk** in the **File** menu). Experiment with it to see what is on your **c:** disk.

2

The World of Messages, Receivers, and Selectors

What You Will Learn

You will learn that Smalltalk can be used as a powerful calculator. We will start with traditional calculator-style operations and explore where that leads us. We will find, for example, that expressions can be as simple (or as complicated) as we like and that we can build complicated expressions out of very simple expressions—much like a complicated structure can be built out of an erector set that contains different kinds of wooden, metallic, and plastic parts. The analogy can be carried further. Even though we can build interesting composites out of the parts, the parts usually cannot be randomly connected. It might be the case, for example, that a plastic part can be connected only to a metallic part. Moreover, perhaps only special kinds of metallic parts can be connected to wooden parts and only in a certain way. By analogy, we must learn the rules for constructing expressions so that we will know what is legal (what will work) and what is not. The best way to develop this understanding is by looking at a substantial number of examples.

2.1   Introduction

One simple form of programming makes use of Smalltalk and the Smalltalk environment as a calculator—as an evaluator for simple expressions, such as the following:

```
1+2
1+2+3+4
1*2+3*4
```

Several questions come to mind. In particular,

- Exactly how can we get the answers to the above expressions?
- How is the answer computed; e.g., is
  $$1*2+3*4 = (1*2)+(3*4) = 2+12=14 \text{ or is}$$
  $$1*2+3*4 = ((1*2)+3)*4 = (2+3)*4 = 5*4 = 20?$$
- How rich is the set of expressions that we can use (what are all the operators and what possible values can be used for computations)?

One way to answer those questions would simply be to try out different possibilities. Unfortunately, we don't yet have enough experience with the Smalltalk environment to be able to perform such experiments confidently. So, we digress for a moment to gain a better understanding of the transcript window, where such expressions can be evaluated.

2.2   The Mechanics of the Transcript Window

In the Smalltalk environment, text can be typed in many different kinds of windows; e.g., transcript windows, workspace windows, or the bottom pane of browser windows. From the point of view of manipulating text, however, all these windows behave the same way, so we don't have to consider each one separately. Here, we will focus on transcript windows.

The transcript window is unique because it is always open in the Smalltalk environment. Moreover, there is only one transcript window. Our immediate goal is to learn to use the transcript window (see Figure 2.1) as a substitute for a typewriter.

2.2.1 Moving the I-beam

We can begin by playing with the I-beam in the transcript window. Recall from the last chapter that an **I-beam** is a vertical line inside a text window (any window that can accept text). It marks the spot where text is to be inserted or deleted. By contrast, the position of the mouse (in a text pane) is represented by a text cursor. As we can see from Figure 2.1, the two are very similar. The text cursor will move when the mouse is moved; the I-beam, by contrast, will not move until the mouse is clicked.

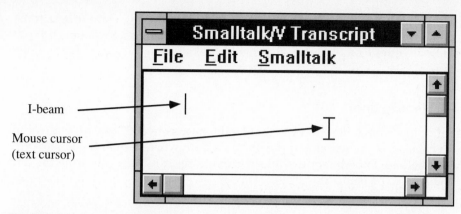

Figure 2.1 A transcript window.

Using the mouse, click anywhere in the transcript window. The I-beam will disappear from its current location and reappear at the location of the mouse cursor.

2.2.2 Typing and Deleting Characters

Now try typing **Hello** after positioning the I-beam in the center of the transcript window. Note that the I-beam moves each time a character is typed—after typing **H**, for example, the I-beam moves to the right of the **H**; after typing **e**, it moves to the right of the **e**, and so on. Once you complete typing the entire word **Hello**, try pressing the **Backspace** key—on most keyboards, this is a left arrow key that is rightmost in the numerics row. The last character typed, in this case **o**, is removed from the transcript window. Pressing the Backspace key again will cause the last **l** to be removed. By pressing the Backspace key repeatedly, it is possible to delete the entire word.

You might wish to try the experiment again, this time moving the I-beam to the center of the word **Hello**, between the two **l**s. Now try pressing the **Delete** key—this key is normally labeled with the word Delete. This time, the character to the right of the I-beam is removed—in this case, the second **l**. Press the Delete key a second time to remove the **o**.

In summary, the Backspace key removes the character on the left side of the I-beam, and the Delete key removes the character on the right. In practice, you might find the Backspace key more convenient to use.

2.2.3 Selecting Words

Now begin by typing a number of spaces. A **space** is the character obtained by pressing the **spacebar**—the large unlabeled key at the bottom of the keyboard. Next, type "**Hello, how are you?**". Note what happens when you place the mouse cursor over any part of a word such as **how** and double-click. The word **how** is highlighted, as shown in Figure 2.2. When that happens, the word is said to be **selected**. If you double-click on a second word, such as **are**, then **how** is deselected—**how** loses its highlighting and **are** is selected instead. Try double-clicking on other words to select them, too.

2.2.4 Selecting Lines

The entire line containing the sentence "**Hello, how are you?**" can be selected by double-clicking at the left end of the line. Click anywhere else in the window to deselect the line. Experiment with the system to see how far away from the left end you have to be before this stops working.

What happens if you double-click at the extreme right of a line? You'll find that the cursor moves to the rightmost character. For example, if you double-click to the extreme right of the line containing "**Hello, how are you?**", the cursor will move to the right of the **?** character. If you double-click on a line above, it will move to the extreme left, since that line contains no characters. How about double-clicking several lines below your sample line? In this case, the cursor moves back to the right of the **?** character once again—not to the left of the line you double-clicked on. Apparently, Smalltalk will not place the I-beam past the last character typed in the window. Double-clicking on a space will highlight exactly one character no matter how many spaces are there. Try double-clicking on the space between **how** and **you**, for example, or a space to the left of **Hello**.

Of course, you can extend your line by hitting the **Enter** key which moves the cursor to a new line. Notice that if you double-click below this point, the cursor will move back to the beginning of the new line rather than to the **?** character. Apparently, an Enter character is treated just like a normal character even though you can't see it. Now hit Enter one more time, type enough spaces so that the cursor is below and to the left of the **H**, and then type "**Fine, thanks.**", as shown in Figure 2.3.

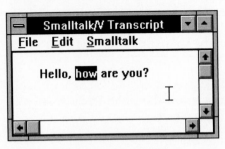

Figure 2.2 Selected text "how".

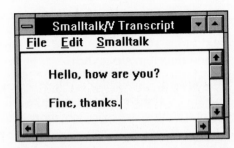

Figure 2.3 Typing multiline text.

2.2.5 Selecting Arbitrarily Long Text

Now suppose we want to select only a part of the existing text; e.g., portion "**how are**" of "**Hello, how are you?**" (see Figure 2.4). Three approaches are possible:

Direct Selection

Four steps are involved in direct selection:
- Move the I-beam to either end of "**how are**".
- Press and hold the left mouse button.
- Without releasing the mouse button, move the mouse cursor to the other end of "**how are**".
- Release the button.

Note that it doesn't matter how the cursor gets to the other end, as long as it eventually gets there (you could draw a figure eight if you wished as long as you ended up at the other end).

Shift-Click Selection

This technique is appropriate for selecting very large amounts of text; e.g., when you can't see all the text without scrolling (see the previous chapter for details about scrolling). Three steps are involved:
- Move the I-beam to either end of "**how are**".
- Move the mouse cursor to the other end of "**how are**" (without pressing the mouse button).
- While holding the Shift key down, click the mouse.

Extending a Selection

Suppose that you have already selected some text; e.g., say you have double-clicked on one of the two words **how** or **are**. You can extend the selection to include the other word as follows:
- Hold the Shift key down.
- Move the cursor to a point that includes the other word.
- Click.

If done properly, the previous selection will be lengthened to include the new characters. Note that this is just a variation of shift-click selection.

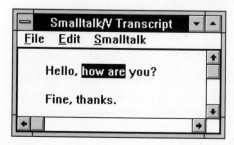

Figure 2.4 Selected text "how are".

2.2.6 Replacing Selected Text

Suppose we want to change only part of the sentence "**Hello, how are you?**", say portion "**how are**". Two approaches are possible:

Replacing Selected Text With New Text

To replace "**how are**" by "**is that**" so that the final sentence is "**Hello, is that you?**", first select "**how are**" and then type the replacement text "**is that**". There is no need to touch the Delete key.

Replacing Selected Text With Nothing (i.e., Deleting It)

To remove "**how are**" so that the final sentence is "**Hello, you?**", first select "**how are**" and then press either the Backspace key or the Delete key. You will note that there are now two spaces after the comma because the space was not part of the selected text. We can get rid of one of these spaces by pressing the Backspace key a second time. Alternatively, we could have included a space with the selected text and avoided the need for pressing the Backspace key a second time.

2.2.7 Executing Simple Commands

Now, we're ready to try evaluating something simple. Type "1+2" somewhere in the transcript window, select it, and then choose **Show It** in the **Smalltalk** menu, as explained below:

- Press the left mouse button over the word **Smalltalk** in the menu bar (below the label bar). This causes a pull-down menu (see Figure 2.5) to appear. This menu will remain as long as the mouse button remains depressed.
- To select an item from the menu (in this case, the **Show It** item), move the cursor over the item desired and release the mouse button (the result is shown in Figure 2.6). Alternatively, you could click on **Smalltalk** to freeze the menu bar and then select the menu item at your leisure.

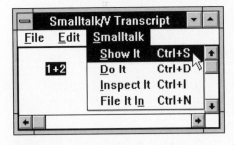

Figure 2.5 A transcript window's Smalltalk pull-down menu.

Figure 2.6 After choosing **Show It**.

We're now ready for more interesting experiments that make use of the transcript window as a work area.

2.3   Experimentation as a Key to Learning

The key to successful learning is directed experimentation; i.e., experimentation for the sake of finding out something that wasn't known before. In this section, we'll adopt this approach for learning basic Smalltalk programming concepts and the associated terminology (as a side effect).

2.3.1   Finding Out about Integers

Now that we know how to execute "1+2" to get "3", we might wonder if spaces are significant. Will we get the same answer if we execute " 1 + 2 " instead of "1+2"? As we can see from Figures 2.7 and 2.8, it doesn't seem to matter.

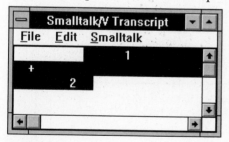

Figure 2.7 Selecting an expression with extra spaces.

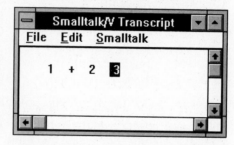

Figure 2.8 Executing the expression shows that spaces are not significant.

In fact, as we can see from Figures 2.9 and 2.10, it doesn't seem to matter if we spread the expression across multiple lines.

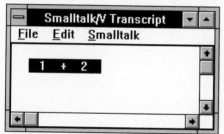

Figure 2.9 Selecting an expression spread across multiple lines.

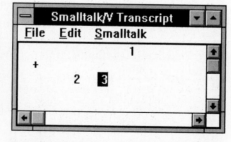

Figure 2.10 Executing the expression shows that expressions can be spread across multiple lines.

However, we have to be careful not to split large numbers across lines. Apparently, such split numbers are interpreted as two consecutive numbers without an intervening operator (see Figures 2.11 and 2.12).

Figure 2.11 Selecting an expression in which a number is split across lines.

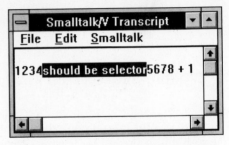

Figure 2.12 Executing the expression shows that numbers can't be split across lines.

So spaces and line boundaries are permitted only between numbers and operators. Now let's try some other experiments. To indicate that the result of evaluating "1+2" is 3, we will write

$1 + 2 \Rightarrow 3$ (addition)

Let's consider other operators.

$4 - 1 \Rightarrow 3$ (subtraction)
$2 * 2 \Rightarrow 4$ (multiplication)
$6 / 2 \Rightarrow 3$ (division)

Some operations don't exist on standard calculators.

$25 \mathbin{/\!/} 3 \Rightarrow 8$ (division with truncation—discards remainder 1 in $8^1/_3$)
$25 \mathbin{\backslash\!\backslash} 3 \Rightarrow 1$ (remainder—just the 1 in $8^1/_3$; also known 25 modulo 3)

Presumably, we can use more complex expressions.

$1 + 1 + 1 \Rightarrow 3$ $2 * 2 * 2 \Rightarrow 8$
$5 - 1 - 1 - 1 \Rightarrow 2$ $12 / 3 / 2 \Rightarrow 2$

What about the converse of complexity? What is the simplest expression? Can we write just a simple number? Clearly, we can (see Figures 2.13 and 2.14).

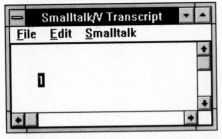

Figure 2.13 Selecting "1" for execution.

Figure 2.14 Executing "1" shows that numbers evaluate to themselves.

We would indicate this as follows:

$1 \Rightarrow 1$

What about negative values?

-1 ⇒ -1

They work, too! Presumably, we can also write more complex expressions that evaluate to negative numbers.

4 - 6 ⇒ -2   2 * -3 ⇒ -6   -6 / 2 ⇒ -3

But we have to be careful. Is "4-3", with no spaces, 4 minus 3 or is it 4 followed by "-3"? Apparently (see Figures 2.15 and 2.16), it's the latter. To compute 4 minus 3, we have to write "4- 3" with a space before the 3, or perhaps "4 - 3", which is equivalent but looks a little better.

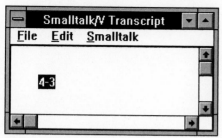
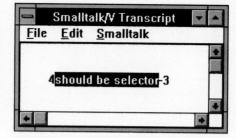

Figure 2.15 Selecting "4-3" for execution.

Figure 2.16 "4-3" is interpreted as integer "4" followed by integer "-3".

Finally, what happens if we start mixing operators. For example, do the following expressions lead to the same answer?

1 + 2 * 3   2 * 3 + 1

The answer is no! The two expression evaluate to different results.

1 + 2 * 3 ⇒ 9   2 * 3 + 1 ⇒ 7

Before we explain why this is the case, let's consider some simple terminology. In an expression such as "1+2", + is termed the **operator** and 1 and 2 are termed **operands** of the operator. The number 1 is the **left operand** of + whereas 2 is the **right operand** of +. In a two operator expression like "1+2*3", it is easy to identify the operators + and * but their operands are more difficult to identify. The reason is that the operators must be evaluated in some order and consequently an operand might be the result of a previous evaluation. For example, consider two possible scenarios.

- If + is evaluated first, "1+2*3" simplifies to "3*3" which in turn simplifies to 9. Hence it should be clear that the left operand of * is not 2 but rather "1+2" (which evaluates to 3).
- If * is evaluated first, "1+2*3" simplifies to "1+6" which in turn simplifies to 7. In that case, "2*3" or 6 would be the right operand of +.

So which is it? As it turns out, the usual order of operation observed in mathematics is not observed in Smalltalk. Evaluation in Smalltalk is strictly **left-to-right**. The leftmost operator is evaluated first with its immediate operands and the result replaces both the operands and the operator; then the process is repeated until no operators remain. Consequently, the above two expressions evaluate as follows:

$$1 + 2 * 3 \Rightarrow 3 * 3 \Rightarrow 9 \qquad\qquad 2 * 3 + 1 \Rightarrow 6 + 1 \Rightarrow 7$$

This process is more evident when an extremely complex expression is evaluated. Consider the following expression. We will underline the part of the expression that is evaluated at each step. In the steps that follow, the result replaces the underlined part.

$$
\begin{array}{l}
\underline{1+2} \;\; *3 \; -4 \; +5 \; *6 \; -7 \; -8 \; /9 \;\Rightarrow \\
\underline{3} \qquad *3 \; -4 \; +5 \; *6 \; -7 \; -8 \; /9 \;\Rightarrow \\
\underline{9} \qquad\quad -4 \; +5 \; *6 \; -7 \; -8 \; /9 \;\Rightarrow \\
\underline{5} \qquad\qquad\; +5 \; *6 \; -7 \; -8 \; /9 \;\Rightarrow \\
\underline{10} \qquad\qquad\qquad *6 \; -7 \; -8 \; /9 \;\Rightarrow \\
\underline{60} \qquad\qquad\qquad\quad -7 \; -8 \; /9 \;\Rightarrow \\
\underline{53} \qquad\qquad\qquad\qquad\;\; -8 \; /9 \;\Rightarrow \\
\underline{45} \qquad\qquad\qquad\qquad\qquad\;\; /9 \;\Rightarrow \\
5
\end{array}
$$

But what if we want the *"operator to evaluate before the + operator in the expression "1+2*3"? Is there any way to force a different evaluation order? The answer is *yes*. Use **round brackets** (also called **parentheses**) to group expressions that must be evaluated as a unit.

$$1 + (2 * 3) \Rightarrow 1 + 6 \Rightarrow 7 \qquad\qquad (2 * 3) + 1 \Rightarrow 6 + 1 \Rightarrow 7$$

As we can see, the round brackets have definitely changed the result in the first expression. In the second case, however, the brackets were superfluous—the result would have been 7 even without the brackets.

Can we use superfluous brackets anywhere? For example, are the following expressions **legal** (is it permissible to attempt to evaluate them)?

(1 + 2 + 3)	(1) + 2
(((1 + 2) + 3) + 4) + 5	(((((1)))))

Yes, all of them are legal. In general, brackets can surround any expression that can serve as an operand for some operator. They are **illegal** when used in any other way. Examples of illegal expressions are the following:

(1+2	missing right round bracket
1+2)	missing left round bracket
1)+(2	missing left and right bracket
(1+)2	1+ cannot be used as an operand

If you attempt to evaluate an illegal expression, an appropriate error message will be generated. For example, consider Figure 2.17. If this happens, just hit **Backspace** to remove the error message and continue as if nothing happened.

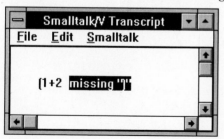

Figure 2.17 Attempting to evaluate "(1+2".

This isn't meant to indicate that you shouldn't make mistakes. On the contrary, you'll make mistakes quite regularly and you'll learn from them. What's important is that the environment is tolerant of errors. In other words, its OK to make mistakes. You won't break anything.

2.3.2   Finding Out about Instances and Classes

So far, all our examples have dealt with numbers like 1, 2, and 3. You might wish to be more precise and call them integers. We can say that 1 is an integer or, more precisely, that 1 is an **instance** of the integer **class**. Presumably, it is also the case that 1 is an **instance** of the number **class**. Since 2 and 3 are also instances of integers and numbers, it is clear that a class has many instances in general and that an instance can be a member of many classes. Just to make sure we understand this basic notion, let's review it one more time:

> ..., -3, -2, -1, 0, 1, 2, 3, ... are integers; i.e., instances of the integer class.
> ..., -3, -2, -1, 0, 1, 2, 3, ... are also numbers; i.e., instances of the number class.
> There are many integers (the integer class has many instances).
> The number class has many numbers (the number class has many instances).

If we focus on a particular instance such as 1, we can agree—based on intuition and common sense—that 1 is both an integer and a number. It would be fortuitous if Smalltalk used the same intuitive terminology. Does it? There are two ways to resolve this question—skip ahead to the summary section and look it up, or use the Smalltalk environment as an exploratory tool to find out. But how can we ask? It would be nice if we could explicitly ask 1 what kind of object it is. Fortunately, this is possible. It is simply a matter of executing the following expression:

1 **class** ⇒ SmallInteger

In essence, we asked 1—"what is your class?" and it replied *SmallInteger*. That's instructive. The answer was not *Integer* as, we might have expected, but it was close!! What else could we ask to find out more? We asked an instance what its class was. Maybe we can ask a class if there is something more general than itself, something above it—the word *super* comes to mind.

> SmallInteger **superclass** ⇒ Integer

Here, we are asking the class SmallInteger, "what is your **superclass** (what class is above or more general than you)?" It replied *Integer*. So a small integer is an integer! Can we continue this line of questioning?

> Integer **superclass** ⇒ Number
> Number **superclass** ⇒ Magnitude
> Magnitude **superclass** ⇒ Object
> Object **superclass** ⇒ nil

What does this all mean? It means that 1 is simultaneously a small integer, an integer, a number, a magnitude, and an object. And the buck stops at Object—it has no superclass. This can be shown in a diagram, as in Figure 2.18. Our initial intuitive understanding was correct—1 is both an integer and a number. But that was only a small part of the story.

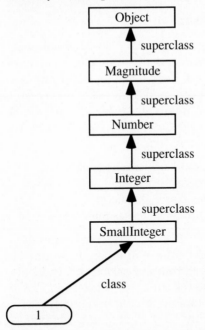

Figure 2.18 Instance "1" and the classes that consider "1" to be a member.

Of course, this raises some other questions. If 1 is a small integer, does that mean there are large integers? Let's try asking some larger instances.

> 123 **class** ⇒ SmallInteger
> 12345 **class** ⇒ SmallInteger
> 1234567890 **class** ⇒ LargePositiveInteger

That's instructive. The answer was not *LargeInteger*, as we might have expected, but once again, it was close! Moreover, this suggests there may be small negative integers and large negative integers. Let's find out.

-1 **class** ⇒ SmallInteger
-1234567890 **class** ⇒ LargeNegativeInteger

Apparently, there is no such thing as a class devoted to small negative integers—both 1 and -1 are small integers. On the other hand, there is a class devoted to large positive and large negative integers, since 1234567890 and -1234567890 are respective instances. Now more questions come to mind. What is 0? Is there a superclass of LargePositiveInteger and LargeNegativeInteger called LargeInteger?

0 **class** ⇒ SmallInteger
LargePositiveInteger **superclass** ⇒ Integer
LargeNegativeInteger **superclass** ⇒ Integer

For small integers, there is no class differentiation between negative, 0, and positive integer instances. There is no such thing as a LargeZero class. Moreover, we can see that a large positive or large negative integer is an integer. There is no such thing as a LargeInteger. Clearly, there must be a dividing line between small integers and either large positive or large negative integers. You may wish to experiment further to find out where it is.

All this information can be represented diagrammatically, as in Figure 2.19. Note that the classes are organized so that the more general classes are at the top with the more specialized classes at the bottom. Since such an organization is a hierarchy, we call such a diagram a **class hierarchy** diagram.

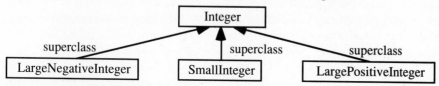

Figure 2.19 The Integer class hierarchy.

Now that we know how to ask (1) an instance for its class and (2) a class for its superclass, we might wonder if we can be sloppy. For example, can we ask an instance for its superclass or a class for its class?

0 **superclass** ⇒ (error—this is not legal)

This time a special window appears—a **walkback** window (see Figure 2.20)—with an error message indicating that 0 does not understand **superclass**. Now we know what happens when we make a mistake. For now, simply close the window by clicking on the close box—the small rectangular button in the top left corner of the window (see the previous chapter for more details). Note: Never close the window without at least reading the error message in the label bar—this could be your only clue to your mistake.

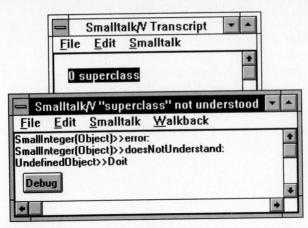

Figure 2.20 A walkback window.

Apparently, you have to know the difference between a class and an instance. Instances don't understand **superclass**—only classes do. Now consider the same scenario for **class**.

    1 **class** ⇒ SmallInteger
    SmallInteger **class** ⇒ SmallInteger class
    Number **class** ⇒ Number class
    Object **class** ⇒ Object class

In this case, you can ask a class for its class but the answer is not very instructive. A proper explanation for this is quite complex and also confusing when you're first learning Smalltalk. In essence, a class is an object—so it must be a member of a class too. But that's more than we need to know. For the moment, it is sufficient to realize that both instances and classes understand **class**. However, if we ask a class what its class is, it seems to regurgitate its own name followed by the word *class*. The word *class* is not part of the answer if you ask an instance such as 1 what its class is!

Perhaps there is another way to learn the same thing; for example, by asking a more direct question.

    2 **isKindOf**: SmallInteger ⇒ true
    2 **isKindOf**: Integer ⇒ true

Presumably, we could check the entire class hierarchy shown in Figure 2.18.

    2 **isKindOf**: Number ⇒ true
    2 **isKindOf**: Magnitude ⇒ true
    2 **isKindOf**: Object ⇒ true

We could also ask questions that we know to be false.

    2 **isKindOf**: LargePositiveInteger ⇒ false
    2 **isKindOf**: LargeNegativeInteger ⇒ false

As expected, the answers should be different for a large positive integer.

    1234567890 **isKindOf**: SmallInteger ⇒ false
    1234567890 **isKindOf**: Integer ⇒ true
    1234567890 **isKindOf**: LargePositiveInteger ⇒ true
    1234567890 **isKindOf**: LargeNegativeInteger ⇒ false

So we conclude that a large positive integer is an integer. If we bothered to ask, we would also find out that a large negative integer is an integer. You might even suggest that we also ask other questions, such as the following:

    2 **isKindOf**: PositiveInteger ⇒ (error—not legal)
    -2 **isKindOf**: NegativeInteger ⇒ (error—not legal)
    1234567890 **isKindOf**: LargeInteger ⇒ (error—not legal)

Unfortunately, you have to know what you are doing to ask the question correctly. In particular, you have to know what a legal class is. For example, we previously asked 1, 1234567890, and -1234567890 what kind (or class) of objects they were by evaluating "1 **class**", "1234567890 **class**", and "-1234567890 **class**", respectively. The answers were SmallInteger, LargePositiveInteger, and LargeNegativeInteger, respectively. These must clearly be legal classes. What about class Integer? Is it a legal class? You should be able to provide a definitive answer from our discussion so far.

2.3.4 Finding Out about Messages

Until now, we have been talking about asking questions of instances and classes much as we ask questions of people. Obviously, instances and classes are not little people but it is convenient to treat them as if they were. This is known as **anthropomorphizing** the objects—ascribing human characteristics to the objects (**anthropos** denotes human and **morphe** denotes form). More than any other programming language, Smalltalk lends itself to this **anthropomorphic** view of programming.

On the other hand, the colloquial term "asking an object" is replaced in Smalltalk by a more technical expression *"sending a message to an object."* In the following examples, we are sending the message "class", "+ 2", and "isKindOf: Integer" respectively to the integer 1.

    1 **class** ⇒ SmallInteger
    1 + 2 ⇒ 3
    1 **isKindOf**: Integer ⇒ true

Indeed, all messages have one of these three forms. In general, we refer to these as

- Unary messages; e.g., "**class**"
- Binary messages; e.g., "+2"
- Keyworded messages; e.g., "**isKindOf**: Integer"

Of these, only the latter has more complicated variations. For example, we might ask

 5 **between**: 1 **and**: 10 ⇒ true

Here, "**between**: 1 **and**: 10" is a keyworded message—"**between**:" is a **keyword** and "**and**:" is a keyword. By analogy with "1+2", we can see that 5, 1, and 10 are the operands. What is the operator? The answer is "**between:and**:". Note that the colons are part of the operator. In general, there is no limit to the number of operands permitted by a keyworded message, but between each operand, there must be a word that terminates in a colon—there must be a keyword. So, for example, the following are illegal:

 5 **between** 1 10   (illegal—missing keyword)
 5 **between** 1 **and** 10   (illegal—missing two colons)
 5 **between**: 1 **and** 10   (illegal—missing one colon)

In addition to the role played by "**between**:" and "**and**:" as separators for operands, it is clear that they also serve to name the operand they immediately precede. This is why they are called **keywords**. Thus, "**between**:" is a keyword for 1, whereas "**and**:" is a keyword for 10.

Although this operator/operand terminology is acceptable for understanding Smalltalk, it is usually replaced by more specialized terminology. In general, an expression such as

 1 **class**
 1 + 2
 1 **between**: 0 **and**: 10

consists of a **receiver** (the integer 1) and a **message** (respectively "**class**", "+2", and "**between**: 0 **and**: 10"). The message is itself composed of a **selector** (respectively, "**class**", "+", and "**between:and**:") and **parameters**; namely, operands other than the receiver (in this case, there are respectively, no parameters, one parameter 2, and two parameters 0 and 10). A summary is provided in Figure 2.21.

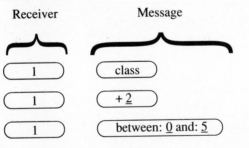

Figure 2.21 Smalltalk terminology. Message selector (normal text) and message parameter (underlined).

We can also refer to the three kinds of selectors as

- Unary selectors; e.g., "**class**"
- Binary selectors; e.g., "+"
- Keyworded selectors; e.g., "**between:and**:"

2.3.5 Finding Out about Message Priority (Mixing Messages)

In the previous section, we introduced three different kinds of selectors: unary, binary, and keyworded selectors, illustrated by the following examples:

        1 **class**
        1 + 2
        1 **between**: 0 **and**: 10

We already know that evaluation proceeds strictly left-to-right for binary selectors such as +, -, *, and /. Does the same rule apply when we mix different kinds of selectors? Before we can answer that, let's have a look at a few more unary messages: **negated** and **factorial**.

        1 **negated** ⇒ -1
        -1 **negated** ⇒ 1
        0 **factorial** ⇒ 1
        1 **factorial** ⇒ 1
        2 **factorial** ⇒ 2 (i.e., 1×2)
        3 **factorial** ⇒ 6 (i.e., 1×2×3)
        4 **factorial** ⇒ 24 (i.e., 1×2×3×4)
        5 **factorial** ⇒ 120 (i.e., 1×2×3×4×5)
        6 **factorial** ⇒ 720 (i.e., 1×2×3×4×5×6)

Perhaps you can guess that 10 factorial would be 1×2×3×4×5×6×7×8×9×10— whatever that works out to be. Can we send the **negated** message to the result of a previous **negated** message? For example,

        1 **negated negated** ⇒ 1

It may not be obvious why the answer is 1. It would be nice if we could see the evaluation proceed step by step.

        1   **negated**   **negated** ⇒
        -1 **negated** ⇒
        1

Clearly, the result of the first (leftmost) **negated** is -1. Further, negating -1 with the second (rightmost) **negated** results in positive 1. Presumably, we could mix different unary selectors.

        3   **factorial**   **negated** ⇒
        6   **negated** ⇒
        -6

So the rule for unary selectors seems to be the same as the rule used to evaluate binary selectors—**left-to-right** evaluation. Now, let's try mixing unary and binary selectors to see what we get.

        1 **negated** + 2 ⇒ 1
        1 + 2 **negated** ⇒ -1

The rule here doesn't seem to be the standard left-to-right rule. If it were, the second example "1+2 **negated**" would have evaluated to "-3". The situation is more complex. In more detail, evaluation proceeds as follows for the second example:

1 + <u>2 **negated**</u> ⇒
<u>1 + -2</u> ⇒
-1

Basically, all selectors are assigned a degree of importance, or **priority**. Unary selectors, in particular, are assigned a higher priority than are binary selectors.

Higher priority selectors seem to be executed first. But is this precise enough? For example, what message is evaluated first in the following example:

1 + 2 + 3 **factorial**

Is it **factorial** because it has a higher priority, or is it the leftmost +? In this case, evaluation proceeds as follows:

<u>1 + 2</u>   + 3 **factorial**   ⇒
3   + <u>3 **factorial**</u> ⇒
<u>3   + 6</u> ⇒
9

The rule might best be described as follows: given two consecutive selectors, the leftmost selector is evaluated first if they both have the same priority; otherwise, the highest priority selector is evaluated first. For reference purposes, let's give this notion a name—the **priority rule**.

The priority rule applies in all cases, even when keyworded selectors are used, under the following priority scheme:

- Unary selectors—highest priority
- Binary selectors—next highest priority
- Keyworded selectors—lowest priority

Consequently, you should be able to determine whether the following evaluation order is correct:

25 **between**: 10 + <u>3 **factorial**</u> **and**: 5 **factorial** + 3 ⇒
25 **between**: <u>10 + 6</u> **and**: 5 **factorial** + 3 ⇒
25 **between**: 16 **and**: <u>5 **factorial**</u> + 3 ⇒
25 **between**: 16 **and**: <u>120</u>   + 3 ⇒
<u>25 **between**: 16</u> **and**: <u>123</u>   ⇒
true

In this case, it is correct. However, it is complex enough to deserve an explanation. We might proceed as follows for the first line:

25 **between**: 10 +   3 **factorial** **and**: 5 **factorial** + 3 ⇒

The first selector is **between:and:** and the second selector is +. Which has a higher priority? The answer is +, since binary selectors have a higher priority than keyworded selectors. Hence, + must execute before **between:and:**. However, we must also take the next selector **factorial** into account. Which has a higher priority, + or **factorial**? The answer is **factorial**, since unary selectors have a higher priority than binary selectors. So **factorial** must execute before +. Should we consider what comes after the **factorial** operator? If we do, we find that it is the second keyword in the keyworded selector **between:and:**. Selector **factorial** has a higher priority and we conclude that it is the very first message to be sent. Who is the receiver? It is 3; hence, the answer is 6.

The next step in the analysis is similar. Consider

    25 **between**: 10 +   6   **and**: 5 **factorial**   + 3 ⇒

The first selector is **between:and:** and the second is +. Since binary operators have a higher priority than keyworded operators, + must be evaluated first. What comes after +? The second keyword of keyworded operator **between:and:**, which has a lower priority. Hence, "+ 6" is the second message sent. The receiver is 10; hence, the answer is 16.

Hopefully, the rest is easier. Consider

    25 **between**: 16   **and**: 5 **factorial**   + 3 ⇒

The first selector is **between:and:**, the second is **factorial**, and the third is +. Selector **factorial** in this case has a higher priority. Hence, message **factorial** is sent to 5. The answer is 120.

Now, consider

    25 **between**: 16   **and**: 120   + 3 ⇒

The only remaining selectors are **between:and:** and +. Since + has a higher priority (it's a binary operator), message "+ 3" is sent to 120 to get 123.

Finally, the last step sends the "**between**: 16 **and**: 123" message to 25. The answer is true, since 25 really is between 16 and 123.

    25 **between**: 16   **and**: 123   ⇒
    true

Clearly, determining the evaluation order is a complicated task the first time you encounter it. However, it is crucial that you understand the concept of priority. When a complex expression is evaluated, only one message at a time is evaluated. At each step, it is sufficient to be able to determine the next message to be evaluated. To give you a little more practice with this notion, see if you can determine which message is evaluated first in each of the following expressions. The answers are shown immediately afterward (you might wish to hide them temporarily).

1+2+3 **factorial**
10 **factorial factorial** + 1
1 + 2 **factorial negated**
1 **between:** 0+0 **and:** 2 **factorial**
1 **negated between:** 0+1 **and:** 5
2 **factorial** + 3 **factorial**

The answers are shown below. The first message sent along with the receiver is underlined.

<u>1+2</u>+3 **factorial**
10 <u>**factorial**</u> **factorial** + 1
1 + <u>2 **factorial**</u> **negated**
1 **between:** <u>0+0</u> **and:** 2 **factorial**
<u>1 **negated**</u> **between:** 0+1 **and:** 5
2 <u>**factorial**</u> + 3 **factorial**

In all the above examples, we avoided the use of brackets. Does the addition of round brackets (parentheses) change the evaluation order? Certainly, that's what brackets are for. Consequently,

1 + (2*3) ⇒	(1+2) * 3 ⇒
1 + 6 ⇒	3 * 3 ⇒
7	9

How does this affect the priority rule? In this case, there is no effect as long as we observe the **bracketing rule**: "A bracketed expression cannot be used as an operand unless all messages inside have been evaluated." Consequently, the following bracketed expression would evaluate as follows:

```
1 + 2     * (3 - 4  + (5 * 6))   + 3    ⇒
3         * (3 - 4  + (5 * 6))   + 3    ⇒
3         * (-1     + (5 * 6))   + 3    ⇒
3         * (-1     + (30))      + 3    ⇒
3         * (29)    + 3 ⇒
87                  + 3 ⇒
90
```

2.3.6 Calculating with Other Kinds of Numbers

Smalltalk supports two other kinds of numbers: fractions and floats. For example, 1/3 is a **fraction** consisting of **numerator** 1 and **denominator** 3, whereas 3.14159 is a **float** (short for **floating point number**). Fractions are **exact**; i.e., there is no bound on the numerator or denominator. By contrast, floats are **approximate**; i.e., the number of digits maintained by floats is bounded. Attempts to use floats with large numbers of digits are tolerated but excess digits are discarded. The number of digits retained is a function of the computer being used to execute Smalltalk. To find out how many digits are retained by Smalltalk on your computer, you might try typing a float with many digits.

3.14159268939 ⇒ 3.14159

In this case, the result indicated that only 6 digits are retained[1]. Of course, we might want to investigate the class hierarchy, as we did for integers, to uncover the relationships among these new classes. We would find the numeric class hierarchy to be as shown in Figure 2.22.

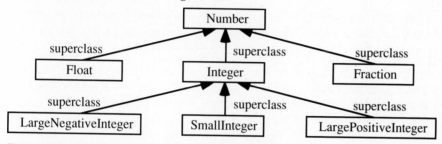

Figure 2.22 The complete numeric class hierarchy.

Getting back to fractions, we might be tempted to try out a few examples.

1/3 ⇒ 1/3	2/3 ⇒ 2/3	3/3 ⇒ 1
4/3 ⇒ 4/3	5/3 ⇒ 5/3	6/3 ⇒ 2

We've seen 6/3 before and we interpreted it as 6 divided by 3. It seems as if we've encountered a confusing situation. Is 1/3 short for "one-third" or is it "1 divided by 3"? It may seem like we're splitting hairs but it's an important difference. "One-third" is a single object, whereas "1 divided by 3" consists of the objects 1 and 3 operated on by the divide operation. How can we resolve the issue?

First, let's be clear that / is a divide operation. For example, we can try out more complex expressions using /.

(2+3) / 4 ⇒ 5/4
2 * 2 **negated** / 3 ⇒ -4/3
1 / 3 **factorial** ⇒ 1/6
10 **factorial** / 9 **factorial** ⇒10

However, this can't be the whole story. When we try to evaluate "1 divided by 3", it's as if nothing happened.

1/3 ⇒ 1/3

---

[1]Actually, floats are represented internally as **bits** (zeros and ones)—the details are of little interest to us. Since 5 bits can be used to represent a number between 0 and 32 and 4 bits can represent a number between 0 and 16, it should be clear that dropping one bit does not correspond to dropping one decimal digit. Hence, saying that Smalltalk (in the above example) returns 7 digits is really just an approximation of the truth—but one that is good enough for our purposes.

Did we get back "1 divided by 3" again? Let's find out using message **class**. For example,

> 1 **class** ⇒ SmallInteger
> 3 **class** ⇒ SmallInteger
> (1/3) **class** ⇒ Fraction

So, the result was a fraction. Hence, to be precise, we should be saying "when 1 is divided by 3, the result is a fraction—one-third." Consequently, when we say that 1/3 is a fraction, we implicitly mean "after it is evaluated."

Obviously, the divide operation is special. In some cases, the result is an integer; e.g., 4 / 2 ⇒ 2. In other cases, it is a fraction; e.g., 2 / 6 ⇒ 1 / 3. Also, the result is as simple as possible—it is **reduced**. Another way to think of it is that / is a conversion operator. When division is not exact, rather than compute an approximation, it converts the operands into a more complicated object—a fraction. In the next section, we'll provide another view on this issue.

Operations +, -, *, /, //, \\, and **negated** that apply to integers also apply to fractions and floats. Consider the following:

> (1/3) + (1/3) ⇒ 2/3   1.3 + 7.1 ⇒ 8.7

Indeed, it is even allowable to mix different numeric values.

> 1 + (1/3) ⇒ 4/3   1 + 1.3 ⇒ 2.3
> 1/3 + 1.3 ⇒ 1.6333333   2.5 + 0.5 ⇒ 3.0

The operators are sophisticated enough to convert one of the operands if they are not both instances of the same class. Moreover, conversion occurs in the order

> integer ⇒ fraction ⇒ float

Once the result is computed, fractions (but not floats) are simplified to integers where possible. Consequently, to evaluate "1 + 1.3", the 1 is converted to 1.0 in order to add 1.3.

It is also possible to explicitly request a conversion using messages **rounded**, **truncated**, and **asFloat**.

> 5.4 **rounded** ⇒ 5   5.7 **rounded** ⇒ 6
> 8.3 **truncated** ⇒ 8   8.8 **truncated** ⇒ 8
>
> 5.4 **rounded** ⇒ 5   5.7 **rounded** ⇒ 6
> 8.3 **truncated** ⇒ 8   8.8 **truncated** ⇒ 8
>
> (5/4) **rounded** ⇒ 1   (7/4) **rounded** ⇒ 2
> (5/4) **truncated** ⇒ 1   (7/4) **truncated** ⇒ 1
>
> 7 **asFloat** ⇒ 7.0
> (1/4) **asFloat** ⇒ 0.25

Floats, unlike integers or fractions, have limited range and an error results if an attempt is made to use (or compute) one that is too large (positive or negative). This limit is a function of the hardware. On a typical computer, the limit might be

99999999999999999999999999999999999999999999999999999999999999999.0
-99999999999999999999999999999999999999999999999999999999999999999.0

Such large numbers are difficult to copy accurately. To help alleviate this problem, a more flexible notation, called the **engineering** or **exponent** notation, is used. Essentially, a number—the **mantissa**—is multiplied by a power of 10—the **exponent**.

$$1\times10^{-20} \qquad 2\times10^{-3} \qquad 3\times10^{3} \qquad 4\times10^{20}$$

In the last case, for example, 4 is the mantissa and 20 is the exponent. Special character × and the superscript integers cannot be used in Smalltalk. Instead, the following notation is used:

$$1e\text{-}20 \qquad 2e\text{-}3 \qquad 3e3 \qquad 4e20$$

Note that the notation is nonunique; e.g., all the following are equivalent:

0.000000000314159e10
0.0314159e2
0.314159e1
3.14159
3.14159e0
31.4159e-1
314.159e-2
31415.9e-4
314159000000000.0e-14

Also, no spaces are allowed. If there is a point, at least one digit is required before and after the point. The **e** must be in lowercase. Only negative exponents have a sign. Additionally, it is easy to mentally transform from the exponent notation to the notation without exponents.

Mathematically
0.0314159e2 means $0.0314159\times10^{2} = 0.0314159\times100 = 3.14159$
314.159e-2 means $314.159\times10^{-2} = 314.159/10^{2} = 314.159/100 = 3.14159$

Intuitively
0.0314159e2 means "move the decimal point right 2" = 3.14159
314.159e-2 means "move the decimal point left 2" = 3.14159
3.14159e0 means "do not move the decimal point" = 3.14159

2.4   The Use of Inspectors as Investigation Tools

Up until now, we haven't had a tool that allowed us to look at the details of an object—to actually see what is inside. We'll call such a tool an **inspector**. If we had known about inspectors, we might have been able to resolve the question "what is 1/3?" with much less cleverness on our part, and without using message **class**.

2.4.1   Inspecting Calculated Results

An **inspector** is a special kind of window that appears when the **inspect** message is sent to an object. This window permits all internal details of the object to be viewed and modified. For example, executing the following results in the corresponding inspectors shown in Figure 2.23. All inspectors that appear remain until you close them by double-clicking on the inspector's close box (see Chapter 1 for a discussion).

> 27 **inspect**
> (1/3) **inspect**
> 32.1 **inspect**

Note the title at the top of each inspector. It tells you what kind of object is being inspected. We can click on any one of the names on the left side. Three situations are shown in Figure 2.24 for object 1/3; namely, where we clicked on **self** (the entire object 1/3), **numerator** (1), and **denominator** (3), respectively.

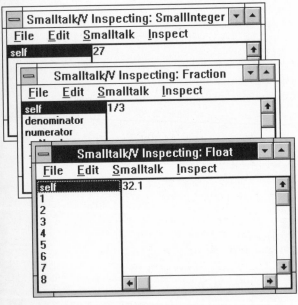

Figure 2.23 Inspectors for (a) 27, (b) (1/3), (c) 32.1.

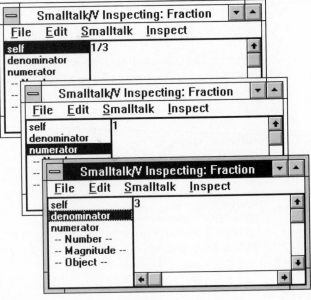

Figure 2.24 Inspectors showing (a) self 1/3, (b) numerator 1, (c) denominator 3.

Inspectors allow us to see an object's **parts** by clicking on the appropriate part name. The object associated with the part is printed in the right pane. In addition to looking at a part's printed representation, we can also create a new inspector specifically for the selected part. For example, double-clicking on **numerator** in the top inspector of Figure 2.25 *after **numerator** has already been selected* causes an inspector for the numerator (in this case, the bottom inspector for 1) to appear.

Alternatively, we could have used the **Inspect** pull-down menu to create an inspector for **numerator** (*once again, after **numerator** had already been selected*), as shown in Figure 2.26. Even though (1) double-clicking on the part name and (2) selecting menu item **Inspect** in the **Inspect** menu item both have the same effect, the former is more convenient.

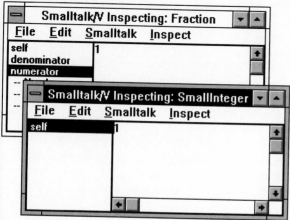

Figure 2.25 Inspecting a part by clicking on the part name after it has been selected. Shown are inspectors for (a) 1/3 and (b) the numerator 1.

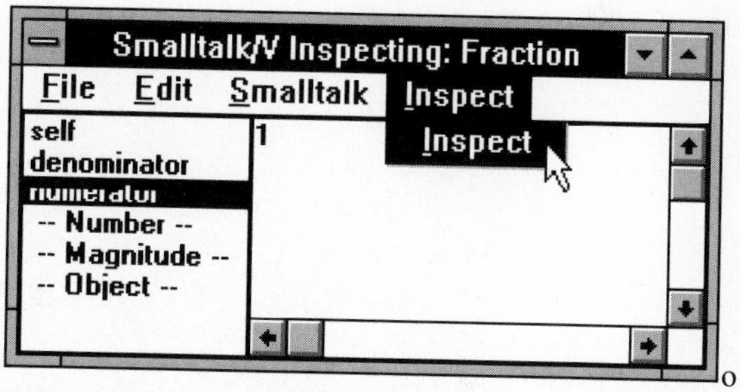

Figure 2.26 Creating an inspector for **numerator** via a menu selection.

Although objects are displayed with all their part names in an inspector, there is sometimes superfluous information (see "— Number —", "— Magnitude —", and "— Object —" in Figure 2.26). If you click on one of these items, nothing is displayed. Clearly, these items have something to do with the fact that a fraction is a number, a magnitude, and an object, so we can use them to determine the class hierarchy associated with an object (we'll investigate this aspect in detail in section 6.1.3 after we know substantially more about class hierarchies). Unfortunately, the class hierarchy information is not always provided. As can be seen in Figure 2.27, it is missing when an object has no part names.

In general, the results of evaluating an expression in any window can be inspected (rather then printed) by choosing **Inspect It** instead of **Show It** in the **Smalltalk** menu (see Figure 2.28). Then, instead of the printed result, an inspector appears. Of course, the printed result can be viewed in the inspector by clicking on **self**.

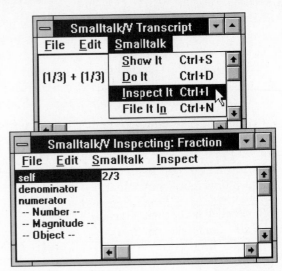

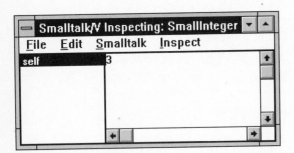

Figure 2.27 An inspector for a small integer has no class hierarchy information.

Figure 2.28 Inspecting the object which is a result of a computation.

Inspectors, in general, are more than just facilities for viewing objects. They can also be used for changing objects. For example, suppose we were inspecting 2/3 (as in Figure 2.28) and we wanted to replace the denominator 3 by 4. By selecting **denominator** in the left pane, changing the 3 into a 4 in the right pane, and selecting menu item **Save** under the **File** menu, we would permanently replace the 3 by 4 (see Figure 2.29).

Subsequently clicking on **self** will show that 2/3 has changed into 2/4 (see Figure 2.30). Notice that the fraction has not been simplified to 1/2. This is because we have changed one of the fraction's parts without the fraction itself being made aware of the modification.

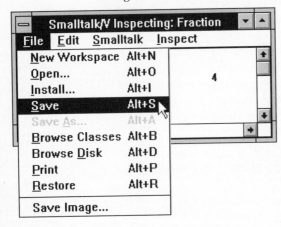

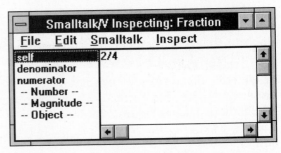

Figure 2.29 Changing denominator 3 into 4.

Figure 2.30 After changing denominator 3 into 4, fraction 2/3 has changed to 2/4.

To summarize, inspectors can be used to

- View an object's parts
- Change an object's parts

2.4.2 Objects with Parts versus Objects without Parts

Now that we're familiar with inspectors, we should be able to use them as tools to investigate objects; e.g., to determine whether specific objects have parts, and, if they do, what they are called, or (in those cases where we can) to determine the class hierarchy associated with an object. So far, we have a reasonable understanding of numbers, a little experience with true and false, but very little exposure to other classes of simple objects. So let's consider a small sample of simple objects to round out our background knowledge.

2001	2/3	3.1415926
true	false	nil
$a	'hello'	

First, let's see if inspectors can confirm what we already know. Consider Figure 2.31. As we can see, 2001 is a small integer with no parts (the class hierarchy isn't evident); 2/3 is a fraction with two parts **numerator** and **denominator** (here, the class hierarchy can be deduced); and 3.14159 is a float with eight parts, none of which are named (once again, the class hierarchy isn't evident). The parts in the floating point number are **indexed** parts to differentiate them from **named** parts. They are referenced by means of an index

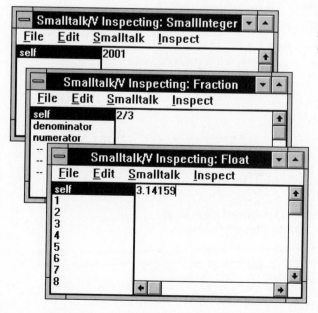

Figure 2.31 Inspecting a small integer, a fraction, and a float.

or offset from the beginning. If we click on any of the indexed parts, we will find that they are small integers in the range 0 to 255. Evidently, floating point numbers are encoded in some peculiar way that is understood by the computer—this encoding would be of interest to us if we were studying machine language (but we're not).

If we investigate true, false, and nil, we find (see Figure 2.32) that none of these objects have parts and, consequently, the class hierarchy isn't revealed by the inspector. However, we can see that true (in lowercase) is an instance of class True (capitalized), false is an instance of False, and nil is an instance of class UndefinedObject.

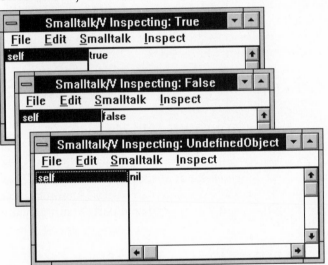

Figure 2.32
Inspecting true, false, and nil.

To learn more about the class hierarchy, we are going to have to do what we've done in prior sections; namely, send messages to the objects.

true **class** ⇒ True   false **class** ⇒ False
True **superclass** ⇒ Boolean   False **superclass** ⇒ Boolean
Boolean **superclass** ⇒ Object

nil **class** ⇒ UndefinedObject
UndefinedObject **superclass** ⇒ Object

Finally, let's inspect the last two candidates on our list (see Figure 2.33). We can see that $a is a character with one part called **asciiInteger**, and that a character is a magnitude and also an object. By contrast, 'hello' is a string with five indexed parts but no class hierarchy information is revealed. Both of these merit further study.

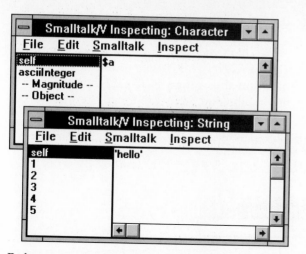

Figure 2.33 Inspecting a character and a string.

Before we consider their parts, however, let's determine the missing class hierarchy information using messages. We'll do it for both kinds of objects even though we already have the information for characters.

$a **class** ⇒ Character
Character **superclass** ⇒ Magnitude
Magnitude **superclass** ⇒ Object

'hello' **class** ⇒ String
String **superclass** ⇒ IndexedCollection
IndexedCollection **superclass** ⇒ FixedSizeCollection
FixedSizeCollection **superclass** ⇒ Collection
Collection **superclass** ⇒ Object

The class hierarchy information for the kinds of objects we know about so far is summarized by the diagram in Figure 2.34.

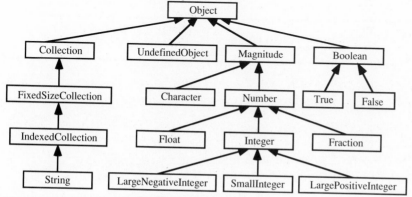

Figure 2.34 An extensive class hierarchy diagram.

To continue our investigation of characters, if we inspect $+ and click on its one and only part, called **asciiInteger** (see Figure 2.35), we find that it contains 43. This is the integer representation of the character; we call it its **ASCII** value. Each character has a unique ASCII value. However, ASCII values are not arbitrary integers—on most machines, the allowable range is 0—255 because most machines are byte-oriented (1 byte = 8 bits) and 8 bits can exactly represent the integers from 0 to 255.

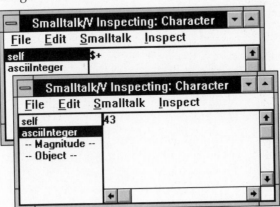

Figure 2.35 Inspecting the character $+.

We could create a table of correspondences between characters and their ASCII values using inspectors but it would be tedious. Nevertheless, a table for selected character (see Table 2.1), might prove interesting. We can see, for example, that the ASCII values for the uppercase characters are less than those of the lowercase characters. The ASCII values for the digits are smaller than those of all alphabetic characters. Moreover, the character $0 (just to pick one) has an ASCII value, not of 0, but of 48. Additionally, characters like "$", ".", and "," are legitimate characters

Table 2.1 Some characters and their ASCII values.

Character	ASCII value	
$a ... $z	97 ... 122	
$A ... $Z	65 ... 90	
$0 ... $9	48 ... 57	
$(	40	
$)	41	
$$	36	\<space\> is obtained by hitting the spacebar;
$.	46	
$,	44	
$\<space\>	32	\<enter\> is obtained
$\<enter\>	13	by hitting the Enter key.

with their own ASCII values. Even the space and Enter characters have ASCII values.

Now, let's continue our investigation of strings. Recall from Figure 2.33 that strings have indexed parts. We don't really know what the parts are—they might be integers (as in floats) or perhaps characters—so, let's inspect a string such as 'ghostly' and double-click on the second entry (as shown in Figure 2.36). As you can see, the second indexed part is the character $h.

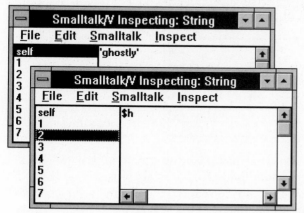

Figure 2.36 Inspecting the string 'ghostly' and the second indexed part.

Hence, strings are collections of characters. With further checking, we could verify that the first indexed part is $g, the second is $h, and the last is $y. Note in particular that the quotes in the string 'ghostly' are not part of the string. When we type 'ghostly', there is both a **leading** quote and a **trailing** quote so that we can tell where the string starts and where it ends. Thus, we can distinguish between a string with one word such as 'hello'; a string with two words such as 'hello there' (the space is actually part of the string); and two consecutive strings such as 'hello' 'there'.

Characters are similar in that there is a leading dollar sign but no trailing character—it is assumed that the character immediately following the dollar sign is the character being specified. That is why $; is a semicolon character, $) is a right parenthesis character, and $ is a space character (even though you can't see anything after the leading character).

Now, let's change a few of the characters just to see what happens. In particular, let's change the last two characters to $' and $s, as shown in the top two inspectors of Figure 2.37. Then by clicking on **self**, we'll be able see what a string looks like when one of its parts really is a quote character. Recall that to make this change, you have to select the part in the left pane, type the replacement in the right pane, and choose **Save** from the **File** menu.

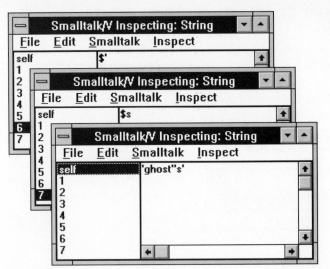

Figure 2.37 Modifying the string 'ghostly'.

The string prints as 'ghost''s'. The quote has been duplicated but the quote is not in the string twice—look at the individual characters again with the inspector. You'll find $g, $h, $o, $s, $t, $', and $s. Moreover, there is no character corresponding to the leading or trailing quote in the string.

We have learned an important concept—*to include a quote character in a string, it is necessary to type it twice*. This feature turns out to be quite useful because it enables us and the Smalltalk environment itself to be able to differentiate between consecutive strings, even when some of them contain quotes. For example, consider

'ghost' 's' 'ghost''s'

In this case, there are three strings in a row: 'ghost', 's', and 'ghost''s'. The first string ends at the second quote because that quote is followed by a space. Just to make sure that you understand this concept, you might try inspecting the following strings:

'Wilf''s car'
'It''s a boy!'
'''hi'''

Going further, we might ask "what is the shortest string? A string with one character? With zero characters?" Let's experiment.

'fine' ⇒ 'fine'
'fin' ⇒ 'fin'
'fi' ⇒ 'fi'
'f' ⇒ 'f'
'' ⇒ ''

Apparently, they are all legal. We call a string with no characters an **empty** string. You might wish to inspect one (see Figure 2.38).

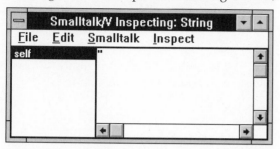

Figure 2.38 Inspecting an empty string.

To summarize, small integers, nil, true, and false have no parts. Characters and fractions have named parts; **asciiInteger** is the part name for characters, and **numerator** and **denominator** are the part names for fractions. Floats and strings have indexed parts; floats have eight indexed parts. and strings have any number from zero upward.

2.4.3 Operations on nil, Booleans, Characters, and Strings

In the previous section, we inspected many different kinds of objects. Typically, we would type a character or a string, select it, and then click on **Inspect It** in the **Smalltalk** menu to cause an inspector to appear. In this section, we would like to go over the same objects with a different purpose in mind—finding out which messages (if any) they understand. We're not going to be comprehensive—we just want a quick tour in preparation for later chapters. In keeping with the spirit of this section, we will first begin by investigating a message that all objects understand, a message that can be used to invoke an inspector without having to use menus: an **inspect** message. Type

'ghostly' **inspect**

and select **Do It**, as in Figure 2.39. Menu item **Do It** is similar to **Show It** except that no answer is printed in the originating window (in this case, the transcript window). This makes sense if we are about to inspect an object because we can print the object in the inspector itself—there is no need to additionally print it in the transcript window.

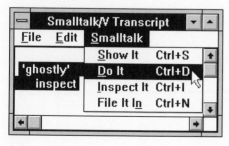

Figure 2.39 Evaluating "'ghostly' **inspect**" and selecting **Do It**.

To summarize, **Smalltalk** menu item **Show It** is used both to evaluate an expression and to print the result in the same window. Menu item **Do It** is used to evaluate an expression without printing the result. This could be particularly useful if the expression caused some picture to be drawn on the display (and we didn't care about the answer).

Now, let's consider special object nil. We know that it is an instance of class UndefinedObject. It understands a few special messages, but not many.

> nil **isNil** ⇒ true
> nil **notNil** ⇒ false

If we ask the same questions of other objects, we get the opposite answer, as you might perhaps expect.

> 25 **isNil** ⇒ false
> 25 **notNil** ⇒ true

Next, let's consider operations understood by booleans (objects that denote truth or falsity). This list also is relatively short. Examples include the following:

> true & false ⇒ false
> false | true ⇒ true
> false **not** ⇒ true
> false **and**: [5 **between**: 3 **and**: 7] ⇒ false
> true **or**: [5 **between**: 3 **and**: 7] ⇒ true

Operators &, |, and **not** denote "and" and "or" respectively. The rule is simple.

> aBoolean & anotherBoolean ⇒ true if both are true; false otherwise
> aBoolean | anotherBoolean ⇒ true if at least one is true; false otherwise
> aBoolean **not** ⇒ true if aBoolean is false; false if aBoolean is true

Operators & and | are the standard boolean operations whereas **and**: and **or**: are the **short-circuit** boolean operators. The short-circuit operators totally ignore the message parameter (the second operand) if the result can be determined solely from the receiver. For example, what do the following evaluate to?

> true **and**: [?] ⇒ don't know (depends on ?)
> false **and**: [?] ⇒ false (both must be true for the result to be true; ? is irrelevant)

The same applies for selector **or**:.

> true **or**: [?] ⇒ true (either one must be true for the result to be true; ? is irrelevant)
> false **or**: [?] ⇒ don't know (depends on ?)

The standard operators, on the other hand, always consider both the receiver and the parameter (the second operand). This becomes important only when complicated expressions need to be computed.

For illustration purposes, consider the following two cases. Keep in mind that computing "1000 **factorial**" takes a long time (say, more than 10 seconds).

```
$A  notNil  |  (1000 factorial between: 900 factorial and: 1100 factorial) ⇒
true        |  (1000 factorial between: 900 factorial and: 1100 factorial) ⇒
true        |  (largeNumber1 between: 900 factorial and: 1100 factorial) ⇒
true        |  (largeNumber1 between: largeNumber2 and: 1100 factorial) ⇒
true        |  (largeNumber1 between: largeNumber2 and: largeNumber3) ⇒
true        |  true ⇒
true
```

Hence, the above might take over 30 seconds to compute. By contrast, the following expression takes less than a second because the results of the message with selector **or:** can be determined without computing the second operand.

```
$A notNil   or: [1000 factorial between: 900 factorial and: 1100 factorial] ⇒
true        or: [1000 factorial between: 900 factorial and: 1100 factorial] ⇒
true
```

Now, let's have a quick tour of character operations.

```
$A isUppercase ⇒ true          $A isLowercase ⇒ false
$a isUppercase ⇒ false         $a isLowercase ⇒ true
$+ isUppercase ⇒ false         $+ isLowercase ⇒ false

$A asLowercase ⇒ $a            $a asLowercase ⇒ $a
$+ asLowercase ⇒ $+

$a asUppercase ⇒ $A

$a asciiValue ⇒ 40             40 asCharacter ⇒ $a
```

We can test the **case** of a character; i.e., whether it is uppercase or lowercase ($+ is neither). It is perfectly legitimate to ask for the uppercase of $A or $+; the character provided is simply the original. We can also ask a character for its ASCII value, or conversely, obtain the character equivalent of an ASCII value. The following more complex example computes character $b from character $a.

```
($a asciiValue + 1) asCharacter ⇒ $b
```

Lastly, let's have a quick tour of string operations. Consider the following:

```
'yes', 'ter', 'day' ⇒ 'yesterday'
'yes' at: 1 ⇒ $y
'yes' at: 2 ⇒ $e
'yes' at: 3 ⇒ $s
'frankly' copyFrom: 2 to: 5 ⇒ 'rank'
'banana' size ⇒ 6
```

The comma "," is an operator that performs string **concatenation**; i.e., creates a new string with the same characters as the operands and in the same order. The **at:** selector permits character extraction when the index of the desired character is specified—index 1 for the first character, 2 for the second, and so on. It's an important operation because it permits indexed parts to be retrieved. The **copyFrom:to:** selector performs **substring** extraction where the index of the first and last characters are specified; i.e., creates a new string containing only the characters between the given indices. Finally, the **size** message tells us how many characters are in a string.

We might inquire about the limits of these operations. For example, are any of the following legal?

```
25, ' cents'
'no' at: 3
'yes' copyFrom: 2 to: 4
```

The answer is no. Concatenation is valid only for strings. Character and substring extraction must be provided with a legal index. For example, if the string contains 10 characters, the index must be an integer from 1 to 10. Consider a few more cases.

```
'me', '', '', 'et' ⇒ 'meet'
'yes' copyFrom: 2 to: 2 ⇒ 'e'
'yes' copyFrom: 2 to: 1 ⇒ ''
```

The last example, in particular, is perplexing. If the end point for the copy occurs before the start, we get back an empty string. Can we be more arbitrary?

```
'yes' copyFrom: 1 to: 0 ⇒ ''
'yes' copyFrom: 4 to: 3 ⇒ (error)
'yes' copyFrom: 3 to: 1 ⇒ (error)
```

Apparently, the first index must specify the position of an existing character. The second index can be 1, but not 2, less than the first index.

Finally, let's consider using double quotes instead of single quotes:

```
"hello" ⇒ nil
25 "hello" ⇒ 25
1 "and" + "and" 2 ⇒ 3
```

Can you guess what is happening? As it turns out, anything in double quotes is a **comment**—it is ignored by Smalltalk. The first case is equivalent to selecting nothing and then attempting to print the result. In the two other cases, the information inside the double quotes (including the double quotes themselves) is simply ignored (discarded). *This technique allows us to comment on what we are doing*. For example, we might have written the following:

```
$+ isAlphabetic "find out if + is an alphabetic character" ⇒ false
```

2.4.4 Immutable Symbols and Mutable Array Literals

Some objects, such as strings and fractions, can be modified—they are said to be **mutable** objects. Other objects, such as characters and small integers, cannot be changed—they are **immutable** objects. It should be clear that the small integer 3 is immutable. It cannot be changed into a 4. Of course, that doesn't mean that you can't compute the 4 from the 3 by adding 1, as in "3+1". But 4 is a totally new object, distinct from 3. After the computation, the 3 is still the same 3.

In general, there are very few immutable objects in Smalltalk. Consequently, it is important to consider the most obvious candidates with this property—symbols. A **symbol** could be defined as an immutable string. Of course, we'll should check this property for ourselves. An example is shown below.

#hello

This is a symbol containing the characters $h, $e, $l, $l, and $o. The special character "#" introduces the symbol, which normally consists of alphabetic characters, although numeric characters are permitted anywhere except the beginning. Symbols end as soon as some other kind of character is encountered, such as a space or a + character.

By contrast, a generalization of a string that permits arbitrary objects in place of characters is called an **array**. The fact that it is a generalization implies that arrays can be used just like strings, but we'll have to check this property for ourselves, too. An **array literal** is a representation for an array in which all the elements are specified explicitly (without computation). An array literal is shown below.

#(10 20 30)

This is an array literal containing the integers 10, 20, and 30. The only elements permitted in an array literal are numbers, characters, strings, symbols, and other array literals. Moreover, each occurrence of a word beginning with an alphabetic, such as "hello", or round brackets, such as "(1 2 3)", is assumed to be **implicitly** preceded by "#"; i.e., to be a symbol or another array literal respectively. Thus, true, false, and nil cannot be part of an array literal, because they get interpreted as symbols. A more complex example of an array literal is shown below.

#(10 $a 'hi there' red green true (5 6 7) false (() (1) (1 2)) nil)

This literal consists of integer 10; character $a; string 'hi there'; symbol #red (the "#" implicitly precedes "red"); symbol #green; symbol #true (not the literal true denoting "truth"); array literal #(5 6 7) containing integers 5, 6, and 7; symbol #false (once again, not the literal false denoting "falsity"); array literal #(() (1) (1 2)), which consists of three array literals #()—an empty array literal, #(1)—an array literal containing 1, and #(1 2)—an array literal containing 1 and 2; and, finally, the symbol #nil. An array literal with no elements is called an **empty array literal**; e.g., #().

But what if you want an array literal containing nil, true, or false? What can be done? The answer is quite straightforward—nothing. You simply cannot type an array literal containing those special objects.

The difference between the string 'nil', the symbol #nil, and the undefined object nil can be seen easily by inspecting each one, as shown in Figure 2.40. Both the string and the symbol contain the characters $n, $i, $l; the undefined object, on the other hand, has no parts.

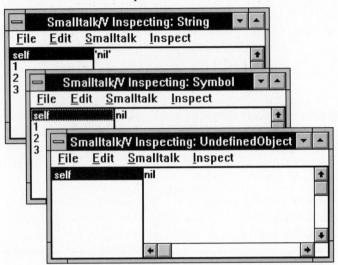

Figure 2.40 The difference between 'nil', #nil, and nil.

Let's begin investigating symbols and arrays. If we query class Symbol, we can determine (as we have done earlier) that Symbol's superclass is String. We can also determine that Array's superclass is FixedSizeCollection. When combined with what we already know about strings, the resulting hierarchy diagram can be summarized as shown in Figure 2.41.

The fact that symbols are strings is important, because it allows us to predict what we can do with symbols. But first, consider how they are printed. Strings print their quotes (we already knew that), but symbols don't print the leading "#" character.

```
'hello' ⇒ 'hello'
#hello ⇒ hello
```

Because of the inheritance hierarchy, string messages are presumably understood by symbols. Nevertheless, there must be some important differences. Let's try out some typical string operations to see what happens and then form some conclusion.

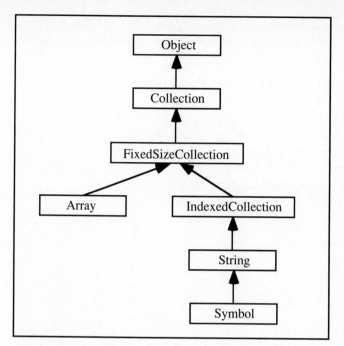

Figure 2.41 A hierarchy diagram for Array and Symbol.

    #hello = #hello ⇒ true
    #hello = 'hello' ⇒ false

Other examples include

    'hello' = #hello ⇒ false
    #hello = #bye ⇒ false
    #hello, #bye ⇒ 'hellobye'
    #hello **at**: 1 ⇒ $h
    #hello **copyFrom**: 1 **to**: 4 ⇒ 'hell'
    #hello **size** ⇒ 5

For the most part, symbols appear to behave just like strings. But they are not the same. Symbols and strings with the same characters are not equal. Note, also, that any operation such as concatenation; i.e., ",", or **copyFrom:to:** that might have been able to return a symbol returns a string instead. Similar operations also apply to array literals.

    #(2 hello $+) = #(2 hello $+) ⇒ true
    #(2 hello $+) = #(2 hello $-) ⇒ false
    #(2 hello $+) = #(2 hello) ⇒ false
    #(2 hello $+), #(4 bye $-) ⇒ #(2 hello $+ 4 bye $-)
    #(2 hello $+) **at**: 1 ⇒ 2
    #(2 hello $+) **at**: 2 ⇒ hello
    #(2 hello $+) **copyFrom**: 1 **to**: 2 ⇒ #(2 hello)
    #(2 hello $+) **size** ⇒ 3

If we can access an element of a string, symbol, or array literal using **at:**, we must also be able to change it with a similar operation. This operation is the **at:put:** operation. Let's try it on each of the three classes of objects.

'hello' **at**: 1 **put**: $j ⇒ $j
#hello **at**: 1 **put**: $j ⇒ (error)
#(1 2 3) **at**: 1 **put**: $j ⇒ $j

The **at:put:** message returns the object that was inserted—the character $j in each case—so we can't tell if the receiver has been modified. Additionally, there is a error message when an attempt is made to modify a symbol (see Figure 2.42).

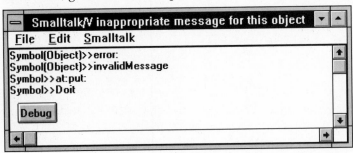

Figure 2.42 After attempting to execute "#hello **at**: 1 **put**: $j".

To be able to verify that a change has occurred for the other two cases, we could simply inspect the original objects and make the modifications in the inspector. We would be able see the changes to the objects.

Clearly, strings and array literals can be modified but symbols cannot. If we use symbols, we know for sure that they will not be modified, even if we are less than careful. We can also use strings and array literals in a manner that deliberately avoids modifying them but nothing prevents accidental modifications. Symbols, small integers, characters, nil, true, and false are all immutable objects. The fact that symbols are **immutable** is an important property but there is an even more important property of symbols that we will discuss in a later chapter.

2.5 Summary

This chapter has introduced the fundamentals needed for writing and executing simple commands. More specifically, we have discussed several notions, including:

- The syntax (form) and semantics (meaning) of Smalltalk expressions
- The components of message expressions: messages, receivers, selectors, and parameters
- The different kinds of messages: unary, binary, and keyworded messages
- The order of evaluation in multiselector expressions and the evaluation priority

- The differences between instances and classes
- The differences between an instance and its parts
- The use of inspectors as tools for investigating objects
- A sampling of the messages understood by classes, integers, fractions, floats, booleans, strings, symbols, characters, arrays, and undefined objects
- The internal structure, or parts, of integers, fractions, floats, booleans, strings, symbols, characters, arrays, and undefined objects
- The difference between immutable and mutable objects
- Typing, editing, and executing commands in text windows
- Inspecting objects

2.6 What You Did and Did Not Learn

This chapter has provided you with the basic skills needed to solve simple programming tasks. You have learned some very intricate and important details about messages and the terminology associated with them. You have also learned the order in which expressions are evaluated. You should be able to take advantage of this in the future.

You have also learned to distinguish between instances and their classes. Being able to answer the simple question "is this an instance or a class?" may seem trivial and obvious if you understand the difference. However, failure to understand this notion can lead to confusion and difficulty later.

Although you have been exposed to a variety of different kinds of objects and the messages they understand, you have only barely scratched the surface. You have yet to learn to use these messages to solve interesting problems.

You have also further developed your skills with text windows by learning how to type, edit, and execute commands. You may not remember all the details that you learned but you will have the opportunity to relearn them as you make more use of the Smalltalk environment.

You have learned a great deal about objects and their parts, about inspectors for investigating objects and their parts, and about the fact that some objects can be changed and others cannot.

Finally, you have learned to be curious, to experiment, to ask questions, and to attempt to answer them—prerequisites for any successful learning.

2.7   Important Facts

Operations on Objects

anObject **class**	The receiver's class
anObject **isKindOf**: aClass	True if a member of aClass; false, otherwise
anObject **isNil**	True if anObject is nil; false, otherwise
anObject **notNil**	The opposite of the above
anObject **inspect**	To view an object and its parts

Operations on Classes

aClass **superclass**	The superclass of the receiver

Operations on Numbers

aNumber + aNumber	Addition
aNumber - aNumber	Subtraction
aNumber * aNumber	Multiplication
aNumber / aNumber	Division without truncation for floats; conversion to fraction, otherwise
aNumber // aNumber	Division with truncation; e.g., discards 1 in $8\frac{1}{3}$
aNumber \\ aNumber	Remainder; e.g., just the 1 in $8\frac{1}{3}$
aNumber **negated**	The negative of aNumber
aNumber **between**: a **and**: b	Between a and b (inclusive)

Operations on Integers

anInteger **factorial**	5 factorial is 5×4×3×2×1; 0 factorial is 1
anInteger **asFloat**	The float equivalent
anInteger **asCharacter**	The character equivalent

Operations on Floats

aFloat **rounded**	Converting to the nearest integer that is either equal or larger by at most 0.5
aFloat **truncated**	Converting to the nearest integer that is smaller or equal

Operations on Booleans

aBoolean & anotherBoolean	True if both are true; false, otherwise
aBoolean | anotherBoolean	True if at least one if true; false, otherwise
aBoolean **not**	True if false and false if true
aBoolean **and**: aBlock	Short-circuit equivalent of &; aBlock is an expression in square brackets
aBoolean **or**: aBlock	Short-circuit equivalent of |

Operations on Strings, Symbols, and Arrays

container **size**	How many elements it contains
container, anotherContainer	Concatenates the two containers

Operations on Strings, Symbols, and Arrays (continued)

container **at**: anInteger   Extracts the object at position anInteger
container **copyFrom**: a **to**: b   Substring or subarray extraction

Operations on Characters

aCharacter **isUppercase**   True if capital letter; false, otherwise
aCharacter **isLowercase**   True if noncapital letter; false, otherwise
aCharacter **asciiValue**   The character's equivalent

The bracketing rule: A bracketed expression cannot be used as an operand unless all messages inside have been evaluated.

The priority rule: Given two consecutive selectors, the leftmost selector is evaluated first if they both have the same priority; otherwise, the highest priority selector is evaluated first. From highest to lowest, the selector priorities are the following:

- Unary
- Binary
- Keyworded

Object parts: Small integers, nil, true, and false have **no parts**. Characters and fractions have **named parts**; asciiInteger is the part name for characters and **numerator** and **denominator** are the part names for fractions. Floats, strings, symbols, and arrays have **indexed parts**; floats have eight indexed parts while strings, symbols, and arrays have any number from zero onward.

Instance versus class: An instance is a member of one of more classes. Conversely, a class is a category for its members or instances.

Undefined object: nil, an instance of class UndefinedObject

Booleans: Instances true and false are members of classes True and False respectively, both with superclasses Boolean.

Integer: An integral number without a decimal point; e.g., 8 or -24.

Fraction: A number such as 1/3 consisting of **numerator** 1 and **denominator** 3.

Float: A number such as -3.14159 or 50.5e3 (also called a **floating point number**) consisting of a **mantissa** 50.5 multiplied by 10 raised to some **power** or **exponent** 3 (in -3.1415, the **exponent** is implicitly 0). A float is an **approximate** value; i.e., there is a bound on the number of digits maintained.

Character: An object representing one of the keys on the keyboard. A character literal is represented by "$" followed by the actual character represented; e.g., $a, $+, or $).

String: A collection of characters represented by a leading and trailing quote that is not part of the string and arbitrary characters between the quotes. Quotes that are part of the string are specified with two single quotes in a row; e.g., 'isn''t' is a string with five characters: $i, $s, $n, $', and $t. The shortest possible string is an **empty string**, a string with no characters; e.g. ''.

Symbol: An immutable string represented by the special character "#" and immediately followed by alphanumeric characters (numeric characters are permitted anywhere except the beginning). Symbols end as soon as some other kind of character is encountered, such as a space or a "+" character. Examples are #red, #aircraft29, #true.

Array literal: A representation for an array where all the elements are specified explicitly (without computation). The only elements permitted are numbers, characters, strings, symbols, and other array literals; true, false, and nil are not permitted; e.g., #(10 $a 'hi' red true (5 6 7) nil) contains symbols #true and #nil along with internal array literal #(5 6 7). The shortest possible array literal is an **empty array literal**; e.g., #().

Comment: A collection of characters surrounded by double quotes; e.g., "hi you". Comments are completely ignored by Smalltalk.

2.8   Keywords

class/instance terminology: approximate, array, array literal, class, class hierarchy diagram, concatenation, denominator, empty array literal, empty string, engineering notation, exponent, exponent notation, float, floating point number, fraction, instance, immutable object, indexed part, mantissa, mutable object, named part, numerator, part, power, reduced, superclass, symbol, short-circuit operator

evaluation rules: bracketing rule, left-to-right evaluation, priorities, priority rule

keyboard terminology: Enter key, Backspace key, Delete key, parentheses, round brackets, space, spacebar, square brackets

message sending terminology: anthropomorphic, binary message, keyword, keyworded message (selector), message, selector, sending a message, parameters, receiver, unary message (selector)

mouse interaction terminology: direct selection, double-clicking, moving the I-beam, shift-click selection

operator terminology: left operand, operand, operator, right operand

pull-down menu commands: Do It, Inspect, Inspect It, Save, Show It

windows: inspector window, transcript window

2.9 Exercises

1. Select everything in the transcript window and delete it. Next, write a small multisentence paragraph such as this one. Finally, delete the second sentence.

2. After typing a short sentence in the transcript window, click on **Save** in the transcript window's **File** menu and then delete your sentence. Then click on **Restore** in the transcript window's **File** menu to see what effect it has.

3. Investigate the class hierarchy associated with date objects. An interesting date object can be obtained by evaluating "Date **today**". Determine whether date objects can be compared and whether they can be compared with strings.

4. Can you inspect the class Number? If so, can you determine the superclass from the inspector? The subclasses?

5. What is the largest possible small integer?

6. How can you include the double quote character " inside a comment? Hint: consider how single quotes are included in strings.

7. Is it an error to divide 1 by 0? Devise a simple expression (if possible) that leads to an error message (if the above doesn't).

8. Determine the integer equivalent of character $0 both by using an inspector and by sending $0 an appropriate message.

9. Is there a difference between "4-3" without spaces and "4 - 3" with spaces? If so, why? Is "4-(3)" legal? Explain your answer.

10. Investigate the parts of large positive and large negative integers. Are they named or indexed?

11. Create a "truth table" for operations & and | (fill in the following tables by experimentally computing the results).

&	true	false		|	true	false
true				true		
false				false		

12. Devise an expression that will construct an array containing the undefined object nil—not the symbol #nil.

13. If you borrowed $100,000.00 at an interest rate of $9^1/_4\%$ per year and you paid $20,000.00 at the end of each year, how much would you owe after 1 year? After 2 years? Compute the answer in the transcript window.

3

Simple Problem Solving Using Workspaces, Transcripts, and Variables

What You Will Learn

In Chapters 1 and 2, we learned to control the programming environment so that we could create our own workspaces, move them around, resize them, and destroy them. We also learned about the simplest Smalltalk objects in the environment and the textual messages to which they respond.

We are now able to use such objects for something more interesting than just learning the syntax of messages or the typical messages they understand. We can now use Smalltalk in simple problem-solving situations. However, we don't yet have enough experience with the basic tools: workspaces and transcripts.

We'll solve our first problem by using the workspace as an advanced calculator. Next, we'll learn to use the transcript, a window often used by the system to inform us of interesting activity, as a "receiver" for dictation—in our case, a letter. Although the text of the letter will appear on the transcript, the instructions for composing and sending the dictation will be written and executed in a workspace. As a side effect, we'll learn how to display various kinds of objects in windows.

As we work on more interesting tasks, we will need to keep track of objects as we perform different computations on them—we will need to name them. Some names directly represent the objects they refer to—we called them **literals** in the Chapter 2; e.g., $a is literal representing the object known as the character "lowercase a". Other names can reference any object whatsoever and the references can be changed over time—these names are called variables. To learn more about variables, we will consider two distinct problems: an algebra problem and a graphics problem.

3.1   Using a Workspace as a Calculator

Let's begin by solving an elementary verification problem. There is a rumor started by a mathematician friend that the value of **pi**, approximately 3.1415, can be computed by summing the terms of an infinite series of fractions. She suggests, for instance, that we try examples such as:

$$1 + \frac{1}{2} + \frac{1}{3} + \frac{1}{4} + \ldots$$
$$1 - \frac{1}{3} + \frac{1}{5} - \frac{1}{7} + \frac{1}{9} - \ldots$$
$$1 - \frac{1}{2} + \frac{1}{4} - \frac{1}{8} + \frac{1}{16} - \ldots$$
$$1 + \frac{1}{4} + \frac{1}{9} + \frac{1}{16} + \ldots$$

where the rule for obtaining the next term is obvious. Notice that the first and last examples only add terms, while the second and third alternately add and subtract. Our goal is to find out which series is related to pi and in what way.

Let's begin by opening a new workspace and typing a few terms of the first candidate series $1 + \frac{1}{2} + \frac{1}{3} + \frac{1}{4} + \ldots$ to see what we get (see Figure 3.1).

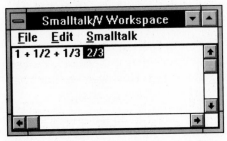

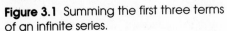

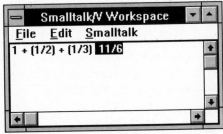

Figure 3.1 Summing the first three terms of an infinite series.

Figure 3.2 Correctly summing the first three terms of an infinite series.

Fortunately, we can easily compute the sum by hand to verify the answer. In particular, $1 + \frac{1}{2} + \frac{1}{3} = \frac{6}{6} + \frac{3}{6} + \frac{2}{6} = \frac{11}{6}$. But wait! That's not the answer shown in Figure 3.1. Did you spot the obvious mistake on our part? We forgot to take into account the order in which expressions are evaluated—the left-to-right rule, which causes the expression in Figure 3.1 to evaluate as $((1 + 1) / 2 + 1) / 3 = (2 / 2 + 1) / 3 = (1 + 1) / 3 = 2/3$. We need round brackets (parentheses) around the fractions, as shown in Figure 3.2.

Now we get the correct answer but we can't tell if it's related to pi because it's a fraction rather than a float. We need to convert the result. One approach is to send the message **asFloat** to $^{11}/_6$. Alternatively, we can surround the infinite series expression by brackets and follow it by the message **asFloat**, as shown in Figure 3.3. The result so far doesn't seem to be related to pi. Let's try a few more terms (see Figure 3.4).

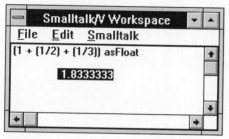

Figure 3.3 The sum of the first three terms of an infinite series as a float.

Figure 3.4 More terms in the infinite series.

This brings us a little closer! Perhaps another three terms will do the trick (see Figure 3.5). Still not enough. Perhaps we should try a large number of terms, say, 16 (see Figure 3.6). In this case, we've gone beyond 3.1415. Something must be wrong. Indeed, a little reflection should convince us that each time we add another term, the result increases. Perhaps we should leave this particular series and try another?

Figure 3.5 Even more terms in the infinite series.

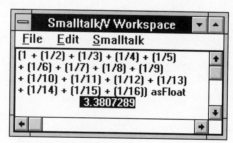

Figure 3.6 A large number of terms in the infinite series.

With the next series, $1 - {}^1/_3 + {}^1/_5 - {}^1/_7 + {}^1/_9 - ...$, let's be a little more methodological. Specifically, let's show the result of including more and more terms to try to determine if there is a pattern to the results (see Figure 3.7 for a summary). Before we start analyzing these results, what is 6.66666666667e-1? Recall from Chapter 2 that we can eliminate the exponent -1 by shifting the decimal point left by 1 position (left because the exponent is negative). Hence, 6.66666666667e-1 (truncated) is approximately 0.66. The successive results are therefore 1.0, 0.66, 0.86, 0.72, 0.83, 0.74, and 0.82. These numbers are not exactly close to pi, are they?

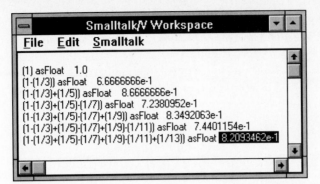

Figure 3.7 Including successive terms in another infinite series.

Perhaps the answers are off by a simple integer multiple. For instance, 0.8 * 2 is 1.6, 0.8 * 3 is 2.4, 0.8 * 4 is 3.2, and 0.8 * 5 is 4.0. The number 4 seems to be the most relevant multiple. Let's recompute the answers by multiplying them by 4, as shown in Figure 3.8. Now we might be able to see a pattern.

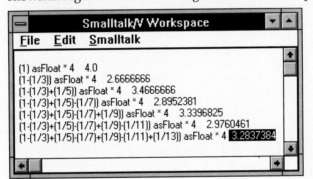

Figure 3.8 Yet more terms in the infinite series.

Indeed, when presented in tabular form (see Table 3.1), we should be able to see a pattern. Every time we add a positive term, we get a result that is greater than pi, but also getting closer. Similarly, each time we add a negative term, the result is

Table 3.1 Investigating the pattern in the successive results.

Terms * 4	Result	Greater than pi	Less than pi
1	4.0	√	
$1 - 1/3$	2.6		√
$1 - 1/3 + 1/5$	3.4	√	
$1 - 1/3 + 1/5 - 1/7$	2.8		√
$1 - 1/3 + 1/5 - 1/7 + 1/9$	3.3	√	
$1 - 1/3 + 1/5 - 1/7 + 1/9 - 1/11$	2.9		√
$1 - 1/3 + 1/5 - 1/7 + 1/9 - 1/11 + 1/13$	3.2	√	

less than pi but also getting closer. It's as though we were saying "it's below **4**, above **2.6**, below **3.4**, above **2.8**, below **3.3**, above **2.9**, below **3.2**."

The more terms we have, the closer the result should be to pi. As a last experiment, let's try adding a large number of terms (see Figure 3.9). With 21 terms, we get approximately **3.18**—correct to two digits. You might like to carry on and see how many terms are needed to yield a result that is correct to three or four digits.

3.2   Using the Transcript Remotely

A **transcript** window (see Figure 3.10) is a workspace that can be used by the programmer or the system as a remote display board for displaying messages. Unlike standard workspaces, however, the transcript window cannot be closed. It has one very important property—a name, **Transcript**, that can be used to reference the window.

Since a transcript window is just another kind of workspace window, we could use it as a replacement for a workspace. For example, the experiments we just performed dealing with infinite series could just as well have been done in the transcript window. In this section, however, we will learn to use the transcript window remotely.

Let's choose a simple task—writing a letter to a friend. Now, rather than type our letter in the transcript window, we will instead do all our typing in a workspace window. More specifically, we will execute Smalltalk messages in the workspace to instruct the transcript as to what it should display. Of course, we won't be able to do this unless we know what messages we can send to the transcript.

Messages Relevant to Transcript Windows

aWindow **cr**	Starts a new line
aWindow **space**	Displays a space
aWindow **nextPut**: aCharacter	Displays a character
aWindow **nextPutAll**: aString	Displays a string (only the parts)
anObject **printOn**: aWindow	Displays an object

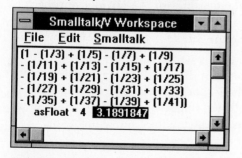

Figure 3.9 The more terms, the closer the result is to pi.

Figure 3.10 A transcript window.

Since **Transcript** is just a special kind of window, it can be a suitable receiver for each of the first four messages. It is also a suitable parameter for the last message. What kind of object is provided as a parameter is very important. Selector **nextPut:**, for example, requires a character object as a parameter. A string or a number will not work. Similarly, selector **nextPutAll:** requires a string as a parameter—in this case, a character or a number is illegal. On the other hand, there is no restriction on the receiver for selector **printOn:**—any object will do.

To get started on our letter-writing task, first activate the transcript window and delete all characters in it. You might also want to position it in the bottom half of the screen. Now create a workspace window and position it in the top half. We are now ready to start writing in the workspace. Normally, we start a letter with the words "Dear ...", skip a line, maybe indent three spaces, and then start a paragraph. So we might write the following in the workspace:

```
Transcript nextPutAll: 'Dear friend'.
Transcript cr.
Transcript space.
Transcript nextPutAll: 'I am learning to '.
Transcript nextPutAll: 'use the Transcript.'.
```

Of course, writing this in the workspace (see Figure 3.11) has no effect on the transcript window. For the transcript window to be affected, it is necessary to execute one or more of the messages. We could select "Transcript nextPutAll: 'Dear friend'" and evaluate it in the usual way. Alternatively, we could select several messages at once, as shown in Figure 3.12. If we do that, however, it is essential that the distinct messages be separated by a period.

> *The period can either be viewed as an expression separator or an expression terminator, since the period is optional after the last expression.*

Normally, we would select **Show It** in the **Smalltalk** menu to cause the expressions to be executed. Of course, this causes some answer to be printed immediately after the selection. In this case, we really don't care about the answer because we are interested only in printing something in the transcript window. To avoid printing the answer, we can select **Do It** instead of **Show It**.

Next, we would like to add three spaces to the transcript. An obvious approach is to execute "Transcript **space**" three times. By the time we did it for the third time, the transcript would appear as shown in Figure 3.13.

As you can see, we can't tell where the spaces went. However, as soon as we execute the next two messages, we will see that the words "I am learning to use the transcript." are indeed preceded by three spaces (for example, look ahead to Figure 3.14). Before we continue, however, we might wonder if there are other ways to output spaces. For example, are the following messages equivalent?

```
Transcript space
Transcript nextPut: $
Transcript nextPutAll: ' '
```

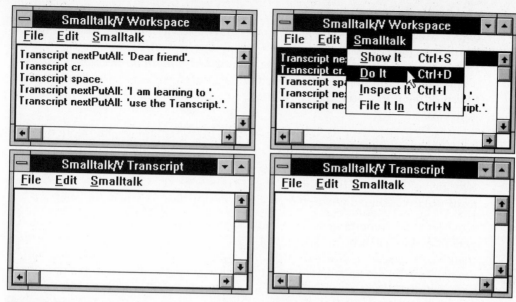

Figure 3.11 After typing commands in the . workspace.

Figure 3.12 Selecting two commands for execution.

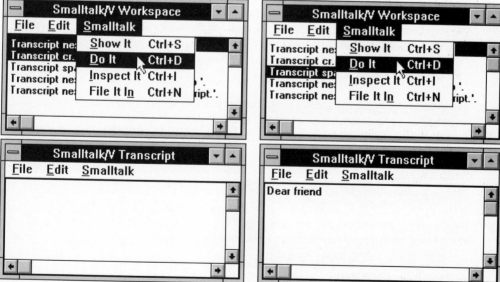

Figure 3.12 Selecting two commands for execution.

Figure 3.13 After sending **nextPutAll:**, **cr**, and three **space** messages to Transcript.

The parameter in a **nextPut:** message must be a character object. Since a character object is any character preceded by "$"—such as $+, $?, $q, $$—it should be possible to follow the $ by an actual space (the character obtained by pressing the spacebar.) Similarly, the parameter in a **nextPutAll:** message must be a string object. Since a string object begins and ends with a single quote, it must be possible to provide a space between the quotes. Indeed, all three messages are legitimate and equivalent. Of course, the first is preferable because it is more concise and less ambiguous. With the third approach, for example, a reader might find it difficult to distinguish between a string with only one space and a string with two.

Let's carry on then and execute the last two **nextPutAll:** messages. Note that the transcript contains the words "I am learning to use the Transcript." as an unbroken sentence even though we provided the transcript with the sentence in two pieces. Since we did not execute "Transcript **cr**" in between, the second **nextPutAll:** continued where the previous one finished.

Now let's try something a little more complicated. In particular, let's try to generate "I can compute 10 factorial = ???." on a new line where the question marks are replaced by the correct result. To begin with, we need a message, **cr**, to cause a new line to be initiated and a message to output the initial portion of the sentence.

    Transcript **cr**.
    Transcript **nextPutAll:** 'I can compute 10 factorial = '.

Note that the equal character is both preceded and followed by exactly one space. We want to get things exactly as requested. Now, how can we output 10 factorial? One way is to compute it (the result is 3628800), and then output it as follows:

    Transcript **nextPutAll:** '3628800'

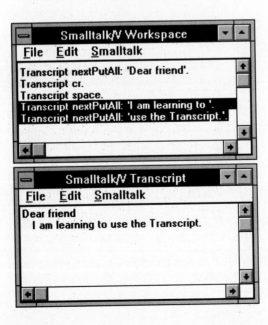

Figure 3.14 After sending another two **nextPutAll:** messages to Transcript.

With **nextPutAll:**, we must provide a parameter that is a string—the number 3628800 would be illegal. This entire approach, however, is unsatisfactory. There is no need for us to see the answer before it appears in the transcript. A much better way would be to ask the number we want displayed to print itself on the transcript. Then we can output the final period to get the result shown in Figure 3.15.

```
10 factorial printOn: Transcript.
Transcript nextPut: $.
```

For the last message, we could have alternatively executed

```
Transcript nextPutAll: '.'
```

However, **nextPut:** is preferred over **nextPutAll:** when only one character is to be sent because it is more efficient. Indeed, "**nextPutAll:** aString" is equivalent to a succession of "**nextPut:** aCharacter" messages, one for each character in aString. It is even legitimate to execute

```
Transcript nextPutAll: ''
```

where there are no characters between the quotes. Its effect is exactly what you would expect—no characters are added to the transcript.

If all objects can print themselves, why do we need **nextPut:** and **nextPutAll:**? Why not just use **printOn:** for characters and strings too? That's an interesting question. Perhaps we should try an experiment to find out. Let's execute the following:

```
Transcript cr.
Transcript nextPutAll: 'The character '.
Transcript nextPut: $+.
Transcript nextPutAll: ' is '.
$+ printOn: Transcript.
Transcript nextPut: $.
```

Note that the first + is output with **nextPut:**, and the second with **printOn:**. The result of this experiment is shown in Figure 3.16.

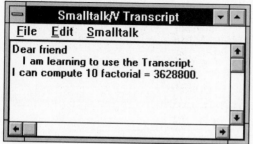

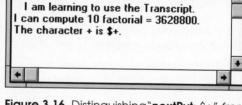

Figure 3.15 Causing 10 factorial to print itself. **Figure 3.16** Distinguishing "**nextPut:** $+" from "$+ **printOn:**".

Clearly, **nextPut**: does not output $ as part of the character, whereas **printOn**: does. Do you expect a similar behavior for strings? We could do a corresponding experiment. This time, however, you might wish to guess what the result will be before you look at it.

```
Transcript cr.
Transcript nextPutAll: 'The string with '.
Transcript nextPutAll: 'hello'.
Transcript nextPutAll: ' in it is '.
'hello' printOn: Transcript.
Transcript nextPut: $.
```

The result of this experiment is shown in Figure 3.17.

Clearly, for characters and strings, **printOn**: displays more than the specified characters. For characters, **printOn**: displays the leading $—**nextPut**: does not. For strings, **printOn**: displays the leading and trailing quote—**nextPutAll**: does not.

Do we understand enough now to try a more complicated sentence? For example, how would we display "I'm showing you character $' and string ''''.", as shown in Figure 3.18?

Let's be creative and attempt several solutions to see if we understand. First, let's try doing it with just one **nextPutAll**:. Recall from Chapter 2 that single quotes in strings must be doubled. For example, the characters $I, $', and $m must be specified as 'I''m' in a string. If you've forgotten, you might wish to inspect the string 'I''m' by executing 'I''m' **inspect** to verify for yourself that the double quote occurs only once in the string. For our first solution, our commands will have to be written as follows:

```
Transcript cr.
Transcript nextPutAll: 'I''m showing you character $'' and string ''''''.'.
```

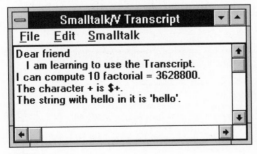

Figure 3.17 Distinguishing message "**nextPutAll**: 'hello' "from "'hello' **printOn**:".

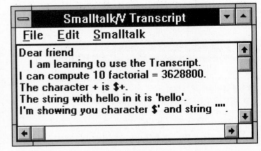

Figure 3.18 Displaying "I'm showing you character $' and string ''''.".

Note that each internal quote had to be doubled. For our second solution, let's try using only **nextPut:** and **nextPutAll:** with the additional restriction that we avoid all single quotes in strings.

```
Transcript cr.
Transcript nextPutAll: 'I'.
Transcript nextPut: $'.
Transcript nextPutAll: 'm showing you character $'.
Transcript nextPut: $'.
Transcript nextPutAll: ' and string '.
Transcript nextPut: $'.
Transcript nextPut: $'.
Transcript nextPut: $'.
Transcript nextPut: $'.
Transcript nextPut: $..
```

Note that the last message is terminated by a period just like every other message. For the third and final solution, let's insist on using **printOn:** wherever we can. Will the following work?

```
Transcript cr.
'I"m showing you character $" and string """"'.' printOn: Transcript.
```

No! This will output an extra quote at the beginning and the end of the sentence. We have to be more careful.

```
Transcript cr.
Transcript nextPutAll: 'I"m showing you character '.
$' printOn: Transcript.
Transcript nextPutAll: ' and string '.
'""""""' printOn: Transcript.
Transcript nextPut: $..
```

Does this look right? As it turns out, it isn't. The transcript should contain a string with one doubled quote in it. The above produces a string with four quotes in it. Why four? Because there are eight single quotes inside the string '""""""' — each one is doubled. To get one single quote inside, we have to double one single quote to get '""'. So the above has to be changed to

```
Transcript cr.
Transcript nextPutAll: 'I"m showing you character '.
$' printOn: Transcript.
Transcript nextPutAll: ' and string '.
'""' printOn: Transcript.
Transcript nextPut: $..
```

Until now, each expression has been terminated by a period. This is sometimes repetitious. For example, in the following closing statements of our letter, the receiver is repeated eight times.

```
Transcript cr.
Transcript nextPutAll: 'Hope to see you soon. '.
Transcript nextPutAll: 'Please drop by any time.'.
Transcript cr.
Transcript cr.
Transcript nextPutAll: '        Your friend'.
Transcript cr.
Transcript nextPutAll: '        Brannon'.
```

One way to avoid such repetition is to use cascaded messages. **Cascaded messages** are messages to the same receiver where the messages are separated by semicolons instead of periods and the receiver is specified only in the first message. For example, the above can be rewritten with cascaded messages as follows:

```
Transcript
    cr; nextPutAll: 'Hope to see you soon. ';
    nextPutAll: 'Please drop by any time.';
    cr; cr; nextPutAll: '        Your friend';
    cr; nextPutAll: '        Brannon'.
```

As we can see, the first **nextPutAll:** message is sent to the same receiver that the previous message, **cr**, was sent to—in this case, it happens to be the transcript.

> *A semicolon encountered in commands indicates that the message immediately after the semicolon is to be sent to the same receiver as the previous message.*

This wording is carefully crafted to apply to all possible cascaded message situations. So, if you really understand it, you should be able to predict the result of the following expression. Note that intuition is not likely to work, but deduction will!

```
3 + 2 - 1; * 100
```

What is the result? Would you believe 500? Why? The semicolon indicates that "* 100" is to be sent to the same receiver as the previous message. The previous message is - and its receiver is the result of executing "3 + 2"; i.e., 5. Hence "* 100" is sent to 5. So the result is 500.

Notice that the result of sending message "- 1" to 5, namely 4, was ignored. This is an example of a tricky piece of code that we would never want to write in practice. Nevertheless, in later chapters, we will encounter more natural examples that require the same degree of understanding.

3.3   What's a Name, a Literal, a Variable?

We all have names. At various times, I've been called Wilfrid, Wilf, Willy, Fred, Mr. LaLonde, Wilf Lalonde, Wilf Roger LaLonde, Emile's boy, Marie's son, but no matter which name is used to refer to me, there is only one me. What is a name? In one sense, a **name** is just a sequence of characters. But there is more to it. We generally attach meaning to names—we use names to refer to people or things. In the above examples, each name referred to a unique individual—me. However, other names are not so unique. For example, "the boss" might refer either to Professor John Pugh when I'm at the university or to my wife Marla Doughty when I'm at home. In this case, to understand who I mean by "the boss," you have to know the context.

The name concept is so useful that some variation exists in all programming languages. In Smalltalk, literals and variables are names for objects. Literals always refer to the same unique object, whereas variables may change which object they refer to over time. In each case, the characters used to specify the names must satisfy certain restrictions—not all characters are allowed.

More specifically, a **literal** is a name (a sequence of special characters—generally specific to each special kind of object) denoting (representing, or referring to) a unique object for all time; for example:

$a is a literal denoting the single character a.
'I"m' is a literal denoting a string containing three characters: I, ', and m.
#red is a literal denoting a symbol containing three characters: r, e, and d.
2000 is a literal denoting integer two thousand.
1.2e2 is a literal denoting the number 1200.0.
true and false are literals denoting truth and falsity.
nil is a literal denoting the undefined object.
#(10 20 30) is a literal denoting an array of integers.

You should already be familiar withthese different kinds of literals, which we investigated in Chapter 2. Recall, for example, that an array literal can contain any other literal except true, false, and nil and cannot contain character "#" internally. Moreover, each occurrence of a word beginning with an alphabetic, such as "hello", or round brackets, such as "(1 2 3)", is assumed to be **implicitly** preceded by "#"; i.e., to be a symbol or another array literal, respectively. Thus,

#((0 1 2 3) (4 5 6) (7 8) (9) ())
#(true false nil red)
#($h $e $l $l $o)

are legitimate array literals. The first is an array literal containing five internal array literals of size 4, 3, 2, 1, and 0, respectively. The second is an array literal containing the symbols #true, #false, #nil, and #red. The third contains the characters spelling "hello".

The examples above illustrate each of the different kinds of literals that exist in Smalltalk—there are no other kinds. You might wonder, however, why there is no fraction literal or why you could not create a literal containing the result of a simple computation such as "1+2". Let's try constructing and inspecting an array literal containing such characters:

#(1/2 nil 1+2)

As you can see from the top inspector in Figure 3.19, it's possible to obtain an array containing this information. But note that the array prints itself with spaces before and after the / and + operators. Is this significant? To see what is going on, you need to investigate the individual elements. If you click on successive elements, you will find that the first element is "1", the second is "/", and the third is "3". The middle inspector in Figure 3.19 shows what you see when the second element is selected. But is this a character, a symbol, or a string? By inspecting this element, we get the bottom inspector, whose title tells us that a symbol is being inspected. So an operator in a literal is interpreted as a symbol, just as nil is, for example. The operator + was implicitly preceded by "#". Does that mean that we can specify symbols like #/ and #+? Experiment to find out (consider, #+, #++, #+++).

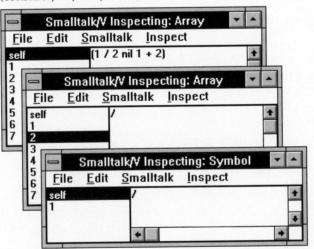

Figure 3.19 Inspecting #(1/2 nil 1+2).

A **variable** is a name (the first character must be alphabetic and the others must be either alphabetic characters or digits) that refers to one arbitrary object. Unlike literals, variables can at one time refer to one object and at another time refer to a completely different object. But a variable can refer only to one object at a time.

By this definition, several of the names used above are invalid as variables because they contain either a space or a quote character. However, we could rewrite the names to satisfy the additional requirement imposed by variables. In that case, the following (in no particular order) are valid:

Wilfrid	Wilf	Willy	Fred	MrLaLonde
EmilesBoy	MariesSon	WilfLalonde	theBoss	WilfRogerLaLonde

In Smalltalk, there are two categories of variables: **global** variables (or **globals**) intended to be universally known and **local** variables (or **locals**) intended for use in specific contexts. By convention, global variables start with an uppercase (capital) letter, and local variables start with a lowercase letter. Hence, "Wilf" would be a global variable, and "theBoss" would be a local variable.

We have already encountered some global variables. For example, the classes are referenced by global variables such as Integer, Number, Magnitude, and Object. Another global variable is Transcript, which refers to the unique window that is always in the Smalltalk environment.

Most of the new variables that we will want to introduce will be local variables. Hence, the names will start with a lowercase letter. Moreover, we will endeavor to use names that indicate what kind of objects they refer to; e.g., aBird, aHorse, aCar. When the name needs to be more descriptive, it can consists of several words concatenated together without intervening spaces. It is conventional to start each word (except the first) with a capital letter; e.g., redBird, movingBall, and colorPicture are preferable to redbird, movingball, and colorpicture, respectively.

Generally, a Smalltalk variable can be used to refer to any object. Moreover, we can generally change which object it refers to when we wish to do so (as we will see). Of course, the fact that we **can** change what a variable refers to doesn't mean that we necessarily want to. For instance, we want the name "Transcript" to permanently refer to the transcript window and names such as "Object", "Magnitude", and "Number" to refer to their respective classes. We don't want to change what these variables refer to. As we will see, it will be up to us to avoid making such changes—we will have to be careful.

To summarize, names are sequences of characters; literals and variables are names that refer to objects. A literal always refers to the same object, but a variable can refer to different objects over time. The names for literals and variables must satisfy special requirements. For literals, the character representation for the name is unique to each kind of object that has literals; i.e., it depends what kind of object it denotes. For variables, the first character must be alphabetic and all the others must be either alphabetic characters or digits. Locals start with a lowercase character and globals start with an uppercase. As we will see, all variables can be changed in one way or another. However, there are a few that won't permit changes by the standard technique; e.g., self, super, and method parameters. We'll encounter these in a more appropriate context in another chapter.

3.4   Local Variables

Objects that need to be remembered for use in a later computation can be saved by associating them with variables. However, before we can make such an association, we need to tell the Smalltalk environment that we intend to use a specific name for that purpose. We need to **declare** our variables. The following template can be used:

```
I variable₁ variable₂ variable₃ ... I
expression₁.
expression₂.
expression₃.
    ⋮
```

In this case, three (or more) variables are being declared: $variable_1$, $variable_2$, $variable_3$, and so on. Once declared, it is legitimate to use the variables in subsequent expressions.

An expression that **binds** a variable to an object has the following form:

```
variable := expression
```

Operator := is called a **binding** (or **assignment**) operator because it binds (or assigns) the variable on the left to the object computed by the expression on the right. Correspondingly, the whole—variable := expression—is called a **binding** (or **assignment**) expression. Once a binding has been performed, *evaluating the variable* retrieves the object to which it is bound. As an example, we might write

```
I temperatureToday temperatureYesterday I
temperatureYesterday := 10. "degrees centigrade"
temperatureToday := 22. "degrees centigrade"
Transcript
    cr;
    nextPutAll: 'The average of yesterday"s and today"s temperature is '.
(temperatureYesterday + temperatureToday) / 2 printOn: Transcript.
```

We would vocalize the first two expressions as "temperatureYesterday is bound to 10" and "temperatureToday is bound to 22." The comment "degrees centigrade" (which is completely ignored by Smalltalk) is provided for the reader's benefit—to make it clear that we mean centigrade degrees rather than, say, fahrenheit degrees.

A subsequent expression using these two variables has access to the objects that the variables are bound to. When "(temperatureYesterday + temperatureToday) / 2" is evaluated, temperatureYesterday is replaced by 10 whereas temperatureToday is replaced by 22. Consequently, 16 is printed in the transcript since "(temperatureYesterday + temperatureToday) / 2" is (10+22) / 2 = 32/2 = 16.

We mentioned before that variable bindings can be changed. A variable that is bound to one object can be bound to a different object later; for example,

```
| temperature |

temperature := 10.
Transcript cr; nextPutAll: 'Yesterday''s temperature is '.
temperature printOn: Transcript.

temperature := 22.
Transcript cr; nextPutAll: 'Today''s temperature is '.
temperature printOn: Transcript.
```

The information printed on the transcript uses the binding that is current at the time of the printing (see Figure 3.20).

Now, what happens if we forget to make a binding? For example, suppose we had said the following:

```
| temperature |

Transcript cr; nextPutAll: 'The temperature is '.
temperature printOn: Transcript.
```

As we can see in Figure 3.21, all variables are initially bound to nil. This should make sense, because nil is an instance of class UndefinedObject. In rare situations, we might want our variables to be nil. However, it is more likely that we will want them to be bound to some other, more relevant objects. Forgetting to initially bind or **define** our variables is a common mistake.

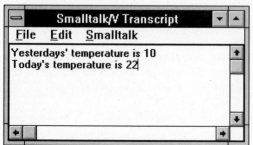

Figure 3.20 When a variable is evaluated, its current binding is used.

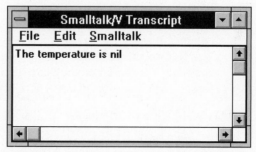

Figure 3.21 When an unbound variable is evaluated, its current binding is nil.

Local variables exist only for the duration of a computation; they disappear immediately afterward. For example, if we execute the following, we should expect to see red as the answer.

```
| color |                                          (1)
color := #red.
color
```

However, when we subsequently reexecute only the part consisting of

| color |
color   (2)

the answer obtained is nil. The system doesn't remember that the last binding to color was #red. Indeed, each time a piece of text is selected and executed, new variables are created specifically for that context and then immediately discarded. In case (1) above, the variable color is totally distinct from the variable color in case (2). They are two different variables with the same name—they exist at two different times in two different contexts. Because of this, local variables are often referred to as **temporary** variables.

The effect of the := operator is rather unique: it binds the variable on the left to the object computed by the expression on the right and it returns the object to which the variable was bound. The second property permits some interesting (though sometimes perverse) examples to be written; for example,

```
| temperatureToday temperatureYesterday |
Transcript cr; nextPutAll: 'Yesterday''s temperature is '.
(temperatureYesterday := 10) printOn: Transcript.
Transcript cr; nextPutAll: 'Today''s temperature is '.
(temperatureToday := 22) printOn: Transcript.
Transcript
    cr;
    nextPutAll: 'The average of yesterday''s and today''s temperature is '.
(temperatureYesterday + temperatureToday) / 2 printOn: Transcript.
```

As you can see, temperatureYesterday is bound to 10 and the same 10 is returned as the result of the := operation. This 10 then serves as the receiver for the **printOn:** message. When such assignments are part of larger expressions, they are termed **inline** assignments. Complex expressions with inline assignments can be more compact but they can also be more difficult to understand. Are inline assignments permitted anywhere? For example, is the following allowed?

```
| sonAge fatherAge |
fatherAge := 25 + sonAge := 10.
```

A quick test (see Figure 3.22) indicates that it is not! On the other hand, it is legal if brackets surround the rightmost assignment (see Figure 3.23).

Presumably, it must therefore be legal to write

```
| fatherAge twinUncleAge |
fatherAge := (twinUncleAge := 10).
```

In fact, we might question whether brackets are needed in this case. Of course, what we think and what we know are two different things. If we try it out, though, we find that the brackets are not needed with consecutive assignment operators (see Figure 3.24).

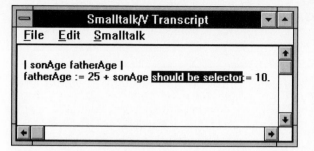

Figure 3.22 Inline assignments are not allowed arbitrarily.

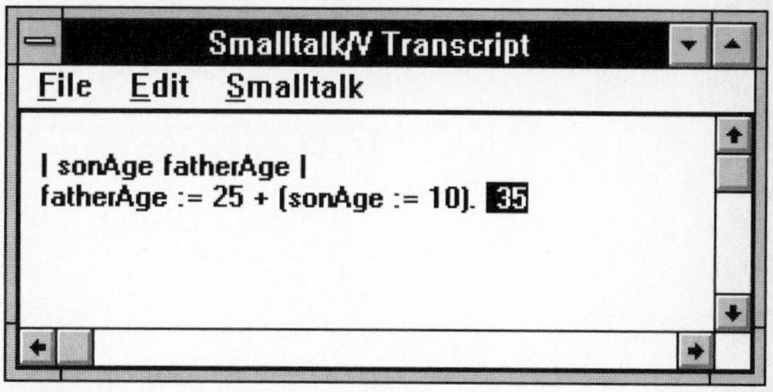

Figure 3.23 Inline assignments are allowed if bracketed.

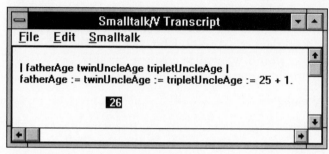

Figure 3.24
Consecutive right-to-left assignments don't need brackets.

The assignments must be performed from right-to-left; otherwise, there wouldn't be an object for the first variable to bind to. Are there any other strange possibilities? As it turns out, no.

Perhaps now we might be in a position to answer a rather complicated question. We know from previous experience that + is an operator and a message selector. In particular, if we write

```
| smallInteger largeInteger |
smallInteger := 1.
largeInteger := 100000000000.
smallInteger + largeInteger
```

we know that both operands of + in the last expression must be evaluated before the message with selector + is sent. Consequently, "+ 100000000000" is being sent to 1. If we had written the following instead, would ":= 100000000000" be sent to 1 (is ":= 100000000000" a message)?

```
| smallInteger largeInteger |
smallInteger := 1.
largeInteger := 100000000000.
smallInteger := largeInteger          "We used := here, instead of +."
```

An appropriate answer here requires a bit of thinking. First, if ":=□100000000000" is actually sent to 1, it would be impossible to ever change variable smallInteger. Hence, it cannot be sent to 1. Clearly, := does not work like

+. There cannot be an arbitrary expression to the left of :=. Only a variable is allowed.

> := is a special operator. *It is not a message.*

If := were a message, a receiver (which can be an arbitrary object) would have been permitted.

3.5   Global Variables

Unlike local variables, global variables (remember—they must be capitalized) are intended to refer to objects that need to be remembered across activations of the Smalltalk environment. When you bind a global variable to an object, save the image, and then reactivate Smalltalk a next week later, the global variable will still be bound to that object. So, you if wanted to create a variable, say to keep track of your best friend, you might write something like

> MyBestFriend := 'Myrna Jones'

Afterward, you could eliminate all visible references to this variable, save the image, and leave. Some time later, you might reactivate the Smalltalk environment and try the following:

> MyBestFriend ⇒ 'Myrna Jones'

Since globals really are variables, we should, of course, be able to make changes.

> MyBestFriend := 'Paul Smith'

Presumably, the latest binding will be remembered if we save the image again. But wait, didn't we forget something? To use local variables, we had to declare them first. Don't we have to do something similar for global variables. Indeed, we do. Before we use global variables, we do need to declare them. Because they are global, we also need to do something special if we want to get rid of them permanently. The process is illustrated below:

> Smalltalk at: #MyBestFriend **put**: 'Sample Object'   "to declare a variable"
> Smalltalk **removeKey**: #MyBestFriend   "to undeclare the variable"

Note that it is important that #MyBestFriend be specified as a symbol. It is the name #MyBestFriend that we want to declare, not the object that is referenced by variable MyBestFriend. **Smalltalk** itself is a global variable that, like **Transcript**, is permanently known.

An alternative approach is to use the variable as if it had already been declared. A confirmation window, as illustrated in Figure 3.25, will appear. Simply click on **Yes**.

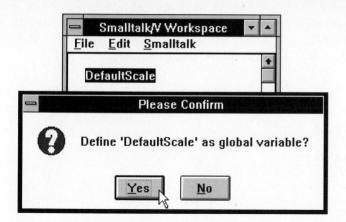

Figure 3.25 Class variables cannot be accessed from a workspace.

Sometimes we mistakenly capitalize local variables and get the same confirmation window. In those circumstances, the proper thing to do, of course, is to click on **No**.

Having used both local and global variables, we might wonder whether we should start to use more globals in preference to local variables. As a rule, the answer is no.

> *Local variables are preferred over global variables. In Smalltalk, there is rarely a need for globals. The unneccessary use of globals is generally consider poor style.*

Most completed applications get their data from files (or external databases—an advanced topic that we won't pursue here); consider text-formatting programs or paint programs. Consequently, there is no need to keep text or graphics information in global variables. On rare occasions, we might obtain a complex picture from the clipboard (a topic considered in Chapter 9). So as not to have to do it again each time we want to use the picture, we might create a global variable—say, Picture—to keep track of it. Alternatively, we might create a global—say called PictureLibrary—that keeps track of a whole collection of pictures.

An exception to the rule is the practical use of globals for pool dictionaries (discussed in Chapter 4). I have rarely used more than a few global variables per year, and most of those weren't really needed (with the exception of pool variables). We'll see later that important data really belongs with important classes. Consequently, it is usually kept in class variables. We'll encounter such variables in Chapter. 4.

Just out of curiosity, what might we expect to see if we inspected **Smalltalk**? Let's try it. As you can see in Figure 3.26, it is an instance of SystemDictionary (we'll investigate dictionaries later), whose main purpose is to group names with their associated values. If we scroll enough, we should be able to find every single global in the system. Figure 3.26 shows what happens when we click on a name in the leftmost pane. The value associated with the variable is displayed in the right pane. In this case, we clicked on **Smalltalk**, but we could just as well have clicked on **SmallInteger**.

So **Smalltalk** is a global variable container. As we can see, it contains all the class names, including itself, in addition to special variables such as **Transcript**.

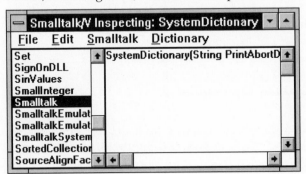

Figure 3.26 Inspecting Smalltalk itself.

So we now know how to declare variables, how to bind them to objects, and how to retrieve the objects to which they are bound. We need more experience with variables.

3.6   Debugging and Typical Mistakes Made by Beginners

We have said before that programming is an art. The best programmers and designers can program "solutions" that solve simple problems in no time at all. But most of us don't have the knowledge or experience that the experts have. Our solutions often don't work. When that happens, we have no choice but to find out what is wrong—a process that we call **debugging**, or locating the **bug**, the cause of the problem.

Actually, debugging is not just relegated to novices. Experts do it all the time. But they are much better at it. An expert can walk behind rows of novice programmers and with a simple glance at their work exclaim: "there's a bug, there's another one, there's a problem." Sometimes, bugs are a result of simple slips. Sometimes, there are a result of deep misunderstandings. But almost always, they're unexpected.

There's no point in giving up when a bug appears. We need to get our bug sprays, so to speak, and **debug** our programs. To do that well, we need some experience. In fact, debugging experience is precisely what a novice needs to improve his or her programming capabilities. *It's not that experts don't make mistakes, it's that they've made them all—at least once.* And he doesn't often repeat his mistakes.

In this section, we'll deliberately make some errors in a simple algebra problem. Your goal is simple. Try to guess what we are about to do wrong. You might also wish to guess the consequences of the mistake; i.e., what kind of error message (if any) will we get? After this experience, you'll have a better chance of being able to spot potential problems by yourself.

Let's imagine that a small company whose main job is to design satellites has come to us with a simple problem. For some scientific experiment involving observations of the sun, they need to place a plain carbon steel rod in a container that is made of material that does not expand—some special plastic. They expect the interior of the satellite to reach a maximum temperature of 500°C. They want to know the length of the rod at that temperature if the rod is 30 inches at 0°F. Presumably, they want the rod to be as tight-fitting as possible in the container but yet have enough room so that it won't crack the container during expansion.

They know we aren't physicists so they gave given us all the information we need to solve the problem. In particular, they told us that the size (or length) of the steel rod could be computed from the formula

$$s = s_0 (1 + \alpha f)$$

where s_0 is the size in inches at 0°F, α (the coefficient of expansion, alpha) is 6.7×10^{-6} inches of expansion per Fahrenheit degree per inch of metal, and f is the temperature in degrees Fahrenheit. You can find this information, they said, in any physics encyclopedia. Fortunately, we know the following relationship between f (in Fahrenheit degrees) and c (in Centigrade degrees).

$$f = 32 + \frac{9}{5} c \qquad \text{"Fahrenheit degrees"}$$

Our goal is to program a Smalltalk solution that will enable us to work out the rod's size at 500°C. So let's open a workspace and proceed to try a sample solution. Being relatively knowledgeable about Smalltalk, we know that the temperature in fahrenheit degrees cannot be computed as

$$32 + \frac{9}{5} c$$

because there is an operation missing between $\frac{9}{5}$ and c. Neither can it be computed as

$$32 + \frac{9}{5} * c$$

because 5 is not intended to divide 32+9. Since evaluation is strictly left to right, brackets are needed, as in

$$32 + ((9/5) * c)$$

Actually, the brackets around the fraction 9/5 are superfluous. It is sufficient to write

$$32 + (9/5 * c)$$

because evaluation inside the brackets is strictly left to right; i.e., / executes before *. On our first attempt to find a complete solution, we might try executing the following (as shown in Figure 3.27):

```
c = 500
f = 32 + (9/5 * c)
s = 30 * (1 + (6.7e-6*f))
```

The result is shown in Figure 3.28.

Figure 3.27 Attempting to use three equations.

Figure 3.28 Variables must be defined.

This is the error message we get if we forget to declare our variables. We need to add, to the beginning, a declaration such as the following:

```
| c f s |
```

If we make this addition and try to execute the expressions in the workspace, an error is encountered, as shown in Figure 3.29.

The comment at the top doesn't seem to be very instructive. It tells us that the message "f" was not understood by some object. What object? An unspecified

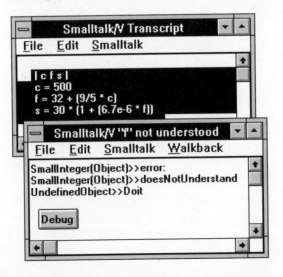

Figure 3.29 Independent expressions must be separated by a period.

small integer, as indicated by the following line in the error window:

"SmallInteger(Object)>>doesNotUnderstand:"

But isn't "f" a variable? Why is "f" being misunderstood as a message? Perhaps this is due to the integer 500 that immediately precedes the "f" on the previous line. Remember that Smalltalk doesn't care how many lines we use to specify the expression. We could, for example, have typed everything on one line:

| c f s | c = 500 f = 32 + (9/5 * c) s = 30 * (1 + (6.7e-6 * f))

In this case, it seems that the subexpression "500 f" consists of the receiver 500 and selector "f". We are sending message f to 500, which doesn't make sense—integers don't understand "f"! What's our mistake? We forgot to separate each equation with a period (recall the Transcript examples in the previous section). We need to rewrite the above as

| c f s | c = 500. f = 32 + (9/5 * c). s = 30 * (1 + (6.7e-6 * f)). s

To make it clear that we want to see s as the result, we might also add expression "s" at the end. However, this should be superfluous because the value returned from an assignment is the value being bound to the variable. After making this change and trying again, we get still another error message, as shown in Figure 3.30.

This one is more difficult to understand. In this case, some undefined object did not understand the message "numerator"—see the title at the top of the window and also the second line, "UndefinedObject(Object)>>doesNotUnderstand:". This seems to be a mystery; we don't have a message called "numerator" anywhere in the workspace. However, there are additional clues. In particular, the third line, "Fraction>>*", indicates that message "*" was sent to a fraction just prior to the

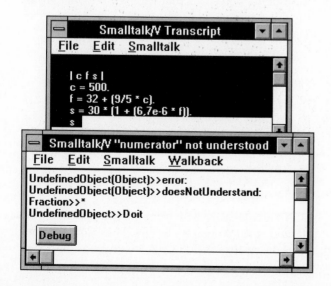

Figure 3.30 Operator = is a comparison, not a binding.

message that wasn't understood. If we look at the workspace, we can see that the first multiply message was sent to fraction 9/5 along with parameter c. Perhaps there is a problem with "c"? As far as we can tell, c should be 500, but is it? Let's find out by evaluating just the first part of our solution, the portion consisting of

```
| c f s |
c = 500.
```

The result, shown in Figure 3.31, is false rather than the expected 500! Clearly, something is being compared—presumably, c is being compared with 500 and the two are not equal.

But what is c? As we can see by selecting just the portion

```
| c f s |

c
```

c is nil (see Figure 3.32).

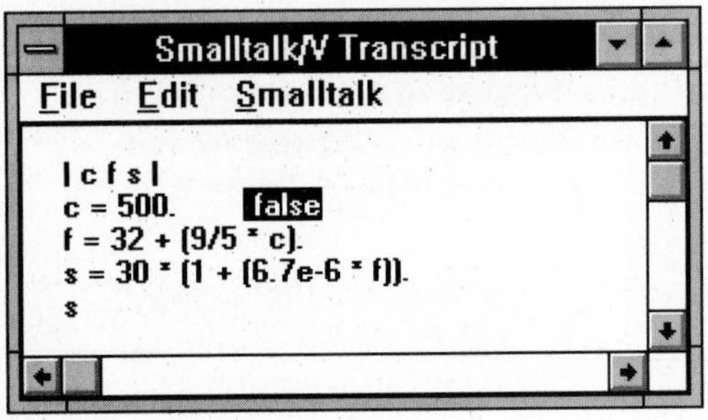

Figure 3.31 Investigating the value of "c = 500".

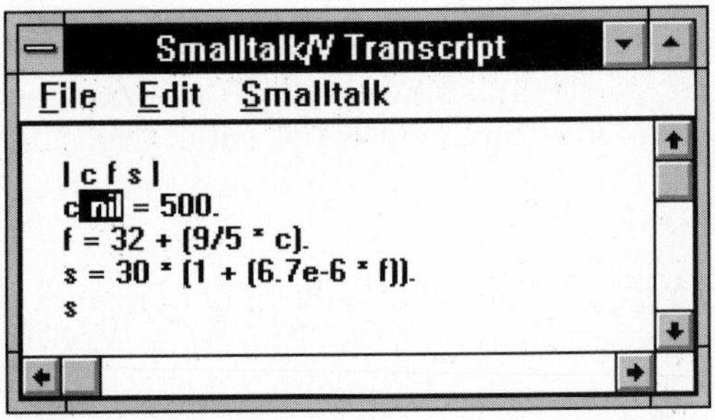

Figure 3.32 Investigating the value of "c".

The problem (as you might have already guessed) is that we used = instead of :=. We don't want to compare c with 500; we want to **bind** c to 500. The solution, as we all know, is to write

```
c := 500.
```

Subsequently, when we write

```
f := 32 + (9/5 * c).
```

we are binding f to the object obtained by evaluating 32 + (9/5 * c). Since c is bound to 500, 32 + (9/5 * c) is really 32 + (9/5 * 500), or 32 + 900 (in other words, 932). Finally, we can evaluate the expression

```
s := 30 * (1 + (6.7e-6 * f)).
```

and return s, the answer, as shown in Figure 3.33. One advantage of using variables is that they make it relatively easy to make changes. For example, if we want to see the result when the temperature is 100°C, it is simply a matter of changing one number, as shown in Figure 3.34.

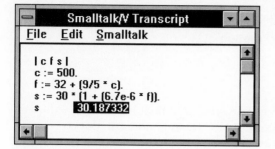
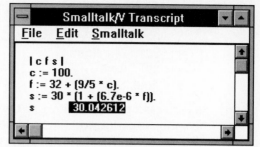

Figure 3.33 Computing the required answer.

Figure 3.34 Computing the result for a new centigrade temperature.

Had we attempted to avoid variables, we would have had to compute a more complicated expression, such as that shown in Figure 3.35. As we can see, finding and changing the 500 to 100, in this case, is not much harder. But it is much more difficult to determine what all the constants represent.

If we subsequently change the 100 shown in Figure 3.35 to yet another value, say 30, as shown in Figure 3.36, making an even further change is problematic—there are now two 30's in the expression. It's easy to forget that one is a temperature and the other is the initial size in inches. We might even accidentally change the wrong one.

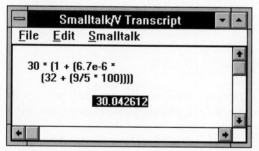

Figure 3.35 Computing a lengthy expression without variables.

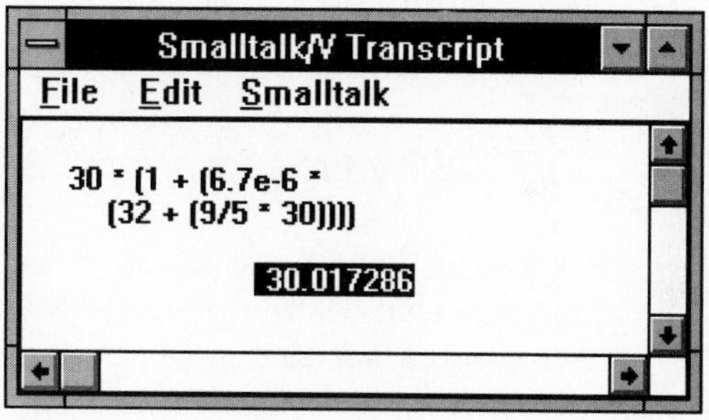

Figure 3.36 Computing another lengthy expression without variables.

Clearly, variables can often make expressions more understandable. As we indicated earlier, it is often useful to introduce variables specifically to make the expressions more readable for others.

In our examples, we are performing arithmetic between two different kinds of objects, integers and floats, so there is some inefficiency associated with the computation. Since inefficiency is not an error, only an expert would recognize it. Consider our best solution:

```
| c f s |
c := 500.                    "The result is an integer."
f := 32 + (9/5 * c).         "The result is an integer or a fraction."
s := 30 * (1 + (6.7e-6 * f)). "The result is a float."
```

If we analyze the last assignment, we will note

$$s := 30 * (1 + (6.7e\text{-}6 * \textbf{integerOrFraction}^{\dagger})) \Rightarrow$$
$$s := 30 * (1^{\dagger} + \textbf{float}) \Rightarrow$$
$$s := 30^{\dagger} * \textbf{float} \Rightarrow$$
$$s := \textbf{float}$$

In each case, the item indicated by † is converted to a float before the arithmetic operation is performed. Since this is automatic, we don't notice it. But converting an integer or a fraction to a float is an expensive operation (many hundreds of messages are unnoticeably executed). If we are interested in efficiency, we might rewrite our solution as follows:

```
l c f s l
c := 500.                       "The result is an integer."
f := 32 + (9/5 * c).            "The result is an integer or a fraction."
s := 30.0 * (1.0 + (6.7e-6 * f)).   "The result is a float (only f is converted to float)."
```

We can avoid all conversions entirely if we use floats everywhere, as in the following:

```
l c f s l
c := 500.0.                     "The result is a float."
f := 32.0 + (1.8 * c).          "The result is a float."
s := 30.0 * (1.0 + (6.7e-6 * f)).   "The result is a float."
```

3.7   Why Programming is Not Mathematics

What we have done so far raises an extremely important issue with respect to style—what we might call the **mathematical** or **algebraic perspective** versus the **computer science** or **programming perspective**. Mathematics is primarily concerned with conciseness. The previous section, for example, illustrates the typical mathematical perspective.

From the programming perspective, the programming examples of the last section are **very poor** examples. Although conciseness is a goal, understandability is more important. Programming in computer science is very much concerned with choosing variable names that are **self-explanatory** in nature. Rather than use variable names such as c and f to denote Centigrade and Fahrenheit degrees, we should use the more obvious names. The example

```
l c f s l
c := 500.0.
f := 32.0 + (1.8 * c).
s := 30.0 * (1.0 + (6.7e-6 * f)).
```

is considered poor style from the programming perspective. It could be redone as follows:

```
| centigrade fahrenheit length |
centigrade := 500.0.
fahrenheit := 32.0 + (1.8 * centigrade).
coefficientOfExpansion := 6.7e-6. "in inches per Fahrenheit degree per inch"
length := 30.0 * (1.0 + (coefficientOfExpansion * fahrenheit)). "in inches"
length
```

Indeed, computer scientists are less likely to debate whether centigrade is a better name than c than to debate whether the name length is precise enough. For example, we might be tempted to use the name ironBarLength instead of length. We might also be tempted to replace the 30 by initialIronBarLength.

For the remainder of this book, we will never again use names like c, f, and s. We encourage the eager student to keep this in mind when choosing variable names. The difference between poor names and well-chosen names is the difference between laziness and keenness, between mediocrity and excellence—between the novice and the expert!

3.8 Preparing for Interaction

Because Smalltalk is an interactive system, it provides facilities for prompting, informing, and displaying information on the screen. Let's investigate some of these basic facilities.

3.8.1 Prompters, Message Boxes, and Menus

Prompters provide facilities that permit a user to supply textual information, **message boxes** provide facilities to inform the user and to solicit true/false responses, and **menus** provides lists of entries for selection. A summary of the relevant messages (primarily class messages) is illustrated below.

A title (in bold) precedes and groups illustrated messages for a specific kind of object. Within a group, italic categorization further groups expressions with similar purpose and provides one line of detail about this purpose. Note that menus are illustrated with a two-message expression.

Operations on Prompters

querying (a textual response or nil expected)

Prompter **prompt**: messageString **default**: initialReplyString

querying (an object response or nil expected)

Prompter **prompt**: messageString **defaultExpression**: initialReplyString

Operations on Message Boxes

informing (no response expected)

MessageBox **message**: aString

querying (a boolean response expected)

MessageBox **confirm**: aString

Operations on Menus

querying (a menu item or nil response expected)

(Menu
    labelArray: anArrayOfStringsOrSymbols
    lines: anArrayOfDividerLineIndices
    selectors: anArrayOfReplies)
      popUp

Some examples will help clarify this protocol. To begin with, suppose we wish to prompt for a name. We might execute the following, which results in the prompter shown in Figure 3.37. Clicking on OK returns the string typed in the entry field (the square text box in the center of the prompter window). If nothing new is typed, the default—the initial reply string—is returned. Alternatively, if Cancel is selected, nil is returned. This allows us to determine if the user changed his mind.

Prompter **prompt**: 'Your name?' **default**: 'Wilf' ⇒ 'Wilf'　"If OK is clicked on."
Prompter **prompt**: 'Your name?' **default**: 'Wilf' ⇒ nil "If Cancel is clicked on."

A variation (see Figure 3.38) permits the user's typed response to be executed and returned; for example:

Prompter
    prompt: 'Compute something?'
    defaultExpression: '10 factorial + 1'
      ⇒ '3628801

An error message results if the expression typed by the user is not a valid Smalltalk expression.

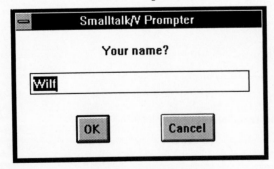

Figure 3.37 Prompting for a name.

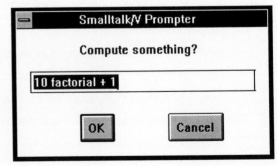

Figure 3.38 Prompting for an expression that is to be computed.

Message boxes, by contrast, can be used to display simple status information or warning messages as shown in Figure 3.39. The user must click on OK to make the message box disappear. Nothing useful is returned. Alternatively, message boxes can be used to request a true/false response, as shown in Figure 3.40. The user must click on either Yes (for true) or No (for false), or hit return as an alternative to clicking on Yes.

MessageBox **message**: 'You can''t do that' ⇒ aMessageBox
MessageBox **confirm**: 'Continue' ⇒ true

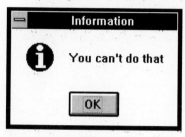

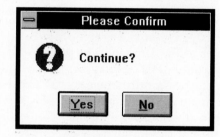

Figure 3.39 Informing the user via a message box.

Figure 3.40 Querying the user for a true/false (yes/no) response.

Menus (see Figure 3.41) provide the user with the capability of providing a list of entries for selection. Three pieces of information must be supplied:

- **List entries**, an array of strings or symbols.
- List-entry **dividing bars**, an array of indices indicating the list entries *after which* a dividing bar is required.
- **List replies**, an array of reply symbols or strings corresponding to the list entries.

The menu can be constructed without making it appear on the display screen. It is made to appear by sending it a **popUp** message. The user must click either on an entry, in which case the corresponding list reply is returned, or outside the list in which case nil is returned. In the following example, it is assumed the user clicked on #Orange, which causes the symbol #orange to be returned.

```
(Menu
    labelArray: #(Red Green Blue Orange Yellow Black White)
    lines: #(3 5)
    selectors: #(red green blue orange yellow black white))
        popUp ⇒ orange
```

Figure 3.41 Requesting a list item from the user.

3.9   Case Study: Smalltalk Pens

Computer graphics is an interesting and rich domain for investigating variables and computation. In this section, we will be concerned with a subset of Smalltalk's graphical capabilities; namely, those dealing with the line drawing capabilities of pens.

3.9.1   An Introduction to Smalltalk Pens

Smalltalk **pens** are objects that can draw from one point to another on the display. More generally, a **pen** is a graphics **tool** that permits drawing on a graphics **medium** such as the display or the printer. **Display** is a global that permanently refers to the monitor's display screen. A **point** is a pair consisting of an **x-coordinate** and a **y-coordinate**; e.g., 10@20 denotes a point with x-coordinate 10 and y-coordinate 20. The Smalltalk display's coordinate system (see Figure 3.42) has its **origin** (the location of point 0@0) at the top-left corner with the x-axis increasing to the right and the y-axis increasing downward. The **x-axis** is an imaginary line at the y-coordinate 0. Similarly, the **y-axis** is an imaginary line at the x-coordinate 0.

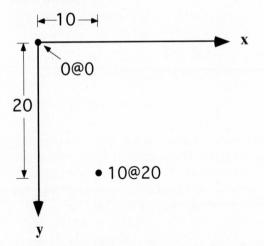

Figure 3.42 The display's coordinate system.

Smalltalk **pens** have
- A **nib**, a drawing tip that can draw when it is **down** (on the surface of the display) but not when it is **up** (off the surface)
- A **location** specified as a point
- A **direction** specified as an angle relative to the x-axis, positive for clockwise and negative for counterclockwise. Thus a direction of 0° points to the right, 90° points down, and -90° points up.

Additionally, a pen can be **placed** at an arbitrary point or made to **go to** a specified point. In the latter case, a line is drawn from the current location to the destination point if the nib is down. A pen can also be made to **go** forward an arbitrary distance in whatever direction it is currently pointing. Each distance unit, either in the x-direction or y-direction corresponds to one **pixel**—one perceivable dot on the screen.

Although Smalltalk pens are similar to the writing pens we are all familiar with, there are some glaring differences. Writing pens don't have direction nor can they "remember" their status; e.g., whether their nib is up, their current location, and their current direction.

The display has both a **width** and a **height** maintained as a point called its **extent**; the x-coordinate of the extent is the width and the y-coordinate is the height. This information can be important when drawing pictures because not all displays are the same size. If you wish to draw a picture at the bottom-right corner, for example, you will need to know the display's extent.

As we did when we learned about the transcript operations, we will first provide a reasonable sample of the operations available to points, pens, and the display and then we will endeavor to make use of those operations.

Operations on Numbers

aNumber @ aNumber	Obtains a new point

Operations on Points

aPoint **x**	Obtains the x-coordinate of the point
aPoint **y**	Obtains the y-coordinate of the point

Operations on Pens

aPen **down**	Enables the nib to draw
aPen **up**	Makes the nib unable to draw
aPen **north**	Points toward the ceiling
aPen **direction**	Gets angle in degrees, 0° points right; 90° down
aPen **direction**: degrees	Sets the angle where 0° points right, 90° down
aPen **turn**: degrees	Turns the specified degrees; clockwise for +ve
aPen **go**: distance	Moves a number of pixels, draws if pen is down
aPen **home**	Positions the pen at the center of the display
aPen **location**	Gets the position as a point
aPen **goto**: aPoint	Moves to the specified point; draws if pen is down
aPen **place**: aPoint	Moves to the specified point without drawing

Operations on global Display

Display **pen**	Gets the display's pen
Display **extent**	Gets the display's extent; i.e., width@height

3.9.2 Using Pens for Line Graphics

In general, to draw something simple like a rectangle, we need to obtain a pen (e.g., from global Display), position it at an appropriate place, and then move it four times to draw each of the sides.

Recall that expressions in transcript or workspace windows must have the following structure:

> | optional local variables |
> expressions

Also, if we wish to be able to draw, the pen's nib must be **down**. To ensure that this is the case, we might wish to execute

> Display **pen down**

Note that this obtains the pen from Display and then sends the **down** message to it. In general, if we adopt the convention that we always bring the pen's nib **down** when we are done with a pen, we won't need to continually execute such code.

For our first example, let's consider drawing a 100-pixel-wide square. Presumably, we can use a variable to refer to our pen. Consequently, it will be easy to use the pen to draw four sides on the display.

```
| aPen |
aPen := Display pen.
aPen place: 100@100.      "Starting point."
aPen goto: 200@100.   "Go right 100 pixels."
aPen goto: 200@200.   "Go down 100 pixels."
aPen goto: 100@200.   "Go left 100 pixels."
aPen goto: 100@100.   "Go up 100 pixels."
```

When the expressions are executed—for example, in the workspace shown in Figure 3.43—the result should appear as shown in Figure 3.44. Note that the square is drawn over whatever happens to be on the display at the time.

Actually, Figure 3.44 illustrates what we expect to happen. What actually happens is illustrated in Figure 3.45. The square of Figure 3.44 appears momentarily as the commands are executed. However, once the instructions finish executing, the Smalltalk environment deselects the selected expressions. This causes the expressions to be redisplayed over the drawing of the square, obliterating the top part.

We can easily get around this problem by moving the workspace to some other part of the display and executing the expressions again. This time, the square will be displayed where our workspace used to be and nothing will be obliterated.

If we want to draw a square of a different size or the same square at different coordinates, we'll have to make substantial changes to our instructions. It would

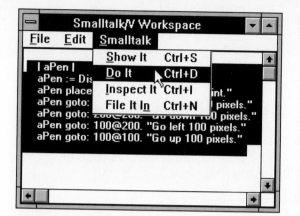

Figure 3.43 Using a pen to draw a square with 100-pixel-wide sides.

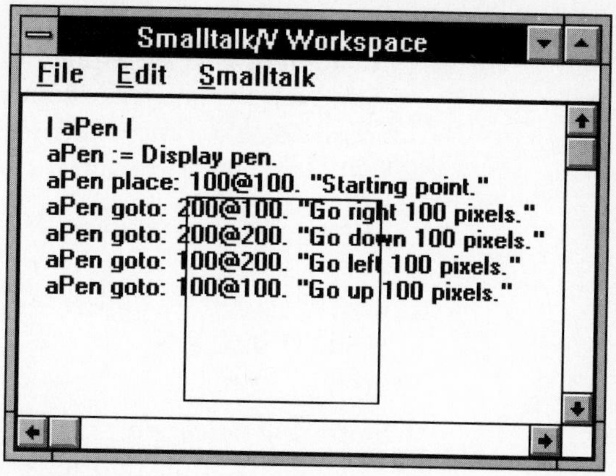

Figure 3.44 The square we expected to see drawn.

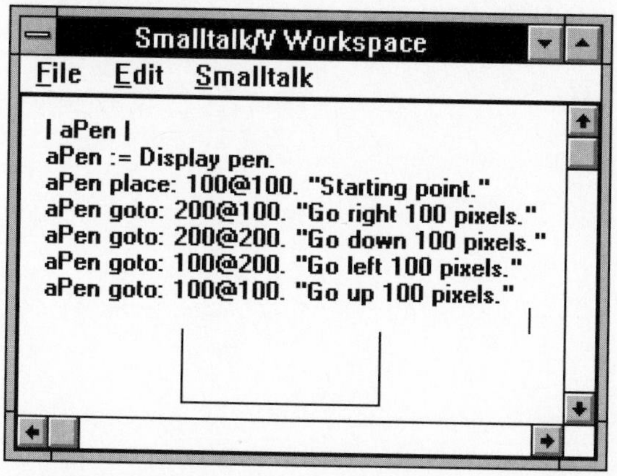

Figure 3.45 The square that is actually drawn.

have been much easier if we had used variables for those things that we might have wanted to change. Presumably, we could start by adding two new variables. We could initialize them to values that will provide the same square as above (for comparison purposes).

```
I aPen start size I
aPen := Display pen.
start := 100@100. "Starting point."
size := 100. "Pixels."

aPen place: start.                          "Top-left corner of square."
```

Now, how do we determine where to go? One way is to compute it.

```
aPen goto: (start x + size) @ (start y).           "Go right the required amount."
aPen goto: (start x + size) @ (start y + size).    "Go down the required amount."
aPen goto: (start x) @ (start y + size).           "Go left the required amount."
aPen goto: start.                                  "Go up to the top-left corner."
```

To look at more detail at the way that point computations work, consider the evaluation of the first expression, "(start **x** + size) @ (start **y**)", which is attempting to add size to the x-coordinate but not to the y-coordinate (to go right by the amount "size"). Since start is 100@100 and size is 100, we would like to have 200@100 when we are done.

(<u>start **x** + size</u>) @ (start **y**) ⇒	(start is 100@100, so the x-coordinate is 100)
(100 + <u>size</u>) @ (start **y**) ⇒	(but size is 100)
(<u>100 + 100</u>) @ (start **y**) ⇒	(adding size to this x-coordinate gives 200)
200 @ <u>start **y**</u> ⇒	(the y-coordinate of start is also 100)
200 @ 100	(so the final result is 200@100)

Computing with points in this way is difficult because we first have to decompose a point into its x and y components, perform the ordinary integer arithmetic on the pieces, and then put the pieces back together into another point using operation "@". Maybe there is an easier way? What would happen if we tried to do arithmetic on points? Let's try some experiments.

```
start ⇒ 100@100
start + 1 ⇒ 101@101
start + (1@2) ⇒ 101@102
start - 10 ⇒ 90@90
start - (10@20) ⇒ 90@80
start * 2 ⇒ 200@200
start * (2@3) ⇒ 200@300
start // 10 ⇒ 10@10
start // (10@20) ⇒ 10@5
start / 10 ⇒ (error)                    Note
start / (10@20) ⇒ (error)               Note
start negated ⇒ (-100@-100)
```

The first observation is that +, -, *, // (divide with truncation), and **negated** all work on point receivers. However, / (divide without truncation or conversion to fraction) does not. Moreover, when the parameter is an integer (as in "start + 1"), the integer is applied to both the x- and y-coordinates. When the parameter is another point (as in "start + (1@2)"), the corresponding x- and y-coordinates are operated on independently. In other words,

(x1 @ y1) op anInteger	means	(x1 op anInteger) @ (y1 op anInteger)
(x1 @ y1) op (x2 @ y2)	means	(x1 op x2) @ (y1 op y2)

Perhaps we can use this new knowledge to rewrite our square-drawing instructions. Additionally, let's use cascading to avoid repeating "aPen".

```
| aPen start size |
aPen := Display pen.
start := 100@100. "Starting point."
size := 100. "Pixels."
```

```
aPen
    place: start;              "Top-left corner of square."
    goto: start + (size @ 0);  "Top-right corner."
    goto: start + size;        "Bottom-right corner."
    goto: start + (0 @ size);  "Bottom-left corner."
    goto: start.               "Top-left corner again."
```

Since drawing squares is a useful thing to do, we might wish to extend pens to enable us to draw squares with a simple command. For example, it would be nice if we could say

```
aPen displaySquareAt: 100@100 side: 200+1
```

To do this, we will have to make use of a browser—a topic for Chapters 4 and 5.

3.9.3 Windows and Graph Panes

One problem with the above examples is that lines are drawn arbitrarily on the screen. A better alternative is to draw directly into a window. As it turns out, it is relatively simple to create a window and get access to its pen.

Graph panes permit rudimentary windows to be constructed and used. A summary of the relevant messages are shown below.

Operations on Graph Panes

opening windows and obtaining graph panes

```
GraphPane openWindow: titleString
GraphPane openWindow: titleString extent: aPoint
```

obtaining pens

```
aGraphPane pen
```

A simple window can be opened by asking the GraphPane class to both create and open a window that contains a graph pane. The contained graph pane is returned. The first message below creates a window whose size is some arbitrary default. This size, however, can be controlled by specifying the extent, as in the second example—it results in the window shown in Figure 3.46. As we can see, it is a little too small—there is no room for the title. The next example creates a window that is more reasonable (see Figure 3.47). Note that the extent is the size of the window, not the size of the graph pane inside the window.

```
GraphPane openWindow: 'Testing' ⟹ aGraphPane
GraphPane openWindow: 'Testing' extent: 100@100 ⟹ aGraphPane
GraphPane openWindow: 'Testing' extent: 220@220 ⟹ aGraphPane
```

Figure 3.46 Opening a window (extent 100@100) with a graph pane.

Figure 3.47 Opening a larger window (extent 220@220) with a graph pane.

It is a simple exercise to modify the previous pen example to query for the start point and the size and also to use graph panes rather than Display's pen.

```
I aPen start size I
aPen := (GraphPane openWindow: 'Sample square') pen.
start := Prompter
    prompt: 'Start of square?' defaultExpression: 100@100.
size := Prompter
    prompt: 'Size of square?' defaultExpression: '100'. "Pixels."

aPen
    place: start;              "Top-left corner of square."
    goto: start + (size @ 0);  "Top-right corner."
    goto: start + size;        "Bottom-right corner."
    goto: start + (0 @ size);  "Bottom-left corner."
    goto: start.               "Top-left corner again."
```

3.10 Summary

This chapter has introduced you to simple problem solving and has extended your knowledge about the Smalltalk environment. We have

- Solved a simple problem using infinite series
- Learned what messages are understood by the transcript
- Written a letter using messages to the transcript
- Learned about variables and their use in computing results in a workspace or a transcript

- Learned the distinction between global variables and local variables and the fact that the former are in uppercase whereas the latter are in lowercase
- Investigated a simple algebra problem that required variables to make the solution understandable
- Investigated a simple graphics problem for further experience using variables

3.11 What You Did and Did Not Learn

Although we solved a small number of relatively unimportant problems, we learned a great deal. We learned (in fact, relearned) that experimentation is important. We also learned how to display objects including strings and characters in the transcript. As a side-effect, we learned about the period as an expression terminator (or separator) and about the semicolon for indicating message cascading.

We also learned that variables are fundamental to computation because they are used pervasively. The remaining chapters will provide us with much more experience with variables. After a while, using variables will become second nature. Although we have provided hints in this chapter , there are many other kinds of variables besides local and global variables. We'll encounter these as we proceed further.

Additionally, we learned a little bit about graphics, a topic that can be quite interesting and exciting because of the immediate visual effects that result.

3.12 Important Facts

Operations on Objects

anObject = anotherObject   Compares the two objects and returns true if they are equal; otherwise, false

Operations on Numbers

aNumber @ aNumber   Obtains a new point

Operations on Points

aPoint **x**	Obtains the x-coordinate of the point
aPoint **y**	Obtains the y-coordinate of the point
aPoint + anotherPoint	Adds corresponding x- and y-coordinates
aPoint + anInteger	Adds anInteger to both the x- and y-coordinates
aPoint - anotherPoint	Subtracts corresponding x- and y-coordinates
aPoint - anInteger	Subtracts anInteger from both coordinates

Operations on Points (continued)

aPoint * anotherPoint	Multiplies corresponding x- and y-coordinates
aPoint * anInteger	Multiplies anInteger with both coordinates
aPoint // anotherPoint	Divides, with truncation, corresponding x- and y-coordinates
aPoint // anInteger	Divides, with truncation, both the x- and y-coordinates of aPoint by anInteger
aPoint **negated**	Negates corresponding x- and y-coordinates

Operations on Pens

aPen **down**	Enables the nib to draw
aPen **up**	Makes the nib unable to draw
aPen **north**	Points towards the ceiling
aPen **direction**	Gets angle in degrees, 0° points right; 90° down
aPen **direction**: degrees	Sets the angle where 0° points right, 90° down
aPen **turn**: degrees	Turns the specified degrees; clockwise for +ve
aPen **go**: distance	Moves a number of pixels; draws if the pen is down
aPen **home**	Positions the pen at the center of the display
aPen **location**	Gets the position as a point
aPen **goto**: aPoint	Moves to the specified point; draws if the pen is down
aPen **place**: aPoint	Moves to the specified point without drawing

Operations on Prompters

Prompter **prompt**: messageString **default**: initialReplyString
Prompter **prompt**: messageString **defaultExpression**: initialReplyString

> Creates a prompter requesting a textual response. The first message returns the text provided; the second also evaluates the text and returns the result.

Operations on Message Boxes

MessageBox **message**: aString
MessageBox **confirm**: aString

> Creates a message box. The first message requires a Yes response to make it go away. Nothing useful is returned. The second requires a Yes or No response which is returned as true or false.

Operations on Menus

(Menu
    labelArray: anArrayOfStringsOrSymbols
    lines: anArrayOfDividerLineIndices
    selectors: anArrayOfReplies)
      popUp

	Creates a pop-up menu of entries from the label array with lines after the indices in the lines array. Selecting a label entry causes the corresponding entry in the selectors array to be returned; nil is returned if no entry is selected

Operations on global Display

Display **pen**	Gets the display's pen
Display **extent**	Gets the display's extent; i.e., width@height

Operations on Windows; e.g., Transcript

aWindow **cr**	Displays a carriage return; starts a new line
aWindow **space**	Displays a space
aWindow **nextPut**: aCharacter	Displays a character
aWindow **nextPutAll**: aString	Displays a string—only the parts (the characters inside)
anObject **printOn**: aWindow	Displays an object

Globals

Smalltalk	A container for all other globals (including itself)
Transcript	The one unique transcript window
Display	The monitor's display screen

Binding and Evaluating

:=	A special operator, not a message
variable := expression	Binds, or assigns, the variable on the left to the object computed by the expression on the right and returns this object
variable$_1$:= variable$_2$:= expr	Evaluates from right-to-left; may be imbedded in a more complex expression if surrounded by round brackets (parentheses)
variable	Retrieves the object to which the variable is bound; initially, the variable is bound to nil

Period versus semicolon: The period can be viewed as either an expression separator or an expression terminator, since the period is optional after the last expression. The semicolon is a message separator for situations in which each message is intended for the same receiver. When encountered, it can be interpreted as "the message immediately after the semicolon is sent to the same receiver as the previous message."

Locals versus globals: As a rule, globals are rarely needed and should be avoided. If you believe you need one, you should have a strong supporting reason.

Short message names: As programmers, we should always strive for short message names like new and extent rather than corresponding longer names like getMeANewOne and whatIsYourExtent. On the other hand, short forms and acronyms, such as f (for Fahrenheit), int (integer), temp (temperature), or gcd (greatest common denominator) are to be avoided.

The Smalltalk coordinate system: The origin of the display is the top-left corner (coordinate 0@0), with the x-axis increasing to the right and the y-axis increasing downward.

3.13 Keywords

graphics: direction, extent, location, nib, origin, pen, pixel, point, x-axis, x-coordinate, y-axis, y-coordinate

interactive querying: graph pane, menu, message box, prompter

names, literals, and variables: assignment, binding, declaration, define, global variable, inline assignment, literal, local variable, name, temporary variable, variable

programming language syntax: assignment operator, binding operator, cascaded messages, period, semicolon

programming terminology: bug, debugging

window varieties: transcript, workspace

3.14 Exercises

To obtain proper feedback, these exercises should be done in an actual Smalltalk environment—not on paper.

1. What value does $\cfrac{1}{2 - \cfrac{1}{2 - \cfrac{1}{2 - \ldots}}}$ approach?

2. How many terms of $4 * (1 - \frac{1}{3} + \frac{1}{5} - \frac{1}{7} + \frac{1}{9} \ldots)$ are needed to compute pi to three digits of accuracy?

3. Using only strings in a workspace, place the following into the transcript (each on a new line):

        hello   I'm   'hi'

4. Using only **printOn:** in a workspace, place the following into the transcript (each on a new line):

| 'please' | $+ | nil |
| true | #true | 'true' |

5. Using cascaded messages in a workspace, place the following into the transcript:

```
        10
   +    30
       - -
        40
```

6. Explain the difference between the following two expressions:

> 3 **factorial factorial factorial**
> 3 **factorial**; **factorial**; **factorial**

7. Predict the result of the following:

> 1 + 10; * 3 **factorial**
> 1 + 10 **factorial**; * 2

8. How many different kinds of literal representations are there? Why is "1/3" not a literal? Why can't true, false, and nil be part of an array literal?

9. What kinds of objects are true, 'true', and #true? Are they equal to each other?

10. A gardener has to make a circular tulip bed to hold 2,000 tulip bulbs planted 36 to a square meter. Find the diameter of the bed rounded to the nearest meter. Hint: The area of a circle is πr^2.

11. Determine the area of a triangle with sides 10, 15, and 20 meters? Hint: Use Heron's formula $\sqrt{s(s-a)(s-b)(s-c)}$ where $s = \dfrac{a+b+c}{2}$. The square root operation in Smalltalk is **sqrt**.

12. Use graph panes and draw complex line drawings representing primitive houses or simple 3-D blocks.

4

The Mechanics of Browsers

What You Will Learn

In the previous chapter, we gained experience with workspaces and transcripts and learned how to program with variables. The next step is to create our own classes and provide both the classes and the instances with the ability to respond to messages unique to them. Such responses will have to be programmed with instructions that we will refer to as methods.

But to do that, we need to know more about browsers, the facility that provides us with the capability to create methods and classes. As part of this process, we will create a simple Banana class with the capability to respond to the message "are you edible?". Two methods will be added to the Banana class: an instance method and a class method.

In addition to providing us with the capability of creating classes and methods, browsers permit us to look at existing methods and classes in the Smalltalk environment, a process we call browsing. Collectively, we'll refer to all the methods and classes in the Smalltalk environment as the Smalltalk library. We will have little opportunity to browse the Smalltalk library in this chapter, but we will begin to explore it in Chapter 6.

Finally, we will investigate how to use browsers to file out classes and methods; i.e., store them in files. We'll also investigate how to file them back in.

Browsers are so fundamental to Smalltalk that we've devoted this entire chapter to their study. Although you might not use all the facilities we cover here immediately, it is useful to know about them early. The next chapter will provide you with a deeper understanding of methods and classes as we illustrate the creation of more complex methods and classes.

4.1 Using Browsers

Browsers are windows that permit methods and classes in the Smalltalk environment to be created, deleted, and viewed. Collectively, the methods and classes in the Smalltalk programming environment make up the **Smalltalk library**. The process of looking at this library is termed **browsing**.

Since browsers are best understood by actually creating classes and methods, we will need a specific example to illustrate their use. As it turns out, it is important to understand the difference between instances and classes when using browsers because we must continually distinguish between instance methods and class methods. Of course, we already know the difference between an instance and a class; e.g., between instance 23 and its class SmallInteger. Moreover, we also know that instances and classes usually understand different messages. For example, instance 23 understands message "+1" but class SmallInteger does not. Conversely, class SmallInteger understands message **"superclass"** but the instance 23 does not.

We can better appreciate this distinction by getting experience creating our own classes and providing both instance and class methods. For simplicity, we will create a class called Banana. Once the class exists, we should be able to obtain an instance as follows:

Banana **new**

Additionally, we would like to provide both the instance and the class with the capability to respond to messages, say a message such as "are you edible?". If instances of class Banana are things we can eat, we would expect to get back the answer **true**. Alternatively, we might ask the same question of the class. But a class is just a concept and we can't eat concepts. So we might expect the response **false** in that case. We can eat bananas (instances of class Banana) but we can't eat the concept Banana (the class itself).

If we are going to send a message to get a response, we need a name for the selector. Recall that selectors cannot have imbedded spaces. So we can't use "are you edible" as the selector name. However, we could use a name such as **areYouEdible**. This would allow us to subsequently write

Banana **new areYouEdible** ⇒ true
Banana **areYouEdible** ⇒ false

There is nothing wrong with a name like **areYouEdible**. However, it does seem a little lengthy.

As programmers, we should always strive for short message names!

Indeed, if such was not an implicit goal of all programmers, messages in Smalltalk would be considerably longer. For example, instead of message **new**, we might have had to use a message like **getMeANewOne**. In that case, our example would have had to be rewritten as

Banana **getMeANewOne areYouEdible**⇒ true
Banana **areYouEdible**⇒ false

Each of these long names is effectively a short sentence with at least a verb and a predicate. We can eliminate the excess words if we implicitly read them in; for example,

Banana **new**   can be mentally read as   Banana "get me a" **new** "one"

We could use the same approach for our new message if we truncate it to just plain **edible**.

Banana **edible**   can be mentally read as   Banana "are you" **edible**

With this slight change in naming convention, our examples would be revised as follows:

Banana **new edible** ⇒ true
Banana **edible** ⇒ false

Of course, if we try to execute the above at this point, we will get error messages (as shown in Figure 4.1), because **edible** is not yet understood.

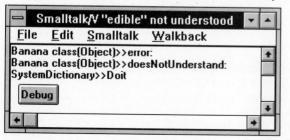

Figure 4.1 Sending a message that isn't understood.

To remedy this, several steps are required. First, we need to obtain a browser—a special kind of window that permits us to create and "look at" or browse a class. Second, we need to create the class itself. Third, we need to add two variations of message **edible**—one version that is understood by instances and another that is understood by the class. These operations are called **methods** since they determine what the reply will be when the receiver is sent the message **edible** (they are methods for computing the answer).

More specifically, we will need to add the following two methods:

> an instance method
> **edible**
>> ^true

> a class method
> **edible**
>> ^false

The former **method** (or set of instructions) specifies that true should be the reply whenever message **edible** is sent to an *instance* of Banana. Thus

> Banana **new edible** ⇒ true

The latter indicates that false should be the reply whenever message **edible** is sent to the *class*. Thus

> Banana **edible** ⇒ false

Any expression preceded by "^" is termed a **reply expression**. It is used to indicate that the answer to a message is the result of the expression that follows "^". It is also permitted in arbitrary expressions in workspaces, transcripts, and inspectors; for example,

> ^1 + 2

is valid in a workspace.

4.1.1 Obtaining a Browser

Any number of browsers can be obtained. Usually, only one is needed, but advanced programmers typically use two or three simultaneously. A **browser** consists of four panes and two switches, as shown in Figure 4.2.

The **class list pane** contains class names, the **method list pane** contains selectors for messages understood either by the class or its instances, and the **code** (or **method**) **pane** contains information retrieved by selections in the other two panes. At any one time, either the **instance switch** or the **class switch** is selected but not both. (The selected switch is darker; a new selection can be made by clicking on the unselected switch.) The switches indicate what information is displayed in the method list pane—instance selectors or class selectors. When the instance switch is selected, the **part names pane** contains the names of an instance's parts. This pane is also called the **instance variables list pane**.

As we begin to use browsers, the significance of these components will become clearer. Don't worry if you forget the terms—we'll redefine them many times in the sections and chapters to come.

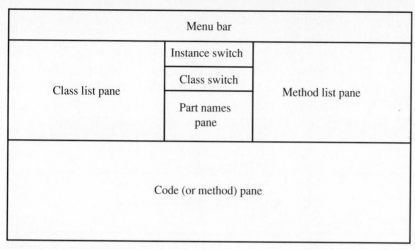

Menu bar		
Class list pane	Instance switch	Method list pane
	Class switch	
	Part names pane	
Code (or method) pane		

Figure 4.2 Browser components.

A browser is obtained by selecting menu item **Browse Classes** in the **File** menu (see Figure 4.3). The browser that subsequently appears is shown in Figure 4.4.

A browser is most useful when it completely fills the screen. This can be accomplished by manually moving and resizing it. Alternatively, the browser can be resized in one step by clicking the **maximize box**—the rightmost box at the top-right corner of the window.

Initially, only the browser's class list pane (the top-left pane) contains information—specifically, a list of class names beginning with Object. Notice that Object is flush-left, while AnimatedObject, Behavior, Boolean, ClassReader, etc. are indented by one character. This indicates that these latter classes are subclasses of Object. If we scroll the pane, we might be able to locate class

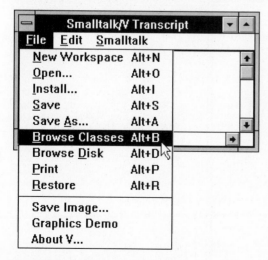

Figure 4.3 Obtaining a browser.

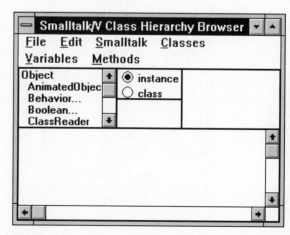

Figure 4.4 The browser obtained.

Magnitude, as shown in Figure 4.5. Notice that Magnitude is indented by one character, indicating that it is a subclass of Object.

If we click once on Magnitude, it will be selected, as shown in Figure 4.6. Note that Magnitude's definition appears in the code pane. For the moment, it is sufficient to observe that superclass Object appears first and that Magnitude, the class we selected, is described as a subclass of Object.

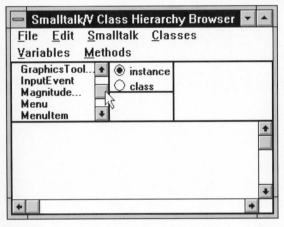

Figure 4.5 Scrolling to view Magnitude.

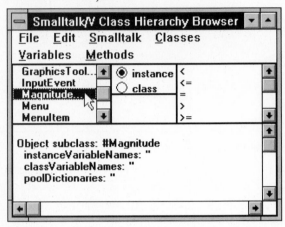

Figure 4.6 Selecting Magnitude.

Double-clicking on Magnitude **opens up the selection** to show all the subclasses (see Figure 4.7). From the indentation, we can see that SmallInteger (partially hidden by the scroll bar) has superclass Integer, which has superclass Number—which in turn has superclass Magnitude. Clicking on Magnitude a second time

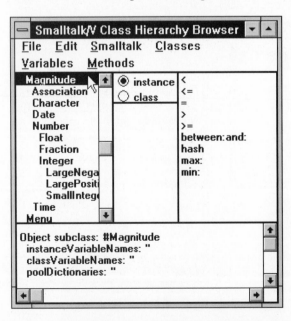

Figure 4.7 Opening up the Magnitude class to show all subclasses.

will **close up the selection** restoring it to its previous state. The three dots after Magnitude (see Figure 4.6) indicate that Magnitude has subclasses and that it can therefore be opened. If we care to investigate, we can see that GraphicsTool (see Figure 4.6) must also have subclasses, since it too can be opened. You might wish to browse around for yourself and see what classes exist.

4.1.2 Viewing a Class Definition

A class definition (as shown in the bottom pane of Figure 4.8) can be viewed simply by clicking on the class name in the class list (top-left) pane. Alternatively, clicking on the instance or class swith has the same effect.

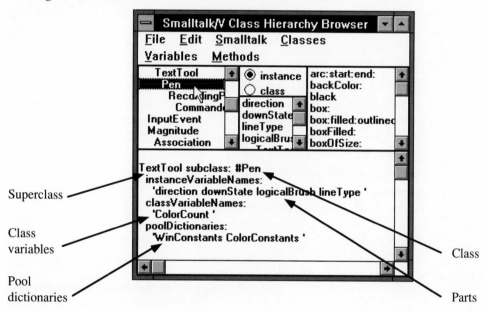

Figure 4.8 Viewing a class definition.

In general, classes are fairly complex objects with several important components. The most important components in the definition are the **class name** and the **superclass**. In this case, Pen is a subclass of TextTool. Hence, TextTool is the superclass of Pen. Next are the **instance variable names** (the names of the variables in an instance) or **part names**. In this case, there are four: direction, downState, logicalBrush, and lineType. Additionally, this class has one **class variable**, called ColorCount, and two **pool dictionaries**, called WinConstants and ColorConstants. We will discuss these components in Chapter 5, after we've had more experience with classes.

Notice that the contents of the code (bottom) pane is actually a four-keyword message with parameters #Pen, 'direction downState logicalBrush lineType', 'ColorCount', and 'WinConstants and ColorConstants'. The first of these parameters (#Pen) must be a symbol (a string will not do) and the others must be strings containing names. Part names must start with lowercase characters while class variables and pool dictionaries must be capitalized.

This message with four-keyword selector **subclass:instanceVariableNames:–classVariableNames:poolDictionaries:** could be executed anywhere—in the browser, in a transcript, or in a workspace. Indeed, we could easily create yet another class—say, Pear—by changing the word TextTool to Object, changing Pen to Pear, replacing the three string parameters by the empty string '', and executing the edited message; e.g., by selecting the entire Smalltalk expression and choosing **Do It** in the **Smalltalk** menu.

However, we don't normally create classes in this way, because it would be difficult to remember such a long and complicated message selector. The next section illustrates how we typically create new classes.

4.1.3 Creating a New Class

When creating a new class, we must first decide what the superclass should be. Recall, for example, that 23 is a SmallInteger whose superclass is Integer. Integer, in turn, has superclass Number, which has superclass Magnitude, which, in turn, has superclass Object. Class Object has no superclass. When in doubt, it is best to choose Object as the superclass. Proceed as follows:

- Select the class that is to become the superclass for the new class.
- Select menu item **Add Subclass...** in the **Classes** menu as illustrated in Figure 4.9. A query window, as shown in Figure 4.10, will appear.
- Type in the name of the new class and then click on the **OK** button. The default switch settings provide us with what we need.

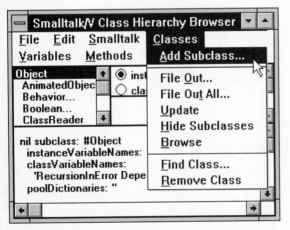

Figure 4.9 Creating a new subclass.

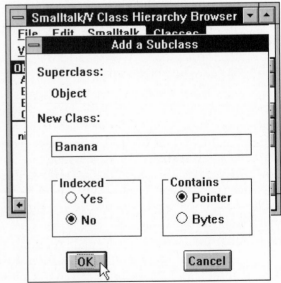

Figure 4.10 Naming the class.

The new class (Banana in this case) will appear, as shown in Figure 4.11.

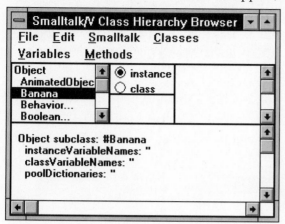

Figure 4.11 The new Banana class, selected.

4.1.4 Deleting a Class

Deleting a class is simpler than creating one. Proceed as follows:

- Select the class that is to be deleted.
- Select menu item **Remove Class** in the **Classes** menu, as illustrated in Figure 4.12. A confirmation window, as shown in Figure 4.13, will appear.
- Click on **Yes** or hit **Enter** on the keyboard, unless you changed your mind.

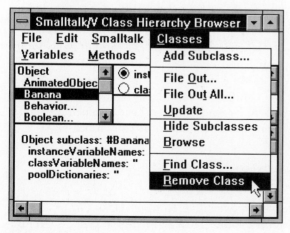

Figure 4.12 Deleting class Banana.

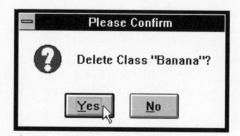

Figure 4.13 Confirming that you really wish to delete class Banana.

4.1.5 Updating a Browser

When several browsers are open at once, it is possible to create a class in one browser that is not visible in the others. This is because the unused browsers are out of date. Technically, creating a class in one browser can leave the other ones out of date because they are not informed of the new information. This can also happen if you create a class from a workspace; as we suggested class Pear might be created in the section "Viewing a Class Definition." In this case, all the browsers would be out of date.

It is a simple matter to update a browser by selecting menu item **Update** in the **Classes** menu, as illustrated in Figure 4.14.

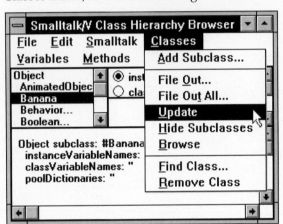

Figure 4.14 Updating a browser.

4.1.6 Locating an Existing Class

One way of locating a class is to scroll the class list pane—the top-left pane, which contains all the class names—opening and closing selections until we find the class we want. This can take quite a while if we don't know where the class is located. For example, suppose we wanted to find class Pen. After searching unsuccessfully for some time, we might be ready for another approach. We could interrogate class Pen for the class hierarchy information, as shown below.

    Pen **superclass** ⇒ TextTool
    TextTool **superclass** ⇒ GraphicsTool
    GraphicsTool **superclass** ⇒ Object

This would allow us to conclude that we have to open class GraphicsTool. Presumably, class Pen will then be visible. However, this explicit searching approach is quite cumbersome.

The easiest way to find a class is to proceed as follows:

- Select menu item **Find Class...** in the **Classes** menu, as shown in Figure 4.15.
- Click on **Find Class...** to cause a prompter to appear, as shown in Figure 4.16. This prompter requests the name of the class to be located. The class name must be typed correctly; otherwise, it will not be found. In particular, it must start with an uppercase letter.
- Once the class name—Pen, in this case—is typed, either click on **OK** or hit **Enter** on the keyboard. Class Pen will then be selected automatically, as shown in Figure 4.17.

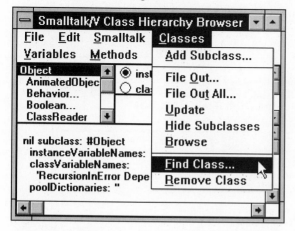

Figure 4.15 Using the browser to find class Pen.

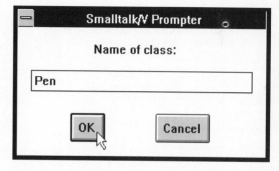

Figure 4.16 The prompter requesting the name of the class to be located.

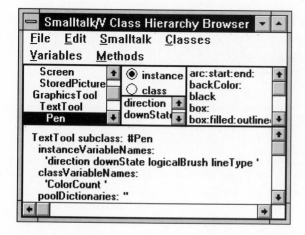

Figure 4.17 Class Pen, in the browser.

4.1.7   Editing an Existing Class

You can edit a class by simply clicking on the class name in the class list pane (the top-left pane). At that point, the class definition will appear in the bottom pane. This definition can be changed and then saved to effect the change.

For example, assume we had not yet defined class Banana. An alternative approach to defining class Banana would be to find an existing class to edit. A suitable candidate, in this case, is class Boolean. Select it to see the definition for class Boolean in the bottom pane, as shown in Figure 4.18. Next, modify the definition by changing the word **Boolean** to the word **Banana**, as shown in Figure 4.19. Finally, either select the entire expression and execute it, or, without worrying about what is already selected, click on menu item **Save** in the **File** menu, as illustrated in Figure 4.20. If a new class was actually constructed, this new class will appear in the browser only after the browser is updated, as explained in the previous section.

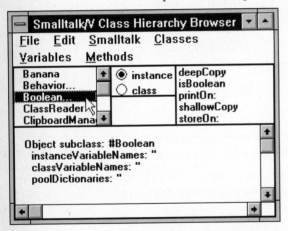

Figure 4.18 Selecting class Boolean for editing purposes.

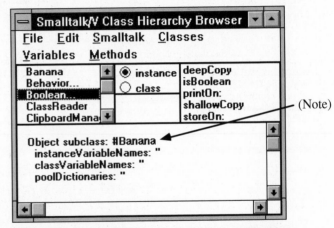

Figure 4.19 The definition of Boolean modified to define class Banana.

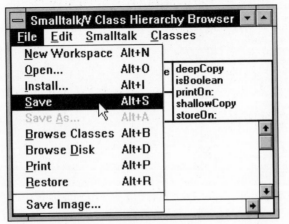

Figure 4.20 Saving the new definition.

In general, we can make more substantial changes to a class; e.g., by changing the structure of its instances. In particular, we can specify that new instances have more or fewer parts by simply adding or removing part names in the definition and saving it. (We will do this quite often in sections and chapters to come; we'll provide details as they are needed.) In most cases, we can make such changes at any time. However, once in a while, a problem arises. This problem is associated with changing class definitions in browsers, so we'll document it here.

For the sake of illustrating the problem, suppose we inspect an instance of Banana (see Chapter 2 if you've forgotten how to do that). The inspector shown in Figure 4.21 should appear. Add a new part to instances of Banana by typing the part name **color** in the string that follows keyword **instanceVariableNames**: (as shown in Figure 4.22), and try to **Save** the definition. The error window shown in Figure 4.23 will appear.

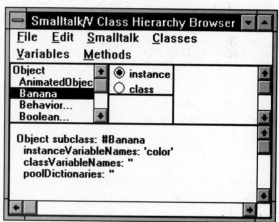

Figure 4.22 Trying to save a Banana definition for which new instances have a **color** part.

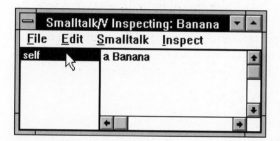

Figure 4.21 Inspecting a banana with no parts.

Figure 4.23 A message indicating that the structure of Banana instances cannot be changed while old instances exist.

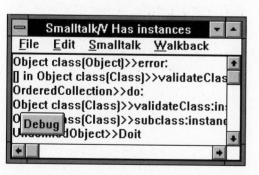

The message at the top, "Smalltalk/V Has instances", is significant. The problem is that old and new Banana instances have a different number of parts. In this particular case, old instances have no parts and new instances are supposed to have a part called **color**. As long as old instances exist, it will not be possible to save the new definition.

The solution is to find all windows that might be "holding on" to an instance (such as the inspector in Figure 4.21) and close them, and all global variables that might be referring to an instance of Banana and rebind them to some other object, such as nil. In the worst case, you might not be able to find all the instances. One way of getting rid of them (even if you don't know where they are) is to destroy them as follows:

> Banana **allInstances do**: [:element | element **become**: nil]

(This expression will make more sense after we discuss **do**: in Chapter 6; **become**: is discussed in detail in Chapter 9.) You'll most likely have to look back at this chapter to recall what to do.

4.1.8   Creating a New Method

Having created a new class Banana, we can now obtain instances of the class by executing

> Banana **new** $\Rightarrow$ a Banana

but we can do very little with these new instances. For example, we might be tempted to ask if the class Banana is edible or if an instance of Banana is edible. As we saw earlier, this might be accomplished by sending a message such as **edible** to an appropriate receiver—to the class or an instance. Unfortunately, if we attempt to execute

> Banana **edible**

right now, we get the error message shown in Figure 4.1, indicating that the class does not understand message **edible**. The same problem occurs if we attempt to execute

> Banana **new edible**

because Banana instances don't understand message **edible**, either. We need to add message **edible** to the repertoire of messages that are understood by the class (and its instances). Recall that we need to add two methods as follows:

> *an instance method*
> > **edible**
> > > ^true

> *a class method*
> > **edible**
> > > ^false

The first method specifies that true should be the reply whenever message **edible** is sent to an *instance* of Banana. The second indicates that false should be the reply whenever **edible** is sent to the *class*.

To add an instance method such as **edible**, proceed as follows (adding a class method differs only in that the class switch must be selected instead of the instance switch):

- In the browser, select the class to be edited. The definition of the class will appear in the code (bottom) pane, as shown in Figure 4.24.
- Make sure that the instance switch is selected if an instance method is to be constructed. For a class method, select the class switch instead.
- Select menu entry **New Method** in the **Methods** menu, as shown in Figure 4.25. A method template then appears in the method pane (the bottom pane), as shown in Figure 4.26.
- Edit the template, as shown in Figure 4.27; i.e., replace "messagePattern" by "**edible**", delete the middle two lines, and replace "statements" by "^true".
- Select menu item **Save** from the **File** menu, as illustrated in Figure 4.28. The message selector **edible** will then appear in the method list pane (the top-right pane), as shown in Figure 4.29.

If a method already exists in the class, an alternative (and simpler) approach consists of the following steps:

- Select either the instance switch if an instance method is to be constructed or the class switch if a class method is desired.
- Select any method in the method list pane; e.g., method **edible**, as shown in Figure 4.29.
- Edit the method in the method pane; e.g., by changing the name **edible** to **areYouEdible**.
- Select menu item **Save** from the **File** menu, as illustrated in Figure 4.28. This method is saved under the new name **areYouEdible**, if this name does not already exist. Otherwise, the older version of method **areYouEdible** is replaced by the new one. Method **edible** is not affected, even though this is the method we originally modified.

In general, the **method template**, a sample that illustrates what methods should look like, consists of the following:

```
messagePattern
        "comment"
        | temporaries |
        statements
```

The **message pattern** indicates what message the method reponds to, the **comment** (optional) describes what the method is supposed to do, the **temporary variables** (also optional) are intended for use in the statements that follow, and the actual statements compute the object to be returned. (Complex methods that contain all these components will be illustrated in the Chapter 5.)

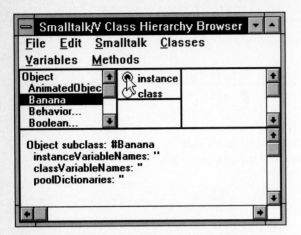

Figure 4.24 Prior to creating a new instance method, select the instance or class switch.

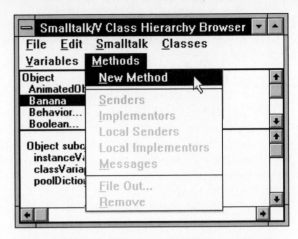

Figure 4.25 Creating a new instance method.

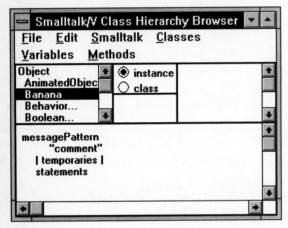

Figure 4.26 The method definition template that results.

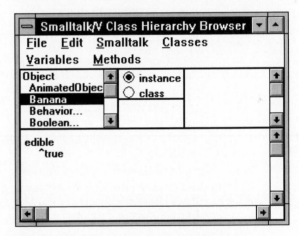

Figure 4.27 The new instance method.

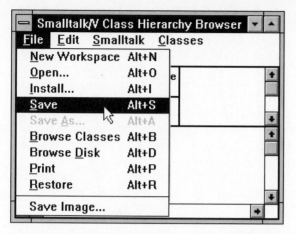

Figure 4.28 Saving the new instance method.

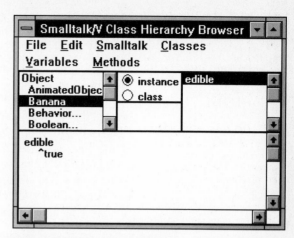

Figure 4.29 The completely finished instance method.

4.1.9 Deleting a Method

To delete a method, proceed as follows:

- In the method list pane, select the method to be deleted, as shown in Figure 4.30.
- Select menu item **Remove** in the **Methods** menu, as shown in Figure 4.31. Be careful! In this case, no confirmation window appears; i.e., if you accidentally click on **Remove**, the currently selected method will be deleted.

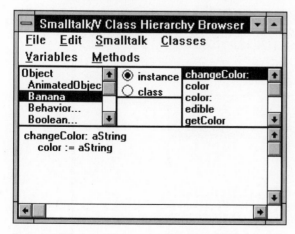

Figure 4.30 Selecting a method to delete.

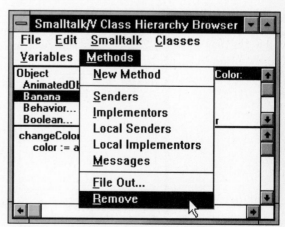

Figure 4.31 Deleting the selected method.

4.1.10 Filing Out a Class or Method

Filing out is the process of saving a method or class on disk in a format that can be retrieved later. To file out a class or method, perform the following steps:

- In a browser, select the method or class you wish to file out.
- For a method, select **File Out...** in the **Methods** menu. For a class, select either **File Out...** or **File Out All...** (as shown in Figure 4.32) in the **Classes** menu. Menu item **File Out...** saves only the selected class (with all instance and class methods), whereas **File Out All...** saves the selected class and all subclasses (with their corresponding methods).
- A file dialog box, as shown in Figure 4.33, will appear with a generated file name. Select the desired drive and directory, replace the generated file name by a new name (if desired), and click on **Save**.

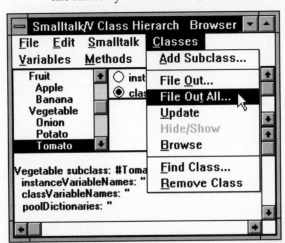

Figure 4.32 Saving a class and its subclasses for later retrieval.

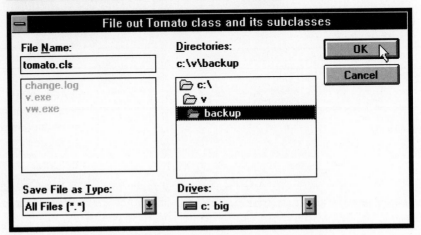

Figure 4.33 Specifying the file name to be used for saving the Tomato class.

As shown in the dialog box in Figure 4.33, the current directory is called **backup** and contains three files: **change.log**, **v.exe**, and **vw.exe**. If we click on [-a-], [-b-], or [-c-], we change the selected disk drive. If we click on [..], we climb the **directory hierarchy** to a directory called **v** (see the current directory information in the dialog box). This directory contains [..], [-a-], [-b-], and [-c-], just as the current **backup** directory, but it also contains the **backup** directory itself. By clicking on [..], we climb further up the hierarchy. By clicking on **backup**, we return to the directory currently being displayed.

4.1.11 Filing In a Class or Method

Filing in is the converse of filing out; i.e., the process of retrieving a method or class from disk. In general, we can either **open** a file, which causes a workspace to appear with a copy of the contents of the file, or we can **install** the file, which causes the contents of the file to be processed and integrated with the programming environment. For example, if a file contains a class definition and two methods, installing the file will create the class (if it did not already exist) and add the two methods to the class.

To **open** a file, execute the following steps:

- Click on **Open...** in the **File** menu in any window (see Figure 4.34). A file dialog box similar to the one that appeared when we filed out the information will then appear (see Figure 4.35).
- Select the desired file and either double-click on it or click on the **OK** button. A workspace, as shown in Figure 4.36 will then appear. You can then look at the text, make changes to it, and save it into the file (thus permanently altering it) by clicking on **Save** in the **File** menu, if you wish.

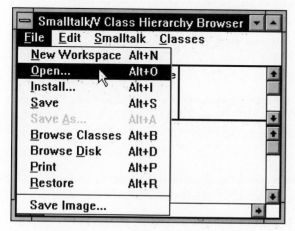

Figure 4.34 Opening a file.

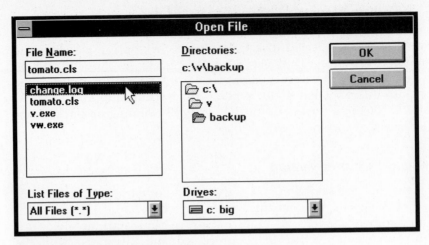

Figure 4.35 Selecting the desired file.

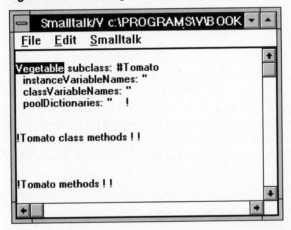

Figure 4.36 The workspace with a copy of the text that is in the file.

Any text file can be opened and investigated. If you attempt to open a file that does not contain text—say, the image **v.exe**—you will be presented with a workspace full of unintelligible characters.

By contrast, you can **install** a file only if it contains Smalltalk code that was previously filed out. You can install directly from a file or from selected parts of a workspace. The following steps should be followed:

Installing from a File

- Click on **Install...** in the **File** menu (see Figure 4.37) in any window. A file dialog box will allow you to select the appropriate file (as in Figure 4.35).
- Select the desired file and either double-click on it or click on the **OK** button. As the file is processed, error messages and recompilation messages will appear in the transcript.

Installing from a Workspace That Is Opened from a File

- Click on **Open...** in the **File** menu (see Figure 4.34) and respond as above to the file dialog box. A workspace will appear with a copy of the text in the file.
- Select all the text in the workspace (e.g., by clicking on **Select All** in the **Edit** menu) and click on **File It In** in the **Smalltalk** menu, as shown in Figure 4.38.

When installing from a workspace, it is possible to select specific portions of the text. However, you must make sure that the extra exclamation marks (see Figure 4.38) are included. These exclamation marks are used by the file-in mechanism to break the file into method-sized chunks. They are absolutely crucial to the proper functioning of the Install facility. Section "Recovering Lost Work and Compressing the Image", in Chapter 1, provides a brief explanation of this special format.

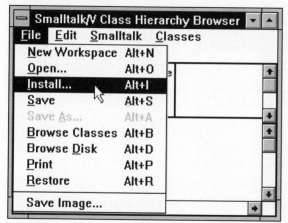

Figure 4.37 Installing a file.

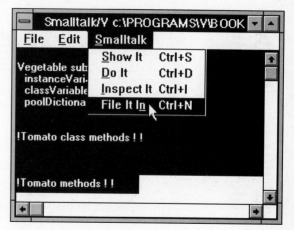

Figure 4.38 Filing in (installing) all the selected text.

4.1.12 Renaming a Class or Changing the Superclass

Renaming a class is the process of changing its name. Currently, Smalltalk/V has no convenient facility for renaming classes. One solution is simply to create a new class with the desired name and physically copy the methods (using Copy and Paste) from the old class to the new. Afterward, the old class can be deleted. If there are many methods, this is a tedious and error-prone approach. It's easy to forget a method or two; e.g., you could copy all the instance methods but forget the class methods.

The only fail-safe solution is to file out the class, delete it from the Smalltalk environment, open the file to obtain a workspace with the text, change the class name in the text to the desired name (using **Find/Replace ...** in the **Edit** menu), save the workspace to place the modified text back into the file, and then install the modified text. The process is cumbersome but necessary, particularly if you are working with a class that has a large number of methods.

Changing the superclass of an existing class is just as difficult as renaming the class. Unexpectedly, attempting to change the definition, for example, from

Object **subclass**: #Banana
    instanceVariableNames: ''
    classVariableNames: ''
    poolDictionaries: ''

to

Magnitude **subclass**: #Banana
    instanceVariableNames: ''
    classVariableNames: ''
    poolDictionaries: ''

results in the error message shown in Figure 4.39.

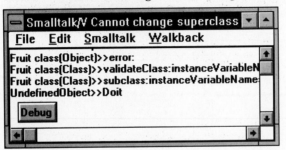

Figure 4.39 The consequence of attempting to change Banana's superclass.

If the class itself has subclasses, care must also be taken to ensure that the subclasses are not lost. Whether you need to rename a class or change its superclass, the same steps must be followed:

Renaming a Class or Changing the Superclass

- File out the class and all subclasses into a file such as **junk** using **File Out All...** rather than **File Out...** in the **Classes** menu (see the special section on filing out classes if you need more details).
- Delete the filed out classes from the programming environment. Note: You cannot delete a class if it has subclasses—you will have to delete the subclasses first.
- Open file **junk** by clicking on **Open...** in the **File** menu of any window. After you respond appropriately to the resulting file dialog box, a workspace with the text of the filed out classes will appear.
- Edit the text appropriately. For example, if you are renaming the class, use **Find/Replace...** in the **Edit** menu to change each occurrence of the old class name to the new name. Don't change the occurrences one by one—there will be too many and you will miss some. If you are changing

the superclass, simply replace it by the new superclass—you can do this by hand, since you will need to change only one name.

- Save the modified workspace text into the file by clicking on **Save** in the **File** menu, and then install the file as explained in the section on filing in classes. An alternative is to select all the text in the workspace and use **File It In...** in the **Smalltalk** menu (this files in only the selected portion, which, in this case, should be the whole workspace).

4.2 Summary

This chapter has introduced you to many details about browsers. We have learned

- About the components of browsers
- How to use a browser for creating, editing, and deleting simple classes and methods, and generally looking around (browsing)
- How to file out methods and classes and how to retrieve them, either to inspect them in workspaces or to install them into the Smalltalk environment
- How to make structural changes to classes—changes that involve adding or removing parts in the instances and changing the superclass

4.3 What You Did and Did Not Learn

We learned how to use browsers to create classes and methods (both instance and classes methods), to edit these classes and methods, and also to delete them. We also provided important details about the file in and file out processes. We don't expect you to remember all the browser details until you've created three or four classes yourself but this is just a matter of time! We will be creating dozens of classes in the chapters to come.

This chapter was devoted primarily to browser mechanics; namely, the basics of what you can do with browsers. Consequently, important details about methods, and the classes that contain them, were glossed over. Chapter 5 will be devoted to clarifying these concepts and examining them in great detail. Real experience with browsers will be provided.

4.4 Important Facts

Replying

^expression   A reply expression; causes the object computed by the expression to be returned to the sender of

the message that caused the containing method
to be executed

Browser Components

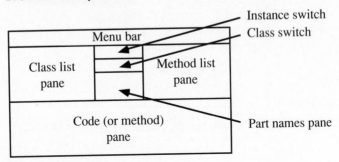

Figure 4.40 Browser components.

menu bar	Contains menus such as **File**, **Classes**, and **Methods** along with corresponding menu items
class list pane	Contains class names
method list pane	Contains selectors for instance or class messages, depending on which of the switches is selected
instance switch	Indicates that instance information is selected
class switch	Indicates that class information is selected
parts name pane	Contains the names of the parts for the instances of the selected class (also called the **instance variables list pane**)
code (or **method**) **pane**	Contains information retrieved by selections in the other two panes; e.g., when class Pen is selected in the class list pane, method **home** is selected in the method list pane, and the instance switch is selected, the text for instance method **home** is shown in the code pane

Method template: a sample illustrating the structure of a method.

```
messagePattern
        "comment"
      I temporaries I
      statements
```

A method consists of four components: a **message pattern** that indicates what
message the method reponds to, an optional **comment** that normally describes
what the method is supposed to do, an optional list of **temporary variables** that
are to be used in the statements that follow, and statements that compute the
object to be returned.

Six Key Steps to Changing the Superclass or Renaming a Class

- File out the class (and all its subclasses) into a file by selecting the class and clicking on **File Out All...** in the **Classes** menu.
- Delete the class from the Smalltalk environment by selecting the class and clicking on **Remove Class** in the **Classes** menu (subclasses will have to be removed first).
- Open the file that was originally filed out above by selecting **Open...** in the **File** menu. This will create a workspace containing the contents of the file.
- Find and modify the definition of the class in the workspace to have the new (desired) superclass. To change the class name, use **Find/Replace....** in the **Edit** menu—there are too many occurrences to change each one individually.
- Finally, perform one of the following:
  - Select all the text in the workspace and click on **File It In** in the **Smalltalk** menu.
  - Save the workspace by clicking on **Save** in the **File** menu, close the workspace, and then reopen the file that was just saved by clicking on **Install...** instead of **Open....**

4.5   Keywords

class components: class name, class variable names, instance variable names, part names, pool dictionaries, superclass

files: directory hierarchy, filing in, filing out, installing, opening

programming terminology: reply expression, browsing, method, Smalltalk library

window varieties: browser

4.6   Exercises

1. Create three browsers and then close all but two.
2. Create a new class Milk using **Add Subclass...** in the **Classes** menu. Note: Click on **Object** before you do this to ensure that Object is the superclass.
3. Create a similar class Hamburger by editing the definition for class **Boolean** and using **Save**. Don't forget to update the browser after you do this.
4. Create yet another class Marble by editing the definition for class Boolean. This time, however, select everything in the window and execute it (using **Do It** or **Show It**) rather than using **Save**.
5. Add instance methods **edible** and **liquid** to each of these classes so that you can query them—have them return the appropriate boolean value. Note that some of these objects are edible and some are not; some are liquid and some are not.
6. File out one of the above classes, delete it, and then recreate it by installing it.

7. Find class String and class Character.
8. Experiment with the disk browser (use menu item **Browse Disk** in the **File** menu).

5

The More Complex World of
Methods, Classes, and
Debuggers

What You Will Learn

In the previous chapter, we gained experience with browsers and surveyed technique for creating, editing, and deleting very simple classes and methods. However, we didn't make use of methods and classes in any interesting way.

To gain a deeper understanding of methods and the messages that cause them to execute, our first goal will be to extend the graphics case study of Chapter 3. Recall that the section finished with an expression that could not be executed because the message used was not understood by pens. We will solve that problem by adding a new method to class Pen. As part of this process, we will learn about parameters (a new kind of variable) and we will examine in greater detail the mechanism by which messages and methods are matched. We will develop a deeper understanding of the basic execution cycle.

The next goal will be to create a slightly more complex class than we did when learning about browsers; specifically, a Truck class. We'll start by reviewing the basic components of a class definition and get a quick introduction to class variables and pool dictionaries. The first version of this class will have instances with no parts. But we will subsequently add a part that can record the color of each truck. Next we will add methods that will permit us to access and modify this color. Finally, we will extend the Truck class so that instances can print themselves with their colors. Such capabilities will ultimately have to be provided whenever new classes are created. So it is useful to learn how to do it early.

To put everything into perspective, we will try to recall what we learned by considering two fairly complex case studies: one involving a Temperature class and another one involving a Money class. In the process, we will review many of the browser fundamentals, the process of defining classes and methods, and the use of the various types of variables that were introduced in both this chapter and the previous chapters. We will get substantially more experience with classes, methods, and variables.

Last, we will be learn how to use the debugger as a tool for tracing execution, for understanding how execution actually works, and for viewing the contents of variables as they change during execution. In particular, we will use it to understand why copies of methods are used during execution, how messages in expressions are matched with variables in the method copies, and how identical names in different contexts can—without ambiguity—refer to different variables.

5.1   Experience with Methods

In this section, we will try to gain a deeper understanding of methods and the corresponding messages that cause them to execute. We will extend class Pen by adding a new method and then we will perform some experiments to discover how this new method works. More specifically, we will investigate the process that matches messages with the methods that respond to the messages.

5.1.1   Revisiting Pens

In Chapter 3, we typed the following square-drawing instructions in a workspace and tested it:

```
| aPen start size |
aPen := Display pen.
start := 100@100. "Starting point."
size := 100. "Pixels."

aPen
    place: start;              "Top-left corner of square."
    goto: start + (size @ 0);  "Top-right corner."
    goto: start + size;        "Bottom-right corner."
    goto: start + (0 @ size);  "Bottom-left corner."
    goto: start.               "Top-left corner again."
```

We finished the chapter by suggesting that we might be able to add a method in class Pen that would permit us to write the same thing on one line; namely,

Display **pen displaySquareAt**: 100@100 **side**: 100

Drawing a smaller square to the right might be achieved by writing

Display **pen displaySquareAt**: 300@100 **side**: 50

5.1.2 Adding a Method to an Existing Class

Since message "**displaySquareAt**: 300@100 **side**: 50" is intended to be understood by an instance of Pen (not by the class itself), we must first select class Pen in the browser and then click on the instance switch. (Review the section "Creating a New Method" if you've forgotten the details and need to see some figures that illustrate the basic steps.) In our case, a simple way to create a new method is to click on any of the message selectors in the method list pane—the top-right pane—and modify the text of the method that is subsequently displayed in the method pane—the bottom pane. Once finished, simply save the new method. Remember: The new method is saved under the new name leaving the old method unmodified.

Because our new method is to be invoked as "aPen **displaySquareAt**: 100@100 **side**: 100", the message pattern (also called the method header) must provide for the parameters. Consequently, our method could be written as follows:

```
displaySquareAt: aPoint side: anInteger
    "Display a square at the specified point with width and height 'anInteger'."
    | topLeft topRight bottomRight bottomLeft |
    topLeft := aPoint.
    topRight := aPoint + (anInteger @ 0).
    bottomRight := aPoint + anInteger.
    bottomLeft := aPoint + (0 @ anInteger).
    self
        place: topLeft;
        goto: topRight;
        goto: bottomRight;
        goto: bottomLeft;
        goto: topLeft.
```

Notice the comment at the top that explains what the method does. In this case, the comment is not very useful because it is merely a rewording of the method header. In general, a comment should explain what the method does if it is not immediately obvious from the method header.

We introduced four variables to make it clear how the four corners of the square are computed. They serve to document the computation—to tell the reader what is going on. Sometimes, variables can be eliminated without loss of information if we are careful about providing suitable comments. For example, we could rewrite the method as follows:

displaySquareAt: aPoint **side**: anInteger
   self
      place: aPoint;   "Top-left corner of square."
      goto: aPoint + (anInteger @ 0);   "Top-right corner."
      goto: aPoint + anInteger;   "Bottom-right corner."
      goto: aPoint + (0 @ anInteger);   "Bottom-left corner."
      goto: aPoint.   "Top-left corner again."

The revised version is shorter and just as understandable. If we have to compromise, however, it is better to create a method that is long yet understandable rather than short but difficult to decipher.

> *Our goal is always to have a method that is as short as possible, uses as few variables as possible, and is as understandable as possible.*

As we can see, the above two methods conform to the method template introduced in the Chapter 4. However, we can now add slightly more detail.

messagePattern
     "comment"
  | temporaries |
  statements

Let's review the terminology and elaborate further where appropriate. A method consists of four components:

- A **message pattern** (also called **method header**) that contains the name of the selector that identifies the method along with parameter names called **method parameters**
- A **comment** that usually describes what this particular method is supposed to do
- A list of **temporary variables** for use in the statements that follow
- The actual statements that respond to the message that was sent

That part of the method excluding the message pattern is often referred to as the **method body**.

5.1.3   Understanding Method Execution

When "aPen **displaySquareAt**: 100@100 **side**: 200+1" is executed, the corresponding method defined in the previous section is executed. Clearly, there must be a correspondence between a message that is sent and the method designed to respond to that message. For example, there must be some kind of connection between expression "aPen **displaySquareAt**: 100@100 **side**: 200+1" and the message pattern "**displaySquareAt**: aPoint **side**: anInteger" in the method. Since the message pattern is missing any mention of the receiver, the special variable "self" is provided for this purpose. Thus, when the **place**: message is sent to "self" in the method, it is really being sent to "aPen"—the actual receiver of the message. Table 5.1 summarizes the correspondence between the expression and the message pattern for the above example.

Table 5.1 Correspondence between an expression and its message pattern.

Expression	Message Pattern
aPen **displaySquareAt:side:** 100@100 201	self **displaySquareAt:side:** aPoint anInteger

This matching process is only one of the steps that occurs when a message is executed. A summary of all the steps involved in sending a message, computing a response, and receiving a reply, is provided below.

The Basic Execution Cycle for One Message.

1. *All parameters in the message are evaluated*; e.g., "100@100" and "200+1" are evaluated. Note: 100@100 is now a single point object; i.e., it is no longer the message "@100" being sent to integer "100". Similarly, "200+1" is now 201.
2. *The message is sent to the receiver*; e.g., "**displaySquareAt:** 100@100 **side:** 201" is sent to "aPen".
3. *The corresponding method for that particular receiver is located and a copy, the **method copy**, is made.*.
4. *The message is matched with the message pattern in the method copy as follows:*
    a) *The receiver in the expression is matched with special variable **self** which denotes the receiver at the time the method copy is executed;* e.g., "aPen" is matched with "self". This special variable is sometimes called a **pseudo-variable** since no specific declaration is provided for it.
    b) *The selector in the expression is matched with the selector in the method copy's header;* e.g., "**displaySquareAt:side:**" in the expression is matched with "**displaySquareAt:side:**" in the method copy's header.
    c) *The parameters in the expression, the **message parameters**, are matched with the corresponding parameters in the method copy's header, the **method parameters**;* e.g., point 100@100 in the expression is matched with method parameter "aPoint" and integer 201 in the expression is matched with method parameter "anInteger" in the method copy.
5. *The method body in the method copy is executed until a reply expression is encountered. If all expressions in the method body execute without encountering a reply expression, default reply expression "^self" is executed.*
6. *The object computed in the reply expression is returned to the sender of the message for use in further computation.*

Notice that a copy of the method is made before execution. This has important implications for the variables in the method; namely, "self", the method parameters, and the local variables. In particular, if we send the same message twice to the same receiver, different variables are involved in each case—even though the variables have the same name. We'll examine this later in more detail.

Additionally, pseudo-variable "self" and method parameters such as "aPoint" and "anInteger" have one very important property:

> *Pseudo-variable "self" and method parameters cannot be changed by the programmer.*

For example, it is illegal to execute assignments like "self := 0", "aPoint := 0@0", or "anInteger := 1".

Now that we have introduced one method, let's try to design another one that permits the square to be rotated at an angle so that we can say the following:

> aPen **displaySquareAt**: 100@100 **side**: 200+1 **angle**: 45

If we reconsider the last method we introduced,

> **displaySquareAt**: aPoint **side**: anInteger
>   self
>   **place**: aPoint;   "Top-left corner of square."
>   **goto**: aPoint + (anInteger @ 0);   "Top-right corner."
>   **goto**: aPoint + anInteger;   "Bottom-right corner."
>   **goto**: aPoint + (0 @ anInteger);   "Bottom-left corner."
>   **goto**: aPoint.   "Top-left corner again."

there seems to be no obvious way to change the method to permit an arbitrary angle. To deal with an arbitrary angle, we'll have to use a totally different approach. We'll need to point the pen in the desired direction and move forward in that direction using **go**: instead of **goto**:. We might begin as follows:

> **displaySquareAt**: aPoint **side**: size **angle**: angle
>   self
>   **place**: aPoint;   "Top-left corner of square."
>   **direction**: angle.   "The angle of the top line."

Note that we decided to name our method parameters "size" and "angle" instead of "anInteger" and perhaps "anotherInteger".

> *We normally like to use names that indicate the classes of objects they refer to. But sometimes, it's better to use a name that indicates the function of the variable rather than its class.*

Note that we used "size" rather than "aSize" because there is no class called "Size". Now, how do we draw a line of the required length? Let's try

> self **go**: size.

The next step seems relatively obvious. We need to turn right by 90°:

>   self **turn**: 90.

Now we have the pattern. Simply repeat this three times. Our complete method would appear as follows:

>   **displaySquareAt**: aPoint **side**: size **angle**: angle
>   self
>
> | | |
> |---|---|
> | **place**: aPoint; | "Top-left corner of square." |
> | **direction**: angle; | "0 degrees is to the right." |
> | **go**: size; | "top" |
> | **turn**: 90; | "and turn" |
> | **go**: size; | "right side" |
> | **turn**: 90; | "and turn" |
> | **go**: size; | "bottom" |
> | **turn**: 90; | "and turn" |
> | **go**: size. | "left side" |

As written, the method is a little long. Perhaps it would be better if we placed a few of the messages on the same line.

>   **displaySquareAt**: aPoint **side**: size **angle**: angle
>   self
>   **place**: aPoint; **direction**: angle; "Initialize at the top-left corner."
>   **go**: size; **turn**: 90; "Display top and turn."
>   **go**: size; **turn**: 90; "Display right side and turn."
>   **go**: size; **turn**: 90; "Display bottom and turn."
>   **go**: size. "Display left side."

Another way of simplifying the method is to use a message that permits repetition—more specifically, to use what we call a **times-repeat-expression**. The times-repeat-expression has the following form:

>   anIntegerExpression **timesRepeat**: repetitionBlock

The receiver of the **timesRepeat**: message must be an integer and the parameter must be a **block** (a sequence of zero or more expressions separated by "." and surrounded by square brackets). A times-repeat-expression is also known as a **control structure** because it permits the path of execution to be controlled; e.g., by controlling the number of times a series of expressions is to be executed. For a simple example, consider the following:

>   5 **timesRepeat**: [Transcript **space**; **nextPutAll**: 'I love you.']

In this case, "I love you." is added to the transcript five times. Since **timesRepeat**: is a message, it too must return a value. Let's find out what that value is. Consider the following series of experiments:

>   5 **timesRepeat**: [1. 2. 3] $\Rightarrow$ 0
>   5 **timesRepeat**: [] $\Rightarrow$ 0

As we can see, a times-repeat-expression always returns 0. Hence it is not particularly useful for the answer it provides. It is much more important for its **side-effects**; i.e., the effect it has on the computation. The 'I love you.' example above, for instance, has the side-effect of writing 'I love you.' in the transcript five times.

Let's use it to simplify our method.

> **displaySquareAt**: aPoint **side**: size **angle**: angle
>   self **place**: aPoint; **direction**: angle. "Initialize at the top-left corner."
>   3 **timesRepeat**: [
>   self **go**: size; **turn**: 90 "Display one side and turn a right angle."].
>   self **go**: size. "Display the left side, the only side remaining."

Instead of repeating **go**: followed by **turn**:, we could have just as easily switched the order and repeated **turn**: followed by **go**:.

> **displaySquareAt**: aPoint **side**: size **angle**: angle
>   self
>   **place**: aPoint; **direction**: angle; "Initialize at the top-left corner."
>   **go**: size. "Display the top."
>   3 **timesRepeat**: [
>   self **turn**: 90; **go**: size "Turn right and display another side."].

Now that we have a general method for displaying a square, we might wonder if our original method is still needed. Surely, rather than say

> aPen **displaySquareAt**: 200@200 **side**: 200

we could say

> aPen **displaySquareAt**: 200@200 **side**: 200 **angle**: 0

The former message assumes an angle of 0 by default but the latter requires the angle explicitly. We should keep the original method but we might want to rewrite it. Given that we have a more general method, it is a good idea to make use of it as follows:

> **displaySquareAt**: aPoint **side**: size
>   self **displaySquareAt**: aPoint **side**: size **angle**: 0

As a general rule, it is a poor programming practice to have similar methods implemented completely differently, particularly when one can be viewed as a special case of another. Since one goal is to create the shortest possible method, replacing the six lines of the original implementation by one line is clearly better.

> *We should strive to reuse methods whenever possible and avoid creating methods with common or similar portions.*

5.2   Experience with Classes

Now that we know how to create both a class and a method, we should attempt to create a simple class with a reasonable number of methods. In addition to getting a bit more experience with the process, we should also learn about the new kinds of variables that can be associated with classes and their instances; namely, class variables and variables maintained by pool dictionaries.

We should also learn about those kinds of methods that typically should be provided with new classes; e.g., methods for accessing and modifying parts and a method for printing instances of the class. Let's consider a simple Truck class to illustrate the new notions.

5.2.1   Class Variables and Pool Dictionaries

Following the steps described in Chapter 4, we should be able to create a Truck class as a subclass of Object. The resulting definition should appear as follows:

```
Object subclass: #Truck
    instanceVariableNames: ''
    classVariableNames: ''
    poolDictionaries: ''
```

Instance variable names are the names of the variables maintained in the instances; i.e., they are part names. Our Truck class is initially defined so that Truck instances have no parts. If we were to replace the string '' after the **instanceVariableNames**: keyword by 'color owner', then all instances would have parts **color** and **owner**. As we will see, *only the individual instances can access their own parts*.

Class variable names, by contrast, are the names of variables maintained in the class—they must be capitalized. As a consequence, there is only one instance of each of these variables. On the other hand, *the class (its subclasses, their subclasses, and so on) and every instance of the class (and the subclasses) can access the class variables*.

A class BankAccount, for example, might use a class variable InterestRate for keeping track of the current interest rate. Assuming this interest rate applies to all instances of BankAccount, there is no need for the instances to have individual instance variables to keep track of this rate. They can simply access the interest rate in class variable InterestRate. We will be illustrating the use of class variables in the case studies that follow this section.

Pool dictionaries are variable containers. *All variables maintained by pool dictionaries can be accessed by the instances and the class that has the pool dictionary in its definition*. They are not accessible by subclasses or their instances.

Recall from the previous chapter that **Smalltalk** is a special global variable container (there is only one). If we actually inspect **Smalltalk**, we find that it is an instance of a special Dictionary class. At this point, we don't know anything about dictionaries (they are discussed in detail in Chapter 7). Nevertheless, we can still create them, inspect them, and change them in the inspectors. For example, to create two global dictionaries, such as VehicleColors and VehicleMakers, to serve the role of pool dictionaries, we can simply execute

```
VehicleColors := Dictionary new.
VehicleMakers := Dictionary new.
```

We can then replace the empty string '' after the **poolDictionaries**: keyword in the definition by 'VehicleColors VehicleMakers'. It is then a simple matter of using inspectors to add names and their associated objects to each of new pool dictionaries. For example, we might add the following associations to pool dictionary VehicleMakers:

```
'Ford' ⇒ 'Ford Motor Company, Inc.'
'Toyota' ⇒ 'Toyota, Inc.'
```

Once we have created such a pool dictionary and included it in the list of pool dictionaries in the class definition, methods in our class (both instance and class methods) can refer to the "variables" Ford and Toyota. Note: Although the pool dictionary VehicleMakers is global, the variables Ford and Toyota are not; it is possible to refer to Ford and Toyota only in the methods of classes that have VehicleMakers in their list of pool dictionaries. A sample class method in Truck could now be written as follows:

```
sample
    "Illustrating how variables in pool dictionaries may be used."
    Transcript
        cr; nextPutAll: 'Two well-known auto makers include ';
        cr; nextPutAll: Ford; nextPutAll: ' and '; nextPutAll: Toyota
```

Executing "Truck **sample**" should result in the following output:

```
Two well-known auto makers include:
Ford Motor Company, Inc. and Toyota, Inc.
```

We glossed over a number of details when we said that we could add names and associated objects to the pool dictionaries. So let's consider the step involved in creating a pool dictionary in more detail:

Creating a Pool Dictionary

- Create a global and bind it to a dictionary; e.g., make VehicleMakers global and execute "VehicleMakers := Dictionary **new**".
- Inspect the global (in this case, VehicleMakers), as shown in Figure 5.1. Note the existence of menu **Dictionary** in the inspector.
- Select pull-down menu item **Add** in menu **Dictionary**, as shown in Figure 5.2. This will cause the prompter shown in Figure 5.3 to appear.
- Type a string containing a capitalized name; e.g., 'Ford'. Note that a string literal is required—the name alone will not work. Click on **OK** or hit **Enter** to satisfy the prompter's request.
- At this point, the inspector should contain the string 'Ford' in the left pane (see Figure 5.4) and nil in the right pane. Replace nil by a Smalltalk expression that will compute the value to be associated with 'Ford'; e.g., in this case, the string 'Ford Motor Company, Inc.'.
- Save this value by clicking on either **Save** in the **File** menu or **Save** in the pop-up menu that appears when you click the right mouse button in the right pane (as shown in Figure 5.5).

This process can be repeated for each name you wish to enter into your pool dictionary. There is no limit to the number of names you can provide.

Pool dictionaries are normal dictionaries used specifically for associating long lists of names with their corresponding values; i.e., for naming long lists of constants. For example, the pool dictionary **ColorConstants** contains the names of all the colors that can be used by pens for line graphics. Figure 5.6, for example, shows an inspector on dictionary **ColorConstants**. We selected **ClrBlue** (**Clr** is short for **Color**). (Those short forms were not chosen arbitrarily—they are the names used by the Microsoft Windows operating system. If it had been our choice to make, we would have used names without short forms.) Independent of that, we can see why the pool dictionary is needed. Who could possibly remember that 16777232 represents the color blue?

Note that the names ClrBlack, ClrBlue, ClrBrown, etc. are not global. They cannot be accessed in a method unless the class for that method specifies ColorConstants as one of the pool dictionaries in its list. But what if you accidentally use ClrRed without providing ColorConstants in the class definition? In that case, you will be prompted with the usual message, shown in Figure 5.7. *Do not click on* **Yes**. If

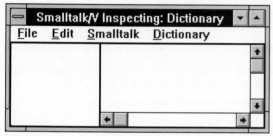

Figure 5.1 Inspecting global dictionary VehicleMakers.

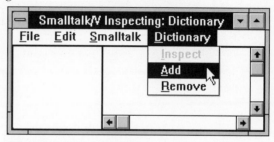

Figure 5.2 Selecting **Add** to enter an entry into global VehicleMakers.

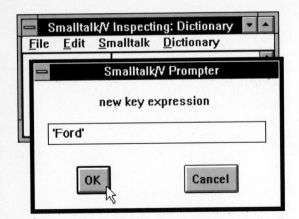

Figure 5.3 After clicking on **Add**, type a string containing a capitalized name.

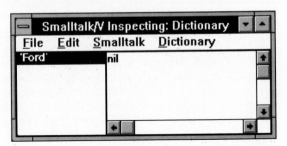

Figure 5.4 It is now possible to replace nil by any valid Smalltalk expression and save it.

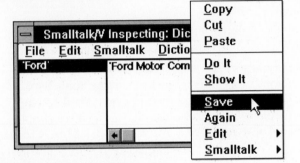

Figure 5.5 Replacing nil by 'Ford Motor Company, Inc.' and saving it.

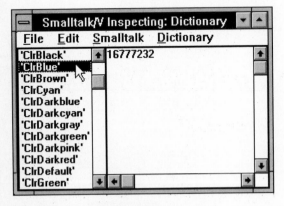

Figure 5.6 Inspecting pool dictionary ColorConstants.

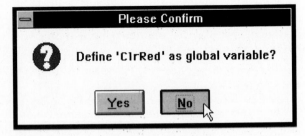

Figure 5.7 Using ClrRed in a method whose class does not have ColorConstants in its list of pool dictionaries.

you do, there will now exist a global called **ClrRed** which is completely different from the **ClrRed** variable kept by the pool dictionary. The value associated with **ClrRed** in ColorConstants is 16777229. By contrast, the value associated with the global **ClrRed** is nil—this global was never initialized. If you do click on **Yes** by mistake, make sure you delete the global; e.g., by executing

Smalltalk **removeKey**: #ClrRed

5.2.2 Adding Parts to Objects without Parts

In general, trucks might have many parts; e.g., the licence number, the model, the year, the load capacity, the engine size, the owner, the color. For illustrative purposes, let's just choose one of these properties—say, the color—and consider the implications.

We begin by modifying the Truck class definition to include color as an instance variable (or part)—by inserting the name **color** between the single quotes after keyword **instanceVariableNames**:. The modified definition is shown below.

Object **subclass**: #Truck
    instanceVariableNames: 'color'
    classVariableNames: ''
    poolDictionaries: ''

After the new definition is saved, the browser will appear as shown in Figure 5.8. Note the introduction of **color** in the part names pane.

Now color is part of all Truck instances. This can be easily verified by inspecting an instance. If we do, however, we will find that the **color** part is nil, as shown in Figure 5.9.

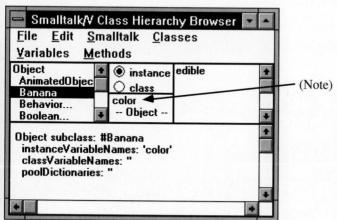

(Note)

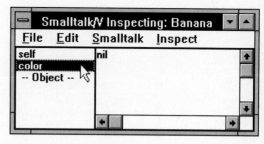

Figure 5.8 The browser after part color has been added.

Figure 5.9 An instance of banana with a nil color.

5.2.3 Adding Accessing and Modification Methods

It should be obvious that the **color** part can't automatically be a legitimate color since we haven't done anything specific to ensure that it is. The computer can't read our minds—how can it possibly know what color a truck should be? We need to provide methods that will allow us to change the color associated with a truck, and then later on, if we've forgotten the color of a particular truck, to determine what it is. In particular, we need to introduce two methods—say, with selectors called **setColor:** and **getColor** (for now)—that allow us to execute the following:

> Truck **new setColor:** 'green'; **inspect** ⇒ (causes an inspector to appear)
> Truck **new setColor:** 'red'; **getColor** ⇒ 'red'

Notice that **setColor:** is a one-parameter selector—the parameter indicates what the new color should be. Notice also the use of the semicolon to indicate cascaded messages. The **inspect** message in the first example is sent to the same object that the "**setColor:** 'green'" message was sent to—namely, the new instance of Truck. Assuming the **setColor:** method has been properly written, the inspector will allow us to confirm that part **color** is properly initialized to 'green'. In the second example, rather than inspect the new instance, we simply ask it for its color. Since we changed it to 'red', we should get 'red'.

A method such as **getColor**, which is designed to return information about an object, is called an **accessing** method (or an **accessor**). Correspondingly, a method such as **setColor:**, which is designed to set or change an object, is called a **modification** method (or a **modifier**).

Before we implement the two methods, let's be clear about an important issue. We can't ask an object for its part by executing, for example,

> Truck **new color**

If we try it, we get the standard error message shown in Figure 5.10. You can get information from an object only by sending it a message. Clearly, **getColor** is a message, but not **color** is not—**color** is just a part name.

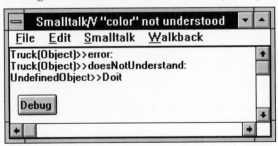

Figure 5.10 Trucks understand messages only if there is a corresponding method.

Surely, at some point, we will have to refer to the part name to get the information. Indeed, we will, within a method—not outside. The two methods that will achieve our aim can be written as follows:

> **setColor**: aString
>   color := aString

> **getColor**
>   ^color

It is a simple process to add these two instance methods to class Truck with a browser. (Review the section "Creating a New Method" if you've forgotten how.) It's important to remember to select the instance switch in the browser (rather than the class switch) when adding the methods, because they are intended to be instance methods. Let's consider each method in turn.

Method **setColor:** is provided with one parameter—we called it aString to indicate the kind of object to be provided. During execution, aString could either be 'green' or 'red', for example, and the **receiver** could be any truck to which the **setColor:** message was sent (see Figure 5.11). Inside the method, we use the assignment operator := to change the part called color. This part is the color part of the receiver. If there exists many trucks in the system, they will each have a color part but only the color part of the receiver is accessed in the method.

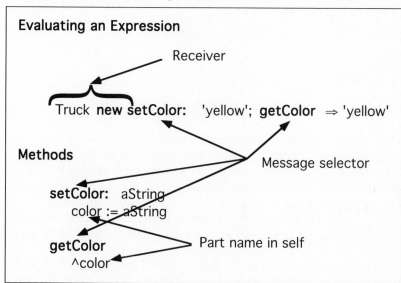

Figure 5.11 Distinguishing messages (and their selectors) from part names.

It is important to note, however, that **color** here is not a message, since there is no receiver preceding it—it is a variable (in this particular case, an instance variable).

> *Inside (but not outside) methods, the assignment operator ":=" can be used to change a part; e.g., by writing "color := 'brown'".*

Method **getColor**, on the other hand, simply returns the color part of the receiver—notice the "^" indicating this. By contrast, there is no "^" in method **setColor:**. Since nothing has been explicitly returned, the receiver (the truck instance) is returned by default in method **setColor:**.

> *All methods reply with (or return) one object using "^". If it is omitted, the receiver is returned.*

Figure 5.11 illustrates the fact that part names are never mentioned in expressions, only in methods. Additionally, the part names (in these methods) always refers to parts associated with "self", the receiver of a specific message.

5.2.4 Following Conventions

The only problem with method names such as **setColor:** and **getColor** is that they don't conform to the names used by typical Smalltalk programmers. By convention, good programmers generally use accessing and modification method names that correspond to the part names directly. In other words, they would use the names **color:** and **color** instead of **setColor:** and **getColor**, respectively. Consequently, the above examples and methods would be rewritten as follows:

> Truck **new color:** 'green'; **inspect** ⇒ (causes an inspector to appear)
> Truck **new color:** 'red'; **color** ⇒ 'red'

and the corresponding methods would be revised as

> **color:** aString
>   color := aString

> **color**
>   ^color

This can be confusing if you don't understand the difference between a message (and its selector) and a part name. As can be seen in the top part of Figure 5.12, only messages (and their selectors) occur in external expressions; e.g., in transcripts or workspaces. The message selector also occurs in the first line of each method definition (bottom part of Figure 5.12). But most important is the fact that part names can be referenced only inside a method. You can tell that it is a part name and not a message because there is no receiver in front of it. Figure 5.12 revises Figure 5.11 with the above changes taken into account. Initially, you will find it more difficult to distinguish a message such as **color** from a part name such as **color**. The more experienced you become, however, the less difficulty you will have. An expert will have no difficulty.

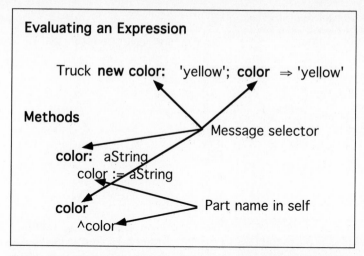

Figure 5.12 Distinguishing messages (and their selectors) from part names.

To make sure that we can distinguish part names from messages with the same name, let's consider this hypothetical method:

testMethod
        color := color **color color**: color **color**

Clearly, the first "color" must be a variable (or part name) because it's to the left of an assignment operator. The second "color" must also be a variable; otherwise, it would have a receiver in front of it. Since the second "color" is a variable, it must be a receiver for a message that follows it; namely, the third "color". The fourth "color" is followed by ":" implying that it must be a keyword. Consequently, "color:" must be a keyword message. There must be a complete expression after a keyword. Therefore, the fifth occurrence of "color" must be a variable, since it has no receiver. The last occurrence must be a message since it is preceded by a variable, its receiver.

Because we used boldface for the message names but not the part names, it is easy to distinguish the two in the above example. But the browser doesn't use boldface to highlight messages in its methods. If you can't distinguish the messages from the part names by context, you will have difficulty using part names and message names that are the same. In that case, you should reread this section before proceeding.

Now, if we change method selector name **getColor** to **color** and method selector name **setColor**: to **color**: and save the modified methods, we will be conforming to convention. But note that the old methods are not removed—class Truck now has four instance methods: **color**, **color**:, **getColor**, and **setColor**:, as shown in Figure 5.13.

To get rid of an unwanted method, select it and click on **Remove** in the **Methods** menu, as shown in Figure 5.14.

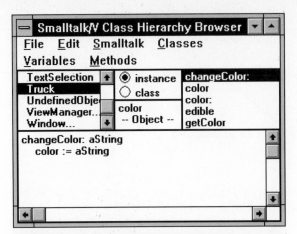

Figure 5.13 Class Truck with five instance methods.

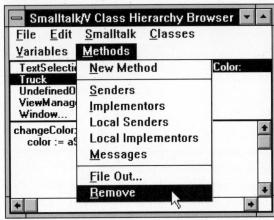

Figure 5.14 Removing the selected method.

5.2.5   Making Sure That Instances Can Print Themselves

One of the problems with the Truck class as defined is that we can't determine a truck's color by printing it. More specifically, each of the following expressions simply prints "a Truck":

> Truck **new** ⇒ a Truck
> Truck **new color**: 'red' ⇒ a Truck
> Truck **new color**: 'green' ⇒ a Truck

Of course, we can use an inspector to look at the color part or we can ask the truck for its color information directly using the **color** accessing method. But this is extra work. It would much nicer if a truck were able to indicate what its color was when it printed itself. If it did, we might get the following result instead:

> Truck **new** ⇒ a nil Truck
> Truck **new color**: 'red' ⇒ a red Truck
> Truck **new color**: 'green' ⇒ a green Truck

The first example is a little strange; what's a nil truck, anyway? At the very least, it provides an indication that we forgot to specify the color. The other two examples, on the other hand, are precisely what we want.

To be able to make this change, we need to add another instance method to class Truck. But what instance method should it be? We can't tell by looking at the examples. A leading question might help: How would we get a truck to print itself on the transcript (even if we were working in a workspace)? Remember now? We simply ask it to print itself as follows:

(Truck **new color**: 'red') **printOn**: Transcript

In the earlier examples, we didn't use **printOn**: directly. Instead, we selected the expression to be evaluated, clicked on **Show It** in the currently active window, and had the answer print there.

> **Show It** *is a request to have the object print itself (using **printOn:**) in the same window that contains the selected expression.*

So now our task is simple. We need to write a **printOn**: method that prints the necessary information in the parameter provided. We need to add a method such as the following:

printOn: aWindow
    aWindow **nextPutAll**: 'a '.
    aWindow **nextPutAll**: color.
    aWindow **nextPutAll**: ' Truck'.

There are two small points about this method. First, the period that terminates the first two expressions is optional for the third expression. Second, we could have used cascading to simplify the method. Notice also that we were very careful to make sure that a space was supplied both after "a" and before "Truck". The revised method appears as follows:

printOn: aWindow
    aWindow **nextPutAll**: 'a '; **nextPutAll**: color; **nextPutAll**: ' Truck'

Yet another variation sends a message to obtain the color. To which object should the color query be directed? To self, of course. No other object understands this message. The result is the following:

printOn: aWindow
    aWindow **nextPutAll**: 'a '; **nextPutAll**: self **color**; **nextPutAll**: ' Truck'

If this seems confusing, don't worry. We'll be considering this again in the case studies below and in subsequent chapters. For now, use whichever method makes the most sense to you.

Having made a number of interesting additions to the Smalltalk system, it might now be a good time to save the image. Most Smalltalk programmers periodically save their images in case of unexpected problems.

5.3   Case Studies

So far, we have seen global variables such as Pen and Display, local variables in transcript and workspace windows and in methods, pseudo-variables such as "self", variables for parameters that cannot be changed (parameters are **immutable**), and instance variables referencing the parts of an object (see Chapter 2 for a discussion of indexed and named parts). We have also seen variables that are intermediate between local variables and global variables; namely, class variables, that are known only to the class and its immediate instances (although subclasses also have access). Finally, we have seen how variables in pool dictionaries can be used and how the pool dictionaries themselves can be defined and constructed.

What we need now are opportunities to use one or more of these different kinds of variables. More specifically, we need case studies dealing with somewhat more complex examples that illustrate many of the things we already know—as well as one or two new ideas.

5.3.1   Case Study: Temperature

Let's design a class for keeping track of temperatures. In the previous sections, we used variables like **c** and **f** to keep track of temperature values. We subsequently decided that it would be better to use names like **centigrade** and **fahrenheit**. Nevertheless, these variables were bound to numbers and if we printed one, it simply printed a number like 32 or 32.0 with no indication as to whether the temperature was in centigrade or fahrenheit units. We would like our temperature objects to know what they are and know how to print themselves. We would like to be able to write the following:

```
I aTemperature I
aTemperature := Temperature centigrade: 100.
aTemperature ⇒ 100 degrees centigrade
```

Of course, if we actually tried to execute the above, it wouldn't work because we haven't created a class called Temperature yet. Nevertheless, even if we don't know how to implement the class or what the operations should be, it is still a good idea to get started. We can start simply by making a subclass of Object called Temperature, as shown in Figure 5.15.

One good way of proceeding is to consider examples that might help us decide what kinds of operations we will need. Rather than write our examples in the transcript or a workspace, it is more convenient to write them as **example** methods. After a few examples are written, we will begin to understand what operations we want. Then we can figure out some way to implement them. Of course, after we partially implement our class in the most obvious way, we could change our minds and make rather dramatic changes. If the example methods

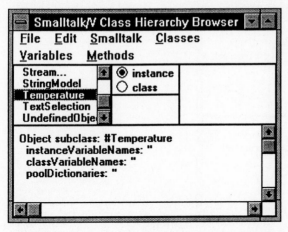

Figure 5.15 The initial (temporary) definition of class Temperature.

still exist, we can subsequently re-execute them to see if the new implementation still works. So example methods are useful for us, as designers. Example methods are also useful for others because they illustrate how the class is intended to be used.

For example, the simplest method that we might think of initially is one that simply constructs a temperature object and returns it. Our class definition (so far) would consist of the following:

class	Temperature
superclass	Object
instance variables	"none (so far)"

class methods

examples

example1
    "Obtain an instance of Temperature specified in centigrade degrees."
    | aTemperature |
    aTemperature := Temperature **centigrade**: 100.
    ^aTemperature
    "Temperature example1"

There are several interesting aspects to note. First, the example method is a class method—not an instance method. Moreover, the last line is a comment whose contents can be executed, as shown in Figure 5.16, to test the method. This is particularly important for people browsing the class because it is cumbersome for a reader to have to type out "Temperature **example1**" just to try it out.

As mentioned at the beginning of this section, we expect the temperature to print as "100 degrees centigrade". But what if you prefer to have your temperature objects print in fahrenheit degrees? Wouldn't it be convenient if you could set

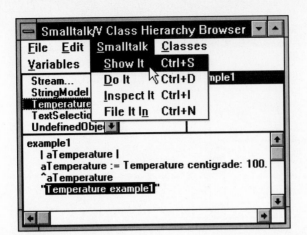

Figure 5.16 Testing class method **example1**.

some default that specifies the temperature scale to to be used for printing purposes? What would be a nice name for this method? Should it be a class method (where the class somehow keeps track of the default) or an instance method (where each instance keeps track of it)?

In general, there could be many instances of class Temperature. If there were ten temperature objects, for example, there would be no need to keep the default in each of these instances—so it should be a class method. To come up with a good name, we need to mentally try out a handfull of potential names. For example, we might consider the following:

> Temperature **printAs**: #centigrade.
> Temperature **default**: #centigrade.
> Temperature **scale**: #centigrade.
> Temperature **defaultScale**: #centigrade.
> Temperature **printDefault**: #centigrade.

The two selector names that I like best are the first and last. The name **printAs**: might give a reader the impression that we are asking the class to print itself. The name **default**: seems too short; if we see it out of context, we might ask, "does this indicate that all temperature objects must now be given in centigrade degrees?" Selectors **scale**: and **defaultScale**: have the same problem—what does setting the scale have to do with printing? In the end, I decided to use the last selector.

> *Finding appropriate names for selectors is a design task that even experts find difficult.*

It's not unusual to think of even better names as the implementation progresses and to revise the names.

Do we need another example method to illustrate the default setting capability, or is it sufficient to provide additional tests in the **example1** method itself? Consider the following revision to **example1**, in which we have added three additional comments at the bottom:

example1
        "Obtain an instance of Temperature specified in centigrade degrees."
        | aTemperature |
        aTemperature := Temperature **centigrade**: 100.
        ^aTemperature

        "Temperature example1"
        "Temperature printDefault: #centigrade. Temperature example1"
        "Temperature printDefault: #fahrenheit. Temperature example1"
        "Temperature printDefault: #kelvin. Temperature example1"

If the default is set to #centigrade, we expect the answer to print as "100 degrees centigrade"; if it's set to #fahrenheit, we expect "212 degrees fahrenheit". Note that the default is specified as a symbol rather than a string. Because we don't expect to ever change the characters in the default, an immutable object might as well be used.

We might now consider implementing the **printDefault**: class method. We already decided that this default information should not be saved in an instance because we want all instances to have the same default. So the class will have to save the default information in a variable that is accessible to both the instances and the class, a class variable. (Don't forget, such variables must be capitalized.) A global variable would also work, but it's a poor solution because it permits all objects—pens, points, and strings just to name a few—to access the variable.

But first things first. What should we call this class variable? As we did before, the best approach is to mentally run through a number of potential names and then pick the best one. Some possibilities include

Scale	ScaleName	Default
DefaultScale	TemperatureScale	DefaultTemperatureScale

Let's choose DefaultScale, since it is the shortest name that makes it clear that it is both a default and a default for some scale. (All the better for you if you can think of an even better alternative.) Now we can revise the definition of the class and implement the **printDefault**: method. Revising the class definition requires three steps:

- Clicking on the class in the class list pane of the browser
- Adding "DefaultScale" inside the string immediately following the keyword **classVariableNames**: (as shown in Figure 5.17)
- Clicking on **Save** in the **File** menu

Now we can implement the **printDefault**: class method. Its task is very simple—to initialize class variable "DefaultScale", as shown below.

class	Temperature
superclass	Object
instance variables	"none (so far)"
class variables	DefaultScale

class methods

class initialization

printDefault: aSymbol
    DefaultScale := aSymbol
    "Temperature printDefault: #centigrade"
    "Temperature printDefault: #fahrenheit"
    "Temperature printDefault: #kelvin"

Since "DefaultScale" is a class variable and not a global, it is not possible to access the variable from a workspace. If we try, we will get an obvious message, as shown in Figure 5.18. Be sure to click on **No**; if you don't, the system will create a global variable called "DefaultScale" which of course, will be different from the class variable that happens to have the same name. This would no doubt cause some confusion: "DefaultScale" in a Temperature method would be the class variable, whereas "DefaultScale" in a workspace or in a method associated with any other class, such as Number, Point, or Pen, would be the global variable. If you accidentally create a global, you can get rid of it by executing

    Smalltalk **removeKey:** #DefaultScale

But how could you access the class variable from a workspace? You couldn't—not directly, at least. But you could send a message to the class and have the class provide you with the contents of the class variable, *provided you added a class method to do it*. What should we call this method? If the method to change the class variable is called **printDefault:** (notice the colon), presumably the method to

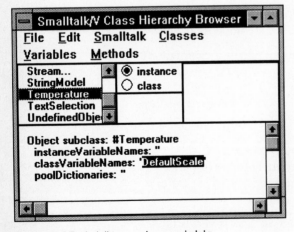

Figure 5.17 Adding a class variable "DefaultScale" to class Temperature.

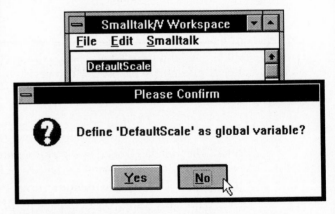

Figure 5.18 Class variables cannot be accessed from a workspace.

retrieve the contents of the class variable should be called **printDefault** (with no colon). It could be implemented as follows:

```
class                            Temperature
superclass                       Object
instance variables               "none (so far)"
class variables                  DefaultScale

class methods

class querying

printDefault
    "Return the current print default."
    ^DefaultScale
    "Temperature printDefault"

class initialization

printDefault: aSymbol
    "Change the current print default."
    DefaultScale := aSymbol
    "Temperature printDefault: #centigrade"
    "Temperature printDefault: #fahrenheit"
    "Temperature printDefault: #kelvin"
```

Now we can execute "Temperature **printDefault**" in a workspace to obtain the default, even though we can't execute "DefaultScale". Note also that we can later change the name of the class variable without impacting users. They don't have to know the name of the class variable. However, users, do have to know what message to use (in this case, **printDefault**) to retrieve it.

What else might we expect to do with temperatures? Compare them, perhaps? We could write another example method to test that capability:

```
example2
    "An example that compares two different temperatures and returns false."
    | temperature1 temperature2 |
    temperature1 := Temperature centigrade: 100.
    temperature2 := Temperature fahrenheit: 100.
    ^temperature1 = temperature2
    "Temperature example2"

example3
    "An example that compares two different temperatures and returns true."
    | temperature1 temperature2 |
    temperature1 := Temperature centigrade: 100.
    temperature2 := Temperature fahrenheit: 212.
    ^temperature1 = temperature2
    "Temperature example3"
```

What if we want to use the temperature as a number in degrees centigrade, say to double it? Should we simply write "aTemperature * 2"? If the temperature is 100 degrees centigrade, do we get 200 as the answer, or 200 degrees centigrade—do we get back a number or another temperature object? Also, what if the default is set to fahrenheit? Since 100 degrees centigrade is equivalent to 212 degrees fahrenheit, do we correspondingly get 424, or 424 degrees fahrenheit?

If a temperature object were retrieved from a sophisticated thermometer, we should be able to ask this temperature object "what is the temperature in degrees centigrade?" independent of what it might print as the default. (Indeed, we should be able to ask a temperature object "what is the temperature in degrees kelvin?") If we ask for the temperature in degrees centigrade, it seems more reasonable to get back a number rather than a string or yet another temperature object. Also, it should be possible to have the same temperature object return different values depending on the query. What might these potential queries be? Once again, let's try some candidates.

aTemperature **centigrade**	versus	aTemperature **fahrenheit**
aTemperature **inCentigrade**	versus	aTemperature **inFahrenheit**
aTemperature **centigradeReading**	versus	aTemperature **fahrenheitReading**
aTemperature **centigradeUnits**	versus	aTemperature **fahrenheitUnits**

We would like to use short names such as **centigrade** or **inCentigrade**, but we suspect that we might get confused later—will we expect a temperature object that contains the information in centigrade degrees or a number? With a name like **centigradeReading**, we are more likely to expect a number. Our first implementation used messages **centigradeReading**, **fahrenheitReading**, and **kelvinReading** but a few days later, we had second thoughts about it. Ultimately, we decided to use shorter names **centigrade**, **fahrenheit**, and **kelvin** because it looked better even though there is a potential for confusion. We argued that if we could create a temperature object using a message such as "**centigrade**: 100", we should be able to retrieve that number with the corresponding message "**centigrade**". Method **example4**, below, illustrates how we might retrieve the number in units different from the one used to create the temperature object.

```
example4
    "An example that returns 0 degrees centigrade as a number in fahrenheit
    units."
    | aTemperature |
    aTemperature := Temperature centigrade: 0.
    ^aTemperature fahrenheit
    "Temperature example4"
```

Why didn't we just tell you about our final solution to begin with? Because we want you to realize something extremely important

> *Changing your mind is part of designing—experts do it all the time.*

Now we have to find a way to record temperature values in temperature objects. If the same temperature object can be queried for centigrade, fahrenheit, and kelvin temperatures (as shown below),

aTemperature **centigrade**
aTemperature **fahrenheit**
aTemperature **kelvin**

should we record all three temperatures in the object? If we do, all three values will have to be set when a temperature object is created—even though users create temperature objects by providing only one value, as in "Temperature **centigrade**: 0". Alternatively, we could just record one temperature and convert it to the appropriate temperature scale when required. This seems simpler, since we have to deal with only one recorded value.

Now, we have to decide whether to store the information in centigrade, fahrenheit, or kelvin units. Does it matter? Suppose we created a temperature objects by executing

aTemperature := Temperature **centigrade**: 0

What would be the three possibilities?

if recorded in centigrade units ⇒ 0 is recorded
if recorded in fahrenheit units ⇒ 32 is recorded
if recorded in kelvin units ⇒ 273.16 is recorded

If we subsequently execute "aTemperature **centigrade**", the centigrade and fahrenheit units will easily convert back to 0, but the kelvin units will convert to 0.0 (a float rather than an integer because a float added to an integer gives a float). The conversion process is summarized below:

if centigrade units requested and temperature value is recorded in
    centigrade units ⇒ return recorded value
    fahrenheit units ⇒ return 32 + 9/5 * recorded value
    kelvin units ⇒ return 273.16 + recorded value

If we record the temperature in kelvin units, some users will claim that the class is badly designed. "I used an integer to specify the temperature in centigrade units. Why can't I get it back as an integer?" It is a poor solution to truncate the result

if centigrade units requested and temperature value is recorded in
    kelvin units ⇒ return (273.3 + recorded value) truncated

because users can also specify the temperature using floats, as in "Temperature **centigrade**: 0.75". Clearly, you should get 0.75 back when the temperature in centigrade units is requested, not 0.

So the best design records temperature values in either centigrade units or fahrenheit units, but not in kelvin units. So let's pick one—say, centigrade units. Now we need to extend the definition of class Temperature so that the instances have a part for recording this temperature value in centigrade units. What do we call the part name? Consider the following candidates:

number	value	amount
degrees	temperature	temperatureAmount
temperatureValue	centigrade	centigradeValue
centigradeAmount	centigradeDegrees	

Let's eliminate some of the candidates. Clearly, temperature is a poor choice because the value to be recorded is not a temperature object—it's a number. So temperatureAmount and temperatureValue are better names, but amount and value (or, for that matter, number) are shorter. However, there is nothing in these choices to indicate whether the value recorded represents centigrade or fahrenheit units. What if we change our minds and decide to record the information in fahrenheit units instead? Will we be able to tell if the conversions used in the methods are correct? If the part name is simply amount, we will not be able to tell unless we provide explicit commentary about the units used. It seems best to use a part name that has the word "centigrade" in it. If we later decide to record the information in fahrenheit units instead, then we'll change the part name to reflect the new units. The most accurate term, even though it is relatively long, is centigradeDegrees.

Now we need to add this new part name to temperature objects. Recall that a part name is called an instance variable in Smalltalk. We must edit the class definition, as shown in Figure 5.19; i.e., we must type the new instance variable name **centigradeDegrees** between the two quotes of the empty string that follows the keyword **instanceVariableNames:**.

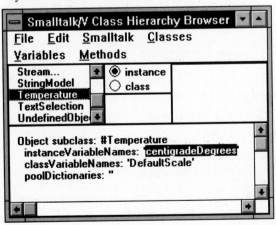

Figure 5.19 Redefining class Temperature so that instances have a part called centigradeDegrees.

Now we can implement the three instance methods for querying temperature objects.

class	Temperature
superclass	Object
instance variables	centigradeDegrees
class variables	DefaultScale

instance methods

querying

centigrade
    ^centigradeDegrees

fahrenheit
    ^32 + (9 / 5 * centigradeDegrees)

kelvin
    ^centigradeDegrees + 273.16

Recall from Chapter 4 that part names (instance variables) in instance methods always refer to the parts of the receiver. Consequently, an expression like "temperature1 **kelvin**" will access the "centigradeDegrees" part of object temperature1. Similarly, expression "temperature2 **kelvin**" will access the "centigradeDegrees" part of object temperature2—the receiver is different in this case.

The only thing missing now is the implementation of a class method to create a properly initialized temperature object; i.e., a method that allows us to say "Temperature **centigrade**: 100". Here's a start at the implementation. What's missing?

class method

instance creation

centigrade: aNumber
    "Obtain an instance of Temperature specified in centigrade degrees."
    | aTemperature |
    aTemperature := Temperature **new**.
    ^aTemperature

    "Temperature centigrade: 100"

If you inspect the temperature object returned, you will see that part "centigradeDegrees" is nil. The part has never been bound; we didn't do anything with parameter "aNumber". Can we simply add an assignment expression to bind instance variable "centigradeDegrees" to "aNumber", as shown in the next variation of the method?

centigrade: aNumber
"Obtain an instance of Temperature specified in centigrade degrees."
| aTemperature |
aTemperature := Temperature **new**.
centigradeDegrees := aNumber.
^aTemperature

"Temperature centigrade: 100"

Unfortunately, this cannot work! If we try to save the method, we get an error message, as shown in Figure 5.20. The problem is that "centigradeDegrees" is part of an instance, not part of the class. Although it can be referenced in an instance method, it cannot be referenced in a class method because only the class is a receiver in a class method.

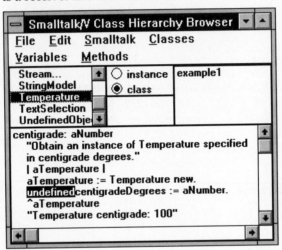

Figure 5.20 Attempting to access an instance part in a class method.

We need to introduce an instance method such as **setCentigradeDegrees**: (see below) that can reference the "centigradeDegrees" part of the instance. Once this instance method exists, our class method can use it to send a message to the instance to change itself.

instance method

setCentigradeDegrees: aNumber
"Modify my centigradeDegrees part."
centigradeDegrees := aNumber

class method

centigrade: aNumber
"Obtain an instance of Temperature specified in centigrade degrees."
| aTemperature |
aTemperature := Temperature **new**.
aTemperature **setCentigradeDegrees**: aNumber.
^aTemperature

"Temperature centigrade: 100"

In Chapter 4, we noted that Smalltalk programmers generally don't use method names such as **setCentigradeDegrees**:. Instead, they prefer names such as **centigrade**:. Of course, if we make this change, we will have two methods with the same name: an instance method and a class method. By now, however, you should know the difference between an instance and a class and so you shouldn't be confused by this.

We will then have three methods dealing with centigrade values:

Temperature **centigrade**: aNumber	To get a temperature instance from the class with the temperature properly recorded
aTemperature **centigrade**	To get the recorded temperature amount in the instance
aTemperature **centigrade**: aNumber	To change the recorded temperature amount in the instance

Continuing with this approach, we would also have to add the corresponding methods for fahrenheit and kelvin values. The fahrenheit methods, for example, would appear as follows:

instance methods

accessing

fahrenheit
```
    "Provide my temperature value in fahrenheit degrees."
    ^32 + (9 / 5 * centigradeDegrees)
```

changing

fahrenheit: aNumber
```
    "Modify my temperature value given the new value in fahrenheit
    degrees."
    centigradeDegrees := (aNumber - 32) * 5 / 9
```

class methods

instance creation

fahrenheit: aNumber
```
    "Obtain an instance of Temperature specified in fahrenheit degrees."
    | aTemperature |
    aTemperature := Temperature new.
    aTemperature fahrenheit: aNumber.
    ^aTemperature

    "Temperature fahrenheit: 100"
```

What's missing now? We haven't yet provided a method that allows temperature objects to be compared for equality. When are two temperature objects equal? Presumably, when their parts are equal. Since all temperature objects record their temperature values in degrees centigrade, we can just compare these corresponding numbers. This suggests a method with the following pattern:

instance methods

comparing

= aTemperature
    If my centigrade value is the same as aTemperature's centigrade value
    then I'll reply that we are equal
    otherwise, I'll reply that we are not equal

Basically, we need to know how to make a test and choose between one of two possible courses of action. We need to know about **if-expressions**, which have the following form:

aBooleanExpression
    ifTrue: trueBlock
    ifFalse: falseBlock

The receiver of the **ifTrue:ifFalse:** message must be either true or false. Hence, any expression that evaluates to a boolean will be valid. Each parameter must be a **block**; i.e., a sequence of zero or more expressions separated by "." and surrounded by square brackets. We encountered blocks earlier when we discussed the **times-repeat-expression**. Like a times-repeat-expression, an if-expression is also known as a **control structure** because it permits the path of execution to be controlled; e.g., by controlling which one of two paths is to be executed. For a simple example, consider the following:

5 **factorial odd**
    ifTrue: [5 **factorial printOn:** Transcript. Transcript **nextPutAll:** ' is odd']
    ifFalse: [5 **factorial printOn:** Transcript. Transcript **nextPutAll:** ' is even']

We could have just as easily written the following instead.

5 **factorial printOn:** Transcript.
5 **factorial odd**
    ifTrue: [Transcript **nextPutAll:** ' is odd']
    ifFalse: [Transcript **nextPutAll:** ' is even']

Alternatively, we could have used variables to avoid recomputing "5 **factorial**".

| result |
result := 5 **factorial**.
result **printOn:** Transcript.
result **odd**
    ifTrue: [Transcript **nextPutAll:** ' is odd']
    ifFalse: [Transcript **nextPutAll:** ' is even']

Since **ifTrue:ifFalse:** is a message, it must return a value. Let's find out what that value is. In particular, consider the following series of experiments:

> 2 > 1 **ifTrue:** [1. 2. 3] **ifFalse:** [10. 20. 30] ⇒ 3
> 1 > 2 **ifTrue:** [1. 2. 3] **ifFalse:** [10. 20. 30] ⇒ 30
> 2 > 1 **ifTrue:** [] **ifFalse:** [] ⇒ nil

Clearly, when the boolean receiver is true, the last expression in the true block is provided as the answer. Similarly, when the receiver is false, the last expression in the false block is the answer. If the corresponding block contains no expression at all, nil is the answer.

Consequently, an **if-expression** might be described as an **ifTrue:ifFalse:** message sent to a boolean receiver. If the receiver is true, the true block is executed and the last value computed in the block is the answer—unless there was no expression at all in the block, in which case, nil is the answer. If the receiver is false, the false block is executed with similar consequences.

Because an **ifTrue:ifFalse:** message returns an answer, the factorial example above could be rewritten as follows:

> | result |
> result := 5 **factorial**.
> result **printOn:** Transcript.
> Transcript **nextPutAll:** (result **odd ifTrue:** [' is odd'] **ifFalse:** [' is even'])

Note: The parameter to keyword **nextPutAll:** must be surrounded by round brackets (not square brackets). If the round brackets were omitted entirely, we would be attempting to send a **nextPutAll:ifTrue:ifFalse:** message to the transcript.

As a first attempt, we could use an if-expression to implement the desired = method as follows:

> instance methods
>
> *comparing*
>
> = aTemperature
>   "Return true if and only if I'm equal to aTemperature."
>   centigradeDegrees = aTemperature **centigrade**
>   **ifTrue:** [^true]
>   **ifFalse:** [^false]

We might read this as follows: "If my centigrade degrees is equal to aTemperature's centigrade degrees, return true; otherwise, return false." Why did we send message **centigrade** to aTemperature instead of just referring to its part name "centigradeDegrees" directly? Because we can't refer to aTemperature's part name directly—aTemperature is not the receiver of the method we are in. So "centigradeDegrees" is self's part, not aTemperature's part.

We might expect such a method from a novice but not from an expert. Although the method provides the desired answer, it is too complex. It's like saying, "if it's true, return true; otherwise, return false." Why not simply return the result of the comparison? If the comparison result happens to be true, that's what we return. If it happens to be false, we return that instead. More specifically, we can rewrite the method as follows:

instance methods

comparing

= aTemperature
    "Return true if and only if I'm equal to aTemperature."
    ^centigradeDegrees = aTemperature **centigrade**

This suggests a useful rule:

> *Results of comparisons can be used directly; e.g., "^a = b" is equivalent to "a = b ifTrue: [^true] ifFalse: [^false]".*

Now, if we can ask aTemperature for the desired information by sending it the message **centigrade**, can we not ask the receiver in the same way? (The receiver can be referenced using pseudo variable "self".) If we do, our method would appear as follows:

= aTemperature
    "Return true if and only if I'm equal to aTemperature."
    ^self **centigrade** = aTemperature **centigrade**

This version of the method seems more balanced because the temperature value is obtained from receiver "self" and parameter "aTemperature" in the same manner. As a general rule,

> *Sending a message to obtain a part is preferable to accessing the part name directly (if an associated method exists).*

Indeed, if we went to all the trouble of providing a method to access a part, we should at least use it. Not using it causes the reader to suspect that there is something wrong with the method—perhaps the method returns a result that can't be used for our purposes! Additionally, there are two other important reasons for using messages instead of accessing a part directly:

- Assuming that the accessing method is retained, methods that use messages to access parts won't need to be changed when the part name is changed in the future
- It permits future subclasses to override the method should they wish the result to be computed slightly differently. (This will be discussed in Chapter 6.)

Of course, if we don't want users to have access to the part at all, we won't provide a method that returns it. In that case, the only way to access the part would be to reference it directly in the method, but that works only if the part we want belongs to the receiver. In the above situation, for example, that would not be a good idea because there would be no way to access the temperature value associated with parameter aTemperature. If that were the case, we wouldn't be able to implement method =.

If it's a good idea to send a message rather than access the part name directly, we might want to look back at some of the methods we've already written to see if they might be revised. Consider the following:

instance methods

querying

centigrade
    ^centigradeDegrees

fahrenheit
    ^32 + (9 / 5 * centigradeDegrees)

kelvin
    ^centigradeDegrees + 273.16

Should we just revise all three?:

instance methods

querying

centigrade
    ^self **centigrade**

fahrenheit
    ^32 + (9 / 5 * self **centigrade**)

kelvin
    ^self **centigrade** + 273.16

These changes turn out to be appropriate for **fahrenheit** and **kelvin**, but not for **centigrade**. As rewritten above, sending the message **centigrade** to a temperature object causes an infinite number of messages to be sent. Fortunately, the problem is detected by the Smalltalk environment; an error message, as shown in Figure 5.21, is generated.

The problem is obvious after the fact. When message **centigrade** is sent to a temperature object, the object sends the message **centigrade** back to itself to determine the answer. But to determine the answer to the second message, it must send a third one, which in turn causes a fourth message to be sent, and so on. Clearly, the method should be restored to its former state—it should simply return the contents of part "centigradeDegrees".

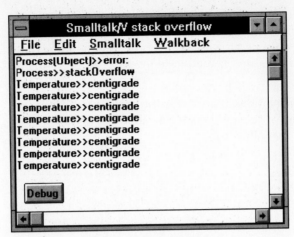

Figure 5.21 Sending a message that results in an infinite number of messages.

Now back to the "=" operation. As written, it doesn't always work. For example, consider the following simple test:

```
| aTemperature |
aTemperature := Temperature centigrade: 0.
^aTemperature = 'hello'
```

In this case, we compared a temperature object to a string. Instead of getting the answer false—and it should be false because temperature objects are not equal to strings—we get an error message indicating that strings do not understand message **centigrade**. Looking back at our method, we can see why.

```
= aTemperature
    "Return true if and only if I'm equal to aTemperature."
    ^self centigrade = aTemperature centigrade
```

Our method expects the parameter to be a temperature object, but it wasn't. Of course, we already know how to determine if a variable is a temperature object—simply execute "variable **isKindOf**: Temperature". Depending on the answer, we need to perform different computations. We need something like

```
If aTemperature is a temperature object
    then I'll reply with the usual response discussed above
    otherwise, I'll reply that we are not equal; i.e., with false
```

Now we have an opportunity to use an if-expression in a more useful situation (in fact, there probably isn't any better way of doing it). It should now be easy to revise the "=" method.

```
= aTemperature
    "Return true if and only if I'm equal to aTemperature."
    (aTemperature isKindOf: Temperature)
        ifTrue: [^self centigrade = aTemperature centigrade]
        ifFalse: [^false]
```

If parameter aTemperature can be a string or a number, for example, it shouldn't be called aTemperature at all. We should find a better name. How about "anObject"?

```
= anObject
    "Return true if and only if I'm equal to anObject."
    (anObject isKindOf: Temperature)
        ifTrue: [^self centigrade = anObject centigrade]
        ifFalse: [^false]
```

Anything else? Yes: Temperature objects print simply as "a Temperature". We need to implement our own **printOn:** method. Of course, there is a bit of a complication; the print default must be taken into account. Let's start off with an implementation that seems quite complicated but that works. Then, we'll try to simplify and improve it.

```
printOn: aWindow
    "I print myself in the form 'xxx degrees yyy' where yyy is either 'kelvin',
    'fahrenheit', or 'centigrade'."
    I degrees I
    DefaultScale = #kelvin
        ifTrue: [degrees := self kelvin]
        ifFalse: [
            DefaultScale = #centigrade
                ifTrue: [degrees := self centigrade]
                ifFalse: [
                    DefaultScale = #fahrenheit
                        ifTrue: [degrees := self fahrenheit]
                        ifFalse: [self error: 'incorrect default scale']]].
    degrees printOn: aWindow.
    aWindow nextPutAll: ' degrees '; nextPutAll: DefaultScale
```

With respect to formatting style, notice that each **ifTrue:** and **ifFalse:** keyword is indented under the boolean expression that precedes it. If the entire block, along with the **ifTrue:** or **ifFalse:** keyword, fits on one line, the combination is kept on the same line; e.g., see the first **ifTrue:** keyword. On the other hand, if there is too much to fit on a line, the first line starts below the keyword and it is indented under it; e.g., see DefaultScale indented below the first **ifFalse:** keyword. In either case, the "[" stays on the same line as the **ifTrue:** or **ifFalse:** keyword. The corresponding "]" terminates the block as soon as possible, with no prior spaces.

This indentation style allows you to figure out what belongs with a block by looking only at the indentation. (You should be able to ignore the square brackets "[" and "]" when reading the code.) As shown in Figure 5.22, code that is part of a keyword parameter should never appear at the same indentation level as the keyword. Code that appears to the left of a keyword signals that it is not part of the keyword.

```
printOn: aWindow
    "I print myself in the form 'xxx degrees yyy' where yyy is either 'kelvin',
    'fahrenheit' or 'centigrade'."
    | degrees |
    DefaultScale = #kelvin
        ifTrue: [degrees := self kelvin]
        ifFalse: [
            DefaultScale = #centigrade
                ifTrue: [degrees := self centigrade]
                ifFalse: [
                    DefaultScale = #fahrenheit
                        ifTrue: [degrees := self fahrenheit]
                        ifFalse: [self error: 'incorrect default scale']]].
    degrees printOn: aWindow.
    aWindow nextPutAll: ' degrees '; nextPutAll: DefaultScale
```

Figure 5.22 Sending a message that results in an infinite number of messages.

Note that proper indentation is obtained by hitting the appropriate number of tabs, not by typing spaces. If we follow the imaginary indentation line under the first **ifFalse:** keyword or under the first character in DefaultScale under it, we ultimately encounter the expression "degree **printOn:** aWindow". By starting it to the left of the indentation line, we convey to a reader that it is not part of the false block.

Because of the indentation style used, we can tell that the first false block consists of an entire **ifTrue:ifFalse:** message whose false block in turn contains another one. Contrast this with the same method without proper indentation and try to figure out where the first false block ends.

```
printOn: aWindow
    "I print myself in the form 'xxx degrees yyy' where yyy is either 'kelvin',
    'fahrenheit' or 'centigrade'."
    | degrees |
    DefaultScale = #kelvin
    ifTrue: [degrees := self kelvin]
    ifFalse: [
    DefaultScale = #centigrade
    ifTrue: [degrees := self centigrade]
    ifFalse: [
    DefaultScale = #fahrenheit
    ifTrue: [degrees := self fahrenheit]
    ifFalse: [self error: 'incorrect default scale']]].
    degrees printOn: aWindow.
    aWindow nextPutAll: ' degrees '; nextPutAll: DefaultScale
```

As a rule, messages that are too long to fit onto one line are formatted as follows:

```
receiver1
    keyword1: ...
    keyword2: ...
    keyword3: ...
receiver2
    keyword1: ...
    keyword2: ...
    keyword3: ...
```

By ensuring that the keywords are indented, rather than lined up with the receiver, we can indicate when a new message starts. Formatting conventions for **if-expressions** fall into this general framework.

Clearly, proper indentation is essential for understandability. But even with good indentation, our latest **printOn**: method still looks too complicated. One way of simplifying the method is to break up it up into two simpler ones and to use control structure messages with a simpler nesting structure. We could use **ifTrue**: messages (with no **ifFalse**: keyword) in place of **ifTrue:ifFalse**: messages. (Presumably, there must exist such a variation.)

```
defaultUnits
    DefaultScale = #kelvin ifTrue: [^self kelvin].
    DefaultScale = #centigrade ifTrue: [^self centigrade].
    DefaultScale = #fahrenheit ifTrue: [^self fahrenheit].
    self error: 'incorrect default scale'

printOn: aWindow
    "I print myself in the form 'xxx degrees yyy' where yyy is either 'kelvin',
    'fahrenheit', or 'centigrade'."
    self defaultUnits printOn: aWindow.
    aWindow nextPutAll: ' degrees '; nextPutAll: DefaultScale
```

With the new method **defaultUnits**, we can ask a temperature object for its temperature in the default units. More important, note the simplicity of the nesting structure. Because we can fit each **ifTrue**: expression on one line, we don't need to bother nesting at all. If the default scale is #kelvin, the kelvin temperature is computed and returned without performing any other tests. When a temperature object is asked to print itself, it obtains the temperature in default units (a number) and the number is asked to print itself. Subsequently, the string 'degrees' is provided along with the default scale which could, for example, be #kelvin. Of course, a symbol is a string; so it can be printed with **nextPutAll**:. Our method should produce the desired effect.

Couldn't we have done this in one method in the first place? Let's try. If we combine the two methods naively, we get the following:

```
printOn: aWindow
    "I print myself in the form 'xxx degrees yyy' where yyy is either 'kelvin',
    'fahrenheit', or 'centigrade'."
    DefaultScale = #kelvin ifTrue: [^self kelvin].
    DefaultScale = #centigrade ifTrue: [^self centigrade].
    DefaultScale = #fahrenheit ifTrue: [^self fahrenheit].
    self error: 'incorrect default scale'.
    self defaultUnits printOn: aWindow.
    aWindow nextPutAll: ' degrees '; nextPutAll: DefaultScale
```

In this case, if the default scale is #kelvin, the temperature in kelvin degrees is obtained and returned without printing anything. Clearly, we have to save the information for later printing. Our next variation of the method might be the following:

```
printOn: aWindow
    "I print myself in the form 'xxx degrees yyy' where yyy is either 'kelvin',
    'fahrenheit', or 'centigrade'."
    | degrees |
    DefaultScale = #kelvin ifTrue: [degrees := self kelvin].
    DefaultScale = #centigrade ifTrue: [degrees := self centigrade].
    DefaultScale = #fahrenheit ifTrue: [degrees := self fahrenheit].
    self error: 'incorrect default scale'.
    degrees printOn: aWindow.
    aWindow nextPutAll: ' degrees '; nextPutAll: DefaultScale
```

Now the problem is more obvious. We always print an error message. Can we change the last **ifTrue:** message to an **ifTrue:ifFalse:** message and place it in the **ifFalse:** part?

```
printOn: aWindow
    "I print myself in the form 'xxx degrees yyy' where yyy is either 'kelvin',
    'fahrenheit', or 'centigrade'."
    | degrees |
    DefaultScale = #kelvin ifTrue: [degrees := self kelvin].
    DefaultScale = #centigrade ifTrue: [degrees := self centigrade].
    DefaultScale = #fahrenheit
        ifTrue: [degrees := self fahrenheit].
        ifFalse: [self error: 'incorrect default scale'].
    degrees printOn: aWindow.
    aWindow nextPutAll: ' degrees '; nextPutAll: DefaultScale
```

But now we get the error message if the default scale is either #kelvin or #centigrade. In fact, we'll find that the only way we can avoid the error message is to use the complicated nesting structure of the very first version of this method.

On the other hand, one could argue that an error test is needed only when an attempt is made to change the default scale—the error test should be moved to method **printDefault**:. If that were the case, the class method could be revised as follows:

```
printDefault: aSymbol
    "Change the current print default."
    DefaultScale := aSymbol.
    DefaultScale = #kelvin ifTrue: [^self "It's OK."].
    DefaultScale = #centigrade ifTrue: [^self "It's OK."].
    DefaultScale = #fahrenheit ifTrue: [^self "It's OK."].
    self error: 'incorrect default scale'.

    "Temperature printDefault: #centigrade"
    "Temperature printDefault: #fahrenheit"
    "Temperature printDefault: #kelvin"
```

Although this works, the method is not well designed because the default scale is changed even if it is incorrect. A better solution would make the change only if it were correct. We need to change the logic a bit.

```
printDefault: aSymbol
    "Change the current print default (if it is legal)."
    (aSymbol = #kelvin) | (aSymbol = #centigrade) | (aSymbol = #fahrenheit)
        ifTrue: [DefaultScale := aSymbol]
        ifFalse: [self error: 'incorrect default scale']

    "Temperature printDefault: #centigrade"
    "Temperature printDefault: #fahrenheit"
    "Temperature printDefault: #kelvin"
```

Operation "|" is the "or" operation. Hence, the above boolean expression can be read as "aSymbol = #kelvin or aSymbol = #centigrade or aSymbol = #fahrenheit". Now we can assume the print default will be correct and no test will be needed in the **printOn**: method. Method **defaultUnits** becomes superfluous and can be removed. The **printOn**: method can then be written simply as follows:

```
printOn: aWindow
    "I print myself in the form 'xxx degrees yyy' where yyy is either 'kelvin',
    'fahrenheit', or 'centigrade'."
    | degrees |
    DefaultScale = #kelvin ifTrue: [degrees := self kelvin].
    DefaultScale = #centigrade ifTrue: [degrees := self centigrade].
    DefaultScale = #fahrenheit ifTrue: [degrees := self fahrenheit].
    degrees printOn: aWindow.
    aWindow nextPutAll: ' degrees '; nextPutAll: DefaultScale
```

One difference between this method and the complex nested version (or even the simple two-method variation) is that superfluous tests are performed. No matter what the default scale might be, three tests are performed. The other variations performed as few tests as they could to determine the unique default scale. So this version is less efficient. Nevertheless, the decrease in efficiency is so slight that it may not be worth the extra effort of making it more efficient. (That might not be the case, however, if there were a substantially larger number of tests.)

One more issue remains. We argued that it was better style to access an instance variable (an object's part) via a message than to reference the variable directly if there was a message available that could be used. Should the same apply to class variables? In our case, there is a message **printDefault**, which can be used to obtain the default scale. Taking this into account, our method looks slightly more complex but conforms to our style guidelines.

```
printOn: aWindow
    "I print myself in the form 'xxx degrees yyy' where yyy is either 'kelvin',
    'fahrenheit', or 'centigrade'."
    I degrees scale I
    scale := self class printDefault.
    scale = #kelvin ifTrue: [degrees := self kelvin].
    scale = #centigrade ifTrue: [degrees := self centigrade].
    scale = #fahrenheit ifTrue: [degrees := self fahrenheit].
    degrees printOn: aWindow.
    aWindow nextPutAll: ' degrees '; nextPutAll: scale
```

We made so many changes during the development of the Temperature class that it is worthwhile having all the pieces in one place.

```
class                         Temperature
superclass                    Object
instance variables            centigradeDegrees
class variables               DefaultScale

class methods

class querying

printDefault
    "Return the current print default."
    ^DefaultScale
    "Temperature printDefault"

class initialization

printDefault: aSymbol
    "Change the current print default (if it is legal)."
    (aSymbol = #kelvin) I (aSymbol = #centigrade) I (aSymbol = #fahrenheit)
        ifTrue: [DefaultScale := aSymbol]
        ifFalse: [self error: 'incorrect default scale']

    "Temperature printDefault: #centigrade"
    "Temperature printDefault: #fahrenheit"
    "Temperature printDefault: #kelvin"
```

examples

example1
"Obtain an instance of Temperature specified in centigrade degrees."
| aTemperature |
aTemperature := Temperature **centigrade**: 100.
^aTemperature

"Temperature example1"
"Temperature printDefault: #centigrade. Temperature example1"
"Temperature printDefault: #fahrenheit. Temperature example1"
"Temperature printDefault: #kelvin. Temperature example1"

example2
"An example that compares two different temperatures and returns false."
| temperature1 temperature2 |
temperature1 := Temperature **centigrade**: 100.
temperature2 := Temperature **fahrenheit**: 100.
^temperature1 = temperature2
"Temperature example2"

example3
"An example that compares two different temperatures and returns true."
| temperature1 temperature2 |
temperature1 := Temperature **centigrade**: 100.
temperature2 := Temperature **fahrenheit**: 212.
^temperature1 = temperature2
"Temperature example3"

example4
"An example that returns 0 degrees centigrade as a number in fahrenheit units."
| aTemperature |
aTemperature := Temperature **centigrade**: 0.
^aTemperature **fahrenheit**
"Temperature example4"

instance creation

centigrade: aNumber
"Obtain an instance of Temperature specified in centigrade degrees."
| aTemperature |
aTemperature := Temperature **new**.
aTemperature **centigrade**: aNumber.
^aTemperature

"Temperature centigrade: 100"

fahrenheit: aNumber
"Obtain an instance of Temperature specified in fahrenheit degrees."
| aTemperature |
aTemperature := Temperature **new**.
aTemperature **fahrenheit**: aNumber.
^aTemperature

"Temperature fahrenheit: 100"

kelvin: aNumber
"Obtain an instance of Temperature specified in kelvin degrees."
| aTemperature |
aTemperature := Temperature **new**.
aTemperature **kelvin**: aNumber.
^aTemperature

"Temperature kelvin: 100"

instance methods

querying

centigrade
^centigradeDegrees

fahrenheit
^32 + (9 / 5 * self **centigrade**)

kelvin
^self **centigrade** + 273.16

modifying

centigrade: aNumber
centigradeDegrees := aNumber

fahrenheit: aNumber
self **centigrade**: (aNumber - 32) * 5 / 9

kelvin: aNumber
self **centigrade**: aNumber - 273.16

comparing

= anObject
"Return true if and only if I'm equal to anObject ."
(anObject **isKindOf**: Temperature)
    ifTrue: [^self **centigrade** = anObject **centigrade**]
    ifFalse: [^false]

printing

printOn: aWindow
    "I print myself in the form 'xxx degrees yyy' where yyy is either 'kelvin',
    'fahrenheit', or 'centigrade'."
    | degrees scale |
    scale := self **class printDefault**.
    scale = #kelvin **ifTrue**: [degrees := self **kelvin**].
    scale = #centigrade **ifTrue**: [degrees := self **centigrade**].
    scale = #fahrenheit **ifTrue**: [degrees := self **fahrenheit**].
    degrees **printOn**: aWindow.
    aWindow **nextPutAll**: ' degrees '; **nextPutAll**: scale

5.3.2 Case Study: Money

Money objects should be able to represent such things as amounts in a bank account or the cost of cars or groceries. Typically, money objects can be either positive or negative—positive, for example, to represent a profit, and negative for a loss. They should print themselves in the standard manner; e.g., $230.52 (or perhaps -$0.99 for negative amounts). Because the total number of different kinds of literals is fixed in Smalltalk, we won't be able to write $25.77 to get a money object. Instead, we'll have to write something like

    Money **dollars**: 25 **cents**: 77

Once we have a money object, however, it should print itself in the standard manner; e.g., $25.77, in this case. It also makes sense to be able to add and subtract money objects, but it doesn't make much sense to multiply or divide them. (What does $2.00 * $3.00 mean, for example? Six squared dollars!) Of course, we do want to be able to multiply a money object by a number—$27.44 * 2 makes sense.

The solution that most people think of first allows money objects to maintain both the number of dollars and the number of cents. The class might be defined as follows with corresponding methods for accessing and modifying the two parts. Let's also introduce a very simple method for printing money objects.

class   Money
instance variables   dollars cents

class methods

instance creation

dollars: anInteger **cents**: anotherInteger
    ^self **new**
        dollars: anInteger;
        cents: anotherInteger

instance methods

accessing and modifying

dollars
  ^dollars
dollars: anInteger
  dollars := anInteger

cents
  ^cents
cents: anInteger
  cents := anInteger

printing

printOn: aWindow
  "I print myself in the form '$4322.51'."
  aWindow **nextPut**: $$.
  self **dollars printOn**: aWindow.
  aWindow **nextPut**: $..
  self **cents printOn**: aWindow.

The **printOn**: method is not quite right. In particular, the money object

"Money **dollars**: 2 **cents**: 5"

prints as $2.5 rather than $2.05. Can you see what's wrong? Consider what happens at each step of the computation.

aWindow **nextPut**: $$.	produces	$
self **dollars printOn**: aWindow.	produces	$2
aWindow **nextPut**: $..	produces	$2.
self **cents printOn**: aWindow.	produces	$2.5

If the number of cents is less than or equal to 9, we clearly need an extra zero in front. So we need an additional test to determine whether to add an additional zero just before we print the number of cents in the window. The new method might appear as follows:

printOn: aWindow
  "I print myself in the form '$4322.51'."
  aWindow **nextPut**: $$.
  self **dollars printOn**: aWindow.
  aWindow **nextPut**: $..
  self **cents** <= 9 **ifTrue**: [aWindow **nextPut**: $0].
  self **cents printOn**: aWindow.

But there is still a problem. Negative amounts print as $-4.10, rather than the more obvious -$4.10. We need to make a small change to the method to force the negative sign to appear before the $ sign. After the $ sign, the absolute value of the amount needs to be printed.

```
printOn: aWindow
    "I print myself in the form '$4322.51' or  '-$4322.51'."
    self dollars < 0 ifTrue: [aWindow nextPut: $-].
    aWindow nextPut: $$.
    self dollars abs printOn: aWindow.
    aWindow nextPut: $..
    self cents <= 9 ifTrue: [aWindow nextPut: $0].
    self cents printOn: aWindow.
```

Now let's consider introducing a method for adding two money objects. An incorrect but very simple solution is shown below:

```
arithmetic

+ aMoney
    ^Money
        dollars: self dollars + aMoney dollars
        cents: self cents + aMoney cents
```

One problem is that parameter aMoney might not be a money object. We could change the name of the parameter and add an explicit test to get the following:

```
+ anObject
    (anObject isKindOf: Money)
        ifTrue: [
            ^Money
                dollars: self dollars + aMoney dollars
                cents: self cents + aMoney cents]
        ifFalse: [^self error: 'illegal money']
```

Of course, if the parameter is not a money object, the error message that we generate—'illegal money'—is not that different from the error message that would result otherwise ('dollars not understood'). An alternative is to avoid the explicit test but to document that the test is not performed, as follows:

```
+ aMoney
    "Assumes a money object as a parameter."
    ^Money
        dollars: self dollars + aMoney dollars
        cents: self cents + aMoney cents
```

This way, a user does not have to read the actual code to determine whether an integer, for example, might be a suitable parameter (it isn't).

But there is an even more important problem with this implementation. When two money objects that print as $2.55 are added together, we don't get $5.10.

Instead, we get $4.110 (four dollars and one hundred and ten cents). Should we fix the method as follows?

```
+ aMoney
    "Assumes a money object as a parameter."
    | totalCents |
    totalCents := self cents + aMoney cents.
    totalCents >= 100
        ifTrue: [
            ^Money
                dollars: self dollars + aMoney dollars + 1
                cents: totalCents - 100
        ifFalse: [
            ^Money
                dollars: self dollars + aMoney dollars
                cents: totalCents]
```

A little thought should convince you that it is not a good idea. First of all, it is too complicated compared to the original method. Second, we are also going to get similar problems when we subtract one money object from another or multiply a money object by a number. For example, $2.50 - $1.90 should not give $1.-40 (one dollar and minus forty cents), nor should $2.50 * 4 gives $8.200 (eight dollars and two hundred cents). A better solution is to make the class method for creating dollar instances more general; i.e., to extend it to permit the following:

```
Money dollars: 3 cents: -10 ⇒ $2.90
Money dollars: -3 cents: 10 ⇒ -$2.90
Money dollars: 3 cents: 110 ⇒ $4.10
Money dollars: 3 cents: -110 ⇒ $1.90
```

The easiest solution is to convert everything to cents and then convert it back to dollars and cents. In the above case, that would give us

```
3*100 + -10 = 290 cents ⇒ $2.90
-3*100 + 10 = -290 cents ⇒ -$2.90
3*100 + 110 = 410 cents ⇒ $4.10
3*100 + -110 = 190 cents ⇒ $1.90
```

To extract the number of dollars and cents from 290 cents, for example, we need to divide the total by 100 (with truncation) to get the dollar amount and also determine the remainder to get the number of cents. The operators for doing this are variants of the divide operator, either // or \\. We investigated these operators in Chapter 2, but you probably won't remember which is which. The best approach is to try both operators on a number that is illustrative.

```
290 // 100 ⇒ 2
290 \\ 100 ⇒ 90
```

Does it work for negative amounts?

-290 // 100 ⇒ -3	(we would have liked to obtain -2)
-290 \\ 100 ⇒ 10	(we would have liked to obtain 90)

Taking this little quirk with negative values into account when we write the method, we might get the following:

```
dollars: anInteger cents: anotherInteger
    I totalCents neededDollars neededCents I
    totalCents := anInteger * 100 + anotherInteger.
    totalCents >= 0
        ifTrue: [
            neededDollars := totalCents // 100.
            neededCents := totalCents \\ 100]
        ifFalse: [
            neededDollars := (totalCents negated // 100) negated.
            neededCents := totalCents negated \\ 100]
    ^self new
        dollars: neededDollars;
        cents: neededCents
```

We can develop a method that is slightly shorter (and therefore nicer) if we compute the amounts needed from the absolute value of the total cents. The number of dollars needed can be negated later if the total number of cents was negative. The resulting method is shown below:

```
dollars: anInteger cents: anotherInteger
    I totalCents neededDollars neededCents I
    totalCents := anInteger * 100 + anotherInteger.
    neededDollars := totalCents abs // 100.
    neededCents := totalCents abs \\ 100.
    totalCents < 0 ifTrue: [neededDollars := neededDollars negated].
    ^self new
        dollars: neededDollars;
        cents: neededCents
```

This solution suggests a much simpler representation for money objects in general. It appears that there is no need to keep two parts, one for dollars and another for cents. It is sufficient to keep just the total number of cents. If some user asks for the number of dollars or the number of cents, we can simply compute it from the total number of cents.

Let's go back and change things completely. (Remember, experts make substantial changes all the time. It indicates a willingness to simplify and improve—attributes that should be commended.) While we are at it, we should also include a few example methods for testing purposes. But wait, there may be a problem! What will happen if we change the existing definition

| class | Money |
| instance variables | dollars cents |

to the following?

| class | Money |
| instance variables | totalCents |

Will there be a problem with those methods that refer to "dollars" and "cents"? Let's try it.

As it turns out, error messages are generated in the transcript for each method that refers to the deleted instance variables "dollars" and "cents" (see Figure 5.23). This clutters up the transcript but it doesn't cause any serious problems. Of course, before we can use the new version of this class, we will have to change all the methods one by one.

A better way to proceed that avoids generating error messages in the transcript is to temporarily change the class definition so that it refers to both the old part names and the new, as in the following:

| class | Money |
| instance variables | dollars cents totalCents |

Now we can take advantage of the browser to first locate all the methods that reference "dollars" and change them. We do this by clicking on the name "dollars" in the parts name pane (the pane below the instance and class switches). The method list pane then enumerates all the methods (and only those methods) that refer to part name "dollars". In our case, there are only two: **dollars** and **dollars:**, as shown in Figure 5.24.

We can then select each method, one by one, and change it. Method **dollars** could be changed as follows:

```
dollars
    | amount |
    amount := totalCents abs // 100.
    totalCents < 0 ifTrue: [^amount negated] ifFalse: [^amount]
```

Method **dollars:** is more of a problem. Since "dollars" will no longer be an instance variable, there will be no need to set it. Instead, we'll need a method that plays the same role for the new instance variable "totalCents"; for example,

```
totalCents: anInteger
    totalCents := anInteger
```

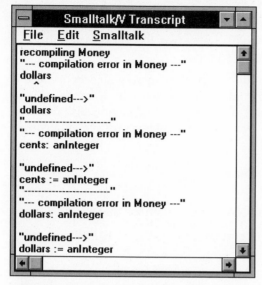

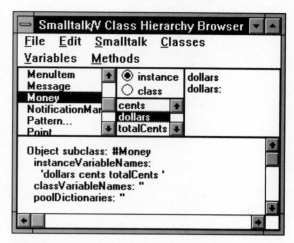

Figure 5.23 Transcript error messages that result from removing instance variables in a class definition.

Figure 5.24 Determining which instance methods refer to part name "dollars".

So our best bet is to delete method **dollars**: entirely by clicking on **Remove** in the **Methods** menu. If we now click on the name "dollars" again in the parts name pane, we get an updated view of the methods that reference this part. As we can see from Figure 5.25, there are no more references to this name.

We can repeat the process with part name "cents" to find that only methods **cents** and **cents**: refer to this instance variable. Method **cents** should be changed to the following; method **cents**: should be deleted.

```
cents
    ^totalCents abs \\ 100
```

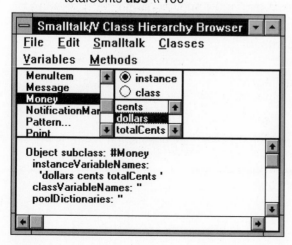

Figure 5.25 A new view of the instance methods referring to part name "dollars".

We can now remove the names "dollars" and "cents" from the definition of the class and save it. No error messages will appear in the transcript, since no methods refer to the part names that were removed.

We'll need to revise the class method for constructing money objects because it needs to store the amount provided in "totalCents" rather than in "dollars" and "cents". The revised method is substantially simpler than the version that had to take into account the possibility that the parameters could be positive or negative, greater or less than 100 (even for cents).

> **dollars**: anInteger **cents**: anotherInteger
> ^self **new totalCents**: anInteger * 100 + anotherInteger

While we're at it, we might want to consider minor variations that exclude one of the two keywords; namely,

> **dollars**: anInteger
> ^self **dollars**: anInteger **cents**: 0

> **cents**: anInteger
> ^self **dollars**: 0 **cents**: anInteger

With the addition of a few example methods that use these new instance creation methods, our new class might appear as follows:

class	Money
instance variables	totalCents

class methods

class initialization

instance creation

dollars: anInteger **cents**: anotherInteger
    ^self **new totalCents**: anInteger * 100 + anotherInteger

dollars: anInteger
    ^self **dollars**: anInteger **cents**: 0

cents: anInteger
    ^self **dollars**: 0 **cents**: anInteger

examples

example1
    "An example that compares two equal money objects; i.e., returns true."
    | money1 money2 |
    money1 := Money **dollars**: 100 **cents**: 23.
    money2 := Money **cents**: 10023.
    ^money1 = money2
    "Money example1"

example2
"An example that returns the number of dollars in 923 cents."
| money1 |
money1 := Money **cents**: 923.
^money1 **dollars**
"Money example2"

example3
"An example that returns the number of cents in 923 cents (after the dollars are removed)."
| money1 |
money1 := Money **cents**: 923.
^money1 **cents**
"Money example3"

instance methods

accessing and modifying

totalCents
^totalCents

totalCents: anInteger
totalCents := anInteger

dollars
| amount |
amount := self **totalCents abs** // 100.
self **totalCents** < 0 **ifTrue**: [^amount **negated**] **ifFalse**: [^amount]

cents
^self **totalCents abs** \\ 100

comparing

= anObject
(anObject **isKindOf**: Money)
    ifTrue: [^self **totalCents** = anObject **totalCents**]
    ifFalse: [^false]

arithmetic

+ anObject
(anObject **isKindOf**: Money)
    ifTrue: [^Money **cents**: self **totalCents** + anObject **totalCents**]
    ifFalse: [^self **error**: 'illegal money']

- anObject
(anObject **isKindOf**: Money)
    ifTrue: [^Money **cents**: self **totalCents** - anObject **totalCents**]
    ifFalse: [^self **error**: 'illegal money']

printing

printOn: aWindow
    "I print myself in the form '$4322.51' or '-$4322.51'."
    self **dollars** < 0 **ifTrue:** [aWindow **nextPut:** $-].
    aWindow **nextPut:** $$.
    self **dollars abs printOn:** aWindow.
    aWindow **nextPut:** $..
    self **cents** <= 9 **ifTrue:** [aWindow **nextPut:** $0].
    self **cents printOn:** aWindow.

There is still the * and / methods to do but, we'll leave those for the exercise.

5.4   Using a Debugger for Understanding Variables in Depth

To properly understand how variables and methods are related, we need to be able to look at the variables and their bindings in the methods during execution. If we could "look for ourselves," we wouldn't have to rely on an outside explanation as to why something does or does not work. We would probably be able to discover the explanation ourselves. A **debugger** is a tool provided especially for this purpose.

A debugger can be invoked in one of two ways:

- By clicking on **Debug** in an error window
- By executing "self **halt**".

Both approaches will be illustrated in this section.

5.4.1 The Mechanics of Using the Debugger

We argued before that it would be easier to understand how execution actually works if we could see it happening in slow motion. The debugger permits us to **single-step** the execution; i.e., to execute one message at a time and see the consequences. This is extremely useful, particularly when we don't get the answer we expect. It is also useful if we want to discover the execution order. To gain some experience with the debugger, let's single-step through **example1** of our Money class (shown below to refresh your memory).

example1
    "An example that compares two equal money objects; i.e., returns true."
    | money1 money2 |
    money1 := Money **dollars:** 100 **cents:** 23.
    money2 := Money **cents:** 10023.
    ^money1 = money2
    "Money example1"

Let's start by adding "self **halt**" to **example1**, in front of the assignments to the variables (as shown in Figure 5.26). Next, let's execute "Money **example1**" by highlighting it and clicking on **Show It** in the **Smalltalk** menu.

A walkback window appears, as shown in Figure 5.27. The message in the title bar indicates that **halt** has been encountered—something that we deliberately caused. Simply click on **Debug** in the **Walkback** menu to get the debugger to appear, as shown in Figure 5.28. The alternative, clicking on **Resume**, allows the halt to be ignored and execution to continue.

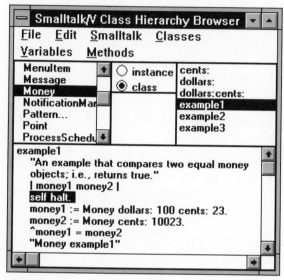

Figure 5.26 Adding "self **halt**" to class method **example1**.

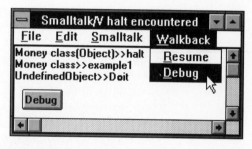

Figure 5.27 Clicking on **Debug** in the walkback window.

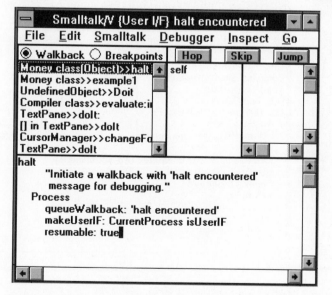

Figure 5.28 The debugger after clicking on **Debug** in the walkback window.

Note that the debugger appears with "Money class(Object)>>halt" selected in the top left pane. The bottom pane displays the method that implements the **halt** message. This will not make any sense until you realize that it deals with instructions for creating the original walkback window. On the other hand, there is an entry immediately below this one that might make sense; namely, the entry "Money class>>example1". If we click on this entry in the pane, the bottom pane displays our **example1** method as shown in Figure 5.29. As you can see, the expression "self **halt**" is highlighted, indicating that we are currently in the process of executing this expression.

By clicking on the **Skip** switch (as shown in Figure 5.29), the **halt** message completes and the next expression to be executed; i.e., "Money **money**: 100 **cents**: 23", is subsequently highlighted (see Figure 5.30).

Clicking again on **Skip** allows execution to proceed to the next message; i.e., "Money **cents**: 10023", which is highlighted, as shown in Figure 5.31.

By now, you should realize that further clicking on **Skip** will cause this highlighted expression, "Money **cents**: 10023", to execute. However, there are other things that we can look at in this browser before executing further. For example, we can look at the receiver "self" by clicking on it in **the part names pane**. However, you should make a habit of predicting what you will see before you actually look. If you study Figure 5.31 once again, you should be able to determine that "self" is the receiver of the **example1** message and you should recall that this message was sent to the Money class. Once you have decided that "self" should be class Money, click on it to verify your prediction. The result is shown in Figure 5.32.

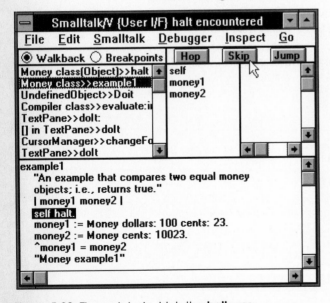

Figure 5.29 The point at which the **halt** was encountered.

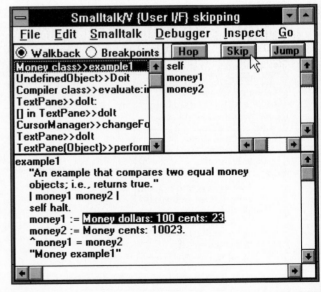

Figure 5.30 Skipping over "self **halt**".

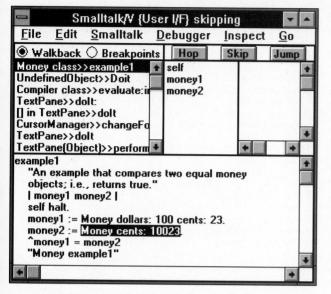

Figure 5.31 Before executing "Money **cents**: 10023".

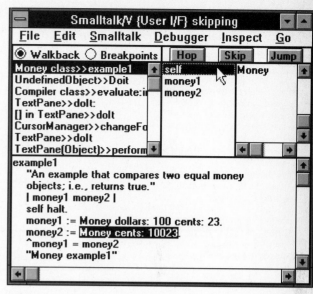

Figure 5.32 Determining the receiver for this method.

In addition to looking at the receiver, we can also look at the local variables in this method; namely, "money1" and "money2". Once again, before looking at the results by clicking on the corresponding names in the parts name pane (as shown in Figures 5.33 and 5.34), guess what they should be. It should be obvious, but be careful! The first assignment has already been executed, since the debugger is about to execute the expression that follows it; namely, "Money **cents**: 10023". So "money1" should be "$100.23". On the other hand, since the current expression has not yet been executed, the assignment to "money2" has not yet been made. Remember: Everything to the right of the assignment must be evaluated before the variable on the left is bound to the result. So "money2" must not yet have a value; i.e., it must be nil. Now look at Figures 5.33 and 5.34 to see if this is the case.

Before we proceed any further, let's quickly review what has been happening. First, expression "self **halt**" was highlighted. We clicked on **Skip**, which caused the debugger to execute the expression and then highlight the expression that follows; i.e., "Money **dollars**: 100 **cents**: 23". By clicking on **Skip** once again, the debugger executed this highlighted expression and proceeded to highlight the next expression, "Money **cents**: 10023". If we clicked on **Skip** one more time, we would expect this expression too to be evaluated and execution to proceed to the next message; namely, "money1 = money2".

Although we might not have noticed it, an important observation can be made.

The debugger never highlights an actual assignment.

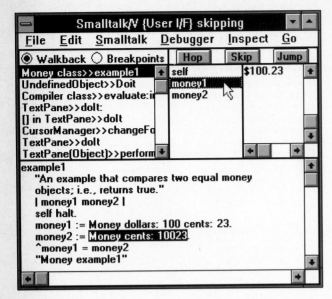

Figure 5.33 Determining what "money1" is bound to.

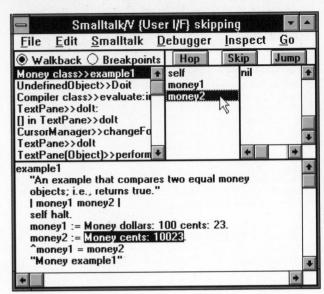

Figure 5.34 Determining what "money2" is bound to.

The debugger highlights only expressions that contain messages. Recall that ":=" is not a message—it is a special operator for binding objects to variables. Of course, the *assignments are executed* because the variables actually get bound (as we saw in Figures 5.33 and 5.34). When an expression is evaluated, the debugger must also evaluate those assignments that immediately follow the evaluated expression, until the next expression containing an actual message is encountered. For example, if we were to click on **Skip** in the debugger of Figure 5.34, we would find the debugger actually performing a three-step sequence:

- Evaluating the expression "Money **cents**: 10023"
- Evaluating the assignment "money2 := the last computed expression"
- Highlighting the next expression "money1 = money2" since it contains the message "= money2" being sent to "money1"

Knowing that assignments are never highlighted is important to understanding how the debugger works.

Now let's explore more interesting aspects of the debugger. Rather than click on **Skip**, as we have been doing so far, let's click on **Hop**. The debugger of Figure 5.34 changes to that of Figure 5.35.

The debugger has reached class method **cents**: in class Money. Consequently, we can deduce that "self" must be the class Money. So message "**dollars**: 0 **cents**: anotherInteger" is about to be sent to the class. Although we haven't shown it, if we click on "anotherInteger", we will see that it is bound to 10023. Let's click on **Hop** one more time. The result is shown in Figure 5.36.

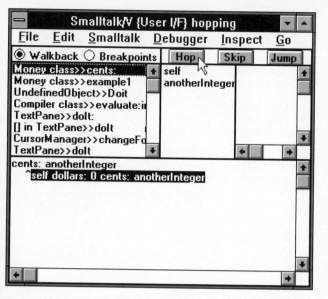

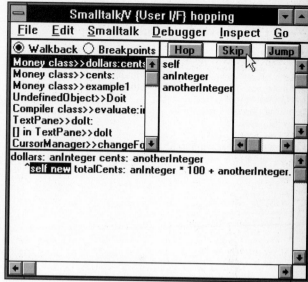

Figure 5.35 After clicking on **Hop** (instead of **Skip**) to reach class method **cents:**.

Figure 5.36 After clicking on **Hop** again to see the consequences of sending message "**dollars:** 0 **cents:** anotherInteger" to "self".

The debugger has now reached class method **dollars:cents:** in class Money and "self **new**" is about to be executed. Since "self" is class Money, we are, in effect, about to execute the equivalent of "Money **new**" to get back an uninitialized instance. Since we have now had experience with both **Skip** and **Hop**, we should be able to predict what will happen in either case. Let's consider the possibilities. If we click on **Skip**, we will expect the next message—in this case, "self **new**"—to be evaluated and the subsequent message to be highlighted; i.e., "anInteger * 100". On the other hand, if we click on **Hop**, we will expect to reach the first expression inside class method **new** itself. This time, let's click on **Skip** instead of **Hop** to get to the next expression, as shown in Figure 5.37.

Although we didn't bother doing it, if we had clicked on "anInteger", we would have found it to be 0. Further clicking on **Skip** should cause the expression "anInteger * 100" to be executed (presumably, the result is 0) and the next expression, which happens to be "anInteger * 100 + anotherInteger", is highlighted as shown in Figure 5.38.

So far, we've led you to believe that the debugger always highlights the very next expression to be evaluated. This is correct. However, you might be confused in this situation, because the highlighted expression, "anInteger * 100 + anotherInteger" contains two operators, "*" and "+". You have to remember that an expression consists of a receiver, a selector, and one or more parameters. If the highlighted portion is one expression (rather than two, for example), the receiver must be "anInteger * 100", the selector must be "+", and the parameter must be

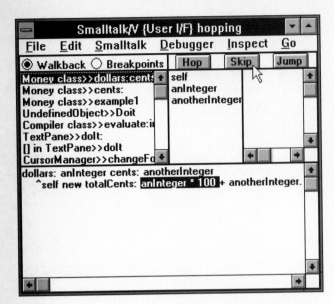

Figure 5.37 After clicking on **Skip** to cause "self **new**" to be executed.

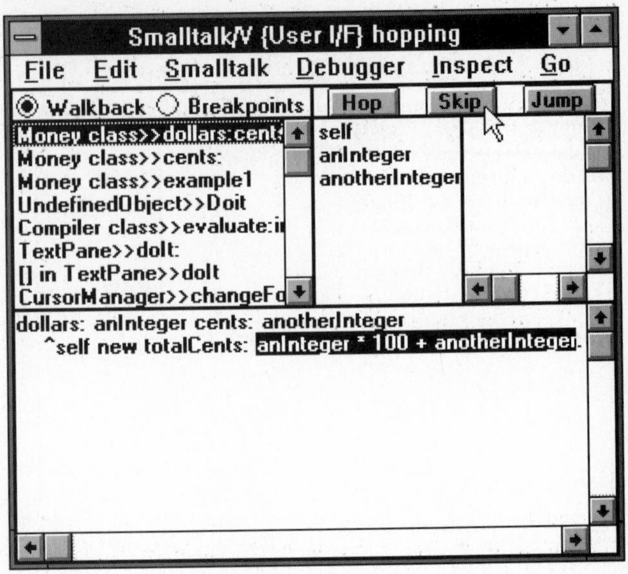

Figure 5.38 After clicking on **Skip** to cause "anInteger * 100" to be executed.

"anotherInteger". In other words, the expression to be evaluated next involves selector "+", not selector "*". Of course, the expression involving selector "*" ("anInteger * 100"), has already been evaluated in the previous step.

If we click on **Skip** one more time, the expression with selector "+" is evaluated and the next message to be evaluated—the message with selector "**totalCents:**"— is highlighted, as shown in Figure 5.39.

Because the debugger always highlights the very next expression to execute, we should be able to tell from the highlighted expression alone that the receiver is "self **new**", the selector is "**totalCents:**", and the parameter is "anInteger * 100 + anotherInteger". It is important to be able to determine what is to execute next in order to be able to predict what will happen. If we now click on **Hop**, we would expect to reach the method with selector "**totalCents:**", as shown in Figure 5.40.

Since method **totalCents:** has no expressions containing messages to be executed—only assignments, execution proceeds all the way to the end. The end of the method is highlighted to indicate that nothing remains to be executed. This is the first time we've reached the end of a method in the debugger. There are several interesting aspects to investigate. First of all, the top left pane contains the following entries:

Money>>totalCents:
Money class>>dollars:cents:
Money class>>cents:
Money class>>example1
UndefinedObject>>Doit

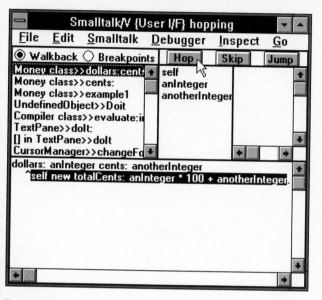

Figure 5.39 After clicking on **Skip** , which executes the expression with selector "+".

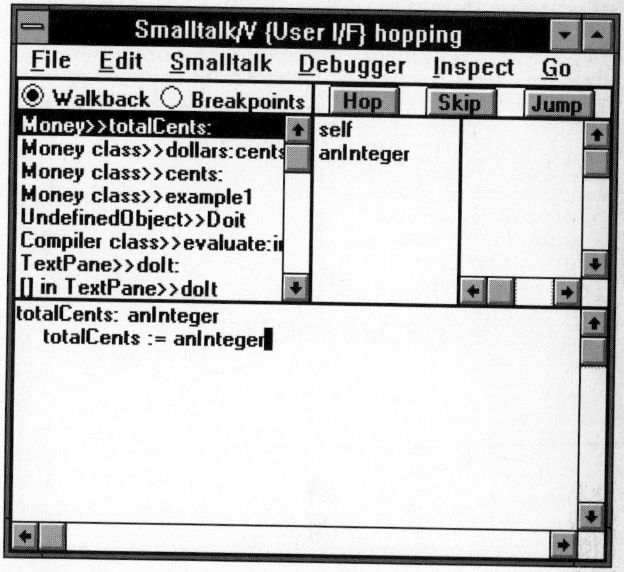

Figure 5.40 After clicking on **Hop** to reach the method with selector "**totalCents:**".

If we successively click on each entry and on "self" to see what it is bound to, we get the results shown in Figures 5.41 through 5.45.

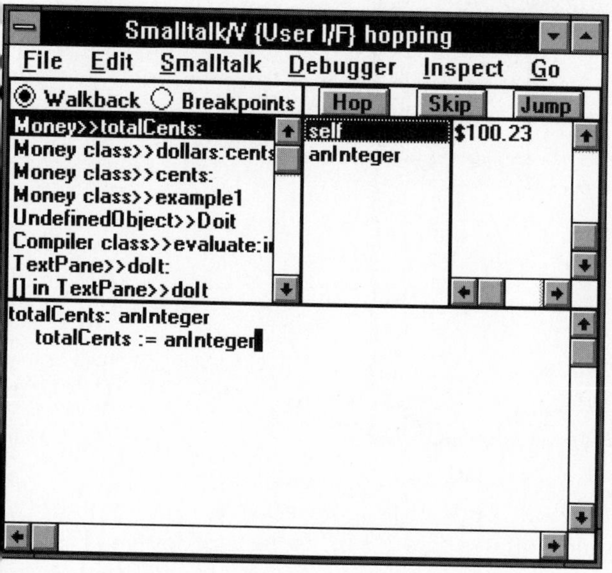

Figure 5.41 Looking at "self" in method "**totalCents:**".

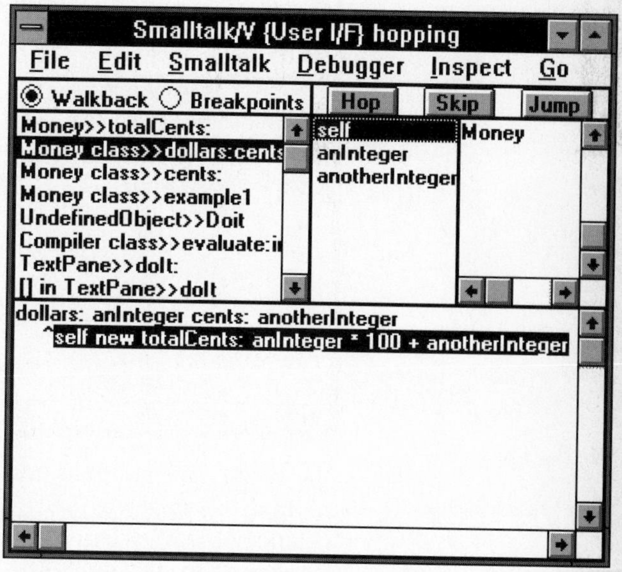

Figure 5.42 Looking at "self" in method "**dollars:cents:**".

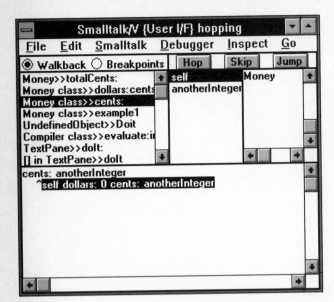

Figure 5.43 Looking at "self" in method "**cents:**".

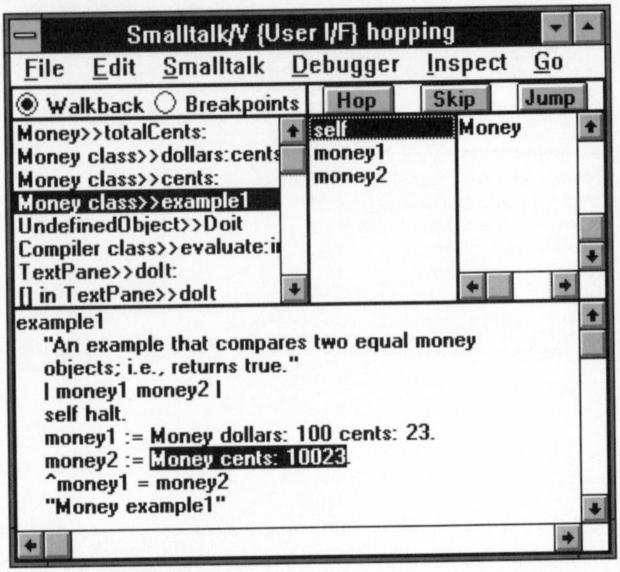

Figure 5.44 Looking at "self" in method "**example1**".

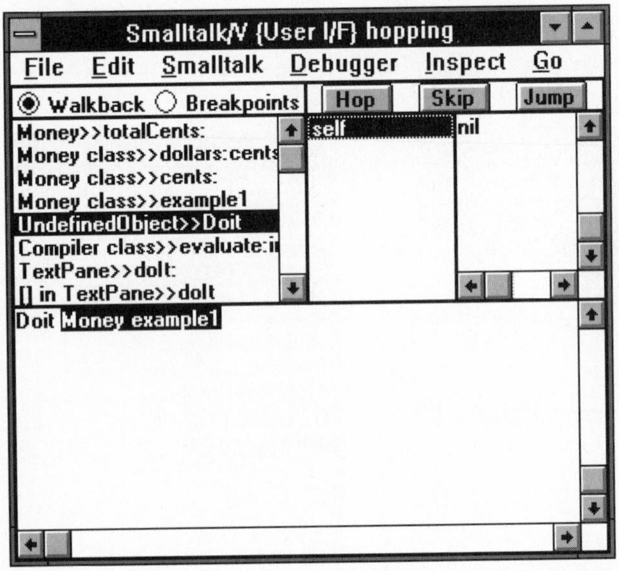

Figure 5.45 Looking at "self" in method "**Doit**".

The results are summarized in Table 5.2. We should have observed that each method has its own "self". In method **totalCents:**, for example, "self" is the instance $100.23, whereas in method **dollars:cents:**, "self" is the class Money. We didn't need to click on "self" to find this out, however—we can tell from the entry in the debugger's left pane. For example, "Money class>>dollars:cents:" indicates that **dollars:cents:** is a "Money class" method, whereas "Money>>totalCents:" indicates that **totalCents:** is a "Money" method; i.e., a method for a Money instance. Now we can tell that **Doit** (the last entry in the table) must be a method for an instance of UndefinedObject. There is only one such instance; namely, nil. If it had been a method for class UndefinedObject, on the other hand, the entry would have been "UndefinedObject class>>Doit".

Table 5.2 Methods in the debugger and their corresponding receivers.

Debugger Selections	self	Type of Object
Money>>totalCents:	$100.23	(an instance)
Money class>>dollars:cents:	Money	(a class)
Money class>>cents:	Money	(a class)
Money class>>example1	Money	(a class)
UndefinedObject>>Doit	nil	(an instance)

Every message to a Smalltalk object results in a computation that determines the answer to be returned to the sender of the message. Even something as simple as sending the message "+ 2" to 1 results in a computation that computes the answer 3 and returns it. The selections in the debugger's left pane provide us with two very important bits of information:

- Which messages are in the process of computing their respective answers
- The order in which these messages were sent

This information is summarized in Table 5.3, which repeats the debugger selections and interprets them in more detail:

Table 5.3 Interpreting the debugger selections.

Debugger Selections	What It Means
Money>>totalCents:	The method below sent a message with selector **totalCents:** to *an instance of Money*.
Money class>>dollars:cents:	The method below sent a message with selector **dollars:cents:** to *class Money*.
Money class>>cents:	The method below sent a message with selector **cents:** to *class Money*.
Money class>>example1	The method below sent a message with selector **example1** to *class Money*.
UndefinedObject>>Doit	Started the entire computation because someone selected an arbitrary Smalltalk expression with the mouse and clicked on **Do It** or **Show It** in the **Smalltalk** menu.

5.4.2 Summarizing Execution State: The Execution Stack History

Clearly, the debugger allows us to look at the entire execution state of the Small-talk environment. The topmost selection is the method currently executing. It will return an answer to the method below it, which, in turn, will return its answer to the method below it, and so on. So the sequence of message sends that lead to the current method are stacked one on top of the other. For this reason, the execution state is often called the **execution stack**. The debugger selections provide us with a simplified view of the contents of the execution stack.

This simplified view of the execution stack is so useful that it is also displayed in walkback windows where it is sometimes called the **walkback** information because it allows a programmer to see how execution would proceed "back" if each method were allowed to continue and return its answer. If we look at the walkback window that caused us to invoke this debugger in the first place (Figure 5.46), we can see the same debugger-like information. But now we should be able to interpret this information. First, the walkback information indicates that message **DoIt** was sent to an instance of UndefinedObject—nil. In turn, this resulted in message **example1** being sent to the class Money. Finally, this resulted in **halt** being sent to class Money.

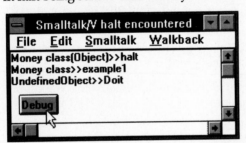

Figure 5.46 Clicking on **Debug** in the walkback window.

The debugger permits us to look at all the important information in the execution stack. But trying to show all this information via diagrams is extremely cumbersome and takes a substantial amount of space. In this and later sections, we will present the information in a more concise manner. One way is to show the **execution stack history**, as follows:

```
Money>>totalCents:
    self ⇒ $100.23  anInteger  ⇒ 10023

    totalCents: anInteger
        totalCents := anInteger□
```

```
Money class>>dollars:cents:
    self ⇒ Money        anInteger ⇒ 0        anotherInteger ⇒ 10023

    dollars: anInteger cents: anotherInteger
        ^self new totalCents: anInteger * 100 + anotherInteger
```

```
Money class>>cents:
    self ⇒ Money        anInteger ⇒ 10023

    cents: anInteger
        ^self dollars: 0 cents: anInteger
```

```
Money class>>example1
    self ⇒ Money        money1 ⇒ $100.23        money2 ⇒ nil

    example1
        "An example that compares two equal money objects; i.e., returns
        true."
        | money1 money2 |
        money1 := Money dollars: 100 cents: 23.
        money2 := Money cents: 10023.
        ^money1 = money2
        "Money example1"
```

```
UndefinedObject>>Doit
    self ⇒ nil

    Doit
        Money example1
```

Notice that the execution stack history shows the message-sending order (the callback information), the expressions involved when a message was sent (the underlined expressions), and the current values of all variables.

Now let's get back to what we were doing initially; tracing the execution of the original message "Money **example1**". First, click on the top entry in the list of debugger selections (the top left pane) so that the debugger is in its original state (see Figure 5.40). Since this method has no **reply** expression, the object returned is "self" by default—in this case, the Money instance that prints as $100.23. Because the debugger is at the end of the **totalCents:** method, clicking on **Skip** (or **Hop**—both have the same effect at the end of a method) will cause this instance to be returned to the sender, the method below it in the list of debugger selections. The debugger subsequently appears as shown in Figure 5.47.

Since the highlighted expression includes the "^", the expression to be executed next is a **reply** expression that must be returning the object just received from the previous message—the Money instance that prints as $100.23. By clicking on **Hop** or **Skip** once again, the Money instance is returned to method **cents:**, as shown in Figure 5.48.

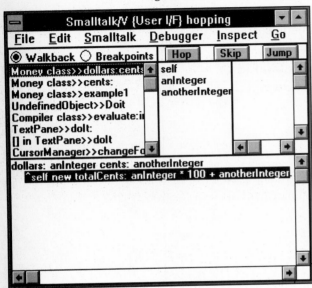

Figure 5.47 After returning from instance method **totalCents:** with the Money instance that prints as $100.23.

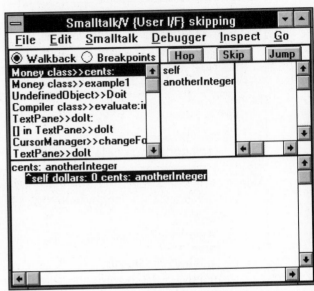

Figure 5.48 After returning from instance method **dollars:cents:** with the Money instance that prints as $100.23.

Once more, the **reply** expression is to be evaluated next. It returns the object obtained from the previous message send, the same money object. One more **Hop** or **Skip** leads to the debugger, as shown in Figure 5.49.

 Now, we are ready to compare the two money objects. By clicking on "money1" and "money2", we can tell that they both print as $100.23 (the latter is shown in Figure 5.49). If we want to find out how the two money objects are actually compared, we would click on **Hop** to trace the messages executed in method "=". We might want to do that, for example, if the result of the comparison turns out to be incorrect. Assuming it will work properly, we might as well click on **Skip**, which leads to the situation shown in Figure 5.50.

One more click on **Hop** or **Skip** (either one will work because we're at the end of the method) should lead to the browser, as shown in Figure 5.51.

Recall that we started this whole process by selecting "Money **example1**" in the browser and clicking on **Show It** in menu **Smalltalk**. The walkback window appeared because expression "self **halt**" was inserted into method **example1**. Clicking on **Debug** caused the debugger to appear and we used it to trace all the

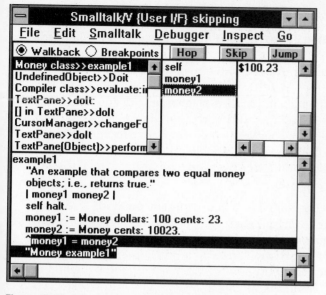

Figure 5.49 After obtaining both money objects.

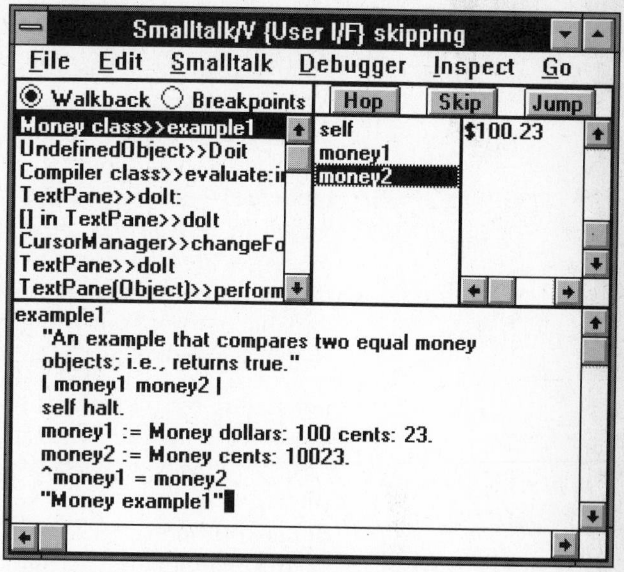

Figure 5.50 After comparing the money objects.

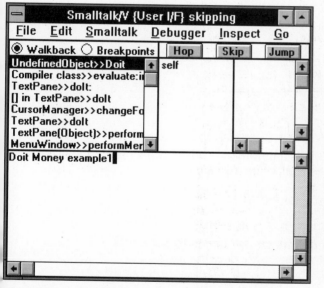

Figure 5.51 After returning from method **example1** with true (presumably).

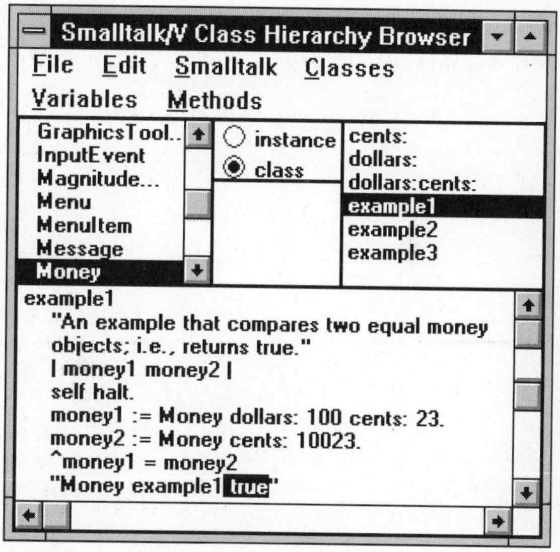

Figure 5.52 The result of executing "Money **example1**".

messages of interest. All we need to do now is to continue the computation as if the debugger had never been used by clicking on **Jump**. The answer "true" will finally be printed after selection "Money **example1**", as shown in Figure 5.52.

5.4.3 Using a Debugger for Understanding the Execution Cycle in Detail

To understand the basic execution cycle, we need to know exactly what happens when a message is sent to an object. For example, is the associated method used directly to compute an answer in response to the message, or is a copy of the method used? Does it matter? Additionally, suppose a message—say, **message1**—is sent to an object, which in turn sends **message2** to another object, which in turn sends **message3**. The methods corresponding to this **chain of messages** are clearly in the middle of computing their respective responses. What if all three methods make use of a temporary variable called "result"? Is this one variable or three? Once again, does it matter? We need to investigate this in detail so that we understand what is going on.

Let's start by investigating what happens when different methods use local variables with the same name—a name such as "result". Let's make a small change to the Money class by introducing an **example4** class method that simply returns a money object, $9.55, constructed from two other money objects, the dollars portion of $9.23 and the cents portion of $3.55. We'll write the method in such a manner that variable "result" is bound to $9.23. Let's also revise class method **dollars:cents:** and instance method **dollars** by changing the name of their local variable to "result". The revised methods are shown below:

```
class                                          Money
instance variables                             totalCents

class methods

class initialization

examples

example4
    "An example that constructs a new money object by extracting the dollars
    and cents parts out of two other money objects."
    | result anotherResult |
    result := Money dollars: 9 cents: 23.
    self halt.
    anotherResult := Money dollars: 3 cents: 55.
    ^Money dollars: result dollars cents: anotherResult cents
    "Money example4"

instance creation

dollars: anInteger cents: anotherInteger
    | result |
    result := self new totalCents: anInteger * 100 + anotherInteger.
    ^result
```

instance methods

accessing and modifying

dollars
>| result |
>result := self **totalCents abs** // 100.
>self **totalCents** < 0 **ifTrue**: [^result **negated**] **ifFalse**: [^result]

Note that method **example4** contains the expression "self **halt**". When we test our **example4** method by executing "Money **example4**", a walkback window should appear. We can use the debugger to look at the execution stack. The execution history that we should see is summarized below:

```
Money class>>example4
    self ⇒ Money        result ⇒ $9.23        anotherResult ⇒ nil

    example4
        "An example that constructs a new money object by extracting the
        dollars and cents parts out of two other money objects."
        | result anotherResult |
        result := Money dollars: 9 cents: 23.
        self halt.
        anotherResult := Money dollars: 3 cents: 55.
        ^Money dollars: result dollars cents: anotherResult cents
        "Money example4"
```

```
UndefinedObject>>Doit
    self ⇒ nil

    Doit
        Money example4
```

So far, "result" has been bound, but not "anotherResult". Let's click on **Skip** to go past the **halt**, click on **Hop** to go into the code for the **dollars:cents:**, and proceed to the point where the return is about to be executed. We should have the following:

```
Money class>>dollars:cents:
    self ⇒ Money   anInteger ⇒ 3   anotherInteger ⇒ 55   result ⇒ $3.55

    dollars: anInteger cents: anotherInteger
        | result |
        result := self new totalCents: anInteger * 100 + anotherInteger.
        ^result
```

```
Money class>>example4
     self ⇒ Money        result ⇒ $9.23        anotherResult ⇒ nil

     example4
          "An example that constructs a new money object by extracting the
          dollars and cents parts out of two other money objects."
          | result anotherResult |
          result := Money dollars: 9 cents: 23.
          self halt.
          anotherResult := Money dollars: 3 cents: 55.
          ^Money dollars: result dollars cents: anotherResult cents
          "Money example4"
```

```
UndefinedObject>>Doit
     self ⇒ nil

     Doit
          Money example4
```

We can see that the "result" variable in method **dollars:cents:** is $3.55, whereas the "result" variable in method **example4** is still $9.23. Since they have different bindings, they must surely be different variables. If this were not the case, a serious problem would arise on returning from the top method because both "result" and "anotherResult" in method **example4** would end up being $3.55— and we know just by looking at the method that "result" should be $9.23. The debugger allows us to verify the following fact:

> *All local variables in methods are local to the methods that contain them.*

So each method has its own copy of the variable. This is extremely important because it allows us to name our variables in a method without having to know what names other methods are using.

We could verify this fact one more time by proceeding further with the debugger. See what happens when "result **dollars**" is executed in **example4**. What are the variables bound to just before execution returns from method **dollars**? By now, you should be able to deduce what you will have to do in the debugger to get to this point. Take a break for a moment and see if you can figure it out. Then read the next paragraph for the solution.

First, select the top method in the debugger and use **Skip** or **Hop** to return to method **example4**. Expression "result **dollars**" is the next one to be executed. Use **Hop** to enter the **dollars** method and then use **Skip** several times in a row until the return expression is the next one to be executed. The execution history should then appear as follows:

```
Money>>dollars
     self ⇒ $9.23          result ⇒ 9

     dollars
          | result |
          result := self totalCents abs // 100.
          self totalCents < 0 ifTrue: [^result negated] ifFalse: [^result]
```

```
Money class>>example4
     self ⇒ Money        result ⇒ $9.23        anotherResult ⇒ $3.55

     example4
          "An example that constructs a new money object by extracting the
          dollars and cents parts out of two other money objects."
          | result anotherResult |
          result := Money dollars: 9 cents: 23.
          self halt.
          anotherResult := Money dollars: 3 cents: 55.
          ^Money dollars: result dollars cents: anotherResult cents
          "Money example4"
```

```
UndefinedObject>>Doit
     self ⇒ nil

     Doit
          Money example4
```

We can see that "result" in method **dollars** is 9, whereas it is $9.23 in method
example4, illustrating once again that variables declared in a method are local to
the method.

> *Parameter variables, too, are local to the method in which they occur.*

We can verify that this also applies to parameters by executing "Money
example1" under the debugger. It would then be straightforward to check that
parameter "anInteger" in method **dollars:cents:** is 0, whereas the corresponding
parameter with name "anInteger" in method **cents:** is 10023.

```
Money>>dollars:cents:
     self ⇒ Money        anInteger ⇒ 0        anotherInteger ⇒ 10023

     dollars: anInteger cents: anotherInteger
          ^self new totalCents: anInteger * 100 + anotherInteger
```

```
Money class>>cents:
     self ⇒ Money        anInteger ⇒ 10023

     cents: anInteger
          ^self dollars: 0 cents: anInteger
```

```
Money class>>example1
    self ⇒ Money        money1 ⇒ $9.23        money2 ⇒ nil

    example1
        "An example that compares two equal money objects; i.e., returns
        true."
        | money1 money2 |
        money1 := Money dollars: 100 cents: 23.
        money2 := Money cents: 10023.
        ^money1 = money2
        "Money example1"
```

```
UndefinedObject>>Doit
    self ⇒ nil

    Doit
        Money example1
```

5.4.4 Understanding Multiple Occurrences of a Method in the Same Execution Stack

So far, we haven't encountered a situation in which the same method occurs more than once in the execution stack. How could that even happen? We can illustrate it by designing a method—say, called **superiors**—that returns a count of the number of superclasses above the receiver. Assuming the hierarchy of Figure 5.53,

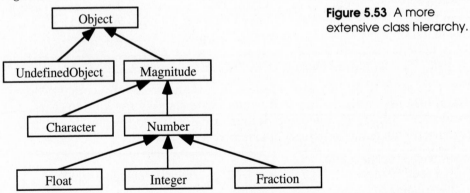

Figure 5.53 A more extensive class hierarchy.

we would like to be able to send the following messages and get the answers shown:

```
Object superiors ⇒ 0
UndefinedObject superiors ⇒ 1
Magnitude superiors ⇒ 1
Character superiors ⇒ 2
Integer superiors ⇒ 3
```

To design a suitable method, we'll need a technique that we all use, called **passing the buck**. For example, if Steve steps out of the bathtub and needs a towel, he might ask his dad Robert to get one. Robert, similarly, might ask his wife Diane, who might actually find one. Diane would give it to Robert, who in turn would give it to Steve, as shown in Figure 5.54.

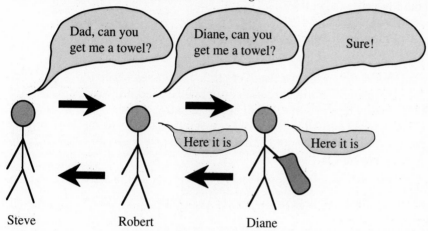

Figure 5.54 Passing the buck.

In each case, the response is similar and of the same form:

    if I know where the towel is and it's easy to get
        then I'll get it and give it to whoever asked me
        otherwise, I'll pass the buck and ask someone else

We're now ready to write method **superiors**. The above form, with minor modifications, can be used as follows:

    if I'm class Object
        then I'll reply with 0
        otherwise,
            I'll ask my superclass what his count is and
            I'll reply with 1 more than his answer.

In Smalltalk, the method might appear as follows:

```
superiors
    self = Object
        ifTrue: [^0]
        ifFalse: [^self superclass superiors + 1]
```

Unfortunately, the method as written, though correct, is a little too simple. With the addition of one variable, however, we will be able to illustrate all the important points. The revised method (which doesn't really need this extra variable) uses an **ifTrue:ifFalse**: expression to determine which integer to assign to count.

```
superiors
    | count |
    count := self = Object
        ifTrue: [0]
        ifFalse: [self superclass superiors + 1].
    ^count
```

Since this method is intended for receivers that are classes, we'll add it as a class method (see Figure 5.55) rather than as an instance method. More specifically, we'll add it to class Object so that it will apply to many classes. Since Magnitude, for example, inherits from Object, it will be possible to send this message to both Magnitude and Object. Of course, the receiver represented by "self" in the method will be different in each case.

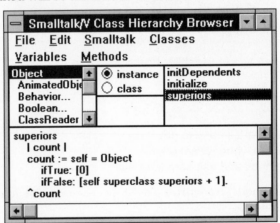

Figure 5.55 The superiors method.

Now let's trace the execution of expression "Character **superiors**". We know from the diagram of Figure 5.53 that the answer should be 2. But it might be difficult to work out the details in our heads. Conceptually, the execution sequence is the following:

Character superiors
   Since I'm not Object, I'll ask Magnitude.

> **Magnitude superiors**
>   Since I'm not Object, I'll ask Object.
>
> > **Object superiors**
> >   Since I'm Object, I'll reply with 0.
>
>   Since Object replied with 0, I (Magnitude) will add 1 and reply with 1.

   Since Magnitude replied with 1, I (Character) will add 1, and reply with 2.

Now let's use the debugger to look at the execution more closely. In particular, let's execute "self **halt**. Character **superiors**" and trace the execution using **Skip** and **Hop** until we get to the point where "self" is bound to "Object"; i.e., use **Hop** whenever expression "self **superclass superiors**" is about to be evaluated and **Skip** everywhere else. The execution stack history will appear as follows:

```
Object class>>superiors
    self ⇒ Object          count ⇒ 0

    superiors
        | count |
        count := self = Object
            ifTrue: [0]
            ifFalse: [self superclass superiors + 1].
        ^count
```

```
Magnitude class>>superiors
    self ⇒ Magnitude          count ⇒ nil

    superiors
        | count |
        count := self = Object
            ifTrue: [0]
            ifFalse: [self superclass superiors + 1].
        ^count
```

```
Character class>>superiors
    self ⇒ Character          count ⇒ nil

    superiors
        | count |
        count := self = Object
            ifTrue: [0]
            ifFalse: [self superclass superiors + 1].
        ^count
```

```
UndefinedObject>>Doit
    self ⇒ nil
    Doit
        self halt. Character superiors
```

As you can see, the same method appears to be used three times. However, the receiver is different in each case. The top method is also at a different execution point compared to the other two and it's version of variable "count" is 0, whereas the others are nil. Clearly, we can't be executing the same method in each case. Rather, each method must be a variation of the original with its own unique variables "self" and "count" and its own execution point. The only rational explanation is that each method is a copy of the method originally defined in the browser. (Technically, what little more there is to it is a subject for compiler writers—those people interested in the details required to translate a Smalltalk method into machine language and in how execution works at the detailed machine language level. Such issues are beyond the scope of this book.)

We can summarize our findings by making the following observation:

> *Methods are never executed directly. Only copies of methods are executed and the variables in each copy are local to the copy.*

Having seen an example of a method for which multiple copies can be used simultaneously, we might wonder whether this is a normal phenomenon or something that occurs very rarely. As it turns out, it is quite normal. Passing the buck is known under various names: **top-down refinement, hierarchical decomposition**, and **recursion** (which is a special case in which the receiver doesn't change). To get a bit more experience with the concept, let's consider an extension of class Money so that large amounts print with commas between each third digit; e.g., $1,232,544.99 rather than just simply $1232544.99. Recall the **printOn:** method as it currently exists.

```
printOn: aWindow
    "I print myself in the form '$4322.51' or '-$4322.51'."
    self dollars < 0 ifTrue: [aWindow nextPut: $-].
    aWindow nextPut: $$.
    self dollars abs printOn: aWindow.
    aWindow nextPut: $..
    self cents <= 9 ifTrue: [aWindow nextPut: $0].
    self cents printOn: aWindow.
```

The problem with the above method is the line

> **self dollars abs printOn:** aWindow.

which prints the dollar amount without commas. Adding commas is not easy, because the number of commas required depends on the dollar amount; e.g., $3.44 requires no commas, $2,333.44 requires one, $1,222,333.44 requires two, and so on. Moreover, the commas have to go between the digits and not every digit at that. This looks like a difficult problem. But, of course, the whole idea about passing the buck is to avoid doing the difficult problems yourself. We can simply have some other method do all the work. Naturally, we do have to know what information this other method will need—in this case, the dollar amount to be printed with commas and the window it should be printed on. We could change the problem line to the following:

> self **print**: self **dollars abs on**: aWindow.

The new method is needed only to make the **printOn**: method work. By contrast with method **printOn**: which is called a **public** method because we expect anyone to use it, method **print:on**: is a **private** method, since it is provided for use only by method **printOn**:. We might begin the method as follows:

```
print: positiveInteger on: aWindow
    "A private method needed by printOn:."
    "Too hard to do without some thinking"
```

How do we proceed when we don't know how to proceed? The answer is simple. Try to determine whether there are some cases that are easy. For example, when are there no commas to be printed? Clearly, when there are three digits or less. This suggests the following:

```
print: positiveInteger on: aWindow
    "A private method needed by printOn:."
    positiveInteger <= 999
        ifTrue: [
            "This is the simple case."
            positiveInteger printOn: aWindow]
        ifFalse: [
            "This is the more complicated case."
            "Too hard to do without some thinking"]
```

The complicated case must consist of at least four digits; e.g., a positive integer such as

> 123456789

which can be broken into two pieces

123456789 \\ 1000 is 789	rightmost three digits
123456789 // 1000 is 123456	other digits after 789 is removed

If we could pass 123456 to some other method to do the work; i.e., pass the buck again, all we would have to do after the other method has done its job is print the 789 with a comma in front. How do we pass the buck again? Simply send a message such as "**print**: otherDigits **on**: aWindow" to self again. The method might appear as follows:

```
print: positiveInteger on: aWindow
    "A private method needed by printOn:."
    | rightmostThreeDigits otherDigits |
    positiveInteger <= 999
        ifTrue: [
            "This is the simple case."
            positiveInteger printOn: aWindow]
        ifFalse: [
            "This is the more complicated case."
            rightmostThreeDigits := positiveInteger \\ 1000. "the remainder"
            otherDigits := positiveInteger // 1000. "dividing with truncation"
            self print: otherDigits on: aWindow. "pass the buck again"
            aWindow nextPut: $,.
            rightmostThreeDigits printOn: aWindow]
```

As it is, this method looks complicated! Can it be simplified? What would have happened, for example, if we had computed the two local variables even for the simple case; i.e., if we had taken advantage of the fact that

789 \\ 1000 is 789	rightmost three digits
789 // 1000 is 0	other digits after 789 is removed

In this special case, the positive integer and the rightmost three digits are equal. So we can replace positiveInteger in the simple case by rightmostThreeDigits. The method would then appear as follows:

```
print: positiveInteger on: aWindow
    "A private method needed by printOn:."
    | rightmostThreeDigits otherDigits |
    rightmostThreeDigits := positiveInteger \\ 1000. "the remainder"
    otherDigits := positiveInteger // 1000. "dividing with truncation"
    positiveInteger <= 999
        ifTrue: [
            "This is the simple case."
            rightmostThreeDigits printOn: aWindow]
        ifFalse: [
            "This is the more complicated case."
            self print: otherDigits on: aWindow. "pass the buck again"
            aWindow nextPut: $,.
            rightmostThreeDigits printOn: aWindow]
```

But now, both cases end with the same expression which we can remove from the if-expression as follows:

```
print: positiveInteger on: aWindow
    "A private method needed by printOn:."
    | rightmostThreeDigits otherDigits |
    rightmostThreeDigits := positiveInteger \\ 1000. "the remainder"
    otherDigits := positiveInteger // 1000. "dividing with truncation"
    positiveInteger <= 999
        ifTrue: [
            "This is the simple case."]
        ifFalse: [
            "This is the more complicated case."
            self print: otherDigits on: aWindow. "pass the buck again"
            aWindow nextPut: $,].
    rightmostThreeDigits printOn: aWindow
```

The true part doesn't do anything, so we can remove it entirely. But to make the test more understandable, it is better to replace

```
positiveInteger <= 999
    ifFalse: [
        "This is the more complicated case."
        self print: otherDigits on: aWindow. "pass the buck again"
        aWindow nextPut: $,].
```

by

```
positiveInteger > 999
    ifTrue: [
        "This is the more complicated case."
        self print: otherDigits on: aWindow. "pass the buck again"
        aWindow nextPut: $,].
```

The revised method can then be simplified as follows:

```
print: positiveInteger on: aWindow
    "A private method needed by printOn:."
    | rightmostThreeDigits otherDigits |
    rightmostThreeDigits := positiveInteger \\ 1000. "the remainder"
    otherDigits := positiveInteger // 1000. "dividing with truncation"
    positiveInteger > 999
        ifTrue: [
            self print: otherDigits on: aWindow. "pass the buck again"
            aWindow nextPut: $,].
    rightmostThreeDigits printOn: aWindow
```

Before we quit, let's try one final test. Let's print one million dollars.

Money **dollars**: 1000000 $\Rightarrow$ $1,0,0.00

Oops! We clearly made a major mistake. Since rightmostThreeDigits can be any number between 0 and 999, it will print with 1, 2, or 3 digits depending on the value. With fewer than 3 digits, we need to provide leading zeros. Of course, we must also be careful not to provide leading zeros for the leftmost digit. Let's study what we have so far.

```
printOn: aWindow
    "I print myself in the form '$4322.51' or  '-$4322.51'."
    self dollars < 0 ifTrue: [aWindow nextPut: $-].
    aWindow nextPut: $$.
    self print: self dollars abs on: aWindow.
    aWindow nextPut: $..
    self cents <= 9 ifTrue: [aWindow nextPut: $0].
    self cents printOn: aWindow.

print: positiveInteger on: aWindow
    "A private method needed by printOn:."
    | rightmostThreeDigits otherDigits |
    rightmostThreeDigits := positiveInteger \\ 1000. "the remainder"
    otherDigits := positiveInteger // 1000. "dividing with truncation"
    positiveInteger > 999
        ifTrue: [
            self print: otherDigits on: aWindow. "pass the buck again"
            aWindow nextPut: $,].
    rightmostThreeDigits printOn: aWindow
```

We might begin by introducing a method that can print numbers between 0 and 999 with extra zeros, if requested.

```
print: positiveInteger withLeadingZerosOn: aWindow
    "A private method needed (indirectly) by printOn:. It is designed to work
    only with numbers between 0 and 999 and to print enough leading zeros
    to ensure that exactly three digits are printed. The number of zeros
    needed is 0 for a number between 100 and 999, 1 for a number between
    10 and 99, and 2 for a number between 0 and 9."
    positiveInteger < 100 ifTrue: [0 printOn: aWindow].
    positiveInteger < 10 ifTrue: [0 printOn: aWindow].
    positiveInteger printOn: aWindow
```

If the number we wish to print is small, we won't need extra zeros. We need extra zeros only after we print a comma. To take this into account, we probably should revert to an earlier version of our **print:on:** method (which we copied below for convenience).

```
print: positiveInteger on: aWindow
    "A private method needed by printOn:."
    | rightmostThreeDigits otherDigits |
    rightmostThreeDigits := positiveInteger \\ 1000. "the remainder"
    otherDigits := positiveInteger // 1000. "dividing with truncation"
    positiveInteger <= 999
        ifTrue: [
            "This is the simple case."
            rightmostThreeDigits printOn: aWindow]
        ifFalse: [
            "This is the more complicated case."
            self print: otherDigits on: aWindow. "pass the buck again"
            aWindow nextPut: $,.
            rightmostThreeDigits printOn: aWindow]
```

The simple case doesn't need extra zeros—only the more complicated case does. So we simply need to revise the method as follows:

```
print: positiveInteger on: aWindow
    "A private method needed by printOn:."
    | rightmostThreeDigits otherDigits |
    rightmostThreeDigits := positiveInteger \\ 1000. "the remainder"
    otherDigits := positiveInteger // 1000. "dividing with truncation"
    positiveInteger <= 999
        ifTrue: [
            "This is the simple case."
            rightmostThreeDigits printOn: aWindow]
        ifFalse: [
            "This is the more complicated case."
            self print: otherDigits on: aWindow. "pass the buck again"
            aWindow nextPut: $,.
            rightmostThreeDigits
                print: positiveInteger
                withLeadingZerosOn: aWindow]
```

Let's try our million-dollar test one more time. As we can see below, it seems to work. Are we sure?

Money **dollars**: 1000000 $\Rightarrow$ $1,000,000.00

Consider the execution sequence for the following example, which was specifically chosen to make it easy to differentiate between the digits:

Money **dollars**: 1002003 **cents**: 45 $\Rightarrow$ $1,002,003.45

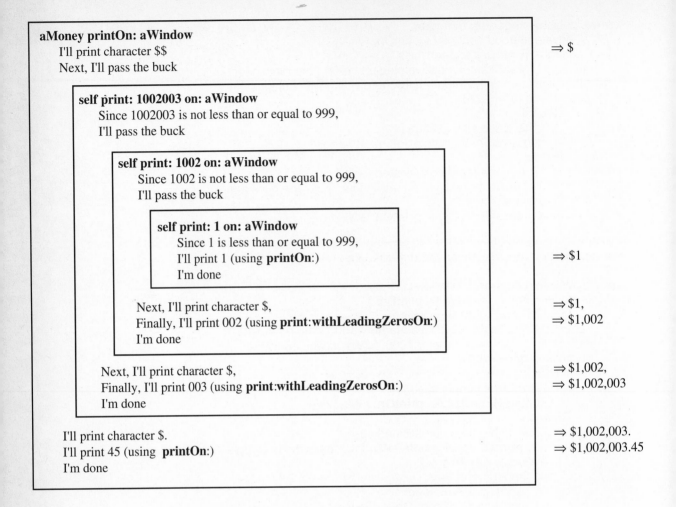

5.5   More on Recursive Techniques

In the previous section, we introduced the concept of passing the buck as a technique for implementing methods that were too complex to implement by themselves. The approach can be summarized as follows:

> when asked to compute something
>> if it's very simple to do
>> then I'll do it myself and return the obvious answer;
>> otherwise,
>>> I'll decompose the request into simpler requests.
>>> Next, I'll ask others to perform the simpler requests and I'll use their answers to figure out the answer to the original request.
>>> Finally, I'll return this answer.

When passing the buck leads to a subcomputation that is identical to the original (although with different data), we are said to be using a **recursive technique**. In this section, we will provide more experience with recursive techniques. More specifically, we will consider a number of simple problems that can be solved recursively. We will leave it to the reader to use the debugger if a better understanding of the execution sequence is needed.

Let's begin with computing the factorial of a number. We know, of course, that this operation can be defined as follows:

n **factorial** = n×n-1×...×3×2×1; 0 **factorial** = 1

Since it applies only to integers, it must be an instance method in Integer.

instance method in class Integer

```
factorial
    self < 0 ifTrue: [self error: 'cannot use negative numbers'].
    self <= 1 ifTrue: [^1].
    ^self * (self - 1) factorial
```

An abbreviated execution sequence for "4 **factorial**" is provided below.

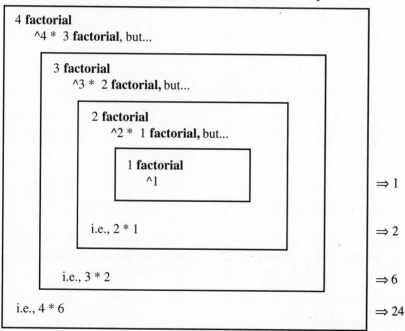

For comparison purposes, two other solutions are also provided below. They are interesting equivalents but they are not quite as elegant as the above. The first one uses control structures that are unnecessarily complex (too deeply nested). The second handles too many special cases unnecessarily.

instance method in class Integer (control structures too complex)

factorial
    self < 0
        ifTrue: [self **error**: 'cannot use negative numbers']
        ifFalse: [
            self <= 1
                ifTrue: [^1]
                ifFalse: [^self * (self - 1) **factorial**]]

instance method in class Integer (too many special cases handled)

factorial
    self < 0 **ifTrue**: [self **error**: 'cannot use negative numbers'].
    self <= 1 **ifTrue**: [^1].
    self = 2 **ifTrue**: [^2].
    self = 3 **ifTrue**: [^6].
    self = 4 **ifTrue**: [^24].
    ^self * (self - 1) **factorial**

Another simple problem is that of reversing a string. Consider adding a method **reverse** that permits the following to execute:

    'hello' **reverse** $\Rightarrow$ 'olleh'
    'erutuf' **reverse** $\Rightarrow$ 'future'
    '' **reverse** $\Rightarrow$ ''

Several solutions are possible. Each solution makes use of concatenation operator ",", and the **copyFrom:to:** operation. Recall that the following are legal:

    'hello' **copyFrom:** 2 **to**: 4 $\Rightarrow$ 'oll'
    'hello' **copyFrom:** 2 **to**: 3 $\Rightarrow$ 'ol'
    'hello' **copyFrom:** 2 **to**: 2 $\Rightarrow$ 'o'
    'hello' **copyFrom:** 2 **to**: 1 $\Rightarrow$ ''

In particular, asking for a copy of size 0 is legal—an empty string is returned.

instance method in class String (focus on rightmost character)

reverse
    "The simple case involves a string of zero or one characters. The more complex case breaks the string into two parts: all characters but the last (which can be reversed recursively) and the last one."
    self **size** <= 1 **ifTrue**: [^self].
    ^(String **with**: self **last**), (self **copyFrom**: 1 **to**: self **size** - 1) **reverse**

instance method in class String (focus on leftmost character)

reverse
    "The simple case involves a string of zero or one characters. The more complex case breaks the string into two parts: the first character and all the other characters (which can be reversed recursively)."
    self **size** <= 1 **ifTrue**: [^self].
    ^(self **copyFrom**: 2 **to**: self **size** - 1) **reverse**, (String **with**: self **first**)

instance method in class String (focus on two halves)

reverse
> "The simple case involves a string of zero or one characters. The more complex case breaks the string into roughly two halves (each piece can be reversed recursively)."
> | midpoint |
> self **size** <= 1 **ifTrue**: [^self].
> midpoint := self **size** // 2.
> "If the size is odd, the left half (from 1 to midpoint) could be shorter than the right half (from midpoint + 1 to the extreme right). Neither half can be empty because midpoint is at least 1 (since the size is at least 2)."
> ^(self **copyFrom**: midpoint + 1 **to**: self **size**) **reverse**,
> (self **copyFrom**: 1 **to**: midpoint) **reverse**

The first two approaches are the simplest. However, the third is more interesting because it passes the buck twice. In that situation, the string self is broken into two halves (roughly)—each is reversed and the order is switched. Even-sized strings such as 'ginger' break into equal-size pieces 'gin' and 'ger', whereas odd-sized strings such as 'great' break into unequal-size pieces 'gr' and 'eat'. Although it is beyond the scope of this book, it turns out that solutions that break problems into equal-sized subproblems are generally preferred over solutions that break them into unequal-sized pieces, because they tend to be more efficient. A sample execution sequence for the last implementation of **reverse** is shown on the next page.

A similar strategy could be used for summing an array. Although we are implementing **sum**, the recursive technique is actually used in private method **sumFrom:to:**. An alternative nonrecursive approach is also presented in Chapter 7.

instance method in class Array

sum
> "Sample use: #(10 20 30 40) sum"
> ^self **sumFrom**: 1 **to**: self **size**

sumFrom: start **to**: end
> | midpoint |
> start > end **ifTrue**: [^0].
> start = end **ifTrue**: [^self **at**: start].
> midpoint := (start + end) // 2. "the midpoint is the average"
> ^(self **sumFrom**: start **to**: midpoint) + (self **sumFrom**: midpoint + 1 **to**: end)

Many problems lend themselves to recursive solutions; e.g., sorting, parsing, problems dealing with trees (ancestry relationships) and lists (natural language processing). Often, recursive solutions develop naturally as a result of attempting to pass the buck.

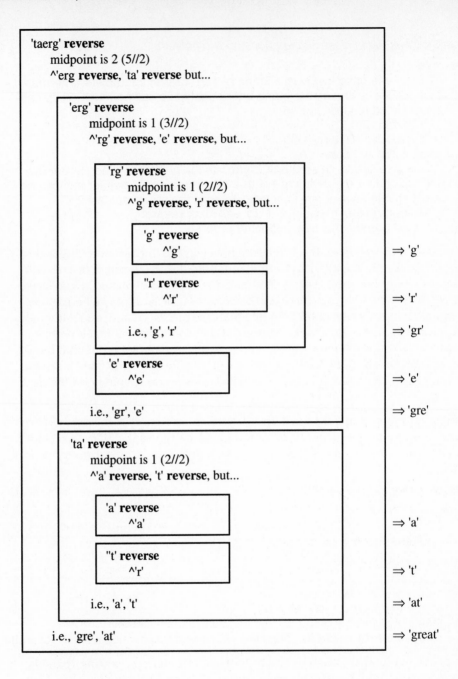

5.6   Summary

This chapter has introduced you to methods and classes in detail, to various types of special variables, and to debuggers. We have

- Investigated a simple graphics problem that required us to add methods to an existing class Pen. The methods made use of pseudo-variable "self", local variables, and method parameters
- Investigated the construction of a simple class Temperature that had special methods for accessing and changing the temperature of its instances, for comparing its instances, and for printing them. Class variables were introduced for keeping track of a default printing scale
- Investigated the construction of another class, Money, that also had special methods for adding, subtracting, comparing, and printing its instances. We saw that revising a class in order to simplify it is a natural thing to do
- Learned how to use the debugger for tracing execution using **Hop** and **Skip**, investigating variable bindings during execution, and inspecting those bindings
- Learned about pseudo-variable "self" which is bound automatically by the system to the receiver of a message
- Learned that temporary variables can be used not only for computing results in workspaces or the transcript but also in methods
- Learned about the distinction between instance variables (also called parts), class variables, and globals
- Learned about pool dictionaries and how they can be created
- Learned the distinction between method parameters and message parameters
- Learned how messages are executed, including how expressions and message patterns in method headers are matched during execution
- Learned how each copy of a method during execution has its own variables local to itself and how different variables with the same name can exist in different copies and be bound to different objects
- Investigated recursive techniques as a special case of passing the buck

5.7   What You Did and Did Not Learn

We reinforced our conviction that variables are fundamental to computation because we saw them used in so many different ways: in workspaces (local and global variables), in methods (pseudo-variable "self", method parameters, instance variables, class variables, local and global variables, and variables defined in pool dictionaries), and in objects (instance variables—also called parts). It may be difficult at this point to remember all the different kinds of variables but no matter. The remaining chapters will provide us with more experience. After a while, you'll be creating and using variables without having to think about what kind of variable you need.

We also learned how to use the debugger—a capability that will help us find our bugs when we consider more difficult tasks later on. In addition to using the debugger to determine what was wrong at an error point, we also used it to trace the execution of code that worked perfectly well; i.e., we used it to better understand working code. We didn't delve into all of the capabilities of the debugger but we did consider all of the important ones.

We learned a little bit about the kinds of methods all classes need to provide; e.g., methods for accessing, modifying, and printing instances. We also learned about the conventions for writing accessing and modification methods. Such basic methods are particularly important because all the new classes that we create in the future will need to provide the same fundamental capabilities. Of course, having created only a few simple classes isn't sufficient to make you feel confident about the process. This will change as you get more experience in subsequent chapters.

We also uncovered a bit more about the execution cycle; e.g., how copies of methods are made when messages are sent, and how the messages are matched with the message patterns in the method copies during execution. However, we have not yet explained how a method is found in the first place. We'll be reviewing this process in the next chapter when we consider problems that make use of inheritance. By then, the execution cycle, will be straightforward and obvious.

Finally, we investigated recursive techniques. More specifically, we used recursion in a **superiors** method for classes, a **printOn**: method for Money objects, a **factorial** method for integers, a **reverse** operation for strings, and a **sum** operation for arrays. Of course, we can't expect to be experts on recursion yet. We need even more experience—experience that will come as a side-effect of new things to be learned in future chapters. Nevertheless, we should have enough of an understanding to be able to duplicate the last three methods from memory since they are relatively small. If you can't, you might want to use the debugger to trace the versions we developed together and actually see what is going on.

5.8   Important Facts

Operations on Objects

anObject **halt**   Causes a walkback window to appear,
                                                     permitting the user to invoke a debugger;
                                                     usually used in the form "self **halt**"

Operations on global Smalltalk

Smalltalk **compressChanges**

Makes the change file smaller (used in Chapter 1)

Smalltalk **removeKey**: #Global

Afterward, variable "Global" no longer exists

Control Structures

aBooleanExpression
    ifTrue: trueBlock
    ifFalse: falseBlock

A message sent to a boolean receiver. If the receiver is true, the true block is executed and the last value computed in the block is the answer—unless there was no expression at all in the block, in which case, nil is the answer. If the receiver is false, the false block is executed with similar consequences. Variations without the **ifTrue**: or **ifFalse**: keywords are also permitted

anIntegerExpression
    timesRepeat: aBlock

A message sent to an integer that permits repetition. The block is executed the number of times specified by the integer. The value returned, 0, is useless for further computation

Replying

^expression

A reply expression; causes the object computed by the expression to be returned to the sender of the message that caused the containing method to be executed

Variables and bindings: All variables, except method parameters, must be declared to be used. Variables that are not initialized are nil. Neither pseudo-variable "self" nor method parameters can be changed by the user. Operator := is not a message; it is a special operator that binds variables to objects. Operations = and := are different; = is a comparison operation and := is a binding operation.

Method template: a sample method such as the following:

```
messagePattern
        "comment"
        | temporaries |
        statements
```

A method consists of four components: a **message pattern** (also called **method header**) that contains the name of the selector identifying the method (along with parameter names, called **method parameters**), an optional **comment** that normally describes what the method is supposed to do, an optional list of **temporary variables** that are to be used in the statements that follow, and statements that compute the object to be returned.

Method execution: When a message is sent, a copy of the corresponding method is made (which includes a copy of all the variables initialized to nil); a match is made between the message and the copy's method header (or message pattern), binding all the method parameters to the message parameters; and execution begins in the copy.

The Basic Execution Cycle

1. All parameters in a message are evaluated.
2. The message is sent to the receiver.
3. The corresponding method for that particular receiver is located and a copy, the method copy, is made. This makes a copy of all variables in the method.
4. The message is matched with the message pattern in the method copy as follows:
   a) The receiver in the expression is matched with special variable "self".
   b) The selector in the expression is matched with the selector in the method copy's header.
   c) The parameters in the expression, the message parameters, are matched with the corresponding parameters in the method copy's header, the method parameters.
5. The method body in the method copy is executed until a reply expression is encountered. If all expressions in the method body execute without encountering a reply expression, default reply expression "^self" is executed.
6. The object computed in the reply expression is returned to the sender of the message for use in further computation.

Methods can return only one answer: All methods reply with (or return) one object using "^". If a reply expression is omitted, the receiver, "self", is returned.

You can access only self's parts: The only object whose parts (instance variables) you can directly reference by name are the parts of "self" in a method body.

Recursion: A special case of passing the buck which leads to a subcomputation that is identical to the original (although with different data).

5.9   Helpful Hints

Use understandable names: Variables names should be self-explanatory. In the majority of the cases, what the variable is intended to be bound to should be evident from the name. Use names like "aPoint" to indicate the kind of object permitted or "position" to indicate the purpose of the variable. Method names should be designed so that when you use them, you can predict what the parameters should be and what will happen; e.g., "5 **between**: 1 **and**: 2" is more predictable than "5 **test**: 1 **and**: 2".

Avoid unnecessary variables: Always eliminate superfluous variables unless they contribute to making the code more understandable.

Results of comparisons can be used directly: An expression such as "^a = b" is equivalent to "a = b ifTrue: [^true] ifFalse: [^false]".

Simplify your methods: Create methods that are as short as possible, that use as few variables as possible, and that are as understandable as possible.

Follow conventions for access and modification methods: If an object with an instance variable—say, called "color"—must have methods for accessing and changing this variable, the accessing method should be called **color** (the same name as the instance variable) and the modification method should be called **color:** (where the parameter provides the new value for the instance variable).

Identify parameters: A parameter name should indicate what kind of object it refers to or what the variable is intended to represent; e.g., aPen, aPoint, size, angle.

Access parts with messages: Once a method has been created to access a particular part, always use a message to access that part; i.e., never access the instance variable directly; e.g., use "self **color**" rather than "color" to allow for potential future changes. If you ever encounter a method that accesses a part directly, ask yourself why.

Make sure your objects can print themselves: All objects should be able to print themselves in a reasonable way. If the default is not sufficient (and it usually is not), a method with message pattern "**printOn:** aWindow" must be added.

Reuse existing methods: Avoid creating methods with common or similar sections.

Be prepared to change your mind: Changing your mind is part of designing — experts do it all the time.

Experts make mistakes, too: It's not that experts don't make mistakes, it's that they've made them all—at least once. The more mistakes you make now, the fewer you'll make later.

5.10 Keywords

class components: class name, class variable names, instance variable names, part names, pool dictionaries, superclass

control structures: block, control structure, if-expression, side-effects, times-repeat-expression

debugging: debugger, single-stepping

globals: ColorConstants, Smalltalk

method components: comment, local variables, message parameter, message pattern, method body, method header, method parameter, reply expression, statements, temporary variables

options in a walkback window: Debug, Resume

options in a debugger: Hop, Skip, Jump

programming techniques: passing the buck, recursion

programming terminology: accessing method, accessor, modification method, modifier, private method, public method

variables: class variable, global variable, instance variable, local variable, message parameter, method parameter, pool dictionary, pseudo-variable, self, temporary variable

window varieties: browser, debugger

5.11 Exercises

1. Design a method to create a five-sided star centered at the current location of the pen.
2. Redesign method **displaySquareAt:side:angle:** so that it displays the square centered at the current location of the pen; i.e., eliminate the first parameter. To do this, you will have to change the name of the method.
3. Create a class called "Drink" with an instance variable called "kind" that can contain symbols such as #milk, #apple, #water, #beer, and so on. Additionally, provide methods for accessing and changing this instance variable.
4. Create a class Wine with a part called **age** (an integer representing the age in years) along with corresponding accessing and modification methods. Additionally, add a class variable to represent the default age at which you consider wines to be old. Provide class messages that allow you to access and modify this variable. Finally, provide a **printOn:** method that either prints 'a New Wine' or 'an Old Wine' depending on the age of the wine.
5. Create a class called "Person" with two instance variable called "age" and "name". Also, provide methods for accessing and changing these variables along with methods for comparing, and printing the instances.
6. Create a class called "Balloon" with an example method that illustrates how a red balloon of radius 10 centimeters might be created. Provide suitable instance methods.

7. Create a more complex class called "Person" that can keep track of a name, an age, a sex, an address, and two phone numbers (one for home and one for work). Use a **printOn:** that specifies only the person's name. Make sure the home phone is referenced if no specific phone is mentioned. Create an **example1** method that creates an interesting Person object and use the debugger to trace it.

8. Create a Distance class that can be used to specify distances in miles, feet, and yards in addition to kilometers, meters, and centimeters. It should be possible to create distance objects in any units and have them print in any other unit. It should also be possible to compare such objects, to add them, and subtract them. It is possible to add convenient methods, say in Number, that permits you to write "6 **miles**", "7 **kilometers**", or "3 **meters**", for example, to obtain instances.

9. Create a method **isPalindrome** in class String that determines whether or not a string is a palindrome. A palindrome is a string that reads the same forward and backward; e.g., "ere". Use a recursive technique. Additionally, trace its execution using the debugger.

10. Use the browser to find an interesting Pen method; i.e., one that can be used to draw an interesting picture. Alternatively, use one of the methods you developed earlier. Trace its execution so that you can control the drawing as it proceeds.

6

Hierarchies of Classes

What You Will Learn

As we have seen in previous chapters, Smalltalk can be used as a calculator for computing numeric quantities, as a word processor for drafting letters, and as a tool for drawing on the display. When illustrating each of these uses, we focused primarily on a single object—the sum of a series, the transcript, a pen. We specifically avoided objects that were minor variations of each other. Of course, many related objects exist in the real world. Cars, for example, are very similar to trucks. When we say that two objects are similar, we mean that there exists another kind of object that represents the common aspects—here, a vehicle. Thus, classes Car, Truck, and Vehicle are highly interrelated classes. The fact that we consider cars and trucks to be different kinds of vehicles suggests that Vehicle is more general than Car or Truck.

The view that many different classes of objects are related leads to the notion of hierarchies of interrelated classes. These hierarchies are reminiscent of family trees, for example, whose goal it is to specify ancestor relationships or classification hierarchies in biology that serve to group animals and plants into related species and subspecies. As we will see, comparable relationships exist between classes.

Hierarchies are natural. People can be classified as either males or females. Living objects can be partitioned into plants and animals. Corner stores and local pizza takeouts can be categorized as small businesses. Sometimes, the hierarchies are relatively shallow because few classes are involved. At other times, it can be fairly deep—consider the number hierarchy.

This chapter focuses on the design and implementation of hierarchies of classes. In the process, we will learn about inheritance of methods and inheritance of instance variables, about the framework for properly initializing instances of hierarchically related classes, about the use of super as a substitute for self, and about techniques that maximize reuse of methods in a hierarchy. We will also uncover the missing details about the one remaining unknown in the method lookup mechanism—how the mechanism works in the presence of inheritance.

Additionally, we will learn how to make use of browser facilities to help us search for unknown classes and operations that suddenly arise during the implementation of a new class; i.e., how to take advantages of the users and implementors of specific selectors. Finally, we will have a brief introduction to techniques for ensuring that different kinds of objects know about each other; e.g., to ensure that libraries know about their books and that books know about their libraries.

We will begin by learning about is-a relationships—a particular hierarchical relationship between classes. Then we will create a hierarchy of food classes that mirrors this is-a relationship. In the process, we will learn about the important aspects of hierarchies of classes. Next, we will design a hierarchy of bank account classes to provide experience with the new notions. As part of the implementation, we will find the need to seek out supporting operations from the Smalltalk library. This will lead us to the use of the above mentioned browsing facilities that enable us to determine the senders and implementors of a particular method selector. Finally, we will implement a bank class that maintains the bank accounts designed earlier. This will introduce the concept of objects that have mutual knowledge of each other, and also introduce four implementation techniques that can be used to implement such objects.

6.1 Case Study: A Hierarchy of Food Classes

A **hierarchy** is an organization (or ranking) of items for the purpose of highlighting the relationships between the items. One such relationship is the **is-a** (also called **is-kind-of**) relationship on classes. If class X is a specialized version of class Y, we say that an X **is-a** Y (or X **is-a-kind-of** Y). This relationship is indicated in the corresponding hierarchy by drawing a line from X to Y. Figure 6.1 illustrates the is-a relationship between two categories of objects, cows and animals.

In this section, we wish to investigate the consequences of designing a hierarchy of classes. More specifically, we would like to create a number of classes dealing with different kinds of foods and organize the classes into a reasonable hierarchy. A typical is-a hierarchy for a very small subset of the possible different kinds of foods is shown in Figure 6.2. Our goal is to create a class hierarchy to mirror this is-a hierarchy.

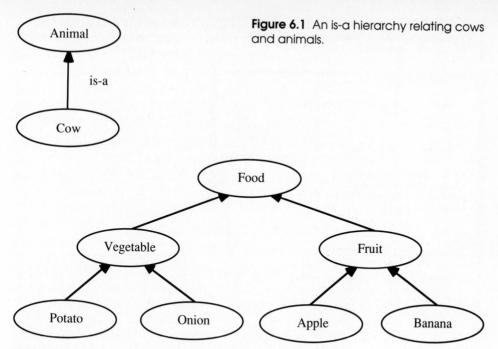

Figure 6.1 An is-a hierarchy relating cows and animals.

Figure 6.2 An is-a hierarchy relating different kinds of foods.

6.1.1 Creating an Initial Class Hierarchy

We have already seen that we can't create a new class without first specifying the superclass. Consequently, we can't define class Apple without having first defined class Fruit. Similarly, we can't define Fruit until class Food is defined. So we should start by defining class Food with Object as its superclass, then define classes Vegetable, Fruit, Potato, Onion, Apple, and Banana. When we are done, we should have the classes defined as shown in Figure 6.3. Of course, none of these classes have instance or class methods yet.

Even though we have not provided any methods, we can obtain instances. Consider the following:

```
Food new ⇒ a Food
Vegetable new ⇒ a Vegetable
Fruit new ⇒ a Fruit
Potato new ⇒ a Potato
Onion new ⇒ an Onion
Apple new ⇒ an Apple
Banana new ⇒ a Banana
```

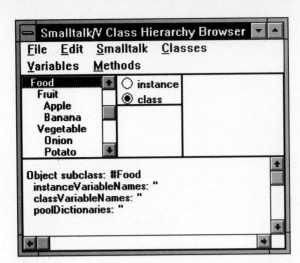

Figure 6.3 A class hierarchy relating different kinds of foods.

To proceed further, we should try to come up with attributes or properties of our foods. To begin, consider the **color** property. Is this a property of apples alone or does it also apply to bananas? If it applies to both, then it is a property of all fruits. But, of course, potatoes and onions also have **color** and therefore it is also a property of vegetables. Going one step further, **color** clearly applies to all foods.

Is it possible to come up with properties that are unique to vegetables—or unique to fruits? Vegetables, for example, can be pod bearing (beans and peas), have edible leaves (cabbages and lettuce), have bulbs (onions and leeks), be suitable for pickling (beets and cucumbers), be primarily roots (carrots and turnips), or be tubers (potatoes and yams). Apparently, no fruits are tubers, so let's focus on the **tuberous** property for illustration purposes in this section. Fruits, similarly, have many properties of their own. One particularly noticeable property is that they can be sour. We've had occasion to eat both sour apples and sweet apples. So we might consider **sweetness** to be a useful property of fruits to focus on.

Although it is much more difficult, it is also possible to find properties unique to individual vegetables and fruits; e.g., some potatoes have edible skins (others have skins that are just too thick or gritty to eat), some onions cause your eyes to water (others are just too mild), some apples are termed cooking apples because they are a lower quality than so-called eating apples, and, lastly, some bananas are too ripe to eat, although they can still be used for making bread.

All this can be summarized in an is-a hierarchy diagram by specifying each property beside the class that it should be associated with. Figure 6.4 summarizes the properties we discussed above.

In general, these are instance properties, not class properties. Hence they must be recorded in the parts of the instances of the individual classes. To provide these parts, we need to add corresponding instance variables to the classes. Making the

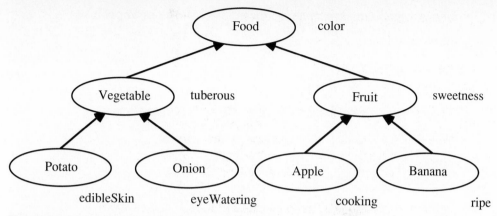

Figure 6.4 Properties of different kinds of foods.

change is easy. Just click on the class to see the definition, change it, and save the new definition. In the case of Food, change

```
Object subclass: #Food
    instanceVariableNames: ''
    classVariableNames: ''
    poolDictionaries: ''
```

to

```
Object subclass: #Food
    instanceVariableNames: 'color'
    classVariableNames: ''
    poolDictionaries: ''
```

Now imagine that we have done this to each and every single class in our hierarchy. Of course, having added instance variables to our classes, we must now consider the need for corresponding accessing and modification methods. Additionally, we must make it clear exactly what kind of object each property maintains. For example, **color** might just be a symbol such as #red, #green, or #blue. On the other hand, **ripe** might be a boolean (true or false) rather than a symbol. Taking this into account, we might come up with the following methods:

```
accessing and modification (instance methods in class Food)
color
    ^color
color: aSymbol
    "Example colors are #red, #green, #blue, #yellow."
    color := aSymbol
```

accessing and modification (instance methods in class Vegetable)

tuberous
    ^tuberous
tuberous: aBoolean
    tuberous := aBoolean

accessing and modification (instance methods in class Potato)

edibleSkin
    ^edibleSkin
edibleSkin: aBoolean
    edibleSkin := aBoolean

accessing and modification (instance methods in class Onion)

eyeWatering
    ^eyeWatering
eyeWatering: aBoolean
    eyeWatering := aBoolean

accessing and modification (instance methods in class Fruit)

sweetness
    ^sweetness
sweetness: aSymbol
    "Example sweetness values are #sweet, #bland, #sour."
    sweetness := aSymbol

accessing and modification (instance methods in class Apple)

cooking
    ^cooking
cooking: aBoolean
    cooking := aBoolean

accessing and modification (instance methods in class Banana)

ripe
    ^ripe
ripe: aBoolean
    ripe := aBoolean

6.1.2 Instance Variables Are Inherited

The class hierarchy is more than just a technique for relating the different classes. It actually affects the **structure** (also called the **representation**) of the instances; i.e., what instance variables they will contain. To see how the class hierarchy affects the structure of the instances, let's create four instances from a subset of the classes in the hierarchy. For ease of reference, Figure 6.5 summarizes that portion of the hierarchy we will be concerned with.

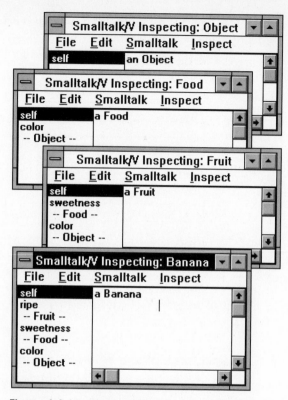

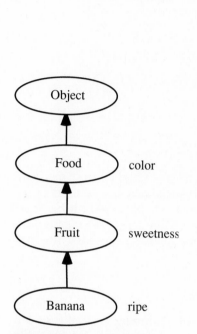

Figure 6.5 Properties of the different kinds of foods.

Figure 6.6 Inspectors for instances of Object, Food, Fruit, and Banana.

In particular, we'll simply inspect four instances by executing

```
Object new inspect
Food new inspect
Fruit new inspect
Banana new inspect
```

The result is shown in Figure 6.6. Two things are noteworthy about the inspectors. Not only do they provide information about the parts (instance variables) of the objects, but they also indicate which class that information comes from. We'll consider each of these aspects in turn.

First, let's construct an equivalent diagram (see Figure 6.7) that more concisely describes the part information. Notice from the inspectors that instances of Object have no parts, instances of Food have one part (color), instances of Fruit have two parts (color and sweetness), and instances of Banana have three parts (color, sweetness, and ripe). This is quite important.

> *When a new class is defined, the instance variables provided in the new class are added to the instance variables automatically obtained from all the classes higher up in the hierarchy.*

We summarize this by saying that *instance variables are inherited*; equivalently, *representation is inherited*.

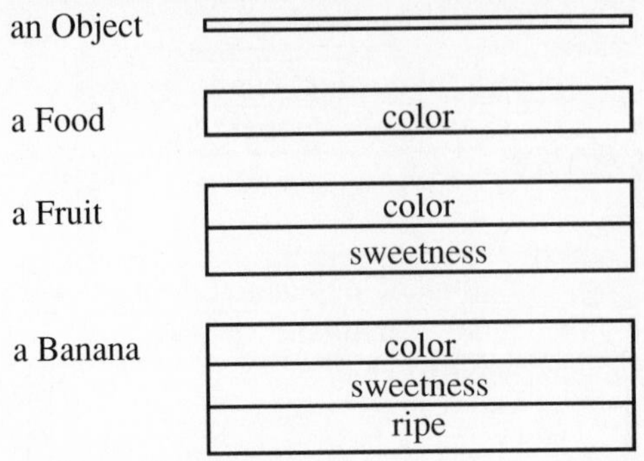

an Object

a Food

	color	

a Fruit

	color	
	sweetness	

Figure 6.7 Instance variables in instances of Object, Food, Fruit, and Banana.

a Banana

	color	
	sweetness	
	ripe	

A new class always inherits the representation from classes higher up. Thus, if we were to create a special class—say, called MidgetBanana—as a subclass of Banana, it follows that instances of MidgetBanana would have at least three instance variables called color, sweetness, and ripe. More instance variables can be added to instances of MidgetBanana, but none of those provided through inheritance can be removed.

6.1.3 Inspectors Indicate Where Parts Inherit From

We indicated earlier that inspectors provide us with more than just information about the instance variables in an instance. They also indicate where these instance variables come from. To see this, consider Figure 6.8, where we have focused on the inspector for a banana. One way of interpreting the inspector is to view it as providing inheritance information in the downward direction (the inspector is considered to be upside down). From this point of view, as we proceed downward from **self**, we are really proceeding up the inheritance hierarchy.

In the context of a banana, this inspector is telling us

- That **ripe** is provided in the definition of class Banana
- That Fruit is next encountered in the class hierarchy (notice "-- Fruit --", immediately below)
- That **sweetness** is inherited from the last class encountered; namely, Fruit
- That Food (notice "-- Food --") is next encountered in the class hierarchy
- That **color** is inherited from this last class, Food
- That Object is next encountered in the class hierarchy
- Tthat nothing is inherited from Object

> *Inspectors provide useful inheritance information.*

In summary, instances of classes inherit representation. This is particularly important because it means that it is impossible to create a subclass of Food, for example, that does not have a color. Representation inheritance is strictly additive; a subclass can never eliminate parts provided by the superclasses.

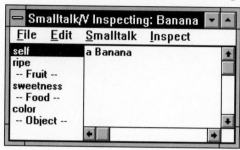

Figure 6.8 Inspectors tell us where the instance variables are inherited from.

6.1.4 Methods Are Inherited

In this section, let's consider inheritance from the perspective of the methods. So far, we have created a small community of classes, each with two methods for accessing and modifying some important property of the class. Figure 6.9 summarizes the methods associated with the classes we investigated in the previous section.

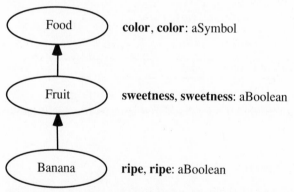

color, color: aSymbol

sweetness, sweetness: aBoolean

ripe, ripe: aBoolean

Figure 6.9 Summarizing the accessing and modifying methods.

We can try some very simple experiments to see which methods are understood by distinct instances. In particular, we can obtain an instance of Food, Fruit, and Banana and try sending them messages from the list supplied in Figure 6.9:

Food **new color**: #yellow ⇒ a Food
Fruit **new color**: #yellow ⇒ a Fruit
Banana **new color**: #yellow ⇒ a Banana

As we can see, all the instances understand message "**color**: #yellow". Instances of Food should understand the message because **color**: is defined in Food. Since fruits and bananas are foods, corresponding instances should also understand the message. Let's try the same experiment with **sweetness**:.

Food **new sweetness**: true ⇒ (error—not understood)
Fruit **new sweetness**: true ⇒ a Fruit
Banana **new sweetness**: true ⇒ a Banana

The situation is different. Why? First of all, we defined foods in such a manner that they don't have the sweetness property. Fruits do and so do bananas, because bananas are fruits. Sweetness is a property of fruits but not of vegetables, so foods (in general) don't have the property. If this is confusing, let's try the same experiment on the next property in the hierarchy.

Food **new ripe**: false ⇒ (error—not understood)
Fruit **new ripe**: false ⇒ (error—not understood)
Banana **new ripe**: false ⇒ a Banana

Since only bananas have the ripeness property, it follows that only bananas should understand message "**ripe**: false".

We can summarize the results of these experiments as follows:

All instances of Food understand
   color, color:
All instances of Fruit understand
   color, color:, sweetness, sweetness:
All instances of Banana understand
   color, color:, sweetness, sweetness:, ripe, ripe:

Alternatively, we might say the following:

> *Subclasses inherit all the methods of the superclasses.*

Of course, we performed our experiments only with instance methods. Does the same principle apply to class methods? It turns out that it does but we'll leave that for you to check.

6.1.5 The Method Lookup Mechanism

Although we considered the execution cycle in detail in previous chapters, the mechanism used to find the method associated with the message being sent, called the **lookup mechanism**, was never elaborated upon. We now know that methods are inherited, but we don't know precisely how the process works. The question that we want to answer is the following: "*When a message is sent to an object, how is the method that matches it located?*" For example, when we execute

aNumber + 1

how does the Smalltalk environment decide whether the method should be the + method for integer, the + method for float, the + method for fraction, or even the + method for point?

A simple (but as far as we know, incorrect) answer is that the environment searches for the method in the class of the receiver. It is part of a class' behavior to keep track of the methods of its instances. If the method is found, a copy is made for execution. If it isn't found, an error message is generated—the message explaining that the receiver does not understand the message.

But now, let's look at an example for which this simplistic answer isn't sufficient:

```
| aBanana |
aBanana := Banana new.
aBanana color: #yellow
```

Consider what happens when message "**color**: #yellow" is sent to the banana. If the previous explanation is correct, a search is made in class Banana for a method that matches. But class Banana has no method called **color**:. Hence, we should get the standard "doesNotUnderstand" error message. Of course, that's not what happens. The method called **color**: is found and nothing is wrong! Why? Since bananas are fruits, fruits are foods, and foods have the color property, method **color**: was defined in class Food, not class Banana.

So we might revise the above explanation of the lookup mechanism as follows:

> *When a message is sent to an object, the receiver's class is searched for the corresponding method. If found, a copy is made and the copy is executed. If not found, the process is repeated in the superclass.*

Now let's see if this explanation is sufficient to explain a subsequent message such as

```
aBanana inspect
```

First, a search for a method matching **inspect** in class Banana is made. None is found, so a further search is made in the superclass Fruit, followed by a search in class Food. None is found here, either! What now? Give up with an error message or keep searching. We know, of course, that it is possible to inspect bananas, so the corresponding method must ultimately be found. Since Food has a superclass, Object, the search must continue in class Object. Since Object has no superclass, we must conclude by deduction that the method for **inspect** is found in class Object (see Figure 6.10). The explanation above is correct as far as it goes, but it's missing the stopping condition:

> *If no superclass exists, an error message is generated, explaining that the receiver does not understand the message.*

When a class such as Banana has access to methods in the classes above it in the hierarchy, the class is said to **inherit** the methods from the superclasses. Thus, Banana inherits instance method **inspect** from class Object. Similarly, Banana inherits instance methods **color** and **color**: from Food and instance methods **sweetness** and **sweetness**: from Fruit.

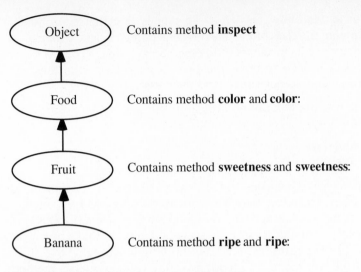

Figure 6.10 Searching for method **inspect**.

In the previous chapter, we said that all objects should be able to print themselves. However, we didn't introduce any printing methods into our food hierarchy example—an oversight on our part. So why does the following work?

```
Object new ⇒ an Object
Food new ⇒ a Food
Fruit new ⇒ a Fruit
Banana new ⇒ a Banana
```

Presumably, it's because all objects print themselves using method **printOn**: which exists in class Object. We could have been more explicit and tried the following instead to illustrate the same point:

```
Object new printOn: Transcript
Food new printOn: Transcript
Fruit new printOn: Transcript
Banana new printOn: Transcript
```

Let's introduce a new **printOn**: instance method into class Food. As we did once before in the previous chapter, we could make sure all foods print their names by providing the following implementation:

```
printing (in class Food)

printOn: aWindow
    "I print myself with my color."
    aWindow nextPutAll: 'a '.
    self color printOn: aWindow.
    aWindow nextPutAll: ' Food'
```

Figure 6.11 contains a summary of what we have so far with respect to methods with selector **printOn:**. Notice that classes Fruit and Banana have no **printOn:** methods of their own. However, they can inherit the **printOn:** method from Food.

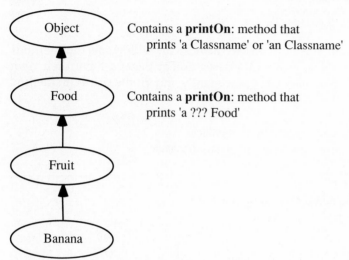

Contains a **printOn:** method that prints 'a Classname' or 'an Classname'

Contains a **printOn:** method that prints 'a ??? Food'

Figure 6.11 A summary of classes containing a method called **printOn:**.

Let's try our four test cases again.

```
Object new ⇒ an Object
Food new ⇒ a nil Food
Fruit new color: #red ⇒ a red Food
Banana new color: #yellow ⇒ a yellow Food
```

Why does each instance print this way? Let's consider the cases, one by one. When an instance of Object is asked to print itself, the search for method **printOn:** starts in class Object. Hence the **printOn:** in class Object is found and used. So "Object **new**" prints as "an Object". When an instance of Food is asked to print itself, the search starts in Food and the **printOn:** there is found and used. Since we didn't give a color to the food, it must still be uninitialized. So "Food **new**" prints as "a nil Food". In the last two cases, the search starts in classes Fruit and Banana, respectively, but neither has a method called **printOn:**. The search ultimately reaches the superclass Food and the **printOn:** in that class is used. This method always prints "a ??? Food", no matter what the receiver. So both the fruit and the banana print themselves without indicating what specific kind of object they are.

As it is, we can't tell the difference between the fruit and the banana because the information they print is not specific enough. We'll have to fix that. One way is to add a more specific method to each of these classes. Let's start by adding a **printOn:** method such as the following to class Fruit.

printing (in class Fruit)

printOn: aWindow
"I print myself with my color."
aWindow **nextPutAll**: 'a '.
self **color** printOn: aWindow.
aWindow **nextPutAll**: ' Fruit'

Figure 6.12 contains a summary of what we have so far with respect to methods with selector **printOn:**. Notice that all classes except Banana have their own **printOn:** method. Class Banana must, consequently, inherit the **printOn:** method from Fruit.

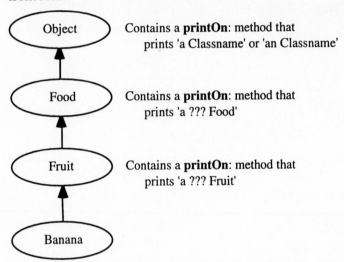

Figure 6.12 A summary of classes containing a method called **printOn:**.

Executing our four examples once more should give us the following:

Object **new** ⇒ an Object
Food **new** ⇒ a nil Food
Fruit **new color:** #red ⇒ a red Fruit
Banana **new color:** #yellow ⇒ a yellow Fruit

Since bananas don't print the way we would like them to, we could also add a special **printOn:** instance method to class Banana. However, there is another way—we could **generalize** the **printOn:** method in class Fruit so that it works for both fruits and bananas. For example, we could rewrite it as follows:

printing (in class Fruit)

printOn: aWindow
    "I print myself with my color."
    aWindow **nextPutAll**: 'a '.
    self **color printOn**: aWindow.
    (self **isKindOf**: Banana)
        ifTrue: [aWindow **nextPutAll**: ' Banana']
        ifFalse: [aWindow **nextPutAll**: ' Fruit']

One problem with the above is that it will no longer be correct if we add new subclasses to Fruit; say, a class called Pear or Orange. We need an approach that avoids testing the class of the receiver. Since the class has a name, we can simply use the class name and avoid using an if-expression, as follows:

printing (in class Fruit)

printOn: aWindow
    "I print myself with my color."
    aWindow **nextPutAll**: 'a '.
    self **color printOn**: aWindow.
    aWindow **space**; **nextPutAll**: self **class name**

Actually, we should be able to simplify this a little. We already know that classes can print themselves.

Object ⇒ Object
Food ⇒ Food
Fruit ⇒ aFruit
Banana ⇒ Banana

We shouldn't have to ask the class for its name.

printing (in class Fruit)

printOn: aWindow
    "I print myself with my color."
    aWindow **nextPutAll**: 'a '.
    self **color printOn**: aWindow.
    aWindow **space**.
    self **class printOn**: aWindow

There is still a problem with this last version. Can you spot it? To illustrate the problem, let's consider using new colors.

Object **new** ⇒ an Object
Food **new color**: #green ⇒ a green Food
Fruit **new color**: #orange ⇒ a orange Fruit
Banana **new color**: #yellow ⇒ a yellow Banana

Although "a green Food" sounds alright, "a orange Fruit" does not—clearly, it should be "an orange Fruit". Let's leave this problem for now. There is a more important issue. The **printOn**: in class Food does the same job as the **printOn**: in class Fruit; i.e., it is superfluous. We should replace the **printOn:** in Food by the **printOn:** in Fruit and remove the **printOn:** from Fruit entirely. In this case, there would be only one **printOn:** in Food and all the subclasses would inherit this one.

Another entirely different approach is to have Fruit print both the color and sweetness information, and have Banana additionally print the ripeness information. If we were to do that, we might get something like the following:

Food **new color**: #green ⇒ a green Food
Fruit **new color**: #orange; **sweetness**: #sour ⇒ a sour orange Fruit
Banana **new color**: #yellow; **sweetness**: #bland; **ripe**: false
    ⇒ a bland unripe yellow Banana

> *As a general rule, the **printOn:** method should not try to print everything known about an object.*

The **printOn:** should print only a small amount of information—enough to allow the receiver to be differentiated from other objects. Should more information be needed, the receiver can always be inspected. The solution we have so far (namely, one **printOn:** method in class Food) is best.

6.1.6 Reorganizing the Hierarchy

As we develop a hierarchy of classes, we will sometimes encounter situations where we need to change the hierarchy. For example, we can easily imagine adding a new class of vegetables, Tomato, to end up with the hierarchy shown in Figure 6.13.

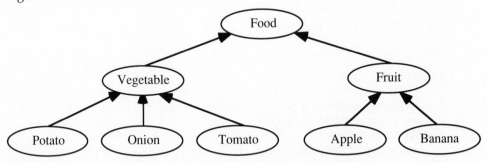

Figure 6.13 Integrating class Tomato with the existing hierarchy.

But, of course, we made a terrible mistake. Tomatoes are actually fruits, not vegetables. If we attempt to fix this mistake by changing the definition from

Vegetable **subclass**: #Tomato
    instanceVariableNames: "
    classVariableNames: "
    poolDictionaries: "

to

Fruit **subclass**: #Tomato
  instanceVariableNames: 'color'
  classVariableNames: ''
  poolDictionaries: ''

we end up with an error message, as shown in Figure 6.14.

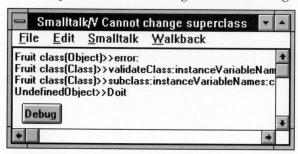

Figure 6.14 The consequence of attempting to change Tomato's superclass.

Of course, if the class has no methods, it is easy to delete the class and start again. It is not so simple, however, if you managed to add dozens of methods to the class. You don't want to lose those methods. As it turns out, there is no easy way to change the class and keep the methods in Smalltalk/V. The solution is described in detail in Chapter 4 in "Renaming a Class or Changing the Superclass." In this case, it involves filing out class Tomato (say, in a file call **junk**), deleting class Tomato from the programming environment, opening file **junk** and editing the definition (as illustrated above) so that Tomato inherits from Fruit instead of Vegetable, saving the changes back into file **junk**, and then installing the file. Alternatively, instead of saving the modified file, we could have selected all the text and then installed the selected portion by clicking on **File It In** in the **Smalltalk** menu.

Filing out classes is an excellent way of creating a **backup**—a copy that can be used to re–create your work should something go wrong with the Smalltalk environment. In our case, we should probably file out the Temperature and Money classes that we developed in Chapter 5 along with the Food classes developed in this chapter. We should be able to create a complete backup with just three files, such as **temperut.cls**, **money.cls**, and **foods.cls**. Note that file names are restricted to eight characters, so we couldn't use a file name such as **temperature.cls**.

6.1.7 The Distinction between self and super

Having had experience designing a **printOn:** method that works for all subclasses of Food, we might find it relatively easy to repeat the process for a new set of classes. For example, if we were to create a small hierarchy of animal classes that might be of use to a farmer, we might come up with a hierarchy such as that shown in Figure 6.15. In this case, all animals would have names and cows would have a milk capacity (we won't bother showing the methods for accessing and modifying these properties).

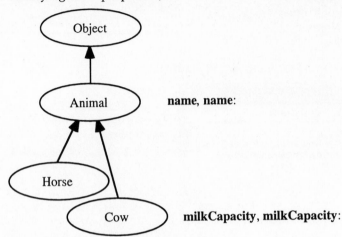

Figure 6.15 A hierarchy of animal classes.

It's a simple task to make available three **printOn:** methods (rather than four): one in Object, one in Animal, and one in Cow. Horses, for example, could inherit the **printOn:** from Animal and cows could have their own unique version. One implementation might be the following:

printing (in class Object)

printOn: aWindow
    "I print myself in a generic manner; e.g., 'an Object' or 'a Horse'."
    "Details not shown."

printing (in class Animal)

printOn: aWindow
    "I print myself with my name; e.g., 'a Horse named Trigger'."
    aWindow **nextPutAll:** 'a '.
    self **class printOn:** aWindow.
    aWindow **nextPutAll:** ' named '.
    self **name printOn:** aWindow

printing (in class Cow)

printOn: aWindow
    "I print myself with my name and milk capacity; e.g., 'a Cow named Betsy with milk capacity 10 liters'."
    aWindow **nextPutAll:** 'a Cow named '.
    self **name printOn:** aWindow
    aWindow **nextPutAll:** ' with milk capacity '.
    self **milkCapacity printOn:** aWindow.
    aWindow **nextPutAll:** ' liters'.

One problem with the above approach is that each **printOn:** method duplicates the work of the others in the superclass—*there is no method reuse.* We already decided in the previous chapters that we should avoid duplicating code. To see how we failed to do that, let's investigate the consequences of using each of the **printOn:** methods on the same object, a cow.

```
| aCow |
aCow := Cow new name: #Betsy; milkCapacity: 10.
aCow ⇒ ???
```

What prints will depend on which **printOn:** is used. To ensure that the Object **printOn:** is used, for example, it is sufficient to (temporarily) delete the **printOn:** in Animal and Cow. Similarly, to ensure that the Animal **printOn:** is used, we can delete the **printOn:** in Cow. We get

```
a Cow                                      (if Object's printOn: is used)
a Cow named Betsy                          (if Animal's printOn: is used)
a Cow named Betsy with milk capacity 10 liters   (if Cow's printOn: is used)
```

Note what is common to the three results. Each successive **printOn:** adds a bit more to the output of the previous one. Is there a way to take advantage of this commonality?

One possibility is to use different names for each **printOn:**—to name the three methods **printOn1:**, **printOn2:**, and **printOn3:** respectively. Then we can make sure that **printOn2:** uses **printOn1:** and that **printOn3:** uses **printOn2:**. We'll also need a **printOn:** in Object that uses **printOn1:**, a **printOn:** in Animal that uses **printOn2:**, and a **printOn:** in Cow that uses **printOn3:**. The details are provided below.

printing (in class Object)

```
printOn1: aWindow
    "I print myself in a generic manner; e.g., 'a Cow'."
    "Details not shown."

printOn: aWindow
    self printOn1: aWindow
```

printing (in class Animal)

```
printOn2: aWindow
    "I print myself with my name; e.g., 'a Cow named Betsy'."
    self printOn1: aWindow. "Print 'a Cow'."
    aWindow nextPutAll: ' named '.
    self name printOn: aWindow

printOn: aWindow
    self printOn2: aWindow
```

printing (in class Cow)

printOn3: aWindow
    "I print myself with my name and milk capacity; e.g., 'a Cow named Betsy
    with milk capacity 10'."
    self **printOn2**: aWindow. "Print 'a Cow named Betsy'."
    aWindow **nextPutAll**: ' with milk capacity '.
    self **milkCapacity printOn**: aWindow.
    aWindow **nextPutAll**: ' liters'.

printOn: aWindow
    self **printOn3**: aWindow

As it turns out, this will work quite well. When a **printOn**: message is sent to the cow, the **printOn**: in class Cow is found by the method lookup mechanism. It sends the **printOn3**: message to itself, which causes the **printOn2**: message to be sent, which in turn results in the sending of the **printOn1**: message, as shown in the execution stack history below:

Object>>printOn1:
    self ⇒ aCow

    printOn1: aWindow
        "I print myself in a generic manner; e.g., 'a Cow'."
        "Details not shown."_

Animal>>printOn2:
    self ⇒ aCow

    printOn2: aWindow
        "I print myself with my name; e.g., 'a Cow named Betsy'."
        <u>self **printOn1**: aWindow</u>. "Print 'a Cow'."
        aWindow **nextPutAll**: ' named '.
        self **name printOn**: aWindow

Cow>>printOn3:
    self ⇒ aCow

    printOn3: aWindow
        "I print myself with my name and milk capacity; e.g., 'a Cow
        named Betsy with milk capacity 10 liters'."
        <u>self **printOn2**: aWindow</u>. "Print 'a Cow named Betsy'."
        aWindow **nextPutAll**: ' with milk capacity '.
        self **milkCapacity printOn**: aWindow.
        aWindow **nextPutAll**: ' liters'.

Cow>>printOn:
    self ⇒ aCow
    printOn: aWindow
        <u>self **printOn3**: aWindow</u>

Unfortunately, it's a poor solution for two reasons:

- We have to double the number of methods needed
- We actually have to change existing methods; to make the **printOn:** in Animal reuse the corresponding **printOn:** in the superclass Object, we had to make changes to class Object. We shouldn't have to change the superclass just because a subclass wants to use a method in the superclass.

Why not use the standard name **printOn:** instead of **printOn1:**, **printOn2:**, and **printOn3:** as in the following?

printing (in class Object)

printOn: aWindow
    "I print myself in a generic manner; e.g., 'a Cow'."
    "Details not shown."

printing (in class Animal)

printOn: aWindow
    "I print myself with my name; e.g., 'a Cow named Betsy'."
    self **printOn:** aWindow. "Print 'a Cow'."
    aWindow **nextPutAll:** ' named '.
    self **name printOn:** aWindow

printing (in class Cow)

printOn: aWindow
    "I print myself with my name and milk capacity; e.g., 'a Cow named Betsy with milk capacity 10 liters'."
    self **printOn:** aWindow. "Print 'a Cow named Betsy'."
    aWindow **nextPutAll:** ' with milk capacity '.
    self **milkCapacity printOn:** aWindow.
    aWindow **nextPutAll:** ' liters'.

As it turns out, this doesn't work at all. Let's see why by trying to execute and print

    Cow **new**

We should get the error message shown in Figure 6.16. Opening the debugger (see Figure 6.17) is quite instructive.

As we can see, message **printOn:** is sent over and over again until we run out of computer memory for the computation. This is an example of a **nonterminating** computation—a computation that can never finish. Why is this? When message **printOn:** is sent to the cow, the **printOn:** method in Cow is located by the method lookup mechanism. A copy is made and the copy begins execution. But the first message it must execute is "self **printOn:** aWindow". Since "self", the receiver, is an instance of class Cow, the method lookup mechanism again finds the **printOn:**

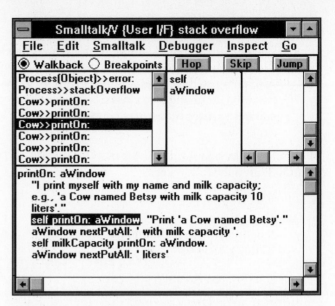

Figure 6.16 The walkback window that appears if we try to print "Cow **new**".

Figure 6.17 Using the debugger to investigate why "Cow **new**" doesn't print.

method in class Cow, makes another copy, and starts to execute it. This process will repeat until we run out of memory—and we *will* run out of memory, because a copy of the method is made each time the **printOn:** message is sent. This is an example of a **loop**, a situation that keeps repeating. We call it an **infinite loop** because there is no possibility of it ever ending—at least, not without an error.

What we really want to be able to say in the **printOn:** method for class Cow is "use the **printOn:** in class Animal." There is no way to say that directly in Smalltalk. However, there is a way of saying "use the **printOn:** higher up in the hierarchy" as follows:

> super **printOn:** aWindow

Recall that the word super means above—we encountered it when we discussed the word superclass.

> *In general, "super" is equivalent to "self" but has the side-effect of causing the method lookup mechanism to start searching for the relevant method in the class above that of the current method.*
>
> *Note that the search does not start in the superclass of the receiver.*

The wording here is potentially confusing. So let's repeat it in the context of a trivial example. Suppose we added a method called **experiment1** to class Animal. Somewhere in the body, message **testing** is sent to **super**, as shown below. Now

synonym for **self**; namely, the cow. The description above indicates that the method lookup mechanism will start searching for method **testing** in the superclass of **Animal** (the class that contains method **experiment1**)—not in the superclass of **Cow** (which is the receiver's class). Consequently, **Correct** is printed in the transcript—not **Wrong**.

a method in class Object

testing
    Transcript **nextPutAll**: 'Correct'

methods in class Animal

experiment1
    "Cow new experiment1"
    ...
    super **testing**.
    ...

testing
    Transcript **nextPutAll**: 'Wrong'

To make sure you get this subtle but very important point, let's describe the method lookup mechanism once more. But this time, let's provide both an incorrect and a correct description.

Incorrect description: When a message is sent to super, method lookup begins in the superclass of the receiver.

If this latter description were correct, sending **experiment1** to a cow would result in a search for **testing** that begins in the superclass of Cow, which is Animal. Hence **Wrong** would be printed.

Correct description: *When a message is sent to super, method lookup begins in the superclass of the class containing the method that has "super" in it.*

A complete solution to our original printing problem—one that properly **reuses** existing methods (and thereby avoids duplication)—is shown below. It makes use of **super** instead of **self** to refer to the **printOn**: higher up in the hierarchy.

printing (in class Object)

printOn: aWindow
    "I print myself in a generic manner; e.g., 'a Cow'."
    "Details not shown."

printing (in class Animal)

printOn: aWindow
  "I print myself with my name; e.g., 'a Cow named Betsy'."
  super **printOn**: aWindow. "Print 'a Cow'."
  aWindow **nextPutAll**: ' named '.
  self **name printOn**: aWindow

printing (in class Cow)

printOn: aWindow
  "I print myself with my name and milk capacity; e.g., 'a Cow named Betsy
  with milk capacity 10 liters'."
  super **printOn**: aWindow. "Print 'a Cow named Betsy'."
  aWindow **nextPutAll**: ' with milk capacity '.
  self **milkCapacity printOn**: aWindow.
  aWindow **nextPutAll**: ' liters'.

Table 6.1 summarizes where the search begins when "super **printOn**: aWindow"
is executed in a Cow method and in an Animal method. In each case, the receiver
(namely, **super**) is a cow; the receiver does not change.

Table 6.1 Where method lookup begins when "super **printOn**: aWindow" is executed.

Where "super **printOn**:" Is	Where Search Starts	What super Is
In a Cow method	Animal (superclass of Cow)	a Cow
In an Animal method	Object (superclass of Animal)	a Cow

This technique, in which a method such as **printOn**: does part of the work itself
and passes on the rest to another method with the same name higher up the
hierarchy, perhaps to repeat the technique once again, deserves a name. We'll call
it **hierarchical buck-passing** since it is an example of passing the buck.

Remember that **super** really is a synonym for **self**. It is not a message. Hence, it
makes no sense to say "self **super**" or "Banana **new super**", for example.

In the examples above, each **printOn**: method used "super **printOn**: ..." to
reference the **printOn**: higher up in the hierarchy. But of course, you don't have
to be in a **printOn**: method to say "super **printOn**: ...". We illustrated this when
we used "super **testing**" in method **experiment1**. But there is another important
point.

Suppose we wanted to add a **halt** message to one of our methods to invoke the
debugger. Normally, we would add "self **halt**" to the method, but we could just
as easily add "super **halt**" instead, as in the following example:

printing (in class Animal)

printOn: aWindow
    "I print myself with my name; e.g., 'a Cow named Betsy'."
    super **halt**.
    super **printOn**: aWindow. "Print 'a Cow'."
    aWindow **nextPutAll**: ' named '.
    self **name printOn**: aWindow

What would be the difference if we had asked to print a horse, say? With "self **halt**", the method lookup mechanism would have started searching for **halt** in class Horse (since the receiver is a horse). Since the method is not there, it would continue searching in Animal. Because it's not there either, it would continue in Object and ultimately find it there. With "super **halt**", the search would start in class Object instead, the class above Animal. We get the same result in both cases because method **halt** is in class Object.

Nevertheless, we should never use "super" unless we really have to because it "informs the reader" that we are trying to bypass the equivalent method in our own class. Of course, you might argue that it is more efficient because there is less to search. But the method lookup mechanism uses very sophisticated "memorization" techniques that eliminate the real search 95% of the time. The very small gain in efficiency obtained by doing this won't be noticed. More important, if you later add a method that you are bypassing with **super**, you will have to find all your occurrences of **super** and change them back to **self**.

> *Avoid using "super message" when "self message" works. The use of "super message" informs the reader that "self message" is problematic.*

In the above example, the only time we would consider it good style to say "super **halt**" is if there already existed a **halt** method in class Animal and we didn't want to use this particular method; i.e., we wanted to bypass it to get the version in Object.

6.1.8 Creating Initialized Instances

One problem with our implementation of the food hierarchy is that we have to initialize all our instances explicitly:

Potato **new color**: #white; **tuberous**: true; **edibleSkin**: true
    ⇒ a white Potato
Onion **new color**: #white; **tuberous**: false; **eyeWatering**: true
    ⇒ a white Onion
Apple **new color**: #red; **sweetness**: #sweet; **cooking**: false
    ⇒ a red Apple
Banana **new color**: #yellow; **sweetness**: #sweet; **ripe**: false
    ⇒ a yellow Banana

If we forget to initialize some aspect of our food, that property will be nil—the default for uninitialized instance variables. It would be much better if we had an **initialize** method that initialized everything to some useful default. If we didn't want the default, we could simply change it. With such a method, we could create fully initialized instances as follows:

> Potato **new initialize** ⇒ a white Potato
> Onion **new initialize** ⇒ a white Onion
> Apple **new initialize** ⇒ a red Apple
> Banana **new initialize** ⇒ a yellow Banana
> Banana **new initialize; color:** #green ⇒ a green Banana

Of course, we will now have to add this **initialize** method to our food hierarchy. Clearly, it should be an instance method. How many do we need? One solution that comes to mind is to have four—one for each of our basic foods.

> *instance initialization (in class Potato)*
>
> **initialize**
>   self **color:** #white; **tuberous:** true; **edibleSkin:** true
>
> *instance initialization (in class Onion)*
>
> **initialize**
>   self **color:** #white; **tuberous:** false; **eyeWatering:** true
>
> *instance initialization (in class Apple)*
>
> **initialize**
>   self **color:** #red; **sweetness:** #sweet; **cooking:** false
>
> *instance initialization (in class Banana)*
>
> **initialize**
>   self **color:** #yellow; **sweetness:** #sweet; **ripe:** false

Although this works, it is not considered very good style. If we added a new property to our foods, say **weight**, we would have to change each of these **initialize** methods to provide a useful default. We need a technique that helps isolate future changes to fewer methods—in the best case, just one. The philosophy that we want to follow is very simple.

> *The class that introduces a new part (or property) is responsible for initializing it to some useful default. Subclasses are allowed to redefine the default only if it is not appropriate for them.*

To see how we need to proceed, look at Figure 6.18. Class Food is responsible for initializing **color**; class Vegetable is responsible for **tuberous**; Fruit, for **sweetness**; Apple, for **cooking,** and so on.

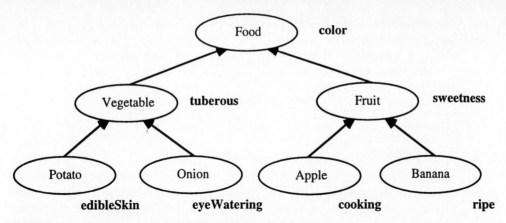

Figure 6.18 Properties of the different kinds of foods.

If each class is responsible for initializing its own parts, and apples, for example, inherit the instance variables higher up in the hierarchy, how do we get an apple to initialize all three instance variables **color**, **sweetness**, and **cooking**? The best approach is to make use of hierarchical buck-passing. The **initialize** for Apple needs to make use of the **initialize** for Fruit, which in turn must make use of the **initialize** for Food. A first solution is provided below.

instance initialization (in class Food)

initialize
    self **color**: #green

instance initialization (in class Vegetable)

initialize
    super **initialize**.
    self **tuberous**: false

instance initialization (in class Fruit)

initialize
    super **initialize**.
    self **sweetness**: #sweet

instance initialization (in class Potato)

initialize
    super **initialize**.
    self **edibleSkin**: true

instance initialization (in class Onion)

initialize
    super **initialize**.
    self **eyeWatering**: true

instance initialization (in class Apple)

initialize
    super **initialize**.
    self **cooking**: false

instance initialization (in class Banana)

initialize
    super **initialize**.
    self **ripe**: false

The hard part is coming up with defaults that make sense. For example, in Food, we decided to use #green as the default because the majority of foods in the world are green—consider broccoli, peas, green beans, lettuce, etc. Of course, in the simplistic food hierarchy that we are using, only onions can make use of this default, since most potatoes, apples, and bananas are white, red, and yellow, respectively. In anticipation of future extensions to the hierarchy, we would like to keep the chosen defaults. So potatoes, apples, and bananas need to **override** the defaults provided by their superclasses—they need to substitute better defaults, as shown below:

instance initialization (in class Potato)

initialize
    super **initialize**.
    self **color**: #white.
    self **edibleSkin**: true

instance initialization (in class Apple)

initialize
    super **initialize**.
    self **color**: #red.
    self **cooking**: false

instance initialization (in class Banana)

initialize
    super **initialize**.
    self **color**: #yellow.
    self **ripe**: false

Note that it matters where "super **initialize**" is executed. For example, if we executed it last, as in

instance initialization (in class Banana)

initialize
    self **color**: #yellow.
    self **ripe**: false.
    super **initialize**.

we would find that the banana would be green, since that is the default provided by the **initialize** method which is higher up.

> *It's a good rule of thumb to (1) initialize the defaults from higher up the hierarchy first, (2) override those defaults if necessary, and finally, (3) provide initialization for instance variables supplied directly by the class.*

Now let's stand back and see if this entire approach is a good one. What would we need to do, for example, if a **weight** were added as a new instance variable in class Food? It should be sufficient to change the **initialize** method in Food and only that one. The same would apply if we were to add a new property, like **greenhouseGrown**, to Fruit. If a subclass of Fruit were added—say, called Tomato—with no new instance variables, we wouldn't even need to supply an **initialize** method if the defaults were correct. In this case, they wouldn't be, so we would probably add a method like the following:

instance initialization (in class Tomato)

initialize
    super **initialize**.
    self **color**: #red.
    self **sweetness**: #sour.

Of course, if we look back at Figure 6.18, we might argue that we have overridden every single default, so "super **initialize**" is not needed. From the point of view of programming style, however, it should be kept. It certainly would be needed if either **weight** or **greenhouseGrown** were added. We should always be designing with future extensions in mind.; we have to keep in mind that it might be needed later.

> *As a rule, all parts should be initialized to defaults that are of the appropriate type.*

If **weight** is to be a number, for example, care should be taken to provide a default that is a number rather than nil or a string such as 'not yet known'. But what is a good default weight? It depends on the units used. It might be 0.1 kilograms or 10 ounces. If you can't think of any reasonable default, a weight of 0 is still preferable to nil.

If animals on a farm are named by the farmer and the names are symbols such as #Betsy, default names should consequently be symbols. In this case, a default such as #Cow or #Unknown might be reasonable. You might have to think a bit to come up with a good default. It's not always easy.

Now that we have a technique for initializing instances, we can obtain initialized instances very simply. To repeat an earlier example, we could write

    Potato **new initialize** $\Rightarrow$ a white Potato
    Onion **new initialize** $\Rightarrow$ a white Onion
    Apple **new initialize** $\Rightarrow$ a red Apple

> Banana **new initialize** ⇒ a yellow Banana
> Banana **new initialize**; **color**: #green ⇒ a green Banana

But this is still cumbersome. We need to send two messages! Why not write a method—say, called **initializingNew**—that combines **new** and **initialize**?

> Potato **initializingNew** ⇒ a white Potato
> Onion **initializingNew** ⇒ a white Onion
> Apple **initializingNew** ⇒ a red Apple
> Banana **initializingNew** ⇒ a yellow Banana
> Banana **initializingNew color**: #green ⇒ a green Banana

Is this an instance method or a class method? Since the receiver is a class, it must surely be a class method. Let's implement it for class Apple first. Then we'll consider it for the other classes.

instance creation (class method in class Apple)

initializingNew
    ^Apple **new initialize**

It seems too simple! We just get a new apple, initialize it, and then return the initialized instance. We could have done the same thing using a local variable, as shown below, but it seems unnecessary to use such a variable.

instance creation (class method in class Apple)

initializingNew
    | anApple |
    anApple := Apple **new**.
    anApple **initialize**.
    ^anApple

If it's so simple, what can go wrong? Several things! Let's rewrite this method in a number of different ways to illustrate potential problems. Your task is to determine (1) if the method is correct and (2) if it isn't, what is wrong with it.

instance creation (class method in class Apple)

initializingNew
    ^self **new initialize**

In this case, it should work fine. The receiver is the class Apple, so "self **new**" is equivalent to "Apple **new**".

instance creation (class method in class Apple)

initializingNew
    Apple **new initialize**

This doesn't work! Since "^" is missing, the receiver is returned by default. But the receiver is the class. Rather than returning an instance of an apple, class Apple is returned instead.

instance creation (class method in class Apple)

initializingNew
    ^Apple **new initialize**; **color**: #green

This works correctly. However, it is odd for **initializingNew** to provide an instance with a color different from the default color, which is #red.

instance creation (class method in class Apple)

initializingNew
    ^Apple **new**; **initialize**

This does not work. The **initialize** method (because of the cascading caused by the semicolon) is sent to class Apple rather than to the instance. Does the class have an **initialize** method? There might very well be one in class Object. If so, the system will be reinitialized and the class will be returned as the answer—not what we wanted. If the class has no **initialize** method, we will get a walkback window reporting an error.

instance creation (class method in class Apple)

initializingNew
    | anApple |
    anApple := Apple **new**.
    color := #red.
    sweetness := #sweet.
    cooking := false.
    ^anApple

It's not even possible to save this method, let alone use it. If you try to save it, you will get an error message, as shown in Figure 6.19.

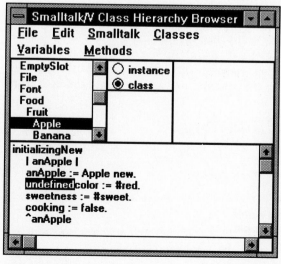

Figure 6.19 Trying to save a class method that references instance variables.

The least important problem is a style problem. You shouldn't be trying to initialize the parts individually if you already have a method to do this; namely, method **initialize**. The second, more important problem is that you can't access the color part of an instance in a class method. Part color can be accessed only in an instance method where it refers to the color part of self, the receiver. In this case, self is the class and the class does not have a part called color.

How do we fix it? Not by defining it. Making color a local variable is wrong because that will only change the binding of the local variable. The color part of anApple will be unaffected. The only way you can change the color part of anApple is to send it a message, as we have done in a prior example; e.g., by executing "anApple **color**: #red". The same holds for the other parts, sweetness and cooking.

instance creation (class method in class Apple)

initializingNew
    ^Apple **initialize new**

This method first attempts to initialize the class. If it works, the class is probably returned by the **initialize** method. Then **new** is sent to the class to obtain an uninitialized instance. Clearly, order matters.

To review, we have seen several ways of implementing method **initializingNew** incorrectly. One of the correct ways is shown below (so you won't have to look back). Now, we have to decide how to provide an **initializingNew** method in all the other classes.

instance creation (class method in class Apple)

initializingNew
    ^Apple **new initialize**

The worst possible way is to repeat the approach seven times, once for each class. The best way is to place the above method as high up the hierarchy as we can so that we can reuse it in all the subclasses; i.e., have it available through inheritance. Of course, if we just put this method in class Food and delete it from class Apple to get

instance creation (class method in class Food)

initializingNew
    ^Apple **new initialize**

we will find that it doesn't work:

Potato **initializingNew** ⇒ a red Apple
Onion **initializingNew** ⇒ a red Apple

Even though we are sending **initializingNew** to Potato, the method insists on obtaining a new apple. You should already know how to fix this method. If you don't, simply determine what **self** is in method **initializingNew**. When the message is sent to Potato, **self** is Potato; when it is sent to Onion, **self** is Onion; when it is sent to Apple, **self** is surely Apple. Rather than say "Potato **new**", "Onion **new**", and "Apple **new**", respectively, it is sufficient to say "self **new**". So the method, which exists only once in class Food, can be revised as follows:

instance creation (class method in class Food)

initializingNew
    ^self **new initialize**

There is still the possibility that we might forget to initialize our instances—we might just use **new** by mistake rather than **initializingNew**. And, of course, **initializingNew** is such a long message to type. It would be more convenient if **new** gave us an initialized instance. Then we could just write the following:

Potato **new** ⇒ a white Potato
Onion **new** ⇒ a green Onion
Apple **new** ⇒ a red Apple
Banana **new** ⇒ a yellow Banana
Banana **new color**: #green ⇒ a green Banana

The obvious solution is to write our own **new**. But what should our **new** do? Exactly what our **initializingNew** does. Do we copy or reuse the code? For example, would the following be a reasonable solution?

instance creation (class method in class Food)

initializingNew
    ^self **new initialize**

new
    ^self **initializingNew**

You should now be able to predict that this will not work. The first thing that happens, perhaps surprisingly, when you attempt to save class method **new** is that a **caution** window appears, as shown in Figure 6.20. It simply is informing you that **new** already exists higher up in the hierarchy—presumably in class Object. In fact, the same caution window should have occurred when you created your own **printOn:** method, since there already existed one in Object. Simply click on **OK** and carry on.

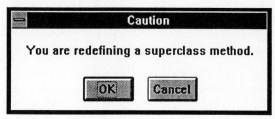

Figure 6.20 It's ok to redefine a method that exists higher up in the class hierarchy.

Now if you try to obtain an instance by executing "Apple **new**", a walkback window (see Figure 6.21) appears. A **stack overflow** indicates that we ran out of space. It's the standard infinite loop problem. Method **initializingNew** sends the message **new** to class Apple while **new** sends **initializingNew**, which causes the cycle to repeat again.

The problem is that method **initializingNew** should be using the **new** in Object, not the **new** in Food. The solution is quite simple. Use "super **new**" instead of "self **new**" to get the **new** higher up. The two class methods then appear as follows:

instance creation (class method in class Food)

initializingNew
    ^super **new initialize**

new
    ^self **initializingNew**

Figure 6.21 Another infinite loop.

Now that we have a solution that works, we might as well simplify it. We don't need two methods. A revised **new** is sufficient.

instance creation (class method in class Food)

new
    ^super **new initialize**

This is really quite a simple solution. We are saying that the **new** for all foods works by using the **new** defined higher up the class hierarchy. The instance that we get back is then initialized and also returned as the answer.

We conclude this section by placing all the methods that we developed together to make it easier to reference later.

class methods

instance creation (in class Food)

new
   ^super **new initialize**

instance methods

instance initialization (in class Food)

initialize
   self **color**: #green

instance initialization (in class Vegetable)

initialize
   super **initialize**.
   self **tuberous**: false

instance initialization (in class Fruit)

initialize
   super **initialize**.
   self **sweetness**: #sweet

instance initialization (in class Potato)

initialize
   super **initialize**.
   self **color**: #white.
   self **tuberous**: true.
   self **edibleSkin**: true

instance initialization (in class Onion)

initialize
   super **initialize**.
   self **eyeWatering**: true

instance initialization (in class Apple)

initialize
   super **initialize**.
   self **color**: #red.
   self **cooking**: false

instance initialization (in class Banana)

initialize
 super **initialize**.
 self **color:** #yellow.
 self **ripe:** false

The technique needed to properly create and initialize a hierarchy of classes is so fundamental that you will have many opportunities to apply it to new classes as you gain experience with Smalltalk. Because there is a rough pattern to be followed for generating a well-designed set of initialization methods, we refer to the technique as an **initialization framework**.

6.1.9 The Concept of Abstract Classes

We can divide the classes in our food hierarchy into two groups: abstract classes, which include Food, Vegetable, and Fruit; and concrete classes, which include Potato, Onion, Apple, and Banana. In general, an **abstract class** is a class for which we don't expect to have instances. By contrast, a **concrete class** is expected to have instances.

In the real world, all our objects are concrete. Consequently, it is not possible to have a pet that is an animal without it also being a specific kind of animal. The same applies to foods. It's not possible to have a food that is not one of the concrete foods. With our somewhat finite food hierarchy, we are saying that there are only four concrete foods: potatoes, onions, apples, and bananas. So you can't have one that isn't one of those four.

Abstract classes are extremely useful because they provide instance variables and methods that can be inherited by the instances of concrete classes. Is there any way to ask a class if it is abstract? As it turns out, there isn't. Moreover, there is no general rule for determining whether a class is abstract. In practice, a class is abstract if the original designer did not intend instances to be created.

Although we can't ask a class a direct question like "are you abstract?", we may still be able to deduce whether a class is abstract by looking at the hierarchy it belongs to. For example, if we look at the hierarchy shown in Figure 6.22, we can generally agree that the classes at the bottom must be concrete. Otherwise, what would be the point of having them? So Float, LargeNegativeInteger, SmallInteger, LargePositiveInteger, Fraction, and Symbol must all be concrete.

By contrast, classes higher up the hierarchy are candidates for abstract classes. For example, is Integer an abstract class? If it is, then the original designers intended instances of the subclasses to exist but not direct instances of Integer. Similarly, Number is also a good candidate for an abstract class. Do we really expect to be able to get an instance of Number that is neither a float, an integer, or a fraction? But we have to be careful. Just because a class has subclasses doesn't mean that it is abstract. Consider String, for example. Even though it has subclass

Symbol, it is still a concrete class because instances are available; e.g., 'hello there' is a string.

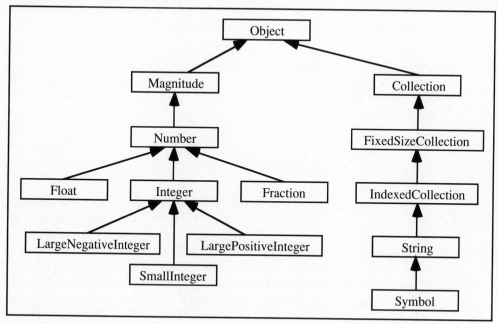

Figure 6.22 Looking for abstract classes in a hierarchy of classes.

There must exist some tests that will help resolve the issue. Consider the following possibilities:

- If a class has no instances, it *might* be an abstract class—by contrast, if there are instances, it is definitely concrete. We can get a class' instances by sending it the message **allInstances**.
- If we can't make an instance of a class, it is *likely* to be abstract. We must be careful, however, because some objects are constructed with messages other than **new** or **new**:.

Let try using first test. Some results are indicated below.

```
Object allInstances ⇒ ()
Magnitude allInstances ⇒ ()
Number allInstances ⇒ ()
Integer allInstances ⇒ ()
Fraction allInstances ⇒ (1/2 1/3 ...)

Collection allInstances ⇒ ()
FixedSizeCollection allInstances ⇒ ()
IndexedCollection allInstances ⇒ ()
String allInstances ⇒ ('hello' 'just a test' ...)
```

This really has not resolved very much. We already know that all classes at the bottom of the hierarchy are concrete and that class String is also concrete. None of the other classes have instances, so they are likely to be abstract, but we can't be sure. The next step is to attempt to make instances.

```
Object new ⇒ an Object
Magnitude new ⇒ a Magnitude
Number new ⇒ (error)
Integer new ⇒ (error)
Fraction new ⇒ (error)

Collection new ⇒ (error)
FixedSizeCollection new ⇒ FixedSizeCollection ()
IndexedCollection new ⇒ (error)
String new ⇒ "
```

A typical error message is shown in Figure 6.23. This is the message that resulted when we executed "Number **new**". Assuming that **new** is the correct message to use to construct instances, we might argue that only Object, Magnitude, and FixedSizeCollection are potential concrete classes. So the others must be abstract. If **new** is not the correct message to use for obtaining instances of these classes, however, we should be getting an error message anyway and so we don't learn anything. This is the case, for example, for fractions. Fractions are not constructed by executing "Fraction **new**". Rather, they are constructed by sending a divide message to an integer; e.g. 1/2 or 1/(1+1).

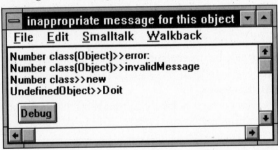

Figure 6.23 Attempting to create an instance of abstract class Number.

Even though we can obtain instances of classes Object, Magnitude, and FixedSizeCollection, it might be just an oversight on the part of the designers. In other words, if the designers intended these to be abstract, they might have assumed that we would not try to make instances. And so they might not have done anything to prevent instances from being created in the first place.

However, if they were intended to be concrete, not only would we be able to make instances, but we would also be able to send messages appropriate to the instances and get reasonable responses. In the case of Magnitude, for example, we might expect to be able to compare magnitudes using >, <, and =.

```
Magnitude new > Magnitude new ⇒ (error)
Magnitude new = 1 ⇒ (error)
```

As it turns out, we can't. However, we can compare instances of subclasses that are concrete; e.g., 1.2 > 1.1 or 6 > 5. By contrast, objects in general are not magnitudes but we should be able to compare them using =. The same presumably applies to fixed-size collections. Since a fixed-size collection is a collection, we should also be able to ask it what its size is.

```
Object new = 1 ⇒ false
FixedSizeCollection new = 1 ⇒ false
FixedSizeCollection new size ⇒ 0
```

In general, anything that objects understand will work on instances of Object. Similarly, anything that fixed-size collections understand will work on instances of FixedSizeCollection—at least, on empty ones. Maybe we should try operations on a slightly larger fixed-size collection.

```
FixedSizeCollection new: 2 ⇒ (error)
```

Interesting! We can't get a fixed-size collection larger than size 0. So now we know that the designers did not intend FixedSizeCollection to have instances. Clearly, FixedSizeCollection is abstract. Now only Object is unresolved. In this case, we could continue to experiment with instances of Object, but we wouldn't ever find any problem using them. In the end, we would conclude that Object is concrete because we can create and manipulate instances without restriction.

To summarize, classes Object, String, and all the classes at the bottom of the hierarchy in Figure 6.22 are concrete. All other classes are abstract.

6.1.10 Case Study Extension: Making Food and Fruit Abstract

As currently implemented, all the classes in the food hierarchy are concrete because we can obtain instances and manipulate them. For example,

```
Food new ⇒ a green Food
Vegetable new ⇒ a green Vegetable
Fruit new ⇒ a green Fruit
Food new color: #red ⇒ a red Food
Fruit new color: #yellow ⇒ a yellow Fruit
```

What would we have to do so that we *couldn't* obtain instances? In particular, what would we have to do so that the following would occur:

```
Food new ⇒ (error; see Figure  6.24)
Vegetable new ⇒ (error; see Figure  6.24)
Fruit new ⇒ (error; see Figure  6.24)
Potato new ⇒ a white Potato
Onion new ⇒ a green Onion
Apple new ⇒ a red Apple
Banana new ⇒ a yellow Banana
Banana new color: #green ⇒ a green Banana
```

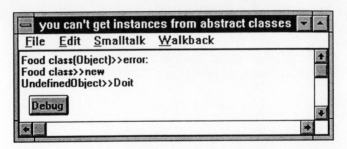

Figure 6.24 The walkback window if **new** in Food generates an error message.

Recall that **new** is currently implemented only in class Food.

instance creation (class method in class Food)

new
          ^super n**ew initialize**

This implementation can be paraphrased as "use the new higher up (presumably in Object) to get an actual instance and then initialize that instance before returning it." We need an implementation that makes it illegal to make an instance of class Food; for example, a method such as the following:

instance creation (class method (n class Food)

new
          ^self **error**: 'you can''t get instances from abstract classes'

This will result in the same kind of walkback window that we normally get when we make a mistake during execution; e.g., a walkback window, as shown in Figure 6.24. Unfortunately, it also introduces a very serious bug. Now, we can't even get a concrete object like a potato or a banana. If we try "Potato **new**", for example, we get the same walkback window.

Perhaps we can take the method we used to have in Food and put it lower down in each of the concrete classes. Then we would end up with the following five methods.

instance creation (class method in class Food)

new
          ^self **error**: 'you can''t get instances from abstract classes'

instance creation (class method in class Potato)

new
          ^super n**ew initialize**

instance creation (class method in class Onion)

new
          ^super n**ew initialize**

instance creation (class method in class Apple)

new
    ^super n**ew initialize**

instance creation (class method in class Banana)

new
    ^super n**ew initialize**

If we try again, we find that it still doesn't work. Why? Because the **new** method in Apple, for example, uses the **new** method above it and it's the **new** method in Food that gives us the error message. We want the **new** method in Apple to use the **new** method in Object—we want to be able to jump around the **new** method in Food. As it turns out, there is no simple way of doing that in Smalltalk; you can't just say "super super **new**". Why not? Because the second super would be a message, but **super** is not a message. We need to try something more complex, like the following:

instance creation (class method in class Food)

new
    ^self **error**: 'you can''t get instances from abstract classes'

privateNew
    ^super n**ew**

instance creation (class method in class Potato)

new
    ^self **privateNew initialize**

instance creation (class method in class Onion)

new
    ^self **privateNew initialize**

instance creation (class method in class Apple)

new
    ^self **privateNew initialize**

instance creation (class method in class Banana)

new
    ^self **privateNew initialize**

This does seem to solve the problem. To see why, consider executing "Banana **new**". Method **new** in Banana sends itself the message **privateNew** which is found by the method lookup mechanism in class Food. When "super **new**" is executed in the **privateNew** method, the method lookup mechanism begins the search for **new** in a class above the class that contains **privateNew**; i.e., in Object.

So we end up getting a new instance, as we should. This instance is, of course, returned to the original **new** method in class Banana, which then proceeds to **initialize** it before returning it. This approach seems to work but it doesn't seem to be as simple as we could make it. For example, we could simplify these methods a bit more by moving **initialize** up into method **privateNew**. Then it would occur only once rather than four times.

Nevertheless, there is still something unsatisfactory about this solution. It seems a little contorted. Indeed, this particular problem was anticipated by the Smalltalk designers. To solve it, they decided that method **new** (the one that actually does the work of creating an uninitialized instance) was not adequate by itself. So they provided another method, called **basicNew** that is equivalent to **new**. The idea was that programmers might redefine **new** but they would never, by convention, redefine **basicNew**. If we rewrite our solution to use **basicNew** instead of **privateNew**, we will get an uninitialized instance that we can then proceed to initialize. A revised solution can then be written as follows:

instance creation (class method in class Food)

new
        ^self **error:** 'you can''t get instances from abstract classes'

instance creation (class method in class Potato)

new
        ^self **basicNew initialize**

instance creation (class method in class Onion)

new
        ^self **basicNew initialize**

instance creation (class method in class Apple)

new
        ^self **basicNew initialize**

instance creation (class method in class Banana)

new
        ^self **basicNew initialize**

Note that we did not provide a **new** method in Vegetable or Fruit because the **new** method inherited from Food is the one needed by both of these subclasses.

Now we have a reasonably well-designed solution. But it is still too complex. Consider, for example, what we would have to do if we were to introduce a new class—say, called Pear—into the hierarchy. We would have to provide a **new** method that looks just like the other **new** methods in the other concrete classes. In other words, we would have to duplicate code. And we know that code duplication is a bad idea, in general. One approach that might eliminate the need to continually add a variation of **new** when new subclasses are created is to merge all these methods into one. We might consider designing a **new** method in class Food that executes something like the following:

> if I'm class Food, Vegetable, or Fruit
> > then I will generate an error message
> > otherwise, I will obtain a basic object and initialize it

In Smalltalk, this might translate to something like

instance creation (class method in class Food)

new
>(self **class** = Food) | (self **class** = Vegetable) | (self **class** = Fruit)
>> **ifTrue:** [^self **error:** 'you can''t get instances from abstract classes']
>> **ifFalse:** [^self **basicNew initialize**]

Now, we don't need a variation of **new** in the concrete classes. If we add a new concrete class such as Pear, it can inherit the **new** method from Food. Note that we no longer need to use **basicNew**. A cleaner and simpler solution would just use "super **new**", as follows:

instance creation (class method in class Food)

new
>(self **class** = Food) | (self **class** = Vegetable) | (self **class** = Fruit)
>> **ifTrue:** [^self **error:** 'you can''t get instances from abstract classes']
>> **ifFalse:** [^super **new initialize**]

Now let's summarize what we have learned. Classes Food, Vegetable, and Fruit are abstract classes and Potato, Onion, Apple, and Banana are concrete classes. We expect users to make instances of the concrete classes but not of the abstract classes. As a rule, whenever we create an abstract class, we need to decide who is responsible for preventing instances from being created. There are two possibilities:

- *The class is responsible* for explicitly preventing instances from being created. This is the solution we used above and also appears to be the solution used for some classes such as Number.
- *The user is responsible* for not creating instances. If the user insists on creating instances, it is the user's fault when something goes wrong. This seems to be the solution used for other classes such as Magnitude.

Is there a solution that is most popular in Smalltalk? We haven't really experimented enough to provide a definitive answer to this question. But if we did, we would find that few abstract classes in Smalltalk actually complain when we try to obtain instances. Clearly, it's easier to do nothing than to take great pains to prevent instances from being constructed. So it is normally the user who is responsible for not creating instances of abstract classes.

Whether we can obtain instances from a class is not really what determines whether it is abstract. More realistically, a class is abstract if the instances are not intended for use by an application. We might want to try to obtain an instance for experimentation purposes, but we really wouldn't want to use one for real.

6.2   Case Study: Bank Accounts

In the previous section, we dealt with a hierarchy of food classes in order to understand the intricacies of inheritance—how method lookup works, how instance variables are inherited, how initialization should be implemented, what abstract classes are for, and so on. Now we need to exercise this newly discovered knowledge so that we will be more comfortable with the concepts.

Let's consider applying our knowledge to the banking domain. In particular, let's create a hierarchy of bank account classes such as we might need if we were to manage bank accounts in Smalltalk.

6.2.1   Creating an Initial Hierarchy

Before we can create a class for bank accounts, it might be useful to consider the typical things you can do with bank accounts. For example, we might **open** an account or **close** one. When we **open** an account, we might expect to have to supply a name and an address. Once we have a bank account, we will likely want to make **deposits** and **withdrawals**. Presumably, we should always be able to find out what the bank account's current **balance** is. Then, there is the issue of **interest rates**. Once a month, perhaps, the bank computes how much interest is accumulated on your savings and adds that interest to the current balance. But there are some bank accounts that don't get interest at all—they are called **checking**[1] accounts. The others are **savings** accounts.

This process of determining how many classes we need, what operations or methods must be supported by the classes, and the relationship between the classes and the instances is called **designing**. Our goal here is to design a set of banking account classes that might serve as the starting point for a more elaborate banking application.

To begin with, we have concluded that we need at least two classes. Let's call them **SavingsAccount** and **CheckingAccount**. Our first task is to organize these classes into a hierarchy. With only two classes, you might think that the solution is trivial. But there are at least three ways of organizing two classes. Figure 6.25 illustrates the possibilities. Let's consider each one in turn.

---

[1]In fact, there are dozens of different types of bank accounts. Some variations of checking accounts yield interest and others don't. For simplicity, we'll assume that checking accounts do not yield interest. This shouldn't detract from the more important points being considered in this section.

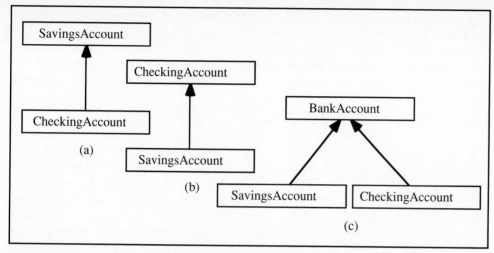

Figure 6.25 Three ways of organizing two classes.

There are two ways to help us decide which is the best choice:

- The **implementation perspective**, in which we take inheritance into account
- The **user perspective**, in which we consider what makes the most sense intuitively—generally, by considering the **is-a** relationship

From the implementation point of view, it is useful to try to determine which class has the most operations. Recall that savings accounts need the ability to compute interest on their balances but checking accounts do not. So savings accounts have more operations than checking accounts.

If we use design choice (a), we will find that the operations in savings accounts for managing interest calculations will automatically be inherited by checking accounts. But we don't want this because checking accounts should not support interest calculations. So choice (a) is a poor choice from the implementation perspective.

If we use design choice (b), checking accounts (at the top) will not support interest calculations (if done properly). However, they will support all the expected bank account operations such as opening and closing, depositing and withdrawing amounts, and so on. Savings accounts could inherit all these checking account operations and also introduce their own for computing interest. So choice (b) is a good choice from the implementation perspective.

From the user's point of view, we need to compare the two kinds of accounts with respect to the **is-a** relationship. For example, is a checking account also a savings account? This is what is suggested by choice (a) if we interpret the connection from CheckingAccount to SavingsAccount as an **is-a** relationship. I think we would all agree that a checking account is not a savings account, so choice (a) is a poor choice from the user's perspective, too. Conversely, we probably would not want to say that a savings account is a checking account, either, although someone might argue that a savings account is really a special kind of checking account in which interest-rate calculations are allowed. Choice (b), then, might be barely acceptable, but it is not a good choice from the user's perspective since not everyone would agree.

The third choice is interesting. It should be clear that all operations common to both savings accounts and checking accounts can be kept in BankAccount. SavingsAccount would consequently inherit **most** of its operations from BankAccount, although it would provide its own unique operations for handling interest calculations. CheckingAccount, by contrast, would inherit **all** its operations from BankAccount—unless we could think of a few new operations unique to checking accounts. With this design, SavingsAccount and CheckingAccount would be concrete classes and BankAccount would be an abstract class. So from the implementation perspective, choice (c) is a good choice because it takes advantage of inheritance. From the user's perspective, everyone would agree that both savings accounts and checking accounts are bank accounts;—choice (c) is a correct **is-a** relationship. Consequently, choice (c) is also a good choice from the user's viewpoint.

> *As a rule of thumb, the best designs are good choices both from the implementation viewpoint and the user's viewpoint.*

Having decided on choice (c), let's start by defining three classes. At this early stage, we might not be able to guess what kind of instance variables we will need. However, we do know that a bank account will need to keep track of the name and address of the owner of the account and, as a minimum, keep the account balance. So we might begin with the following.:

class	BankAccount
superclass	Object
instance variables	name address balance
class	SavingsAccount
superclass	BankAccount
instance variables	"none (so far)"
class	CheckingAccount
superclass	BankAccount
instance variables	"none (so far)"

6.2.2 Adding Behavior (Methods)

Having designed a hierarchy of banking account classes, the next step might be to provide each class with methods that will determine the **behavior** of the objects; i.e., what the object can do. A bank account's behavior is dictated solely by the messages it understands and by the manner in which it reacts to those messages.

Our first task, then, might be to choose names for the methods that we believe will be needed.

> *When we choose names for methods, we should always strive to use domain-relevant terminology.*

For bank account objects, we should use banking terminology, just as we would use architecture terminology for an architecture application. We already reviewed most of the terms when we first introduced bank accounts. Nevertheless, a few are worth considering in more detail.

In particular, if we didn't care about using domain-specific terms, we might create bank accounts by asking for a **new** one rather than **opening** an account, we might **add** money to our account rather than make a **deposit**, and we might **subtract** money from the account rather than make a **withdrawal**. Of course, if we didn't know anything about banking in the first place, it would be difficult to use domain-specific terms. But we could always interview a banker to find out which terms to use, or locate a book that summarizes what banking is all about.

As we have done in previous chapters, perhaps the best way to get started is to create an example method that uses a sampling of the messages we might expect bank accounts to understand.

class	BankAccount
superclass	Object
instance variables	name address balance

class method

examples

example1
```
    "BankAccount example1"
    | account1 account2 |
    account1 := SavingsAccount open
        name: 'Wilf LaLonde';
        address: '24 Fall Down Lane, Ottawa, Canada'.
    account2 := CheckingAccount open
        name: account1 name;
        address: account1 address.
    account1 deposit: (Money dollars: 100).
    account2 deposit: (account1 withdraw: (Money dollars: 25)).
    Transcript cr; nextPutAll: 'Savings account is '.
    account1 printOn: Transcript.
    Transcript cr; nextPutAll: 'Checking account is '.
    account2 printOn: Transcript.
```

Now, we can go on to provide

- Accessing and modification methods for those instance variables that are intended to be public (the balance, for example, should change only as a consequence of depositing or withdrawing monetary amounts—so we shouldn't provide a method to change the balance)
- An **initialize** method that sets meaningful defaults for the instance variables
- A **printOn**: method that prints the essentials of a bank account (without printing too much)
- Domain-specific operations such as **open**, **close**, **deposit:**, and **withdraw:**

The **open** method, for example, must be a class method, presumably in BankAccount, but it should work for both savings and checking accounts. The corresponding **close** method should be an instance method, since we have to be able to close existing accounts—not the class. But what should we do to close an account? If it were a real bank account, the bank itself would be asked to close the account. We could create a class called **Bank** whose sole role would be to keep track of all the opened bank accounts. When an existing account is closed, this account could simply be removed from its list of accounts. For the moment, let's adopt a simpler solution. Since an account that is closed has nothing in it, we will simply reinitialize it. If our **initialize** method is properly implemented, this will reset all the instance variables to standard defaults.

As a rule, the initialization framework that we described in great detail in the first part of this chapter suggests that we should provide an **initialize** method in each of our three classes. Since we have not yet provided instance variables in the two subclasses of BankAccount, there is no point having an **initialize** method whose sole purpose is to send a message to the **initialize** method higher up the hierarchy. We'll just omit the **initialize** method in the subclasses for now and have them automatically inherit the one in BankAccount.

Similarly, we should be able to design a single **printOn**: method in BankAccount that can differentiate between savings and checking accounts.

Tthe **withdraw**: method should provide some sort of error message if there is insufficient funds to make the withdrawal. Also, as we have used it in method **example1** above, message "**withdraw**: amount" seems to return the amount of money withdrawn. This makes it convenient for cross-account transfers. Should **deposit**: similarly return the amount deposited? In both of these methods, we have the option of returning either the receiver (the bank account) or the amount withdrawn or deposited. As designers, we need to make a choice. It is also important to make that choice known to users of the class in a comment at the beginning of the method. Let's make both **withdraw**: and **deposit**: return the amount withdrawn or deposited.

Taking all of this into account, we might end up with the following methods:

class	BankAccount
superclass	Object
instance variables	name address balance

class methods

instance creation

new
>"Construct a fully initialized bank account."
>^super **new initialize**

open
>"Construct a fully initialized bank account."
>^self **new**

examples

example1
>"BankAccount example1"
>... see above ...

instance methods

instance initialization

initialize
>"Provide meaningful defaults."
>self **name**: 'Unknown'; **address**: 'Unknown'.
>balance := (Money **cents**: 0).

instance finalization

close
>"In the absence of a bank, reinitialize."
>self **initialize**

accessing and modification

name
>^name

name: aString
>name := aString

address
>^address

address: aString
>address := aString

balance
>^balance

printing

printOn: aWindow
"Prints like 'Wilf LaLonde's SavingsAccount (balance $50.00)'."
aWindow
nextPutAll: self **name**; **nextPutAll**: '''s ';
nextPutAll: self **class name**;
nextPutAll: ' (balance '.
self **balance printOn**: aWindow.
aWindow **nextPut**: $)

domain-specific operations

deposit: aMoney
"Deposits aMoney and also returns the amount deposited."
balance := balance + aMoney.
^aMoney

withdraw: aMoney
"Withdraws aMoney and also returns the amount withdrawn."
balance >= aMoney
ifTrue: [balance := balance - aMoney].
ifFalse: [self **error**: 'insufficient funds'].
^aMoney

Notice that **deposit**: and **withdraw**: respectively execute the following:

balance := balance + aMoney.
balance := balance - aMoney.

You should read this as

bind the new balance to the sum of the old balance and aMoney.
bind the new balance to the difference between the old balance and aMoney.

If the old balance was $100.00 and aMoney was $10.00, the corresponding new balances would be the following:

balance := $100.00 + $10.00 (or $110.00)
balance := $100.00 - $10.00 (or $90.00)

Having defined and implemented class BankAccount, let's now consider the first subclass, SavingsAccount. Since savings accounts need to be able to periodically add interest to the account, say once a month, there is a need to record the interest rate somewhere. Is this rate different for each instance or is it the same for all savings accounts? If the former is the case, we will need to introduce a new instance variable. Otherwise, a class variable will be sufficient.

In general, the interest rate can change but there is only one interest rate in effect at any particular time. When the interest is computed, it is always computed using the current interest rate. So the best solution (so far, at least) is to use a class variable. A name like InterestRate might be sufficient but an even better name such as CurrentInterestRate, would be more informative. Note that we don't have interest objects that print themselves, for example, as 12%. It seems like too much work to create an entire class just for this purpose. So we'll just use fraction 12/100 to represent 12%.

So that we can change the interest rate, we will need a method—say, called **interestRate:**. But we shouldn't need an instance just to change the interest rate. Consequently, this method should be a class method. A class method for accessing this interest rate—say, called **interestRate**—should also be provided. To compute and add the interest to our savings account, we will need an instance method (since a savings account is an instance). Generally, interest is computed once a month rather than on a yearly basis (at 1/12 of the current interest rate). So a name like **addMonthlyInterest** would be a better choice than **addInterest**.

class	SavingsAccount
superclass	BankAccount
instance variables	"none (so far)"
class variables	CurrentInterestRate

class methods

interest rate accessing and modifying

interestRate
    "Returns the interest rate as a fraction; e.g., 12/100 means 12%."
    ^CurrentInterestRate

interestRate: aFraction
    "Sets the interest rate, which is recorded as a fraction; e.g., 12/100 means 12%."
    CurrentInterestRate := aFraction

    "SavingsAccount interestRate: 12/100"

instance methods

interest rate calculation

addMonthlyInterest
    "Computes the monthly interest on the current balance and deposits it."
    self **deposit:** self **balance** * (self **class interestRate** / 12)

Before we use this class, we'll have to be sure to set the interest rate. Otherwise, class variable CurrentInterestRate will be uninitialized; i.e., nil. To make this convenient, we added a comment at the end of method **interestRate:**. Anyone can select the code inside the comment (without selecting the quotes) to initialize the interest rate. Alternatively, we could have created an **initialize** method (a class method) whose sole purpose is to set the interest rate as follows:

class methods

class initialization

initialize
"Must be executed once after the class is constructed"
"SavingsAccount initialize"
self **interestRate**: 12/100

Finally, let's consider subclass CheckingAccount. Checking accounts don't provide interest but they do provide another service. They keep a record of the checks made out to the account. Every time a check made out to your account is processed by a teller, a short descriptive string describing the check is inserted into your checking account. It should then be possible to ask for a complete list of all the checks made out to the account.

We can anticipate the need for a new instance variable for keeping track of this information. But we need an appropriate domain-specific name. For example, names like comments or list are totally inappropriate. A name like checkList would be better. Better yet would be a name like checkingHistory.

We should begin by constructing an example method since it will allow us to determine how checks should be submitted to the checking account and how the checking history can be retrieved. Note that we don't have to know how to implement the methods that we'll need to use. We can leave that for later.

class   CheckingAccount
superclass   BankAccount
instance variables   checkingHistory

class methods

examples

example1
"CheckingAccount example1"
| aCheckingAccount |
aCheckingAccount := CheckingAccount **open**.
aCheckingAccount
    deposit: (Money **dollars**: 500);
    check: (Money **dollars**: 100) **comment**: 'Check #1: J.C. Penny';
    check: (Money **cents**: 1023) **comment**: 'Check #2: Joe''s Gas';
    check: (Money **dollars**: 120) **comment**: 'Check #3: Woolworth'.
Transcript **cr**.
aCheckingAccount **printOn**: Transcript.
Transcript **nextPutAll**: ' made the following checks: '.
aCheckingAccount **checkingHistory printOn**: Transcript

We can now attempt to add the two instance methods that we used in **example1**. Clearly, there is a problem—we don't know how to manage lists.

instance methods

instance initialization

initialize
    super **initialize**.
    ... NOW INITIALIZE checkingHistory SOMEHOW ...

checking history manipulation

check: aMoney **comment:** aString
    "Make a withdrawal for the amount of the check and record the string in
    the checking history."
    self **withdraw:** aMoney.
    "Insert aString into the checking history."
    ... WE DON'T KNOW HOW TO DO THIS ...

checkingHistory
    ^checkingHistory

The problem now is to figure out what to do when we don't know how to do it. Before we come up with a solution, we need a bit of experience using the system as a source of knowledge. Surely, there must be some classes and operations on the instances of those classes that will allow us to finish our implementation. We just need to know how to look for such a class and for such operations. So let's take a short detour to find out how to use Smalltalk to help us find answers.

6.2.3 Browsing the Smalltalk Library

Let's take a very simple problem and ask how we would go about solving it, given that we have access to the Smalltalk environment. For example, suppose we built an ice rink that was 100 feet long by 10 feet wide (or 100 meters long by 10 meters wide) and we wanted to know the distance between opposite corners. There is a simple formula for finding the answer; namely,

$$\sqrt{\text{length}^2 + \text{width}^2}$$

A partial solution might consist of the following:

```
| length width solution |
length := 100.
width := 10.
solution := ((length * length) + (width * width)) squareRootPlease.
^solution
```

Few of us will know how to find the square root of a number in Smalltalk. We could make a guess and try **squareRoot**. If we do, we will get an error message, because numbers simply do not understand **squareRoot**. Presumably, we have just used the wrong name for the message. But another possibility is that there is no message that will allow us to determine the square root of a number in Smalltalk. To find out, we have to go searching. Of course, we can't just search arbitrarily. We have to know where to start. *To know where to start searching, we need to ask what kind of object is a likely receiver for this message*. In our case, the receiver is (100*100) + (10*10) = 10000 + 100 = 10100, which is an integer (more precisely, a small integer). Of course, 10100 is also a number, a magnitude, and an object.

In general, *we should always begin our search at the most specific class*—in this case, SmallInteger. *If we fail to find it there, we should consider the next class higher up in the hierarchy*; i.e., superclass Integer, in this case. Continuing in this manner, we would next search Number, then Magnitude, and finally Object. Of course, during our search, it is always possible to find something that will cause us abandon this search direction; i.e., to search elsewhere if we find a better clue to the probable location of the method we are looking for.

Recall that this process of looking at classes and methods in the Smalltalk environment is called **browsing**. In this case, we are browsing with a purpose since we are looking for a method that will enable us to find the square root of an integer. Let's start by selecting class SmallInteger in a browser, making sure that the instance switch has been selected since we are looking for an instance method, not a class method. In general, the methods in the method list pane are sorted. So we should only need to look at methods beginning with "s"—assuming that "square root", whichever way it is spelled, at least begins with "s". The browser, in this case, might appear as shown in Figure 6.26.

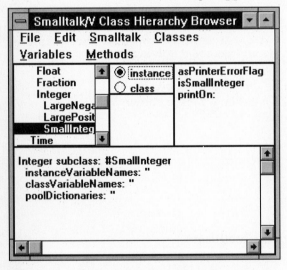

Figure 6.26 Browsing class SmallInteger.

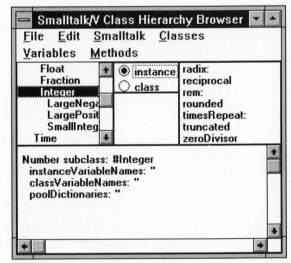

Figure 6.27 Browsing class Integer.

In this case, there are only three methods. None of them seem relevant because their names have nothing to do with finding a square root. So we might as well repeat the process on class Integer that is immediately above this class in the hierarchy. In that case, we will find (see Figure 6.27) that there are a large number of methods. In fact, we have to scroll to get to see them all. If we scroll to the section beginning with "s", we again fail to find a relevant method.

Repeating this process one more time, we do find something interesting in class Number (see Figure 6.28). We find a method called **sqrt**, which suspiciously appears to be a short form for "square root". It is worthwhile clicking on **sqrt** in the method list pane to see the code for the method in the code pane. The comment indicates that it is indeed the method for finding the square root of a number.

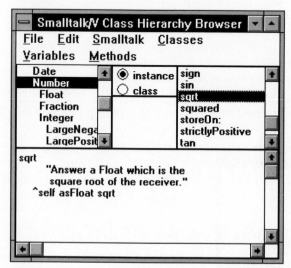

Figure 6.28 Browsing class Number.

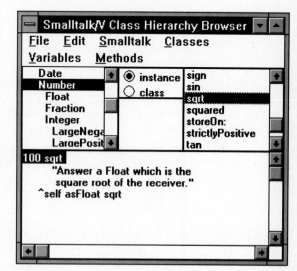

Figure 6.29 Testing the method by sending **sqrt** to an integer.

Just to be sure that it is the correct method, we should try it out by typing a suitable receiver (100, in this case) directly in the browser, as shown in Figure 6.29.

We should find that

    100 **sqrt** ⇒ 10.0

As we can see by reading the code, the real work is actually done in a float method also called **sqrt**. Consequently, if we ask 100.0 for its square root, we should expect to get the same answer. Notice that we get a floating point answer regardless of whether the receiver is an integer or a float.

    100 **sqrt** ⇒ 10.0
    100.0 **sqrt** ⇒ 10.0

So now, we can revise our solution as follows:

```
| length width solution |
length := 100.
width := 10.
solution := ((length * length) + (width * width)) sqrt.
^solution
```

Whenever we browse for something specific, such as **sqrt**, it is nearly always the case that accidental discoveries are made. For example, our solution was written in such a manner that length and width were multiplied by themselves to get their squares. But if we look immediately below **sqrt** in the browser's method list pane, we notice the method **squared**. If it actually squares the receiver, we might want to use it in our solution. We should at least click on it to see if the comment and perhaps even the code indicates that this is the case. Having made a slight change to the method in the browser, you might be surprised to find the sudden appearance of a prompter, as shown in Figure 6.30. Simply click on **No** because the modification made in the browser was not intended to cause the method to be modified. By now, you should have already encountered this prompter a number of times.

Figure 6.30 A request about what to do with the previously modified method.

As we can see from Figure 6.31, message **squared** will cause the receiver to be multiplied by itself. So we can revise our previous solution. The new solution can also be simplified by removing brackets that are now superfluous.

```
| length width solution |
length := 100.
width := 10.
solution := (length squared + width squared) sqrt.
^solution
```

Getting back to the **sqrt** method (see Figure 6.28), we were able to deduce that some variation must exist in class Float. Is there a third variation? The easiest way to answer such a question is to ask for all the **implementors** of the selector of the method being viewed; i.e., to ask for every **sqrt** method in the system. We do this by clicking on **Implementors** in the **Methods** menu, as shown in Figure 6.32.

The result is a new window (see Figure 6.33), with the title **Implementors of sqrt** and two subpanes: The top pane contains a list of method names and the bottom pane contains the source code for the selected method name. For example, "Float>>sqrt" in the top pane is the name of method **sqrt** in class Float. The bottom pane is the actual code for this method. We now know that there are

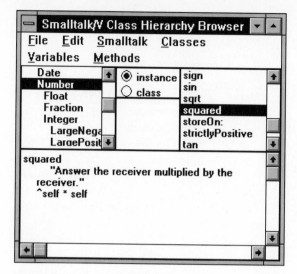

Figure 6.31 The **squared** method.

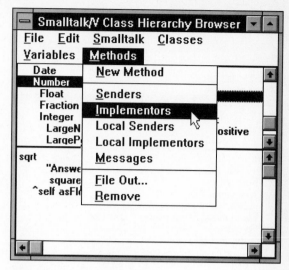

Figure 6.32 Asking for the implementors of **sqrt**.

exactly two implementations of method **sqrt**, one in Number, which we have already seen in Figure 6.28, and one in Float, seen here in Figure 6.33. The float implementation is not particularly decipherable because it is primitive. The best strategy for a novice, at this stage, is to ignore the code.

In general, when investigating new methods in the browser, four pieces of information are available to help us determine what a method does:

- The **method header**. Sometimes, the name is sufficient to tell us what the method does; e.g., the name **squared** is illuminating on its own
- The **comment**. It further explains what the method is intended to do
- The **code**. It provides further information (when it can be understood) that is sometimes missing from the comment
- **Examples** of code that use the method. Sometimes, examples help us to understand the method in more detail

The easiest way to find examples that use a method is to ask for the **senders** of the method being viewed—technically, the senders of messages with the same selector as the selected method. The senders of method **sqrt** consist of every method in the system that contains a **sqrt** message. We do this by clicking on **Senders** in the **Methods** menu as shown in Figure 6.34.

The result is a new window (see Figure 6.35) with the title **Senders of sqrt**. Since there are only two method names in the top pane, we know that only two methods in the entire system send the message **sqrt**; namely, method **arcSin** in Number and method **sqrt** in Number. We don't really care what **arcSin** does (it's a trigonometric operation) but we can discover something about **sqrt** if we look at the method. As we can see from Figure 6.35, the receiver of the **sqrt** message

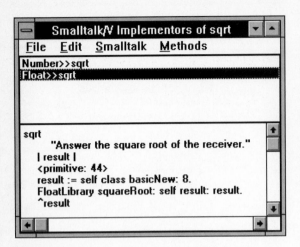

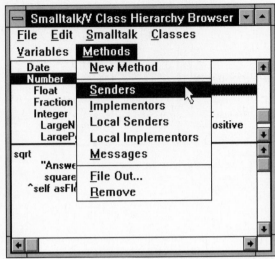

Figure 6.33 The implementors of **sqrt** (the Float implementation is being viewed).

Figure 6.34 Asking for the senders of **sqrt**.

is "(1 - (self * self))". Since **arcSin** is a Number method, self must be a number—however, we can't tell if it's an integer, float, or fraction. Consequently, the receiver for **sqrt** must be a number. If we didn't know this already, this might have turned out to be useful information.

Note that if we wanted to look further at the senders or implementors of **arcSin**, we would simply have to click on **Senders** or **Implementors** in the new window's **Methods** menu. The process can be repeated to search as many methods as we care to investigate.

Let's briefly review what we learned. When we click on a message selector like **sqrt** in a browser's method list pane, the code for the **sqrt** method is displayed in the code pane. We can ask *for the senders or implementors of this selector* by clicking on **Senders** or **Implementors,** respectively, in the **Methods** menu. This will cause a new window to appear that contains a complete list of all the methods that are implementations or users of the original **sqrt** method. We can browse this list and perhaps discover interesting and useful information.

> *We can only ask for the senders or implementors of the selector of the method that is currently selected.*

What if we wanted to look at the senders or implementors of a message selector in the code? For example, what if we wanted to investigate the senders or implementors of message **error:**, **pi**, **negated**, or **arcTan** in method **arcSin**? Clicking on **Senders** or **Implementors** , respectively, in the **Methods** menu will give us only the senders or implementors of **arcSin**—not the senders or implementors of **pi**, for example.

To be able to investigate the messages used in a method body, we first have to get a list of all the selectors in the method body by clicking on **Messages** in the **Methods** menu. For example, to investigate the messages used in the **arcSin** method body, we would click on **Messages**, as shown in Figure 6.36.

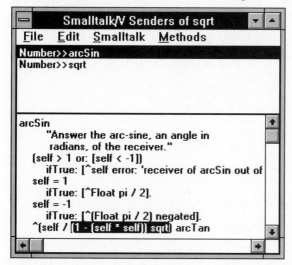

Figure 6.35 The senders of **sqrt** (the **arcSin** method in Number is being viewed).

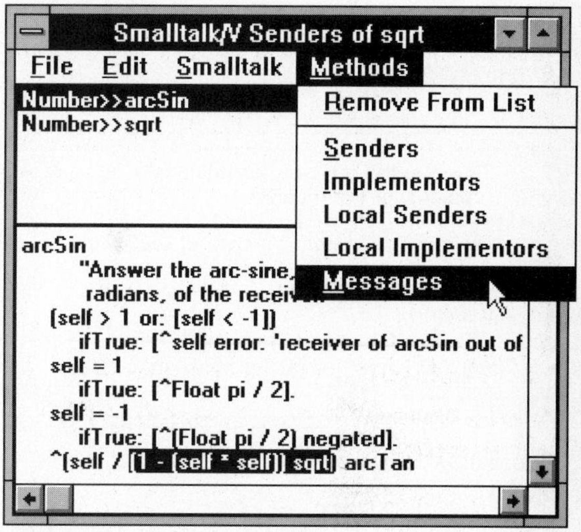

Figure 6.36 Asking for the list of messages used in **arcSin**'s method body.

The result is another window (see Figure 6.37) that contains the message selectors in the top left pane. The code pane at the bottom indicates where the chosen selector is used in method **arcSin**.

Having selected **pi**, we can then ask for either the senders or the implementors of **pi** by clicking on the appropriate item in the **Selectors** menu as shown in Figure 6.38.

The list of implementors is then shown in the top right pane (see Figure 6.39). In this case, we find out that there is exactly one implementor of **pi**. Moreover, the method name in the top right pane, "Float class>>pi", indicates that method **pi** is a class method. If it had been an instance method, the method name would have been "Float>>pi". If you know trigonometry, you will understand that

$$\tan \pi/4 = 1$$

so that $\pi/4 = \tan^{-1}1$ and hence $\pi = 4 \times \tan^{-1}1$. In trigonometry, function $\tan^{-1}$ is called the arc tangent function. In Smalltalk, $4 \times \tan^{-1}1$ is computed by asking 1 for the arc tangent and multiplying the result by 4. If you don't know trigonometry, simply ignore the code for the method. Our real goal was simply to locate method **pi** and in order to do that, we needed to understand how to ask for the messages used by a selected method.

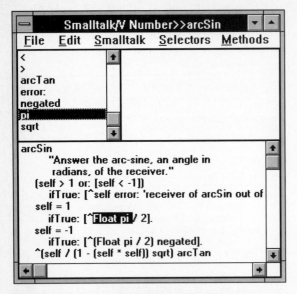

Figure 6.37 The messages used by method arcSin.

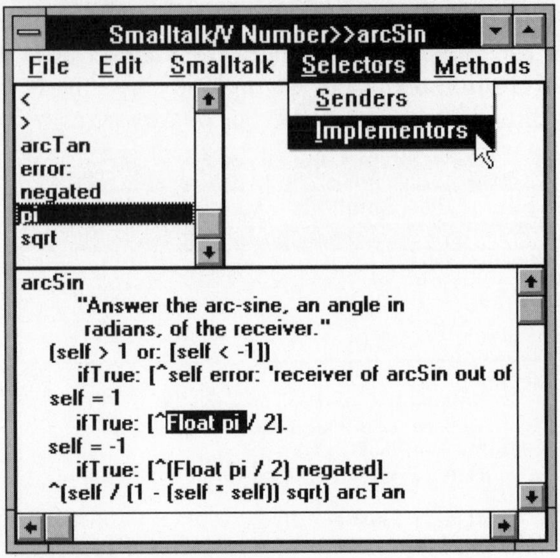

Figure 6.38 Asking for the implementors of **pi**.

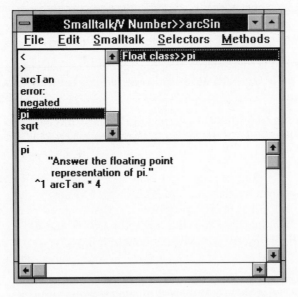

Figure 6.39 The implementors of method **pi**.

6.2.4 Completing the Implementation

Now let's get back to our bank account implementation. The checking account class needs to properly initialize the **checkingHistory** instance variable so that commentary information can be inserted by the teller when processing checks on the account. Presumably, we need some kind of object that can maintain an arbitrary number of commentary strings—a collection of some sort, but what kind? Since we know very little about collections, perhaps we should just be told that an ordered collection would work well in this case and that we can get one by executing "OrderedCollection **new**". Nevertheless, we don't know how to use ordered collections. In particular, we don't know how to insert a string into the collection. We will need to use a browser to search for a method that will permit us to make insertions into an ordered collection. So let's open a browser on class OrderedCollection by selecting **Find Class...** in the **Class** menu and typing OrderedCollection. If we look at the class methods (see Figure 6.40), we can see that ordered collections are created with **new** or **new:**. The comment in method **new** suggests that ordered collections will automatically grow when more room is needed for additional objects.

When we look at the instance methods (see Figure 6.41), we should immediately notice a method (second from the top, called **add:**). The method comment, "Answer anObject. Add anObject after the last element of the receiver collection", indicates that the object added is returned. Moreover, the new object is added at the end of the existing list of objects.

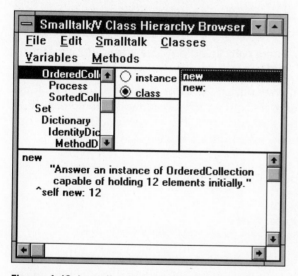

Figure 6.40 Investigating OrderedCollection class methods.

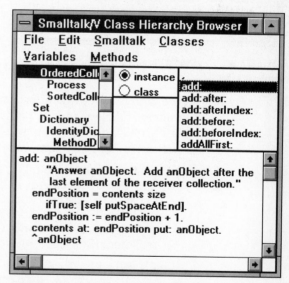

Figure 6.41 Investigating OrderedCollection instance methods; specifically, **add:**.

We might want to click on **Senders** in the **Methods** menu (see Figure 6.42) to find out how others use this method. The result is a long list of methods that we can click on one by one until we get one that makes some sense. The first one that was understandable was method **allSuperclasses**, shown in Figure 6.43.

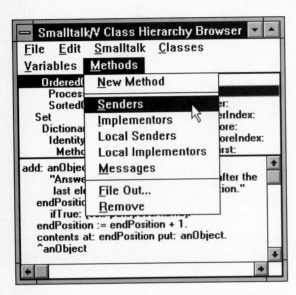

Figure 6.42 Querying about the senders of method **add**:.

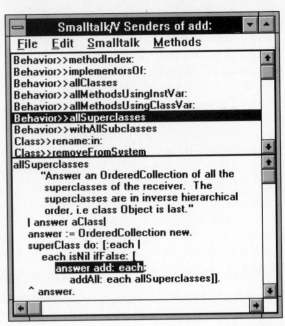

Figure 6.43 Investigating the senders of method **add**:.

We don't have to understand the entire method in order to gain some understanding of **add**:. In particular, it is quite clear how a new ordered collection is created and how a new object is added to the collection. To verify our understanding, we might want to try executing a simple test of our own.

```
| anOrderedCollection |
anOrderedCollection := OrderedCollection new.
anOrderedCollection add: 2001.
anOrderedCollection add: 'hello'.
anOrderedCollection add: Object new.
anOrderedCollection ⇒ OrderedCollection (2001 'hello' anObject)
```

If we scroll a little further in the original browser of Figure 6.41, we might notice method **do**: (see Figure 6.44). The comment is not particularly understandable, so we might be tempted to find out once again how others use this method.

By asking for the senders of this message, we get another long list of methods which we can browse. Ignoring methods that don't make any sense, we might first pause on method **includes**: as shown in Figure 6.45.

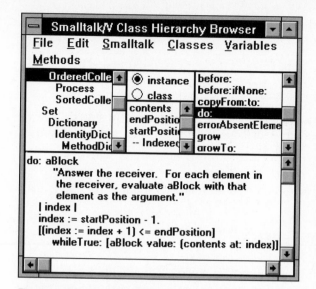

Figure 6.44 Investigating instance method **do:** in class OrderedCollection.

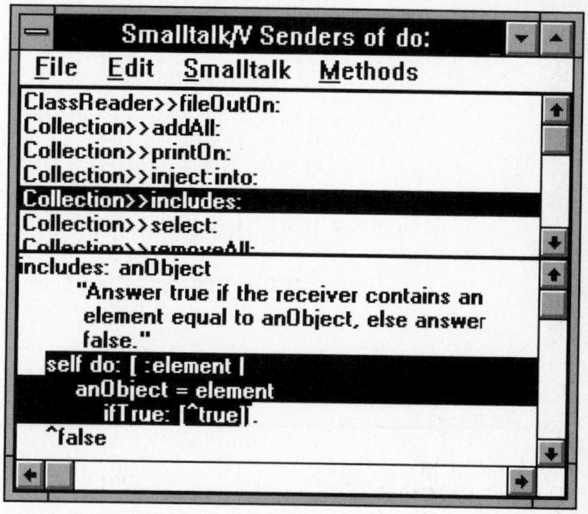

Figure 6.45 Investigating the senders of method **do:**.

This method is intended to be used to determine whether a particular ordered collection contains an object. We might try it out by adding the following line to our test code above to get

anOrderedCollection **includes**: 2001 ⇒ true

or, alternatively,

anOrderedCollection **includes**: 2000 ⇒ false

But now, let's focus on the body of the **includes**: method. Message **do:** is sent to self, which is an ordered collection in our case. The **do:** parameter is a block; i.e., a sequence of zero or more expressions separated by "." and surrounded by square brackets. However, this block is different from the blocks we encountered in previous chapters, because it contains a **block parameter**, called element. The interpretation we should place on the **do:** message used in an example such as

anOrderedCollection **do:** [:loopVariable | ... loop body ...].
Transcript **nextPutAll**: 'Message do: is done'

is the following: *Sequence through all the objects in anOrderedCollection and for each one, bind loopVariable to the object and then execute the code in the loop body. Continue with the next message after all objects have been considered.* The colon immediately after the opening square bracket indicates that the next name is a block parameter. The bar after the loop parameter indicates that there are no more block parameters. If there were, there would be another colon followed by another name.

For example, the following illustrates blocks with different numbers of block parameters:

[1+2]	a zero-parameter block
[:data I data]	a one-parameter block
[:object1 :object2 I object1 + object2]	a two-parameter block

Message **do**: requires a one-parameter block; i.e., it is an error to supply a zero-parameter block or a two-parameter block. Now, let's consider method **includes**: in more detail.

```
includes: anObject
    "Answer true if the receiver contains an element equal to anObject, else
    answer false."
    self do: [:element I
        anObject = element ifTrue: [^true]].
    ^false
```

If we execute "anOrderedCollection **includes**: 'hello'", for example, anObject is bound to 'hello' and message **do**: is sent to self, which happens to be "anOrderedCollection". Since anOrderedCollection contains three elements, the block will attempt to execute three times. The first time, element is bound to 2001 and the block body is executed. The second time, element is bound to 'hello' and the block body executed again. The third time, it is bound to the object that prints as "anObject" for a third execution of the block body.

So **do**: is used to iterate through the elements of the collection—to **sequence** through the collection. Let's consider each iteration in turn.

When element is bound to 2001, the block body is executed. So anObject (which is 'hello') is compared with element (which is 2001). Since the two are not equal, the true block is not executed. The **do**: block is now finished executing.

When element is bound to 'hello', the block body is executed a second time. This time, anObject (which is still 'hello') is compared with element (which is now 'hello'). Since the two are equal, the true block is executed and so true is returned as the final answer for this method. As a consequence, we never get to execute the loop body for the third time.

If we had sent the message "anOrderedCollection **includes**: 2000" instead, the **do**: block would have executed three times, since anObject, which is 2000, is never equal to any of the elements. Consequently, the next expression after the **do**: would finally execute, causing false to be returned as the final answer.

Our original intention, in this section, was to complete our implementation of the CheckingAccount class. We used the browser to investigate three methods that instances of ordered collections understand; namely, **add:**, **do:**, and **includes:**. As it turns out, we will be investigating ordered collections in much more detail in the next chapter. Nevertheless, this preview of ordered collections, although relatively brief, should be sufficient for our current needs. The three related classes can now be completed as follows:

instance methods

instance initialization

initialize
    super **initialize**.
    checkingHistory := OrderedCollection **new**

checking history manipulation

check: aMoney **comment**: aString
    "Make a withdrawal for the amount of the check and record the string in the checking history."
    self **withdraw**: aMoney.
    "Insert aString into the checking history."
    checkingHistory **add**: aString

checkingHistory
    ^checkingHistory

6.2.5 Adding a Bank Class

We mentioned earlier that opening and closing an account is something that is normally done in the context of a bank. If there were more than one bank, it is possible to have a savings accounts at each bank. So presumably, we would open an account at a specific bank. Conversely, when we close an account, it is somehow eliminated or forgotten by the bank. This suggests that a bank knows about its bank accounts and that bank accounts know about their banks; i.e., given a bank, we can obtain the list of accounts and given an account, we can obtain the associated bank.

Before we go on to define a bank class, it might be wise to investigate this relatively general phenomenon of **mutual knowledge**. A library might know about all the books it contains and each book might know which library it comes from. A small business might know about its owner and the owner presumably would know about the small business. We will say that an object **knows** about another object if it can provide that object upon request. We will also say that it knows **explicitly** about the object if it has an instance variable bound to the object; otherwise, it knows **implicitly** about the object—in this case, it might have to go through some sort of search or computation to find the requested object.

As it turns out, there are four completely different ways of implementing two classes of objects with mutual knowledge. Let's consider the possibilities in the context of a husband and wife pair, where the husband (the first object) knows about his wife and the wife (the second object) knows about her husband.

Implementing objects with mutual knowledge

- **Only the first object knows explicitly about the second**: e.g., the husband knows explicitly about the wife.
- **Only the second object knows explicitly about the first**: e.g., the wife knows explicitly about the husband.
- **Both know explicitly about each other**: ; e.g., the husband and wife know explicitly about each other.
- **Neither knows explicitly about each other; rather, a separate object maintains a list of related pairs**: e.g., a global WeddingRegistry keeps track of all husbands and wives.

This could be illustrated using a diagram, as shown in Figure 6.46. For each of these cases, we can provide a **wife** instance method in the Husband class that can retrieve the wife and a **husband** instance method in the Wife class that can retrieve the husband.

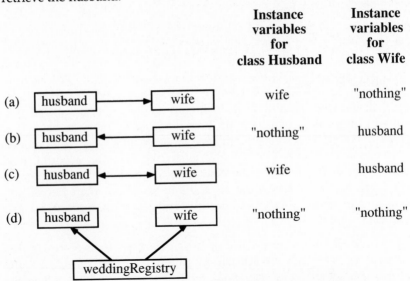

		Instance variables for class Husband	Instance variables for class Wife
(a)	husband → wife	wife	"nothing"
(b)	husband ← wife	"nothing"	husband
(c)	husband ↔ wife	wife	husband
(d)	husband wife (weddingRegistry)	"nothing"	"nothing"

Figure 6.46 Different implementations of mutual knowledge.

When an instance variable is bound to the object requested, it is easy to return the instance variable. When there is no instance variable providing the object, a more sophisticated computation—in most cases, a search—is required. We will illustrate how we can do this for each of the above four cases.

For case (a), asking a husband for his wife is trivial but asking a wife (the receiver) for her husband requires a search through all the existing husbands until one is found whose wife is equal to the receiver. Note that **allInstances** provides us with a list of all the existing husbands and **do:** allows us to sequence through this list; i.e., iterate through the husbands.

Case (a): Only the husband knows explicitly about the wife

class   Husband
instance variables   wife

instance methods

querying

wife
    ^wife

class   Wife
instance variables   "nothing"

instance methods

querying

husband
    ^Husband **allInstances do**: [:aHusband |
        aHusband **wife** = self **ifTrue**: [^aHusband]].
    self **error**: 'wife has no corresponding husband'

The next case is very similar—only the roles have been switched. To find the wife of a husband (the receiver), it is necessary to search all wives for one whose husband matches the receiver.

Case (b): Only the wife knows explicitly about the husband

class   Husband
instance variables   "nothing"

instance methods

querying

wife
    ^Wife **allInstances do**: [:aWife |
        aWife **husband** = self **ifTrue**: [^aWife]].
    self **error**: 'husband has no corresponding wife'

class   Wife
instance variables   husband

instance methods

querying

husband
    ^husband

The next case is the simplest of all because the requested information is immediately available from instance variables.

Case (c): Both the husband and wife know explicitly about each other

class	Husband
instance variables	wife

instance methods

querying

wife
   ^wife

class	Wife
instance variables	husband

instance methods

querying

husband
   ^husband

The last case assumes the existence of a global WeddingRegistry that is an ordered collection of husband and wife pairs. Each pair might be an instance of a Registry object. To find the wife of a husband (the receiver), for example, we need to search the wedding registry for a pair in which the husband matches the receiver. The corresponding wife is returned.

Case (d): Neither the husband nor the wife know explicitly about each other

class	Registry
instance variables	husband wife

instance methods

querying

husband
   ^husband
wife
   ^wife

class	Husband
instance variables	"nothing"

instance methods

querying

wife
   WeddingRegistry **do:** [:aRegistry |
      aRegistry **husband** = self **ifTrue:** [^aRegistry **wife**]].
   self **error:** 'husband not in registry'

```
class                                    Wife
instance variables                       "nothing"

instance methods

querying

husband
    WeddingRegistry do: [:aRegistry |
        aRegistry wife = self ifTrue: [^aRegistry husband]].
    self error: 'wife not in registry'
```

Even though all four implementation techniques provide essentially the same functionality, they are not all equivalent in terms of efficiency. Clearly, those implementations that have to search must be dramatically slower. So case (c) is almost always preferred. Case (d) could occur when information is made available through relational databases, which are simply collections of pairs, triples, quadruples, and so on. Case (a) might occur in a particular application if there is no need to ever ask a wife for her husband. Case (b) is similar, but focuses on wives rather than on husbands.

The lesson to learn here is that there are many objects with mutual knowledge. Moreover, the simplest implementation is one in which that knowledge is explicit. If we were to draw an **object diagram**, a diagram showing the instance variables of an object along with the objects the instance variables are bound to, we would find the mutual knowledge quite evident (see Figure 6.47).

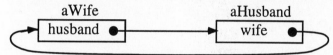

Figure 6.47 Object diagrams for objects with explicit knowledge of each other.

Getting back to our main topic, it ought to be possible to ask banks about bank accounts and, conversely, to ask bank accounts about banks.

- **What we might ask a bank**: Can you give me all the bank accounts for 'Wilf LaLonde'?
- **What we might ask a bank account**: Can you give me the bank that this bank account is associated with?

Before we worry about specific implementation techniques, let's create an example method in a new class called Bank that illustrates (1) the new protocol (new messages) for **opening** and **closing** accounts and (2) messages that illustrate the above example queries.

As the example method indicates, we now create bank accounts with **openAt:** rather than **open**, we query a bank with **accountsBelongingTo:**, we ask an account for its bank with **bank**, and we close an account just like before, using **close**. Method **close**, however, must now have different semantics. After we close account1, for example, it should no longer be possible to obtain the account by sending bank1 the message "**accountsBelongingTo**: 'Wilf LaLonde'" because it should no longer exist.

```
class                                    Bank
superclass                               Object
instance variables                       "unknown yet"

class methods

examples

example1
    "Bank example1"
    | bank1 bank2 account1 account2 accounts |

    "Get two banks each with one account."
    bank1 := Bank new name: 'Bank of Switzerland'.
    account1 := (SavingsAccount openAt: bank1)
        name: 'Wilf LaLonde';
        address: '24 Fall Down Lane, Ottawa, Canada'.

    bank2 := Bank new name: 'Bank of Japan'.
    account2 := (CheckingAccount openAt: bank2)
        name: 'Marie Hervieux';
        address: 'Matachewan, Ontario, Canada'.

    "Query a bank for specific accounts."
    Transcript cr; nextPutAll: 'Bank of Switzerland contains '.
    accounts := bank1 accountsBelongingTo: 'Wilf LaLonde'.
    accounts printOn: Transcript.

    "Query an account for a specific bank."
    Transcript cr.
    account2 bank printOn: Transcript.
    Transcript nextPutAll: ' contains '. account2 printOn: Transcript.

    account1 close. account2 close
```

If banks and bank accounts have mutual knowledge of each other, we know that this knowledge is best represented explicitly; i.e., banks should explicitly keep track of bank accounts and bank accounts should explicitly keep track of banks. Since there are fewer banks than bank accounts, it may be convenient to keep track of the actual banks in global variables, as follows:

```
Bank1 := Bank new name: 'Bank of Switzerland'.
Bank2 := Bank new name: 'Bank of Japan'.
```

When new accounts are opened, they would be opened at one of the global banks. For example, we might execute the following:

```
| account1 account2 |
account1 := (SavingsAccount openAt: Bank1)
    name: 'Wilf LaLonde';
    address: '24 Fall Down Lane, Ottawa, Canada'.
```

```
account2 := (CheckingAccount openAt: Bank2)
    name: 'Marie Hervieux';
    address: 'Matachewan, Ontario, Canada'.
```

Even though the bank accounts above were bound to local variables that existed only during execution of the above code, it is still possible to recover these bank accounts as follows:

```
| wilfsAccounts mariesAccounts |
wilfsAccounts := Bank1 accountsBelongingTo: 'Wilf LaLonde'.
mariesAccounts := Bank2 accountsBelongingTo: 'Marie Hervieux'.
```

To continue our implementation, instances of Bank would need at least two instance variables—say, **name** and **accounts**. Instance variable **accounts** is the key. It would consist of an ordered collection of bank accounts. Additionally, we need facilities to add bank accounts to the bank and to remove them. In the previous section, we used the browser to search for a method that allowed objects to be inserted into an ordered collection—it turned out to be called **add:**. We can use the browser in the same way to find the method that permits objects to be removed or deleted from the collection. It turns out to be called **remove:**.

Assuming that accounts are properly initialized to an empty ordered collection, we could implement two Bank instance methods **insert:** and **delete:**, using ordered collection messages **add:** and **remove:**, as follows:

```
initialize
    self name: 'Unknown'.
    accounts := OrderedCollection new

insert: aBankAccount
    "Record the bank account."
    accounts add: aBankAccount

delete: aBankAccount
    "Remove the bank account from the record."
    accounts remove: aBankAccount
```

Consider method **insert:**. When we execute "aBank **insert:** aBankAccount", the bank (the receiver) adds it to the ordered collection kept in accounts.

Of course, names like **insert:** and **delete:** could be confusing to a user because they are synonyms for **add:** and **remove:**. It would be better if we used the same name, as follows:

```
add: aBankAccount
    "Record the bank account."
    accounts add: aBankAccount

remove: aBankAccount
    "Remove the bank account from the record."
    accounts remove: aBankAccount
```

This works just as well. When we execute "aBank **add**: aBankAccount", the bank (the receiver) adds it to the ordered collection kept in accounts. Of course, these names are not very domain-specific. What if we later need to add or remove personnel or add and remove savings bonds? Perhaps names such as **addAccount**: and **removeAccount**: would be better.

Now all we need is a way of implementing method **accountsBelongingTo**:. Consider the following:

```
accountsBelongingTo: oldName
    "Returns an ordered collection of accounts with the same name as
    oldName."
    | result |
    result := OrderedCollection new.
    accounts do: [:aBankAccount |
        aBankAccount name = oldName
            ifTrue: [result add: aBankAccount]].
    ^result
```

We need to make use of **do**: to sequence through all the bank accounts. Once we get one, we need to compare the name of the account with the name provided as a parameter. If they match, the corresponding account is saved in variable result. After we have processed all accounts, we can return the final ordered collection in result.

The complete Bank class can then be summarized as follows:

```
class                                 Bank
superclass                            Object
instance variables                    name accounts

class methods

instance creation

new
    ^super new initialize

instance methods

instance initialization

initialize
    self name: 'Unknown'.
    accounts := OrderedCollection new

accessing and modifying

name
    ^name
name: aString
    name := aString
```

account management

addAccount: aBankAccount
    "Record the bank account."
    accounts **add**: aBankAccount

removeAccount: aBankAccount
    "Remove the bank account from the record."
    accounts **remove**: aBankAccount

accountsBelongingTo: oldName
    "Returns an ordered collection of accounts with the same name as
    oldName."
    | result |
    result := OrderedCollection **new**.
    accounts **do**: [:aBankAccount |
        aBankAccount **name** = oldName
            ifTrue: [result **add**: aBankAccount]].
    ^result

The corresponding BankAccount class must be revised to add one instance variable called bank and to incorporate the revised **openAt**: and **close** methods.

class	BankAccount
superclass	Object
instance variables	name address balance bank

class methods

instance creation

openAt: aBank
    "Construct a fully initialized bank account."
    | anAccount |
    anAccount := self **new bank**: aBank.
    aBank **addAccount**: anAccount.
    ^anAccount

instance methods

querying

bank
    ^bank
bank: aBank
    bank := aBank

instance finalization

close
    "Remove from all bank records."
    self **bank removeAccount**: self.
    self **initialize**

6.3 Summary

This chapter has introduced you to classes that are hierarchically related and to classes that are related through mutual knowledge. More specifically, we have

- Introduced the concept of a hierarchy as an organizational tool for relating items that share some interesting commonality
- Introduced the concept of an is-a (also called is-kind-of) relationship and showed how it can be used to guide the design of a hierarchy of classes
- Determined that instance variables (also called parts or representation) defined in a class were inherited by subclasses
- Learned that this representation inheritance is additive; i.e., an instance variable inherited from a superclass cannot be removed from the subclass
- Determined that methods in a class (both instance methods and class methods) are inherited by subclasses
- Learned that inheritance forces new classes to be defined by providing only those methods and instance variables that are extra to those provided by the superclasses
- Uncovered the one missing ingredient about the method lookup mechanism; i.e., how it works in the presence of inheritance
- Discovered that methods can be redefined in subclasses; i.e., overridden, to provide behavior that the original method did not provide
- Discovered that **new** can be overridden by a variation that initializes the instances
- Discovered that instance methods like **initialize** and **printOn:** can take advantage of the corresponding methods higher up in the hierarchy to provide a portion of the required functionality
- Introduced the concept of hierarchical buck-passing, which was illustrated in the two methods mentioned above
- Discovered the distinction between "self" and "super"
- Learned how to have methods in a subclass make use of a method in the superclass with the same name; i.e., we learned how to use "super"
- Learned how to avoid duplicating functionality in a subclass by creating a method higher up in the hierarchy that the subclasses could inherit
- Learned how to extend a class in a hierarchy so that it could create initialized instances; i.e., learned about the initialization framework
- Investigated and compared abstract classes with concrete classes
- Learned how to implement abstract classes that refuse to provide instances
- Found out how to generate our own error messages
- Discovered that inspectors not only provide information about an instance's instance variables but also indicate where these instance variables come from in the inheritance hierarchy

- Discovered how to use the browser to determine the senders, receivers, and messages associated with a method and its selector
- Learned that objects that know about each other can be implemented in four distinct ways, depending on whether one has explicit or implicit knowledge of the other
- Investigated to a few of the operations applicable to ordered collections; e.g., messages **add:**, **remove**, **includes:**, and **do:**
- Studied the design of a hierarchy of bank account classes and a bank class to provide experience with the notions learned in this chapter
- Learned that the best designs use method names that are domain-specific rather than generic and make use of class hierarchies that maximize method and instance variable inheritance while simultaneously mirroring an is-a hierarchy

6.4 What You Did and Did Not Learn

In this chapter, we learned a great deal about individually simple but nevertheless interrelated notions associated with classes in a hierarchy; e.g., the notion of "super", method overriding, abstract classes, etc. Perhaps the most important concept that we learned was the notion of the initialization framework and the principle of reusability that helped us determine when a design was better or worse. In our case studies, we used all this knowledge in an effort to design our classes in as simple a manner as possible. Yet we always tried to provide the most general facilities that we could think of at the time.

We spent a great deal of time trying to choose understandable names for our methods. We also tried to make these names domain-specific. In the previous chapter, we argued that choosing names was one of the hardest parts about designing. If choosing names seems simple to you already, it's probably because we have given you too many of our solutions. It won't be so easy when you have to make up the names on your own.

After studying the examples used to illustrate the chapter's concepts, you should have gained some intuition about the process of designing a method, a class, or a group of related classes. In particular, the simple fact that a method is "evolved" and "improved" rather than simply developed correctly by clever reasoning was illustrated many times. It should help you understand that you don't have to know how to get it right in order to attempt to do it. The attempt itself will serve as a starting point for the next modification or improvement.

The issues of reusability and duplication avoidance dominated many of our discussions because they are fundamental to all design. To better appreciate why they are important, we had to go into a great deal of detail about instance initialization, and about inheritance of instance methods such as **initialize** and class methods such as **new**. We had to understand about "super" and how it differs from "self" and we had to learn how to give our own error messages if we wanted to make sure a user couldn't create instances of an abstract class. And, of course, we learned about the distinction between concrete classes and abstract classes.

The Bank class introduced the need for an object that could maintain a collection of other objects; e.g., an ordered collection. When we started, we didn't know anything about ordered collections. So we had to use the browser's facilities for finding the senders and implementors in order to search for and understand the few important operations that we needed to complete the banking application. In the end, we had to make use of some relatively complicated methods like **add:**, **remove:**, and **do:**. We certainly didn't have much of an opportunity to understand these operations very well. The minimal level of understanding that we were able to get was at least sufficient to allow us to complete the implementation of the Bank class.

It is important to realize that the above scenario is a relatively normal phenomena. There will be many situations in the future where there will be a need to use classes that you don't understand very well. At first, this can be scary. After you've done it a few times, however, it becomes a challenge. It's fun to learn something new.

Of course, our use of ordered collections, in this chapter, was rather incidental. We barely explored the complexities and intricacies of ordered collections and their operations. Indeed, since Smalltalk has a very large hierarchy of collection classes, we will need to explore collections in much more detail—a topic for the next chapter.

6.5 Important Facts

Operations on Classes

aClass **allInstances**

Obtains all the instances of the class and returns it in a collection

Operations on Objects

anObject **error**: aString

Brings up an error window with aString as the error message

Operations on Class OrderedCollection

OrderedCollection **new**

Obtains an instance of the ordered collection that contains no elements; any number of elements can be added subsequently

Operations on OrderedCollections

anOrderedCollection **add**: anObject	Adds anObject to the receiver. Returns anObject
anOrderedCollection **remove**: anObject	Removes an element equal to anObject from the receiver if such an element exists and returns anObject. If no such element exists, an error is reported
anOrderedCollection **includes**: anObject	Returns true if the receiver contains an element equal to anObject; otherwise, false
anOrderedCollection **do**: [:element	…]	Requests the receiver to successively bind the block parameter to each of its elements and execute the block after each binding has been performed; **do**: requires a one-parameter block

Blocks Can Have Block Parameters

Blocks can have block parameter; some examples include:

[1+2]	a zero-parameter block
[:data	data]	a one-parameter block
[:object1 :object2	object1 + object2]	a two-parameter block

Browsing for Information (Locating Messages)

- To know where to start searching, determine what kind of object is a likely receiver for the message of interest.
- Once known, begin the search at the most specific potential class and investigate the instance methods while proceeding slowly up the class hierarchy.
- Most of the time, the name of the method is sufficient information but sometimes the comment associated with the method is necessary for understanding the method.
- When a specific candidate is promising, use the **senders** to find out how to use the method and the **implementors** to find out if variations on other, potentially more relevant, classes also exist.

Inheritance

- **Instance variables are inherited**; equivalently, **representation is inherited**; i.e., when a new class is defined, the instance variables specified in the new class automatically include the instance variables specified in the classes higher up in the hierarchy. Consequently, instances of the new class contain all these instance variables.
- **Methods are inherited**; i.e., instances of a subclass inherit all the instance methods of the superclasses; the subclass itself inherits all the class methods of the superclasses.
- **Methods can be overridden**; i.e., a subclass can have a method (an instance or class method) with the same name as a corresponding method in a superclass.

The Method Lookup Mechanism: When a message is sent to an object, the receiver's class is searched for the corresponding method. If found, a copy is made and executed. If not found, the process is repeated in the superclass. If no superclass exists, an error message is generated, explaining that the receiver does not understand the message.

Using "super": "super" is equivalent to "self", but when used in a method belonging to class C, has the side-effect of causing the method lookup mechanism to start searching for the corresponding method in the superclass of C; e.g., if the message "super **test**" is in a method belonging to class Pen, the search for **test** begins in the superclass of Pen.

Ways of Implementing Mutual Knowledge

There are four ways of implementing two classes of objects that know about each other. One may know **explicitly** about the other; i.e., have an instance variable bound to the other, or it may know about the other only **implicitly**; i.e., it can determine the other object through some elaborate computation or search. The four possibilities are

- **Only the first knows explicitly about the second**: e.g., the first has an instance variable referencing the second
- **Only the second knows explicitly about the first**: e.g., the second has an instance variable referencing the first
- **Both explicitly know about each other**: e.g., both have instance variables referencing each other
- **Neither explicitly knows about each other; rather a separate object maintains a list of related pairs**: e.g., some other object maintains references to both

Preventing Instances of Abstract Classes from Being Created

As a rule, whenever we create an abstract class, we need to decide who is responsible for preventing instances from being created. There are two possibilities:

- *The class is responsible* for explicitly preventing instances from being created—this is the solution used for some classes like Number.
- *The user is responsible* for not creating instances—if the user insists on creating instances, it is the user's fault when something goes wrong. This seems to be the solution used by the great majority of abstract classes.

The Initialization Framework

This framework is the pattern to be followed for generating initialized instances. It includes the use of a **new** defined as "super **new initialize**" and **initialize** methods that conform to the rules of style. In particular, each **initialize** method should (1) initialize the defaults from higher up the hierarchy first, (2) override those defaults if necessary second, and finally, (3) provide initialization (of the right type) for instance variables supplied directly by the class.

The Principle of Reusability

This principle is the notion that code duplication can be avoided by careful use of existing code; e.g., other methods in the same class, methods higher up the class hierarchy, or instances of existing classes.

6.6 Helpful Hints

The best designs are good choices both from the implementation viewpoint and the user's viewpoint: The implementation perspective tries to maximize reusability by taking inheritance into account (to reuse inherited methods and inherited representation) and the user perspective tries to maximize intuition by ensuring that the subclass hierarchy is also a proper is-a relationship.

Strive to use domain-relevant terminology: Method names should be chosen to reflect the terminology appropriate to the domain of application.

Objects should print a minimal amount about themselves: In practice, an object should print only enough information to distinguish it from other instances; i.e. the **printOn:** method should not try to print everything known about an object.

Classes should provide initialized instances: Instances that are initialized with useful defaults are preferable to uninitialized instances.

Defaults should be of the right type: If a particular part is intended to be bound to a string, it should be bound to some reasonable default string—not to nil or some other kind of object.

Each class should initialize only the parts it is explicitly aware of: A class is entirely responsible for initializing its parts, is permitted to reinitialize the parts inherited from superclasses if the defaults are inappropriate, and is not permitted to initialize the parts of subclasses. Moreover, this initialization should be performed by an instance initialization method.

Never use "super" to speed up method lookup: It doesn't speed it up enough to make a noticeable difference. More important, the use of "super" tells a reader that an attempt is being made to bypass an equivalent local method with that name. This makes the reader want to know why the local method is being bypassed, where the local method resides, and what the local method does.

6.7   Keywords

abstraction: abstract class, behavior, concrete class, generalization

browsing: senders of a method selector, implementors of a method selector, messages of a method

execution: infinite loop, nonterminating computation

files: backup, file, filing in, filing out

hierarchies: hierarchy, is-a hierarchy, is-kind-of hierarchy

inheritance: hierarchical buck-passing, implementation perspective, inheritance, initialization framework, overriding, user perspective

mutual knowledge: explicit knowledge, implicit knowledge, mutual knowledge

programming terminology: designing, representation, reusability

6.8   Exercises

1. Verify that class methods are inherited just like instance methods.
2. Inspect a pen and determine which class each instance variable is inherited from.
3. Find all the implementors of **printOn:** and investigate those that are relatively simple; e.g., the version for Point, Fraction, Rectangle.

4. Use the browser's facilities to help you determine what **printString** does. Hint: Create a method—say, called **experiment1**—in any class that simply sends the message **printString** to any object. Then ask the browser for the messages used in this method. The resulting window that appears can then be used to find the senders and the implementors of **printString**. You might also try experiments on your own.

5. Create a subclass of Object called Ticket with one instance variable called ticketNumber. After adding accessing and modification methods **ticketNumber** and **ticketNumber:** and a class creation method that permit you to get an instance by executing "Ticket **number:** 517", change the superclass to Magnitude. Hint: Make sure the approach you use would work even if there were hundreds of methods in the class. Then complete the class by making sure that tickets can be compared and printed.

6. Devise a reasonable is-a hierarchy for houses, barns, and shacks. If necessary, introduce suitable abstract objects.

7. Extend the **openAt:** method in class Bank so that it is not possible to open a second account (of the same kind) under the same name.

8. Create a small hierarchy of animal classes such as you would find on a typical single-family farm. Be sure to include at least one property unique to each class. Provide suitable initialization and printing facilities.

9. Create a small set of classes for the objects you might buy at a local supermarket. Hint: Since all possible foods in the world are represented, you will not be able to classify based on food names. Focus on what the supermarket needs to know about those foods in order to keep them fresh, to be able to sell them, and to be able to replace them. Provide suitable initialization and printing facilities.

7

Object Containers

What You Will Learn

As we have seen in previous chapters, Smalltalk can be used as a calculator for computing numeric quantities, as a word processor for drafting letters, and as a vehicle for drawing on the display. When illustrating each of these uses, we focused primarily on a single object; e.g., the sum of a series, the transcript, a pen. The same applied when we considered case studies dealing with temperature and money objects. However, when banks were considered, we saw the need for a bank to keep track of its accounts. We were very briefly exposed to ordered collections.

Many applications need to keep track of large numbers of objects at once—sometimes an unbounded number. In some cases, the objects to be managed must be ordered; e.g., when it consists of instructions for putting together a new bicycle. At other times, the ordering is immaterial; e.g., when we are simply keeping track of the countries visited in the past. In other situations, we may need to deal with correlated objects. A phone book, for example, consists of names and correlated phone numbers.

In each of these cases, we are dealing with container objects—objects that can contain other objects. We need to understand in detail how to create such objects, how to add elements to these objects, and how to retrieve the elements. To expand our knowledge in this area, we will first focus on the two most important kinds of container objects: ordered collections and dictionaries.

Next, we will apply our new knowledge by considering two case studies. The first will focus on the development of a phone book class that makes simultaneous use of both kinds of collections. The second will focus on the development of a tic-tac-toe game. It will make use of a number of container objects for both the game board itself and for encoding whether there is a winning horizontal, vertical, or diagonal line in the game. As a side effect, you will gain additional experience with drawing facilities.

7.1 Using Objects as Containers

A **container** is an object that can contain an arbitrary number of other objects. Strings and symbols, for example, are character containers. Each string is a fixed size but different strings, such as 'hi' and 'hello', can contain different numbers of characters. Arrays, as in #('hello' there 3.14159), are containers for mixtures of different kinds of objects—in this case, a string, a symbol, and a float.

An **ordered collection** is a container for arbitrary objects—one that maintains the relative insertion ordering of the objects. If we add the words of a sentence such as "Good morning all you eager programmers" to an ordered collection, we can be sure that we will be able retrieve the words in the same order—they will not be jumbled up when we retrieve them.

Sometimes, we are more interested in correlating information rather than just storing it. A good example is a personalized phone book. Yours might contain ten names but mine might contain only three. We should be able to get a new phone book, add new names and their associated phone numbers, and then be able to look up the numbers (by specifying the names).

Another object that is very similar to a phone book is a dictionary. In this case, of course, the meaning of a word is associated with the word. If we want to know the meaning of a word such as "programming", we look it up and perhaps retrieve something like "the art of transcribing commands onto a medium that can be read."

This notion of correlating or associating one object with another is so fundamental that a special class of objects called a Smalltalk **dictionary** supports it. A Smalltalk dictionary contains both **keys**—objects that serve as indicators for the information we are really interested in, and **values**—the information itself. Thus, a Smalltalk dictionary contains key-value pairs and provides access to the values, given the keys. Smalltalk dictionaries are more general than everyday dictionaries because they can be used for correlating arbitrary things. For example, they could be used for correlating colors with fruits, or cars with their owners. As a special case, Smalltalk dictionaries could be used to create phone books—the keys could be strings and the values could be numbers.

To investigate container objects, let's first enumerate the typical operations applicable to ordered collections and dictionaries. Then, we'll examine the individual container types in more detail. We'll also categorize the operations so that we can better "differentiate" between them.

Operations on Collections

obtaining instances

Dictionary **new**
OrderedCollection **new**

adding objects

anOrderedCollection **add**: anObject
anOrderedCollection **addFirst**: anObject
anOrderedCollection **addLast**: anObject
anOrderedCollection **at**: anInteger **put**: anObject
aDictionary **at**: anObject **put**: anotherObject

querying

aDictionary **size**
anOrderedCollection **size**
aCollection **isEmpty**

anOrderedCollection **includes**: anObject
anOrderedCollection **at**: anInteger
anOrderedCollection **first**
anOrderedCollection **last**
aDictionary **at**: anObject
aDictionary **at**: anObject **ifAbsent**: aBlock

removing objects known to be in the container

anOrderedCollection **remove**: anObject
anOrderedCollection **removeFirst**
anOrderedCollection **removeLast**
aDictionary **removeKey**: anObject

removing objects thought, but not known, to be in the container

anOrderedCollection **remove**: anObject **ifAbsent**: aBlock
aDictionary **removeKey**: anObject **ifAbsent**: aBlock

accessing all objects contained

anOrderedCollection **do**: [:element | ...]
aDictionary **do**: [:element | ...]
aDictionary **keysDo**: [:key | ...]

Operations on Objects

asking for the receiver

anObject **yourself**

There are several interesting notions dealing with the messages that make use of blocks that are not self-evident. Moreover, message **yourself** seems unnecessary (it simply returns the receiver)—we'll get to those soon. For now, let's start with ordered collections.

7.1.1 Ordered Collections

An **ordered collection** is a container that maintains the order of the elements as they are added. Moreover, the elements can be added at either end of the collection. We can add at the beginning using **addFirst:** and at the end using **addLast:** (**add:** is a synonym for **addLast:**). For example, to add the words of the sentence "Once upon a time, there lived a bear." (including punctuation) to an ordered collection, we might proceed as follows:

```
| sentence |
sentence := OrderedCollection new.
sentence add: 'Once'.
sentence add: 'upon'.
sentence add: 'a'.
sentence add: 'time'.
sentence add: ','.
sentence add: 'there'.
sentence add: 'lived'.
sentence add: 'a'.
sentence add: 'bear'.
sentence add: '.'.
sentence ⇒ OrderedCollection ('Once' 'upon' 'a' 'time' ',' 'there' 'lived' 'a' 'bear' '.')
```

The **size** of an ordered collection is the number of elements it contains. Thus, a new ordered collection would have a size of 0. The size of the ordered collection referenced by "sentence" is 10.

```
OrderedCollection new size ⇒ 0        OrderedCollection new isEmpty ⇒ true
sentence size ⇒ 10                    sentence isEmpty ⇒ false
```

Typically, ordered collections are created in one expression, using cascading as follows:

```
| sentence |
sentence := OrderedCollection new
    add: 'Once'; add: 'upon'; add: 'a'; add: 'time'; add: ',';
    add: 'there'; add: 'lived'; add: 'a'; add: 'bear'; add: '.';
    yourself.
sentence ⇒ OrderedCollection ('Once' 'upon' 'a' 'time' ',' 'there' 'lived' 'a' 'bear' '.')
```

Message **yourself** simply returns the receiver of the message; e.g., 5 **yourself** is 5, 'hello' **yourself** is 'hello'. It is interesting to analyze why **yourself** is needed at all. Basically, it's a consequence of the semantics of message **add**:. Recall that every message results in an object being returned. The **add**: message, in particular, returns the object added, not the collection. Consider

```
| experiment |
experiment := OrderedCollection new.
experiment add: 'OK' ⇒ 'OK'
experiment add: 'NOW'; yourself ⇒ OrderedCollection ('OK' 'NOW')
```

Because of cascading, message **yourself** is sent to experiment (actually, the ordered collection that experiment is bound to) rather than to the result of the **add**:. We have to be careful when we use **yourself** because it is easy to forget about the necessity for cascading. For example, neither of the following work:

```
experiment add: 'OK' yourself ⇒ 'OK'
(experiment add: 'NOW') yourself ⇒ 'OK'
```

Now, let's consider the other add operations, **addFirst**: and **addLast**:. Operationally, **addFirst**: adds a new object at the beginning; i.e., once it is done, the newly added element is first in the collection; **addLast**: is similar but deals with the opposite end.

```
experiment addFirst: 'LEFT'.
experiment first ⇒ 'LEFT'
experiment ⇒ OrderedCollection ('LEFT' 'OK' 'NOW')
experiment addLast: 'RIGHT'.
experiment last ⇒ 'RIGHT'
experiment ⇒ OrderedCollection ('LEFT' 'OK' 'NOW' 'RIGHT')
```

With respect to our earlier example, we could have constructed the sentence "Once upon a time, there lived a bear." by adding words and punctuation in a totally different order. For example, we could start with the comma and then proceed to add on both the left and right sides.

```
| sentence |
sentence := OrderedCollection new
    add: ',';
    addFirst: 'time'; addFirst: 'a'; addFirst: 'upon'; addFirst: 'Once';
    addLast: 'there'; addLast: 'lived'; addLast: 'a'; addLast: 'bear';
    addLast: '.';
    yourself.
sentence size ⇒ 10
sentence ⇒ OrderedCollection ('Once' 'upon' 'a' 'time' ',' 'there' 'lived' 'a' 'bear' '.')
```

Notice that we had to add the words in the sentence fragment "Once upon a time," in the reverse order. If we could have seen the ordered collection grow as we added elements, we would have seen it change as follows:

```
OrderedCollection ()
OrderedCollection (',')
OrderedCollection ('time' ',')
OrderedCollection ('a' 'time' ',')
OrderedCollection ('upon' 'a' 'time' ',')
OrderedCollection ('Once' 'upon' 'a' 'time' ',')
OrderedCollection ('Once' 'upon' 'a' 'time' ',' 'there')
OrderedCollection ('Once' 'upon' 'a' 'time' ',' 'there' 'lived')
OrderedCollection ('Once' 'upon' 'a' 'time' ',' 'there' 'lived' 'a')
OrderedCollection ('Once' 'upon' 'a' 'time' ',' 'there' 'lived' 'a' 'bear')
OrderedCollection ('Once' 'upon' 'a' 'time' ',' 'there' 'lived' 'a' 'bear' '.')
```

An ordered collection is very much like a dictionary because the elements can be accessed using keys (we'll discuss dictionaries in more detail later). However, the keys are not arbitrary. They must be integers in the range 1 to the size of the collection. When a new element is added, either at the left or right end, the keys are renumbered so that the leftmost element is always accessed using key 1 and the rightmost with a key that is the size of the collection. Such keys are often called **subscripts** in other programming languages. We'll use the terms keys and subscripts interchangeably.

The operations for accessing and modifying existing elements of ordered collections are the same ones used for strings; namely, **at**: and **at:put**:, as illustrated below:

```
'hello' at: 2 ⇒ $e.
'hello' at: 2 put: $u; yourself ⇒ 'hullo'
```

For example, the elements of the above ordered collection could be accessed as follows:

```
sentence at: 1 ⇒ 'Once'
sentence at: 2 ⇒ 'upon'
sentence at: 3 ⇒ 'a'
sentence at: 4 ⇒ 'time'
sentence at: 5 ⇒ ','
sentence at: 6 ⇒ 'there'
sentence at: 7 ⇒ 'lived'
sentence at: 8 ⇒ 'a'
sentence at: 9 ⇒ 'bear'
sentence at: 10 ⇒ '.'
```

Any other key is illegal.

```
sentence at: 0 ⇒ (error)
sentence at: 11 ⇒ (error)
```

It can be modified as follows:

```
sentence at: 9 put: 'rabbit' ⇒ 'rabbit'
sentence ⇒ OrderedCollection ('Once' 'upon' 'a' 'time' ',' 'there' 'lived' 'a' 'rabbit' '.')
```

But note that **at:put:** has the same restrictions as **at:**.

    sentence **at**: 0 **put**: 'start' ⇒ (error)
    sentence **at**: 11 **put**: 'end' ⇒ (error)

Thus, the size of a collection can be changed only by using **add:**, **addFirst:**, and **addLast:**—not by using **at:put:**.

The use of an illegal key is such a common error that we refer to it as **subscripting out of bounds**.

To illustrate that adding elements causes the position of the elements to change, consider element #pear below.

    | foods |
    foods := OrderedCollection **new add**: #pear; **yourself**.
    foods **at**: 1 ⇒ pear

    foods **addFirst**: #apple ⇒ apple
    foods **at**: 1 ⇒ apple
    foods **at**: 2 ⇒ pear

    foods **addFirst**: #orange ⇒ orange
    foods **at**: 1 ⇒ orange
    foods **at**: 2 ⇒ apple
    foods **at**: 3 ⇒ pear

Searching can be important requirement in some applications using containers. Fortunately, it is easy to determine if an ordered collection contains a particular element.

    sentence **includes**: 'rabbit' ⇒ true
    sentence **includes**: 'rab', 'bit' ⇒ true
    sentence **includes**: 'dog' ⇒ false

Semantically, the result of sending message "**includes**: anObject" to an ordered collection is true if the collection contains an element equal to anObject. The ordered collection need not contain the actual object to return true. That's why we get the same answer for both 'rabbit' and 'rab', 'bit'. In the last case, concatenating 'rab' with 'bit' results in an entirely new string that happens to be equal to 'rabbit'.

Elements are removed just as easily.

    sentence **remove**: 'rabbit' ⇒ 'rabbit'

Note that the container replies with the parameter to the message; i.e., with string 'rabbit' in this case. Thus the semantics of **remove:** are similar to the semantics of **add:**. In particular, you do not get the container back as the answer. Presumably, even though a string has been returned, the container must have been modified as a side-effect. This is easily checked as follows:

    sentence ⇒ OrderedCollection ('Once' 'upon' 'a' 'time' ',' 'there' 'lived' 'a' '.')

Presumably, we can keep removing elements until a container is empty. But what happens if we try to remove an element that isn't there? For example, let's try to remove 'day' from ordered collection sentence or foods.

    sentence **remove**: 'day' ⇒ (error)
    foods **remove**: 'day' ⇒ (error)

The actual message appears in Figure 7.1. Clearly, you can remove only elements that are already there.

Figure 7.1 Attempting to remove something that is not in a container.

When we're not sure if a container has a specific element, we can always test for it explicitly. For example, we could have written the following, instead:

    (sentence **includes**: 'day') **ifTrue**: [sentence **remove**: 'day']

Of course, this is rather cumbersome. A better alternative is to use the message

    aContainer **remove**: anObject **ifAbsent**: aBlock

The meaning, or **semantics**, of this message is rather straightforward. If aContainer contains an element equal to anObject, remove it and return anObject. Otherwise, execute aBlock and return the last value computed. Using this message, we could have safely executed the following, instead.

    sentence **remove**: 'day' **ifAbsent**: [nil] ⇒ nil
    sentence **remove**: 'zoo' **ifAbsent**: [1 + 5 **factorial**] ⇒ 121

If we had tried to remove an element such as 'upon' that was still in the collection, the block would not have executed.

>   sentence **remove**: 'upon' **ifAbsent**: [nil] ⇒ 'upon'

In addition to **remove**: and **remove:ifAbsent:**, two other removal operations are available—**removeFirst** and **removeLast**.

```
| colors |
colors := OrderedCollection new add: #red; add: #green; add: #blue; yourself.
colors ⇒ OrderedCollection (red green blue)

colors removeFirst ⇒ red
colors removeLast ⇒ blue
colors ⇒ OrderedCollection (green)
```

We have to be careful, however. Attempt to remove an element if there are no elements left, results in an error.

```
colors removeFirst ⇒ green
colors removeLast ⇒ (error)
```

In general, using **addFirst**: three times in a row followed by three corresponding **removeFirst** operations provides a **last-in first-out (LIFO)** behavior. For example, after adding "1", then "2", and finally "3", we can subsequently retrieve "3", "2", and "1" in that order. LIFO behavior is what happens when cars go down a dead-end street that is wide enough for only one car to pass. This same LIFO, or **stacking**, behavior can also be provided using **addLast**: in conjunction with the corresponding **removeLast** operation.

The related **first-in first-out (FIFO)**, or **queuing**, behavior that we encounter when going to a movie, for example, can be provided by pairing operations **addLast**: with **removeFirst** (or equivalently, **addFirst**: with **removeLast**).

Because of this LIFO and FIFO behavior, ordered collections are often used as stacks and queues. These have important applications in language translation and simulation, domains we might wish to investigate in the future.

Finally, we can sequence through all the elements of a container and do something with each element using message **do:** as in

```
aContainer do: aBlock
```

However, unlike all previous block examples in this chapter, this block requires a **block parameter**,. a special variable that is declared at the beginning of the block by preceding it with character ":" and following it with character "|". (We encountered block parameters in the previous chapter. But let's review it here in more detail.) Any number of spaces are permitted both before and after the special characters. However, by convention, we usually omit the spaces around the ":" character and we provide only one space both before and after the "|" character, as shown below.

```
aContainer do: [:member | ...]
```

In this case, "member" is the block parameter—the name is chosen by the programmer. The block parameter is for exclusive use inside the square brackets; i.e., the variable should not be accessed outside the block.

The **do**: message requests the container to successively bind the block parameter to each of its elements and execute the block after each binding has been performed. For ordered collections, the elements are bound in the first-to-last order. In the above situation, "member" is bound to the first element of aContainer and the block is executed. Then, member is bound to the second element of aContainer and the block is executed again, and so on until the block has been executed for all elements in aContainer. Let's consider a specific example.

```
| directions |
directions := OrderedCollection new
    add: #left; add: #right; add: #up; add: #down; yourself.

Transcript cr; nextPutAll: 'Directions: '.
directions do: [:direction | Transcript cr. direction printOn: Transcript].
```

The resulting transcript window will then appear, as shown in Figure 7.2.

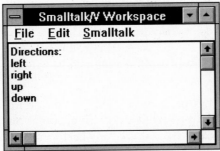

Figure 7.2 After sequencing through and displaying all elements of directions.

By now, it should be obvious that we can insert anything into ordered collection. We used strings and symbols above for illustration purposes. But we can have more complex examples, such as the following:

```
| complicatedOrderedCollection simpleOrderedCollection |
simpleOrderedCollection := OrderedCollection new.
simpleOrderedCollection add: 'Hi.'; add: 'Bye.'.

complicatedOrderedCollection := OrderedCollection new.
complicatedOrderedCollection
    add: Display pen; add: 5 factorial; add: simpleOrderedCollection.
complicatedOrderedCollection
    ⇒ OrderedCollection (a Pen 120 OrderedCollection ('HI.' 'Bye.'))
```

This complicated ordered collection is clearly of size 3, since it contains three elements: a pen, an integer, and another ordered collection. As we can see, *containers can even contain other containers.*

Relationship to Strings

We might now summarize an ordered collection as a container that permits elements to be added and removed easily from either end and that also permits element access and modification using integer subscripts. The latter part of this description applies just as well to strings. But strings are fixed-size and permit only character elements. So an ordered collection can be described as a generalization of strings that permits arbitrary objects as elements and that can grow and shrink over time. Presumably, we should be able to use ordered collections in place of strings.

```
I aString anOrderedCollection I
aString := 'red'.
anOrderedCollection := OrderedCollection new add: $r; add: $e; add: $d; yourself.

aString ⇒ 'red'
anOrderedCollection ⇒ OrderedCollection ($r $e $d)

aString do: [:aCharacter I Transcript nextPut: aCharacter].
anOrderedCollection do: [:aCharacter I Transcript nextPut: aCharacter].
Transcript nextPutAll: anOrderedCollection
```

In Chapter 2, we were exposed to the fact that we could extract substrings from strings. We repeat that information here as a review. However, we might be tempted to try out the same message on an ordered collection to see what happens.

```
aString copyFrom: 2 to: 3 ⇒ 'ed'
anOrderedCollection copyFrom: 2 to: 3 ⇒ OrderedCollection ($e $d)
```

It seems to work for both. Is the receiver modified? It's easy to find out by printing the original string and ordered collection.

```
aString ⇒ 'red'
anOrderedCollection ⇒ OrderedCollection ($r $e $d)
```

Apparently, message **copyFrom:to:** has no side-effects on the receiver. It results in the construction of a new container of the same class as the receiver. Of course, that's why the message name starts with the word **copy**—it makes a copy of the receiver rather than modify it.

In general, many but not all of the string operations apply to ordered collections. For example, concatenation via "," applies, but not **asSymbol**. Nevertheless, the close relationship between strings and ordered collections permits us to make good guesses that can be checked out easily.

Relationship to Arrays

Ordered collections are also related to arrays. We encountered arrays when we discussed literals; e.g., #(10 20 30) is an array literal containing the three elements 10, 20, and 30. **Arrays** are fixed-size containers for arbitrary objects. They can be viewed as extensions of strings that permit arbitrary elements or as restrictions of ordered collections that don't permit size changes. Because the size cannot change, they must be constructed with the required size. For example,

```
| anArray |
anArray := Array new: 20.
```

constructs an array with twenty elements. Initially, each element is nil but can be replaced with **at:put:**. However, you can't use any of the **add:**, **addFirst:**, **addLast:**, **remove:**, **removeFirst**, or **removeLast** messages because these require the receiver to grow or shrink. Nevertheless, you can use any of the other ordered collection or string operations; e.g., **at:**, **copyFrom:to:**, **do:**. Our first ordered collection example could be redone with arrays as follows:

```
| sentence |
sentence := (Array new: 10)
    at: 1 put: 'Once';
    at: 2 put: 'upon';
    at: 3 put: 'a';
    at: 4 put: 'time';
    at: 5 put: ',';
    at: 6 put: 'there';
    at: 7 put: 'lived';
    at: 8 put: 'a';
    at: 9 put: 'bear';
    at: 10 put: '.';
    yourself.

sentence size ⇒ 10
sentence ⇒ ('Once' 'upon' 'a' 'time' ',' 'there' 'lived' 'a' 'bear' '.')
```

As you can see, arrays are the only containers that print without the class name in front. An empty ordered collection prints as "OrderedCollection ()", for example, whereas an empty array prints as "()". How do we get an empty array? Try "Array **new**: 0".

Notice that we used brackets around "Array **new**: 10" above. Was this necessary? If you can't decide, rewrite the expression on one line without the brackets.

```
| sentence |
sentence := Array new: 10 at: 1 put: 'Once'; at: 2 put: 'upon'; ... ; yourself.
```

What's the first message? As we can see, it's the **new:at:put:** message being sent to the class (a three-parameter message). Clearly, no such message exists—so it wouldn't be understood. We need the brackets.

7.1.2 Dictionaries

Since dictionaries (in the Smalltalk sense) permit us to associate one object with another, two pieces of information must be provided: a key and its correlated value. For example, consider the construction of a dictionary that associates colors (strings) with respective fruits (symbols); i.e., the fruits are keys and the colors are the values.

```
| aDictionary |
aDictionary := Dictionary new
    at: #apple put: 'red';
    at: #pear put: 'yellow';
    at: #banana put: 'yellow';
    at: #orange put: 'orange';
    at: #cherry put: 'red';
    yourself.

aDictionary size ⇒ 5
aDictionary ⇒ Dictionary ('red' 'yellow' 'orange' 'yellow' 'red')
```

As you can see, dictionaries print only their values, not their keys. Moreover, because the values are printed in arbitrary order, we can't attach too much importance to a dictionary's printed representation; i.e., we can't really tell what's in a dictionary by printing it. If we inspect it, however, we will see that all the information is in the dictionary. But we do have to look at the individual keys one by one, as shown in Figure 7.3.

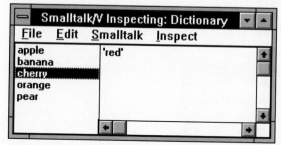

Figure 7.3 Inspecting a dictionary.

Clearly we used message **at:put:** above for its side-effects; i.e., for its effect in adding both a key and an associated value to the dictionary. In keeping with the semantics of all the other **at:put:** operations for strings, arrays, and ordered collections, the result returned is the value provided via the **put:** keyword.

To retrieve the value associated with a key in a dictionary, we only need to provide the key using message **at:**.

```
| aDictionary |
aDictionary := Dictionary new
    at: 'chicken' put: 'bird';
    at: 'elm' put: 'tree';
    at: 'sparrow' put: 'bird';
    at: 'maple' put: 'tree';
    at: 'robin' put: 'bird';
    yourself.

aDictionary at: 'sparrow' ⇒ 'bird'
aDictionary at: 'robin' ⇒ 'bird'
aDictionary at: 'turkey' ⇒ (error)
```

However, we have to be sure that an equal key exists. The error that results is shown in Figure 7.4. Note that the same error would also have occurred if we had said something that is clearly wrong, such as "aDictionary at: nil".

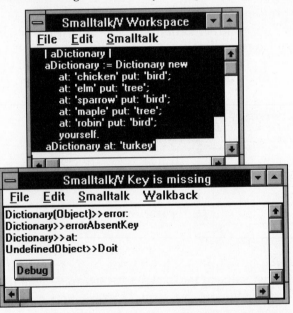

Figure 7.4 Querying a dictionary for a non-existent key.

Since it is an error to query a dictionary about a key that doesn't exist, some alternative message must be available when we're not sure about the existence of a key. In this case, we can use **at:ifAbsent:**.

aDictionary **at:** 'fire' **ifAbsent:** ['don''t know'] ⇒ 'don''t know'

Message "**at:** key **ifAbsent:** aBlock" obtains the value associated with an equal key if such a key exists; otherwise, the block is evaluated and the last object computed is returned. In the above example, 'don''t know' is returned because there is no key equal to 'fire' in the dictionary. Of course, if an equal key exists, **at:ifAbsent:** behaves just like **at:**.

> aDictionary **at**: 'maple' **ifAbsent**: ['don''t know'] ⇒ 'tree'

Removing an element is as easy as inserting one.

> aDictionary **removeKey**: 'maple' ⇒ 'maple'
> aDictionary ⇒ Dictionary ('bird' 'tree' 'bird' 'tree')
> aDictionary **at**: 'maple' **ifAbsent**: ['maple not there'] ⇒ 'maple not there'

Once again, we can't tell if the specified key was properly removed by simply printing the dictionary. Since both 'elm' and 'maple' have the associated value 'tree', all we can tell by printing the dictionary is that one of these was removed. Of course, we expect the dictionary to have removed the proper key—and it does.

When we aren't sure about the existence of the key, we should use selector **removeKey:ifAbsent:**, as in

> aDictionary **removeKey**: 'fire' **ifAbsent**: [nil] ⇒ nil

In general, the element provided as a parameter to an addition and removal message selector such as **add:**, **remove:**, **remove:ifAbsent:**, **removeKey:**, **removeKey:ifAbsent:** is returned when an equal element is found in the container; e.g., "aDictionary **removeKey**: anObject" returns "anObject" after removing the key equal to "anObject". The key itself isn't returned. It is rare for such a subtlety to be important, however, because we tend to use these messages for their side-effects, not for what they return.

Just as we can sequence through the elements of ordered collection, we can also sequence through the values in dictionaries.

> | aDictionary |
> aDictionary := Dictionary **new**
>   **at**: 'apple' **put**: 'red'; **at**: 'pear' **put**: 'green'; **yourself**.
>
> Transcript **cr**; **nextPutAll**: 'Dictionary elements: '.
> aDictionary **do**: [:element | Transcript **cr**. element **printOn**: Transcript].

However, since dictionaries contain both keys and their associated values, it is often more appropriate to display both as follows:

> Transcript **cr**; **nextPutAll**: 'Dictionary elements: '.
> aDictionary **keysDo**: [:key |
>   Transcript **cr**.
>   key **printOn**: Transcript.
>   Transcript **nextPutAll**: ' is associated with '.
>   (aDictionary **at**: key) **printOn**: Transcript].

The result is shown in Figure 7.5. Note that once we have a key, it is an easy matter to get the associated value using message **at:** (there is no need for message **at:ifAbsent:**, because we know the key is there).

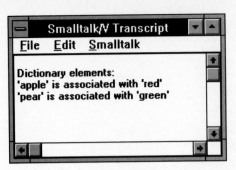

Figure 7.5 After further displaying dictionary elements.

All our examples have used strings and symbols for keys. However, there is no restriction on the kinds of keys allowed. Consider

```
| aDictionary |
aDictionary := Dictionary new
        at: 2001 put: 'great movie';
        at: 100 factorial put: 'wow';
        at: 2/3 put: 'a fraction, ok?';
        at: 3.14 put: 'pi (not pie)';
        at: 5@10 put: 'What''s the point?';
        at: #(10 20 30 40 50) put: 'an array of integers';
        yourself.

aDictionary at: 2001 ⇒ 'great movie'
aDictionary at: 100 factorial ⇒ 'wow'
aDictionary at: 2/3 ⇒ 'a fraction, ok?'
aDictionary at: 3.14 ⇒ 'pi (not pie)'
aDictionary at: 5@10 ⇒ 'What''s the point?'
aDictionary at: #(10 20 30 40 50) ⇒ 'an array of integers'
```

7.1.3 Class Operations and Converting From one Collection to Another

So far, we have explicitly constructed containers with elements using messages such as **add:** and **at:put:**.

```
| aDictionary anOrderedCollection anArray |
aDictionary := Dictionary new
        at: 1 put: 'This'; at: 2 put: 'is'; at: 3 put: 'it'; yourself.
anOrderedCollection := OrderedCollection new
        add: 'This'; add: 'is'; add: 'it'; yourself.
anArray := (Array new: 3)
        at: 1 put: 'This'; at: 2 put: 'is'; at: 3 put: 'it'; yourself.
```

We can even do the same with strings, although it is not likely that we would ever want to do this explicitly... or would we?

```
| aString |
aString := (String new: 3) at: 1 put: $H; at: 2 put: $i; at: 3 put: $!; yourself.
aString ⇒ 'Hi!'
```

On the other hand, there is a convenient *class* message that can be used to simultaneously create new instances and initialize them (if there are only a small number of elements).

```
| anOrderedCollection anArray aString |
anOrderedCollection := OrderedCollection with: 'This' with: 'is' with: 'it'.
anArray := Array with: 'This' with: 'is' with: 'it'.
aString := String with: $H with: $i with: $!.
```

Unfortunately, this doesn't work for dictionaries. Since the keys aren't provided, class dictionary refuses to assume they must be consecutive integers starting at 1. Ordered collections, arrays, and strings, however, do make this assumption because their keys must always be integers starting at 1 anyway.

In general, only four messages are provided to create and simultaneously initialize a container object (any container except a dictionary, that is).

```
aContainerClass with: anObject
aContainerClass with: anObject with: anObject
aContainerClass with: anObject with: anObject with: anObject
aContainerClass with: anObject with: anObject with: anObject with: anObject
```

If we try to construct a larger container, for example, using

```
OrderedCollection with: 1 with: 2 with: 3 with: 4 with: 5
```

we'll find that the message isn't understood.

There are also convenient **conversion** operations that permit new containers to be obtained from existing ones. The originals are not modified. These include

```
aContainer asOrderedCollection
aContainer asArray
```

Once again, dictionaries are special, since no corresponding conversion is provided. There is also no easy way of converting a container to a string—even if it does consist only of characters. A simple example illustrating a conversion operation might be

```
| anOrderedCollection anArray |
anOrderedCollection := OrderedCollection with: 'this' with: 'is' with: 'it'.
anArray := anOrderedCollection asArray.
```

```
anOrderedCollection ⇒ OrderedCollection ('this' 'is' 'it')
anArray ⇒ ('this' 'is' 'it')
```

7.1.4 More on Sequencing through Containers

Since sequencing is fundamental to many applications, let's consider the notion in more detail, by examining short, simple, isolated examples that illustrate some of the important issues and techniques. To begin with, consider a collection of integers that we wish to process; e.g., to find the sum, the product, the maximum, and the minimum. An approach to finding the sum is illustrated below.

```
| data sum |
data := #(1 2 3 4 5 6 7 8 9 10).
sum := 0.
data do: [:element |
    sum := sum + element].
^sum
```

The basic strategy is to accumulate the answer in a variable called "sum". First, "sum" is initialized to 0. Next, the elements in "data" are obtained one by one using **do**:. Each time a new element is obtained, the sum is updated to include the new element using "sum := sum + element". To make sense of this assignment, it should be read as follows:

"new sum" := "old sum" + element

Once all the elements have been processed, the **do**: terminates and the answer is provided in "sum".

Since the **do**: causes block "[:element | sum := sum + element]" to execute once for each object in "data"; i.e., once when "element" is 1, once when it is 2, then 3, then 4, ..., 10, the effect is best understood by observing how sum changes. Table 7.1 summarizes sum's evolution.

Table 7.1 Illustrating the execution steps as sum changes.

Expression	element	"old sum" + element	"new sum"
sum := 0.	—	—	0
sum := sum + element	1	0 + 1	1
sum := sum + element	2	1 + 2	3
sum := sum + element	3	3 + 3	6
sum := sum + element	4	6 + 4	10
sum := sum + element	5	10 + 5	15
sum := sum + element	6	15 + 6	21
sum := sum + element	7	21 + 7	28
sum := sum + element	8	28 + 8	36
sum := sum + element	9	36 + 9	45
sum := sum + element	10	45 + 10	55
^sum			55

To find the product instead of the sum requires only two small semantic modifications. It is necessary to start with 1 instead of 0 (otherwise, the result would be 0). Additionally, operation "+" must be changed to "*". For clarity, we will also want to change variable name "sum" to "product".

```
| data product |
data := #(1 2 3 4 5 6 7 8 9 10).
product := 1.
data do: [:element |
    product := product * element].
^product
```

The following code structure summarizes the basic approach to processing collections of data items:

```
initialization in preparation for looping
 aCollection do: [:element |
     process "element"]
finalization to complete the computation
```

Care is always needed when applying this code structure to new situations. For example, consider applying it to the task of finding the maximum instead of the sum or product. First, we need to be able to find a maximum of two numbers. One approach is the following:

```
| number1 number2 maximum |
number1 := 10.
number2 := 20.
(number1 > number2)
    ifTrue: [maximum := number1]
    ifFalse: [maximum := number2].
```

This seems a little complex but it works. If we interchange 10 and 20, for example, we still get the correct answer. However, a little work on our part browsing class Number and its superclass Magnitude might lead to a simple operation that can find the maximum of two numbers. It turns out that such an operation is called **max**:. Thus, we could write

```
10 max: 20 ⇒ 20
20 max: 10 ⇒ 20
```

Now, we can easily apply the standard code template as follows:

```
| data maximum |
data := #(1 2 3 4 5 6 7 8 9 10).
maximum := 0.
data do: [:element |
    maximum := maximum max: element].
^maximum
```

Of course, we did have to think of some initial value for maximum. Zero works in this case but it is not a general solution. For example, what would be the result if data contained only negative numbers?

    data := #(-1 -2 -3 -4 -5 -6 -7 -8 -9 -10).

It turns out that we would get the answer 0, because all negative numbers are smaller. But the correct answer is -1. One approach to fixing the problem for this special situation is to initialize maximum to a number that is smaller than all existing numbers.

    maximum := -11.

Of course, every time we change the data, we might have to change the initial value. We need a more general solution! One approach that works is to use one of the data elements as the initial value. If it happens to be the maximum, we'll at least return a valid data element. If it is not the maximum, an even larger number will be found and this alternative data element will be returned instead. An easy way to obtain a data element is to ask for either the first or last element.

```
| data maximum |
data := code that obtains a collection.
maximum := data first.
data do: [:element |
    maximum := maximum max: element].
^maximum
```

Now this seems to work, but it still has one flaw that doesn't arise in the case of summing the elements (reproduced below for comparison purposes).

```
| data sum |
data := code that obtains a collection.
sum := 0.
data do: [:element |
    sum := sum + element].
^sum
```

The problem arises when the collection is empty, as in

    data := #()

Clearly, the sum of zero data elements is 0. Fortunately, that's what we get if we execute the "summing" code with an empty collection, because sum is initially set to 0. On the other hand, if we try to execute the corresponding code for finding the maximum, we get an error message. Can you see why? Consider message **first**. If the data collection is empty, there is no first element. So, we get a "subscript out of bounds" error.

But what is the maximum of zero data elements, anyway? There doesn't seem to be any appropriate number. Perhaps a more general solution ought to return nil if there is no maximum. The code might be revised as follows:

```
| data maximum |
data := code that obtains a collection.
data size = 0
    ifTrue: [maximum := nil]
    ifFalse: [
        maximum := data first.
        data do: [:element |
            maximum := maximum max: element]].
^maximum
```

Finding the minimum is analogous to finding the maximum, except that we need to use **min**: instead of **max**:.

Now, let's consider the task of initializing collections. Several approaches are possible:

- Specify the elements using an array; for example,

    ```
    #(1 2 3 4 4 3 2 1)
    ```

- Specify the elements using an array but convert to the desired kind of collection; for example,

    ```
    #(1 2 3 4 4 3 2 1) asOrderedCollection
    ```

- Specify **constructor elements** and use these to construct the desired collection; for example,

    ```
    | constructorElements desiredCollection |
    constructorElements := #(1 2 3 4 4 3 2 1).
    desiredCollection := OrderedCollection new.
    constructorElements do: [:element |
        desiredCollection add: element factorial].
    ^desiredCollection
    ```

- Construct the desired collection directly; for example,

    ```
    | desiredCollection |
    desiredCollection := OrderedCollection new.
    1 to: 4 do: [:index |
        desiredCollection add: index factorial].
    4 to: 1 by: -1 do: [:index |
        desiredCollection add: index factorial].
    ^desiredCollection
    ```

Sometimes, the collections are structured in complex ways. For example, a 3 by 3 tic-tac-toe board with cells that can contain an X, O, or B (for blank) and consisting of three rows and three columns might be defined as follows:

```
| board |
board := #(
    (X B B)
    (B X B)
    (B B X))
```

This is an array with three internal arrays or **subarrays**. The top-left element, X, is in row 1 (the first subarray) and column 1 (the first element in the subarray). The top-right element, B, is in row 1 and column 3. This element might be obtained by first specifying the subarray (in this case, the first one) and then the element within this subarray (namely, the third element) as follows:

```
(board at: 1) at: 3
```

Now, suppose we wanted to clear the board to start a new game; i.e., to fill it with blanks. We would need to sequence through each row and each column.

```
1 to: 3 do: [:row |
    1 to: 3 do: [:column |
        (board at: row) at: column put: #B]]
```

When "row" is 1, "column" ranges from 1 to 3. Similarly, when "row" is 2, "column" also ranges from 1 to 3. The same applies when "row" is 3. So nine Bs are put into the board.

7.2   Case Study: A Phone Book

A **phone book** is an object that can keep track of names and their associated phone numbers. We can use a dictionary for that purpose, as follows:

```
| aPhoneBook |
aPhoneBook := Dictionary new
    at: 'Jim' put: 2135665;
    at: 'Tom' put: 6134112;
    yourself
```

However, phone books are very specialized dictionaries. A PhoneBook class could be designed that uses domain-specific messages rather than general-purpose dictionary messages. There are several issues to be resolved:

- What are the domain-specific messages?
- Should we be able to look up numbers, given the names, and also names, given the numbers?
- How should phone books print themselves?
- Should we be able to compare them for equality?
- Should the names be sorted?

To be more domain-specific, we could use a selector such as **name:number:** instead of **at:put:**. Interrogation messages could have the form **numberForName:** and **nameForNumber:**. A phone book with the information above might be designed to print itself as

```
PhoneBook ('Jim' => 213-5665 'Tom' => 613-4112)
```

Presumably, it makes sense to be able to compare phone books. So why not implement comparison operations such as = and ~=. Sorting the names is a more complex issue. (It turns out that we can do this easily using a special kind of collection called a sorted collection, a container we will consider later.) Here, we'll sort our own names from first principles.

Before we can begin, we need to decide on the instance variables needed by the PhoneBook class. Clearly, we need one instance variable to keep track of a dictionary that associates numbers with the names. But dictionaries do not maintain their keys in any sorted order, so we need another instance variable to keep the names in sorted order. We'll call the ordered collection with sorted name "names" and the dictionary "numbers" since it maps names to numbers.

```
class                            PhoneBook
superclass                       Object
instance variables               names numbers

class methods

instance creation

new
    "Construct a fully initialized phone book."
    ^super new initialize

examples

example1
    "PhoneBook example1"
    ^PhoneBook new
        name: 'Jim' number: 2135665;
        name: 'Tom' number: 6134112

instance methods

instance initialization

initialize
    names := OrderedCollection new.
    numbers := Dictionary new.
```

For **example1** above, we expect names to be bound to an ordered collection consisting of 'Jim' and 'Tom', in that order, and numbers to be bound to a dictionary that associates the corresponding numbers with 'Jim' and 'Tom'. The problem with using only the dictionary is that **keysDo:** is just as likely to provide us with the keys in the order 'Tom' and 'Jim' rather than the desired order 'Jim' followed by 'Tom'. This will be of concern when we implement a **printOn:** method that prints the phone book as

```
PhoneBook ('Jim' => 213-5665 'Tom' => 613-4112)
```

For example, the following preliminary version of **printOn:** prints the names in a totally random order.

printing

```
printOn: aWindow
    "Might print like PhoneBook ('Tom' => 6134112 'Jim' => 2135665 )."
    self class printOn: aWindow.
    aWindow nextPutAll: ' ('.
    numbers keysDo: [:name |
        name printOn: aWindow.
        aWindow nextPutAll: ' => '.
        (numbers at: name) printOn: aWindow.
        aWindow nextPutAll: ' '].
    aWindow nextPut: $)
```

To ensure that the keys are printed in sorted order, we need to replace

```
numbers keysDo: [:name | ...]
```

by

```
names do: [:name | ...]
```

But there are other problems, as well. One that might be obvious is that a space is output before the final right bracket. As a rule, there should never be any spaces immediately inside surrounding brackets. We need to insert a space between each key-value pair to separate them, but we don't want one at the end. A special counter could be introduced to directly prevent the last space from being generated, as follows:

```
counter := 0.
names do: [:name |
    ...
    counter := counter + 1.
    counter < numbers size
        ifTrue: [aWindow nextPutAll: ' ']]
```

But this solution seems cumbersome. A slightly simpler solution is to add the space ahead of a key-value pair rather than after it, preventing the first space from being generated.

```
firstSpace := true.
names do: [:name |
    firstSpace
        ifTrue: [firstSpace := false].
        ifFalse: [aWindow nextPutAll: ' '].
    ...]
```

But the best solution takes advantage of the fact that message "**nextPutAll**: aString" will work for any string—including an empty string.

```
spacer := ''. "no spaces (an empty string) for the first iteration"
names do: [:name |
    Window nextPutAll: spacer.
    spacer := ' '. "one space for the next and all subsequent iterations"
    ...]
```

Another problem with the **printOn**: method is getting a phone number like 2135665 to print as 213-5665. How do we get the dash between the digits?

Clearly, we have to decompose the phone number into parts. We should be able to use / / (divide with truncation) and \ \ (remainder) for this purpose.

```
2135665 // 10000 ⇒ 213
2135665 \\ 10000 ⇒ 5665
```

This leads to a strategy exemplified by the following:

```
(2135665 // 10000) printOn: aWindow.
aWindow nextPut: $-.
(2135665 \\ 10000) printOn: aWindow.
```

If a number has an area code, it is necessary to extract it using 10000000 instead of 10000. But how can we tell if there is an area code? Presumably, if it is missing, the result of the extraction will be zero.

```
areaCode := 2135665 // 10000000.
areaCode > 0 ifTrue: [ "Area code exists." areaCode printOn: aWindow]
```

But all this ignores still another problem. A number such as 5550004 prints as 555-4; i.e., the leading zeros are missing!!

To force leading zeros to be generated, we could convert the number to a string and then pad it with the required number of leading zero characters.

```
number := 0004. "an example"
paddedNumber := number printString.
[paddedNumber size < 4] whileTrue: [
    paddedNumber := '0', paddedNumber].
aWindow nextPutAll: paddedNumber.
```

But concatenation is inefficient if repeated too often. Too many characters are copied multiple times. You can see, from Table 7.2., that character $4 is copied three times when three concatenations are performed.

Table 7.2 Repeated concatenation copies the same character many times.

Iteration	paddedNumber	Number of characters copied
0	'4'	0
1	'0', '4' $\Rightarrow$ '04'	0+(1+1) = 2
2	'0', '04' $\Rightarrow$ '004'	2+(1+2) = 5
3	'0', '004' $\Rightarrow$ '0004'	5+(1+3) = 9

We could introduce a special method that has the same effect but avoids using concatenation.

> **printNumber**: number **zeroPaddedTo**: totalDigits **on**: aWindow
>   (totalDigits - number **printString size**) **timesRepeat**: [
>   aWindow **nextPut**: $0].
>   number **printOn**: aWindow

Putting all this together, we end up with the solution shown at the end of this section.

Now, let's consider the fundamental method for adding a new phone number; namely, **name:number:**. First, consider a solution that doesn't bother sorting the names.

> *inserting*

> **name**: name **number**: number
>   "Adds the new name to the phone book if it is not already there. Also,
>   updates the associated number.
>   (names **includes**: name) **ifFalse**: [names **add**: name].
>   numbers **at**: name **put**: number

Now, if names contains three strings such as 'Boyd', 'George', and 'Manning', sorted as shown below, adding a new name 'Danny' simply requires searching through the list from left to right until a name X is found that either is equal to 'Danny' (it's already there) or satisfies 'Danny' < X.

> 'Boyd' < 'George' < 'Manning'

In this case, since 'Danny' < 'Boyd' is false, we continue moving right to the next name and test again. In this case, 'Danny' < 'George' is true, so 'Danny' is inserted in front of 'George'. We need to modify our method as follows:

> **name**: name **number**: number
>   "Adds the new name to the phone book if it is not already there. Also,
>   updates the associated number."
>   self **privatelyInsert**: name.
>   numbers **at**: name **put**: number

```
privatelyInsert: name
    I containedName I
    1 to: names size do: [:index I
        containedName := names at: index
        name = containedName ifTrue: [^self "already there"].
        name < containedName ifTrue: [^self privatelyInsert: name at: index]].
    "Must go at the end of the list."
    self privatelyInsert: name at: names size + 1
```

Once we have determined where the new name should go, we can insert it at the new position and leave the method (even if more iterations are possible). However, if we managed to exhaust all possibilities, then it should be clear that the new name must go at the end.

Finally, to insert a new name at a specified index, we will have to first grow the collection so that it can hold the new entry. As we will see, it is convenient to create an entry on the right.

```
'Boyd' < 'George' < 'Manning' < nil
```

Next, we can make room for the new name by shifting to the right all the entries to the immediate right of the new element's insertion point. Thus, 'Manning' would be shifted before 'George', as shown below.

```
'Boyd' < 'George' < 'Manning' < nil
'Boyd' < 'George' < 'Manning' < 'Manning'
'Boyd' < 'George' < 'George' < 'Manning'
```

Finally, 'Danny' would be added at the new position to get

```
'Boyd' < 'Danny' < 'George' < 'Manning'
```

This leads to the following method. Note that the loop must proceed from right to left; i.e., it must start with the size of "names" and then decrease until "index" is reached. If it went the other way, we would find that 'George' would be moved right, then this new 'George' would be moved right again, until 'George' replaced every single element to the right.

```
privatelyInsert: name at: index
    "First, grow the collection."
    names addLast: nil.
    "Second, move the existing elements over to the right."
    names size to: index + 1 by: -1 do: [:newIndex I
        names at: newIndex put: (names at: newIndex - 1)].
    "Third, insert the new name."
    names at: index put: name
```

This approach to inserting a new name into a sorted collection of names is relatively slow. If "names" has n entries, for example, n iterations are needed in the worst case to determine where a new entry belongs; e.g., when the new name must be added to the extreme right. It is possible to develop a more efficient approach by considering only the middle entry and determining whether to further search the left or right half. By continually dividing the entries to be searched into successive halves, only $\log_2 n$ entries need to be considered in the worst case (see below for a derivation).

> After processing entry 1, there are $n/2^1$ more entries to consider
> After processing entry 2, there are $n/2^2$ more entries to consider.
> After processing entry 3, there are $n/2^3$ more entries to consider.
>
> ...
>
> After processing entry i, there are $n/2^i$ more entries to consider.

After processing a particular entry in the middle of the list, only half of the entries (either the left half or the right half, but not both) need to be considered. Entry i is the last entry when $n/2^i = 1$.

$$n = 2^i \text{ (or alternatively)}$$
$$2^i = n$$

But	$\log_2(2^i) = \log_2 n$	(taking the log of both sides)
	$i \log_2(2) = \log_2 n$	(since $\log_2 x^y = y \log_2 x$)
	$i = \log_2 n$	(since $\log_2(2) = 1$)

The development of this more efficient approach is known as **top-down decomposition** (or **stepwise refinement**). The basic strategy is to reword the task in such a manner that it can be divided into two or more subtasks that look like the original task but are simpler in some way. At some point, each task will be so simple that it can be completed without breaking it up into subtasks. The special situation where we divide the task into two parts for searching is called **binary search**. We begin by revising method **privatelyInsert:** as shown below:

> **privatelyInsert**: name
>   self **privatelyBinarySearchFor**: name **between**: 1 **and**: names **size**

The initial task has been changed to one that can be decomposed. For example, if "names" already contains 10 items, the task

> self **privatelyBinarySearchFor**: name **between**: 1 **and**: 10

can be decomposed in two roughly equal-sized subtasks by focusing on the midpoint 5 (the average of 1 and 10). Ignoring the fifth element for the moment, the original task can be replaced by one of the following:

> self **privatelyBinarySearchFor**: name **between**: 1 **and**: 4

or

> self **privatelyBinarySearchFor**: name **between**: 6 **and**: 10

Now the task is to determine which one is applicable. If "name" is less than the fifth element, the first possibility applies. If it is equal, we have found the name and we are done. If it is greater than the fifth element, the second possibility applies. So we can pass the buck and ask for a solution to the unique, simpler subtask that applies. This process might repeat itself a number of times, but ultimately, one really simple case will present itself, a case like

    self **privatelyBinarySearchFor**: name **between**: 7 **and**: 7

where "name" is either to be inserted at position 7 if it is less than the seventh element, declared "found" if it is equal, or inserted at position 8 otherwise. A solution is shown below.

```
privatelyBinarySearchFor: name between: start and: end
    I midPoint midName I
    midPoint := (start + end) // 2. "the average"
    midName := names at: midPoint
    start = end
        ifTrue: [
            name = midName
                ifTrue: [^self "already there"].
            name < midName
                ifTrue: [^self privatelyInsert: name at: start]
                ifFalse: [^self privatelyInsert: name at: start + 1]]
        ifFalse: [
            name = midName
                ifTrue: [^self "already there"].
            name < midName
                ifTrue: [
                    ^self privatelyBinarySearchFor: name
                        between: start and: midPoint - 1]
                ifFalse: [
                    ^self privatelyBinarySearchFor: name
                        between: midPoint + 1 and: end]]
```

We could simplify the above method a little, but before we do, we must consider a major shortcoming. When collection "names" is initially empty, message

    self **privatelyBinarySearchFor**: name **between**: 1 **and**: 0

is executed The correct response, in this case, is to insert the name at position 1. We need a special test at the beginning of the method to do this.

    start > end **ifTrue**: [^self **privatelyInsert**: name **at**: start].

But now, there are three cases: start > end, start = end (the **ifTrue**: part), and start < end(the **ifFalse**: part). But both the **ifTrue**: and **ifFalse**: parts are similar— they have identical tests between name and midName but they proceed differently as a result of the tests. The **ifTrue**: part is the end of the search since there is no more buck passing but the **ifFalse**: part further divides the task into subtasks. Nevertheless, intuition tells us that there are too many cases!!

What would happen if we simplified the method by replacing "start = end **ifTrue**: [...] **ifFalse**: [...]" by just the **ifFalse**: part? In particular, any situation in which start and end are equal would potentially be further decomposed. For example, consider the following:

　　　self **privatelyBinarySearchFor**: name **between**: 7 **and**: 7

In this situation, midPoint would be 7. The "name = midName" case would work just like before. However, the case "name < midName" would result in the first decomposition below while the opposite "name > midName" case would result in the second decomposition.

　　　self **privatelyBinarySearchFor**: name **between**: 7 **and**: 6

or

　　　self **privatelyBinarySearchFor**: name **between**: 8 **and**: 7

Because of the new test "start > end **ifTrue**: [...]" added above, each of these results in the name being inserted at position 7 and 8 respectively. But this is what would have happened with the original code. This suggests the above simplification should be done to get the following:

```
privatelyBinarySearchFor: name between: start and: end
    I midPoint midName I
    start > end ifTrue: [^self privatelyInsert: name at: start].
    midPoint := (start + end) // 2. "the average"
    midName := names at: midPoint
    name = midName
        ifTrue: [^self "already there"].
    name < midName
        ifTrue: [
            ^self privatelyBinarySearchFor: name
                between: start and: midPoint - 1]
        ifFalse: [
            ^self privatelyBinarySearchFor: name
                between: midPoint + 1 and: end]
```

Reviewing our search methods one final time, we might be tempted to rename the binary search method to ensure that all three names are similar; i.e., rather than have methods such as

```
privatelyInsert: name
privatelyInsert: name at: index
privatelyBinarySearchFor: name between: start and: end
```

we might replace them by the following (the possibility that the last method might be using the binary search technique could be mentioned inside the method as a comment; an implementer might care but not a user):

```
privatelyInsert: name
privatelyInsert: name at: index
privatelyInsert: name between: start and: end
```

The only other methods to finalize are the querying methods **numberForName:** and **nameForNumber:** along with the comparison operation =. There is no need to implement ~=, since it can be inherited from Object. In fact, ~= is simply implemented as follows in Object.

```
~= anObject
    ^(self = anObject) not
```

A complete implementation is shown below.

class	PhoneBook
superclass	Object
instance variables	names numbers

class methods

instance creation

new
>   "Construct a fully initialized phone book."
>   ^super **new initialize**

examples

example1
>   "PhoneBook example1"
>   ^PhoneBook **new**
>   **name:** 'Jim' **number:** 2135665;
>   **name:** 'Tom' **number:** 6134112

instance methods

instance initialization

initialize
>   names := OrderedCollection **new.**
>   numbers := Dictionary **new.**

inserting

name: name **number:** number
>   "Adds the new name to the phone book if it is not already there. Also, updates the associated number."
>   self **privatelyInsert:** name.
>   numbers **at:** name **put:** number

privatelyInsert: name
>   self **privatelyInsert:** name **between:** 1 **and:** names **size**

privatelyInsert: name **at**: index
    "First, grow the collection."
    names **addLast**: nil.
    "Second, move the existing elements over to the right."
    names **size to**: index + 1 **by**: -1 **do**: [:newIndex |
        names **at**: newIndex **put**: (names **at**: newIndex - 1)].
    "Third, insert the new name."
    names **at**: index **put**: name

privatelyInsert: name **between**: start **and**: end
    "Uses the binary search technique to speed up the search in the sorted
    names collection."
    | midPoint midName |
    start > end **ifTrue**: [^self **privatelyInsert**: name **at**: start].
    midPoint := (start + end) // 2. "the average"
    midName := names **at**: midPoint
    name = midName
        ifTrue: [^self "already there"].
    name < midName
        ifTrue: [^self **privatelyInsert**: name **between**: start **and**: midPoint - 1]
        ifFalse: [^self **privatelyInsert**: name **between**: midPoint + 1 **and**: end]

querying

numberForName: name
    "Returns the associated number if it exists; otherwise, nil."
    ^numbers **at**: name **ifAbsent**: [nil]

nameForNumber: number
    "Returns the associated name if it exists; otherwise, nil."
    numbers **keysDo**: [:name |
        (numbers **at**: name) = number **ifTrue**: [^name]].
    ^nil

printing

printOn: aWindow
    "Prints like PhoneBook ('Jim' => 213-5665 'Tom' => 613-4112)."
    | spacer |
    self **class printOn**: aWindow.
    aWindow **nextPutAll**: ' ('.
    "We need to provide a space between the entries but none at the
    beginning or end."
    spacer := ''. "nothing"
    names **do**: [:name |
        aWindow **nextPutAll**: spacer.
        spacer := ' '. "one space"
        name **printOn**: aWindow.
        aWindow **nextPutAll**: ' => '.
        self **privatelyPrintNumber**: (numbers **at**: name) **on**: aWindow].
    aWindow **nextPut**: $)

```
privatelyPrintNumber: number on: aWindow
    "Prints 6132135665 as 613-213-5665 and 2135665 as 213-5665."
    | areaCode nonAreaCode prefix suffix |
    areaCode := number // 10000000.
    nonAreaCode := number \\ 10000000.
    prefix := nonAreaCode // 10000.
    suffix := nonAreaCode \\ 10000.
    areaCode > 0 ifTrue: [
        self printNumber: areaCode zeroPaddedTo: 3 on: aWindow.
        aWindow nextPut: $-].
    self printNumber: prefix zeroPaddedTo: 3 on: aWindow
    aWindow nextPut: $-.
    self printNumber: suffix zeroPaddedTo: 4 on: aWindow

printNumber: number zeroPaddedTo: totalDigits on: aWindow
    (totalDigits - number printString size) timesRepeat: [
        aWindow nextPut: $0].
    number printOn: aWindow
```

comparing

```
= anObject
    "Equal if anObject is a phone book with the same names and phone
    numbers."
    (anObject isKindOf: PhoneBook) ifFalse: [^false].
    self privateNames = anObject privateNames ifFalse: [^false].
    names do: [:name |
        (self numberForName: name) = (anObject numberForName: name)
            ifFalse: [^false]].
    "Everything matched?
    ^true

privateNames
    ^names
```

7.3   Case Study: A Tic-Tac-Toe Game

Tic-tac-toe is a relatively simple two-person game played on a 3 by 3 board. The players alternatively take turns. One player plays with Xs and the other plays with Os. The first player to create a line (vertical, horizontal, or diagonal) consisting solely of his chosen symbols (all Xs or all Os) wins. A tie results if there is no winner by the time all the board entries are filled.

One requirement for such a game is that it be interactive. Hence, some rudimentary facilities for prompting, informing, and displaying information are needed. You may need to review the basic prompter, message box, and graph pane facilities in Chapter 3 before proceeding. It is also useful to investigate a few additional pen facilities.

7.3.1 Additional Pen Facilities

In addition to the simple pen operations discussed in Chapter 3, we can make use of higher-level operations such as the following:

Operations on Pens

coloring

aPen **backColor**: color   (see ColorConstants for a complete listing)
aPen **foreColor**: color

settling the line size

aPen **setLineWidth**: anInteger

creating filled and unfilled boxes

aPen **boxFilled**: aPoint   Top-left corner at pen location; bottom-right at aPoint
aPen **box**: aPoint

creating filled and unfilled circles

aPen **circleFilled**: radius   Center at pen location
aPen **circle**: radius

ensuring that panes can redraw when uncovered

aPen **drawRetainPicture**: aBlock

writing text

aPen **nextPut**: aCharacter
aPen **nextPutAll**: aString

For example, we can specify the line drawing color (the **foreground** color) and the color to be used in the background when drawing a filled shape (the **background** color). as illustrated in Figure 7.6. **Filled** shapes have interiors colored in the background color. The boundary is in the foreground color. An **unfilled** shape has a transparent interior.

Figure 7.6 Drawing pictures and displaying text in a graph pane.

Colors are **magic** integers—integers that appear to be relatively arbitrary. Dictionary ColorConstants contains a complete list of the available colors. It is a simple matter to inspect this dictionary to browse the list of names (the keys). Some examples include

ClrBlack ClrWhite ClrRed ClrPink ClrBlue ClrYellow ClrGreen

One way to change a pen's foreground color is to indicate the color by directly referencing the ColorConstants dictionary.

aPen **backColor**: (ColorConstants **at**: 'ClrPink')

Of course, it would be much more convenient to write

aPen **backColor**: ClrPink

As it turns out, this is legal in workspaces, transcripts, and, in fact, any expression selected and chosen for execution via **Do It** and **Show It**. However, it is not legal in methods unless the ColorConstants dictionary is declared to be a **pool dictionary** of the class containing the method.

```
Object subclass: #SampleClass
    instanceVariableNames: ''
    classVariableNames: ''
    poolDictionaries: 'ColorConstants'
```

Recall that a **pool dictionary** is simply a global dictionary in which the keys are strings that are legal capitalized names and the values are the constants associated with the names. We will illustrate the use of pool dictionaries again in the next section.

We can also display text using the familiar **nextPut:** and **nextPutAll:** operations. In general, boxes (via **box:** and **boxFilled:**) display their top-left corner at the pen location. The bottom-right corner is the specified message parameter. Similarly, circles (via **circle:** and **circleFilled:**) have centers at the pen location. The radius is specified as the message parameter.

Figure 7.6, for example, was created with the following code:

```
| aPane aPen |
aPane := GraphPane openWindow: 'Tic Tac Toe' extent: 220@220.
aPen := aPane pen.
aPen
    backColor: ClrYellow; foreColor: ClrRed;
    place: 10@10; box: 30@30;
    place: 40@10; boxFilled: 60@30;
    place: 80@20; setLineWidth: 2; circle: 10;
    place: 110@20; circleFilled: 10;
    place: 10@60; backColor: ClrLightgray; nextPutAll: 'Hello'
```

One problem with the above is that the picture in the graph pane disappears if some other window (for example, a prompter) temporarily covers it. The picture is not drawn permanently in the pane.

To ensure that the information displayed is redrawn once the covering window is removed, we must issue the important drawing commands while the pen is *draw-and-retain mode*. This can be achieved as follows:

aPen **drawRetainPicture**: [... code to draw pictures ...]

Taking this into account, we need to change our example to the following:

```
I aPane aPen I
aPane := GraphPane openWindow: 'Tic Tac Toe' extent: 220@220.
aPen := aPane pen.
aPen drawRetainPicture: [
    aPen
        backColor: ClrYellow; foreColor: ClrRed;
        place: 10@10; box: 30@30;
        place: 40@10; boxFilled: 60@30;
        place: 80@20; setLineWidth: 2; circle: 10;
        place: 110@20; circleFilled: 10;
        place: 10@60; backColor: ClrLightgray; nextPutAll: 'Hello']
```

7.3.2 Designing the Tic-Tac-Toe Game

The simplest design requires at least one class—say, called TicTacToeGame—with an instance variable such as "board" to keep track of the status of the game and another instance variable such as "player" to keep track of who the next player is. Even at this stage, "player" is somewhat ambiguous since we can't tell without context whether we mean the "next" player or the "last" player. We should immediately change the name to "nextPlayer" to avoid confusion.

class	TicTacToeGame
superclass	Object
instance variables	board nextPlayer

Our aim is to develop a game that ultimately looks that that shown in Figure 7.7. The best approach to take when we don't know how to proceed is to adopt a **top-down stragegy**; i.e., attempt to develop a method to play a game without worrying if the messages exist or not. In fact, the whole point of the top-down strategy is to discover which messages will be needed.

We might begin with a class message such as **play** to set the stage by getting a new game, opening a window, and getting the associated pen to be used for drawing the Xs and Os.

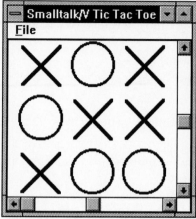

Figure 7.7 The result of playing a tic-tac-toe game.

class methods

playing

play
```
"TicTacToeGame play"
| aGame aPen |

aGame := TicTacToeGame new.
aPen := (GraphPane openWindow: 'Tic Tac Toe' extent: 220@240) pen.
MessageBox message: 'Let''s play'.

"Play the game."

MessageBox message: 'Game over'
```

The next step needs to get into more details of the game. Presumably, we need to prompt for some kind of move that will result in either the game ending or the whole process being repeated. If the game is recording the moves, it should be able to determine whether the game is over. So we might revise our method as follows:

class methods

playing

play
```
"TicTacToeGame play"
| aGame aPen |

aGame := TicTacToeGame new.
aPen := (GraphPane openWindow: 'Tic Tac Toe' extent: 220@240) pen.
MessageBox message: 'Let''s play'.

[aGame over] whileFalse: [
    "Prompt for moves and display the result."].

MessageBox message: 'Game over'
```

Now, how can we prompt for a move. One way is to prompt the next player for the position of the appropriate X or O. The position can be specified by asking the player for the next row and column.

```
row := Prompter
    prompt: 'Player ', aGame nextPlayer printString, ', specify the row'
    defaultExpression: '1'.
column := Prompter
    prompt: 'Player ', aGame nextPlayer printString, ', specify the column'
    defaultExpression: '1'.
```

Alternatively, we might solicit the row and column simultaneously by asking for it as a point in the form row@column.

```
move := Prompter
    prompt: 'Player ', aGame nextPlayer printString, ', "s move?'
    defaultExpression: '1@1'.
```

Having obtained the next move, we should display it in the window. We should also record the move to ensure that we can stop the game if this results in a win. So we might next require

```
aGame displayMove: move using: aPen.
aGame playMove: move
```

Our method, so far, might consist of the following:

```
play
    "TicTacToeGame play"
    | aGame aPen |

    aGame := TicTacToeGame new.
    aPen := (GraphPane openWindow: 'Tic Tac Toe' extent: 220@240) pen.
    MessageBox message: 'Let"s play'.

    [aGame over] whileFalse: [
        move := Prompter
            prompt: 'Player ', aGame nextPlayer printString, '"s move?'
            defaultExpression: '1@1'.
        aGame displayMove: move using: aPen; playMove: move].

    MessageBox message: 'Game over'
```

There are some problems with our design so far. What happens if the move supplied has already been made? Or, if a player hits the **Cancel** button on the prompt? Even more serious, how do you stop in the middle of the game? As it is implemented now, prompting will continue until the game is over.

We can start by replacing the initial information message 'Let"s play' by 'Play as prompted or cancel to quit game' and then add the following expression after the move prompt:

```
move isNil ifTrue: [^self "cancel the game"].
```

Presumably, the game should know if the move is legal, because it is keeping track of the board. It should be as simple as asking

> aGame **isLegal**: move

If it is not, an error message should be generated. But then, we have to repeat the process; i.e., prompt for a move, determine if it is legal, ... Clearly, we need a loop. Moreover, it will have to be structured as follows:

```
Prompt for move
[aGame isLegal: move] whileFalse: [
    MessageBox message: 'Move ', move printString, ' is illegal. Try again.'.
    Prompt for move].
```

Finally, once the game is over, we should be able to say something more specific than 'Game over'. We should be able to tell, for example, who the winner is. Integrating all these changes, we get the following method:

```
playing

play
    "TicTacToeGame play"
    | aGame aPen move |

    aGame := TicTacToeGame new.
    aPen := (GraphPane openWindow: 'Tic Tac Toe' extent: 220@240) pen.
    MessageBox message: 'Play as prompted or cancel to quit game'.

    [aGame over] whileFalse: [
        move := Prompter
            prompt: 'Player ', aGame nextPlayer printString, '''s move?'
            defaultExpression: '1@1'.
        move isNil ifTrue: [^self "cancel the game"].
        [aGame isLegal: move] whileFalse: [
            MessageBox
                message: 'Move ', move printString, ' is illegal. Try again.'.
            move := Prompter
                prompt: 'Player ', aGame nextPlayer printString, '''s move?'
                defaultExpression: '1@1'.
            move isNil ifTrue: [^self "cancel the game"]].
        aGame displayMove: move using: aPen; playMove: move].

    aGame hasWinner
        ifTrue: [
            MessageBox
                message: 'Good game player ', aGame winner printString]
        ifFalse: [MessageBox message: 'It''s a tie']
```

The message boxes and prompters that result in an actual game are shown in Figures 7.8 through 7.11.

Now, we just need to add the methods that make everything work. To begin with, a new game should start with a board of empty squares. An empty square

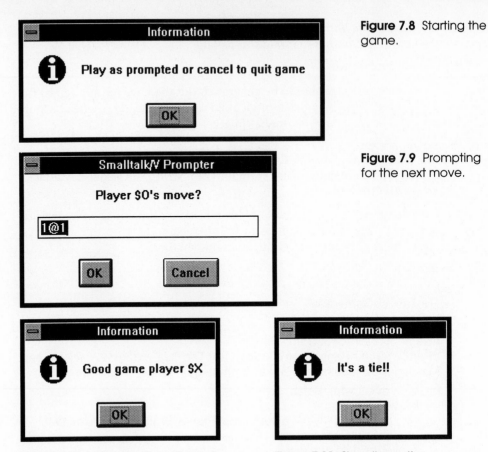

Figure 7.8 Starting the game.

Figure 7.9 Prompting for the next move.

Figure 7.10 Indicating the winner.

Figure 7.11 Signaling a tie.

might be indicated by the character "$ ", an X by "$X", and an O by "$O". We will need the usual class message **new** that creates an initialized instance. The instance method **initialize** might be provided as follows:

instance method

initialize
"Set up the board: 3 rows of 3 empty squares."
board := #(($ $ $) ($ $ $) ($ $ $)).
nextPlayer := $X.

The board here is a three-element array, each representing one row. A row is a three-element array ($ $ $) of empty squares—one for each column. As we play, the board elements will change to $X or $O, depending on which player's turn it is to play.

Unfortunately, there is a major problem with this approach. Moreover, the problem won't show up until we attempt to play a second game. Suppose, for example, that the first game ended in a tie. As we begin to play the second game, we immediately get the message box shown in Figure 7.11. For some reason, the second game believes the game is over even before any player has made a move. Congratulations to anyone who can determine the cause of this very subtle problem.

When a new game is obtained, the second board is bound to the same array literal that the first board was bound to. But the first board modified this array literal by changing the empty squares to $X and $O. The new game starts off with a board that has no empty squares and so the game is over.

The solution is to make sure that a new board is used for each game. So "board" must not bound to a literal; it must be bound to a new array. Before we provide the revised **initialize** method, it might be convenient to create three class variables "X", "O", and "Empty" to contain the corresponding characters "$X", "$O", and "$ ", respectively. The space character, in particular, is very difficult to notice, since it relies on the fact that there is an actual space after the "$". These class variables would have to be initialized once, in a class method called **initialized**.

```
class                          TicTacToeGame
superclass                     Object
instance variables             board nextPlayer
class variables                X O Empty
```

class methods

class initialization

initialize
```
    "TicTacToeGame initialize"
    X := $X. O := $O. Empty := $ .
```

instance creation

new
```
    "Construct a fully initialized game."
    ^super new initialize
```

instance methods

instance initialization

initialize
```
    "Set up the board: 3 rows of 3 empty squares."
    "Using board := #(($ $ $ ) ($ $ $ ) ($ $ $ )). is not enough."
    board := OrderedCollection new
        add: (Array with: Empty with: Empty with: Empty ); "row 1"
        add: (Array with: Empty with: Empty with: Empty ); "row 2"
        add: (Array with: Empty with: Empty with: Empty ); "row 3"
        yourself.
    "Start with player X."
    nextPlayer := X.
```

The next step might be to implement methods to enable "aGame **over**" followed by "aGame **hasWinner**" to execute. In general, a game is over if there is already a winner or if it's not possible to win. The latter is more difficult to determine, so we'll adopt a simpler strategy.

```
over
    "The game is over when there is a winner or there are no more empty
    squares."
    self hasWinner ifTrue: [^true].
    board do: [:row |
        row do: [:square |
            square = Empty ifTrue: [^false]]].
    ^true
```

Determining if a game has a winner requires testing for many cases. For example, row 1 must be tested for all Xs or all Os. A similar test is needed for row 2, row 3, column 1, column 2, column 3, and also the two diagonals. Unless we are clever, the method performing these tests will be extremely long and repetitive. One approach is to set up yet another class variable WinningLines that provides a collection of coordinate triples that can be used to focus the search for a winner. For example, one line or triple might consist of the three points

```
1@1 1@2 1@3
```

denoting the top row. Similarly, one diagonal might be denoted

```
1@1 2@2 3@3
```

This might lead us to adding the following line to class method **initialize**.

```
WinningLines := #(
    ((1@1) (1@2) (1@3))      "row 1"
    ((2@1) (2@2) (2@3))      "row 2"
    ((3@1) (3@2) (3@3))      "row 3"
    ((1@1) (2@1) (3@1))      "column 1"
    ((1@2) (2@2) (3@2))      "column 2"
    ((1@3) (2@3) (3@3))      "column 3"
    ((1@1) (2@2) (3@3))      "diagonal 1"
    ((3@1) (2@2) (1@3)))     "diagonal 2"
```

Unfortunately, we can't create an array literal containing points. An entry such as (1@2) is actually a three element array with 1 as the first element, the symbol #@ as the second element, and the integer 2 as the third element. Still, this might work just fine as long as we are aware of this fact. Consequently, method **hasWinner** might be implemented as follows:

hasWinner
    "Returns true if there are 3 Xs or 3 Os in the same row, column, or diagonal; otherwise, false."
    | entries entry1 entry2 entry3 |
    WinningLines **do**: [:line |
        entries := OrderedCollection **new**.
        line **do**: [:triple | entries **add**: ((board **at**: triple **first**) **at**: triple **last**)].
        entry1 := entries **first**. entry2 := entries **at**: 2. entry3 := entries **last**.
        (entry1 = entry2) & (entry2 = entry3) & (entry3 ~= Empty)
            ifTrue: [^true]].
    ^false

The idea is to use the coordinates in each line for obtaining the corresponding board entries. If these entries are equal and not empty, we must have either three Xs or three Os. We could have simply written

```
triple := line at: 1.
entry1 := (board at: triple first) at: triple last.
triple := line at: 2.
entry2 := (board at: triple first) at: triple last.
triple := line at: 3.
entry3 := (board at: triple first) at: triple last.
```

instead of creating an ordered collection of entries in a loop, but the loop approach seemed more compact. It is a little more difficult to understand, however. Note that our game specifies the winner when it is over. Assuming we added winner as a new instance variable, we could simply change the above method to record this winner as follows:

```
(entry1 = entry2) & (entry2 = entry3) & (entry3 ~= Empty)
    ifTrue: [winner := entry1. ^true]].
```

Additionally, it seems that message "aGame **hasWinner**" is sent twice—once by method **over** and once by method **play** at the end of the game loop. If we initialize "winner" to Empty in the instance method **initialize**, we could add the following test at the beginning of method **hasWinner** to avoid recomputing the winner if it is already known:

```
"If it has already been computed, don't do it again."
winner ~= Empty ifTrue: [^true].
```

Method **isLegal** just needs to make sure that the corresponding board position is empty. We could also provide additional tests to make sure that the parameter is actually a point with coordinates in the range 1 to 3—see the final version for these extensions.

isLegal: aPoint
    ^((board **at**: aPoint **x**) **at**: aPoint **y**) == Empty.

Method **playMove**: simply records the new move on the board and changes the next player.

```
playMove: aPoint
    (board at: aPoint x) at: aPoint y put: nextPlayer.
    nextPlayer := nextPlayer == X ifTrue: [O] ifFalse: [X]
```

But the most complex and most interesting method to implement is method **displayMove:using**. To ensure that the drawing doesn't disappear when a prompter or message box overlaps it, we must use **drawRetainPicture:** as shown:

```
displayMove: aPoint using: aPen
    | center |
    center := ... determine where to place the pen ...
    aPen setLineWidth: 3; backColor: ClrWhite; place: center.
    aPen drawRetainPicture: [
        nextPlayer == O
            ifTrue: [aPen foreColor: ClrBlue; circle: 25]
            ifFalse: [
                aPen
                    foreColor: ClrRed;
                    up; north; turn: 45; go: 30; "top right of X"
                    turn: 180; down; go: 60; "to bottom left of X"
                    up; turn: 180; go: 30; turn: -90; go: 30; "top left of X"
                    turn: 180; down; go: 60 "to bottom right of X"]]
```

Now, the only problem remaining is where to place the pen. If the Xs and Os are to occupy roughly a square 60 pixels by 60 pixels and the pen is to be at the center of the square, then row 1 should have a y-coordinate of 30; row 2, a y-coordinate of 60 + 30 (= 90); and row 3, a y-coordinate of 2 * 60 + 30 (=150). We can compute the y-coordinate for row x as (x - 1) * 60 + 30, or x * 60 - 30. Similarly, column y should be at x-coordinate y * 60 - 30. Thus, given that the new move is specified as aPoint (= x@y), the center of the desired square is

```
x-coordinate y * 60 - 30
y-coordinate x * 60 - 30
```

which can be computed in one expression if we use the browser to locate a point method **transpose** that will switch the x- and y-coordinates.

```
center := aPoint transpose * 60 - 30
```

In practice, the resulting Xs and Os are not quite in the center of the window. We fixed that by adding a small experimentally determined offset. The actual computation was performed as follows:

```
offset := 5@-3. size := 60@60.
center := offset + (aPoint transpose * size) - (size // 2).
```

The complete TicTacToeGame class is shown below:

class	TicTacToeGame
superclass	Object
instance variables	board nextPlayer winner
class variables	X O Empty
pool dictionaries	ColorConstants

class methods

playing

play
```
    "TicTacToeGame play"
    | aGame aPen move |

    aGame := TicTacToeGame new.
    aPen := (GraphPane openWindow: 'Tic Tac Toe' extent: 220@240) pen.
    MessageBox message: 'Play as prompted or cancel to quit game'.

    [aGame over] whileFalse: [
        move := Prompter
            prompt: 'Player ', aGame nextPlayer printString, '''s move?'
            defaultExpression: '1@1'.
        move isNil ifTrue: [^self].
        [aGame isLegal: move] whileFalse: [
            MessageBox
                message: 'Move ', move printString, ' is illegal. Try again.'.
            move := Prompter
                prompt: 'Player ', aGame nextPlayer printString, '''s move?'
                defaultExpression: '1@1'.
            move isNil ifTrue: [^self]].
        aGame displayMove: move using: aPen; playMove: move].

    aGame hasWinner
        ifTrue: [
            MessageBox
                message: 'Good game player ', aGame winner printString]
        ifFalse: [MessageBox message: 'It''s a tie']
```

instance creation

new
```
    "Construct a fully initialized game."
    ^super new initialize
```

class initialization

initialize
"TicTacToeGame initialize"
X := $X. O := $O. Empty := $.
WinningLines := #(
    ((1@1) (1@2) (1@3))   "row 1"
    ((2@1) (2@2) (2@3))   "row 2"
    ((3@1) (3@2) (3@3))   "row 3"
    ((1@1) (2@1) (3@1))   "column 1"
    ((1@2) (2@2) (3@2))   "column 2"
    ((1@3) (2@3) (3@3))   "column 3"
    ((1@1) (2@2) (3@3))   "diagonal 1"
    ((3@1) (2@2) (1@3)))   "diagonal 2"

instance methods

instance initialization

initialize
"Set up the board: 3 rows of 3 empty squares."
"Using board := #(($ $ $) ($ $ $) ($ $ $)) is not enough."
board := OrderedCollection **new**
    add: (Array **with**: Empty **with**: Empty **with**: Empty); "row 1"
    add: (Array **with**: Empty **with**: Empty **with**: Empty); "row 2"
    add: (Array **with**: Empty **with**: Empty **with**: Empty); "row 3"
    yourself.
"Start with player X."
nextPlayer := X.
winner := Empty.

querying

hasWinner
"Returns true if there are 3 Xs or 3 Os in the same row, column, or diagonal; otherwise, false."

| entries entry1 entry2 entry3 |
"If it has already been computed, don't do it again."
winner ~= Empty **ifTrue**: [^true].
WinningLines **do**: [:line |
    entries := OrderedCollection **new**.
    line **do**: [:triple | entries **add**: ((board **at**: triple **first**) **at**: triple **last**)].
    entry1 := entries **first**. entry2 := entries **at**: 2. entry3 := entries **last**.
    (entry1 = entry2) & (entry2 = entry3) & (entry3 ~= Empty)
        ifTrue: [winner := entry1. ^true]].
^false

isLegal: aPoint
(aPoint **isKindOf**: Point) **ifFalse**: [^false].
(aPoint **x between**: 1 **and**: 3) **ifFalse**: [^false].
(aPoint **y between**: 1 **and**: 3) **ifFalse**: [^false].
^((board **at**: aPoint **x**) **at**: aPoint **y**) == Empty.

querying (continued)

over
"The game is over when there is a winner or there are no more blank
squares."
self **hasWinner ifTrue**: [^true].
board **do**: [:row |
    row **do**: [:square |
        square = Empty **ifTrue**: [^false]]].
^true

nextPlayer
^nextPlayer

winner
^winner

playing

playMove: aPoint
(board **at**: aPoint **x**) **at**: aPoint **y put**: nextPlayer.
nextPlayer := nextPlayer == X **ifTrue**: [O] **ifFalse**: [X]

displaying

displayMove: aPoint **using**: aPen
| offset size center |
"Note that row@column corresponds to x@y but when the row
changes, we must move vertically. So as coordinates, a
board location must be transposed; i.e., the x and y interchanged."
offset := 5@-3. size := 60@60.
center := offset + (aPoint **transpose** * size) - (size // 2).
aPen **setLineWidth**: 3; **backColor**: ClrWhite; **place**: center.
aPen **drawRetainPicture**: [
    nextPlayer == O
        ifTrue: [aPen **foreColor**: ClrBlue; **circle**: 25]
        ifFalse: [
            aPen
                foreColor: ClrRed;
                up; **north**; **turn**: 45; **go**: 30; "top right of X"
                turn: 180; **down**; **go**: 60; "to bottom left of X"
                up; **turn**: 180; **go**: 30; **turn**: -90; **go**: 30; "top left of X"
                turn: 180; **down**; **go**: 60 "to bottom right of X"]]

7.4 Summary

This chapter has introduced you to container classes in general and to the collection and stream classes in particular. More specifically, we have

- Investigated the most important Smalltalk container classes; namely, dictionaries, ordered collections, strings, and arrays
- Investigated the operations for creating instances of these container classes; adding, removing, and accessing elements; and sequencing through the elements
- Investigated techniques for creating container classes with large numbers of elements; e.g., "(OrderedCollection **new add:** 1; **add:** 2; **yourself**)", and also more convenient techniques when the number of elements is less than five; e.g. "(OrderedCollection **with:** 1 **with:** 2)"
- Looked at the conversion operations that permitted us to obtain containers of other types with the same elements as the original; e.g. "OrderedCollection **asArray**" provides a new array with the same elements as contained by "OrderedCollection"
- Gained experience with collections via two case studies: a phone book and a tic-tac-toe game

7.5 What You Did and Did Not Learn

In this chapter, we investigated the two major container classes, ordered collections and dictionaries, in considerable detail. Because strings and arrays can be viewed as specialized ordered collections that are fixed length, you should also have a better understanding of these kinds of objects. It is our hope that you can remember the most important messages associated with these container objects; e.g., messages like **add:**, **remove:**, **at:**, and **at:put:**. But it is not necessary that you remember them all. What is more important is that you be able to use a browser to easily find the operations that you have forgotten.

7.6 Important Facts

Operations on Objects

querying the receiver

anObject **yourself**   Returns the receiver; useful for constructing large collections; e.g. "OrderedCollection **new add:** 1; **add:** 2; **yourself**"

Operations on Collections

Note: Indexed collections include ordered collections, arrays, and strings, but not dictionaries.

constructing empty collections

aCollectionClass **new**

> Obtains an instance of the collection class with no elements; e.g., "Dictionary **new**"

constructing non-empty collections

anIndexedCollectionClass **with**: anObject
anIndexedCollectionClass **with**: anObject **with**: anObject
anIndexedCollectionClass **with**: anObject **with**: anObject **with**: anObject
anIndexedCollectionClass **with**: anObject **with**: anObject **with**: anObject **with**: anObject

> Obtains an instance of the collection class with respectively one, two, three, or four elements; e.g., "OrderedCollection **with**: 1" obtains an ordered collection comtaining 1

type conversion

anIndexedCollection **asArray**
anIndexedCollection **asOrderedCollection**

> Obtains a new collection of the specified class and initializes it with the same elements as those in the receiver

querying

aCollection **size** The number of elements in the collection
aCollection **isEmpty** True if the size is 0; false otherwise
anIndexedCollection **includes**: anObject

> True if anelement equal to Object is in anIndexedCollection ; false, otherwise.

anIndexedCollection **first** The element at index 1; illegal if empty
anIndexedCollection **last** The element at the last index; illegal if empty

sequencing

aCollection **do**: aBlock

> Sequences through the elements of the collection (for a dictionary, the elements are the values)

aDictionary **keysDo**: aBlock Sequences through the keys

concatenating

anIndexedCollection, anotherCollection

> A new collection like the receiver with the elements of both; can be different kinds of collections

Operations on Collections (continued)

copying (non-destructive; i.e., does not change the receiver)

anIndexedCollection **copyFrom**: start **to**: stop

A new collection like the receiver is constructed with the specified elements

Operations on OrderedCollections (extra to above)

growing the collection

anOrderedCollection **addFirst**: anObject
anOrderedCollection **addLast**: anObject
anOrderedCollection **add**: anObject   (equivalent to **addLast**:)

Respectively adds anObject to the start or end of anOrderedCollection; i.e., the new element will be at the first or last subscript, respectively. Returns anObject.

shrinking the collection

anOrderedCollection **removeFirst**
anOrderedCollection **removeLast**

Respectively removes the first or last element from anOrderedCollection, if such an element exists, and also returns it. If no such element exists, an error is signaled

anOrderedCollection **remove**: anObject   (error if not there)
anOrderedCollection **remove**: anObject **ifAbsent**: aBlock

Message **remove**: eliminates one element equal to anObject if it exists and signals an error otherwise—anObject is returned. Instead of signaling an error, **remove:ifAbsent**: returns the object computed by the block.

modifying the collection

anOrderedCollection **at**: index
anOrderedCollection **at**: index **put**: anotherObject

Respectively returns the value associated with "index" or associates anotherObject with key "index". The key must be an integer between 1 and the size of the receiver; i.e., it is not legal to use a key outside the bounds of the receiver to attempt to grow the collection. Message **at:put**: returns anObject

Operations on Dictionaries (extra to above)

querying the dictionary

aDictionary **at**: anObject
aDictionary **at**: anObject **ifAbsent**: aBlock

> Returns the value associated with a key equal to anObject if such a key exists; otherwise, **at**: reports an error whereas **at:ifAbsent**: executes the block and returns the last object computed

modifying the dictionary

aDictionary **at**: anObject **put**: anotherObject

> Associates value anotherObject with key anObject in aDictionary. If an equal key already exists, replaces the old association by this new one. Returns anotherObject

aDictionary **removeKey**: anObject
aDictionary **removeKey**: anObject **ifAbsent**: aBlock

> Removes the key equal to anObject and the associated value, if such a key exists, and also returns anObject. If no such key exists, **removeKey**: signals an error whereas **removeKey:ifAbsent**: executes the block and returns the last object computed

Operations on Pens

setting the line size

aPen **setLineWidth**: anInteger   For drawing boundaries

coloring

aPen **backColor**: color
aPen **foreColor**: color

> Respectively sets either the background color (for filling boxes and circles) or the foreground color (for boundaries and text). See ColorConstants for a complete list of colors

creating filled and unfilled boxes

aPen **boxFilled**: aPoint
aPen **box**: aPoint

> The top-left corner is at the pen location; the bottom-right corner is at aPoint

Operations on Pens (continued)

creating filled and unfilled circles

aPen **circleFilled**: radius
aPen **circle**: radius — Draws a circle centered at the pen location

ensuring that panes can redraw when uncovered

aPen **drawRetainPicture**: [...] — All drawing performed in the block is replayed whenever the drawing is covered by some other window and then uncovered

writing text

aPen **nextPut**: aCharacter
aPen **nextPutAll**: aString — Draws the text at the pen location

Operations on Date

creating instances

Date **newDay**: anInteger **month**: aSymbol **year**: anotherInteger
Creates and returns a date of the day anInteger in the month aSymbol for the year anotherInteger

Operations on Time

creating instances

Time **fromSeconds**: anInteger — Returns a time that represents anInteger seconds from midnight

Common Errors

- **Subscripting out of bounds**—for an ordered collection, using a subscript that is either negative or greater than the size of the collection; for a dictionary, using a key that does not exist
- **Trying to grow fixed-size collections**—trying to use **add**: or **remove**: with arrays
- **Assuming collections are not empty**—using **first** or **last** without guaranteeing that the collection is non-empty

Stacks and queues: Ordered collections can be used both for

- Last-in first-out (**LIFO**) behavior (also called stacking behavior) using **addLast**: and **removeLast** (or **addFirst**: and **removeFirst**)
- First-in first-out (**FIFO**) behavior (also called queuing behavior) using **addLast**: and **removeFirst** (or **addFirst**: and **removeLast**)

7.7   Helpful Hints

Constructing Collections: When collections must be constructed, use the "with" notation if possible. For example,

OrderedCollection **new**
OrderedCollection **with**: 1
OrderedCollection **with**: 1 **with**: 2
OrderedCollection **with**: 1 **with**: 2 **with**: 3
OrderedCollection **with**: 1 **with**: 2 **with**: 3 **with**: 4

construct ordered collections with zero, one, two, three, or four elements, respectively. If more elements are needed, use the "yourself" approach.

OrderedCollection **new add**: 1; **add**: 2; **add**: 3; **add**: 4; **add**: 5; **yourself**

Containers can contain other containers: Arrays, ordered collections, and dictionaries (to name a few) can contain other container objects; e.g., consider "Array **with**: (OrderedCollection **with**: Dictionary **new**)".

The sequencing code structure: Sequencing is a familiar operation often used in the following standardized manner. When using this code structure, be sure that the result is correct even if the collection is empty.

initialization in preparation for looping
aCollection **do**: [:element |
    process "element"]
finalization to complete the computation

Strategies for Constructing Collections:

* Use array literals directly; e.g.,
    #(1 2 3).
* Use, but convert, the array literals; e.g.
    #(1 2 3) **asOrderedCollection**.
* Use array literals to construct the elements; e.g.,
    result := OrderedCollection **new**.
    #(1 2 3) **do**: [:element | result **add**: element].
    ^result
* Directly compute the elements; e.g.,
    result := OrderedCollection **new**.
    1 **to**: 100 **do**: [:element | result **add**: element **factorial**].
    ^result

7.8 Keywords

basic terminology: block parameter, pool dictionary

design: binary search, stepwise refinement, top-down decomposition, top-down strategy

graphics: background, color constants, foreground, filled shape, unfilled shape

programming terminology: first-in first-out (FIFO) behavior, last-in first-out (LIFO) behavior, subscripting out of bounds

7.9 Exercises

The following exercises are meant to provide experience with collections and streams.

1. Create an ordered collection containing the steps for making a fried egg sandwich. Each step can be a simple string.

2. Create a dictionary that associates each person's name with the names of his or her friends. Note that some people have no friends, some have one, and some have many.

3. Design a **Song** class (and a corresponding **Verse** class) with a short example method that returns a song like "Old MacDonald Had a Farm" or "One Hundred Bottles of Beer on the Wall." Each song should be a collection of verses and each verse should be a collection of strings—one per statement in the verse. Write a conversion method **asString** that takes a song and converts it to one very long string with carriage returns after each line. Test your conversion operation by printing your song in the transcript. Hint: use CharacterConstants as a pool dictionary to get access to a carriage return character.

4. Implement a Checkerboard class that can be used for keeping track of black and white checkers in a game. Ensure that the board can be displayed in realistic colors.

5. In a large hotel with a series of elevators, a computer screen might be used to indicate which floor each elevator is on by displaying a visual representation of the elevator doors on the appropriate floor. Design an ElevatorDisplay class that can display any number of elevators on any number of floors, with their doors open or closed, in an arbitrary rectangular area on the screen.

Evolutionary Software Development and Design

What You Will Learn

This chapter is an optional chapter illustrating the evolutionary software development process and introducing techniques for designing and documenting large applications. It can safely be skipped by the beginner, since it is concerned with notions that will become important only after several years of programming. Nevertheless, the knowledge gained from reading this chapter now will be valuable, since it makes explicit what we have been learning indirectly throughout the first seven chapters. It is, additionally, a detailed case study that makes use of container objects in a fundamental way.

Because the software development process requires access to the Smalltalk library, the use of the interactive facilities of the programming environment, and the evolving software, the process is best illustrated online; i.e., in an environment with an actual machine. However, we don't have this luxury here because we need to illustrate the approach on paper. As a consequence, this chapter is particularly detailed as it proceeds to show how design and development are inextricably intertwined.

We will find that it is not possible to pursue our many design and development tasks to completion before we go on to new ones. On the contrary, each task will typically generate new ones that must be pursued while they are fresh. We will be doing many things in parallel, going back and forth between tasks that are unfinished, and trying to remember the many tasks held in abeyance. Keep in mind as you read further that it is the approach—the process—that we are illustrating. The end result, in this case, is not the goal.

To illustrate the evolutionary software development process and the associated design concepts, we will partially design and implement an airline reservation system. We will have the opportunity to review such terms such as analysis and design, that were introduced in Chapter 1, and elaborate on them further. We will also introduce new terms such as responsibilities, helpers, use-cases, and is-a hierarchies, to name a few.

The terms and techniques introduced in this section will have wide applicability when complex applications have to be developed from client specifications.

8.1 Case Study: An Airline Reservation System

An **airline reservation system** is a system that can make passenger reservations on specific flights for specific airlines. Normally, designing such a system is a major effort. Our goal in this section will be to design a minimal version—one that can illustrate some important capabilities; e.g., the capability of booking a passenger on a flight. As a consequence, we will learn some important aspects about design itself; i.e., about the creative process that enables us to generate a working system from nothing.

8.1.1 The Analysis and Design Process

To design anything, we need a clear understanding of the **requirements**; i.e., what is needed. For this case study, we chose a domain that is relatively well understood by most people—at least, at a superficial level. We will assume that we understand what an airline reservation system is all about. In general, however, it is often the case that very detailed requirements documents are provided to designer/implementers even before they begin.

The process of determining what is needed (the requirements) is often called **analysis** and the process of determining how to implement it is called **design**. In object-oriented systems, the distinction between the two processes is relatively fuzzy, because determining what is needed is in fact a first pass at the design. For example, determining that the reservation system must keep track of airlines is part of analysis. Deciding that we will have a class called Airline is design, because we might choose not to have airline objects; e.g., we might simply maintain lists of airline names to represent the airlines. However, anything important enough to be highlighted as part of analysis is generally important enough to provide a corresponding class of objects to represent it in the implementation.

Consequently, analysis and design are virtually inseparable in the early stages. In the later stages, when we understand reasonably well what we want, we can make very specific decisions about how to achieve the goals and we are clearly into design; e.g., when we are trying to decide what kind of collection to use to represent a list of passengers.

The key **analysis and design steps** for understanding and ultimately implementing any application include

- **Finding the classes**—determining what classes are needed to account for the requirements of the application
- **Determining the relationships between the classes**—determining how the new classes relate to the classes in the existing library and how they relate to each other
- **Determining the relationships between the instances**—determining how the instances of the classes relate to other instances; e.g., what parts they need to maintain to effectively carry out their tasks
- **Determining the behavior of the classes and instances**—determining what messages they should understand (their **responsibilities**), and consequently what methods they will need

Because these steps focus on objects, their behaviors, and their responsibilities, the analysis and design process is known by various names, including

- **Object-oriented** analysis and design
- **Responsibility-driven**[1] analysis and design
- **Behavior-driven** analysis and design
- **Anthropomorphic**[2] analysis and design (because the objects are viewed as anthropomorphic entities)
- **Need-driven** behavior analysis and design

The description above implies that the steps should be applied in the order listed. But different orderings might be more realistic or it might be impossible to have any one fixed ordering. Alternatively, it might be necessary to leave one step before it is finished to proceed with another. Or, we might have to apply all steps in parallel; i.e., try to develop each step whenever we can but not necessarily work on any one step for a long time.

It is not clear which strategy is best. To begin with, should we find all the classes first or only the most important ones? If the latter, when do we come back to find the remaining classes. In either case, should the last step be done before the second and third steps? After all, how can we find relationships between different objects unless we know their behaviors?

---

[1] R. Wirfs-Brock, B. Wilkerson, and L. Wiener, **Designing Object-Oriented Software**, (Englewood Cliffs: Prentice Hall, 1990).
[2] Mary Beth Rosson and Eric Gold, "Problem-Solution Mapping in Object-Oriented Design," **OOPSLA '89 Conference Proceedings** (New Orleans: October 1989) 7-10. (Also **ACM SIGPLAN Notices 24, Number 10,** October 1989.)

A **methodology** is a clearly specified series of steps, and a partial ordering of those steps, that will achieve a well-defined goal. One methodology that is particularly suited to object-oriented systems and Smalltalk, in particular, is the **iterative refinement** methodology. This methodology acknowledges that all steps are best done in parallel starting with nothing for each step, and then evolving and developing these steps whenever we can. Mistakes are allowed and changes are permitted whenever they can be made.

To get started, however, we need a little bit more direction. Because we are really interested in a behavior-driven iterative refinement methodology, we need to focus on the behaviors of the objects in the application from two perspectives:

1. An **object-centered view** to gain an understanding of the application from the perspective of the individual objects that make up the application
2. A **object-community view** to gain an understanding of the interactions between the individual objects that make up the application

The object-centered viewpoint ignores the second step in the four-step list above and focuses on the remaining three from the point of view of the individual objects. From this perspective, the last three analysis and design steps are often paraphrased less precisely as finding the

- **Classes** (or abstractions)
- **Responsibilities** (or behaviors)
- **Helpers** (the other classes or instances that the object needs to effectively carry out its responsibilities)

We will refer to these three steps as a **CRH** (classes-responsibilities-helpers) **design**, even though there is analysis involved, because it is a first-pass design. An object's **helpers** are those other objects that it explicitly needs access to in order to perform its duty. For example, if object A requires object B to perform its job, then B is A's helper. On the other hand, if B can perform its job all by itself, it has no **helpers**. The helpers of a class generally consist of the superclass and subclasses that it has direct knowledge of and sometimes other global classes that it needs to reference for one reason or another. The helpers of an instance are all its parts, since these are often explicitly referenced, and sometimes more global objects that it needs to reference directly, such as a class.

Other terms for helper have also been used by others[1]; e.g., **colleagues** or **collaborators** leading to the acronym CRC (class-responsibilities-collaborators) as an alternative to CRH. However, using this terminology, you must be aware that an object's collaborators are only those objects it collaborates with—not the objects that collaborate with it. There is no comparable confusion with the term **helper**.

---

[1]Kent Beck and Ward Cunningham, "A Laboratory for Teaching Object-Oriented Thinking," **OOPSLA '89 Conference Proceedings** (New Orleans: October 1989) 1–6. (Also **ACM SIGPLAN Notices 24, Number 10**, October 1989.)

From an object-community viewpoint, we focus primarily on the second and fourth steps in the four-step list above and consequently deal with

- **Use-cases** (example uses of the application that illustrate more detailed inter-object behavior)
- **Class hierarchy integration** (positioning the classes in the existing library of classes and determining whether special varieties of classes identified in the CRH design are needed)

For our airline reservation system, we'll start with a CRH design (an object-centered perspective) and then go on to uses-cases and class hierarchy integration (an object-community perspective).

8.1.2 A First-Pass CRH Design (Object-Centered Perspective)

A CRH (classes-responsibilities-helpers) design focuses on

- **Classes** (or abstractions)
- **Responsibilities** (or behaviors)
- **Helpers** (other objects needed)

from an object-centered perspective. A CRH design is a first-pass design that uncovers the major objects in the application. It is not concerned with determining minor variations of similar objects. In a repair shop management system, for example, we might decide that vehicles are an important class of objects. However, we would not at this stage try to determine the many possible varieties of vehicles—such as cars, trucks, and off-road vehicles.

Additionally, a CRH design focuses on the instances, not the classes, even though the kinds of instances involved must be named (by specifying the class name). The major focus is to determine the behavior of the instances and the helpers of these instances. At this preliminary stage, we won't consider the behavior of the classes themselves—we'll assume that they can create instances, for example. When we determine that the repair shot management system needs to include vehicles, we are saying that the application will need one or more instances of a class that we will call Vehicle but we are primarily interested in the responsibilities and helpers of the vehicle instances.

Finally, a CRH design is concerned with application-specific objects, not low-level objects that can be used for many different applications. We are not interested in specifying objects such as characters, numbers, strings, ordered collections, or dictionaries.

Now, how do we start the process of designing the airline reservation system? First, we'll try to determine what kinds of objects are needed (we'll just name the classes), then we'll try to determine what instances of those classes should be able to do, and finally we'll find out what helpers those instances will need.

Finding the Classes

We start off by simply naming the classes that an airline reservation system will need. The most obvious class (and the one most likely forgotten) should probably be called AirlineReservationSystem. The next most obvious class is Airline. What do airlines consist of? Planes? Flights? Do we need both? What about pilots, flight attendants, cargo, passengers? It is possible to get carried away with an endless list of possibilities, so it is best to be conservative and attempt to have as few classes as possible. We can always add more classes later if we find out that they are really needed.

One way to proceed is to imagine what information you would need in order to fly across the country. You would need to know what airline you would be traveling on, what flight you would have to take, and the boarding date and time. Clearly, Airline and Flight are application-specific objects, but not Date and Time. Note that even though you will be flying on a plane, you probably have no idea what kind of plane it is. Why include a class Plane if it is not needed for booking and cancelling flights?

As a minimum, then, we will need the three classes shown in Figure 8.1. Perhaps we forgot an important class. If we did and we know what it is, we should add it immediately. If we can't tell, perhaps its not that important. We can always come back and add it later when the need for it becomes more obvious.

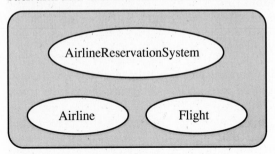

Figure 8.1 The result of "finding the classes".

Determining the Responsibilities

We can determine the responsibilities of the instances of the classes isolated above by simply asking what each object can do for us. We are not concerned with too complex a description here. A few simple English sentences, such as the following, might do fine.

> **Class**: AirlineReservationSystem
> **Responsibilities**:
>   Keeps track of the airlines that it services.
>   Handles bookings and cancellations.

> **Class**: Airline
> **Responsibilities**:
>   Keeps track of the flights that are scheduled.

Class: Flight
Responsibilities:
> Keeps track of the passengers that are on the flight.
> Knows the starting point and destination for the flight, along with the departure and arrival dates and times.

Of course, any time we write down a description, we might need to rethink what we did earlier. Indeed, in this case, the fact that flights keep track of passengers should cause us to at least ask what a passenger is. Is it just a name, which might be maintained simply as a string, or does it include more information, such as a phone number or an address? This latter information might be important if a flight is cancelled and the passengers have to be notified. In the latter situation, we should introduce a new class called Passenger.

While we are at it, passengers might also want to keep track of the bonus miles accumulated. If that's the case, the airline reservation system would have to remember who they were even if they weren't booked on any flight. So we would also have to revise the responsibility of the airline reservation system as follows:

Class: AirlineReservationSystem
Responsibilities:
> Keeps track of the airlines that it services.
> Keeps track of the passengers it has or will service.
> Handles bookings and cancellations.

Class: Passenger
Responsibilities:
> Maintains the passenger name, phone number, address, and bonus miles, if available.

Determining the Helpers

We can often determine the helpers simply by reading the description of the responsibilities. Although a helper is any object that is needed for a given object to get its job done, we typically will consider only application-specific helpers. Moreover, even though a helper for one instance is typically an instance of a class, we generally will list only the name of the class that the helper belongs to (rather than bother indicating that the helper is actually an instance of the class). Adding helpers allows us to finalize the CRH description as follows:

Class: AirlineReservationSystem
Responsibilities:
> Keeps track of the airlines that it services.
> Keeps track of the passengers it has or will service.
> Handles bookings and cancellations.
Helpers: Airline, Passenger

Class: Airline
Responsibilities:
    Keeps track of the flights that are scheduled.
Helpers: Flight

Class: Flight
Responsibilities:
    Keeps track of the passengers that are on the flight.
    Knows the starting point and destination for the flight, along with the
    departure and arrival dates and times.
Helpers: Passenger

Class: Passenger
Responsibilities:
    Maintains the passenger name, phone number, address, and bonus
    miles, if available.
Helpers: None

An airline reservation system must keep track of an arbitrary number of airlines and passengers. These are instances of class Airline and Passenger. Does the airline reservation system also have to know about the classes, as distinct from the instances? In this case, it does, because it will likely have to create new instances whenever new airlines or passengers are to be handled. Nevertheless, we don't normally bother listing the class helpers explicitly. So, by convention, the helpers listed are always instance helpers—never class helpers. Technically, the airlines and passengers must be kept in some kind of collection, so the collection instances are also helpers, but we don't bother mentioning these, either, since they are not application-specific objects.

Airlines, by contrast, are much simpler since all they need to do is keep track of the scheduled flights. Once again, these are all instance helpers and so Flight is listed in the Helper section of the Airline class. Similarly, flights maintain passenger lists and Passenger is included in the Helper section. Passengers are the only object here without helpers since the information they contain is presumably all maintained in simple non-application-specific objects like strings, numbers, and collections.

Before we claim to be done, perhaps we should have one quick look to see if anything obvious is missing. For example, given an airline object, what steps would we have to follow to determine whether it was U.S. Air or Air Canada? Would we just ask the airline object for its name or would we have to ask the airline reservation system for the name of this specific airline object? In the first situation, the airline object would have to keep track of its own name, in which case its list of responsibilities would have to be upgraded. In the second situation, the airline reservation system would need, say, a dictionary that maps airline names to airline objects. Given an airline object, it could look up the corresponding name. In this case, the list of responsibilities of the airline reservation system would have to be upgraded.

Clearly, it is simpler if the airline maintains its own name. So we should upgrade its list of responsibilities. Does this affect the list of helpers? In this situation, there is no change because a name is just a string—it isn't an application-specific object.

The same line of reasoning might apply to flight objects. Who keeps track of the flight number? Is it really a number? Could there be a flight called '212B'—a special overflow flight or a special rescue flight? We're not experts in the airline industry. This is something we should find out about from someone in the business. In the meantime, we can generalize the notion of a flight number to a flight name and maintain it as a string; e.g., flight '212' versus flight '212B'.

If a flight knows about its name (or flight number), can it also know about the airline it belongs to? How else could we answer a simple question such as "what is the name of the airline associated with this flight object?"

It is one small step further to wonder if the airline should know about its airline reservation system. But there might not be any advantage to knowing such a fact. It might even be detrimental if we want to later permit more than one airline reservation system to book flights on the same airline. It makes more sense for a flight to know about its airline, because a flight belongs to exactly one airline.

Another small point: When we say that a flight knows about its airline, do we mean that it keeps track of an actual airline object or does it just keep track of the name of the airline? Surely, some things must be stated unambiguously. We would specifically say that a flight knows about the name of its airline if that's what we really meant. The revised CRH design consists of the following:

Class: AirlineReservationSystem
Responsibilities:
> Keeps track of the airlines it services.
> Keeps track of the passengers it has or will service.
> Handles bookings and cancellations.

Helpers: Airline, Passenger

Class: Airline
Responsibilities:
> Keeps track of its name.
> Keeps track of the scheduled flights.

Helpers: Flight

Class: Flight
Responsibilities:
> Keeps track of its name (flight number) and the airline it belongs to.
> Keeps track of the passengers on the flight.
> Knows the starting point and destination for the flight, along with the departure and arrival dates and times.

Helpers: Passenger, Airline

Class: Passenger
Responsibilities:
    Maintains the passenger name, phone number, address, and bonus
    miles, if available.
Helpers: None

Since they are not an essential part of a simple airline reservation system, we will omit the details of keeping track of bonus miles in the sections to follow.

8.1.3 Creating Classes Corresponding to the CRH Design

The CRH design provides us with an understanding of the application domain and enables us to get started. For each class identified in the CRH design, we can create a corresponding Smalltalk class. The helpers and the list of responsibilities allow us to decide what instance variables to provide. In particular, if an object has a helper, it must be able to refer to that helper; i.e., the helper must be part of the object. And we know that instance variables keep track of an object's parts. Taking all this into account, we could produce the following preliminary class definitions:

class	AirlineReservationSystem
superclass	Object
instance variables	airlines passengers
class	Airline
superclass	Object
instance variables	name flights
class	Flight
superclass	Object
instance variables	name airline passengers
class	Passenger
superclass	Object
instance variables	name address phone

The instance variables that are pluralized must clearly be collections of some sort, but we don't yet know whether they are dictionaries, ordered collections, or even something else. However, we do know that each class containing such methods will need an **initialize** instance method. Will we need accessing and modification methods for airlines, flights, and passengers, in the respective classes? We might assume so at this point, but we might very well be wrong. In the interest of providing a **need-driven** design, let's delay the introduction of all but the most obvious ones. For example, it is reasonably clear that we will need to be able to access both an airline's name and a flight's name (or flight number). Also, the information in a passenger is likely to be needed. Note that we have not provided instance variables in Flight to keep track of the departure and arrival locations, dates, and times. We might need up to six different instance variables to keep track of all that information. It's too early to decide on the specifics at this stage, so let's leave it for the future. The same might apply to the bonus miles in passengers. So we might begin by adding methods such as the following:

class   AirlineReservationSystem
superclass   Object
instance variables   airlines passengers

class methods

instance creation

new
    ^super **new initialize**

instance methods

instance initialization

initialize
    airlines := nil "for now, we'll have to choose some sort of collection later"
    passengers := nil "for now, we'll have to choose some sort of collection later"

---

class   Airline
superclass   Object
instance variables   name flights

class methods

instance creation

new
    ^super **new initialize**

instance methods

instance initialization

initialize
    name := '<unknown>'.
    flights := nil "for now, we'll have to choose some sort of collection later"

accessing and modifying

name
    ^name
name: aString
    name := aString

class	Flight
superclass	Object
instance variables	name airline passengers

class methods

instance creation

new
    ^super **new initialize**

instance methods

instance initialization

initialize
    name := '<unknown>'.
    airline := Airline **new name**: '<unknown>'.
    passengers := nil "for now, we'll have to choose some sort of collection later"

simple accessing and modifying

name
    ^name
name: aString
    name := aString

airline manipulation

airline
    ^airline
airline: anAirline
    airline := anAirline

---

class	Passenger
superclass	Object
instance variables	name address phone

class methods

"none"

instance methods

accessing and modifying

name
    ^name
name: aString
    name := aString
address
    ^address
address: aString
    address := aString

phone
    ^phone
phone: anInteger
    phone := anInteger

The only methods that might possibly be premature are methods **airline** and **airline**: in class Flight. We'll allow them for now and hope we will need them. (Note that we initialized instance variable "airline" to an actual airline object. Presumably, we can explicitly change it later.) We are just following the convention that we should initialize all our instance variables. Moreover, they should be initialized to the right kind of object so that we don't have to have special case tests later; e.g., tests of the form "if its nil, do one thing; otherwise, do another".

8.1.4 Use-Cases (Object-Community Perspective)

The **behavior** of an object; i.e., how it reacts, is dictated by the set of messages that it responds to, along with the precise manner in which it responds to those messages. The behavior is precisely defined by providing the detailed methods. Just as we made a best effort when we came up with the list of responsibilities in our CRH design, we could similarly make a best effort and come up with the detailed methods needed by each class. The problem with this approach is that we are likely to introduce behavior that we don't need; i.e., unnecessary methods, or behavior that isn't quite right; i.e., partially correct methods. This raises a very important question.

> *How do we determine what behaviors are appropriate for our objects?*

One approach that seems to work is to have someone use your classes (yourself, perhaps) and provide methods only if they are needed. We call this **need-driven** behavior design. More specifically, the approach requires that you

1. Find a user for your classes—but don't tell the user exactly what methods are available.
2. Make sure that the user sends messages to the classes and the corresponding instances to exercise them.
3. Add a method for each message that is not understood.

The user will probably try to use your classes for many different purposes or in many different contexts. Each such example, called a use-case, by Ivar Jacobson[1], will lead to the introduction of necessary behavior if that behavior is not already there. A **use-case** is simply a sample use of a class that illustrates how it might be used in one, of perhaps many, typical situations.

---

[1]Ivar Jacobson, **Object-Oriented Software Engineering: A Use Case Driven Approach** (Reading: ACM Press/Addison-Wesley, 1992).

In the airline reservation system, many use-cases come to mind. Consider the following partial list:

- Setting up a simple airline reservation system
- Booking a flight
- Cancelling a reservation
- Inquiring about availability
- Confirming a reservation

To begin with, where should this use-case reside? In class AirlineReservationSystem, Airline, Flight? Presumably, if it's dealing with an airline reservation system, it should reside in class AirlineReservationSystem. On the other hand, if it's dealing exclusively with Flight, it would be more appropriate to provide it in class Flight. Also, should it be a class method or an instance method? The very definition of use-case gives us the answer—it is an example method to illustrate a typical use. All example methods are class methods, because they illustrate how to use both the class and instances of the class.

To start, let's add the following class method to class AirlineReservationSystem:

```
useCase1
    "AirlineReservationSystem useCase1"
    "A use-case to set up a simple airline reservation system."

    "I don't know what to do yet."
```

We chose to call this method **useCase1** in anticipation of further use-cases to be added. You might have preferred to call it **example1** instead. Notice also that the first comment in the method permits us to try it out. Some programmers prefer to place this comment at the end instead of the beginning. If the method is long, however, a reader will have to scroll to find it.

What's a typical airline reservation system? For simplicity, let's consider one that deals with just two airlines. We might try

```
I system airline1 airline2 I
system := AirlineReservationSystem new.
airline1 := Airline new.
airline2 := Airline new.
```

We should be careful to initialize each component. To do this properly, we will have to remember what we wrote earlier in our CRH design. For example, airlines have names, but not airline reservation systems.

```
I system airline1 airline2 I
system := AirlineReservationSystem new.
airline1 := Airline new name: 'U.S. Air'.
airline2 := Airline new name: 'Air Canada'.
```

Next, we have to make sure that the airlines are known by the airline reservation system. Since we are writing the use-case, we can make up any name we want for the message; e.g., consider the following possibilities:

```
system remember: airline1.
system add: airline1.
system insert: airline1.
system addAirline: airline1.
```

Of course, we do want to use names that other readers will understand; i.e., we would like to use application domain names where appropriate. So the last choice is likely the best. In fact, if we anticipate future messages, we might expect to eventually have a message called **addPassenger:**, because the airline reservation keeps track of all past or current passengers (recall the CRH description for class AirlineReservationSystem). Consequently, differentiating between **addAirline:** and **addPassenger:** would be essential.

So far, our use-case would contain

```
| system airline1 airline2 |
system := AirlineReservationSystem new.
airline1 := Airline new name: 'U.S. Air'.
airline2 := Airline new name: 'Air Canada'.
system addAirline: airline1.
system addAirline: airline2.
```

Now, let's consider adding two flights to the second airline. We might need something like

```
| system airline1 airline2 flight1 flight2 |
... see above ...
flight1 := Flight new name: '232'.
flight2 := Flight new name: '552'.
airline2 addFlight: flight1; addFlight: flight2.
```

At first glance, this solution seems reasonable. If we can add airlines to an airline reservation system, we should be able to add flights to airlines. However, there is a subtle flaw. In the future, we might need to add a new flight; e.g., a special flight to Jamaica. Presumably, we'll know about the airline reservation system but we won't likely have direct access to the actual airline object. We would need to execute something like the following:

```
flight := Flight new name: '888'.
airline := system airlineNamed: 'Air Canada'.
airline addFlight: flight
```

Pursuing this further, if we had needed to add a passenger to a flight, we would first have had to ask the airline reservation system for a specific airline, then ask that airline for a specific flight, and then add the passenger to that flight. But why can't the airline reservation system do all the work? Surely, it's in its job description. We should be able to ask the airline reservation system to add a specific flight to a specific airline and expect it to worry about the details. To do this, we would need a message like

```
flight := Flight new name: '888'.
system addFlight: flight toAirlineNamed: 'Air Canada'.
```

Notice that we didn't call the selector **addFlight:toAirline**: because we don't know the airline object—we just know its name. The entire method might then appear as follows:

```
useCase1
    "AirlineReservationSystem useCase1"
    "A use-case to set up a simple airline reservation system."

    | system airline1 airline2 flight1 flight2 |
    system := AirlineReservationSystem new.
    airline1 := Airline new name: 'U.S. Air'.
    airline2 := Airline new name: 'Air Canada'.
    system addAirline: airline1; addAirline: airline2.
    flight := Flight new name: '232'.
    system addFlight: flight1 toAirlineNamed: 'Air Canada'.
    flight := Flight new name: '552'.
    system addFlight: flight2 toAirlineNamed: 'Air Canada'.
    ^system
```

As we have done many times in the past, we can simplify this method by eliminating unnecessary variables. In fact, we could get rid of them all, but we'll keep one because of its central role.

```
useCase1
    "AirlineReservationSystem useCase1"
    "A use-case to set up a simple airline reservation system."

    | system |
    system := AirlineReservationSystem new.
    system
        addAirline: (Airline new name: 'U.S. Air');
        addAirline: (Airline new name: 'Air Canada');
        addFlight: (Flight new name: '232') toAirlineNamed: 'Air Canada';
        addFlight: (Flight new name: '552') toAirlineNamed: 'Air Canada'.
    ^system
```

To really finish this use-case, we'll have to be a bit more specific about the flights. Typically, flights have starting locations, dates, and times as well as destination locations, dates, and times. However, before we can pursue this modification, we need to know how to create dates and times. We would like to be able to create a date corresponding, for example, to February 12, 1999 and a time such as 2:45 p.m. If we browse the two corresponding classes, we will find the following class methods:

Class Methods in Date:

baseDay	private
calendarForMonth: aSymbol **year**: anInteger	
checkDay: dInteger **month**: aSymbol **year**: yInteger	private
currentDateInto: anArray	private
dateAndTimeNow	
dayOfWeek: aSymbol	
daysInMonth: aSymbol **forYear**: anInteger	
daysInYear: anInteger	
errorInDay	private
errorInMonth	private
fromDays: anInteger	
fromString: aString	
indexOfMonth: aSymbol	
initialize	private
leapYear: anInteger	
leapYearsTo: anInteger	
monthNameFromString: aString	
nameOfDay: anInteger	
nameOfMonth: anInteger	
newDay: dInteger **month**: aSymbol **year**: yInteger	
newDay: dInteger **year**: yInteger	
today	

Class Methods in Time:

currentTimeInto: anArray	private
dateAndTimeNow	
fromSeconds: anInteger	
initialize	private
millisecondClockValue	
millisecondsToRun: aBlock	
mouseClockValue	private
now	
startTimer: anInteger **period**: milliSeconds **forWindow**: aWindow	
stopTimer: anInteger **forWindow**: aWindow	
totalSeconds	

Ignoring all the private methods, only method **newDay:month:year:** in Date seems relevant. Similarly, method **fromSeconds:** in Time might apply, although it is difficult to tell from the name. If we look at the comment in the individual methods, we get a little more information.

Class Methods in Date:

newDay: dInteger **month**: aSymbol **year**: yInteger
"Answer a Date of the day dInteger in the month aSymbol for the year yInteger."

Class Methods in Time:

fromSeconds: anInteger
   "Answer a Time which represents anInteger number of seconds from midnight."

A simple test might tell us more.

Date **newDay**: 12 **month**: #February **year**: 1999 ⇒ Feb 12, 1999
Time **fromSeconds**: 13 * 60 * 60 ⇒ 13:00:00

If we inspect the results, we will see that they are actually date and time objects, respectively—not strings, as you might guess from the printout. It's cumbersome to create time objects using **fromSeconds**:. We might want to extend the system and provide a more convenient method. Perhaps we should add a class method like the following:

Class Methods in Time:

hour: integer1 **minute**: integer2 **second**: integer3
   ^self **fromSeconds**: (integer1 * 60 + integer2) * 60 + integer3

Perhaps we should call it **newHour:minute:second**: to match the corresponding Date method. Alternatively, we could provide an equivalent method to Date, as follows:

Class Methods in Date:

day: integer1 **month**: aSymbol **year**: integer2
   ^self **newDay**: integer1 **month**: aSymbol **year**: integer2

Back to our original goal—providing the flights with starting and destination locations, dates, and times. Let's consider some possibilities:

Flight **new**
   name: '232';
   departing: 'Toronto';
   departureDate: aDate;
   departureTime: aTime;
   arriving: 'San Francisco';
   arrivalDate: aDate;
   arrivalTime: aTime

Flight **new**
   name: '232';
   departing: 'Toronto' **date**: aDate **time**: aTime;
   arriving: 'San Francisco' **date**: aDate **time**: aTime

It seems better to package the departure and arrival information in one method. That way, we won't forget any of the pieces. Now, we can complete our use-case as follows:

useCase1
    "AirlineReservationSystem useCase1"
    "A use-case to set up a simple airline reservation system."

    | system airline1 airline2 flight1 flight2 |
    system := AirlineReservationSystem **new**.
    system
        addAirline: (Airline **new name**: 'U.S. Air');
        addAirline: (Airline **new name**: 'Air Canada');

        addFlight: (Flight **new**
           name: '232';
           departing: 'Toronto'
               date: (Date **day**: 12 **month**: #Feb **year**: 93)
               time: (Time **hours**: 8 **minute**: 0 **second**: 0);
           arriving: 'San Francisco'
               date: (Date **day**: 12 **month**: #Feb **year**: 93)
               time: (Time **hours**: 16 **minute**: 0 **second**: 0))
        toAirlineNamed: 'Air Canada';

        addFlight: (Flight **new**
           name: '552';
           departing: 'San Francisco'
               date: (Date **day**: 19 **month**: #Feb **year**: 93)
               time: (Time **hours**: 17 **minute**: 0 **second**: 0);
           arriving: 'Toronto'
               date: (Date **day**: 19 **month**: #Feb **year**: 93)
               time: (Time **hours**: 23 **minute**: 0 **second**: 0))
        toAirlineNamed: 'Air Canada'.
    ^system

Now that we have a completed use-case, we can either carry on with other use-cases or make this particular use-case work; i.e., we could provide the missing methods in the correct classes so that we could execute the use-case.

> *Implementing a use-case requires an object-community perspective.*

An object-community perspective is needed because we will have to add methods to many different classes; i.e., rather than attempt to add all the (hopefully) required methods to one specific class, we will add only those methods needed in the many different classes to make this particular use-case work. So, we will be jumping from class to class in the browser. This is clearly an interactive process. It is easier to do it than it is to describe it on paper. Nevertheless, we will attempt to describe the steps involved this one time.

If we attempt to execute our use-case, the first message that will not be understood is likely to be **addAirline**:. The intended receiver is an airline reservation system, so we will need to add this instance method to class AirlineReservationSystem. Presumably, a new airline object will have to be added to the list of airlines maintained by instance variable "airlines". Since this variable is not yet properly initialized, we will also have to revise method **initialize**. At this point, we can't really tell whether we need an ordered collection or a dictionary, so let's guess an ordered collection. (We'll find out later if we are right.) We end up with the following changes to class AirlineReservationSystem:

instance initialization (instance method in class AirlineReservationSystem)

initialize
    airlines := OrderedCollection **new**.
    passengers := nil "for now, we'll have to choose some sort of collection later"

airline manipulation (instance method in class AirlineReservationSystem)

addAirline: anAirline
    airlines **add**: anAirline

Now we can reexecute our original use-case. This gets us a little further, but not much. At this point, we get an error message indicating that **departing:date:time:** is not understood by a flight object. So we need to add this instance method to class Flight. We'll now have to decide how to store this information. (So much for our efforts to delay making this decision.) While we're at it, we might as well take the next message into account; i.e., **arriving:date:time:**. So far, we have the following:

instance initialization (instance method in class Flight)

initialize
    name := '<unknown>'.
    airline := Airline **new name**: '<unknown>'.
    passengers := nil "for now, we'll have to choose some sort of collection later"

arrival and departure information (instance method in class Flight)

departing: aString **date**: aDate **time**: aTime
    "Don't know what to do yet."

arriving: aString **date**: aDate **time**: aTime
    "Don't know what to do yet."

One approach is to add three new instance variables for departures, three for arrivals, and implement the arrival and departure methods as follows:

departing: aString **date**: aDate **time**: aTime
    departureLocation := aString.
    departureDate := aDate.
    departureTime := aTime

arriving: aString **date**: aDate **time**: aTime
    arrivalLocation := aString.
    arrivalDate := aDate.
    arrivalTime := aTime

However, there is so much similarity between the two different sets of three variables that it is tempting to create a class—say, called FlightEntry—that can explicitly keep track of this information.

class	FlightEntry
superclass	Object
instance variables	location date time

class methods

"none"

instance methods

accessing and modifying

location
    ^location
location: aString
    location := aString
date
    ^date
date: aDate
    date := aDate
time
    ^time
time: aTime
    time := aTime

To be complete, we should really go back to the CRH design and include this new class. (Or should we?). Is the introduction of this new class part of analysis or is it part of design? The answer really depends on your point of view. We clearly did not discover this class during analysis or even design, but rather during implementation. Moreover, it was provided as an alternative to having many instance variables in class Flight. We could argue that we are using it only for convenience, and therefore it is part of design and not part of analysis. On the other hand, perhaps it is a useful application-domain object. If we argue that it ought to have been part of the initial CRH description, we are essentially indicating that it is an analysis-level object. In any event, it is now an application-specific object and consequently should be included in the CRH description.

Taking this new class into account, we would need to introduce only two new instance variables—say, "source" and "destination"—to class Flight. Consequently, our two methods might be implemented as follows:

arrival and departure information (instance method in class Flight)

departing: aString **date**: aDate **time**: aTime
    source := FlightEntry **new location**: aString; **date**: aDate; **time**: aTime

arriving: aString **date**: aDate **time**: aTime
    destination := FlightEntry **new location**: aString; **date**: aDate; **time**: aTime

What's next? Let's try the use-case one more time. Now the airline reservation systems fails to understand message **addFlight:toAirlineNamed:**. If we could only get the airline object corresponding to the supplied parameter name, it would be a simple matter of sending it an **addFlight:** message, as shown below.

flight manipulation (instance method in class AirlineReservationSystem)

> **addFlight**: aFlight **toAirlineNamed**: airlineName
>   (self **airlineNamed**: airlineName) **addFlight**: aFlight

But, of course, **airlineNamed:** doesn't yet exist. So we'll have to add it too! But how do we find the airline with the given name? Since all we are keeping is an ordered collection of airline objects, we would have to search this collection using **do:** and return the answer when we find it. This would result in a method like the following:

flight manipulation (instance method in class AirlineReservationSystem)

> **airlineNamed**: airlineName
>   ^airlines **do**: [:anAirline |
>   anAirline name = airlineName **ifTrue**: [^anAirline]].
>   self **error**: 'airline does not exist'

Of course, this would have been much simpler had we been placing airlines in a dictionary in the first place. The airline name could serve as a key. To make this change, we would have to revise three methods, **initialize**, **addAirline:**, and **airlineNamed:**, as follows:

instance initialization (instance method in class AirlineReservationSystem)

> **initialize**
>   airlines := Dictionary **new**. "instead of OrderedCollection new"
>   passengers := nil "for now, we'll choose some sort of collection later"

airline manipulation (instance method in class AirlineReservationSystem)

> **addAirline**: anAirline
>   airlines **at**: anAirline **name put**: anAirline

flight manipulation (instance method in class AirlineReservationSystem)

> **airlineNamed**: airlineName
>   ^airlines **at**: airlineName

So far, we have been keeping track of everything in our heads. Perhaps we can summarize all the important messages and objects in a **use-case diagram**. Figure 8.2 is a start at such a diagram—it only includes creating an airline reservation system, creating an airline, and adding it to the airline reservation system.

The labels for the majority of the directed lines in a use-case diagram must be message names. The objects are also labeled so that they can be repeated without confusion. A few other directed lines are also needed to indicate an object's parts;

e.g., "name" is part of anAirline and "airlines" is part of anAirlineReservation-System—they are bolder to differentiate them from the messages. Dashed lines indicate the result returned from a message (only indicated here if the result is useful). The messages and returned results are also numbered to indicate the processing order. When a returned result is an existing object, a line connects the object to the dashed result line via a small lasso (see the circle near 2). Message parameters are indicated by a small rectangle; e.g., see **name**: in step 5.

The specific notation used is not as important as the information you are trying to provide. You could use your own notation as long as a reader could decipher what you mean.

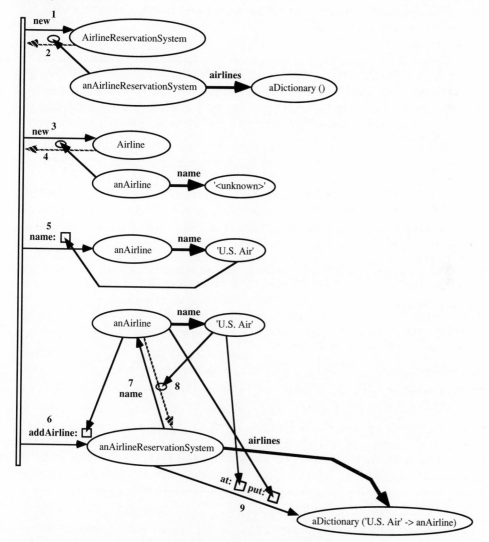

Figure 8.2 A use-case diagram for a portion of **useCase1**.

The use-case diagram in Figure 8.2 indicates that there are four messages sent by some external object (the use-case messages).

- The first message, **new** (step 1), obtains an instance of an airline reservation system with a part called "airlines" (presumably set up in as part of the **new** method but with no details, except the fact that it is an empty dictionary shown in the diagram) and the new instance is returned in step 2.

- In step 3, a **new** airline is requested, which is returned in step 4 (part "name" is initialized to '<unknown>').

- In step 5, the name of the airline is set to a string object—'U.S. Air', which causes the **name** part of the airline to be bound to the string. Nothing useful is returned.

- In step 6, **addAirLine**: is sent (with the airline as parameter) to the airline reservation system which in turn asks the airline for its **name** (step 7 with the result returned in step 8). The airline reservation system then uses string 'U.S. Air' and the airline as parameters of an **at:put**: message, which is sent to its "airlines" part in step 9. Presumably, the message is executed for its side-effect, since nothing useful is indicated as a result.

Normally, use-case diagrams show all the useful object interactions but they are extremely cumbersome to construct by hand. We might be willing to construct a diagram to summarize the entire use-case if we had a tool to do that, but we don't—yet! And if we did have a tool, we might want to be able to see the time evolution of the diagram. This is more akin to video than to a simple static diagram. Of course, once a use-case is generated as part of an example method, we can always use the debugger to trace the interactions in detail. Currently, that is the best way to study the use-case details.

There are many other ways of drawing the diagrams. An alternative, more in keeping with the notation used by Jacobson, is shown in Figure 8.3. It has the advantages of not having to duplicate objects, since they are labeled at the top, and of keeping the order of messages clear, since time flows from top to bottom.

Now, where were we? Let's execute the use-case again. We will find that **addFlight**: isn't understood by some airline object. Oh, yes! We had just finished adding method **addFlight:toAirlineNamed**:, but had not yet implemented **addFlight**:.

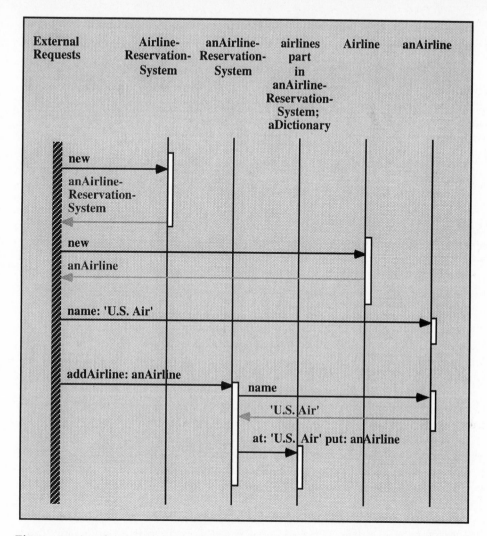

Figure 8.3 An alternative representation for the use-case diagram of Figure 8.2.

Since a flight has a name just like an airline, our previous experience might lead us to use a dictionary rather than an ordered collection to maintain the list of flights in the airline. We will need to add methods like the following:

```
class                          Airline
superclass                     Object
instance variables             name flights
```

instance initialization (instance method in class Airline)

initialize
    name := '<unknown>'.
    flights := Dictionary **new**.

flight manipulation (instance method in class Airline)

addFlight: aFlight
    flights **at**: aFlight **name put**: aFlight

Although airlines keep track of their flights, don't flights also keep track of the airline they belong to? Looking up the Flight class definition ought to make that clear; it has an instance variable called airline and, more important, methods **airline** and **airline**:.

class	Flight
superclass	Object
instance variables	airline name source
	destination passengers

Who should set up the "airline" instance variable? Should the user of the airline reservation system do it? If so, we would have to change the use-case so that it gets done. Actually, a much better solution is to have the **addFlight**: method in Airline do it. This way, adding a flight to an airline automatically ensures that the flight knows about the airline it is added to. The method would be revised as follows:

flight manipulation (instance method in class Airline)

addFlight: aFlight
    flights **at**: aFlight **name put**: aFlight.
    aFlight **airline**: self

We are now ready to carry on. But wait! Once in a while, we'll get an idea while in the middle of **use-case chasing**. In this situation, it might occur to you that flight names (flight numbers) are recycled. Flight 202 leaving next Thursday is not unique. There is another flight 202 leaving one week later. How can we handle that? One way is to use a key that includes the date as shown below; i.e., to use a key that is an array containing both a string and a date. Of course, we could always just ignore this bright idea and wait until later, when we are forced to do something about it. If we do make the change, however, we'll also have to provide a substitute for a method like **flightNamed**:. Additionally, if we are going to use a date, which date is it? The departure (source) date or the arrival (destination) date? In any event, we'll need to ensure that methods exist to retrieve the **source** and **destination** flight entries maintained by the flight.

flight manipulation (instance method in class Airline)

addFlight: aFlight
    "Use both the name and the source date, since the same flight name might be used on different days."
    flights
        at: (Array **with**: aFlight **name** with: aFlight **source date**)
        put: aFlight.
    aFlight **airline**: self

flightNamed: flightName **date**: aDate
^flights **at**: (Array **with**: flightName **with**: aDate)

One last try at the use-case convinces us that we are done, because we get back an airline reservation system object. We could inspect it to look at the airlines and then inspect those in turn to look at the flights.

The most important aspect of the process is the notion of use-case chasing. Just as it is too difficult to multiply large numbers in your head (you use a tool like a pen and paper), it is similarly too difficult to perform use-case chasing on paper (you need an interactive tool like a Smalltalk debugger to help you track the use-cases and add the missing methods to your design).

Now we're back to generating additional use-cases. Let's just look at two more to get a feel for it again.

useCase2
```
"AirlineReservationSystem useCase2"
"A use-case to book a passenger on two flights. Note that the airline
reservation system will ensure that a unique up-to-date passenger object
is used by all its airlines even if distinct passenger objects are provided.
Notice that the second passenger object has an address and the first
does not."

I system I
system := self useCase1.
system
    book: (Passenger new name: 'Long John Silver')
    onAirlineNamed: 'Air Canada'
    flightName: '232'
    date:  (Date day: 12 month: #Feb year: 93);

    book: (Passenger new
        name:'Long John Silver'; address: 'Ottawa, Canada')
    onAirlineNamed: 'Air Canada'
    flightName: '552'
    date:  (Date day: 19 month: #Feb year: 93).
^system
```

useCase3
```
"AirlineReservationSystem useCase3"
"A use-case to print a report on the status of an airline reservation
system."

I system I
system := self useCase2.
system printReportOn: Transcript.
^system
```

Use-case chasing for use-case2 will cause us to add the new booking method to the airline reservation system. In turn, this should causes us to add an **updatePassenger**: method, again to the airline reservation system, which will cause us to add method **book:** to the flight class. We should end up with the following additions:

passenger manipulation (instance method in class AirlineReservationSystem)

book: aPassenger **onAirlineNamed:** airlineName **flightName:** flightName
date: aDate
   | passenger airline flight |
   passenger := self **updatePassenger:** aPassenger.
   airline := self **airlineNamed:** airlineName.
   flight := airline **flightNamed:** flightName **date:** aDate.
   flight **book:** passenger

updatePassenger: aPassenger
   "Update old information about the passenger and return the updated
   one."
   | oldPassenger |
   oldPassenger := passengers
      at: aPassenger name
      ifAbsent: [passengers **at:** aPassenger **name put:** aPassenger].
   aPassenger **address isNil**
      ifFalse: [oldPassenger **address:** aPassenger **address**].
   aPassenger **phone isNil**
      ifFalse: [oldPassenger **phone:** aPassenger **phone**].
   ^oldPassenger

In the case of the Flight class, we have to revise the **initialize** method so that it keeps the passenger list in a dictionary:

instance initialization (instance method in class Flight)

initialize
   name := '<unknown>'.
   airline := Airline **new name:** '<unknown>'.
   passengers := Dictionary **new**

passenger manipulation (instance method in class Flight)

book: aPassenger
   passengers **at:** aPassenger **name put:** aPassenger

The third use-case could be done without use-case chasing. However, we should understand the difference between **printOn:** and **printReportOn:**. In general, **printOn:** is intended to provide a short description of an object, so that we can recognize it when we see it printed. It is not intended for producing nicely formatted documents. As a consequence, there are no **printOn:** methods in the system that provide new lines (carriage returns) or tabs. Even ordered collections print all their elements on the same line. As a rule, reports must be generated with a special method. We called it **printReportOn:** in this application. But there might be a need for different variations such as **printDetailedReportOn:** or

printShortReportOn:. We can better appreciate the differences by comparing **printOn**: and **printReportOn**: for the respective classes.

class	AirlineReservationSystem

printing

printOn: aWindow
    "Prints like 'an AirlineReservationSystem for Air Canada, U.S. Air'."
    | space |
    super **printOn**: aWindow.
    self **airlines size** > 0 **ifTrue**: [
        aWindow **nextPutAll**: ' for '.
        space := ''.
        self **airlines do**: [:anAirline |
            aWindow **nextPutAll**: space; **nextPutAll**: anAirline **name**.
            space := ', ']]

printReportOn: aWindow
    "Prints a report on all the airlines."
    aWindow
        cr; **cr**;
        nextPutAll: 'Airline Reservation System Report'.
    airlines **do**: [:anAirline | anAirline **printReportOn**: aWindow]

---

class	Airline

printing

printOn: aWindow
    "Prints like 'Air Canada Airline'."
    aWindow **nextPutAll**: self **name**; **space**.
    self **class printOn**: aWindow

printReportOn: aWindow
    "Prints a report about all the flights."
    aWindow **cr**; **cr**; **nextPutAll**: self **name**; **nextPutAll**: ' Airline Report'.
    flights **size** = 0 **ifTrue**: [aWindow **cr**; **cr**; **nextPutAll**: 'Nothing to report'].
    flights **do**: [:aFlight | aFlight **printReportOn**: aWindow]

class   Flight

printing

printOn: aWindow
    "Prints like 'Air Canada Flight 232 with 25 passengers'."
    aWindow
        nextPutAll: self **airline name**;
        nextPutAll: ' Flight ';
        nextPutAll: self **name**;
        nextPutAll: ' with '.
    self **passengers size printOn**: aWindow.
    aWindow **nextPutAll**: ' passenger'.
    self passengers size = 1 ifFalse: [aWindow nextPut: $s]

printReportOn: aWindow
    "Prints a report about this particular flight."
    aWindow
        cr; **cr**; **nextPutAll**: 'Flight '; **nextPutAll**: self name;
        cr; **tab**; **nextPutAll**: 'leaving '.
    self **source printOn**: aWindow.
    aWindow
        cr; **tab**; **nextPutAll**: 'arriving at '.
    self **destination printOn**: aWindow.
    aWindow
        cr; **cr**; **nextPutAll**: 'Passengers:'; **cr**.
    passengers **do**: [:aPassenger | aPassenger **printReportOn**: aWindow]

---

class   FlightEntry

printing

printOn: aWindow
    aWindow **nextPutAll**: location; **nextPutAll**: ' on '.
    self **date printOn**: aWindow.
    aWindow **nextPutAll**: ' at '.
    self **time printOn**: aWindow.

---

class   Passenger

printing

printOn: aWindow
    self **class printOn**: aWindow.
    aWindow **nextPutAll**: self name

printReportOn: aWindow
    "Prints a report about this particular passenger."
    aWindow **cr**; **nextPutAll**: self **name**; **space**.
    self **address isNil**
        ifFalse: [aWindow **nextPutAll**: self **address**; **space**].
    self **phone isNil**
        ifFalse: [aWindow **nextPutAll**: ' phone '; **nextPutAll**: self **phone**]

8.1.5 Class Hierarchy Integration (Is-a versus Part-of)

Class hierarchy integration is concerned with determining how our application classes relate to each other and to existing classes in the Smalltalk library. More specifically, we need to design an appropriate **is-a**[1] hierarchy. Figure 8.4 is a specific example illustrating that a cow is an animal and that an animal is an object.

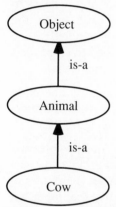

Figure 8.4 An is-a hierarchy relating classes Cow and Animal.

Each of our classes must ultimately inherit from Object. In an application with a large number of classes, we might be tempted to **generalize**—to create classes that capture the essence of a number of existing concrete classes. Sometimes, those generalizations are themselves concrete classes. At other times, they are used as abstract classes for powerful and more useful concrete subclasses. There are few similar classes in our application, so this option doesn't appear to be available (so far). The converse, called **specialization**, introduces specialized variations of existing classes. For example, is there a need to differentiate between propeller-driven flights and jet-driven flights? It may not be necessary today, but it might become an issue in the future if passengers begin to reject propeller-driven flights as old-fashioned or unsafe. In any event, an is-a hierarchy for the airline reservation system developed so far is shown in Figure 8.5.

---

[1]Actually, we would prefer to design a **subtype** hierarchy, but that is an advanced topic best pursued in a more advanced book. Our immediate concern is not to use subclassing for parts.

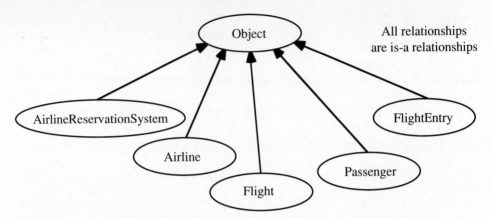

Figure 8.5 The complete is-a hierarchy for our airline reservation system.

By contrast, we might also want to diagram the parts of our objects; i.e., to display a **parts diagram** as shown in Figure 8.6. Note that we have drawn the arrows in the opposite direction to highlight the fact that objects explicitly keep track of their parts. Parts, on the other hand, do not explicitly keep track of their containers. Additionally, the relationships are between instances (not classes).

As a rule, we don't generally bother going into details about the parts in a parts diagram. When such details are important, we'll generally refer to it as an **object ensemble diagram**, since it deals with a group of objects; e.g., see Figure 8.7.

It is very important to be able to distinguish between parts relationships and is-a relationships. A diagram such as that shown in Figure 8.8 might easily confuse a novice. A window is not a building, so this couldn't possibly be an is-a diagram. A window is part of a building. If there were a class called Window that inherited from Building, we would have to conclude that the resulting design (and designer) was totally confused! Parts are specified as instance variables of an object, not by inheriting from the object. This diagram, if meaningful at all, must be indicating that doors, windows, and rooms are parts of buildings—even if the arrows are in the wrong direction and the components are classes rather than instances.

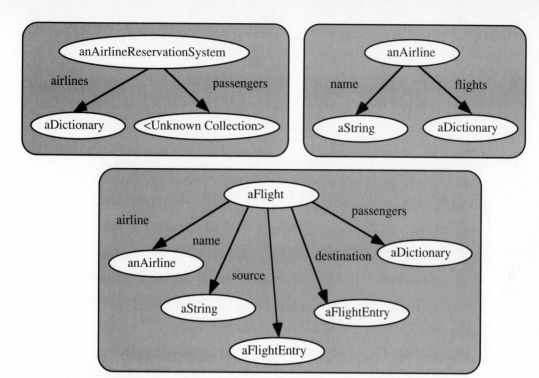

Figure 8.6 Parts diagrams for three of the classes in the airline reservation system.

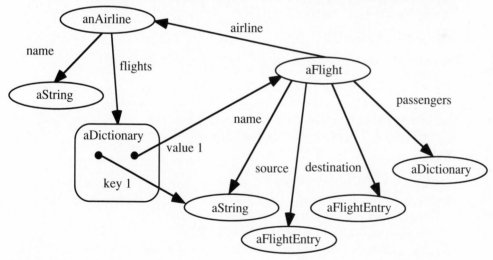

Figure 8.7 An object ensemble diagram showing interrelated airline and flight objects.

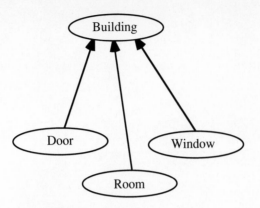

Figure 8.8 An is-a diagram or a parts diagram? (Clearly, the latter)

8.1.6 The Implementation So Far

An airline reservation system is a system that can make passenger reservations on specific flights for specific airlines. This section summarizes the classes and methods developed in the previous sections that partially implement an airline reservation system. Class methods are provided that illustrate three use-cases: The first use-case creates a sample airline reservation system, the second one books a passenger on two flights, and the third prints a detailed summary of the state of the airline reservation system after the second use-case. This detailed report prints as follows:

> Airline Reservation System Report
>
> U.S. Air Airline Report
>
> Nothing to report
>
> Air Canada Airline Report
>
> Flight 232
>   leaving Toronto on Feb 12, 93 at 08:00:00
>   arriving at San Francisco on Feb 12, 93 at 16:00:00
>
> Passengers:
>
> Long John Silver Ottawa, Canada
>
> Flight 552
>   leaving San Francisco on Feb 19, 93 at 17:00:00
>   arriving at Toronto on Feb 19, 93 at 23:00:00
>
> Passengers:
>
> Long John Silver Ottawa, Canada

Five classes were designed: AirlineReservationSystem, Airline, Flight, Flight-Entry, and Passenger.

class   AirlineReservationSystem
superclass   Object
instance variables   airlines passengers

class methods

examples

useCase1
    "AirlineReservationSystem useCase1"
    "A use-case to set up a simple airline reservation system."

    | system airline1 airline2 flight1 flight2 |
    system := AirlineReservationSystem **new**.
    system
        addAirline: (Airline **new name**: 'U.S. Air');
        addAirline: (Airline **new name**: 'Air Canada');

        addFlight: (Flight **new**
            name: '232';
            departing: 'Toronto'
                date: (Date **day**: 12 **month**: #Feb **year**: 93)
                time: (Time **hours**: 8 **minute**: 0 **second**: 0);
            arriving: 'San Francisco'
                date: (Date **day**: 12 **month**: #Feb **year**: 93)
                time: (Time **hours**: 16 **minute**: 0 **second**: 0))
        toAirlineNamed: 'Air Canada';

        addFlight: (Flight **new**
            name: '552';
            departing: 'San Francisco'
                 date: (Date **day**: 19 **month**: #Feb **year**: 93)
                 time: (Time **hours**: 17 **minute**: 0 **second**: 0);
            arriving: 'Toronto'
                 date: (Date **day**: 19 **month**: #Feb **year**: 93)
                 time: (Time **hours**: 23 **minute**: 0 **second**: 0))
        toAirlineNamed: 'Air Canada'.
    ^system

useCase2
    "AirlineReservationSystem useCase2"
    "A use-case to book a passenger on two flights. Note: airline reservation
    system will ensure that a unique up-to-date passenger object is used by
    all its airlines even if distinct passenger objects are provided. Notice that
    the second passenger object has an address and the first does not."

    | system |
    system := self **useCase1**.
    system
        book: (Passenger **new name**: 'Long John Silver')
        onAirlineNamed: 'Air Canada'
        flightName: '232'
        date: (Date **day**: 12 **month**: #Feb **year**: 93).

```
system
    book: (Passenger new
        name: 'Long John Silver'; address: 'Ottawa, Canada')
    onAirlineNamed: 'Air Canada'
    flightName: '552'
    date:  (Date day: 19 month: #Feb year: 93).
^system
```

useCase3
```
"AirlineReservationSystem useCase3"
"A use-case to print a report on the status of an airline reservation
system."

| system |
system := self useCase2.
system printReportOn: Transcript.
^system
```

instance creation

new
```
^super new initialize
```

instance methods

instance initialization

initialize
```
airlines := Dictionary new.
passengers := Dictionary new
```

airline manipulation

airlines
```
^airlines
```
addAirline: anAirline
```
airlines at: anAirline name put: anAirline
```
airlineNamed: airlineName
```
^airlines at: airlineName
```

flight manipulation

addFlight: aFlight **toAirlineNamed:** airlineName
```
(self airlineNamed: airlineName) addFlight: aFlight
```

passenger manipulation

book: aPassenger **onAirlineNamed:** airlineName **flightName:** flightName
date: aDate
```
| passenger airline flight |
passenger := self updatePassenger: aPassenger.
airline := self airlineNamed: airlineName.
flight := airline flightNamed: flightName date: aDate.
flight book: passenger
```

updatePassenger: aPassenger
"Update old information about the passenger and return the updated one."
| oldPassenger |
oldPassenger := passengers
    at: aPassenger name
    ifAbsent: [passengers **at**: aPassenger **name put**: aPassenger].
aPassenger **address isNil**
    ifFalse: [oldPassenger **address**: aPassenger **address**].
aPassenger **phone isNil**
    ifFalse: [oldPassenger **phone**: aPassenger phone].
^oldPassenger

printing

printOn: aWindow
"Prints like 'an AirlineReservationSystem for Air Canada, U.S. Air'."
| space |
super **printOn**: aWindow.
self **airlines size** > 0 **ifTrue**: [
    aWindow **nextPutAll**: ' for '.
    space := ''.
    self **airlines do**: [:anAirline |
        aWindow **nextPutAll**: space; **nextPutAll**: anAirline **name**.
        space := ', ']]

printReportOn: aWindow
"Prints a report on all the airlines."
aWindow
    cr; cr;
    nextPutAll: 'Airline Reservation System Report'.
airlines **do**: [:anAirline | anAirline **printReportOn**: aWindow]

---

class   Airline
superclass   Object
instance variables   name flights

class methods

instance creation

new
    ^super **new initialize**

instance methods

instance initialization

initialize
    name := '<unknown>'.
    flights := Dictionary **new**

accessing and modifying

name
    ^name
name: aString
    name := aString

flight manipulation

addFlight: aFlight
    "Use both the name and the date since the same flight name might be
    used on different days."
    flights **at**: (Array **with**: aFlight **name** with: aFlight **source date**) **put**: aFlight.
    aFlight **airline**: self

flightNamed: flightName **date**: aDate
    ^flights **at**: (Array **with**: flightName **with**: aDate)

printing

printOn: aWindow
    "Prints like 'Air Canada Airline'."
    aWindow **nextPutAll**: self **name**; **space**.
    self **class printOn**: aWindow

printReportOn: aWindow
    "Prints a report about all the flights."
    aWindow **cr**; **cr**; **nextPutAll**: self **name**; **nextPutAll**: ' Airline Report'.
    flights **size** = 0 **ifTrue**: [aWindow **cr**; **cr**; **nextPutAll**: 'Nothing to report'].
    flights **do**: [:aFlight | aFlight **printReportOn**: aWindow]

---

class	Flight
superclass	Object
instance variables	name airline passengers
	source destination

class methods

instance creation

new
    ^super **new initialize**

instance methods

instance initialization

initialize
    name := '<unknown>'.
    airline := Airline **new name**: '<unknown>'.
    passengers := Dictionary **new**

simple accessing and modifying

name
    ^name
name: aString
    name := aString

airline manipulation

airline
    ^airline
airline: anAirline
    airline := anAirline

passenger manipulation

passengers
    ^passengers

book: aPassenger
    passengers **at**: aPassenger **name put**: aPassenger

addPassenger: aPassenger
    self **book**: aPassenger

flight entry manipulation

source
    ^source
destination
    ^destination
itinerary
    ^Array **with**: source **with**: destination
departing: aString **date**: aDate **time**: aTime
    source := FlightEntry **new location**: aString; **date**: aDate; **time**: aTime
arriving: aString **date**: aDate **time**: aTime
    destination := FlightEntry **new location**: aString; **date**: aDate; **time**: aTime

printing

printOn: aWindow
    "Prints like 'Air Canada Flight 232 with 25 passengers'."
    aWindow
        nextPutAll: self **airline name**;
        nextPutAll: ' Flight ';
        nextPutAll: self name;
        nextPutAll: ' with '.
    self **passengers size printOn**: aWindow.
    aWindow **nextPutAll**: ' passenger'.
    self **passengers size** = 1 **ifFalse**: [aWindow **nextPut**: $s]

printReportOn: aWindow
    "Prints a report about this particular flight."
    aWindow
        cr; **cr**; **nextPutAll**: 'Flight '; **nextPutAll**: self **name**;
        cr; **tab**; **nextPutAll**: 'leaving '.
    self **source printOn**: aWindow.
    aWindow
        cr; **tab**; **nextPutAll**: 'arriving at '.
    self **destination printOn**: aWindow.
    aWindow
        cr; **cr**; **nextPutAll**: 'Passengers:'; **cr**.
    passengers **do**: [:aPassenger | aPassenger **printReportOn**: aWindow]

---

class	FlightEntry
superclass	Object
instance variables	location date time

class methods

"none"

instance methods

accessing and modifying

location
    ^location
location: aString
    location := aString
date
    ^date
date: aDate
    date := aDate
time
    ^time
time: aTime
    time := aTime

printing

printOn: aWindow
    aWindow **nextPutAll**: location; **nextPutAll**: ' on '.
    self **date printOn**: aWindow.
    aWindow **nextPutAll**: ' at '.
    self **time printOn**: aWindow.

class	Passenger
superclass	Object
instance variables	name address phone

class methods

"none"

instance methods

accessing and modifying

name
    ^name
name: aString
    name := aString
address
    ^address
address: aString
    address := aString
phone
    ^phone
phone: anInteger
    phone := anInteger

printing

printOn: aWindow
    self **class printOn**: aWindow.
    aWindow **nextPutAll**: ' '; **nextPutAll**: self **name**

printReportOn: aWindow
    "Prints a report about this particular passenger."
    aWindow **cr**; **nextPutAll**: self **name**; **space**.
    self **address isNil**
        ifFalse: [aWindow **nextPutAll**: self **address**; **space**].
    self **phone isNil**
        ifFalse: [aWindow **nextPutAll**: ' phone '; **nextPutAll**: self **phone**]

8.2   Summary

This chapter has introduced you to the analysis and design of groups of classes. More specifically, we have

- Learned the distinction between analysis and design and why it is difficult to separate the two when dealing with object-oriented systems
- Investigated two different viewpoints from which to approach design: the object-centered viewpoint and the object-community viewpoint
- Investitgated responsibility-driven (also called behavior-driven, need-driven, or anthropomorphic) design which is summarized by the CRH methodology (classes, responsibilities, and helpers) and the concept of use-cases
- Investigated the design of an airline reservation system to illustrate many of the important issues and techniques used in evolutionary software development

8.3   What You Did and Did Not Learn

We learned about the major analysis and design terminology, including terms such as anthropomorphic design, behavior, responsibility, helper, and the steps needed to create a design: finding the classes, finding the relationships between the classes, finding the parts (relationships between the instances), and finding the behaviors. We also learned about the object-centered perspective exemplified by the CRH methodology and the object-community perspective exemplified by use-cases.

A design can be documented by providing a CRH description of the classes and by providing class diagrams, parts diagrams (also called object diagrams), object-ensemble diagrams, and use-case diagrams. Of these, the last are the most difficult to produce—they are often replaced by English text describing the details of the use-case. As a rule, it is not as important to be able to physically draw the diagrams in the midst of a design as it is to be able to mentally picture them as you make changes to the structure of the classes and the objects. In the long run, the initial diagrams are likely to be out-of-date anyway. After substantial refinement, it is clear that only the final design needs to be documented.

In situations where documentation is provided only after a project is completed, it is still the case that expert designers develop their software using the CRH methodology and use-cases. Even though they may not document their initial efforts on paper, they still go through the stages mentally. For example, before they define a new class, they mentally determine what the class is for, what behaviors they expect of it, and what parts it is likely to keep track of. Some of the methods may be generated from an object-centered perspective. However, the most important behavior is likely to be generated from the object-community perspective as use-cases are created to help flesh out the needed behavior. The idea of use-case chasing that we illustrated while designing the airline reservation system is a crucial capability that you will have to develop as you design groups of application classes. The ability to jump from class to class as you implement needed methods is something that is best done interactively in a system that supports it. After some experience, you will find that it is actually more difficult watching someone else perform use-case chasing than it is to do it yourself.

8.4   Important Facts

Synonyms for Object-Oriented Analysis and Design

- **Object-oriented** analysis and design
- **Responsibility-driven** analysis and design
- **Behavior-driven** analysis and desig
- **Anthropomorphic** analysis and design
- **Need-driven** behavior analysis and design

Design Viewpoints for Understanding Behaviors

- An **object-centered view** provides an understanding of the application from the perspective of the individual objects that make up the application.
- A **object-community view** provides an understanding of the interactions between the individual objects that make up the application.

The Four Key Analysis and Design Steps

- **Finding the classes**—determining what classes are needed to account for the requirements of the application
- **Determining the relationships between the classes**—determining how the new classes relate to the classes in the existing library and how they relate to each other
- **Determining the relationships between the instances**—determining how the instances of the classes relate to other instances; e.g., what parts they need to maintain to effectively carry out their tasks
- **Determining the behavior of the classes and instances**—determining what messages they should understand; i.e., their **responsibilities**, and consequently what methods they will need

Need-Driven Behavior Design (Use-Case Generation)

1. Find a user for your classes—but don't tell the user exactly what methods are available.
2. Make sure that the user sends messages to the classes and the corresponding instances to exercise them.
3. Add a method for each message that is not understood.

The CRH Design Steps (The Object-Centered Viewpoint)

- **Classes** (or abstractions)
- **Responsibilities** (or behaviors)
- **Helpers** (the other classes or instances that an object needs to effectively carry out its responsibilities)

Useful Diagrams

- **Class hierarchy** diagrams
- **Parts** diagrams (also called **object** diagrams)
- **Object-ensemble** diagrams
- **Use-case** diagrams

8.5   Helpful Hints

Reports require methods other than printOn:: In practice, **printOn:** is intended to provide a short description of an object so that we can recognize it when we see it printed. It is not intended for producing well-formatted documents. As a consequence, there are no **printOn:** methods in the system that provide new lines (carriage returns) or tabs. Even ordered collections print all their elements on the same line. By contrast, reports are generated with special methods such as **printReportOn:**, **printDetailedReportOn:**, or **printShortReportOn:**.

8.6   Glossary

analysis and design: analysis, anthropomorphic design, behavior, behavior-driven design, class hierarchy integration, collaborator, colleague, CRC methodology, CRH methodology, design, generalization, helpers, is-a hierarchy, iterative refinement, methodology, need-driven, object-centered design, object-centered view, object-community view, object ensemble diagram, parts diagram, requirements, responsibilities, responsibility-driven design, reusability, specialization, stepwise refinement, top-down decomposition, top-down strategy, use-case, use-case chasing, use-case diagram

8.7   Exercises

The following exercises are meant to provide experience with collections and the notions of object-oriented analysis and design.

1. Design and implement a garage maintenance system that can keep track of the work orders for the garage.
2. Design and implement an appointment system for dentists who need to schedule their patients for visits.
3. Design and implement a video library system that can keep track of your videos at home.

9

The Smalltalk Library

What You Will Learn

In the previous chapters, we developed a reasonably good understanding of a large number of important objects: numbers, characters, strings, arrays, ordered collections, dictionaries, and pens. We studied the major operations associated with the corresponding classes because they serve as a foundation for future understanding. They are also extremely useful building blocks for developing applications. But the classes involved are only a small subset of the Smalltalk class library.

In this chapter, we provide a more comprehensive view of the basic classes in the class library. In particular, we will look at the inheritance structure in the library and investigate both classes that are new to us as well as classes that we have already seen but that we have not looked at from the perspective of the hierarchy. In the process, we will gain a better understanding of the relationship between the classes and we will uncover some new and interesting notions. For example, we will learn about the distinction between identity and equality, the difference between a shallow copy and a deep copy, the distinction between print strings and store strings, hashing, and the use of blocks for building domain-specific control structures.

This chapter assumes you have, by now, learned how to learn. We present the important concepts, with as few examples as possible, expecting that you are able to use the Smalltalk system itself to explore the issues that require further elaboration. We also cover many operations that we don't expect you to remember. But you will recall the kinds of operations that are available and how to find them when the need arises.

9.1 Class Object and Its Protocol

As can be seen in Figure 9.1, class Object has many subclasses. Some, such as UnderfinedObject, Boolean, Collection, Magnitude, and Point, are already familiar to us. But many others, such as Message, Context, and GraphicsMedium, to name a few, are new. We have grouped Window and ViewManager together because they are interrelated. These two classes (along with a large number of subclasses, not shown) provide facilities for building user interfaces, a topic we will consider in Chapter 10. File and Stream are similarly related. So, too, are the graphical classes Point, Rectangle, ClipboardManager, GraphicsMedium, and GraphicsTool. Although we have already encountered a few of the Collection classes in Chapter 7 (and earlier), we consider the entire hierarchy which includes such additional collection classes as IdentityDictionary, SortedCollection, Set, and Bag. We also consider many advanced collection facilities.

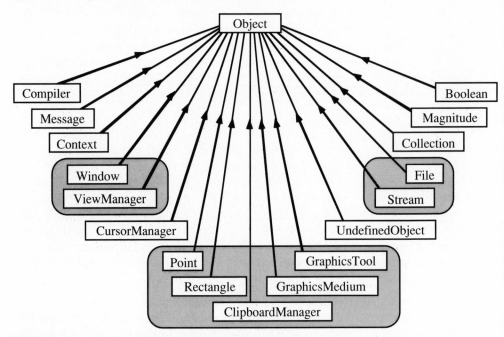

Figure 9.1 A working subset of the Smalltalk class library.

Before we go on to consider the subclasses, let's consider class Object itself. It provides a small number of operations that all objects inherit.

9.1.1 Equality versus Identity

We were introduced to the concept of **equality** in one of the early chapters. Intuitively, two objects are equal if they "look the same." We can test for equality using operations = (**equal**) and ~= (**not equal**).

Operations on Objects

comparing

anObject = anotherObject	Returns true for equal object; false, otherwise
anObject ~= anotherObject	Returns true for unequal objects; false, otherwise
anObject == anotherObject	Returns true for identical objects; false, otherwise
anObject ~~ anotherObject	Returns true for distinct objects; false, otherwise

A similar but distinct notion is the concept of **identity**. Two variables A and B are said to be **identical** if they refer to the same object. The corresponding operations are == (**identical**) and ~~ (**not identical**). As shown below, identity and equality are quite different notions.

```
| name1 name2 |
name1 := 'the management'.
name2 := 'the ', 'management'.
name1 == name2 ⇒ false
name1 = name2 ⇒ true
```

Note that name2 is bound to an object constructed by concatenating two strings together. So variables name1 and name2 are equal; i.e., they are both bound to strings containing the same characters. But they are not identical, because they are bound to two distinct strings. Diagrammatically, the relationships might be pictured as shown in Figure 9.2.

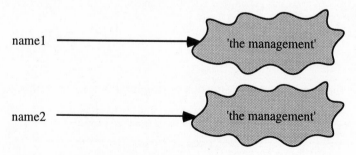

Figure 9.2 Variables name1 and name2 bound to different strings (they are not identical).

Note that we could make sure that name1 and name2 are bound to the same object by rebinding name1 as follows:

```
name1 := name2.
name1 == name2 ⇒ true
name1 = name2 ⇒ true
```

After the assignment, name1 is bound to the same string that name2 is bound to; i.e., name1 and name2 are identical, as shown in Figure 9.3. Clearly, if name1 and name2 are the same object, they must also be equal.

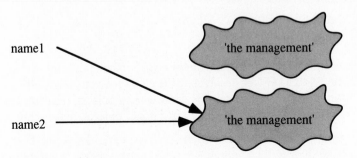

Figure 9.3 Variables name1 and name2 bound to the same strings (they are identical).

This notion of identity is important because distinct objects could have common parts; i.e., parts that are shared. Side-effects on one part could potentially affect another. Additionally, there are many objects that cannot be copied because they are unique in the system; e.g., there is only one instance of nil, true, and false. Consequently, when a new array is constructed; e.g., using "Array **new**: 3", all elements of the array must be bound to the same nil object (see Figure 9.4).

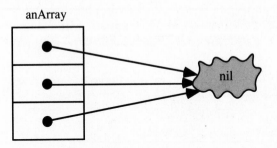

Figure 9.4 The instance resulting from executing "Array **new**: 3".

This illustrates one of the fundamental properties of the Smalltalk programming language.

> *Smalltalk promotes sharing, not copying.*

A more complex example can be used to illustrate sharing in more detail.

```
| aString aFloat aClass anArray |
aString := 'hello'.
aFloat := 19.99.
aClass := Pen.
anArray := Array with: aString with: aFloat with: aClass.
anOrderedCollection := anArray asOrderedCollection.
```

A diagram of the result is illustrated in Figure 9.5. Note that the array elements are bound to the same objects as the respective element variables. Note also that the ordered collection elements are the same as the array elements.

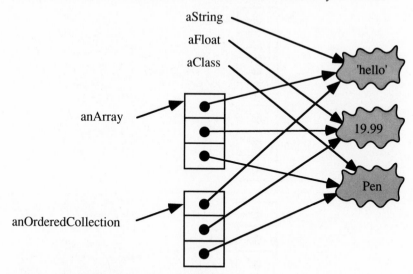

Figure 9.5 Smalltalk promotes **sharing**.

As a consequence, the following results should come as no surprise.

```
(anArray at: 1) == aString ⇒ true
(anArray at: 1) == (anOrderedCollection at: 1) ⇒ true
(anArray at: 1) == (anArray at: 2) ⇒ false     "after all, they are not all the same"
```

9.1.2 Shallow versus Deep Copies

By virtue of the fact that Smalltalk promotes sharing, most requests for objects generally return the originals rather than copies. As we saw in the previous example, asking for the second element of anArray results in the return of the unique 19.99 object—not a copy. If that is the case, how do we get a copy? As rule, copies must be explicitly requested via specific operations such as the following:

Operations on Objects

copying

anObject **copy**	Usually, a shallow copy
anObject **shallowCopy**	A copy that shares the same elements
anObject **deepCopy**	A copy with shallow copies of the elements

Subject to one restriction (see below), a **shallow copy** (see Figure 9.6) makes a copy of the original but does not copy its parts; i.e., the parts are shared by both the original and the copy. By contrast, a **deep copy** makes both a copy of the original and a shallow copy of the parts. However, certain special object, such as nil, true, false, along with classes, refuse to make copies and provide themselves instead of a copy.

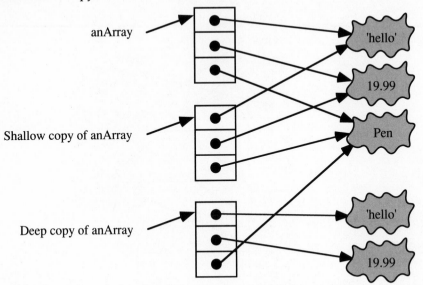

Figure 9.6 Shallow versus deep copies—classes are never copied.

For most uses, shallow copies are preferable to deep copies. Certainly, it is more efficient to obtain a shallow copy, since fewer objects are duplicated. Consequently, **copy** defaults to **shallowCopy** in the great majority of cases. In Figure 9.6, for example, both the shallow and deep copies of "anArray" can be used interchangeably without fear of side-effects. As can be seen in Figure 9.7, changing the first element of the shallow copy to 'goodbye', has no effect on any of the other arrays (or elements).

When do you want a deep copy? Suppose we had designed an application in which factories kept track of their inventory. If we needed a copy of the factory for experimentation and we had already constructed a reasonably complex factory object, would a shallow copy be sufficient? Yes—if we intended never to change the inventory. However, if additions were made to the inventory, both the original factory and its copy would be affected (see Figure 9.8). Under those conditions, a deep copy would be required, since each factory object would need its own collection.

Sometimes, even a deep copy is not adequate. For example, a deep copy of a bank will provide a new bank containing a shallow copy of its parts. But one of its

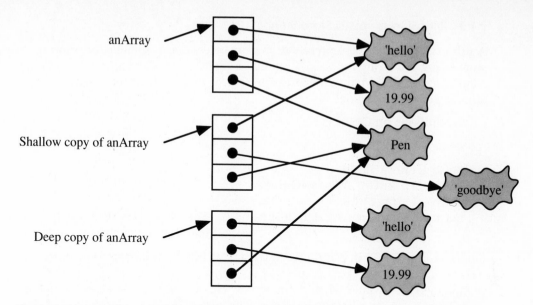

Figure 9.7 Modifying a shallow copy has no effect on the original or a deep copy.

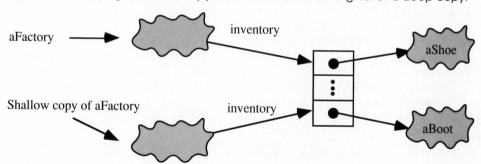

Figure 9.8 A deep copy is needed if parts are themselves containers that can be modified.

parts is a collection of bank accounts. A shallow copy of this collection will share the same bank accounts as the original collection. If a deep copy of a bank is intended to provide a copy of the bank accounts, too, then method **deepCopy** for banks will have to be redefined to create copies of the bank accounts too. The default deep copy operation is not deep enough!

9.1.3 Print Strings versus Store Strings

A **print string** is a string representation of an object that is suitable for printing. A **store string** is a string representation that is suitable for storing; i.e., it is a string containing a valid Smalltalk expression that, if executed, would create another object equal to the original.

Operations on Objects

printing

anObject **printString**
anObject **printOn**: aWindowOrStream
anObject **storeString**
anObject **storeOn**: aWindowOrStream   The Object version doesn't
                                                                            handle circular structures

Operations **printString** and **storeString** are both implemented in terms of **printOn:** and **storeOn:**, respectively. Consequently, there is no need to reimplement the former when defining new classes. To illustrate the distinction, consider an ordered collection with two elements.

```
| aCollection |
aCollection := OrderedCollection with: 1 with: 2.
aCollection printString ⇒ 'OrderedCollection (1 2)'
aCollection storeString ⇒ '(OrderedCollection new; add: 1; add: 2; yourself)'

Transcript nextPutAll: 'The ordered collection print and store strings consist of '.
aCollection printOn: Transcript.
Transcript nextPutAll: ' and '.
aCollection storeOn: Transcript.
```

Note that the store string, but not the print string, can be executed.

```
OrderedCollection (1 2) ⇒ (error; incorrect syntax)
(OrderedCollection new; add: 1; add: 2; yourself) ⇒ OrderedCollection (1 2)
```

So, in general, a store string is a string that when executed constructs an object equal to the original. For simple objects, like booleans and integers, the print and store strings are the same. But they are completely different for more complex objects (as we saw above).

When new classes are created, it is conventional to provide both a **printOn:** and a **storeOn:** method if the versions inherited from Object are not adequate. In class Bank, for example, we introduced our own **printOn:** because the inherited version printed too simply as "a Bank". The revised version printed banks in a more intuitive manner; e.g., "Bank of Switzerland".

Usually, the **storeOn:** in Object can be inherited. For banks, however, the inherited version will not work, because of the mutual references in the objects. In particular, banks keep tracks of their bank accounts and the bank accounts, in turn, keep track of their banks. The **storeOn:** for a bank asks the bank's accounts to store themselves. The **storeOn:** for a bank account will in turn ask the bank to store itself. An infinite loop results. A solution to this problem might require extensions to one or more of these classes. We won't pursue that here but it is an interesting exercise.

On the other hand, recall class Money, which we designed and implemented in Chapter 5. It contained a **printOn:** method (one version is repeated below) but no **storeOn:** method.

printing

printOn: aWindow
    "I print myself in the form '$4322.51' or '-$4322.51'."
    self **dollars** < 0 **ifTrue:** [aWindow **nextPut:** $-].
    aWindow **nextPut:** $$.
    self **dollars abs printOn:** aWindow.
    aWindow **nextPut:** $..
    self **cents** <= 9 **ifTrue:** [aWindow **nextPut:** $0].
    self **cents printOn:** aWindow.

The **storeOn:** method must generate a valid Smalltalk expression. Moreover, to ensure that it integrates properly with the **storeOn:** for other objects, such as ordered collections, we should surround the result in parentheses.

printing

storeOn: aWindow
    "I store myself in the form '(Money cents: 432251)'."
    aWindow **nextPutAll:** '(Money cents: '.
    self **totalCents storeOn:** aWindow.
    aWindow **nextPut:** $).

Now, if we create a collection with money objects, they will be properly integrated. Without the surrounding brackets, messages **add:cents:** would be sent to the ordered collection instead of **add:**.

    (OrderedCollection **with:** (Money **dollars:** 2) **with:** (Money **cents:** 25))
        storeString
            ⇒ '(OrderedCollection new add: (Money cents: 200); add: (Money
                cents: 25); yourself)'

9.1.4 Meta-level Operations for Executing Messages

When we create window based applications in the next chapter, clicking on buttons will cause application-specific messages to be sent to our application. Consequently, it will be necessary for the buttons themselves to be able to keep track of the messages—say, in an instance variable—and then to be able to send this message. Protocol for doing this is provided in class Object.

Operations on Objects

sending messages

anObject **perform**: aSymbol **withArguments**: anArray
anObject **perform**: aSymbol
anObject **perform**: aSymbol **with**: parameter
anObject **perform**: aSymbol **with**: parameter1 **with**: parameter2

The first operation is general purpose; the others are special cases, when the number of parameters is fixed. In the following example, we illustrate how each method can be used for unary, binary, and keyword messages. Note that the messages (and parameters, if we so desire) can be kept in variables.

```
| message1 message2 message3 |
5 factorial ⇒ 120
message1 := #factorial.
5 perform: message1 withArguments: #() ⇒ 120
5 perform: message1 ⇒ 120

1 + 2 ⇒ 3
message2 := #+.
1 perform: message2 withArguments: #(2) ⇒ 3
1 perform: message2 with: 2 ⇒ 3

10 between: 1 and: 20 ⇒ true
message3 := #between:and:.
10 perform: message3 withArguments: #(1 20) ⇒ true
10 perform: message3 with: 1 with: 20 ⇒ true
```

This might have application in a scanner, for example, where the task is to pick up individual tokens or entities in a string. A class variable ScanningMethod could be initialized to contain the name of the method to use to scan for a number, a string, or an array.

```
            ...
'0123456789' do: [:aCharacter |
     ScanningMethod at: aCharacter put: #scanNumber:].
ScanningMethod at: $' put: #scanString:.
ScanningMethod at: $# put: #scanArray:.
            ...
data := ... "string to be scanned"
self perform: (ScanningMethod at: data first) with: data
```

The above **perform**: operations are called **meta-level** operations, because they are operations dealing with operations; messages about messages—they are above the level of normal messages.

9.1.5 Object Mutation and Instance Gathering

Smalltalk is one of the few object-oriented languages that permits object mutation. An important application has to do with object monitoring. An object to be monitored can be mutated into a **gatekeeper** that keeps track of the original. We'll illustrate this in the section devoted to class Message.

Operations on Objects

object mutation

anObject **become**: anotherObject

instance gathering

Object **allInstances**

When object1 becomes object2, all references to object1 are replaced by references to object2, as shown in Figure 9.9. It is not necessary to know where the references to object1 come from in the first place.

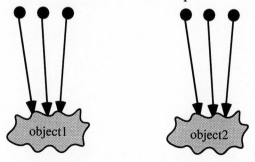

Figure 9.9 Illustrating object mutation

Before "object1 **become**: object2"

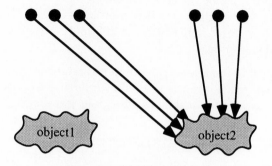

After "object1 **become**: object2"

This operation is very powerful. It allows mice, for example, to be changed into elephants or vice versa. A more mundane example is illustrated below.

```
| aString anotherString |
aString := 1/3. anotherString := aString. "not yet strings, however"
aString == anotherString ⇒ true

aString become: 'hello'.
aString ⇒ 'hello'
anotherString ⇒ 'hello'
aString == anotherString ⇒ true
```

One of the most common uses is to remove out-of-date objects. When a new class is designed—say, a class called, Factory—with no instance variables, it is not unusual for instances to be recorded somewhere and then misplaced. For example, if we executed

```
Junk3 := Factory new
```

we might very well forget some time later that a reference to an instance exists. If we then tried to change the definition of the class (for example, to add an instance variable called name), we would be prompted with the message as shown in Figure 9.10.

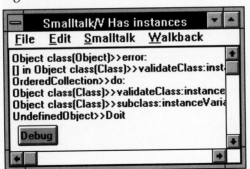

Figure 9.10 Attempting to change the structure of a class with existing instances.

If we know that Junk3 is bound to an instance, it is not difficult to rebind it to something else. However, it will more often be the case that we won't be able to remember the source of the reference. We might have opened on inspector on an instance and then forgotten about it or stored some instance in a more complex object like a dictionary or an ordered collection.

We can easily find all the instances using meta-level operation **allInstances**. But even that is not adequate if what we really need is the object referring to our instance. One solution is to mutate each of the instances into some well-known object such as nil:

```
Factory allInstances do: [:aFactory | aFactory become: nil]
```

9.1.6 Creating Subclasses of Object

When creating subclasses of Object, it is important to realize that most of the inherited operations provide the behavior you expect of them. However, there is one operation that must often be reimplemented because the default behavior is inadequate. In particular, the equal operation in class Object defaults to identity. Thus

Object **new** = Object **new** ⇒ false

In practice, such strange behavior can be eliminated from those subclasses for which equality is important by redefining the equal operation more appropriately. We will find, for example, that strings, numbers, dates, indexable collections, and rectangles (to name a few) provide revised implementations of equal.

Operations on Objects

operations that subclasses must reimplement

anObject = anObject

operations that subclasses can inherit

anObject ~= anObject

Although operations = and ~= are complementary, there is no need to reimplement ~=, because it is defined in terms of = as follows:

~= anObject
    ^(self = anObject) **not**

9.2 Class Message and Its Protocol

When an error is reported in an error window, the object supplied as a parameter to **error:** is called aMessage, an instance of the Message class. Since we just discussed the notion of meta-level operations in the previous section, we might as well introduce class Message itself, which directly inherits from class Object (see Figure 9.11). It provides an alternative technique for relaying messages from one object to another.

Figure 9.11 Class Message provides meta-level facilities.

A **message** object keeps track of a receiver, a selector, and arguments and permits the associated message to be sent to the receiver.

Operations on Messages

accessing and modifying

aMessage **receiver**
aMessage **receiver**: anObject
aMessage **selector**
aMessage **selector**: aSymbol
aMessage **arguments**
aMessage **arguments**: anArray

executing the message

aMessage **perform**

With messages, we can rewrite the examples of the previous section as follows:

```
| message1 message2 message3 |
5 factorial ⇒ 120
message1 := Message new
    receiver: 5; selector: #factorial arguments: #().
message1 perform ⇒ 120

1 + 2 ⇒ 3
message2 := Message new
    receiver: 1; selector: #+ arguments: #(2).
message2 perform ⇒ 3

10 between: 1 and: 20 ⇒ true
message3 := Message new
    receiver: 10; selector: #between:and: arguments: #(1 20).
message3 perform ⇒ true
```

Now, let's consider creating a gatekeeper whose sole role is to record the external messages sent to a specific object. We will make use of the **become:** operation, which we described earlier, as well as a new Object operation called **doesNotUnderstand:**, which we will subsequently discuss.

class	Gatekeeper
superclass	nil
instance variables	object history

class methods

instance creation

on: anObject
    ^self **new on:** anObject

examples

example1
"Gatekeeper example1"
"We will surround an ordered collection by a gatekeeper but we will use
the resulting gatekeeper as if it were the ordered collection. All the
ordered collection messages will fail to be understood. Even so, the
gatekeeper will process them properly, because it has its own version of
doesNotUnderstand: for handling the errors. It will record the messages
and pass them on to the ordered collection as if everything were normal."
| aCollection |
aCollection := Gatekeeper **on**: OrderedCollection **new**.
aCollection **add**: 'hello'; **add**: 'there'; **add**: aCollection **size**.
aCollection **restoreAndProvideHistory**

instance methods

instance initialization

on: anObject
"First, initialize."
history := OrderedCollection **new**.
"Next, store a copy of the object."
object := anObject **shallowCopy**.
"Finally, mutate the object into this gatekeeper."
anObject **become**: self

handling all messages

become: anObject
"The receiver takes on the identity of anObject. All the objects that
reference the receiver will now point to the object."
<primitive: 72>
^self **primitiveFailed**

handling all messages

doesNotUnderstand: aMessage
"Record the message and then reroute it to the object."
history **add**: aMessage
^object
    perform: aMessage **selector**
    withArguments aMessage **arguments**

restore and provide history information

restoreAndProvideHistory
"Extract the information before mutating since it won't be available
afterwards."
| result |
result := history.
self **become**: object.
^result

There are a number of interesting issues in the Gatekeeper class:

- It does not have a superclass, so instances (and the class) understand only the messages provided here.
- We have included a **doesNotUnderstand**: method. The equivalent method in class Object creates an error walkback window. This one records the message that was not understood and then reroutes it to the object for which it is a gatekeeper. *Presumably, this doesNotUnderstand: method is executed each time a message is not understood.*
- We have not stored the original object (see instance method **on:**) but rather a shallow copy. So when the original object is mutated into a gatekeeper, the gatekeeper still has a copy. If "object" had been bound to the original object instead, it would have mutated into the gatekeeper and all semblance of the original object would have been lost.
- When we are done (see method **restoreAndProvideHistory**), we first extract the history information and then mutate the gatekeeper into the stored object. This stored object is actually a copy of the original, but it behaves exactly like the original. It is important to extract the history information first, because after the mutation, there is no history instance variable in the object into which "self" mutated.
- Method **become**: had to be copied from Object because the Gatekeeper class does not inherit from Object.
- When we later inspect the history information, we will find that the message receiver's are the intended receivers (the ordered collection object in our example). Originally, each receiver was the gatekeeper, but it was mutated into the ordered collection when we finished.

There are a few problems with this implementation. First, it can't be used to track objects that cannot make shallow copies; e.g., objects such as nil, true, and false. Second, it cannot be used to track objects that already understand **on:** because it will misinterpret the gatekeeper's **on:** for the object's **on:**—we could simply choose a unique name to get around this problem. Third, there may be some messages that cannot be recorded in the history data because they will be understood; e.g., message == (it is treated specially by the compiler).

9.3 Class Compiler and its Protocol

Class Compiler (see the hierarchy in Figure 9.12) provides facilities for converting methods into corresponding machine instructions; e.g., when the user selects menu item **Save** in the browser. Most of the methods are private and, consequently, the source code is not available. Nevertheless, it is possible to get an instance of a compiler.

Figure 9.12 Class Compiler is involved when methods are saved.

Aside from the major use described above, it can also be used to compile and evaluate expressions contained in strings.

Operations on Compilers

evaluating

Compiler **evaluate**: aString

Consequently, we can execute an expression such as the following:

Compiler **evaluate**: '1+2' $\Rightarrow$ 3

Other classes in the system sometimes make use of this capability. Prompters, for example, make use the compiler to ensure that the supplied result is evaluated.

Prompter **prompt**: 'Specify a coordinate' **defaultExpression**: '1@1'

9.4   Class UndefinedObject and Its Protocol

All uninitialized variables are bound to the unique object denoted by nil, an instance of Class UndefinedObject (see Figure 9.13).

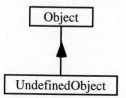

Figure 9.13 Class UndefinedObject provides the unique instance called nil.

As we can see, the protocol for nil is relatively impoverished even though it does inherit all of the Object operations.

Operations on UndefinedObjects (and Objects)

querying

anObject **isNil**   True if the receiver is nil; false otherwise
anObject **notNil**   Converse of the above

Consequently, the following can be executed:

5 **isNil** $\Rightarrow$ false
nil **isNil** $\Rightarrow$ true

What is interesting, however, is the approach used to implement **isNil** and **notNil**. Clearly, it is not adequate to implement these operations in class UndefinedObject. If it were, 5 would clearly not understand the messages. So are they implemented in Object? Surely, we could implement **isNil** in Object as follows:

isNil
    ^self == nil

But we can do better. We could implement the operations in both Object and UndefinedObject as follows:

in class Object
isNil
    ^false

in class UndefinedObject
isNil
    ^true

In this implementation, **isNil** is **polymorphic**; i.e., more than one implementation exists (in different classes). Note that this approach is more efficient. If message "**isNil**" is sent to 2, the version in class Object is found by the method lookup mechanism. The answer, false, can be returned without any further comparisons being made. The first approach required an extra comparison using the identity operation.

There are many polymorphic operations in the system. In particular, there are a few in class Object that we have not considered; e.g., **isArray**, **isNumber**, **isPoint**, and **isInteger**.

9.5   Class Boolean and Its Protocol

Class Boolean (see Figure 9.14) is already well-known. In fact, we learned in Chapter 2 that there are two subclasses, True and False, which are quite distinct from the instances true and false, respectively. The interesting question is why?

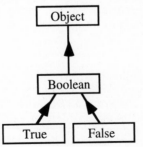

Figure 9.14 Class Boolean has two subclasses.

Presumably, a relevant clue is provided by class UndefinedObject and the technique used to implement **isNil**. Perhaps the boolean operations are polymorphic; i.e., there is one version for true and another for false. We could easily resolve this question by looking at the two subclasses with a browser. However, before doing so, let's see if we can implement polymorphic versions of "&", "|", and **not**. Recall that the "&" result is true only if both the receiver and its parameter are true.

true & true $\Rightarrow$ true   false & true $\Rightarrow$ false
true & false $\Rightarrow$ false   false & false $\Rightarrow$ false

Similarly, the "|" result is false only if both are false.

true | true $\Rightarrow$ true   false | true $\Rightarrow$ true
true | false $\Rightarrow$ true   false | false $\Rightarrow$ false

Finally,

true **not** $\Rightarrow$ false   false **not** $\Rightarrow$ true

All three of these can be implemented as instance methods in class True, as follows:

instance methods in class True

& aBoolean
      ^aBoolean

| aBoolean
      ^true

not
      ^false

In class False, the same operations can be implemented as follows:

instance methods in class True

& aBoolean
      ^false

| aBoolean
      ^aBoolean

not
      ^true

Let's just consider the "&" operations, for example. If the receiver is true, the result is true if the parameter is true, and false otherwise—the parameter must therefore be the correct answer. On the other hand, if the receiver is false, the answer is false regardless of the parameter.

The alternative implementation where only one class Boolean is provided would have to be more complex—perhaps something like the following:

alternative implementations in class Boolean (hypothetical)

```
& aBoolean
    self == false ifTrue: [^false].
    ^aBoolean

| aBoolean
    self == true ifTrue: [^true].
    ^aBoolean

not
    self == true ifTrue: [^false] ifFalse: [^true]
```

Clearly, the approach consisting of two subclasses is simpler and more efficient than this approach. Yet another alternative would provide booleans with an integer part where 0 represents false and any other integer represents true. This implementation, too, is less efficient because integer bit operations would be needed to "and" and "or" the integer bits.

9.6 Class CursorManager and Its Protocol

CursorManager (see Figure 9.15) provides the protocol to control the visual appearance of the cursor. The current cursor is an instance of CursorManager called **Cursor**. Changing cursors is useful, for example, to indicate a busy situation when a long computation is attempted. Without visual feedback, a user might erroneously assume the system is in an infinite loop.

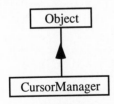

Figure 9.15 Class CursorManager provides facilities for changing the cursor.

Operations on CursorManagers

obtaining new cursors

CursorManager **normal**
CursorManager **arrow**   Same as **normal**
CursorManager **crossHair**
CursorManager **execute**
CursorManager **text**

manipulating cursors

aCursorManager **hide**   Makes the cursor disappear
aCursorManager **display**   Makes the cursor reappear
aCursorManager **changeFor**: aBlock   Uses the new cursor temporarily
                                           while executing the block

Four cursors provided by the class are illustrated in Figure 9.16.

Figure 9.16 A set of cursor icons.

Arrow or normal   Cross hair   Execute   Text

An example of changing the cursor to signal a long computation is shown below. The cursor is changed to the execute cursor during the execution of the block. It is restored to the original cursor (whatever that might have been) once the block finishes executing.

```
CursorManager execute
    changeFor: [2000 factorial printOn: Transcript]
```

9.7   The Magnitude Classes and Their Protocol

Class Magnitude (see Figure 9.17) provides facilities for a large number of subclasses such as Character, Date, Time, and Number.

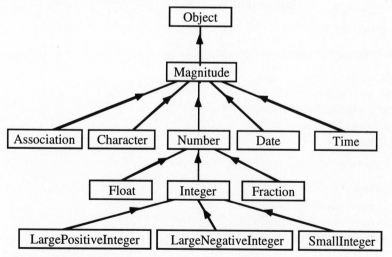

Figure 9.17 Class Magnitude has a large number of subclasses.

9.7.1 Magnitudes

When creating subclasses, the comparison operations <, <=, >, and >= must be reimplemented. The implementation in Magnitude issues an error message indicating that the subclass should have implemented it as illustrated for operation < below.

```
< aMagnitude
      ^self implementedBySubclass
```

It is also necessary to reimplement the **hash** method. A **hash** is simply an integer value that can be computed from its receiver. It should have the property that each time a particular object is hashed, the same integer is computed. It is permissible for different objects to have the same hash but it is better if they are all different. Hashes are used by dictionaries for speeding up the storage and lookup of keys. A key can be found faster if the search is restricted to other keys that have the same hash. Since all objects already understand **hash**, it is straightforward to implement new **hash** methods in terms of existing ones. For example, a **hash** method for class Money that we developed earlier could be implemented as follows:

in class Money

hash
    "Compute a hash from the instance variable totalCents."
    ^totalCents **hash** "works even if totalCents is a fraction"

All the other operations, however, can be inherited as expected. They directly use the reimplemented comparison operations.

Operations on Magnitudes

operations that subclasses must reimplement

aMagnitude < anotherMagnitude
aMagnitude <= anotherMagnitude
aMagnitude > anotherMagnitude
aMagnitude >= anotherMagnitude
aMagnitude **hash**

operations that subclasses can inherit

aMagnitude **abs**
aMagnitude **max:** anotherMagnitude
aMagnitude **min:** anotherMagnitude
aMagnitude **between:** magnitude1 **and:** magnitude2

9.7.2 Associations

An **association** is a key-value pair. Associations are important only if we need to sequence through all the keys and values in dictionaries. As we will see when we discuss collections in more detail, **associationsDo**: provides sequences of associations rather than just the keys or just the values that are provided by **keysDo**: and **do**:, respectively. Once we get an association, we need to be able to extract the key and value components using messages **k e y** and **value**, respectively. It is also possible to modify associations using **key**: and **value**: but such modifications will generally have undesirable side-effects on the dictionaries themselves. Consequently, it is of interest to implementors of dictionaries but not to users.

Operations on Associations

querying operations

anAssociation **key**
anAssociation **value**
anAssociation **key**: anObject   (Has undesirable side-effects if
anAssociation **value**: anObject   used on dictionary associations)

9.7.3 Characters

Class Character provides the typical operations for manipulating characters such as $0, $a, and $?. Associated with each character is a **digit value** (the values 0, 1, 2, ..., 9, 10, 11, ..., 35 for characters $0, $1, $2, ..., $A, $B, ..., $Z, respectively) and an **ASCII value** (an integer between 0 and 255).

Operations on Characters

constructing characters

Character **digitValue**: anInteger   Character for the integer as a digit value
Character **value**: anInteger   Character for the integer as an ascii value

converting

aCharacter **digitValue**   The digit value
aCharacter **asciiValue**   The ASCII value
aCharacter **asInteger**   The ASCII value
aCharacter **asString**   A string containing the character
aCharacter **asLowerCase**   Uppercase characters converted;
    others unchanged
aCharacter **asUpperCase**   Lowercase characters converted;
    others unchanged

querying

aCharacter **isLowerCase**	One of $a, $b, ..., $z
aCharacter **isUpperCase**	One of $A, $B, ..., $Z
aCharacter **isLetter**	One of $a, $b, ..., $z, $A, $B, ..., $Z
aCharacter **isDigit**	One of $0, $1, ..., $9
aCharacter **isAlphanumeric**	Letter or digit
aCharacter **isSeparator**	One of space, tab, carriage return, line feed, form feed
aCharacter **isVowel**	One of $a, $e, $i, $o, $u, $A, $E, $I, $O, $U

9.7.4 Numbers

Classes Number and its subclasses provide all the usual numeric facilities. So far, we have used only a small subset of these facilities. All the traditional mathematical functions, such as sin, cos, log, arc tan, along with less traditional truncation operations, such as rounding to a multiple of some integer, are supported.

Operations on Numbers

querying

aNumber **even**	No remainder when divided by 2
aNumber **odd**	A remainder when divided by 2
aNumber **positive**	aNumber >= 0
aNumber **strictlyPositive**	aNumber > 0
aNumber **negative**	aNumber < 0

simple mathematical operations

aNumber **negated**	0 - aNumber
aNumber **reciprocal**	1 / self
aNumber **// anotherNumber**	$5//3 \Rightarrow 1, -5//3 \Rightarrow -2$
aNumber **quo:** anotherNumber	5 **quo:** $3 \Rightarrow 1$, -5 **quo:** $3 \Rightarrow -1$
aNumber **\\ anotherNumber**	$5\backslash\backslash3 \Rightarrow 2, -5\backslash\backslash3 \Rightarrow 1$
aNumber **rem:** anotherNumber	5 **rem:** $3 \Rightarrow 2$, -5 **rem:** $3 \Rightarrow -2$

complex mathematical operations

aNumber **exp**	$e^{aNumber}$
aNumber **ln**	$\log_e aNumber$
aNumber **log**	$\log_{10} aNumber$
aNumber **log:** anotherNumber	$\log_{anotherNumber} aNumber$
aNumber **exp**	$e^{aNumber}$
aNumber **sqrt**	$\sqrt{aNumber}$
aNumber **squared**	$aNumber^2$

trigonometric operations

aNumber **sign**	-1 for < 0, 0 for 0, +1 for > 0
aNumber **sin**	sin of aNumber provided as an angle in radians
aNumber **cos**	cos of aNumber provided as an angle in radians
aNumber **tan**	tan of aNumber as an angle in radians
aNumber **arcSin**	Angle in radians for aNumber between -1 and 1
aNumber **arcCos**	Angle in radians for aNumber between -1 and 1
aNumber **arcTan**	Angle in radians for aNumber between $-\infty$ and ∞

raising to a power, rounding, truncating

aNumber **raisedTo**: anotherNumber	$aNumber^{anotherNumber}$
aNumber **raisedToInteger**: anInteger	$aNumber^{anInteger}$
aNumber **rounded**	1.4 **rounded** $\Rightarrow$ 1, -1.4 **rounded** $\Rightarrow$ -1
	1.6 **rounded** $\Rightarrow$ 2, -1.6 **rounded** $\Rightarrow$ -2
aNumber **roundTo**: anotherNumber	27 **roundTo**: 5 $\Rightarrow$ 25, -27 **roundTo**: 5 $\Rightarrow$ -25
	28 **roundTo**: 5 $\Rightarrow$ 30, -28 **roundTo**: 5 $\Rightarrow$ -30
aNumber **truncated**	1.4 **truncated** $\Rightarrow$ 1, -1.4 **truncated** $\Rightarrow$ -1
	1.6 **truncated** $\Rightarrow$ 1, -1.6 **truncated** $\Rightarrow$ -1
aNumber **truncateTo**: anotherNumber	27 **truncateTo**: 5 $\Rightarrow$ 25, -27 **truncateTo**: 5 $\Rightarrow$ -25
	28 **truncateTo**: 5 $\Rightarrow$ 25, -28 **truncateTo**: 5 $\Rightarrow$ -25

conversion operations

aNumber **asInteger**	
aNumber **asFloat**	
aNumber **degreesToRadians**	
aNumber **radiansToDegrees**	

operations unique to Float

Float **pi**	3.1415...

bit manipulation operations unique to Integers

anInteger **bitAnd**: anotherInteger	15 **bitAnd**: 3 $\Rightarrow$ 3
anInteger **bitor**: anotherInteger	3 **bitAnd**: 4 $\Rightarrow$ 7
anInteger **bitXor**: anotherInteger	3 **bitAnd**: 6 $\Rightarrow$ 5
anInteger **bitInvert**	0 and 1 bits switched
anInteger **bitAt**: anotherInteger	1 or 0; bits indexed 1, 2, ... from right to left
anInteger **bitShift**: anotherInteger	> 0 $\Rightarrow$ left shift, = 0 $\Rightarrow$ no shift,
	< 0 $\Rightarrow$ right shift

numerical operations unique to Integers

anInteger **factorial**	n **factorial** = n×n-1×...×3×2×1; 0 **factorial** = 1
anInteger **gcd**: anotherInteger	Greatest common divisor; 25 **gcd**: 35 $\Rightarrow$ 5
anInteger **lcm**: anotherInteger	Least common multiple; 25 **gcd**: 35 $\Rightarrow$ 175
anInteger **radix**: anotherInteger	15 **radix**: 2 $\Rightarrow$ '2r1111', 15 **radix**: 16 $\Rightarrow$ '16rF'

9.7.5 Dates and Times

Classes Date and Time were discussed and used in the previous chapter. A more complete protocol is previded here.

Operations on Dates and Times

current date and time objects

Date **today**	A new date that is current
Time **now**	A new time that is current

creating date and time objects

Date **newDay:** dayOfMonthInteger **month:** aSymbol **year:** yearInteger
Date **newDay:** dayOfYearInteger **year:** yearInteger
Date **fromDays:** anInteger   A new date from January 1, 1901

Time **hours:** integer1 **minutes:** integer2 **seconds:** integer3
Time **fromSeconds:** anInteger   A new time from seconds since midnight

querying

Date **dayOfWeek:** aSymbol	1, 2, ..., 7 for #Monday, #Tuesday, ...
Date **indexOfMonth:** aSymbol	1, 2, ..., 12 for #January, #February, ...
Date **daysInMonth:** aSymbol **forYear:** anInteger	Integer between 28 and 31
Date **daysInYear:** anInteger	365 or 366
Date **nameOfDay:** anInteger	#Monday, #Tuesday, ... for 1, 2, ..., 7
Date **nameOfMonth:** anInteger	#January, #February, ... for 1, 2, ..., 12

timing

Time **millisecondsToRun:** aBlock   A timing facility

querying

aDate **asSeconds**	Seconds since January 1, 1901
aDate **dayIndex**	An integer from 1 to 7
aDate **monthIndex**	An integer from 1 to 12
aDate **dayOfMonth**	An integer from 1 to 31
aDate **dayOfYear**	An integer from 1 to 366

aTime **asSeconds**	Seconds since midnight
aTime **hours**	Hours since midnight
aTime **minutes**	Minutes past the hour
aTime **seconds**	Seconds past the minute

mathematical operations

aDate **addDays:** anInteger	A date that is anInteger days later
aDate **subtractDays:** anInteger	A date that is anInteger days earlier
aDate **subtractDate:** anotherDate	The number of days between the dates
aTime **addTime:** anotherTime	(A time from the sum or difference between
aTime **subtractTime:** anotherTime	the respective seconds since midnight)

To time how long it takes to compute an expression, we could evaluate it as follows:

```
Time millisecondsToRun: [100 factorial]
```

To be more accurate, we might wish to execute the expression several times, take into account the cost of the iterations, and then average the result as follows:

```
I iterations time1 time2 time I
iterations := 10.
time1 := Time millisecondsToRun: [iterations timesRepeat: [100 factorial]].
time2 := Time millisecondsToRun: [iterations timesRepeat: []].
time := (time2 - time1) // iterations
```

9.8 Class Block and Its Protocol

A **block** is a sequence of zero or more Smalltalk expressions separated by periods and surrounded by square brackets; e.g., [], ['hi'], ['Transcript **show**: 'welcome'. 10 **factorial**]. In practice, each of these examples is an instance of HomeContext—there is no class called Block. The term **block** is used because of its importance as a building block for control structures. In fact, there are actually two classes involved (see Figure 9.18).

```
[] class ⇒ HomeContext
(Dictionary new at: #purple ifAbsent: [^[]]) class ⇒ Context
```

Top-level blocks are instances of HomeContext and nested blocks (blocks within blocks) are instances of Context.

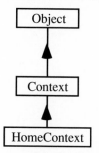

Figure 9.18 Blocks are instances of HomeContext.

Technically, each of the above illustrates a block **literal**—a representation of a block that when executed provides an instance of an appropriate context or home context. Blocks cannot be created by sending message **new** to Context or HomeContext. They can be obtained only from block literals. The example below should make it clear that a block literal is indeed similar to an array literal.

```
I anArray aBlock I
anArray := #(1 2 3 4 5 6 7 8 9 10).
aBlock := [Transcript show: 'inside a block'. 1+2].
^OrderedCollection with: anArray with: aBlock
```

All messages that require blocks as receivers or parameters can be provided either with block literals or with expressions that evaluate to blocks.

Examples with Literals	**Examples with Variables**

```
| result |
result := #(hello there).
result size > 0
    ifTrue: [Transcript cr].
```

```
| aBlock result block1 block2 |
result := #(hello there).
aBlock := [Transcript cr].
result size > 0
        ifTrue: aBlock.
```

```
[result size > 0] whileTrue: [
    result removeLast
        printOn: Transcript].
```

```
block1 := [result size > 0].
block2 := [result removeLast
        printOn: Transcript].
block1 whileTrue: block2.
```

```
1 to: 10 do: [:index |
    index printOn: Transcript.
    Transcript cr].
```

```
aBlock := [:index |
index printOn: Transcript.
    Transcript cr].
1 to: 10 do: aBlock.
```

If we provided class methods—say, in Boolean—consisting of the following:

class methods in class Boolean

trueBlock
  ^[true]

falseBlock
  ^[false]

then we could execute an example like the following:

```
aBoolean := result size > 0
    ifTrue: Boolean trueBlock
    ifFalse: Boolean falseBlock
```

which is equivalent to

```
aBoolean := result size > 0
    ifTrue: [true]
    ifFalse: [false]
```

Clearly, blocks are objects. Consequently, they can be passed around and manipulated like all other objects. In an automotive service center, for example, where customer objects are maintained in a dictionary keyed by the customer's first two initials and last name, we could provide a querying method such as **customer:ifAbsent:**, as shown below:

class	AutomotiveServiceCenter
superclass	Object
instance variables	customers ...

class methods

examples

example1
    "AutomotiveServiceCenter example1"
    "Create a global service center object"
    BytownServiceCenter := self **new**

example2
    "AutomotiveServiceCenter example2"
    "Query the global service center for a specific customer. If not there, add
    the new customer."
    BytownServiceCenter
        customer: 'J.R. Ewing'
        ifAbsent: [BytownServiceCenter **addCustomer**: 'J.R. Ewing'].

instance methods

customer recording

addCustomer: aCustomer
    "Code not shown"

customer querying

customer: aCustomer **ifAbsent**: aBlock
    ^customers **at**: aCustomer **name ifAbsent**: aBlock

Note that the Dictionary object, "customers", is queried with the standard **at:ifAbsent:** message in the last method. The block provided as parameter to the **customer:ifAbsent:** message is simply passed along to the dictionary. It will execute if and only if there is no customer with that name in the dictionary.

9.8.1 Implementing Variations of Existing Control Structures

Although we don't recommend it in practice, it is nevertheless useful as an exercise in understanding blocks to be able to provide alternative names for existing control structures or to provide minor variants of existing ones. For example, suppose that we would like to be able to execute each of the following expressions:

```
| data |
5 > 2 then: [Transcript show: 'true'] else: [Transcript show: 'false'].
[Transcript cr; show: 'hello'] iterate: 5.
data := #(1 2 3 4) asOrderedCollection.
[data removeFirst printOn: Transcript] repeatWhile: [data size > 0].
[Transcript show: 'all done'] when: [10 > 0].
```

Before we can provide methods for any of these messages, we have to be able to determine where in the class hierarchy to add the corresponding methods.

The **then:else:** message, for example, has a receiver that is either true or false; i.e., a boolean. So **then:else:** must be a method in class Boolean or in one of its subclasses True or False. We might as well place the method in the superclass Boolean and have it apply to both instances true and false.

The **iterate:** message has a block as the receiver, so a new method must be added either to Context or HomeContext. Since HomeContext inherits from Context, placing the new method in Context will ensure that it works for all blocks, regardless of whether they are top-level blocks or nested blocks. Similarly, both the **repeatWhile:** and **when:** messages must have blocks as receivers. They, too, should be instance methods in class Context. Note that the block receiving the message is referred to as "self" in each of these three methods. The last two methods also have a second block passed as a parameter—we'll call this one "anotherBlock".

The **repeatWhile:** message, by comparison with the **whileTrue:** message, has the receiver and parameter interchanged; i.e., the receiver is the body and the parameter is the boolean block. In most programming languages, the **repeatWhile:** semantics is slightly different from the **whileTrue:** semantics. The **repeatWhile:** executes the body at least once; the **whileTrue:** might not execute it at all. The only approach that we have discussed (so far) for executing a block is to use it in some control structure that requires its execution—hence, the need for the if statement that is guaranteed to execute.

instance method in class Boolean

then: thenBlock **else:** elseBlock
     ^self **ifTrue:** thenBlock **ifFalse:** elseBlock

instance method in class Context

iterate: anInteger
     ^anInteger **timesRepeat:** self

instance method in class Context

repeatWhile: anotherBlock
     "Must execute block self one or more times. Note that self is the body block and anotherBlock is the boolean block"
     true **ifTrue:** self. "force self to execute once"
     ^anotherBlock **whileTrue:** self "might execute self zero times"

instance method in class Context

when: anotherBlock
     ^anotherBlock **ifTrue:** self

The **repeat:While:** method can be simplified if we know which message to send to the block to cause it to execute. It turns out to be message **value** (one of the few block messages that we will investigate in the next section).

instance method in class Context

repeatWhile: anotherBlock
"Must execute block self one or more times. Note that self is the body block and anotherBlock is the boolean block"
self **value**. "force self to execute once"
^anotherBlock **whileTrue:** self "might execute self zero times"

9.8.2 Using Blocks to Simplify Computation

Blocks are simply "unnamed" functions. They can be invoked (or executed) by sending them one of the following messages, depending on the number of parameters. Normally, the last expression computed in the block is returned to the sender of the **value**, **value:**, or **value:value:** message.

Operations on Blocks

executing blocks

aBlock **value**
aBlock **value:** anObject
aBlock **value:** anObject **value:** anotherObject
> Causes the block parameters to be bound to the supplied parameters and the expressions within the block to execute. If a return expression is encountered, the return expression is returned from the method containing the block; otherwise, the last expression computed is returned to the sender of the appropriate **value**, **value:**, or **value:value:** message.

An error results if the number of parameters expected by the block is different from the number of parameters supplied.

```
| block1 block2 block3 |
block1 := [4 factorial].
block2 := [:integer | integer factorial].
block3 := [:integer1 :integer2 | integer1 factorial + integer2].

block1 value ⇒ 24
block2 value: 3 ⇒ 6
block3 value: 3 value: 1 ⇒ 7

block1 value: 3 ⇒ (error, incorrect number of parameters)
block1 value: 3 value: 1 ⇒ (error, incorrect number of parameters)

block2 value ⇒ (error, incorrect number of parameters)
block2 value: 3 value: 1 ⇒ (error, incorrect number of parameters)

block3 value ⇒ (error, incorrect number of parameters)
block3 value: 3 ⇒ (error, incorrect number of parameters)
```

Blocks can be used as functions in methods when the computation to be performed is repetitive. Consider an example method like the following:

```
example1
    | printFunction |
    printFunction := [:title :object |
        Transcript cr; nextPutAll: title. object printOn: Transcript].
    printFunction value: '-5 / 3 is ' value: -5 / 3.
    printFunction value: '-5 // 3 is ' value: -5 // 3.
    printFunction value: '-5 \\ 3 is ' value: -5 \\ 3.
    printFunction value: '-5 quo: 3 is ' value: (-5 quo: 3).
    printFunction value: '-5 rem: 3 is ' value: (-5 rem: 3).
```

The same idea can be applied to a number of different methods if the code they contain is relatively similar. For example, suppose a friend recently added the following three methods to array to permit the elements to be added, summed, or concatenated.

instance methods in class Array

```
sum
    | sum |
    sum := 0.
    self do: [:element | sum := sum + element].
    ^sum

product
    | product |
    product := 1.
    self do: [:element | product := product * element].
    ^product

concatenation
    | string |
    string := ''.
    self do: [:element | string := string, element].
    ^string
```

Although the methods are different, they have a striking number of similarities. They both provide different initial values and perform different operations in an identical loop. We could design a single method to serve as a base for implementing the above three, as follows:

instance methods in class Array

```
compute: aBlock startingWith: initialObject
    | result |
    result := initialObject.
    self do: [:element | result := aBlock value: result value: element].
    ^result
```

This generic method starts off by setting result to an arbitrary initial value supplied by parameter "initialObject". Next, **do:** is used to sequence through the elements of the receiving array. Each time through the loop, the block is asked to compute some arbitrary expression from result and element. Finally, the answer is remembered in "result"—permitting the process to be repeated the next time around the loop. When the loop is over, "result" is returned.

We should be able to use this general method to reimplement each of the original **sum**, **product**, and **concatenation** methods as one-line expressions.

instance methods in class Array

sum
    ^self **compute:** [:element1 :element2 |
        element1 + element2] **startingWith:** 0
product
    ^self **compute:** [:element1 :element2 |
        element1 * element2] **startingWith:** 1
concatenation
    ^self **compute:** [:element1 :element2 |
        element1, element2] **startingWith:** ''

In method **sum**, for example, the block simply adds the two parameters supplied. The **compute:startingWith:** method repetitively evaluates the block with its own choice of parameter values; namely, "result" and "element".

As it turns out, a method similar to **compute:startingWith:** is already provided in the collection library. It's called **inject:into:**. So we don't need our clever method at all.

9.8.3 Using Blocks to Implement Sophisticated Control Structures

Let's consider implementing a number of control structures in ordered collections that are similar to **do:** but more useful. In particular, let's implement **select:**, **reject:**, and **collect** with semantics that can be deduced from the following examples:

```
| anOrderedCollection |
anOrderedCollection := #(1 2 3 4 5 6 7 8 9 10) asOrderedCollection.
anOrderedCollection select: [:element | element odd]
    ⇒ OrderedCollection (1 3 5 7 9)
anOrderedCollection reject: [:element | element < 6]
    ⇒ OrderedCollection (6 7 8 9 10)
anOrderedCollection collect: [:element | element squared]
    ⇒ OrderedCollection (1 4 9 16 25 36 49 64 81 100)
anOrderedCollection collect: [:element | element printString]
    ⇒ OrderedCollection ('1' '2' '3' '4' '5' '6' '7' '8' '9' '10')
```

Both **select**: and **reject**: return a subcollection of the original elements—those that meet or fail to meet the selection or rejection criteria, respectively. Their associated block parameters return boolean values. Control structure **collect**:, on the other hand, returns only computed objects—never the original elements. Moreover, its associated block can compute arbitrary objects.

To begin with, **select**:, **reject**:, and **collect** must surely be instance methods in class OrderedCollection or in some superclass—let's assume OrderedCollection for now. (We'll consider generalizing the methods to other kinds of collections—moving it up the class hierarchy—later.) Each of these methods requires exactly one parameter—a block. Now, consider **select**:. It must evaluate the block for each element. If the result of the block is true, the element must be kept. Consequently, we must adhere to something like the following template:

```
select: aBlock
    "Keep those elements for which aBlock evaluates to true."
    (aBlock value: element$_1$) ifTrue: ["Keep element$_1$"].
    (aBlock value: element$_2$) ifTrue: ["Keep element$_2$"].
    (aBlock value: element$_3$) ifTrue: ["Keep element$_3$"].
            ...
    (aBlock value: element$_n$) ifTrue: ["Keep element$_n$"].
    ^"The kept elements"
```

We can get the successive elements by using **do**:, we can use an ordered collection to save the elements we want to keep, and we can return this ordered collection as the answer when we are done. Since **select**: is an instance method in OrderedCollection, receiver "self" is the ordered collection whose elements are to be selected.

```
select: aBlock
    "Keep those elements for which aBlock evaluates to true."
    | result |
    result := OrderedCollection new.
    self do: [:element |
        (aBlock value: element) ifTrue: [result add: element]].
    ^result
```

Method **reject**: can be implemented in a similar manner by keeping only those that are not rejected by the block.

```
reject: aBlock
    "Discard those elements for which aBlock evaluates to true; i.e., keep
    those for which aBlock evaluates to false."
    | result |
    result := OrderedCollection new.
    self do: [:element |
        (aBlock value: element) ifFalse: [result add: element]].
    ^result
```

Alternatively, we could just as easily implement **reject**: in terms of **select**:. The result is simpler and more compact.

> **reject**: aBlock
>   "Discard those elements for which aBlock evaluates to true; i.e., keep those for which aBlock evaluates to false."
>   ^self **select**: [:element | (aBlock **value**: element) **=** false]

This is equivalent to the following:

> **reject**: aBlock
>   "Discard those elements for which aBlock evaluates to true; i.e., keep those for which aBlock evaluates to false."
>   ^self **select**: [:element | (aBlock **value**: element) **not**]

Presumably, method **collect**: is very similar. However, rather than store away the elements, we must simply store away the object returned from the block evaluation.

> **collect**: aBlock
>   "Keep the objects returned from evaluating the block."
> | result |
>   result := OrderedCollection **new**.
>   self **do**: [:element |
>   result **add**: (aBlock **value**: element)].
>   ^result

Finally, let's add one more method that simultaneously selects and collects computed objects. The intent is to provide a method that works as follows:

> | anOrderedCollection |
> anOrderedCollection := #(1 2 3 4 5 6 7 8 9 10) **asOrderedCollection**.
> anOrderedCollection
>   **when**: [:element | element **odd**]
>   **collect**: [:element | element **squared**]
>   ⇒ OrderedCollection (1 9 25 49 81)

We need to implement the method in such a manner that if an element satisfies the when (or selection) block, then the collect block value is saved.

> **when**: selectBlock **collect**: collectBlock
>   "Keep the objects returned from evaluating the collect block if it satisfies the select block."
> | result |
>   result := OrderedCollection **new**.
>   self **do**: [:element |
>   (selectBlock **value**: element) "do we want it"
>   **ifTrue**: [result **add**: (collectBlock **value**: element)]].
>   ^result

Of course, we could use this method to implement all the others, either directly or indirectly, as follows:

```
collect: aBlock
    "Keep the objects returned from evaluating the block."
    ^self when: [:element | true "always"] collect: aBlock

select: aBlock
    "Keep those elements for which aBlock evaluates to true."
    ^self when: aBlock collect: [:element | element "the original"

reject: aBlock
    "Discard those elements for which aBlock evaluates to true; i.e., keep
    those for which aBlock evaluates to false."
    ^self
        when:   [:element | (aBlock value: element1) not]
        collect: [:element | element "the original"
```

Alternatively, we could have implemented the original **when:collect:** in terms of **select:** and **reject:** (our current preferred solution).

```
when: selectBlock collect: collectBlock
    "Keep the objects returned from evaluating the collect block if it satisfies
    the select block. Implemented by first selecting the desired elements and
    then collecting the results."
    ^(self select: selectBlock) collect: collectBlock
```

To finish up this section, we should now generalize our methods to apply to many different kinds of collections—even those we might not already be familiar with. If we did, we would be able to execute the following:

```
| anArray |
anArray := #(1 2 3 4 5 6 7 8 9 10).
anArray
    select: [:element | element odd] ⇒ (1 3 5 7 9)
anArray asOrderedCollection
    select: [:element | element odd] ⇒ OrderedCollection (1 3 5 7 9)
anArray asSet
    select: [:element | element odd] ⇒ Set (1 3 5 7 9)
anArray asBag
    select: [:element | element odd] ⇒ Bag (1 3 5 7 9)
anArray asSortedCollection
    select: [:element | element odd] ⇒ SortedCollection (1 3 5 7 9)
```

The idea here is that the receiver determines the resulting kind of collection. If the receiver is an array, for example, the result is an array. If it's a set, the result is a set. Our original implementation is not adequate, because it always returns an ordered collection. The following is a first attempt at a solution. We begin by moving the method higher up in the hierarchy to Collection, the highest collection class.

instance method in class Collection
select: aBlock
    "Keep those elements for which aBlock evaluates to true."
    | result |
    result := OrderedCollection **new**.
    self **do**: [:element |
        (aBlock **value**: element1) **ifTrue**: [result **add**: element]].
    (self **isKindOf**: Array) **ifTrue**: [^result **asArray**].
    (self **isKindOf**: OrderedCollection) **ifTrue**: [^result].
    (self **isKindOf**: Set) **ifTrue**: [^result **asSet**].
    (self **isKindOf**: Bag) **ifTrue**: [^result **asBag**].
    (self **isKindOf**: Dictionary) **ifTrue**: [^result "oh oh, a problem"].
    self **error**: 'unexpected collection class'

There are three problems with this implementation. First, if the receiver is a dictionary, the selected values have corresponding keys that are discarded. The resulting dictionary should contain these old keys. Second, we probably have not considered all the different collection classes, so error messages will result in some cases. Most users will simply assume that the implementation was not fully completed—a black mark for the implementor. Third, **class-based cases** are inadequate and, in fact, totally inappropriate in any implementation that has to be immune to future changes. For example, if class Set is removed from the system, this method will need to be fixed. More important, the addition of a new class (a user-defined collection class, for example) also requires a change to the method. A solution is needed that does not require changes when classes are added or removed.

One solution is to replace the long list of cases with code such as the following:

    ^self **class new addAll**: result

This turns out to work just fine for ordered collections, sets, and bags, but not for arrays and dictionaries. In the case of an array, for example, we get an empty array (an array of size 0) that has no room for elements. Another solution is the following:

    ^(self **class new**: result **size**) **addAll**: result

This turns out to get an array of the correct size (it also works for ordered collections, sets, and bags, since the size is interpreted as a hint or initial guess), but arrays don't understand **add**:, which is used by **addAll**:. Alternatively, we might use the following instead:

    ^(self **class new**: result **size**) **replaceFrom**: 1 **to**: result **size with**: result

Now, it's sets and bags that don't understand **replaceFrom:to:with:**. As it turns out, the solution used in the Smalltalk library is to implement the method three times: once in Collection to handle set-like collections that use **add:**, once in IndexedCollection to handle array-like collections that use **at:put:**, and once in Dictionary to handle dictionary-like collections. (We'll leave it to the reader to look up these individual implementations.) In fact, it is a wonder that three implementations are sufficient for all collections. How, for example, do they handle intervals that permit the following?

(1 **to:** 10) **select:** [:element | (element **odd**) & (element ~= 5)] $\Rightarrow$ (1 3 7 9)

Surely, the result cannot be an interval (it cannot be of the form "a **to:** b **by:** c") because there is a missing integer in the middle of the sequence. The result is actually returned as an array. To handle such possibilities easily, an instance method **species** was added to class Object and Interval (among others), as shown below:

instance method in class Object
species
    "The class for the receiver"
    ^self **class**

instance method in class Interval
species
    "The substitute class for the receiver"
    ^Array

The various implementations of **select:** then make use of code such as the following instead of the equivalent code shown earlier.

^(self **species new:** result **size**) **addAll:** result
^(self **species new:** result **size**) **replaceFrom:** 1 **to:** result **size with:** result

9.8.4 The Effect of Returns on Blocks

In the previous sections, none of the block examples made use of return statements. But such returns are pervasive. For example, consider the following methods taken from the existing Smalltalk library:

instance method in class Collection

includes: anObject
    "Answer true if the receiver contains an element equal to anObject, else answer false."
    self **do:** [:element | anObject = element **ifTrue:** [^true]].
    ^false

instance method in class IndexedCollection

= aCollection
>"Answer true if the elements contained by the receiver are equal to the elements contained by the argument aCollection."
>| index |
>self == aCollection **ifTrue:** [^true].
>(self **class** == aCollection **class**) **ifFalse:** [^false].
>index := self **size**.
>[index ~= aCollection] **whileFalse:** [
>>(self **at:** index) = (aCollection **at:** index) **ifFalse:** [^false].
>>index := index - 1].
>
>^true

instance method in class IndexedCollection

indexOf: anObject **ifAbsent:** aBlock
>"Answer the index position of the element equal to anObject in the receiver. If no such element is found, evaluate aBlock (without any arguments)."
>| index size |
>size := self **size**. index := 1.
>[index <= size] **whileTrue:** [
>>(self **at:** index) = anObject **ifTrue:** [^index].
>>index := index + 1].
>
>^aBlock **value**

Each of these methods illustrates returns in either an **ifTrue:** block or an **ifFalse:** block. Moreover, some of these returns are embedded in enclosing **do:**, **whileTrue:**, and **whileFalse:** blocks. As expected, when a return is encountered, the return value is returned to the sender of the message that caused execution to proceed in the current method.

There are no new concepts to discover, here. A return executed inside method **indexOf:ifAbsent:**, for example, causes a value to be returned to the sender of the **indexOf:ifAbsent:** message—provided that we get to the return in question. You can't return twice from the same method. For example, if "^index" is executed in the body of the **whileTrue:**, control immediately returns to the sender of message **indexOf:ifAbsent:**. We'll never get out of the loop to execute "^aBlock **value**".

But what about "^aBlock **value**"? Is it possible that the block value might not come back? Notice that aBlock is not defined in the current method. It was passed as a parameter. What if it contains a return statement that is executed? In that case, we won't get any answer back, because such an answer comes back from the **value** message only if the end of the block is encountered—at which time, the last value computed is provided as the answer. If aBlock executes an internal return statement, the return result will be returned to the sender of the message for the method that contains the block referenced by "aBlock"—not the **indexOf:ifAbsent:** method above.

To elaborate further on this last point, let's consider a simpler example. We can easily create a number of methods such as the following (say, class methods in

Object). Each method **a**, **b**, **c**, **d:**, **e:**, and **f:** in the list prints a simple message at both the beginning and the end of the method and then sends a message to the next one in the list. In method **d:**, roughly in the middle of the list, a block is passed along to the end. This block is executed in the middle of **f:**. The question is, "What prints on the transcript when expression "Object **a**" is executed?"

```
a
    "Object a"
    Transcript cr; show: 'Start of a'.
    self b.
    Transcript cr; show: 'End of a'
b
    Transcript cr; show: '    Start of b'.
    self c.
    Transcript cr; show: '    End of b'
c
    Transcript cr; show: '        Start of c'.
    self d: [^#anything].
    Transcript cr; show: '        End of c'
d: aBlock
    Transcript cr; show: '            Start of d:'.
    self e: aBlock.
    Transcript cr; show: '            End of d:'
e: aBlock
    Transcript cr; show: '                Start of e:'.
    self f: aBlock.
    Transcript cr; show: '                End of e:'
f: aBlock
    Transcript cr; show: '                    Start of f:'.
    aBlock value.
    Transcript cr; show: '                    End of f:'
```

If the block were of the form "[#anything]" rather than "[^#anything]"; i.e., if the block did not contain a return, the following output would be expected on the transcript:

```
Start of a
    Start of b
        Start of c
            Start of d:
                Start of e:
                    Start of f:
                    End of f:
                End of e:
            End of d:
        End of c
    End of b
End of a
```

With "[^#anything]", however, an entirely different output results. Before we look at this output, consider method "**c**" above. What should happen when the block "[^#anything]" is sent a **value** message? Clearly, #anything should be returned from method "**c**". This should happen in spite of the fact that message **value** is sent to the block by method "**f:**". In other words, when method "**f:**" sends a **value** message to the block, control never comes back, because execution returns from method "**c**". Consequently, the following output results:

```
Start of a
    Start of b
        Start of c
            Start of d:
                Start of e:
                    Start of f:
    End of b
End of a
```

We can summarize all this as follows:

> A **value**, **value:**, or **value:value:** *message sent to a block either returns with the last expression computed in the block (if no return statement is encountered in the block) or returns from the method containing the block (if a return statement is successfully executed inside the block).*

Knowing this, it should be clear why the following examples return the values indicated. In both cases, the **ifAbsent:** block is executed, since there is no #black key. The first example immediately returns nil and the second returns #notThere. In the second case, there is no "^" in the **ifAbsent:** block. Consequently, nil is the result of the block which is returned from the **at:ifAbsent:** message. Hence, answer is bound to nil, and execution proceeds further to return #notThere.

example1
```
"This example returns nil—instead of #notThere or #there."
| answer aDictionary |
... code to initialize aDictionary with keys #red, #green, #blue ...
answer := aDictionary at: #black ifAbsent: [^nil]. "Note the ^."
answer isNil
    ifTrue: [^#notThere]
    ifFalse: [^#there]
```

example2
```
"This example returns #notThere."
| answer aDictionary |
... code to initialize aDictionary with keys #red, #green, #blue ...
answer := aDictionary at: #black ifAbsent: [nil]. "There is NO ^."
answer isNil
    ifTrue: [^#notThere]
    ifFalse: [^#there]
```

Another implication of the above is that *there is no point storing blocks (either in instance variables or global variables) if they contain return statements*. Why not? Consider the following example:

a class method in class Object

example1
    "This example returns a block that is evaluated later."
    | aBlock |
    aBlock := [self **subclasses size** > 20
        ifTrue: [^'Object has more than 20 subclasses']
        ifFalse: [^'Object has 20 subclasses or less']].
    ^aBlock

Now, we could test it as follows:

    "First, store the block obtained from example1 above."
    GlobalVariable := Object **example1**.
    "Next, try to evaluate the block."
    GlobalVariable **value** $\Rightarrow$ (**error**, you can't return twice from the same method)

When the **example1** message is sent to Object, the block is returned from method **example1**. When a **value** message is sent to the block, a return from method **example1** is attempted a second time. We said before that you can't return twice from the same method. Of course, the above would have worked just fine if the block had contained no return statements as shown below.

a class method in class Object

example1
    "This example returns a block that is evaluated later."
    | aBlock |
    aBlock := [self **subclasses size** > 20
        ifTrue: ['Object has more than 20 subclasses']
        ifFalse: ['Object has 20 subclasses or less']].
    ^aBlock

9.9 The Graphical Classes and Their Protocol

As can be seen in Figure 9.19, quite a large number of classes are devoted to graphics. Points are used to indicate positions on the screen or in an application's pane and rectangles are used to delineate rectangular areas. Neither points nor rectangles have the ability to display themselves. However, pens can be used to display circles, ellipses, rectangles, and arbitrarily shaped objects both filled (colored) and unfilled, in addition to displaying bitmaps, which are colored pictures. Bitmaps are easily constructed in paint programs outside the Smalltalk environment, pasted into the clipboard, and then imported into Smalltalk through the unique global called **Clipboard**, an instance of ClipboardManager.

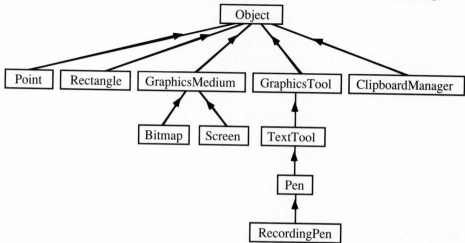

Figure 9.19 The graphical classes.

A point representing both an x-coordinate and a y-coordinate; e.g., 10@20 with x-coordinate 10 and y-coordinate 20, is essentially a two-dimensional vector with associated vector arithmetic. As can be seen below, a large number of operations are supported. Many of the point operations permit numbers and points that we referred to as the **scale**. Both "aPoint + (10@5)" and "aPoint + 1" are legal.

In Smalltalk/V Windows, the **origin** (coordinate 0@0) of the coordinate system for a screen, bitmap, or pane is the top-left corner. The positive x-axis is directed to the right and the positive y-axis is directed downward. The end diagonally opposite of the origin is called the **corner**.

In Smalltalk/V for OS/2, the origin, by contrast, is the bottom-left corner. The positive x-axis is directed to the right (as in Windows) but the positive y-axis is directed upward.

As a consequence, adding an amount like 10@20 to a point in V Windows results in a point that is lower. In V for OS/2, however, it results in a point that is higher. In an effort to make it possible to write code that is portable between the two different dialects of Smalltalk, coordinate system independent methods are provided in Number, Point, and Rectangle. Rather than write

aPoint + (10@20)

with corresponding incompatible semantics in the two different systems, we can instead write

aPoint **rightAndDown**: (10@20)

and be guaranteed of identical results. Note that going right -10 is equivalent to going left 10. Similarly, going down -10 is equivalent to going up 10.

Operations on Numbers

coordinate system independent querying

aNumber **leftMost**: anotherNumber
aNumber **rightMost**: anotherNumber
aNumber **higherOf**: anotherNumber
aNumber **lowerOf**: anotherNumber

aNumber **isAbove**: anotherNumber
aNumber **isBelow**: anotherNumber
aNumber **isLeftOf**: anotherNumber
aNumber **isRightOf**: anotherNumber

aNumber **isAboveEqual**: anotherNumber	Above or equal
aNumber **isBelowEqual**: anotherNumber	Below or equal
aNumber **isLeftEqual**: anotherNumber	Left of or equal
aNumber **isRightEqual**: anotherNumber	Right of or equal

coordinate system independent manipulation

aNumber **left**: anotherNumber
aNumber **right**: anotherNumber
aNumber **up**: anotherNumber
aNumber **down**: anotherNumber

Operations on Points

instance creation

aNumber @ aNumber

instance manipulation

aPoint + scale	aPoint - scale	aPoint * scale
aPoint / scale	aPoint // scale	aPoint \\ scale
aPoint **abs**	aPoint **max**: aPoint	aPoint **min**: aPoint
aPoint **negated**	aPoint **rounded**	aPoint **truncated**
aPoint **transpose**		

aPoint < scale	aPoint = scale	aPoint > scale
aPoint <= scale	aPoint >= scale	aPoint ~= scale

aPoint **between:** point1 **and:** point2
aPoint **moveBy:** anotherPoint   Destructively adds anotherPoint to aPoint
aPoint **dotProduct:** anotherPoint   Sum of the product of corresponding x-
                                        and y-coordinates

coordinate system independent operations

aPoint **isBefore:** aPoint   True if text-wise earlier

aPoint **isLeftAndAbove:** anotherPoint
aPoint **isLeftAndBelow:** anotherPoint
aPoint **isRightAndAbove:** anotherPoint
aPoint **isRightAndBelow:** anotherPoint

aPoint **leftAndDown:** delta
aPoint **leftAndUp:** delta
aPoint **leftMostAndHighest:** anotherPoint   Leftmost x; highest y
aPoint **leftMostAndLowest:** anotherPoint   Leftmost x; lowest y

aPoint **rightAndDown:** delta
aPoint **rightAndUp:** delta
aPoint **rightMostAndHighest:** anotherPoint   Rightmost x; highest y
aPoint **rightMostAndLowest:** anotherPoint   Rightmost x; lowest y

aPoint **up:** anInteger
aPoint **down:** anInteger
aPoint **left:** anInteger
aPoint **right:** anInteger

Rectangles can be specified by providing any two diagonally opposite corner points or by providing one of the two leftmost points along with an **extent** (a width and a height). The top or bottom of a rectangle refers to the highest or lowest y-coordinate. Similarly, the left or right of a rectangle is the leftmost or rightmost x-coordinate. Although it is customary to refer to different points in a rectangle, such as the top-left point or the bottom-right point, by specifying the height first, the messages used to request these points from a rectangle are named using the convention that the x-coordinate is specified first and the y-coordinate second. Thus, we get the top-left point by sending message **leftTop** to the rectangle. Similarly, we get the bottom-right point by sending message **rightBottom**.

Operations on Rectangles

coordinate system dependent instance creation

aPoint **corner**: anotherPoint
aPoint **extent**: anotherPoint

Rectangle **origin**: originPoint **corner**: cornerPoint
Rectangle **origin**: originPoint **extent**: extentPoint

coordinate system independent instance creation

aPoint **rightBottom**: anotherPoint	aPoint must be leftTop
aPoint **rightTop**: anotherPoint	aPoint must be leftBottom
aPoint **extentFromLeftBottom**: anotherPoint	aPoint must be leftBottom
aPoint **extentFromLeftTop**: anotherPoint	aPoint must be leftTop

Rectangle **leftBottom**: leftBottomPoint **extent**: extentPoint
Rectangle **leftBottom**: leftBottomPoint **rightTop**: rightTopPoint
Rectangle **leftTop**: leftTopPoint **extent**: extentPoint
Rectangle **leftTop**: leftTopPoint **rightBottom**: rightBottomPoint

Rectangle **leftBottomUnit**	(Coordinates for
Rectangle **leftTopUnit**	a rectangle of
Rectangle **rightBottomUnit**	width 1 and
Rectangle **rightTopUnit**	height 1)

querying and modifying

aRectangle **top**
aRectangle **center**
aRectangle **bottom**
aRectangle **left**
aRectangle **right**
aRectangle **origin**
aRectangle **corner**

aRectangle **leftTop**
aRectangle **leftTop**: aPoint
aRectangle **leftBottom**
aRectangle **leftBottom**: aPoint
aRectangle **rightTop**
aRectangle **rightTop**: aPoint   (This method is missing)
aRectangle **rightBottom**
aRectangle **rightBottom**: aPoint

aRectangle **width**
aRectangle **width**: anInteger
aRectangle **height**
aRectangle **height**: anInteger

rectangle manipulation

aRectangle **rounded**
aRectangle **truncated**
aRectangle **scaleBy**: delta
aRectangle **translateBy**: delta
aRectangle **containsPoint**: aPoint
aRectangle **intersect**: aRectangle
aRectangle **intersects**: aRectangle
aRectangle **moveBy**: aPoint
aRectangle **moveTo**: aPoint
aRectangle **expandBy**: delta
aRectangle **insetBy**: delta
aRectangle **merge**: aRectangle

Bitmaps are one of the more important graphical objects, because they provide arbitrarily complex color pictures that can be displayed either on other bitmaps or on the screen. Both bitmaps and screens are graphical mediums that keep track of their own extent, their bounding box (a rectangle with origin 0@0 of the same extent), and their own pen. Technically, the **pen** can be any graphics tool, including a text tool (so the word pen is a slight misnomer). Pens, and more generally, graphics tools, keep track of their associated graphics mediums. In other words, correlated graphics mediums and graphics tools know about each other.

Operations on GraphicsMediums

querying

aGraphicsMedium **width**
aGraphicsMedium **height**
aGraphicsMedium **extent**
aGraphicsMedium **boundingBox**
aGraphicsMedium **pen**

Operations on GraphicsTools

querying

aGraphicsTool **graphicsMedium**

Bitmaps can be constructed in paint programs such as Paintbrush which is supplied with Program Manager in Microsoft Windows. Such bitmaps can be selected and either copied into the clipboard or saved in a file with suffix **.bmp**; e.g., a file named **Picture.bmp**. In Smalltalk, the bitmap can be extracted from the clipboard by sending message **getBitmap** to global **Clipboard**, an instance of class ClipboardManager. Alternatively, it can be obtained from the file by executing Bitmap **fromFile**: 'Picture.bmp'.

It is also possible to create bitmaps from pictures already visible on the screen or by obtaining an instance of a specific extent (see below). The bitmap's pen can then be used to draw on the bitmap. Alternatively, it can be used to copy over bits and pieces from other bitmaps (as we will review in more detail below).

Bitmaps must be released when they are no longer needed. Consequently, updating a bitmap, for example, requires a strategy such as the following:

> MyMostPreciousPicture **release**.
> MyMostPreciousPicture := Clipboard **getBitmap**

The space occupied by the bits is not returned until either the bitmap is released or until an exit from Smalltalk is performed.

Operations on ClipboardManagers

copying and pasting bitmaps

Clipboard **getBitmap**
Clipboard **getString**
Clipboard **setBitmap**: aBitmap
Clipboard **setString**: aBitmap

Operations on Bitmaps

instance creation

Bitmap **extent**: aPoint	A new black and white bitmap
Bitmap **screenExtent**: aPoint	A new color bitmap
Bitmap **fromFile**: aBmpBitmapFileName	A file with suffix .bmp
Bitmap **fromScreen**: aRectangle	A copy of a portion of the screen
Bitmap **fromUser**	As above but prompts for rectangle

querying

aBitmap **isColor**	Color?
aBitmap **isMono**	Black and white?

miscellaneous

aBitmap **displayAt**: aPoint **with**: aPen
aBitmap **outputToFile**: aBmpBitmapFileName
aBitmap **release**

Any display medium can be copied to another medium by asking the intended receiver's pen to copy the graphical data. For data on arbitrary mediums, messages of the form **copy:**... should be used. Such messages are necessary for copying information from the screen to a bitmap (or vice versa), for example. Recall that global **Display** is an instance of Screen—not Bitmap. If the data is known to reside in a bitmap, messages of the form **copyBitmap:**... can be used instead.

If the from- and to-rectangles are the same size (or a message specifying only the from-rectangle is used), the information is copied unchanged; otherwise, it is compressed or magnified to fill the new rectangular area. Normally, the rectangular area is the entire area of the medium, which can be obtained by asking the medium for it **boundingBox**.

The **raster** constants (denoted rC below) are special constants indicating how the source and destination bits are to be combined. They include (among others)

Srccopy	use source bits only
Srcand	"and" source and destination bits
Srcpaint	"or" source and destination bit
Srcinvert	"xor" source and destination bits

When not specified, the default raster constant used is Srccopy. Very interesting effects can be achieved by performing boolean operations (and, or, and not) on the source and destination bits.

Operations on GraphicsTools (Pens and TextTools Are Interchangeable)

copying display medium information (works for bitmaps and screens)

toPen **copy**: fromPen **from**: fromRectangle **at**: toPoint
toPen **copy**: fromPen **from**: fromRectangle **at**: toPoint **rule**: rC
toPen **copy**: fromPen **from**: fromRectangle **to**: toRectangle
toPen **copy**: fromPen **from**: fromRectangle **to**: toRectangle **rule**: rC

copying bitmap information (works only for bitmaps)

toPen **copyBitmap**: aBitmap **from**: fromRectangle **at**: toPoint
toPen **copyBitmap**: aBitmap **from**: fromRectangle **at**: toPoint **rule**: rC
toPen **copyBitmap**: aBitmap **from**: fromRectangle **to**: toRectangle
toPen **copyBitmap**: aBitmap **from**: fromRectangle **to**: toRectangle **rule**: rC

An example might serve to indicate how we can construct a bitmap given a file containing a picture of a clock. Suppose our goal was to create a bitmap with two superimposed pictures of different sizes, a small picture of the clock in the middle of a larger picture of the same clock.

```
| originalClockBitmap desiredClockBitmap |
originalClockBitmap := Bitmap fromFile: 'Clock.bmp'.
desiredClockBitmap := Bitmap screenExtent: 300@300. "a color bitmap"
desiredClockBitmap pen "first, get a copy that is full size"
    copyBitmap: originalClockBitmap
    from: originalClockBitmap boundingBox
    to: desiredClockBitmap boundingBox.
```

```
desiredClockBitmap pen "second, place a much smaller copy in the center"
    copyBitmap: originalClockBitmap
    from: originalClockBitmap boundingBox
    to: (desiredClockBitmap boundingBox insetBy: 130@130). "will be 40@40"
desiredClockBitmap outputToFile: 'NewClock.bmp'.
originalClockBitmap release.
desiredClockBitmap release.
```

Graphics-tool operations are partitioned into four classes: abstract class GraphicsTool and the three concrete subclasses TextTool, Pen, and RecordingPen. The abstract class is concerned with managing colors and the location of the tool. Color can be created from red, green, and blue components, where each component is an integer between 0 (indicating no color) and 255 (indicating maximum color). Colors can also be obtained from preset constants in pool dictionary **ColorConstants**; e.g., ClrRed, ClrGreen, ClrBlue, ClrPink, or ClrYellow.

A closed figure such as a circle has a boundary that is colored in the **foreColor** and an interior that is colored in the **backColor**. A pen's medium can be filled by specifying color, the rectangular area to be filled, and a raster constant with the same interpretation as for the copy operations discussed earlier.

Operations on GraphicsTools

color creation and manipulation

GraphicsTool **red**: red **green**: green **blue**: blue
> An integer representing an RGB color value where each of the three color components is in the range 0 to 255.

aGraphicsTool **foreColor**
aGraphicsTool **foreColor**: color
aGraphicsTool **backColor**
aGraphicsTool **backColor**: color

aGraphicsTool **erase**
aGraphicsTool **blank**: aRectangle
aGraphicsTool **fill**: color
aGraphicsTool **fill**: aRectangle **color**: color
aGraphicsTool **fill**: aRectangle **rule**: rasterConstant
aGraphicsTool **fill**: aRectangle **rule**: rasterConstant **color**: color
aGraphicsTool **reverse**: aRectangle
> Fills the specified rectangle (default is the entire medium) with the supplied color (default is the background color) using the specified raster constant (defaults to Srccopy) or reverses the color in the last case.

tool placement

aGraphicsTool **location**
aGraphicsTool **place:** aPoint

Class TextTool provides additional facilities for drawing text at indicated points or at the current location. Fonts are generally specified via special menus in browsers and workspaces. As a user, it is generally sufficient to make use of the font associated with a text tool.

Operations on TextTools

drawing

aTextTool **bell**	Useful for debugging
aTextTool **font**	
aTextTool **font:** aFont	
aTextTool **setTextColor:** color	
aTextTool **centerText:** aString	
aTextTool **centerText:** aString **at:** aPoint	
aTextTool **displayText:** aString	
aTextTool **displayText:** aString **at:** aPoint	
aTextTool **stringWidthOf:** aString	Width in pixels in current font

Pens provide a large number of graphical drawing operations. Some are obvious but others are quite complex.

Operations on Pens

pen manipulations

aPen **up**	
aPen **down**	
aPen **direction**	East is 0°, south is 90°
aPen **direction:** anInteger	
aPen **north**	270°
aPen **turn:** anInteger	+ve is clockwise
aPen **home**	To center of medium
aPen **go:** anInteger	Draws in current direction if down
aPen **goto:** aPoint	Draws if down
aPen **lineWidth**	
aPen **setLineWidth:** anInteger	

drawing (simple operations)

aPen **box:** aBottomRightPoint	Pen located at top-left
aPen **boxFilled:** aBottomRightPoint	Pen located at top-left
aPen **boxOfSize:** extentFromTopLeft	Pen located at top-left
aPen **circle:** radius	Pen located at center
aPen **circleFilled:** radius	Pen located at center

drawing (simple operations — continued)

aPen **polygon**: anArrayOfPoints
aPen **polygonFilled**: anArrayOfPoints
aPen **ellipse**: major **minor**: minor   Pen located at center
aPen **ellipseFilled**: major **minor**: minor   Major is x-radius, minor is y-radius

drawing (complex operations)

aPen **box**: point1 **filled**: boolean1 **outlined**: boolean2 **roundCorner**: point2
    The roundedness of the corner is specified by point2, the major and
    minor radii of an ellipse. Small radii, such as 1@1, have sharper corners
    than larger ones, such as 100@100.
aPen **curveFrom**: p1 **to**: p3 **towards**: p2
aPen **partialArc**: major **minor**: minor **angles**: aPoint   Pen at center
aPen **chord**: major **minor**: minor **angles**: aPoint   Pen at center
aPen **chordFilled**: major **minor**: minor **angles**: aPoint   Pen at center
aPen **pie**: major **minor**: minor **angles**: aPoint   Pen at center
aPen **pieFilled**: major **minor**: minor **angles**: aPoint   Pen at center

All drawing operations except **polygon:**, **polygonFilled:**, and **curveFrom:to:-towards:** assume the pen is located either at the top-left corner (for box-like drawings) or in the center (for elliptical or pie-like drawings). The first case is not coordinate system independent since the pen is assumed to be at the bottom-left corner in Smalltalk/V for OS/2. The following example illustrates all of the simple drawing facilities (see Figure 9.20 for the result):

```
| pen |
pen := (GraphPane openWindow: 'Simple' extent: 220@200) pen.
pen
    foreColor: ClrBlack; backColor: ClrYellow;

    "First line."
    place: 20@0; box: 40@20;
    place: 60@0; boxFilled: 80@20;
    place: 100@0; boxOfSize: 20@20;

    "Second line."
    place: 30@40; circle: 10;
    place: 70@40; circleFilled: 10;

    "Third line."
    place: 30@70; ellipse: 20 minor: 10;
    place: 70@70; ellipseFilled: 20 minor: 10;

    "Fourth line."
    polygon: (Array with: 30@90 with: 40@110 with: 20@110);
    polygonFilled: (Array with: 70@90 with: 80@110 with: 60@110);
    yourself
```

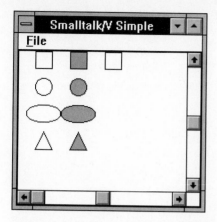

Figure 9.20 Illustrating some of the simple drawing facilities.

The more complex drawing facilities make use of the notion of **drawing angles**, a point in the form startAngle@amountToSweepAsAnAngle. For example, an arc that must be drawn from start angle θ with sweep angle ω would be specified with drawing angles $\theta@\omega$, as shown in Figure 9.21.

The arc to be drawn

Figure 9.21 Illustrating drawing angles $\theta@\omega$.

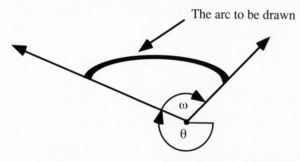

StartAngle θ SweepAngle ω

The distinction between **arcs** (curved lines), **chords** (areas bounded by a curved line and a straight line connecting the start and end points), and **pies** (areas bounded by a curved line drawn from a center and the two lines that connect the center to the end points) is relatively clear once you see an example. Figure 9.22 illustrates an arc at the top-left, a chord immediately below it, and a pie at the bottom-left. Of all the figures drawn, the most difficult to control is the curve constructed from message **curveFrom: to:towards:**.

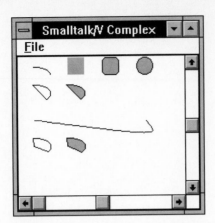

Figure 9.22 Illustrating some of the more complex drawing facilities.

Figure 9.22 was constructed from the code below. Note that the first of the three boxes at the top has no outline and the boxes have corners that are progressively more rounded. In fact, the third box looks more like a circle.

```
I pen I
pen := (GraphPane openWindow: 'Complex' extent: 220@200) pen.
pen
        foreColor: ClrRed; backColor: ClrYellow;

        "First line."
        place: 20@20;
            partialArc: 20 minor: 10 angles: -90@90;
        place: 60@0;
            box: 80@20 filled: true outlined: false roundCorner: 1@1;
        place: 100@0;
            box: 120@20 filled: true outlined: true roundCorner: 10@10;
        place: 140@0;
            box: 160@20 filled: true outlined: true roundCorner: 100@100;

        "Second line."
        place: 20@40; chord: 20 minor: 10 angles: -90@135;
        place: 60@40; chordFilled: 20 minor: 10 angles: -90@135;

        "Third line."
        curveFrom: 20@70 to: 150@70 towards: 170@90;

        "Fourth line."
        place: 20@100; pie: 20 minor: 10 angles: -90@135;
        place: 60@100; pieFilled: 20 minor: 10 angles: -90@135;
        yourself
```

Finally, recording pens have facilities for recording their behavior so that the drawings instructions can be reconstructed when a window is uncovered, for example. Recording pens can be used in one of three different modes: **draw mode**, which draws the figures but does not record it; **retain mode**, which records the figure but does not draw it; and **draw-and-retain mode**, which both draws and records the figure. The default is draw mode. A polygon, for example, would be processed in draw-and-retain mode by executing the associated messages within a draw-and-retain block, as follows:

recordingPen **drawRetainPicture**: [
   recordingPen
       polygon: (Array **with**: 30@90 **with**: 40@110 **with**: 20@110)]

The other modes are similar. Each use of **drawPicture:**, **retainPicture:**, and **draw-RetainPicture**: causes a segment to be created that retains the drawing instructions in a special **stored picture** object. It is possible to reference these segments through segment numbers and force the pen to draw only selected segments. However, such facilities are needed only for relatively advanced applications.

Operations on RecordingPens

drawing

aRecordingPen **segmentIsOpen**	True if a segment is available
aRecordingPen **openSegment**	Creates segment; returns segment number
aRecordingPen **currentId**	The current segment number
aRecordingPen **deleteCurrentSegment**	
aRecordingPen **deleteSegment**: segmentNumber	
aRecordingPen **deleteAllSegments**	
aRecordingPen **drawSegment**: segmentNumber	
aRecordingPen **drawPicture**: aBlock	Execute aBlock in draw mode
aRecordingPen **retainPicture**: aBlock	Execute aBlock in retain mode
aRecordingPen **drawRetainPicture**: aBlock	Execute aBlock in both modes

9.10 The Collection Classes and Their Protocol

The collection classes form a large sublibrary in Smalltalk (see Figure 9.23). Three abstract classes are clearly noticeable: Collection, IndexedCollection, and FixedSizeCollection. Sets are unordered collections that contain no duplicates. They cannot be accessed by indexing—**do**: is typically used to sequence through the elements. Bags are similarly unordered collections, but they keep duplicates. More specifically, bags keep one of the instances along with a count of the actual number of duplicates. Byte arrays are compact arrays restricted to integer elements in the range 0 to 255. Intervals are collections maintained via a starting number, ending number, and increment; e.g., 1 **to**: 10 **by**: 3. Identity dictionaries are similar to dictionaries but base key comparison on == (identity) rather than = (equality). Global variable **Smalltalk** is an instance of SystemDictionary, a variety of dictionaries with special facilities. Finally, sorted collections permit elements to be sorted according to an arbitrary sort criterion.

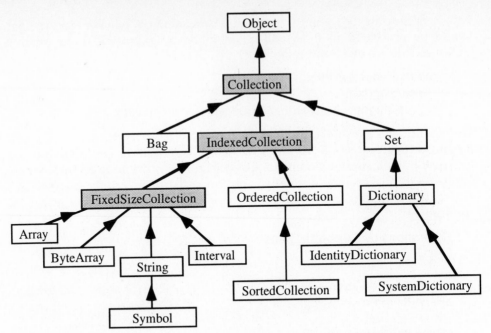

Figure 9.23 Class Collection provides abstract and concrete subclasses.

9.12.1 Instance Creation, Querying, Adding, Removing, and Converting

All collections except intervals can be constructed using **new** and **new:**. Similarly, all collections except intervals and dictionaries can be constructed from class messages **with:**, **with:with:**, **with:with:with:**, and **with:with:with:with:**. Querying (see messages below) is permitted on all collections but adding and removing are allowed only on collections that can grow or shrink. Most collections (dictionaries excepted) can be converted to arrays, ordered collections, sorted collections, sets, and bags. There is no conversion facility for more esoteric collections such as intervals, byte arrays, and strings.

Operations on Collections

instance creation   (illegal on intervals)

aCollectionClass **new**
aCollectionClass **new:** size

instance creation   (illegal on intervals and dictionaries)

aCollectionClass **with:** object1
aCollectionClass **with:** object1 **with:** object2
aCollectionClass **with:** object1 **with:** object2 **with:** object3
aCollectionClass **with:** object1 **with:** object2 **with:** object3 **with:** object4

Operations on Collections (contnued)

querying

aCollection **size**
aCollection **isEmpty**
aCollection **notEmpty**
aCollection **includes**: anObject
aCollection **occurrencesOf**: anObject

adding and removing (illegal on fixed-size collections; restricted in dictionaries)

aCollection **add**: anObject
aCollection **addAll**: anotherCollection
aCollection **remove**: anObject
aCollection **remove**: anObject **ifAbsent**: aBlock
aCollection **removeAll**: anotherCollection

type conversion (illegal on dictionaries)

aCollection **asArray**
aCollection **asOrderedCollection**
aCollection **asSet**
aCollection **asBag**
aCollection **asSortedCollection**
aCollection **asSortedCollection**: aBlock

9.12.2 Sequencing

The Smalltalk library contains quite a large number of sequencing operations. Having had experience with a few case studies that used collections and sequencing operations such as **do**:, we should now be prepared to appreciate the more advanced counterparts.

Advanced sequencing operations are not universally applicable to all collections. Some are allowed only for dictionaries; e.g., **keysDo**:, while others are allowed only on non-dictionaries; e.g., **collect**:.

Operations on Collections

sequencing

aCollection **do**: aBlock
aCollection **select**: aBlock
aCollection **reject**: aBlock
aCollection **collect**: aBlock   (illegal on dictionaries)
aCollection **detect**: aBlock   (error if not there)
aCollection **detect**: aBlock **ifNone**: exceptionBlock
aCollection **inject**: initialValue **into**: aBinaryBlock

Operations on Collections (continued)

aDictionary **keysDo**: aBlock
aDictionary **associationsDo**: aBlock
aDictionary **associationsSelect**: aBlock   (see explanation below)

anIndexedCollection **reverseDo**: aBlock
anIndexedCollection **with**: aCollection **do**: aBlock

anIndexedCollection **findFirst**: aBlock   (error if not there)
anIndexedCollection **findLast**: aBlock   (error if not there)
anIndexedCollection **indexOf**: anObject   (returns 0 if not there)
anIndexedCollection **indexOf**: anObject **ifAbsent**: aBlock
anIndexedCollection **indexOfCollection**: aCollection   (returns 0 if not there)

In the interest of dispensing with detailed semantics (which can be quite lengthy), consider the examples that follow. As a rule, those operations that return collections actually return new collections that share the same elements as the original;. They are **shallow copies**. These resulting collections can be modified without affecting the originals. An exception to this rule is **associationsSelect**: (see below for an explanation).

Both **select**: and **reject**: return a subcollection of the original elements—those that respectively meet, or fail to meet, the boolean test computed by the block. Message **collect**:, on the other hand, returns only the objects computed by the block—never the original elements. Message **detect** (along with **detectifNone**:) is a minor variation of **select**: that is useful for searching. Method **inject:into**: is most unusual—we'll consider it separately. Methods **do**: and **keysDo**: are already quite familiar to us. By contrast, **associationsDo**: provides associations (both the keys and the values) rather than just the keys (as in **keysDo**:) or just the values (as in **do**:). **Associations** are simple objects that respond to messages **key** and **value** (for accessing) along with **key**: and **value**: (for modifying). Method **associationsSelect**:, for dictionaries, is similar in spirit to **select**:; it returns a dictionary with the selected associations. The semantics of **reverseDo**: are relatively obvious. By contrast, **with:do**: is unusual but interesting. An number of additional operations are provided for indexed collections—these typically return indices.

```
| aSet |
aSet := #(1 2 3 4 5 6 7 8 9 10) asSet.
aSet select: [:element | element odd] ⇒ Set (1 3 5 7 9)
aSet reject: [:element | element < 6] ⇒ Set (6 7 8 9 10)
aSet collect: [:element | element squared] ⇒ Set (1 4 9 16 25 36 49 64 81 100)
aSet detect: [:element | element odd & (element > 5)] ⇒ 7
aSet detect: [:element | element < 0)] ⇒ (error, no element found)
aSet detect: [:element | element < 0] ifNone: [nil] ⇒ nil
```

The new dictionary operations include **associationsDo:** and **associationsCollect:**. The first is useful if both keys and values are needed.

```
| aDictionary maximumKey maximumValue |
aDictionary := Dictionary new
    at: 1 put: #10;
    at: 2 put: #20;
    at: 3 put: #30;
    yourself.
maximumKey := maximumValue := 0.
aDictionary associationsDo: [:pair |
    maximumKey  := maximumKey max: pair key.
    maximumValue := maximumValue max: pair value].
Transcript cr; nextPutAll: 'The maximum key and value are '.
(Array with: maximumKey with: maximumValue) printOn: Transcript
```

The two sequencing operations **findFirst:** and **findLast:** are problematic. They generate error messages if no element satisfies the block test. There is clearly a need for methods like **findFirst:ifAbsent:** and **findLast:ifAbsent:**. Message **detect:ifNone:** is a good substitute for **findFirst:**.

```
| anArray |
anArray := #(1 2 3 4 5 6 7 8 9 10).
anArray findFirst: [:element | element > 3 & element odd] ⇒ 5
anArray detect: [:element | element > 3 & element odd] ifNone: [nil] ⇒ 5
anArray findFirst: [:element | element > 30] ⇒ (error, no such element)
anArray detect: [:element | element > 30] ifNone: [nil] ⇒ nil
anArray findLast: [:element | element > 3 & element odd] ⇒ 10
```

Equally problematic is operation **associationsCollect:**. It is particularly dangerous, since both the new dictionary returned and the old dictionary share the common associations. Consequently, changing the value associated with key 1 in one dictionary (see below for example) has the effect of modifying the other dictionary, too!

```
| aDictionary anotherDictionary |
aDictionary := Dictionary new
    at: 1 put: #rouge;
    at: 2 put: #vert;
    at: 3 put: #bleu;
    yourself.

anotherDictionary := aDictionary associationsCollect: [:anAssociation |
    anAssociation key <= 2] ⇒ Dictionary (rouge vert)]

anotherDictionary at: 1 put: #noire.
aDictionary ⇒ Dictionary (noire vert bleu)
```

Searching for specific elements or specific subcollections in indexed collections is relatively easy. All comparisons are based on object equality. Missing elements are indicated by returning index 0.

> #(hello you there) **indexOf:** #you ⇒ 2
> #(hello you there) **indexOf:** #me ⇒ 0
> #(hello you there) **indexOf:** #me **ifAbsent:** [#notThere] ⇒ notThere
> #(once there lived a little rabbit) **indexOfCollection:** #(a little) ⇒ 4
> #(once there lived a little rabbit) **indexOfCollection:** #(a big) ⇒ 0

Message **with:do:** is particularly useful for sequencing over two collections in parallel. The block has two loop variables, permitting the corresponding values to be accessed simultaneously.

> result := OrderedCollection **new.**
> #(1 2 3 4 5 6 7 8 9) **with:** #(1 2 3 4 5 6 7 8 9) **do:** [:array1Element :array2Element
>   result **add:** array1Element + array2Element].
> result ⇒ OrderedCollection (2 4 6 8 10 12 14 16 18)

Finally, as a lead-in to message **inject:into:**, consider successively better ways of summing the elements of an array.

> *the worst technique*
> | anArray |
> anArray := #(1 2 3 4 5 6 7 8 9 10).
> sum := 0.
> 1 **to:** anArray size **do:** [:index | sum := sum + (anArray **at:** index)].
> ^sum

> *a better technique*
> | anArray |
> anArray := #(1 2 3 4 5 6 7 8 9 10).
> sum := 0.
> anArray **do:** [:element | sum := sum + element].
> ^sum

> *a technique used only by the most experienced*
> | anArray |
> anArray := #(1 2 3 4 5 6 7 8 9 10).
> ^anArray **inject:** 0 **into:** [:sum :element | sum + element].

The **inject:into:** message works as follows. First, 0 is injected into "sum" and "element" is bound to 1, the first element of the array. Next, sum and element are added in the block and the result, 1, is reinjected back into "sum" and "element" is bound to 2. These are once again added together to get 3 and the result reinjected into "sum" with the third element 3, and so on. The last time through the loop, 45 and 10 are injected into "sum" and "element", the two are added to get 55, and the result is returned (since there are no more elements to inject into the block).

One convenient property of the **inject:into:** message is the fact that there is no need to declare a special variable to accumulate the result; i.e., the running total, "sum" in the example, is a block variable. Care, however, is required to ensure that the variables are in the right order. Although the collection elements are first and the injected value second, the variables get the injected value first, followed by the collection elements. In other words, the following template is the correct one:

> aCollection **inject:** value **into:** [:valueVariable :collectionElementVariable | ...]

Note that **inject:into:** is more general than the above example suggests. Other examples include

> *finding the product of the elements*
> | anArray |
> anArray := #(1 2 3 4 5 6 7 8 9 10).
> ^anArray **inject:** 1 i**nto:** [:product :element | product * element].

> *concatenating the elements*
> | anArray |
> anArray := #(Once upon a time, there lived a young prince.).
> ^anArray **inject:** " i**nto:** [:string :element | string, element, ' '].

9.12.3 Indexed Collections

IndexedCollection is an abstract class for all those collections such as arrays, strings, and ordered collections that can be indexed. In addition to sequencing operations discussed earlier, a large number of operations are provided for concatenating such collections, comparing them, copying subcollections, and destructively modifying existing collections.

> **Operations on IndexedCollections**
>
> *accessing*
>
> aCollection **first**
> aCollection **last**
>
> *comparing*
>
> aCollection = anotherCollection
>
> *concatenating*
>
> aCollection, anotherCollection   (can be different kinds of collections)
>
> *initializing*
>
> aCollection **atAll:** aCollectionOfIndices **put:** anObject
> aCollection **atAllPut:** anObject

copying (non-destructive; i.e., does not change the receiver)

aCollection **copyFrom**: start **to**: stop
aCollection **copyReplaceFrom**: start **to**: stop **with**: aCollection
aCollection **copyWith**: anObject   Appends at the end
aCollection **copyWithout**: anObject   Has all equal objects omitted
aCollection **reversed**   Elements are interchanged

modifying (destructive; i.e., changes the receiver)

aCollection **replaceFrom**: start **to**: stop **with**: aCollection
aCollection **replaceFrom**: start **to**: stop **with**: aCollection **startingAt**: anotherStart
aCollection **replaceFrom**: start **to**: stop **withObject**: anObject

The initializing operations subscribe to the *sharing philosophy*; i.e., all elements are bound to the object provided as parameter. For example, in the following, each element of the two arrays is bound to one of the three strings 'unspecified', 'first half', and 'second half'.

```
| anArray anotherArray |
anArray := (Array new: 100)
    atAllPut: 'unspecified';
    yourself.
anotherArray := (Array new: 100)
    atAll: (1 to: 50) put: 'first half';
    atAll: (51 to: 100) put: 'second half';
    yourself.
```

In most applications, non-destructive operations are sufficient for creating modified variations of existing indexed collections. In certain special circumstances, however, destructive operations are desirable; e.g., to ensure that all objects referencing an original subsequently reference a modified version.

```
| aCollection |
aCollection := #(an example of a destructive change).
aCollection replaceFrom: 5 to: 6 with: #(dangerous modification).
aCollection ⇒ (an example of a dangerous modification)
```

The non-destructive **replace**... operations are easily distinguishable from the destructive ones, since they all start with the prefix **copy**. The destructive operations are permitted only in situations where the number of replacement elements corresponds exactly to the number being replaced. This restriction is not necessary for the non-destructive variety.

```
#(once upon a time) copyReplaceFrom: 2 to: 3 with: #(there was more)
    ⇒ (once there was more time)
#(once upon a time) replaceFrom: 2 to: 3 with: #(there was more)
    ⇒ (error, incorrect number of replacement elements)
#(here) replaceFrom: 1 to: 1 with: #(everywhere there) startingAt: 2
    ⇒ (there)
```

A few other examples illustrate the remaining operations.

#(once upon a) **copyWith**: #time ⇒ (once upon a time)
#(a man and a woman) **copyWithout**: #a ⇒ (man and woman)
#(big boy) **reversed** ⇒ (boy big)

9.12.4 Intervals

Intervals are compact collections of integers with constant differences; e.g., 1 **to**: 10 (difference 1), 1 **to**: 10 **by**: 3 (difference 3), 10 **to**: 1 **by**: -2 (difference -2). Intervals can be used just like normal collection as far as sequencing and accessing are concerned. However, they are immutable (they cannot be changed).

Operations on Numbers

interval creation

aNumber **to**: anotherNumber
aNumber **to**: anotherNumber by: yetAnotherNumber

Operations on Intervals

arithmetic

anInterval + anInteger
anInterval - anInteger

accessing

anInterval **at**: anInteger

A few examples should clarify the fact that intervals really are a simple kind of collection.

(1 **to**: 10) ⇒ Interval (1 2 3 4 5 6 7 8 9 10)
(1 **to**: 10) **size** ⇒ 10
(1 **to**: 10 **by**: 2) ⇒ Interval (1 3 5 7 9)
(1 **to**: 10 **by**: 2) **size** ⇒ 5
(1 **to**: 10 **by**: 2) **collect**: [:element | element **squared**] ⇒ (1 9 25 49 81)
(1 **to**: 10 **by**: 2) + 1 ⇒ Interval (2 4 6 8 10)
(10 **to**: 1 **by**: -2) ⇒ Interval (10 8 6 4 2)
(10 **to**: 1 **by**: -2) **at**: 3 ⇒ 6

9.12.5 Strings (and Symbols)

Strings (and symbols, since they inherit from String) are provided with a small number of special operations that permit comparisons where case is ignored.

'aB' **equalsIgnoreCase**: 'AB' ⇒ true

They are also provided with special-effects operations and operations for type conversion.

Operations on Strings

comparing

aString **equals**: aString   Same as =; case is significant
aString **equalsIgnoreCase**: aString

special effects

aString **asArrayOfSubstrings**
aString **trimBlanks**
aString **withCrs**   Each "\" character replaced by carriage return
aString **upTo**: aCharacter   Substring that excludes aCharacter; whole string
                                             if aCharacter is not in aString

type conversion

aString **asDate**
aString **asFloat**
aString **asInteger**
aString **asLowerCase**
aString **asUpperCase**
aString **asStream**
aString **asString**   Returns the original; not a copy
aString **asSymbol**

Some examples include the following:

'once upon a time' **asArrayOfSubstrings** ⇒ ('once' 'upon' 'a' 'time')
'   yes   ' **trimBlanks** ⇒ 'yes'
'yes\no' **withCrs** ⇒ 'yes
no'   (the new line for no is intentional)
'abcdef' **upTo**: $c ⇒ 'ab'
'abcdef' **upTo**: $x ⇒ 'abcdef'
'September 1, 1992' **asDate** ⇒ Sep 1, 1992
'1.2e5' **asFloat** ⇒ 120000.0
'2000' **asInteger** ⇒ 2000
'hello THERE' **asLowerCase** ⇒ 'hello there'
'hello THERE' **asUpperCase** ⇒ 'HELLO THERE'
'testing' **asStream** ⇒ a ReadWriteStream
'hi' **asString** ⇒ 'hi'
'hi' **asSymbol** ⇒ hi

9.12.6 Ordered Collections

Ordered collections are already quite familiar to us. We already know most of the basic operations.

Operations on OrderedCollections

adding and removing

anOrderedCollection **addFirst**: anObject
anOrderedCollection **addLast**: anObject

anOrderedCollection **remove**: anObject   The first equal to anObject
anOrderedCollection **removeFirst**
anOrderedCollection **removeLast**

However, there are a number of variations that we may not be aware of. These variations permit us to add many elements at one time and to add elements at relatively precise positions.

Operations on OrderedCollections

adding and removing

anOrderedCollection **addAllFirst**: aCollection
anOrderedCollection **addAllLast**: aCollection

anOrderedCollection **add**: newObject **after**: oldObject
anOrderedCollection **add**: anObject **afterIndex**: anInteger
anOrderedCollection **add**: newObject **before**: oldObject
anOrderedCollection **add**: anObject **beforeIndex**: anInteger

anOrderedCollection **removeIndex**: anInteger

searching

anOrderedCollection **before**: anObject
anOrderedCollection **before**: anObject **ifNone**: aBlock
anOrderedCollection **after**: anObject
anOrderedCollection **after**: anObject **ifNone**: aBlock

For example, we might try some of the following:

```
| anOrderedCollection |
anOrderedCollection := OrderedCollection with: #three
        ⇒ OrderedCollection (three)
anOrderedCollection addAllFirst: #(one two)
        ⇒ OrderedCollection (one two three)
anOrderedCollection addAllLast: #(four five)
        ⇒ OrderedCollection (one two three four five)
```

anOrderedCollection **before**: #(four) ⇒ three
anOrderedCollection **before**: #(ten) ⇒ (**error**, element not found)
anOrderedCollection **before**: #(one) ⇒ (**error**, element not found)
anOrderedCollection **before**: #(one) **ifNone**: [nil] ⇒ nil

anOrderedCollection **removeIndex**: 3
⇒ OrderedCollection (one two four five)

9.12.7 Sorted Collections

Ordered collections are sequences of objects in the order provided by the user. Sorted collections, by contrast, are sequences of objects in an order specified by an additional **sort criterion**—a test supplied via a two-parameter block, termed a **sort block**, that returns true if the two parameters are in sort order. A default sort criterion is provided when none is given. For example, consider the following:

#(there you hello) **asOrderedCollection**
⇒ OrderedCollection (there you hello)
#(there you hello) **asSortedCollection**
⇒ SortedCollection (hello there you)

The ordered collection contains the same elements as the array and in the same order. On the other hand, the sorted collection contains the elements in a non-decreasing sort order. We can see this more clearly by looking at collections of integers where some of the integers are repeated.

#(1 10 2 9 3 8 4 7 5 6 1 10) **asOrderedCollection**
⇒ OrderedCollection (1 10 2 9 3 8 4 7 5 6 1 10)
#(1 10 2 9 3 8 4 7 5 6 1 10) **asSortedCollection**
⇒ SortedCollection (1 1 2 3 4 5 6 7 8 9 10 10)

Since sorted collections inherit from OrderedCollection, we might expect the sorted collection protocol to be very similar to the ordered collection protocol. Indeed, it is, but there are some special exceptions. In particular, it is the sorted collection's responsibility—not the user's—to maintain the sort order. Consequently, operations that might permit a user to place elements at incorrect positions are disallowed; e.g., **addFirst**:, **addLast**:, and **add:after**:.

Operations on SortedCollections

instance creation

SortedCollection **new**
SortedCollection **sortBlock**: aBlock

re-sorting

aSortedCollection **sortBlock**: aBlock

converting

aCollection **asSortedCollection**
aCollection **asSortedCollection:** aBlock

In general, the default sort block is of the form "[:x :y | x <= y]" which indicates that x and y are in the correct sort order if x <= y. So a sorted collection that uses the default sort block must consist of elements that can be compared pairwise using "<="; i.e., compared two at a time.

```
| aSortedCollection |
aSortedCollection := SortedCollection new ⇒ SortedCollection ()
aSortedCollection add: 1 ⇒ SortedCollection (1)
aSortedCollection add: 5 ⇒ SortedCollection (1 5)
aSortedCollection add: 2 ⇒ SortedCollection (1 2 5)
aSortedCollection add: 4 ⇒ SortedCollection (1 2 4 5)
aSortedCollection add: 0 ⇒ SortedCollection (0 1 2 4 5)
```

A sorted collection can be created with a non-standard sort block using class message "**sortBlock:** aBlock". The same message can also be sent to an instance, which will cause the existing elements to be re-sorted according to the new sort block. Consequently, we can easily change the sort to decreasing order (or, to be technically correct, non-increasing order to account for any equal elements) as follows:

```
| aSortedCollection |
aSortedCollection sortBlock: [:x :y | x >= y] ⇒ SortedCollection (5 4 2 1 0)
```

But the most important use of sort blocks is to permit the elements to be sorted based on some special property of the elements; e.g., to sort Personnel objects according to their salary or their seniority.

```
aCollectionOfPersonnel asSortedCollection: [:person1 :person2 |
    person1 salary >= person2 salary]
aCollectionOfPersonnel asSortedCollection: [:person1 :person2 |
    person1 age >= person2 age]
```

We can also sort using more complex criteria. The following example illustrates a sort block that can be used to sort foods so that the heaviest foods come first and foods of equal weight are sorted with smallest volumes first.

```
aCollectionOfFoods asSortedCollection: [:food1 :food2 |
    (food1 weight > food2 weight) or: [
    (food1 weight = food2 weight) and: [food1 volume <= food2 volume])]
```

As a very simple application, consider sorting the subclasses of Object. It turns out that simply asking the class for all its subclasses provides a set—the ordering is totally arbitrary.

```
Object subclasses ⇒ Set (Number Collection ...)
```

To sort the subclasses, it is not adequate just to write the following because classes cannot be compared—classes are not magnitudes.

> Object **subclasses asSortedCollection**
> ⇒ (**error**, can't compare classes)

We need to be more clever! Although we can't compare classes, we can compare class names, because the names are simply strings. So we should be able to write the following:

> Object **subclasses asSortedCollection**: [:class1 :class2 |
> class1 **name** <= class2 **name**]
> ⇒ SortedCollection (... properly ordered ...)

The result is a collection of classes (not a collection of names) that are sorted based on the names.

9.10.8 Sets and Bags

Sets and bags are unordered collections. They can be used much like ordered collections, but the elements cannot be retrieved by indexing the sets or bags. More typically, the elements are retrieved by sequencing through the collections using **do**:. Sets and bags do not re-implement operation "=", which is inherited from Object. Hence, two sets (or bags) are considered equal only if they are the same set (or bag). Sets discard duplicates (equal elements), whereas bags maintain only the first occurrence along with a count of the number of occurrences. A special operation is therefore available for bags that permits a count to be specified.

Operations on Bags

adding

aCollection **add**: anObject **withOccurrences**: anInteger

Sets are often used to remove duplicates, as shown below:

anArray **asSet asArray**

Unfortunately, sets (and bags) also have the property of randomly reordering their elements. Bags are useful for keeping track of large inventories where there are many duplicate items; e.g., 1000 bolts, 600 spark plugs, 5000 washers, etc.

Sets and bags use hashing[1] techniques (associating integers with objects and using the integers as an index to indicate where the object might be) for storing and retrieving elements. This can be an advantage when the sets and bags are large, because few elements will be searched to determine if an equal element already exists. On the other hand, the search can be extremely slow if the hash has too many **collisions**: i.e., too many elements have the same hash.

---

[1]Hashing is discussed in the Magnitude section.

9.10.9 Equality and Identity Dictionaries

Dictionaries provide facilities for associating arbitrary values (objects) with arbitrary keys (also objects). When a value is to be retrieved, a key is supplied to the dictionary. This key is compared with the stored key. If a match is found, the associated value is retrieved; otherwise, a "key not found" error is reported. There are two fundamental operations for matching keys: = and ==. The former leads to an **equality dictionary**; the latter, to an **identity dictionary**.

Equality comparisons (using =) return true if the objects being compared have the same content. **Identity** comparisons (using ==) return true if the objects being compared are the same object. Consequently, if two variables both refer to money objects, we should be able to determine if the money objects are different objects (using ==). If they are different, we should also be able to determine whether they are for the same amount (using =). Consider the following:

```
| jimsMoney franksMoney tomsMoney marysMoney |
jimsMoney := Money cents: 25.
franksMoney := Money cents: 10.
tomsMoney := Money cents: 25.
marysMoney := jimsMoney.

jimsMoney = franksMoney ⇒ false
jimsMoney = tomsMoney ⇒ true

jimsMoney == franksMoney ⇒ false
jimsMoney == tomsMoney ⇒ false
jimsMoney == marysMoney ⇒ true
```

Note that there are three money objects and four variables. Two of the variables—namely, jimsMoney and marysMoney—refer to the same object. We can determine this using operation ==.

Class Dictionary provides equality dictionaries, whereas IdentityDictionary provides identity dictionaries. SystemDictionary provides a special kind of equality dictionary with unique facilities. There is only one instance of SystemDictionary called **Smalltalk**. Smalltalk contains all the globals in the system; the keys are symbols such as #Collection, whereas the values are the corresponding objects, such as the Collection class itself.

In addition to standard dictionary operations like **at:**, **at:ifAbsent:**, **at:put:**, **removeKey:**, **removeKey:ifAbsent:**, **do:**, **keysDo:**, and **associationsDo:**, dictionaries also contain a number of operations that allow all the keys and values to be extracted as well as operations for obtaining the keys given the values. System dictionaries additionally contain operations for compressing the source and changes file and for leaving the Smalltalk environment.

Operations on Dictionaries

querying keys and values

aDictionary **keys**	Returns a set
aDictionary **values**	Returns a bag
aDictionary **keyAtValue**: anObject	Compares objects using =
aDictionary **keyAtValue**: anObject **ifAbsent**: aBlock	

Operations on SystemDictionaries

compressing and exiting

aSystemDictionary **compressChanges**
aSystemDictionary **compressSources**
aSystemDictionary **exit**

We can easily illustrate the distinction between equality (normal) dictionaries and identity dictionaries by associating owners with Money objects.

```
| anIdentityDictionary dime1 dime2 |
anIdentityDictionary := IdentityDictionary new.
dime1 := Money cents: 10.
dime2 := Money cents: 10.
dime1 = dime2 ⇒ true                "equal but"
dime1 == dime2 ⇒ false              "not the same"
anIdentityDictionary at: dime1 put: #Wilf.
anIdentityDictionary at: dime2 put: #John.
anIdentityDictionary at: dime1 ⇒ #Wilf
anIdentityDictionary at: dime2 ⇒ #John
```

Clearly, this wouldn't work if we used a normal (equality) dictionary instead, because there would be only one key. In that case, #John would have replaced #Wilf. Since dime1 = dime2, both keys would retrieve the same value; namely, #John, the last value associated with that key.

9.11 The Stream Classes and Their Protocol

Streams should be familiar because we have been using a subset of the stream protocol for some time. Global Transcript, in particular, is a window that supports such a subset. A **stream** is an indexed collection with a position indicator. Operations are provided that allow elements at the current position in the collection to be accessed or replaced while simultaneously moving the position indicator as a side-effect.

Streams are meant for reading (accessing information), writing (adding or replacing information), or both. Correspondingly, abstract class Stream (see

Figure 9.24) provides the basic facilities for concrete classes ReadStream, WriteStream, and ReadWriteStream.

There are two main categories of streams: streams that reside in main memory (ReadStream, WriteStream, and ReadWriteStream) and streams that reside externally in files (FileStream). Main-memory streams can contain arbitrary objects. File streams, on the other hand, can contain only characters and must be closed when they are no longer needed. Clearly, file streams are quite specialized compared to main-memory streams.

Most of the stream protocol is in abstract class Stream. The read operations, either directly or indirectly, make use of **next** which is defined in ReadStream. Message **next** causes the next object in the stream to be retrieved and additionally increments the position indicator. If no object is available, an error is reported. Similarly, the write operations make use of **nextPut:**, which is defined in WriteStream. Message **nextPut:** causes an object to be inserted into the stream at the current position and also increments the position indicator.

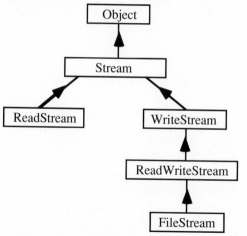

Figure 9.24 Class Stream provides filing protocol.

A stream is obtained by asking for a concrete instance **on:** an indexed collection such as an array, a string, or an ordered collection. The collection is then maintained by the stream. Note that a stream on an array or an ordered collection can contain arbitrary objects. A stream on a string can contain only characters. It is the stream's responsibility (not the user's) to automatically replace fixed-size collections by larger collections whenever circumstances require more room. So there is no need to worry about supplying an inappropriately sized indexed collection.

The most basic approach to using read streams is to first construct one on a collection of existing objects, then to obtain the successive stream objects in a loop using **next** until there are no more. At that point, the stream will reply true to message **atEnd**.

By contrast, write streams are constructed on new collections, then successive objects are placed into the stream using **nextPut:**, and finally the stored information is recovered by asking the stream for its **content**.

File streams are obtained by specifying the name of an external file and are processed like write streams. Of course, only characters are allowed. Instead of recovering the contents when done, the file stream is sent a **close** message to finalize the actual external information. If a **close** message is not sent to a file stream when it is no longer needed, two problems will ultimately result. First, the file will not be complete. Second, an operating system resource limit will ultimately be reached. There is a limit to the number of file streams permitted at any one time. Closing a file stream permits a replacement to be subsequently opened without running out of these "file" resources.

Operations on Strings

instance creation

aString **asStream**   Obtain a read/write stream on aString

Operations on Streams

instance creation

aStreamClass **on**: anIndexedCollection Obtain an instance

instance releasing

aStream **close**   To release access

direct positioning

aStream **reset**	Position at the beginning
aStream **setToEnd**	Position at the end
aStream **position**	Current position; 0 or more
aStream **position**: anInteger	Set to position between 0 and size
aStream **skip**: anInteger	Increment or decrement position
aStream **skipTo**: anObject	Advance beyond anObject if possible; otherwise to end of file; returns true or false, respectively
aStream **countBlanks**	Skip blanks and tabs counting 1 and 4, respectively

querying

aStream **size**	The number of elements
aStream **isEmpty**	Has no elements
aStream **atEnd**	Result is true if at the end
aStream **indexOf**: aCollection	Search forward and return the position if found; 0 otherwise

reading

aStream **peek**	Next object; position not moved
aStream **peekFor**: anObject	True and advance if found; false otherwise
aStream **next**: anInteger	Next "anInteger" elements as a collection
aStream **upTo**: anObject	Subcollection from current position to anObject exclusive; position beyond or at end if not there
aStream **contents**	The entire collection independent of position
aStream **reverseContents**	The reverse of the entire collection independent of position
aStream **copyFrom**: firstIndex **to**: lastIndex	A subcollection

writing

aStream **next**: anInteger **put**: anObject	Insert anObject "anInteger" times while advancing each time
aStream **nextLine**	Characters up to but excluding carriage return; position beyond carriage return

sequencing

aStream **do**: aBlock	Do from current position onward

Operations on ReadStreams

reading

aReadStream **next**	Get next object and advance; reports an error if there isn't one

Operations on WriteStreams

writing

aWriteStream **nextPut**: anObject	Store object and advance
aWriteStream **nextPutAll**: aCollection	As above but elements only
aWriteStream **cr**	Store carriage return character
aWriteStream **space**	Store space character
aWriteStream **tab**	Store tab character

Operations on ReadWriteStreams

writing

aReadWriteStream **truncate**	End stream at current position

Operations on FileStreams

querying

aFileStream **file**	The file associated with the stream
aFileStream **pathName**	(e.g., 'C:\name1\name2\file')

Operations on Files

file stream instance creation

File **newFile**: aNameOrFilePathName	Create new file; overwrites old; returns file stream
File **pathName**: aNameOrFilePathName	Locates old file; creates new only if it does not exist; returns file stream
File **pathNameReadOnly**: aNameOrFilePathName	
	As above but modifications not allowed and file must exist

querying

File **exists**: aFilePathName	True if file exists; false otherwise
File **name**	Name of the file as a string
File **directory**	Directory containing the file

Operations on Directories

querying

aDirectory **drivePathName**	(e.g., 'C:\name1\name2')
aDirectory **fullDirName**	(e.g., 'C:\name1\name2\')
aDirectory **pathName**	(e.g., '\name1\name2')

The most complicated situation involves file streams, since their use simultaneously involves files streams, files, and directories. Files are fully specified by providing a string of the form

$$\text{'drive:\textbackslash directory}_1\text{\textbackslash directory}_2\text{\textbackslash ...\textbackslash directory}_n\text{\textbackslash fileName'}$$

called a **path name**; e.g., 'a:\course\examples\file1'. In this case, "file1" is the name of a file in a directory called "examples" which in turn is in a directory called "course" on drive "a". A file stream is obtained by asking class File for a file stream, rather than asking the file stream directly; e.g.,

```
| aFileStream aFile aDirectory |
aFileStream := File newFile: 'a:\course\examples\file1'.
```

The file stream "knows" about the associated file, which in turn knows about the directory. Under normal circumstances, we don't really care about the file and directory objects, since we typically manipulate the stream. However, as an illustration of the existence of these specialized objects and the querying facilities that can be used to interrogate them, consider the following:

```
aFileStream pathName ⇒ 'a:\course\examples\file1'

aFile := aFileStream file.
aFile ⇒ a File on: 'file1'
aFile name ⇒ 'file1'

aDirectory := aFile directory.
aDirectory ⇒ a Directory on: 'a:\course\examples\'
aDirectory drivePathName ⇒ 'a:\course\examples'
aDirectory fullDirName ⇒ 'a:\course\examples\'
aDirectory pathName ⇒ '\course\examples'
```

Rather than specify the entire path name, it is also possible to specify just the file name. In that case, the file is understood to be in the current directory, a directory maintained by global variable **Disk**. When the Smalltalk environment starts up, **Disk** is initialized to the directory containing the Smalltalk image. So we could have written

```
aFileStream := File newFile: 'file1'.
```

to obtain a file stream that manipulates **file1** in the same directory that contains the Smalltalk image.

Once we have a file stream, we can add characters to the file and then ultimately close it to ensure that the information is physically recorded externally.

```
aFileStream
    nextPutAll: 'This file contains two lines.'; cr;
    nextPutAll: 'The above line and this line.';
    close.
```

The converse—reading the information back in—would be achieved by first creating a file stream on an existing file using **pathName**: rather than **newFile**:, and then reading the data using messages like **nextLine** or **contents**, as follows:

```
aFileStream := File pathName: 'file1'.
aFileStream nextLine ⇒ 'This file contains two lines.'
aFileStream nextLine ⇒ 'The above line and this line.'
aFileStream atEnd ⇒ true
aFileStream close
```

Alternatively, we could have obtained the entire file as one long string, as follows:

```
aFileStream := File pathName: 'file1'.
aFileStream contents ⇒ 'This file contains two lines.
The above line and this line.'     "Note: The string contains a new line character."
aFileStream close
```

Read and write streams permit arbitrary objects, rather than sequences of characters, to be processed. To illustrate the facilities, consider the task of creating a write stream that contains only the numbers contained by some other read stream. We might proceed as follows:

```
I aReadStream aWriteStream I
aReadStream := ReadStream
     on: #(There are 4 doors measuring 4.5 feet by 6.6 feet).
aWriteStream := WriteStream on: OrderedCollection new.
```

```
aReadStream size ⇒ 10              aReadStream position ⇒ 0
aWriteStream size ⇒ 0             aWriteStream position ⇒ 0
```

```
[aReadStream atEnd] whileFalse: [
    nextObject := aReadStream next.
    (nextObject isKindOf: Number)
        ifTrue: [aWriteStream nextPut: nextObject]].
```

```
aReadStream size ⇒ 10             aReadStream position ⇒ 10
aWriteStream size ⇒ 3            aWriteStream position ⇒ 3
```

```
^aWriteStream
```

Note first that the read stream is on an array and the write stream is an ordered collection. Consequently, asking the read stream for its contents would give us an array, whereas asking the write stream would give us an ordered collection.

```
I aReadStream aWriteStream I
aReadStream contents ⇒ (There are 4 doors measuring 4.5 feet by 6.6 feet).
aWriteStream contents ⇒ OrderedCollection (4 4.5 6.6).
```

Note also that **next** reads an object, whereas **nextPut:** writes an object. In both cases, the stream is responsible for advancing the position indicator.

There is a large list of operations for extracting bits and pieces from streams. Let's consider a few just to get a feel for what you can do with them.

```
I aReadStream I
aReadStream := ReadStream
     on: #(There are 4 doors measuring 4.5 feet by 6.6 feet).
aReadStream next ⇒ There
aReadStream next ⇒ are
aReadStream peek ⇒ 4                    "position not advanced"
aReadStream peek ⇒ 4                    "position not advanced"
aReadStream next ⇒ 4
aReadStream next ⇒ doors

aReadStream peekFor: #measuring ⇒ true    "position advanced"
aReadStream next ⇒ 4.5
aReadStream peekFor: #junk ⇒ false        "position not advanced"
aReadStream next ⇒ feet

aReadStream reset                         "reposition to beginning"
aReadStream next ⇒ There
```

aReadStream **skip**: 2	"forward 2 objects"
aReadStream **next** ⇒ doors	
aReadStream **skip**: -2	"backward 2 objects"
aReadStream **next** ⇒ 4	
aReadStream **skipTo**: #feet ⇒ true	"found search object"
aReadStream **next** ⇒ by	
aReadStream **skipTo**: #junk ⇒ false	"did not find search object"
aReadStream **atEnd** ⇒ true	"but reached the end in the process"
aReadStream **reset**	"reposition to beginning"
aReadStream **upTo**: #doors ⇒ (There are 4)	"excludes #doors but past it"
aReadStream **next** ⇒ measuring	
aReadStream **next**: 3 ⇒ (4.5 feet by)	
aReadStream **indexOf**: #(feet) ⇒ 9	"position of next (second) #feet"
aReadStream **reset**	"reposition to beginning"
aReadStream **indexOf**: #(4 doors) ⇒ 2	"position of subcollection"
aReadStream **position**: 2	
aReadStream **next** ⇒ 4	
aReadStream **next** ⇒ doors	
aReadStream **contents** ⇒ There	
aReadStream **position**: 0	
aReadStream **next** ⇒ There	
aReadStream **next** ⇒ are	
aReadStream **contents**	

  ⇒ (There are 4 doors measuring 4.5 feet by 6.6 feet)
aReadStream **reverseContents**
  ⇒ (feet 6.6 by feet 4.5 measuring doors 4 are There)

To finish this section, let's consider a potential implementation of instance method **printString** in Object.

printString
  "Returns a string representation of the receiver that is suitable for printing."
  | aWriteStream |
  aWriteStream := WriteStream **on**: (String **new**: 20).
  self **printOn**: aWriteStream.
  ^aWriteStream **contents**

As we can see, the receiver is simply asked to print itself on the newly created stream. Once done, the contents of the stream—a string consisting of exactly those characters added by the **printOn**: message—is returned. Note that we get a string back because we created a stream on a string (as opposed to a stream on an array, for example). The initial size of the string is simply a default size. If more than 20 characters are added by the **printOn:** message, the stream will get a larger string so that nothing is lost.

Finally, note that the **printOn:** methods that implement the **printOn:** message must actually be provided with a stream parameter. As a consequence, they are all of the form

> **printOn:** aStream
>   ... implementation ...

rather than

> **printOn:** aWindow
>   ... implementation ...

We might wish to keep that in mind when writing **printOn:** methods in the future.

9.12 Case Study: Adding Transactions to BankAccounts

Although we touched on a large number of classes in this chapter, there are a few basic concepts that should be reviewed because they are so fundamental. As a rule, most classes need basic facilities for providing print strings and store strings, deep and shallow copies, and perhaps sequencing and comparison operations. Often, comparisons become important, because the objects are inserted into sorted collections. It would also be interesting if we could illustrate some of the meta-level facilities, such as object mutation.

Another fundamental is that of non-object-oriented programming—more specifically, the style of programming that determines what to do based on a large number of cases that have to do with the type of parameter being processed. We called these **class-based cases** in an earlier section. First, we need to be able to recognize such case-based programming. Next, we need to be able to decide whether an alternative might be better and, if so, what that alternative might be.

To review these concepts, we will consider redesigning our bank accounts to make them transaction-oriented. Rather than make direct deposits from and withdrawals into our bank accounts, we will create deposit transactions and withdrawal transactions and add the transactions to the bank accounts. You do, after all, have to fill in a deposit slip or a withdrawal slip for a teller to process, or, you use an automated teller machine (ATM). ATM requests for money automatically generate withdrawal transactions.

What we have in mind is a system with many different kinds of bank accounts and transactions. For example, a specific bank might have normal savings accounts, high-yield savings accounts (with better interest rates), normal checking accounts (where checks have a service charge), and preferred client checking accounts (that don't have service changes on checks), to name a few. It's in the bank's best interest to keep coming up with new kinds of bank accounts to entice new customers. Similarly, the bank might also have service charge transactions, deposit transactions, check transactions, withdrawal transactions, and bonus transactions.

Our goal is to provide an approach that will allow us to add new kinds of bank accounts and transactions in an extensible fashion. Our aim is to permit the addition of new classes (and new methods to existing classes) without requiring modifications to existing methods.

For simplicity, we are not going to worry about being complete. We know that, among other things, bank accounts need to keep track of the owner, the bank that it belongs to, the balance, and the transactions. We'll just keep track of the transactions and the balance. Transactions will keep track of an amount, a date, and a time. We will, however, provide a sufficient number of different kinds of bank accounts and transactions to ensure that interesting interactions occur. Figure 9.25 summarizes the classes we will introduce. Although the number of concrete classes is fairly large, most of the methods will reside in the abstract classes.

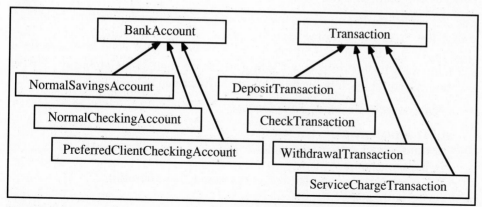

Figure 9.25 A typical set of bank account and transaction classes.

We'll assume that checks are legal only on checking accounts and that they result in a $2.00 service charge on a normal checking account but no charge on a preferred client checking account. Whenever a normal checking account balance goes over $1000.00, it will revert to a preferred client checking account. If a preferred client checking account's balance goes below $1000.00, it will revert to a normal checking account. Deposit transactions will cause the balance to increase; withdrawal, service charge, and check transaction will cause it to decrease.

There are enough special cases that the implementation will be complex and difficult to extend to other kinds of bank accounts and transactions later if we are not careful. The main focus of our efforts is a method that might look like the following if we were to provide a case-based implementation.

instance method in class BankAccount

```
addTransaction: aTransaction
    transactions add: aTransaction.
    (aTransaction isKindOf: DepositTransaction) ifTrue: [
        self balance: self balance + aTransaction amount. ^self].
    (aTransaction isKindOf: WithdrawalTransaction) ifTrue: [
        self balance: self balance - aTransaction amount. ^self].
    (aTransaction isKindOf: ServiceChargeTransaction) ifTrue: [
        self balance: self balance - aTransaction amount. ^self].
    (aTransaction isKindOf: CheckTransaction) ifTrue: [
        (self isKindOf: NormalSavingAccount)
            ifTrue: [self error: 'checks not allowed']
            ifFalse: [self balance: self balance - aTransaction amount].
        self addTransaction: (ServicreCharge amount: (Money dollars: 2)).
        ^self].
    self error: 'unknown transaction'
```

It should be clear that the number of interactions will increase as we introduce new kinds of bank accounts and transactions. What's the alternative?

The answer is simply to pass the buck. Let the transaction itself do the work. Each transaction is capable of doing something different. We can actually do more than that, however. We can also let the transaction know what type of account it is working with by sending it a slightly different message, depending on the account. We could use meta-level facilities to do this, as follows:

instance method in class BankAccount

```
addTransaction: aTransaction
    transactions add: aTransaction.
    aTransaction
        perform: ('applyTo', self class name, ':') asSymbol
        with: self
```

This is equivalent to sending one of the following three messages to the transaction:

```
aTransaction applyToNormalSavingAccount: self
aTransaction applyToNormalCheckingAccount: self
aTransaction applyToPreferredClientSavingAccount: self
```

Of course, we don't really need the meta-level facility to do this. We can simply have three different **addTransaction:** methods—one for each kind of bank account (see listing at the end of this section). This particular technique, in which a message sent to one object is in turn passed to another object while providing information about the parameter being passed, is called **double dispatching**.

Because changing the balance directly is rather heavy-handed, it might be better to introduce methods that are more in the spirit of banking. So, let's introduce two methods called **credit:** and **debit:** that respectively increase and decrease the balance.

instance methods in class BankAccount

credit: aMoney
    self **balance:** self **balance** + aMoney
debit: aMoney
    self **balance:** self **balance** - aMoney

Recall that preferred client checking accounts maintain their preferred status as long as the balance is over $1000.00. As soon as it dips lower, the account should revert to a normal checking account. We can easily do this if we re-implement **debit:** in the preferred client checking account, as follows:

instance methods in class PreferredClientCheckingAccount

debit: aMoney
    super **debit:** aMoney.
    self **balance** < (Money **dollars:** 1000) **ifTrue:** [
        self **become:** self **asNormalCheckingAccount**]

The rest of the methods should be relatively obvious. Note, for example, that the transactions are kept in a sorted collection with the usual default sort block. Because store strings cannot record the sort blocks, we create a store string with an array rather than a sorted collection. Whenever the collection is replaced, we ensure that it is converted to a sorted collection (if it isn't one already). Because we used sorted collection, <= must be defined for transactions. We also implemented a **do:** operation that permits sequencing through a bank account's transactions.

class   BankAccount
superclass   Object
instance variables   ... transactions balance

class methods

"none"

instance methods

instance initialization

initialize
    self **transactions:** SortedCollection **new.**
    self **balance:** Money **dollars:** 0

accessing and modifying

transactions
　　^transactions
transactions: aCollection
　　transactions:= aCollection **asSortedCollection**

balance
　　^balance
balance: aMoney
　　balance := aMoney

printing and storing

printOn: aStream　　"or aWindow"
　　"Prints like 'a $50.00 NormalSavingAccount'."
　　aStream **nextPutAll**: 'a '.
　　self **balance printOn**: aStream.
　　aStream **space**.
　　self **class printOn**: aStream

storeOn: aStream
　　"Stores like '(NormalSavingAccount new
　　　　transactions: SortedCollection new;
　　　　balance: (Money dollars: 20))'."
　　aStream **nextPut**: $(.self **class printOn**: aStream.
　　aStream **nextPutAll**: ' new'.
　　aStream **nextPutAll**: ' transactions: '.
　　　　self **transactions asArray storeOn**: aStream.
　　　　aStream **nextPut**: $;.
　　aStream **nextPutAll**: ' balance: '.
　　　　self **balance storeOn**: aStream.
　　　　aStream **nextPut**: $)

copying

deepCopy
　　^self **class** new
　　　　transactions: self **transactions deepCopy**;
　　　　balance: self **balance**

transaction processing

addTransaction: aTransaction
　　transactions **add**: aTransaction

type conversion

asNormalCheckingAccount
　　"Note: transactions are shared."
　　^NormalCheckingAccount **new**
　　　　transactions: self **transactions**;
　　　　balance: self **balance**

asPreferredClientCheckingAccount
    "Note: transactions are shared."
    ^PreferredClientCheckingAccount **new**
        transactions: self **transactions**;
        balance: self **balance**

crediting and debiting

credit: aMoney
    self **balance**: self **balance** + aMoney
debit: aMoney
    self **balance**: self **balance** - aMoney

sequencing

do: aBlock
    "Permit aBankAccount do: [:aTransaction | ...]."
    self **transactions do**: aBlock

---

class	NormalSavingAccount
superclass	BankAccount
instance variables	...

class methods

"none"

instance methods

transaction processing

addTransaction: aTransaction
    super **addTransaction**: aTransaction.
    aTransaction **applyToNormalSavingAccount**: self

---

class	NormalCheckingAccount
superclass	BankAccount
instance variables	...

class methods

"none"

instance methods

transaction processing

addTransaction: aTransaction
    super **addTransaction**: aTransaction.
    aTransaction **applyToNormalCheckingAccount**: self

crediting and debiting

credit: aMoney
    super **credit**: aMoney.
    self **balance** > (Money **dollars**: 1000) **ifTrue**: [
        self **become**: self **asPreferredCheckingAccount**]

debit: aMoney
    self **balance**: self **balance - aMoney**

---

class	PreferredClientCheckingAccount
superclass	BankAccount
instance variables	...

class methods

"none"

instance methods

transaction processing

addTransaction: aTransaction
    super **addTransaction**: aTransaction.
    aTransaction **applyToPreferredClientCheckingAccount**: self

crediting and debiting

debit: aMoney
    super **debit**: aMoney.
    self **balance** < (Money **dollars**: 1000) **ifTrue**: [
        self **become**: self **asNormalCheckingAccount**]

---

class	Transaction
superclass	Magnitude
instance variables	amount date time

class methods

instance creation

amount: aMoney
    ^self **new amount**: aMoney

instance methods

instance initialization

initialize
    self **amount**: (Money **dollars**: 0).
    self **date**: Date **today**.
    self **time**: Time **now**

accessing and modifying

amount
    ^amount
amount: aMoney
    amount:= aMoney

date
    ^date
date: aDate
    date := aDate

time
    ^time
time: aTime
    time := aTime

printing and storing

printOn: aStream   "or aWindow"
    "Prints like 'a $50.00 DepositTransaction'."
    aStream **nextPutAll**: 'a '.
    self **amount printOn**: aStream.
    aStream **space**.
    self **class printOn**: aStream

storeOn: aStream
    "Stores like '(DepositTransaction new
        date: Date today
        time: Time now;
        amount: (Money dollars: 20))'."
    aStream **nextPut**: $(. self **class printOn**: aStream.
    aStream **nextPutAll**: ' new'.
    aStream **nextPutAll**: ' date: '.
        self **date storeOn**: aStream.
        aStream **nextPut**: $;.
    aStream **nextPutAll**: ' time: '.
        self **time storeOn**: aStream.
        aStream **nextPut**: $;.
    aStream **nextPutAll**: ' amount: '.
        self **amount storeOn**: aStream.
        aStream **nextPut**: $)

comparing

= aTransaction
    ^(self **date** = aTransaction **date**) **and**: [
    (self **time** = aTransaction **time**) **and**: [
    (self **amount** = aTransaction **amount**)]]

```
< aTransaction
    ^(self date < aTransaction date) or: [
    (self date = aTransaction date) and: [
    (self time < aTransaction time) or: [
    (self time = aTransaction time) and: [
    (self amount < aTransaction amount)]]]]

<= aTransaction
    ^(self < aTransaction) or: [self = aTransaction]

> aTransaction
    ^(self <= aTransaction) not

>= aTransaction
    ^(self < aTransaction) not

hash
    ^self time hash
```

transaction processing

```
applyToNormalSavingAccount: aBankAccount
    self error: 'implemented in subclass'
applyToNormalCheckingAccount: aBankAccount
    self error: 'implemented in subclass'
applyToPreferredClientSavingAccount: aBankAccount
    self error: 'implemented in subclass'
```

_____

class	DepositTransaction
superclass	Transaction
instance variables	...

class methods

"none"

instance methods

transaction processing

```
applyToNormalSavingAccount: aBankAccount
    aBankAccount credit: self amount
applyToNormalCheckingAccount: aBankAccount
    aBankAccount credit: self amount
applyToPreferredClientSavingAccount: aBankAccount
    aBankAccount credit: self amount
```

class   WithdrawalTransaction
superclass   Transaction
instance variables   ...

class methods

"none"

instance methods

transaction processing

applyToNormalSavingAccount: aBankAccount
   aBankAccount **debit**: self **amount**
applyToNormalCheckingAccount: aBankAccount
   aBankAccount **debit**: self **amount**
applyToPreferredClientSavingAccount: aBankAccount
   aBankAccount **debit**: self **amount**

---

class   CheckTransaction
superclass   WithdrawalTransaction
instance variables   ...

class methods

"none"

instance methods

transaction processing

applyToNormalSavingAccount: aBankAccount
   self **error**: 'checks not allowed on saving accounts'
applyToNormalCheckingAccount: aBankAccount
   super **applyToNormalCheckingAccount**: aBankAccount
   aBankAccount **addTransaction**: (ServiceChargeTransaction
     amount: (Money **dollars**: 2)).

---

class   ServiceChargelTransaction
superclass   WithdrawalTransaction
instance variables   ...

class methods

"none"

instance methods

transaction processing

"all inherited"

9.13 Summary

This chapter has reviewed a large number of classes and their protocol, and introduced a number of new concepts. More specifically, we have

- Investigated the fundamental operations provided by class Object and the concepts that it supports: equality, identity, object sharing, deep and shallow copies, the distinction between print strings and store strings, meta-level operations, the family of **perform**: operations, and object mutation
- Investigated class Message and its facilities for storing receivers, selectors, and parameters as well as how to get those message to execute on demand
- Looked at class Compiler and its simple facility for evaluating expressions
- Scrutinized class UndefinedObject and the special technique used to implement **isNil** and **notNil**
- Reviewed class Boolean and the polymorphic approach to implementing the boolean operations in subclasses True and False
- Learned how to control the current cursor by investigating global Cursor and its associated class CursorManager
- Reviewed the magnitude classes to gain an appreciation for the protocol provided with associations, characters, numbers, dates, and times, including the concetps of a **hash**, the distinction between a digit value and an ASCII value, the large numeric library, and the possibility of bit manipulation on integers
- Investigated blocks in great detail to understand how they can be created, passed as parameters, executed for their result, and used for constructing sophisticated sequencing operations, as well as how returns work in the presence of blocks
- Reviewed familiar graphical objects such as points, rectangle, and pens and investigated new graphical objects such as the clipboard and bitmaps
- Considered a number of graphical operations that attempt to provide a degree of independence from the coordinate system being used; the notion that bitmaps have associated pens which are used to perform copy operations, both simple and complex graphical primitives; and drawing modes associated with recording pens
- Surveyed the collection and stream classes along with the class hierarchy that they belong to
- Learned about new collection classes such as sets, bags, sorted collections, identity dictionaries, and intervals (among others)
- Learned about abstract classes Collection, IndexedCollection, and FixedSizeCollection

- Investigated collection conversion operations, sequencing operations, the string-like indexed collection protocol for destructively modifying and non-destructively copying indexed collections, the concept of a sort block, and the distinction between identity dictionaries and normal (or equality) dictionaries
- Investigated streams, file streams, and files and how they may be used for sequentially (or randomly) accessing elements of a collection and looked at the implementation of **printString**
- Considered a revised implementation of bank accounts based on transactions that illustrate a number of concepts: meta-level operations, avoiding class-based cases, and double dispatching

9.14 What You Did and Did Not Learn

This chapter has provided an overview of the major classes in the Smalltalk library and all of the major concepts and protocol that they support: identity versus equality, deep versus shallow copies, sophisticated sequencing operations, blocks, bitmap manipulation; as well as advanced collection and stream operations. We also investigated the inheritance structure to gain a better understanding of the relationship between the classes. We should now understand all the Smalltalk fundamentals.

Because we surveyed such a large number of special-purpose classes and operations and illustrated their use in very simple examples, we don't expect you to remember or even try to memorize all the operations associated with these classes. As you proceed with application development in the future, you will require some (and perhaps, many) of these facilities. Having encountered them in this chapter, you will remember they existed even though you might not remember the exact message or messages involved. Nevertheless, you will remember enough to be able to browse the appropriate portion of the hierarchy in search of the facility that you need. There is no need to memorize everything.

In spite of the many classes surveyed in this chapter, we have not provided a comprehensive view of the entire set of Smalltalk classes. There are many other classes in the system that we have not investigated; e.g., class Behavior and the windowing classes. Nevertheless, you do have all the required background to build relatively sophisticated applications that don't require user interfaces. We will get an introduction to these user interface classes in Chapter 10.

9.15 Important Facts

Operations on Library Classes

See chapter contents.

Smalltalk promotes sharing: Assignments bind variables without making copies, shallow copies share common components, operations like **at:put:**, **atAll:put:**, and **atAllPut**: bind many entries to the same object. Indeed, copies are obtained only if explicitly requested for via messages such as **copy**, **shallowCopy**, and **deepCopy**.

Not all objects can be copied: Special objects such as nil, true, false, along with classes, provide themselves unchanged when copies are requested of them.

Blocks are fundamental control structure building blocks: They can be passed as parameters to application specific messages such as **do**: and **collect**:.

Block semantics: A **value**, **value:**, or **value:value**: message sent to a block either returns with the last expression computed in the block (if no return statement is encountered in the block) or returns from the method containing the block (if a return statements is successfully executed inside the block).

Ordering: Dictionaries, sets, and bags are unordered containers; ordered collections, sorted collections, streams, arrays, and strings are ordered containers.

Use collect:, select:, and reject: if possible: Instead of constructing collections using **do**:, as shown below, attempt to use **collect:**, **select:**, and **reject**: instead.

Acceptable

```
| result1 result2 |
result1 := OrderedCollection new.
aCollection do: [:element |
    element odd ifTrue: [result1 add: element]].
^result1

result2 := OrderedCollection new.
aCollection do: [:element |
    result2 add: element squared].
^result2
```

Better alternatives

```
^aCollection select: [:element | element odd]        "result1"
^aCollection reject: [:element | element even]        "result1 again"
^aCollection collect: [:element | element squared]    "result2"
```

9.16 Helpful Hints

Do not confuse classes True and False with the instances true and false: The result of a test can be either true or false but never True or False.

Use shallow copies where possible: Deep copies are expensive (requiring more time and space to construct) and unnecessary in most situations.

Self-referencing objects need to reimplement "deepCopy" and "storeOn:": The default deep copy does not provide a correct implementation for objects such as banks and bank accounts that refer to each other. Similarly, **storeOn**: will result in an infinite loop.

Subclasses of Object and Magnitude need certain operations implemented: Subclasses of Object need to reimplement = (but not ~=), since the inherited version defaults to identity. Subclasses of Magnitude need to reimplement <, <=, >, >=, and hash.

Avoid class-based cases: Avoid code like "if this object's class is X, then do case 1. If it's Y, then do case 2, ..." Use double dispatching instead.

Get rid of old objects to permit recompiling a class definition: Make all instances of the class become nil.

9.17 Keywords

concepts: ascii value, class-based case, collision, digit value, double dispatching, equality, hash, identity, meta-level operation, object mutation, print string, store string

containers: bag, collection, container, dictionary, identity dictionary, interval, key, ordered collection, sequencing, set, sorted collection, subarray, subcollection, subscript, value

special objects: association, block, directory, equality dictionary, file, fixed-size collection, identity dictionary, indexed collection, interval, raster constant, sort block, stream

graphics: backColor, bounding box, drawing mode, foreColor

globals: Clipboard, Cursor, Disk, Display, Smalltalk

9.18 Exercises

1. Are equal characters also identical? What about floats and integers? Do you get the same result for small and large integers?

2. Does binding the first element of a shallow copy of an array affect the original? Should the same semantics apply to a dictionary? Does it?

3. What is the difference between a print string and a store string for integers, for characters, and for arrays? How many classes of objects have their own unique store string? How could you use the compiler to determine whether an object (such as one of the above) implements a correct store string? Implement a store string for Interval—do you have to implement **storeString** or **storeOn**:?

4. Find out how many arrays, sets, and dictionaries are in the Smalltalk environment.

5. Create a Person class with a spouse component that can be used by a man, for example, to keep track of his wife. Design the spouse part to either be nil or another Person—not the name of a person. Implement operations **shallowCopy**, **deepCopy**, and =.

6. Implement a **do**: for integers that permits sequencing through the individual digits of a number. This should allow the following to be executed:

```
| sumOfDigits |
sumOfDigits := 0.
100 factorial do: [:digit |
    sumOfDigits := sumOfDigits + digit].
^sumOfDigits
```

7. Design a three-dimensional point class. It would be nice if an expression such as 1@2@3 would return instances of this class. Make this work or devise an equally convenient solution.

8. Design a sort block that can be used to sort person objects by names. Design another one that ensures that all males come before females. (Presumably, it should be possible to ask a person object if it is **male** or **female**.)

9. Design a new kind of collection called a SortedDictionary that provides access to the keys in sorted order.

10 Design a WordStream class that can sequence over words in a string. All space-like characters, such as tab, carriage-return, and space, should be discarded. Everything else, however, should be provided either as a name (a string, like 'hello') or a special character, such as $;.

11. Design a Tree class that can contain a value and any number of subtrees. Provide a display capability that can draw the tree using an arbitrary pen.

10

Window-Based
Applications

What You Will Learn

All commercial applications provide some sort of user interface to enable users to control the application. Building such a user interface generally requires substantial knowledge of the windowing classes; e.g., classes such as View-Manager, SubPane, Button, ListPane, and TextPane. Additionally, special knowledge is needed to properly interconnect the various components of the user interface and to specify a resizable layout—one that will properly grow and shrink when the window size is changed.

With the introduction of window builders such as Digitalk's PARTS™ (Parts Assembly and Reuse Tool Set), Objectshare Systems' Widgets/V 286™, WindowBuilder/V™ and WindowBuilder Pro™, and VisualWorks™ from ParcPlace Systems, much of this knowledge can be acquired from the tool itself. Layout and resizing specifications are simple and intuitive. As a consequence, it is generally acknowledged that building user interfaces by hand is an extremely tedious and relatively unproductive endeavor. Yet, even if we use a window builder, we must still understand how windows and panes communicate with the application.

In this chapter, we will provide a very brief introduction to the windowing classes and the event-based behavior that they support using the commercial window builder WindowBuilder/V, from Objectshare Systems, Inc. We will also implement a very simple application to demonstrate how events are used to control the application.

This chapter is not intended as a comprehensive tutorial on building user interfaces, but rather as an introduction that should inspire and motivate the reader to go on to more advanced books on the topic.

10.1 The Fundamentals of Applications

When creating a new application, a designer creates a subclass of ViewManager (see Figure 10.1) that manages all the information needed for that application, including the application window and the panes that it, in turn, contains. The application is responsible for interfacing with the application window and for interpane coordination. This coordination is achieved through Smalltalk window events (discussed below).

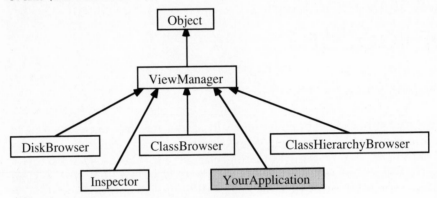

Figure 10.1 Some Smalltalk view managers.

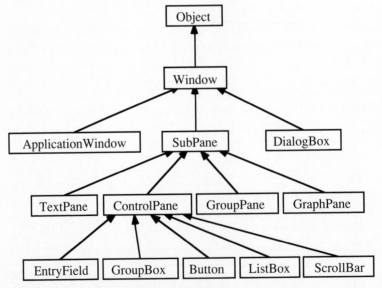

Figure 10.2 A partial window hierarchy.

A sampling of the class library that includes ApplicationWindow and the major Pane classes is shown in Figure 10.2. An application window displays the top-level title bar and other associated information such as the system menu and zoom and collapse boxes, and it contains zero or more panes. Panes (depending on the kind of pane) can display text, lists of selectable items, graphical information, etc. and permit the user to control the application; e.g., by clicking on entries in the list or clicking on a button.

An application is said to be the **owner** of the application window and its panes. When an application window (or pane) needs information specific to the application, it requests it from its owner.

A Smalltalk **event** is generated by a pane either when it needs some information from the application or when it needs to tell the application that something significant has happened. The event names are symbols such as #getContents or #clicked. To generate an event,

> aPane **event**: #eventSymbol

is executed by the Smalltalk environment—but users typically never send this message. In order for the application (or owner) to be able to respond to that event, the application must have provided the pane with a selector for an **event handler**, as follows:

> aPane **when**: #eventSymbol **perform**: #eventHandlerSelector:

The event handler selector must have exactly one parameter which will be the pane generating the event. Hence, the application must have a method such as the following:

> **eventHandlerSelector**: aPane
>   "Code to respond to event #eventSymbol."

The application then explicitly communicates with the pane to either get or change some attribute of the pane. It can also communicate with other panes by explicitly sending them messages. Panes can be named by executing

> aPane **paneName**: 'aName'

and once named, can be referenced by executing

> anApplication **paneNamed**: 'aName'.

Each kind of pane generates its own set of events. There are, however, a small set of common events that all panes generate. A summary of the most important ones, along with the expected application responses, is provided below.

Common Events
#getContents
When generated: A #getContents event is generated each time the message **update** is sent to the pane. It is also generated (but once only) when the application is first opened. More specifically, when **open** is sent to the application, a #getContents event is generated for all panes, then an #opened event is generated, and finally the window appears on the screen.

Response: The pane is out of date. Do whatever is needed to make the pane be completely up to date; e.g., turn on a radio button if it should be on; provide a list pane with the list to be displayed and the item that should be selected; or supply a text pane with the text to be displayed.

#getMenu
When generated: The user attempts to pop-up a menu by clicking with the right mouse button.

Response: Set the pane's menu to an instance of Menu via message **setMenu:**. The system will then use this menu and make it pop-up.

#gettingFocus
#losingFocus
When generated: Only one pane is ever active (has focus) at a time. A pane can lose focus when a user clicks on a new pane which subsequently gets focus (this can also happen if a user tabs to the next pane in a preset sequence).

Response: An application decides what to do in each of these cases.

Text Pane Events
#save
When generated: The user selects **Save** in the default pop-up menu associated with the text pane or the user explicitly sends an **accept** message to the pane.

Response: Get the text from the text pane (by sending message **contents**) and process it in the application. Tell the text pane that it is no longer modified (using message **modified:**), so that it knows the text has been saved.

List Pane Events
#select
When generated: The user clicks on an item in the list.

Response: Obtain the selection from the pane (by sending message **selectedItem**) and respond to it.

#doubleClickSelect
When generated: The user double-clicks on an item in the list.

Response: Obtain the selection from the pane (by sending message **selectedItem**) and respond to it.

Graph Pane Events
#button1Down
#button1DownShift
#button1Up
#button1DoubleClick
#button1Move (moving while button1 is down)
#button2Down
#button2Up
#button2DoubleClick
#button2Move (moving while button2 is down)
#mouseMove
> **When generated**: As indicated.
> **Response**: Respond to mouse movement or button clicking. The pane can be interrogated about the location of the mouse during the last event by sending it the message **mouseLocation**.

Button Pane Events
#clicked
> **When generated**: The user clicks on the button.
> **Response**: React to the button click. Get pane information if desired; e.g., **selection** returns true if the button is on; false, otherwise.

Event names #getContents and #getMenu are actually misnomers; they should be called #update (or #setContents) and #setMenu, respectively. A #getContents event is generated whenever a pane is out of date; e.g., when the window initially opens or when the pane is explicitly told to update itself (by sending it an **update** message).

When an application is opened, the subpanes needed for the application are created and added to the application. Additionally, these panes must be told, by specifying the event handlers, how to communicate with the application when any of the above events are generated. Example code fragments best illustrate what is needed.

```
open
    "Open a sample application."
    self labelWithoutPrefix: 'Sample Application'.
    self addSubpane: (GraphPane new
        owner: self;
        paneName: 'graphPane';
        when: #getContents perform: #graphPaneUpdate:;
        when: #getMenu perform: #setGraphMenu:;
        framingRatio: (0@0 extent: 1/3@1)).
```

```
    self addSubpane: (TextPane new
        paneName: 'textPane';
        owner: self;
        when: #getContents perform: #textPaneUpdate:;
        when: #save perform: #textSave:;
        when: #getMenu perform: #setTextMenu:;
        framingRatio: (1/3@0 extent: 1/3@1)).
    self addSubpane: (ListPane new
        paneName: 'listPane';
        owner: self;
        when: #getContents perform: #listPaneUpdate:;
        when: #select perform: #listSelect:;
        when: #getMenu perform: #setListMenu:;
        framingRatio: (2/3@0 extent: 1/3@1)).
    self openWindow
```

The **framing ratio** specifies where the pane is to be placed, assuming the entire window is a square with sides of length 1; i.e., rectangle 0@0 **extent:** 1@1; 0@0 is the top-left corner and 1@1 is the extent (the width and the height). An alternative is a **framing block** that computes the absolute rectangle of the pane, given the absolute rectangle of the window on the screen.

An example of the sample application's responses to three of these events is shown below. Except for **setTextMenu:**, most of the event handlers should be understandable on their own. In the **setTextMenu:** handler, labels are separated by a backslash character "\". These separators are replaced by carriage returns using message **withCrs**. The "~" character causes the character following it to be underlined and also causes it to become a keyboard speed key. The selectors are the names of methods to be executed when the corresponding menu item is selected. The selector message is sent to the owner of the menu (in this case, self, which is the application view manager).

```
textPaneUpdate: aTextPane
    "Assume that textPaneContents is an instance variable in the application,
    say containing 'Sample String'."
    aTextPane contents: textPaneContents

setTextMenu: aTextPane
    | aMenu |
    aMenu := Menu
        labels: 'Item1 ~1\Item2 ~2\Item3 ~3' withCrs
        lines: #(2)
        selectors: #(itemOne itemTwo itemThree).
    aMenu
        title: 'Text Menu Title';
        owner: self.
    aTextPane setMenu: aMenu
```

itemOne

"Respond to item one selection in the menu; e.g., by changing the contents of the textPaneContents instance variable and telling the text pane to update itself. This will generate a #getContents event for the text pane and cause the corresponding handler **textPaneUpdate**: to execute."
textPaneContents := 'Item 1 Information'.
(self **paneNamed**: 'textPane') **update**

listPaneUpdate: aListPane

"In general, the following collection would have to be something more appropriate for the application."
aListPane **contents**: #('Entry 1', 'Entry 2', 'Entry 3').
aListPane **selection**: 'Entry 2'

listSelect: aListPane

selectedTextEntry := aListPane **selectedItem.**
"Further application specific processing."

A sample of the more interesting messages understood by panes is shown below.

Text Panes

aTextPane **contents**

> Returns the string contained.

aTextPane **contents**: aString

> Set it to the specified string.

aTextPane **modified**: aBoolean

> After changes are made in a text pane, the modified instance variable becomes true. This method is useful for telling the application that the contents have been saved (by setting modified to false) in reaction to a #save event.

List Panes

aListPane **contents**

> Returns the array (or ordered collection) of strings contained.

aListPane **contents**: anIndexableCollection

> Set it to the specified collection.

aListPane **selectedItem**

> Returns the string selected (if one exists) or nil if nothing is selected.

aListPane **selection**: aStringOrNil

> Set the item to be highlighted.

Buttons

aButton **contents**

> Returns the string that is the label for the button.

aButton **contents**: aString

> Sets the label.

aButton **selection**

> Returns true if the button is on; false, otherwise.

aButton **selection**: aBoolean

> Sets the button on (true) or off (false).

Graph Panes
aGraphPane **mouseLocation**
> Returns the current location of the mouse in *pane coordinates*.

In general, there are two mechanisms for telling a pane to update itself: by explicitly sending it an **update** message, as in

(self **paneNamed**: 'textPane') **update**

and by sending the application (the owner of the pane, which is generally "self") a **changed:** message indicating which #getContents event handlers should respond, as in

self **changed**: #getContentsHandler

The former is more intuitive, so we'll use it exclusively.

10.2 Using Window Builders

A **window builder** is a tool that helps a designer create a window-based application. It provides facilities for selecting panes, laying out the panes in the window, and connecting the panes to the application. When WindowBuilder from Objectshare Systems is filed into Smalltalk, the transcript is modified to contain an extra menu, as shown in Figure 10.3.

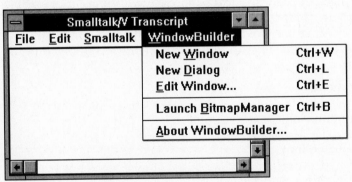

Figure 10.3 The modified transcript window.

When **New Window** is selected in the menu, a window builder appears (see Figure 10.4). We can immediately save this new application window by clicking on **Save As...** in the **File** menu. It will prompt for a class name and define it as a subclass of ViewManager.

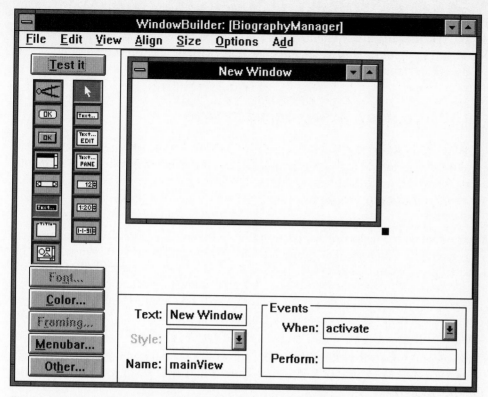

Figure 10.4 The window builder opened on a new window.

We can edit the title for the new window, view the events associated with the window in the **Events group box**, specify event handlers by typing in a new name in the **Perform: entry field**, and add subpanes by choosing them from the rightmost list of buttons under the **Test It** button. Clicking on one of the icons in the leftmost list of buttons (in this case, we clicked on the **Text...** icon—sixth in the list) changes the contents of the rightmost list. Currently, the rightmost list provides us with different kinds of text panes. It is simply a matter of clicking on one of these and then clicking in the new window to get a text pane. An instance of the selected pane will then appear in the new window.

When starting, we might wish to learn what kinds of panes are available by simply getting one of each and placing it in some appropriate place in the new window. By clicking on **Test It**, we can then obtain an actual working window to see what it looks like in practice. The window builder permits the newly added panes to be named, moved, colored, resized, aligned and distributed with respect to each other, and also permits fonts to be chosen for panes that can contain text.

Once we have added all the panes that we want for our application, we can simply **Save** the application and then switch to a browser to see the methods generated by the builder. This particular version will generate an **open** method that builds a window; creates the subpanes, names them, colors them, positions them, specifies their event handlers, adds them to the window; and then starts the application. Menus and a menu bar (if specified) are also generated. Let's consider an actual application.

10.3 Case Study: A Biography Manager

A **biography manager** is an application that keeps track of a number of people and their associated biographical data. The biographical data could be any textual data spanning multiple lines. We'll use the word **biography** to refer to an object that maps names to biographical text. In our case, a biography will be a simple dictionary.

Our intent is to develop an application that can take a biography and display it on the screen in a manner that permits users to view and modify it. We want to be able to use the same application for viewing and editing biographical information associated with different people; e.g., baseball players, hockey players, business associates, or friends. So these dictionaries will be either globals themselves or stored collectively in one global collection. As an extension, we could even permit this biographical data to reside in files (but we won't pursue that here).

To execute our application on specific biographical data, we should be able to create a new biography manager and open it on a specific biography, as shown below.

    BiographyManager **new openOn:** (Dictionary **new**
        at: 'Frank Jones' **put:** 'Likes sports.';
        at: 'John Smith' **put:** 'Enjoys swimming.';
        yourself)

The result should be a window (see Figure 10.5) that has a list pane for scrolling through the names, a text pane for viewing and modifying the biographical data, and four buttons for adding and removing names and for accepting or cancelling biographical text modifications.

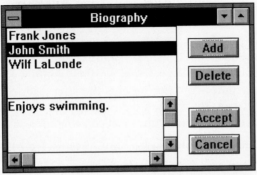

Figure 10.5 A biography manager.

We begin with the window builder to create a class called BiographyManager. Then we add a list pane, a text pane, and four buttons as shown in Figure 10.6.

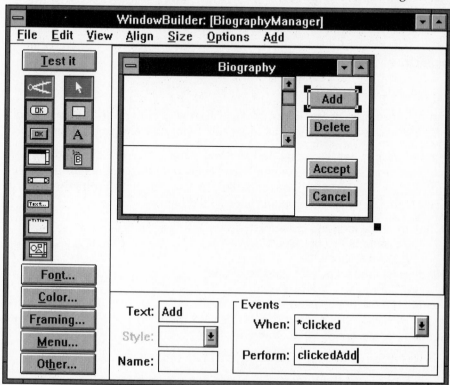

Figure 10.6 Building the user interface for the biography manager.

Next, we need to specify the event handlers for our panes. Figure 10.6, for example, illustrates the process of associating an event handler called **clickedAdd**: with the **Add** button's **#clicked** event.

The application should be designed in such a manner that all the information needed to keep track of the application is kept in instance variables. In our case, it will be sufficient to keep track of two things: the biography itself and the name (or key) of the selected entry. So our application could be defined as follows:

class	BiographyManager
superclass	ViewManager
instance variables	biography selectedName
pool dictionaries	ColorConstants WBConstants

Note that the pool dictionaries specified were provided by the window builder when we first saved the application called BiographyManager. At that time, no instance variables were provided by the window builder. We added them explicitly afterward.

The window builder generates an **open** method but it does not provide an **openOn**: method. An **openOn**: instance method such as the following can be provided to initialize our instance variables. Note that "selectedName" is initialized to nil by default to indicate that no name is initially selected.

> *opening*
>
> **openOn**: aDictionary
>   biography := aDictionary.
>   self **open**

We can also provide an **initialize** method that sets "biography" to an empty dictionary in case someone attempts to execute "BiographyManager **new open**".

During processing, the list pane and the text pane could get out of date; e.g., when a new name is added. So we will need #getContents handlers for these. For the buttons, we will need #clicked handlers to react to clicks on the buttons. A summary of all the specified handlers is provided below.

> **Handlers for the list pane called "listPane"**
>   #getContents ⇒ #updateList:
>   #select ⇒ #selectList:
> **Handlers for the text pane called "textPane"**
>   #getContents ⇒ #updateText:
> **Handlers for the button titled "Add"**
>   #clicked ⇒ #clickedAdd:
> **Handlers for the button titled "Remove"**
>   #clicked ⇒ #clickedRemove:
> **Handlers for the button titled "Accept"**
>   #clicked ⇒ #clickedAccept:
> **Handlers for the button titled "Cancel"**
>   #clicked ⇒ #clickedCancel:

Now, let's consider specific #getContents handlers; e.g., the list pane's **updateList**: handler and the text pane's **updateText**: handler. Recall that the handler's parameter is the pane in which the event occurred. Consequently, the pane for **updateList**: will be a list pane. Similarly, the pane for **updateText**: will be a text pane.

For the list pane (see below), we need to provide an indexed collection of names. We can get these names from instance variable "biography". Since it is a dictionary, message **keys** will give us the required names but it is provided, perhaps surprisingly, as a set. Converting to a sorted collection will ensure that it is indexable by the pane and will also provide it in a more reasonable order. We can give this list to the pane by sending it message **contents**:. Additionally, we have to tell the pane which entry to select by sending it message **selection**:. Note that "selectedName" must be nil to indicate "no selection"—this is the situation when we start, even if we don't initialize "selectedName".

For the text pane, we simply need to supply the text associated with the selected name by sending the pane a **contents:** message. We must be careful, however, to take care of the situation where there is no entry selected. In that case, selectedName will be nil. Since nil is not a valid key, an empty string will be supplied by the **ifAbsent:** block.

handlers for the list pane's #select event

> **updateList**: aPane
>   "The list pane's #getContents handler."
>   aPane **contents**: biography **keys asSortedCollection**.
>   aPane **selection**: selectedName

> **updateText**: aPane
>   "The text pane's #getContents handler."
>   aPane **contents**: (biography **at**: selectedName **ifAbsent**: [''])

Each of the #clicked handlers for the buttons must be handled specially, since they each have a different function. Let's consider the **Add** button first. We begin by prompting the user for a new name. If the user clicks on the prompter's **Cancel** button, nil will be returned. We can easily test for nil and return from the method without doing anything. If the user clicks on the prompter's OK button (or hits carriage return), the new name will be provided. If it is already in "biography", we provide an error message and repeat the process recursively. Otherwise, we associate an empty string with this new name and update the application. To update the application, we simply tell both the list pane and the text pane that they are out of date—by sending them **update** messages.

handler for the Add button's #clicked event

> **clickedAdd**: aPane
>   "The Add button's #clicked handler."
> | newName |
>   newName := Prompter
>   **prompt**: 'New Name' **default**: 'FirstName LastName'.
>   newName **isNil ifTrue**: [^self "user cancelled"].
>   (biography **includesKey**: newName) **ifTrue**: [
>   MessageBox **message**: 'Key ', newName, ' already exists!!'.
>   ^self **clickedAdd**: aPane].
>   biography **at**: newName **put**: ''.
>   selectedName := newName.
>   self **update**

updating all panes

> **update**
>   "Update both the list and text panes."
>   (self **paneNamed**: 'listPane') **update**.
>   (self **paneNamed**: 'textPane') **update**

The #clicked handler for the **Delete** button is similar. However, it must cause the currently selected name to be removed from the biography, as shown below. Note that care must be taken to avoid removing key nil when there is nothing selected. Also, it is good practice to confirm the deletion, in case it was accidental. In addition to removing the current selection from the biography, we also have to deselect it by setting "selectedName" to nil. Of course, it is message **update** that will cause the revised list with no selection to become visible. It will also cause the displayed text to be an empty string.

handler for the Delete button's #clicked event

```
clickedDelete: aPane
    "The Delete button's #clicked handler."
    selectedName isNil ifTrue: [^self "nothing selected"].
    (MessageBox confirm: 'Delete ', selectedName, '?')
        ifFalse: [^self "cancelled"].
    biography removeKey: selectedName.
    selectedName := nil.
    self update
```

The #clicked event handler for the **Accept** button is a little different. Note that the pane provided as parameter is the button pane. We need to take the textual information from the text pane (not the button pane) and store it in the biography. So we must first get the text pane. Assuming that "selectedName" isn't nil, we can subsequently get the text pane's **contents** and associate it with the key maintained in "selectedName" by using an **at:put:** message.

As part of its regular behavior, a text pane keeps track of whether changes have been made; i.e., it considers itself to be modified if the text displayed in the pane is different from its initial contents. Attempts to close the application window when there are text panes containing modified text result in a **Save Current Changes** prompter. Replying with **Yes** or **Cancel** aborts the close. To ensure that such a prompt does not occur, we need to tell the text pane that it should now consider itself to be unmodified by sending it the message "**modified**: false".

handler for the Accept button's #clicked event

```
clickedAccept: aPane
    "The Accept button's #clicked handler."
    | textPane |
    textPane := self paneNamed: 'textPane'.
    textPane modified: false.
    selectedName isNil ifTrue: [^self "nothing selected"].
    biography at: selectedName put: textPane contents
```

When we wrote the **Add** button's #clicked handler, we didn't take into account the fact that text in the text pane might not have been accepted. If, for example, we made changes to a person's biographical data and then clicked on **Add** before accepting it, this modified text would be lost because it would not have been recorded in "biography". To handle this situation, we need to introduce the following at the beginning of the **clickedAdd**: method:

```
textPane := self paneNamed: 'textPane'.
textPane modified ifTrue: [
    (MessageBox confirm: 'Save Changes?')
        ifTrue: [self clickedAccept: nil "pane not needed"]].
```

The **Cancel** button's #clicked handler is similar to the handler for **Accept**. It differs, however, by resetting the contents of the text pane to the information in "biography".

handler for the Cancel button's #clicked event

```
clickedCancel: aPane
    "The Cancel button's #clicked handler."
    | textPane |
    textPane := self paneNamed: 'textPane'.
    textPane modified: false.
    selectedName isNil ifTrue: [^self "nothing selected"].
    textPane contents: (biography at: selectedName)
```

The complete class is shown below. Note that methods **wbCreated** and **open** are generated by the builder. It is possible to learn more about creating windows by studying the **open** method itself. However, it makes use of FramingParameters methods for positioning and resizing that are very cryptic.

class	BiographyManager
superclass	ViewManager
instance variables	biography selectedName
pool dictionaries	ColorConstants WBConstants

class methods

examples

example1
```
    "BiographyManager example1"
    BiographyManager new openOn: (Dictionary new
        at: 'Frank Jones' put: 'Likes sports.';
        at: 'John Smith' put: 'Enjoys swimming.';
        yourself)
```

generated by the window builder

wbCreated
```
    ^true
```

instance methods

instance initialization

initialize
    super **initialize**.
    biography := Dictionary **new**

opening

openOn: aDictionary
    biography := aDictionary.
    self **open**

opening (generated by the window builder)

open
    "WARNING!! This method was automatically generated by WindowBuilder. Code you add here which does not conform to the WindowBuilder API will probably be lost the next time you save your layout definition."
    | v |
    self **addView**: (
       v := self **topPaneClass new**
          owner: self;
          labelWithoutPrefix: 'Biography';
          noSmalltalkMenuBar;
          viewName: 'mainView';
          framingBlock: (FramingParameters **new**
             iDUE: 677 @ 376; **xC**; **yC**;
             cRDU: (14 @ 364 **rightBottom**: 663 @ 50));
          pStyle: #(sysmenu sizable titlebar minimize maximize);
          addSubpane: (
            CPBitmapButton **new**
               owner: self;
               framingBlock: (FramingParameters **new**
                  iDUE: 135 @ 44; **IDU**: 487 **r**: #left; **tDU**: 244 **r**: #top);
               startGroup;
               when: #clicked **perform**: #clickedCancel:;
               contents: 'Cancel';
               backColor: ClrPalegray;
               yourself);
          addSubpane: (
            CPBitmapButton **new**
               owner: self;
               framingBlock: (FramingParameters **new**
                  iDUE: 135 @ 44; **IDU**: 487 **r**: #left; **tDU**: 184 **r**: #top);
               startGroup;
               when: #clicked **perform**: #clickedAccept:;
               contents: 'Accept';
               backColor: ClrPalegray;
               yourself);

```
        addSubpane: (
            CPBitmapButton new
                owner: self;
                framingBlock: (FramingParameters new
                    iDUE: 135 @ 44; IDU: 487 r: #left; tDU: 90 r: #top);
                startGroup;
                when: #clicked perform: #clickedDelete:;
                contents: 'Delete';
                backColor: ClrPalegray;
                yourself);
        addSubpane: (
            CPBitmapButton new
                owner: self;
                framingBlock: (FramingParameters new
                    iDUE: 135 @ 44; IDU: 487 r: #left; tDU: 28 r: #top);
                startGroup;
                when: #clicked perform: #clickedAdd:;
                contents: 'Add';
                backColor: ClrPalegray;
                yourself);
        addSubpane: (
            TextPane new
                owner: self;
                framingBlock: (FramingParameters new
                    iDUE: 457 @ 156; IDU: 0 r: #left;
                    rDU: 457 r: #left; tDU: 158 r: #top; bDU: 314 r: #top);
                paneName: 'textPane';
                startGroup;
                when: #getContents perform: #updateText:;
                yourself);
        addSubpane: (
            ListBox new
                owner: self;
                framingBlock: (FramingParameters new
                    iDUE: 457 @ 160; IDU: 0 r: #left;
                    rDU: 457 r: #left; tDU: 0 r: #top; bDU: 160 r: #top);
                paneName: 'listPane';
                startGroup;
                when: #getContents perform: #updateList:;
                when: #select perform: #selectList:;
                yourself);
    yourself).
    self openWindow
```

handlers for the list pane's #select event

```
selectList: aPane
    "The list pane's #select handler."
    selectedName := aPane selectedItem.
    (self paneNamed: 'textPane') update
```

handlers for the list and text pane's #getContents event

updateList: aPane
    "The list pane's #getContents handler."
    aPane **contents**: biography **keys asSortedCollection**.
    aPane **selection**: selectedName

updateText: aPane
    "The text pane's #getContents handler."
    aPane **contents**: (biography **at**: selectedName **ifAbsent**: [''])

handlers for the buttons' #clicked event

clickedAdd: aPane
    "The Add button's #clicked handler."
    | textPane newName |
    textPane := self **paneNamed**: 'textPane'.
    textPane **modified ifTrue**: [
        (MessageBox **confirm**: 'Save Changes?')
            ifTrue: [self **clickedAccept**: nil "pane not needed"]].
    newName := Prompter
        prompt: 'New Name' **default**: 'FirstName LastName'.
    newName **isNil ifTrue**: [^self "user cancelled"].
    (biography **includesKey**: newName) **ifTrue**: [
        MessageBox **message**: 'Key ', newName, ' already exists!!'.
        ^self **clickedAdd**: aPane].
    biography **at**: newName **put**: ''.
    selectedName := newName.
    self **update**

clickedDelete: aPane
    "The Delete button's #clicked handler."
    selectedName **isNil ifTrue**: [^self "nothing selected"].
    (MessageBox **confirm**: 'Delete ', selectedName, '?')
        ifFalse: [^self "cancelled"].
    biography **removeKey**: selectedName.
    selectedName := nil.
    self **update**

clickedAccept: aPane
    "The Accept button's #clicked handler."
    | textPane |
    textPane := self **paneNamed**: 'textPane'.
    textPane **modified**: false.
    selectedName **isNil ifTrue**: [^self "nothing selected"].
    biography **at**: selectedName **put**: textPane **contents**

clickedCancel: aPane
    "The Cancel button's #clicked handler."
    | textPane |
    textPane := self **paneNamed**: 'textPane'.
    textPane **modified**: false.
    selectedName **isNil ifTrue**: [^self "nothing selected"].
    textPane **contents**: (biography **at**: selectedName)

updating all panes

update
    "Update both the list and text panes."
    (self **paneNamed**: 'listPane') **update**.
    (self **paneNamed**: 'textPane') **update**

10.4 Summary

This chapter has provided a very brief introduction to windows, panes, window builders, and applications. More specifically, we have

- Investigated the basics of windows and panes including the major pane classes and the notion of events supported by these classes
- Looked at a commercial window builder to see how it can be used to generate an initial application
- Developed a simple application, a biography manager, to illustrate how events can be used to handle the interactions between list panes, text panes, and buttons

10.5 What You Did and Did Not Learn

In this chapter, we have provided only a brief introduction to window-based applications. It is possible to carry on from here to design and build larger and more sophisticated applications with substantially more complex objects. Although there are many useful panes and events that have not been illustrated, it is possible to extend your expertise gradually by picking and choosing only those panes and events that make immediate sense; e.g., by browsing the panes and event lists in the builder. Beyond that, you should also have the knowledge and courage to experiment and discover what you need.

10.6 Important Facts

Operations on ViewManagers (Applications)

anApplication **paneNamed**: aString

> Retrieves a pane by name

anApplication **changed**: #getContentsHandler

> Equivalent to telling the pane with the indicated #getContents handler to **update**

Operations on Panes

aPane **paneName**: aString   Gives a name to a pane

aPane **event**: #eventSymbol   Executed by the Smalltalk environment to cause a Smalltalk event to occur

aPane **when**: #eventSymbol **perform**: #eventHandlerSelector:

> Associates a handler with an event

aPane **update**   Generates a #getContents event

Operations on Text Panes

aTextPane **accept**   Generates a #save event

aTextPane **contents**   Returns the string contained

aTextPane **contents**: aString   Sets the displayed text to the specified string

aTextPane **modified**: aBoolean   Indicates whether the visible text is to be considered changed

Operations on List Panes

aListPane **contents**

> Returns the list items, an indexable collection of strings

aListPane **contents**: anIndexableCollection

> Sets the list items to the specified collection

aListPane **selectedItem**

> Returns the string selected (if one exists) or nil if nothing is selected

aListPane **selection**: aStringOrNil   Sets the item to be highlighted

Operations on Buttons

aButton **contents**

> Returns the string that is the label for the button

aButton **contents**: aString   Sets the label

aButton **selection**

> Returns true if the button is on; false, otherwise

aButton **selection**: aBoolean   Sets the button on (true) or off (false)

Operations on Graph Panes

aGraphPane **mouseLocation**

> Returns the current location of the mouse in *pane coordinates*

A Sampling of Events

Common Events
#getContents ⇒ Update the pane to bring it up to date.
#getMenu ⇒ Set the pane's menu to an instance of Menu.
#gettingFocus ⇒ React to gaining control.
#losingFocus ⇒ React to losing control.

Text Pane Events
#save ⇒ React to the pane being told to save.

List Pane Events
#select ⇒ React to single-clicking on an entry.
#doubleClickSelect ⇒ React to double-clicking on an entry.

Graph Pane Events
#button1Down
#button1DownShift
#button1Up
#button1DoubleClick
#button1Move (moving while button1 is down)
#button2Down
#button2Up
#button2DoubleClick
#button2Move (moving while button2 is down)
#mouseMove
  ⇒ React to mouse manipulations.

Button Pane Events
#clicked ⇒ React to clicking on a button.

10.7 Helpful Hints

Use a window builder to create the user interface: Window builders make it easy to develop applications by permitting the designer, or programmer, to select the right kinds of panes, to position them, to resize them, and to associate appropriate event handlers.

10.8 Glossary

windows and panes: application, event, event handler, framing block, framing ratio, owner, window builder

10.9 Exercises

1. Create a Chooser dialog box (click on **New Dialog** instead of **New Window**) that would permit a user to execute

   Chooser **new openOn**: #('red' 'green' 'blue') **title**: 'Choose a color'

   A user should be able to
   • Double-click on an entry—causing the window to close and the selected entry to be returned
   • Click once on an entry and then click on an **OK** button— causing the same effect as above
   • Click on a **CANCEL** button—causing nil to be returned

   After a dialog box opens on the display, execution past the **open** message is suspended until the user does something to cause it to be sent a **close** message. It should be possible to return the selected entry immediately after this **open** message.

2. Create a bank account manager for browsing and editing transactions.
3. Create a bitmap librarian for keeping track of pictures by name.
4. Create a simplified calculator.

Appendix: A Smalltalk Subset

Comments

"Hello, there. This is a comment."

Control Structures

Expression **ifTrue**: [Statements].
Expression **ifFalse**: [Statements].
Expression **ifTrue**: [Statements] **ifFalse**: [Statements].
[Expression] **whileTrue**: [Statements].
anInteger **timesRepeat**: [Statements].
Expression **to**: Expression **by**: Expression **do**: [:loopIndex | Statements].
Expression **to**: Expression **do**: [:loopIndex | Statements].
Variable := Expression   an assignment
^Expression   a return statement

Booleans

true, **false**	constants
Expression = Expression	equal
Expression ~= Expression	not equal
Expression == Expression	identical
Expression ~~ Expression	not identical
Expression > Expression	greater
Expression < Expression	less
Expression <= Expression	less or equal
Expression >= Expression	greater or equal
Expression I Expression	or
Expression & Expression	and
Expression **or**: [Expression]	short-circuit or[†]
Expression **and**: [Expression]	short-circuit and[†]

[†]may not evaluate 2nd expression.

Numbers

23.5e3	float constant (lowercase e)
1999 integer constant	
(2/3)	fraction constant
+,-,*,/	typical operations
Expression // Expression	divide and truncate toward -∞
Expression \\ Expression	remainder after truncation by //
Expression **negated**	
Expression **abs**	absolute value
Expression **sqrt**	square root
Expression **raisedTo**: aNumber	
Expression **squared**	

Note: all expressions are evaluated left to right with *no operator priority*. For example, 1+2*3 means (1+2)*3.

Strings

'hello this is a string, isn"t it?'	string constant (consists of characters)
Expression, Expression	string concatenation
Expression **copyFrom**: start **to**: end	copying a part of a string

Note: array operations also apply to strings and vice versa.

Characters

$a, $x, $;	character constants

Conversion

Expression **asInteger**	valid for numbers
Expression **asFloat**	valid for numbers
Expression **asFraction**	valid for numbers
Expression **asCharacter**	valid for integers
aCharacter **asciiValue**	converse of **asCharacter**
Expression **printString**	valid for anything (gives string)
Expression **storeString**	valid for anything (gives code to recreate)

Transcript Operations

Transcript **nextPutAll**: aString	appends string to Transcript
Transcript **nextPut**: aCharacter	appends character to Transcript
Transcript **cr**	appends carriage return
Transcript **space**	appends a blank
Transcript **tab**	appends a tab

Object Operations

anObject **printOn**: aWindow	appends its print string into the window
anObject **storeOn**: aWindow	appends its store string into the window

Collections (Arrays, Ordered Collections, Dictionaries)

#('hello' 56 1.5e-10 $a)	array constant
Array **new**: sizeOfArray	gets a new array
OrderedCollection **new**	gets a new ordered collection
Dictionary **new**	gets a new dictionary

CollectionClass **with**: object1 [†]	e.g., Array **with**: 10 **with**: 20
CollectionClass **with**: object1 **with**: object2 [†]	
CollectionClass **with**: object1 **with**: object2 **with**: object3 [†]	
CollectionClass **with**: object1 **with**: object2 **with**: object3 **with**: object4 [†]	

aCollection **size**	number of elements
aCollection **at**: key	element at key
aCollection **at**: key **put**: aValue	replace the element at key by a new one
anOrderedCollection **add**: anObject	adds at end (grows collection)
anOrderedCollection **addFirst**: anObject	adds at beginning (grows collection)
anOrderedCollection **addLast**: anObject	same as **add**:
anOrderedCollection **removeFirst**	obtains and removes first element (shrinks collection)
anOrderedCollection **removeLastt**	obtains and removes last element (shrinks collection)

[†]Not allowed on dictionaries.

Note: Arrays and ordered collections must have integer keys between 1 and the size of the collection; dictionaries can have arbitrary keys.

Special Effects

Terminal **bell**	rings the bell

Window Operations

self **halt**	opens a debugger if you choose to debug
anObject **inspect**	opens an inspector
MessageBox **message**: 'continue'	presents a message on the screen (expect no answer)
MessageBox **confirm**: 'continue'	presents a message on the screen (expect a boolean)
Prompter **prompt**: aQuestionString **default**: aDefaultAnswerString	presents a message (expect a string)

Glossary

Analysis and Design

analysis Determining what is needed (the requirements).

anthropomorphic design See **responsibility-driven design**.

behavior How an object reacts to messages.

behavior-driven design See **responsibility-driven design**.

class hierarchy diagram A diagram that represents the relationships between the classes.

class hierarchy integration Determining how application classes relate to each other and to existing classes in the Smalltalk library.

collaborator A synonym for **helper**.

colleague A synonym for **helper**.

CRC methodology Short for **classes-responsibilities-collaborators methodology**.

CRH methodology Short for **classes-responsibilities-helpers methodology** (synonymous with CRC).

design Determining how to implement the requirements.

generalization Making a class more general; i.e., applicable in more circumstances than before; e.g., generalizing a truck to a vehicle.

helpers The other classes or instances that an object needs to effectively carry out its responsibilities.

is-a hierarchy A graph that contains a directed edge from class Y to class X if a Y **is a** (or **is an**) X; i.e., if a Y is a specialized X; e.g., a cow is an animal, so a directed edge would connect class Cow to class Animal in a corresponding is-a hierarchy.

iterative refinement An approach in which small improvements are continually made until no more changes or improvements are possible. An object-oriented iterative refinement methodology evolves analysis, design, and implementation in parallel.

methodology A clearly specified series of steps and a partial ordering of those steps that will achieve a well-defined goal; e.g., the iterative refinement methodology.

need-driven design An approach to design that focuses on what is actually needed rather than on what might be needed.

object-centered design See **responsibility-driven design**.

object-centered view A viewpoint that considers an object to be at the center and everything else to be secondary.

object-community view A viewpoint that rises above all the objects to provide a bird's eye view of the objects.

object ensemble diagram A diagram that deals with a group of connected objects.

parts diagram A diagram that shows the parts (or instance variables) that each instance of a class has; e.g., a parts diagram for Truck might contain parts "cargoCapacity" and "cargo".

requirements What a client wants or desires.

responsibilities The messages a class and its instances should understand and consequently the methods needed to ensure proper replies to those messages.

responsibility-driven design Design driven by the desire to determine what an object's behavior is with respect to other objects; i.e., its responsibilities. Also known as object-centered design, behavior-driven design, anthropomorphic design, or need-driven design.

reusability The notion that something should be used for other things besides what it was specifically built or designed for.

specialization The process of making a class more specific; i.e., applicable in fewer circumstances than before; e.g., specializing a vehicle to a car.

stepwise refinement A synonym for top-down decomposition.

top-down decomposition A technique for developing a method that depends on dividing the task to be performed into two or more subtasks. (See the binary search technique in the phone book case study.)

top-down strategy A technique for developing a method that ignores whether the messages used exist. The whole point of the strategy is to discover which messages are needed.

use-case A sample use of a class that illustrates how it might by used in one, of perhaps many, typical situations.

use-case chasing Tracing or implementing the messages that are part of a use-case.

use-case diagram A diagram that summarizes all the important messages and objects involved in a computation.

Assignments and Binding

assignment A synonym for **binding**.

binding Making a variable refer to an object. What the binding operator ":=" does. Initially, all variables are bound to nil.

declaration Telling the Smalltalk environment that we intend to use a specific name as a variable.

defining Binding a variable to a desired object.

inline assignment An assignment that is part of a larger expression; e.g., "1 + (age := aPerson **age**)".

Browsing

implementors of a method selector All the methods with the same selector; e.g., implementors of "+" are all the "+" methods in the Smalltalk environment including the float "+" , the fraction "+", the integer "+" , etc.

messages of a method All the messages sent by the method—a starting point for tracing other messages.

senders of a method selector Other methods that use that selector; e.g., senders of "+" are all those methods with code containing "+". Senders provide example uses of a method.

Computer Components

cabinet A special enclosure containing the processor and memory.

computer A machine that can interpret commands in a given/specific language; it consists of several components: a **processor** that can execute commands, **memory** that can be used to store information (including commands), a **monitor** that can display information on a screen, a **keyboard** that can be used to type in information, and a **mouse** that can be used to point at and select items on the screen.

family Computers that may (or may not) look different but behave the same way; e.g., the Macintosh or IBM PC family of computers.

keyboard A device that can be used to type (enter) information into a computer.

memory Where information (including commands) can be stored in a computer.

model A particular member of a family of computers, usually by the same manufacturer.

monitor A device that can display information on a screen.

mouse A device that can be used to point at and select items on the screen.

processor That part of a computer that can execute commands.

Computer Terminology

activating Starting up Smalltalk or making a window the current window.

booting the system Turning on a computer (or resetting it) so that the operating system is loaded into memory and executing.

code The colloquial term for **software**.

commanding Providing instructions for something or someone else to follow.

designer A high-level programmer.

designing Organizing for the purpose of solving a problem or building a complicated system of interacting components. When programming, it is the process of determining how many classes are needed, what operations or methods must be supported by the classes, and the kinds of relationship that must exist between the classes and the instances.

evaluating A synonym for **executing**.

executing In the context of commands given to a computer, the act of performing the commands.

hardware The portion of the system that is relatively resilient to change—the physical computer.

machine language A language understood by and unique to each class of processors.

operating system The software that provides a computer with a specific "look and feel."

program A piece of software that can be executed as a unit.

programmer The designer or creator of a set of commands.

programming The art of transcribing commands onto a medium that can be read.

programming environment A facility that provides three capabilities: an interface between a programmer-oriented language such as Smalltalk and a specific machine language, tools that support the programming process in the programmer-oriented language, and a library of preprogrammed instructions that can be used to construct more elaborate commands.

software The portion of the system that is easy to change—the commands.

Control Structures

block A sequence of zero or more expressions separated by "." and surrounded by square brackets; e.g. "[Transcript **cr**. anObject **printOn**: Transcript]". Blocks are often used in control structures.

control structure A message that permits the path of execution to be controlled; e.g., an if-expression or a times-repeat-expression.

do loop A looping construct that supports sequencing over changing values; e.g., "#('hi' 100 dollars) **do**: [:anObject | anObject **printOn**: Transcript].

if-expression An ifTrue:ifFalse: message sent to a boolean receiver; e.g., "anInteger **odd ifTrue**: [Transcript **cr**] **ifFalse**: [Transcript **space**]". Variants also exist with the **ifTrue**: or **ifFalse**: keywords missing or interchanged.

side-effect The effect produced by evaluating an expression independent of the result obtained; e.g., evaluating "5 **timesRepeat**: [Transcript **cr**]" returns 0 but has the much more important side-effect of changing the transcript.

times-repeat-expression A message (**timesRepeat:**) sent to an integer to control the number of times a block is to execute; e.g., "10 **timesRepeat**: [Transcript **nextPutAll**: 'hi ']".

while-expression A **whileTrue**: or **whileFalse**: message sent to a block; e.g., "| counter | counter := 10. [counter > 0] **whileTrue**: [counter **printOn**: Transcript. counter := counter - 1]"

Debugging

bug The cause of a problem.

debugger A tool that permits the user to trace program execution using **Hop** and **Skip**, investigate variable bindings during execution, and inspect those bindings.

debugging Finding out what is wrong.

single stepping Executing one message at a time in a debugger to see the consequences.

Evaluation Rules

bracketing rule A bracketed expression cannot be used as an operand unless all messages inside have been evaluated.

left-to-right evaluation The order in which consecutive operators of the same priority are evaluated.

priorities Selectors are ordered, from highest to lowest priority, as follows: unary selectors, binary selectors, and keyworded selectors.

priority rule Given two consecutive selectors, the leftmost selector is evaluated first if they both have the same priority; otherwise, the highest priority selector is evaluated first.

short-circuit operation An operation such as "**and**:" or "**or**:" that evaluates only the receiver if that is sufficient to determine the answer.

Files

backup A copy of selected methods or classes kept in files rather than in the Smalltalk programming environment.

directory A special file that can contain other files.

directory hierarchy The list of directories from a particular file; i.e., the file, the directory containing it, the directory containing the previous directory, and so on.

disk drive The mechanism that can read from and write to a disk. Usually designated by a special prefix such as **a:**, **b:**, or **c:**.

file Information saved on disk in a format that can be retrieved later.

filing in Retrieving a method or class from disk and adding it to the programming environment.

filing out Saving a method or class on disk in a format that can be retrieved later.

floppy disk A file recording medium that permits files to be transported easily between computers.

hard disk A file recording medium built-in to the computer.

path name A name such as "c:\v20\book\vw.exe" that includes the drive and a complete directory hierarchy.

Globals

Clipboard An instance of ClipboardManager that maintains the information copied from some other application, such as a paint program or a word processing program.

ColorConstants A pool dictionary containing the names of all the colors available for line graphics.

Cursor An instance of CursorManager that provides the current iconic representation for the mouse on the screen.

Disk An instance of Directory that refers to the directory containing the Smalltalk image.

Display An instance of Screen whose pen can be used for drawing and copying bitmaps.

Smalltalk An instance of SystemDictionary that keeps track of all global variables (including itself) and that provides special facilities for managing the Smalltalk image. One member among many computer languages. Other examples are BASIC, Fortran, COBOL, Pascal, C, PL/1, Ada, Snobol, Forth, Prolog, and Lisp.

Transcript A global referring to the transcript window.

Graphics

backColor The color of a closed figure's interior.

background The interior of a picture or window.

bounding box The rectangular area associated with a medium such as a bitmap.

color constants Colors referenced by names such as ClrBlack, ClrWhite, ClrRed, ClrPink, ClrBlue, ClrYellow, and ClrGreen. These color are defined in dictionary ColorConstants.

direction The heading associated with a pen. It is specified as an angle relative to the x-axis, positive for clockwise and negative for counter-clockwise; e.g., a direction of $0°$ points to the right, $90°$ points down, and $-90°$ points up.

drawing mode One of the three modes associated with recording pens. It includes **draw mode**, where figures are drawn but not recorded; **retain mode**, where figures are recorded but not drawn; and **draw and retain mode**, which combines the aspects of both. When a figure is recorded, graph panes can redraw the figures when activated; e.g., aPen **drawRetainPicture**: [... *code to draw*...].

extent A point denoting the width (x-coordinate) and the height (y-coordinate).

filled shape A shape in which the interior is colored in the background color. The boundary is in the foreground color.

foreColor The color of a closed figure's boundary.

foreground The boundary of picture or window.

location The position of a pen specified as a point.

nib A drawing tip that permits a pen to draw when the nib is **down** (on the surface of the display) but not when it is **up** (off the surface).

origin The point 0@0 on the display; the top-left corner.

pen An object that can draw from one point to another on the display. It maintains a nib, a location, and a direction. A pen can be **placed** at an arbitrary point, made to **goto** a specified point, or made to **go** forward an arbitrary distance in whatever direction it is currently pointing (in the last two situations, a line is drawn from the current location to the destination point if the nib is down).

pixel A unit distance, either in the x- or y-direction, on the display

point An x- and y-coordinate pair; e.g., 10@20 is a point with x-coordinate 10 and y-coordinate 20.

unfilled shape A shape in which the interior is not colored (it is transparent). The boundary is colored in the foreground color.

x-axis The imaginary line in which the y-coordinate is 0.

x-coordinate The first component of a point; e.g., the 10 in 10@20.

y-axis The imaginary line in which the x-coordinate is 0.

y-coordinate The second component of a point; e.g., the 20 in 10@10.

Inheritance

class hierarchy diagram A diagram that represents the relationships between the classes.

hierarchical buck-passing A variation of the technique known as passing the buck, whereby a method such as **printOn**: does part of the work itself and passes on the rest of the work to another method with the same name higher up in the hierarchy.

hierarchy An organization (or ranking) of items for the purpose of highlighting the relationships between the items; typically illustrated with a graph.

implementation perspective The view that tries to increase reusability by maximizing the reuse of inherited methods and inherited representation.

inheritance The process that permits methods and representation provided by a superclass to be used automatically by a subclass.

initialization framework An implementation pattern for a set of hierarchically related classes that results in a well-designed set of initialization methods.

is-a hierarchy A graph that contains a directed edge from class X to class Y if an X **is a** (or **is an**) Y; i.e., if each instance of X can play the role of a Y; e.g., a cow is an animal, so a directed edge would connect class Cow to class Animal in a corresponding is-a hierarchy.

is-kind-of hierarchy A synonym for **is-a hierarchy**.

overridding Defining a method in a subclass that happens to have the same name as an existing method in a superclass.

subclass A class that inherits from another immediately above it in the class hierarchy.

user perspective The view that tries to ensure that the subclass hierarchy is also an is-a hierarchy.

Keyboard Terminology

Enter key A key that causes a new line to be started.

Backspace key A key that causes the character to the left of the I-beam to be removed; usually indicated by a left arrow at the extreme right end of the numerics row.

Delete key A key that causes the character to the right of the I-beam to be removed.

parentheses A synonym for **round brackets**.

round brackets Brackets "(" and ")" that can be used to surround an expression so that it can be treated as an operand.

space The character obtained by pressing the **spacebar**.

spacebar The large unlabeled key at the bottom of the keyboard that causes a space character to be typed.

square brackets Brackets "[" and "]" surrounding a sequence of expressions separated by a period. Denotes a block.

Message-Sending Terminology

binary message (selector) A message (selector) with one parameter where the selector consists of nonalphabetic characters; e.g., "+2" ("+") in "1+2".

keyword A word terminated with a colon that precedes a parameter; e.g., both "**between:**" and "**and:**" are keywords in "3 **between:** 1 **and:** 5".

keyworded message (selector) A message (selector) with two or more parameters where the selector consists of keywords; e.g., message "**between:** 1 **and:** 5" (selector "**between:and:**") in "3 **between:** 1 **and:** 5".

message The combination of selector and parameters; e.g., "class" in "25 **class**", "+2" in "1+2", and "**between:** 1 **and:** 5" in "3 **between:** 1 **and:** 5".

selector That part of the message that excludes the parameters; e.g., "**class**" in "25 **class**", "+" in "1+2", and "**between:and:**" in "3 **between:** 1 **and:** 5".

sending a message Requesting that a simple Smalltalk expression consisting of a receiver, a selector, and parameters be evaluated.

parameters That part of the message that excludes the selector; e.g., there are no parameters in "25 **class**", one parameter "2" in "1+2", and 2 parameters "1" and "5" in "3 **between:** 1 **and:** 5".

polymorphic message A message with several implementations in different classes; e.g., "*" is polymorphic because it is understood by different kinds of objects such as fractions and float.

receiver The recipient of a message.

unary message (selector) A message (selector) with no parameters; e.g., "**class**" in "5 **class**" is both a unary message and a unary selector.

Method Components

comment Information inside double quotes that provides an explanation of some sort; often provided at the beginning of a method to explain the purpose of the method.

local variables Variables that exist only during execution; in the context of a method, either variables declared in the method or method parameters.

message parameter A parameter in a message; a subexpression, after it has been evaluated, that is part of a message in an expression; e.g., "2+3" and "4 **factorial**" in "8 **between:** 2+3 **and:** 4 **factorial**".

message pattern A synonym for **method header**.

method body Everything after the method header; includes comments and expressions separated by periods.

method header A pattern on the first line of a method. The pattern describes the message processed by the method.

method parameter A variable in a method header (message pattern); e.g., "aNumber" and "anotherNumber" in a method header such as "**between:** aNumber **and:** anotherNumber".

method template A sample method that illustrates what methods should look like. Consists of a message pattern (also called method header), comment, temporary variables, and statements.

reply expression An expression of the form "^anotherExpression" that causes the result computed by anotherExpression to be returned to the sender of the message that initiated the computation.

Mouse Interaction Terminology

clicking The process of pressing down on a mouse button followed by an immediate release.

direct selection Moving the I-beam to the start of a sequence of characters to be selected, pressing the left mouse button, and moving the cursor to the end of the sequence (without releasing the button), and finally releasing the button.

double-clicking Clicking the mouse twice in rapid succession Double-clicking on a word selects it, double-clicking at the beginning of a line selects the entire line, and double-clicking at the extreme right end of a line causes the cursor to move to the right of the last character. Double-clicking on a part in an inspector causes a new inspector on the part to appear.

moving the I-beam Clicking the mouse once at a new spot in a window already containing the I-beam.

performing a mouse button action *over* **a window component** The act of first moving the cursor to the window component, and then performing the specified action (such as pressing, clicking, or double clicking the mouse button).

pressing and holding Pressing the mouse button for a long time without releasing it.

shift-click selection Moving the I-beam to the start of a sequence of characters to be selected, moving the cursor to the end of the sequence without touching any buttons, and finally pressing the left button while simultaneously pressing the Shift key. Can also be used to extend an existing selection.

Names, Variables, and Parameters

block parameter A special variable at the beginning of a block; e.g., member in "aContainer **do**: [:member | ...]".

class variable A variable that can be accessed by a class (and subclasses) and any of their instances. Class variables should be used in preference to global variables.

global variable A variable that can be accessed anywhere. It starts with an uppercase (capital) letter; e.g., "Transcript", "Object". A global is created by using it and responding yes to a prompt that subsequently results. A global such as "Junk" is removed from the Smalltalk environment by executing "Smalltalk **removeKey**: #Junk".

instance variable A variable used to refer to a part of an instance; e.g., "numerator" and "denominator" are instance variables of fractions.

literal A name denoting a unique object for all time; e.g., $a is a literal denoting the single character that we call "lowercase a". Each name consists of a sequence of special characters—generally, the characters are specific to each kind of literal.

local variable A variable that is used in a specific context. It starts with a lowercase letter; e.g., "temperatureToday", "age", "height". A variable that exists only during execution of instructions in a workspace, transcript, or method; a temporary variable or method parameter.

message parameter An object provided as a parameter to a message; e.g., 3 and 5 are message parameters in "4 **between**: 3 **and**: 5".

method parameter A variable in a method header (message pattern); e.g., "aNumber" and "anotherNumber" in a method header such as "**between**: aNumber **and**: anotherNumber". Method parameters cannot be changed.

name Generally, any sequence of words used to refer to someone or something else; in Smalltalk, a sequence of characters, other than space, that refers to an object.

part A synonym for **instance variable**. Technically, a part is the subobject that an instance variable is bound to. The only object whose parts (instance variables) you can directly refer to by name are the parts of **self** in a method body.

pool dictionary A global dictionary in which the keys are strings that are legal capitalized names and the values are the constants associated with the names. The variables are known and accessible to any method in a class that has the dictionary in its list of pool dictionaries; e.g., any class wanting access to colors such as ClrRed can include ColorConstants as a pool dictionary.

pseudo-variable A variable that doesn't quite behave like a standard variable, because the name was chosen by the system and it doesn't permit changes; e.g., "self" and "super".

self A pseudo-variable denoting the receiver;. It is associated with a specific method copy and cannot be changed.

super A pseudo-variable denoting the receiver but causing method lookup to begin in the superclass of the method containing "super". It cannot be changed.

temporary variable A variable that is created for a specific context and that immediately disappears when that context no longer exists; e.g., variables declared specifically for executing a series of expressions in a workspace, or variables declared in the body of a method.

variable A name that refers to one arbitrary object. The specific object that it refers to at any one time can be changed. For each name, the first character must be alphabetic and all the others must be either alphabetic characters or digits. When evaluated, a variable returns the object to which it is bound; before any binding is explicitly performed, a variable is bound to nil.

Object Terminology

abstract class A class that either has no instances or that could but is not intended to, since the instances are not useful. Useful instances are obtained from subclasses of the abstract class.

anthropomorphic Ascribing human characteristics to things not human— **anthropos** denotes man and **morphe** denotes form. Behaving like a little person.

behavior What an object can do; the set of messages it responds to; the operations (and their semantics) associated with an object.

concrete class A class that is expected to have instances.

generalization The process of making a method or class more general or applicable; e.g., making a **printOn:** method applicable to all subclasses independent of the number of subclasses.

immutable object An object such as a character, small integer, or symbol that cannot be changed.

indexed part A component of an object that can be referenced by an index or position; e.g., string 'hi' has two parts, indexed by 1 and 2.

instance A member of one of more classes; e.g., 5 is an instance of classes SmallInteger, Integer, Number, Magnitude, and Object.

instance variable A variable in an instance; a part.

mutable object An object such as a string, fraction, or array that can be modified.

named part A component of an object that can be referenced by name; e.g., "numerator" and "denominator" are the named parts of a fraction.

part A component of an object; e.g., fraction "1/3" has parts 1 and 3; string 'hi' has parts $h and $i.

reduced A result that is as simple as possible; e.g., "6/3" reduces to 2; "6/4" reduces to "3/2".

representation The structure of an instance (its instance variables).

specialization The converse of generalization. The process of making a method or class more specific; e.g., by eliminating parameters and replacing them by defaults, creating classes that are a special case of the more general class.

subclass A class below a given class in a class hierarchy.

superclass A class above a given class in a class hierarchy.

Operating Systems Terminology (Microsoft Windows)

Program Manager The window by which a programmer can communicate with the Microsoft Windows operating system.

program group An icon in the Program Manager window that contains program items. The icon can be opened by double-clicking on it.

program item An icon that has a program associated with it. The program can be executed by double-clicking on the icon.

Operator Terminology

concatenation Operation "," that permits a new (usually longer) string or array to be constructed from two shorter ones; e.g., 'yester', 'day' $\Rightarrow$ 'yesterday'.

left operand The leftmost operand in an expression; e.g., "1" in "1+2".

operand That portion of the expression consisting of data for the operator; e.g., "1" and "2" in "1+2".

operator That portion of the expression that specifies what to compute; e.g., "+" in "1+2".

right operand The rightmost operand in an expression; e.g., "2" in "1+2".

Options in a debugger

Hop Hops into the method for the next message to be evaluated; i.e., begins the evaluation of the next message by creating a new entry at the top of the debugger's top-left pane and displaying the beginning of the method associated with the next message.

Jump Causes the debugger to disappear and execution to continue from the current execution point.

Skip Evaluates the currently selected text and subsequently positions the debugger at the message immediately following it.

Options in a walkback window

Debug The option that replaces the walkback window by a debugger.

Resume The option that permits execution to continue.

Programming Environment

changes file The file that keeps track of the source for everything that you executed, including the source for all methods.

image The file that keeps track of the programming environment as it existed at the time you saved the image.

Programming Language Syntax

cascaded messages Multiple messages to the same receiver. Technically, each message is separated by a semicolon and the receiver is specified only in the first message; e.g., "Transcript **space**; **space**; **cr**".

engineering notation The notation used by floats; e.g., 55.37e20.

exponent notation A synonym for **engineering notation**.

period An expression separator or an expression terminator (a period is optional after the last expression); e.g., expression1. expression2. expression3.

reply An expression preceded by special character "^" to indicate that the expression is to be the receiver's reply to a message it received.

semicolon A message separator that indicates successive messages are to be sent to the same receiver; e.g., "Transcript **cr**; **space**; **space**".

Programming Techniques

binary search A top-down decomposition technique that breaks the search task into two equal subtasks.

double dispatching A programming technique in which a message sent to one object in turn passes the buck to another object while providing information about the parameter being passed. (See **addTransaction:** in bank accounts.)

first-in first-out (FIFO) behavior Queuing behavior obtained by using **addLast:** and **removeFirst** (or **addFirst:** and **removeLast**) in ordered collections.

last-in first-out (LIFO) behavior Stacking behavior obtained by using **addLast:** and **removeLast** (or **addFirst:** and **removeFirst**) on ordered collections.

passing the buck A programming technique that allows you to compute a value by asking some other object to do most of the work for you.

recursion A variation of passing the buck in which the receiver does not change.

sequencing Running through the successive elements of a container; e.g., **do:** is a sequencing operation.

Programming Terminology

accessor (or **accessing method**) A method that returns the object contained by an instance's part.

ASCII value An integer between 0 and 255 corresponding to each of the 256 unique characters.

browsing Looking at classes and methods in the Smalltalk environment using a browser.

class-based case A case (or situation) that is a function of the type of object being processed.

collision The fact that a particular object's hash is the same as that of some other non-equal object in the same collection.

conversion Obtaining a different type of object from a receiver; e.g., #hello **asString**, #(1 2) **asSet**.

deep copy A copy that should share only objects that cannot be copied; in practice, a copy that provides a shallow copy of the parts.

digit value One of the values 0, 1, 2, ..., 9, 10, 11, ..., 35 for characters $0, $1, $2, ..., $A, $B, ..., $Z, respectively.

equality Two objects are said to be **equal** if they "look the same"; otherwise, they are **not equal**. The corresponding operations are = (**equal**) and ~= (**not equal**). Each class is free to define equality specially.

explicit knowledge Direct reference to an object; an object has explicit knowledge of another object if it has an instance variable bound to the object.

hash An integer value that can be computed from its receiver. It should have the property that each time a particular object is hashed, the same integer is computed. It is permissible for different objects to have the same hash but it is better if they are all different. Hashes are used by sets, bags, and dictionaries for speeding up object searches.

identity Variables A and B are said to be **identical** if they refer to the same object; otherwise, they are **not identical**. The corresponding operations are == (**identical**) and ~~ (**not identical**). There is only one definition of identity.

implicit knowledge Indirect reference to an object; an object has implicit knowledge of another object if the other object can be retrieved through some sort of search or elaborate computation.

infinite loop A nonterminating computation.

meta-level operation An operation dealing with messages; e.g. "1 **perform:** #+ **with:** 2" is a meta-level operation dealing with message "+ 2".

method A set of instructions for an operation or message understood by a class or an instance.

modifier (or **modification method**) A method that permits the object in an instance's part to be changed.

mutual knowledge A phenomenon whereby distinct instances know about each other; e.g., a library might know about all the books it contains and each book might know which library it comes from.

nonterminating computation A computation that can never finish.

object mutation A capability whereby one object changes permanently into another; achieved via the meta-level operation **become:**; e.g., 'hi' **become:** nil.

print string A string representation of an object that is suitable for printing. Generally, print strings print only an interesting subset of the information associated with an object.

private method A method intended only for use inside the class it is defined in; it is not intended for use by outside users.

public method A method that outside users are permitted to use.

reusability The notion that something should be used for other things besides what it was specifically built or designed for.

semantics The meaning (as opposed to the syntax).

shallow copy A copy that shares the parts of the original object.

Smalltalk library The set of all methods and classes in the Smalltalk programming environment.

store string A string representation that is suitable for storing. It contains a valid Smalltalk expression that, if executed, would create another object equal to the original.

subscripting out of bounds Using a subcript in an **at:** or **at:put:** message that is invalid (not between 1 and the size of the receiver).

syntax The form (as opposed to the meaning).

variable A name referencing an object where the reference can change over time.

Pull-Down Menu Commands

Do It (in the Smalltalk menu) Evaluates the currently selected text but doesn't print anything.

Inspect (in the Inspect menu of an inspector) Evaluates the currently selected text and opens an inspector on the result.

Inspect It (in the Smalltalk menu) Evaluates the currently selected text and opens an inspector on the result.

Save (in the File menu) In a inspector, changes the part selected in the left pane to the value typed in the right pane.

Show It (in the Smalltalk menu) Evaluates the currently selected text and displays the result.

Special Objects

array A generalization of a string that permits arbitrary objects in place of characters.

array literal A representation for an array where all the elements are specified explicitly (without computation). The only elements permitted are numbers, characters, strings, symbols, and other array literals; true, false, and nil are not permitted; e.g., #(10 $a 'hi' red true (5 6 7) nil). (Note that true and nil here are symbols while (5 6 7) is an internal array literal.)

association A key-value pair kept by a dictionary.

block A sequence of zero or more Smalltalk expressions separated by periods and surrounded by square brackets; e.g., [], ['hi'], ['Transcript **cr**. 10 **factorial**]. In practice, each of these examples are instances of HomeContext—there is no class called Block. The term **block** is used because it is a building block for control structures.

class The object denoting what kind of object an instance is.

collection A special container that inherits from class Collection.

container An object that can contain an arbitrary number of other objects.

dictionary A container that permits you to correlate or associate one object with another; a container of key-value pairs where the keys are the objects that serve as indicators for the information of interest and the values are the relevant data items.

directory A file containing the names of other files that are maintained in the directory.

empty array literal An array consisting of zero objects; e.g., #().

empty string A string consisting of zero characters; e.g., ''.

equality dictionary The kind of dictionary that compares keys using "=" (equality); a member of class Dictionary (there is no EqualityDictionary class).

float A number such as 3.14159 or 50.5e3 (also called a **floating point number**) consisting of a **mantissa** 50.5 multiplied by 10 raised to some **power** or **exponent** 3 (in 3.1415, the exponent is implicitly 0). A float is an **approximate** value; i.e., there is a bound on the number of digits maintained.

fraction A number, such as 1/3, consisting of **numerator** 1 and **denominator** 3.

file A sequence of characters that resides on disk and that can be referenced via a path name such as 'a:\course\examples\file1'.

fixed-size collection A collection that cannot grow; e.g., a member of Array, String, or ByteArray; a subclass of FixedSizeCollection.

identity dictionary The kind of dictionary that compares keys using "==" (identity); a member of class IdentityDictionary.

indexed collection A set of classes that supports integer indices; e.g., Array, String, OrderedCollection; a subclass of IndexedCollection.

interval A compact collection of integers with constant differences; e.g., 1 **to**: 10 **by**: 3 (difference 3), 10 **to**: 1 **by**: -2 (difference -2).

key An object that can be used to retrieve information stored in a dictionary, an ordered collection, a sorted collection, a string, or an array; a generalization of an index that need not be an integer (although it must be an integer for any collection other than a dictionary).

ordered collection A container that maintains the order of the elements as they are added. The elements can be added either on the left or on the right.

raster constant A special constant indicating how source and destination bits are to be combined during bitmap-copying operations.

sort block A two parameter block that returns true if the parameters supplied are in sorted order; e.g., [:person1 :person2 | person1 **age** >= person2 **age**] is a sort block that sorts person objects by non-increasing age.

sorted collection A container that sorts the elements according to a specified sort block. The default sort block sorts in non-decreasing order.

stream An indexed collection with a position indicator. Operations are provided that allow one or more elements from the current position onward to be accessed or replaced and that simultaneously move the position indicator as a side-effect.

subarray An array that is an element of some other collection; e.g. #(1 2 3) is a subarray in "OrderedCollection **with**: #(1 2 3)". A portion of an array; e.g., the subarray containing only the first two elements of #(1 2 3 4 5),

subcollection A collection that is an element of some other collection; e.g. the ordered collection in "Array **with**: OrderedCollection **new**". A portion of a collection; e.g., the ordered collection containing only the first element of the collection "#(1 2 3 4) **asOrderedCollection**".

subscript A synonym for **key**.

symbol An immutable string.

value An object associated with a key or index.

Window Builders, Applications, and Panes

application An instance of ViewManager that is responsible for interacting with a user through a user interface.

event A special signal generated as a result of mouse interactions, keyboard typing, or as a consequence of starting up (opening) or ending (closing) an application.

event handler A method (requiring a pane as a parameter) that is designed to react to the occurrence of a specific event.

framing block An alternative to a framing ratio that computes the absolute rectangle of a pane given the absolute rectangle of the window on the screen; e.g., [:aRectangle | *... code to compute a rectangle for the pane ...*].

framing ratio A rectangle specifying where a pane is to be placed, assuming the entire window is a square with sides of length 1; e.g., 0@0 **extent**: 1@1.

graph pane A pane that supports the construction of rudimentary windows for graphics and that can be used for drawing.

owner The object, normally an application, that is to respond to the events generated in a window or pane.

window builder A tool that helps a designer create a window-based application.

Window Components

close box A button that causes the window to disappear from the environment when double-clicked.

label bar The rectangular area at the top of a window containing a title.

maximize box A button that causes the window to grow to maximum size when the left mouse button is clicked over it.

menu bar The rectangular area below the label bar containing a list of menu items; a pull-down menu of commands appears under the item when the left mouse button is pressed over it. A command can be selected by releasing the mouse button over the command.

minimize box A button that causes the window to shrink to minimum size when the left mouse button is clicked over it.

pane A subwindow without a label bar or associated window buttons.

pop-up menu A menu that pops up over a pane when the user clicks on the right mouse button.

pull-down menu A menu that drops down from the menu bar.

scroll arrow Special buttons at both ends of a scroll bar that cause text to move in the direction indicated when pressed with the left mouse button.

scroll bar A rectangle indicating that pane data can moved horizontally or vertically. It consists of a shaded area and a small rectangle called the **scroll box**.

scroll box A small rectangle that is part of the scroll bar.

text pane A pane that can hold text.

Window Cursors

arrow cursor A cursor indicating that text cannot be written at that location; e.g., in the label bar.

cursor A special icon (or picture) that indicates the location of the mouse on the screen.

cross hair cursor A cursor indicating that a selection is expected from the user.

execute cursor A cursor indicating that some long computation is being performed.

text cursor A cursor indicating that the mouse is over some portion of a window where text can be written

window resizing cursor A cursor indicating that the edges or corners of a window can be moved.

Window Manipulation

activating a window Clicking the mouse anywhere over a window that is not active.

closing a window Destroying a window. Clicking on the close box.

collapsing a window Iconizing the window. Clicking on the minimize box.

maximizing a window Enlarging the window to full-screen size. Clicking on the maximize box.

moving a window Pressing the left mouse button over the window's label bar and dragging it to its new location.

opening a window Creating a window.

resizing a window Pressing the mouse over either an edge or a corner of the window and moving it.

Window Terminology

active window The window that currently accepts characters written on the keyboard or that responds to mouse clicks. An active window can be recognized by the fact that the top of the window (the **label bar**) is highlighted.

clicking The process of pressing down on a mouse button followed by an immediate release.

collapsed window A window shrunk to minimum size by clicking on the minimize box leaving only a labelled icon visible.

double-clicking Clicking the mouse button twice in rapid succession.

background The area behind the windows.

I-beam A vertical line inside a text window marking the spot where text can be inserted or deleted.

inactive window A window that does not respond to mouse clicks or typed characters.

scrolling The process of moving the contents of a window up, down, right, or left.

window An area on the screen surrounded by a special boundary. It can generally be moved around and resized. Distinct windows can overlap.

Window Varieties

class hierarchy browser (browser for short) A window used to view the class library (methods and classes) and to make additions or modifications to this class library.

debugger A window used to investigate and correct an execution error.

disk browser A window used to view and modify files on disk.

inspector A window used to look at and modify objects in the system. It can display an object and all its parts, including the class that it is a member of in the title. The object is indicated as "self" and the parts are distinguished with individual names (for **named** parts) or indices (for **indexed** parts); e.g., an inspector for a fraction will permit "self", "numerator", and "denominator" to be viewed.

message box A temporary window for either informing or requesting a true/false response.

prompter A temporary window requesting a textual response.

transcript A workspace that cannot be closed; a text window that can be used by the programmer or the system as a display board; a window with the global name "Transcript".

walkback A window that appears when a programming command contains an execution error.

workspace A text window that can be used by the programmer for arbitrary computation.

Index